PARLIAMENTARY HISTORY: TEXTS & STUDIES

16

Anglo-Irish Politics, 1680–1728

The Correspondence of the Brodrick Family

of Surrey and County Cork

VOLUME TWO, 1714–22

Ivory portrait medallion of Thomas Brodrick, by David Le Marchand, c.1714–26.
© The Trustees of the British Museum.

Anglo-Irish Politics, 1680–1728

The Correspondence of the Brodrick Family
of Surrey and County Cork

VOLUME TWO, 1714–22

Edited by

David Hayton and Michael Page

WILEY
for
THE PARLIAMENTARY HISTORY YEARBOOK TRUST

© 2020 The Parliamentary History Yearbook Trust

John Wiley & Sons

Registered Office
John Wiley & Sons Ltd, The Atrium, Southern Gate, Chichester, West Sussex, PO19 8SQ, UK

Editorial Offices
101 Station Landing, Medford, MA 02155, USA
9600 Garsington Road, Oxford, OX4 2DQ, UK
The Atrium, Southern Gate, Chichester, West Sussex, PO19 8SQ, UK

For details of our global editorial offices, for customer services, and for information about how to apply for permission to reuse the copyright material in this book please see our website at www.wiley.com/wiley-blackwell.

The rights of David Hayton and Michael Page to be identified as the editors of the editorial material in this work has been asserted in accordance with the Copyright, Designs and Patents Act 1988.

All rights reserved. No part of this publication may be reproduced, stored in a retrieval system, or transmitted, in any form or by any means, electronic, mechanical, photocopying, recording or otherwise, except as permitted by the UK Copyright, Designs and Patents Act 1988, without the prior permission of the publisher.

Wiley also publishes its books in a variety of electronic formats. Some content that appears in print may not be available in electronic books.

Library of Congress Cataloging-in-Publication Data

Library of Congress Cataloging-in-Publication data is available for this book

ISBN 9781119799931

A catalogue record for this title is available from the British Library
Set in 10/12pt Bembo
by Aptara Inc., India
Printed and bound in Singapore
by C.O.S. Printers Pte Ltd

1   2020

Parliamentary History: Texts & Studies

CONTENTS

ACKNOWLEDGMENTS

Our first acknowledgment must be to the Viscount Midleton, for permission to publish this further selection from his family papers. We are also indebted to the owners and custodians of the other collections of manuscripts cited and quoted: the Marquess Townshend; the Lord Bolton; his grace the archbishop of Armagh; the Castletown Foundation; the keeper of western manuscripts in the Bodleian Library; the British Library Board; the Governing Body of Christ Church, Oxford; the clerk of the records of parliament; the comptroller of Her Majesty's Stationery Office; the Henry E. Huntington Library and Art Gallery; Hertfordshire Archives and Library Services; Kent County Council; the librarian, Lambeth Palace Library; Leicester and Leicestershire Record Office; the keeper, Marsh's Library; the director, National Archives of Ireland; the director, National Library of Ireland; the deputy keeper of the Records of Northern Ireland; the Registry of Deeds, Dublin; the master and fellows of St John's College, Cambridge; the Suffolk Record Office; and the board of Trinity College Dublin. For assistance with particular points we thank Alex Barber, John Curran, Clyve Jones, Robin Eagles, Stuart Handley and John McCafferty. We are especially grateful to Linda Clark, the general editor of the series, for her careful attention to the text. David Hayton also wishes to acknowledge the assistance provided to him by the staff of the McClay Library, Queen's University Belfast. Finally, a special vote of thanks is due to Guz Guzman of the Surrey History Centre for his efforts, beyond the call of duty, in facilitating the checking of the text at a critical time in the production process.

ABBREVIATIONS

Add. MS(S)	Additional Manuscript(s)
Al. Dub.	*Alumni Dublinenses: A Register of the Students, Graduates, Professors and Provosts of Trinity College in the University of Dublin 1593–1860*, ed. G.D. Burtchaell and T.U. Sadleir (new edn, Dublin,1935)
Anglo-Irish Politics, Vol. 1	*Anglo-Irish Politics, 1680–1728, The Correspondence of the Brodrick Family of Surrey and County Cork, Vol. One, 1680–1714* (Parliamentary History Texts & Studies xv, 2019)
Ball, *Judges*	F.E. Ball, *The Judges in Ireland 1221–1921* (2 vols, 1926)
BL	British Library, London
Boyer, *Political State*	Abel Boyer, *The Political State of Great Britain* … (60 vols, 1711–40)
Brady, *Records*	W.M. Brady, *Clerical and Parochial Records of Cork, Cloyne and Ross* … (3 vols, 1864)
Burns, *Politics*	R.E. Burns, *Irish Parliamentary Politics in the Eighteenth-century* (2 vols, Washington, DC, 1989–90)
CTB	*Calendar of Treasury Books*
CTBP	*Calendar of Treasury Books and Papers*
CTP	*Calendar of Treasury Papers*
Carswell	John Carswell, *The South Sea Bubble* (1961)
CJ	*Commons Journals*
CJI	*The Journals of the House of Commons of the Kingdom of Ireland* (2nd edn, 19 vols, Dublin, 1753–76)
Cobbett, *Parl. Hist.*	*Cobbett's Parliamentary History of England from the Earliest Period to the Year 1803* (36 vols, 1805–20)
Cork Council Bk	*The Council Book of the Corporation of the City of Cork, from 1609 to 1643, and from 1690 to 1800*, ed. Richard Caulfield (Guildford, 1876)
Cotton, *Fasti*	Henry Cotton, *Fasti Ecclesiae Hibernicae: The Succession of Prelates and Members of the Cathedral Bodies of Ireland* (5 vols, Dublin, 1847–60)
Coxe, *Walpole*	William Coxe, *Memoirs of the Life and Administration of Sir Robert Walpole, Earl of Orford* (3 vols, 1798)
CSP Dom.	*Calendar of State Papers, Domestic Series*
Dalton, *Army Lists*	Charles Dalton, *English Army Lists and Commission Registers, 1661–1714* (6 vols, 1892–1904)

Dalton, Geo. I's Army	Charles Dalton, *George the First's Army, 1714–1727* (2 vols, 1910–12)
DIB	*Dictionary of Irish Biography* (online edition: https://dib.cambridge.org)
ECI	*Eighteenth-century Ireland*
[E]	England
[GB]	Great Britain
HALS	Hertfordshire Archives and Library Services
Hayton, *Ruling Ireland*	D.W. Hayton, *Ruling Ireland, 1685–1742: Politics, Politicians and Parties* (Woodbridge, 2004)
HC 1690–1715	*The House of Commons 1690–1715*, ed. Eveline Cruickshanks, D.W. Hayton and Stuart Handley (5 vols, Cambridge, 2002)
HC 1715–54	*The House of Commons 1715–1754*, ed. Romney Sedgwick (2 vols, 1970)
Hist. Ir. Parl.	Edith Mary Johnston-Liik, *History of the Irish Parliament 1692–1800: Commons, Constituencies and Statutes* (6 vols, Belfast, 2002)
HL 1660–1715	*The House of Lords 1660–1715*, ed. Ruth Paley (5 vols, Cambridge, 2016)
HMC	Historical Manuscripts Commission (reports)
IHS	*Irish Historical Studies*
ILD	Irish Legislation database (online: http://www.qub.ac.uk/ild/)
[I]	Ireland
K. Inns Adm.	*King's Inns Admission Papers, 1607–1867*, ed. Edward Keane et al. (Dublin, 1982)
Lib. Mun.	*Liber Munerum Publicorum Hiberniæ*, ed. Rowley Lascelles, (2 vols, 1824–30)
LJ	*Journals of the House of Lords*
LJI	*Journals of the House of Lords [of Ireland]* (8 vols, Dublin, 1779–1800)
M. Temple Adm.	*Register of Admissions to the Honourable Society of the Middle Temple from the Fifteenth Century to the year 1944*, ed. H.A.C. Sturgess (3 vols, 1949)
NAI	National Archives of Ireland, Dublin
NLI	National Library of Ireland, Dublin
n.d.	no date
n.p.	no place (of publication)
n.s.	new series
N.S.	New Style
OED	*Oxford English Dictionary* (online edition: http://www.oed.com)
O.S.	Old Style

Oxf. DNB	*The Oxford Dictionary of National Biography* (online edition: http://www.oxforddnb.com)
Phillimore, *Indexes*	*Indexes to Irish Wills*, ed. W.P.W. Phillimore and Gertrude Thrift (5 vols, 1909–20)
PRONI	Public Record Office of Northern Ireland
Reg. Deeds	Registry of Deeds, Dublin
RO	Record Office
SHC	Surrey History Centre
Swift Corr.	*The Correspondence of Jonathan Swift, D.D.*, ed. David Woolley (5 vols, Frankfurt am Main,1999–2014)
TCD	Trinity College Dublin
TNA	The National Archives [of the U.K]
Vicars, *Index*	*Index to the Prerogative Wills of Ireland, 1536–1810*, ed. Sir Arthur Vicars (Dublin, 1897)
Wake	Christ Church, Oxford, Wake MSS

Introduction

'If I am not a whig what am I?' (Alan Brodrick, 1716)

1

After the struggles, tensions and alarms of the last year of Queen Anne's reign, the peaceful accession of George I – what one of the Brodricks' tenants in County Cork called 'this glorious change and happy resolution' in public affairs[1] – was for whigs in England and Ireland the political equivalent of arrival in the promised land. Office and power were theirs. The few English tories who were welcomed at the Hanoverian court all came from the 'Hanoverian' wing of the party, and it did not take long for the leading men among them to become disillusioned and rejoin their erstwhile colleagues in opposition. In London the members of King George's whig government soon began the process of calling their predecessors to account. The previous chief minister, the earl of Oxford, was impeached. Lord Bolingbroke, the former secretary of state, and the duke of Ormond, Marlborough's successor as captain-general, anticipated events and fled to join the jacobite Pretender in France. Their flight, and the involvement of other tories in the jacobite invasion attempt of 1715–16, effectively smeared the party as a whole as jacobite. Tories suffered a major reverse at the polls in the British general election of 1715.[2] In sharp contrast to the whigs, the tory party seemed to have entered the political wilderness.[3]

A similar course of events unfolded in Ireland. Indeed, given that the rise of a 'high church' interest in Ireland had been a relatively recent phenomenon, and that the succession issue was a peculiarly sensitive issue for Irish protestants, it should come as no surprise that the downfall of the tory party in Ireland was even swifter than in England. After the king's arrival in London, tories were quickly removed from the Irish government: Alan Brodrick himself replaced the tory lord chancellor, Sir Constantine Phipps, the great bugbear of the whigs; the privy council was remodelled; and a new commission of whig lords justices installed. But the process went much farther. An inevitable consequence of the crystallisation of 'party politics' in Ireland after 1702 had been the development of a 'spoils system'. Every swing of the political pendulum after 1706, from tory to whig and back again, had been accompanied by wholesale changes in office-holding, a process which reached its zenith in 1714–15, when almost every tory, from high court judges to the most humble revenue

---

[1]SHC, G145/box95/2: Benjamin Garde to Alan Brodrick I, 26 Oct. 1714.

[2]Surveyed in *HC 1715–54*, i, 19–25; and W.A. Speck, 'The General Election of 1715', *EHR*, xc (1975), 507–22.

[3]Linda Colley, *In Defiance of Oligarchy: The Tory Party 1714–60* (Cambridge, 1982), 177–89.

official, was implicated, directly or by association, in the political crimes of the outgoing ministry. It was open season for applications for preferment from those who could claim to have acted 'honestly' during the last four years of Queen Anne's reign, which whigs were now calling 'the worst of times'. The tory Lord Chief Justice Cox reported in September 1714, that 'abundance of whigs are gone over [*to England*] and they make one another believe they shall have all employments'.[4] Even when a tory incumbent could find powerful friends to support him, the iron logic of party allegiance usually prevailed.[5]

In these circumstances, the loyalty of the more moderate – or needier – tories in Ireland was tested to the limit, and in many cases snapped. Sir Richard Levinge, who had been the court candidate for speaker of the Commons in 1713, was a predictable renegade, having a long-established reputation as a moderate, or, as his detractors put it, one who tried to be all things to all men.[6] Others to dive off the sinking ship included the former solicitor-general Francis Bernard, one of the Brodricks' political rivals in County Cork, and Agmondisham Vesey, whose father Archbishop Vesey of Tuam, had served as a lord justice alongside Phipps. As in England, the general election in Ireland in October to November 1715 delivered a further blow to the tory party, resulting in an overwhelming whig majority in the Dublin house of commons. No more than 80 of the 300 seats in the new House were occupied by MPs who could be identified as tories on the basis of their previous parliamentary behaviour. In practice, the active number of tory diehards was probably nearer 30.[7] The party's strength in the Lords seemed stronger to begin with; the tories had, after all, enjoyed a clear majority in the upper house in the 1713 parliament, which they had exploited to defend Phipps from attacks mounted by whigs in the Commons. But a combination of peerage creations, appointments and translations in the episcopate, and defections by the ambitious or penurious, soon put the whigs in the driving seat.[8] Enthusiasm for the 'high church' cause remained for some time a powerful current in the broader 'political nation', even if it had fewer opportunities to make itself felt, and on occasion tories could still foment trouble for government; if the right issue arose, such as a proposal for the relief of protestant dissenters. For the most part, however, they were reduced to impotence.

Inevitably, there was not enough milk and honey to satisfy the needs of all loyal whigs in Ireland, and like every political party whose triumph has been too complete, some among the victors began to feel irritated, and then aggrieved, until dissatisfaction produced personal quarrels and factional conflicts. Tensions were visible even before the general election, with rival whig interests jostling for pre-eminence in some counties, and when the house of commons did assemble, one of the most striking features of the session was the behaviour of a body of whig malcontents, clearly disappointed in their hopes of advancement.[9]

[4]BL, Add. MS 38157, f. 117: Cox to Edward Southwell, 7 Sept. 1714. The phenomenon continued into the winter (TCD, MS 1995–2008/1560: Frederick Hamilton to Archbishop King, 30 Dec. 1714).

[5]D.W. Hayton, 'Ireland and the English Ministers, 1707–16', Oxford DPhil., 1975, pp. 265–7; cf. Patrick McNally, 'The Hanoverian Accession and the Tory Party in Ireland', *Parliamentary History*, xiv (1995), 266–76.

[6]BL, Add. MS 47087, ff. 17–18: Sir John Perceval's journal, 18 Mar. 1713.

[7]McNally, 'Hanoverian Accession and Tory Party', 276–9.

[8]D.W. Hayton, 'Party and Management in the Irish House of Lords 1713–1715', in *Peers and Politics, c. 1650–c. 1850: Essays in Honour of Clyve Jones*, ed. Richard A. Gaunt and D.W. Hayton (Oxford, 2020), 99–125.

[9]TCD, MS 2536, pp. 168–9: Archbishop King to Robert Molesworth, 12 Jan. 1714[/15]; Hayton, *Ruling Ireland*, 219.

The Brodricks not only expected rewards for Alan and his brother, Thomas, but for Alan's elder son St John, whose performances in the Irish parliament in 1711 and 1713 had brought him to the forefront of the whig party. William, Alan's other surviving brother, was also eyeing a return to Ireland from the Caribbean, where his plantation was in financial difficulties and his 'extravagant courses' had made him powerful political enemies.[10] William was returned to the Irish parliament at a by-election for Mallow in County Cork in 1716, and obtained a minor preferment in Ireland as second serjeant in 1718, but had an inflated idea of his abilities and entitlements, and agitated for a place on the judicial bench. Finally, some thought had to be given to the career prospects of Alan's younger son, Alan II, even though he was only in his early teens in 1714, and also to the brothers Arthur and Trevor Hill, the children of Alan's third wife Anne Hill. This was only the immediate family: the Brodricks' acknowledgment of the claims of a very wide kinship and determination to maintain the strength of their local power-base in Munster inevitably involved them in a far greater range of solicitation, on behalf of 'cousins', connections, allies and dependants, efforts which inevitably resulted in frustration as well as gratification.

The anxieties produced by the scramble for advancement under the new viceroy, Lord Sunderland, and his successors, would have tested the patience of any politician. For someone of Alan's temperament it was a severe trial. Disappointment had always brought out the worst in him, for his elevated sense of self-worth was combined with a personality that was over-sensitive, querulous, and ill-tempered. Throughout his career, Alan, and for that matter Thomas, dramatised adversity: every setback was a disaster, and more than once Alan talked of leaving the political stage and returning to the landed estate – either in County Cork or in Surrey – which he managed with great care. He kept a very close eye on property matters throughout his life, even while heavily involved in the great political events of the day. This was of course by no means unusual for someone of his age and class, but the fact that he remained active in the land market, ready to purchase whenever the possibility arose, is suggestive of a man always seeking to build up an insurance against the collapse of his professional and political career.[11]

The family correspondence during the period covered by this volume includes much close discussion of matters of estate management, which for reasons of space has not been reproduced. These letters reveal that both Alan and Thomas were not only preoccupied with the management of their property but were also highly suspicious of agents and tenants, and, at least in Alan's case, determined to minimise expense. A perennial bone of contention between the brothers was Thomas's fondness for racing his own horses, especially at Newmarket, which was not only an extravagance in itself but a pastime that immersed participants in a culture of gambling, and inevitably increased their debts.

It is not difficult to see why Alan's initial relief at the safe accomplishment of the Hanoverian succession, and his subsequent gratification at his appointment as lord chancellor of Ireland in place of Phipps, should soon have given way to unease, and then discontent. His standing as the leader of his party in Ireland, generally acknowledged during and after the parliament of 1713 both in private correspondence and in the public prints, seemed suddenly to evaporate. He may have been lionised in his native county, where the corporation

---

[10] Karst de Jong, 'The Irish in Jamaica during the Long Eighteenth Century (1698–1836)', Queen's University Belfast PhD, 2017, pp. 79–81.

[11] SHC, G145/98/1: Nicholas Grene to Alan I, 29 Feb. 1720/1.

of the city of Cork paid for a portrait of him in his new robes,[12] but from the outset he discovered that his was only one of many voices listened to by the lord lieutenant, Lord Sunderland, who corresponded with a range of different whig politicians in Ireland, and seems to have paid particular attention to the advice of William Whitshed, the new lord chief justice of king's bench, a man of whom the Brodricks were very wary. It was common knowledge that 'good lord chancellor you know likes to have things done thro' himself'.[13]

The fact that Alan was not nominated as one of the lords justices who carried out the business of government in Sunderland's absence was a specially bitter blow: it was highly unusual for a lord chancellor not to be included, and the choice of Archbishop King of Dublin and the young earl of Kildare alongside the continuing Archbishop Vesey was perceived as a snub, as indeed in one sense it may have been, calculated to avoid the impression that government had simply been handed over to the Brodricks. Furthermore, while Alan himself had been given high office, and a few of his intercessions with Sunderland bore fruit, neither Thomas nor St John received anything for themselves, except that Thomas was restored to the Irish privy council. For someone, who had enjoyed a lucrative government employment under a previous whig administration in England (as joint comptroller of army accounts 1708–11), this must have seemed to Thomas a poor return for his labours in the whig cause in the Westminster parliament.

The Irish lord chancellorship also appeared likely to be a burden to Alan, despite the salary and the status it conveyed. In political terms, the office lacked a ready fund of patronage. Its major asset, control over the issuing of commissions of the peace, which in England offered the opportunity to influence county opinion by purging 'undesirable' jp(s), was much less politically useful in Ireland, where the relative scarcity of qualified protestant gentlemen in many counties made it impracticable to pick and choose. Leaving the house of commons in order to preside over the Lords was also an unattractive proposition. The role of the lord chancellor as Speaker in the upper house was ceremonially gratifying but in practice much less significant than the active part played by the Commons Speaker in political management. The chancellor could not, for example, expect to engage frequently in debates in committee. Alan was also nervous about the probable aggressiveness of the tory interest in the upper house, which had been so dominant in Queen Anne's reign. As early as October 1714 he confessed to Thomas that he expected to be made an Aunt Sally for political opponents. Using a colourful (and regrettably obscure), analogy, he wrote:[14]

I consider how fond some people will be of using me in another manner in the house of lords when I am restrained from speaking or debating then they will otherwise; and have fancied that my condition there in the chair would be like that which I have some where read; that the way of treating prisoners is to bind them naked and defenceless to trees and set on their children to kill them, and that the greater cruelty may be exercised upon them, every child is armed with a very blunt weapon without point or edge.

As Alan recognised, he had almost certainly taken a backward step politically, despite the acquisition of a peerage title as Baron Brodrick. He had opened the way for his successor in

---

[12] *Cork Council Bk*, 373.

[13] NLI, MS 12149, f. 88: [William Howard] to [?Sir Paul] Whichcote, 13 Nov. 1715.

[14] See below, Letter 226.

the Commons chair – his quondam friend and ally William Conolly – to build up his own political interest and become indispensable to government. In addition, Conolly had been restored to the revenue board – ironically, at Alan's suggestion[15] – where he was effectively 'first commissioner' and would use his influence over appointments at all levels to build up a strong personal following in the Commons.[16] By contrast, the management of the upper House was seen as less important. Certainly it was necessary to maintain a government majority there, to avoid political embarrassments, something that would become acutely important in the years 1717–20, when a dispute between the Irish and English parliaments over the claim by the Lords at Westminster to an appellate jurisdiction over Ireland threatened a political explosion. But the really important business of the session – the examining of estimates and accounts, and the preparation of money bills – took place in the Commons. Alan soon found himself reduced to the position of an observer of discussions over the supply – quantum, duration and ways and means – which were now carried on by Speaker Conolly and his friends. Previously, under chief governors like Capell, Pembroke or Wharton, Alan had been the key figure in these negotiations; indeed, his role in securing supply legislation in the 1690s was what had put him (and Thomas) at the head of the whig party in Ireland. Now he was outside, looking in.

Before the Irish parliament was called in 1715, Sunderland resigned the lord lieutenancy, under the pretext of ill health (observers in England had always doubted his willingness to leave the centre of power and travel to Ireland to hold a parliamentary session), and the chief governorship was entrusted to two lords justices, the veteran Huguenot soldier Lord Galway, who had served as a lord justice in 1697–1700, and the young duke of Grafton. Galway had not enjoyed a particularly amicable relationship with Alan and Thomas on his previous tour of duty: he had found them difficult to deal with and continued to mistrust Alan. Grafton was very much the junior partner and seems to have followed Galway's lead. The stage was thus set for a difficult relationship between the Brodricks and the new government, which is exactly what developed. While Alan seems to have done everything that was asked of him in terms of managing the upper house, running into difficulties only when the bishops were provoked by a proposal to modify the sacramental test, his followers in the Commons behaved in a manner that government regarded as at best 'whimsical' and at worst maliciously destructive.

By now Thomas had taken up residence permanently in England and had not sought re-election to the Irish parliament. The leadership of the family interest in the Irish house of commons devolved upon St John, who replaced his father as knight of the shire for Cork in the 1715 election and quickly rose to a position of prominence, partly through his own energies and abilities, and also for want of competition: not only his father, but a number of other leading whigs from the previous reign had left the House through being raised to the peerage or the judicial bench. Already, when the session opened, St John's standing was such that he was named first to both the committee of privileges and the committee to prepare the loyal address. He was also one of the earliest nominees listed in the committee of accounts (which was chaired by his uncle James Barry).[17] Observers noted above all

---

[15] BL, Add. MS 61636, f. 114: Alan I to [Sunderland], Oct. 1714.

[16] Patrick Walsh, *The Making of the Irish Protestant Ascendancy: The Life of William Conolly, 1662–1729* (Woodbridge, 2010), ch. 7.

[17] *CJI*, iv, 13, 15, 28.

his 'warmth' in debate, which to begin with was directed at the remnants of the old tory administration.[18] Having in the 1713 parliament led the Commons' investigations into the alleged misdeeds of the tory government, he carried on in 1715 in the same vein, chairing committees of inquiry into the proceedings of the former privy council over the Dublin mayoral election and the supposed failure of the lords justices and council to deal adequately with reports of the activities of jacobite recruiting officers.[19] But at the same time he was proving a thorn in the side of government managers, on one occasion provoking Galway's chief secretary, Martin Bladen, to some sharp words in the House, at which the family took collective offence.[20]

To outside observers, this was all very puzzling. Why should the lord chancellor's son be obstructive in the matter of supply or, in the case of the incident which had infuriated Bladen, make common cause with tories on the issue of relief for protestant dissenters while at the same time going out of his way on other issues to emphasise his whig credentials and seek the punishment of former tory ministers and privy councillors? One obvious explanation was filial obedience; that he was acting on his father's behalf. According to some observers, Alan was dissatisfied with the preferment he had received, angry above all that he had not been made a lord justice, and while discharging his own duties as speaker of the house of lords with perfect propriety, encouraged his son underhand to make trouble for the lords justices in the Commons.[21] There was a degree of plausibility in this analysis: Alan was certainly an unhappy man, convinced that Bladen was his implacable enemy and moreover hand-in-glove with the Speaker and Lord Chief Justice Whitshed, a man whom Alan suspected (in a characteristically paranoid flourish) of having designs on the lord chancellorship for himself. In Alan's view, these three formed an unholy 'triumvirate'. It would thus have been natural for Alan to have encouraged St John in acts of defiance. Yet the fact of collusion is impossible to prove. Throughout the following decade, when Alan was seeking to absolve himself from his son's political misdemeanours, he argued to successive viceroys and English ministers that St John was a headstrong young man, beyond parental control. And from what we know of the Brodricks' individual characters, and turbulent family relationships, this may well have been at least partly true. Nothing in the correspondence printed below enables us to draw a firm conclusion; but one would hardly expect it to, given Alan's obsessive anxiety that his letters to England were being opened by the Irish postmaster-general, Conolly's crony Isaac Manley. Hence the elaborate circumlocutions used to hide the identity of individuals – circumlocutions which are even more effective at this distance of time – and the occasional addressing of letters to other family members – his son, or his first wife's relations – which were clearly intended to be read by his brother.

2

The after-effects of the parliamentary session were all too apparent when Galway and Grafton left Ireland early in 1717. Unlike lords lieutenant, who returned to England as

[18] BL, Add. MS 47028, f. 204: Lord Perceval to Charles Dering, 8 Oct. 1717.
[19] *CJI*, iv, 58, 60.
[20] TNA, SP 63/373/336–7: Charles Delafaye to [Robert Pringle], 17 Dec. 1715.
[21] NAI, M 3036, ff. 31–3: —— to Lord Nottingham, 24 Dec. 1715.

soon as the Irish parliamentary session was over, the two lords justices remained at Dublin Castle until in February 1717, their commission was terminated in favour of one of the secretaries of state, Charles, Viscount Townshend. This change of master must have seemed a positive development, as far as Alan was concerned, since he knew Townshend well and had corresponded with him privately.[22] But it came with a sting: the commission of lords justices appointed to govern Ireland in Townshend's absence, to which Alan was gratified to find himself named, also included Archbishop King and, crucially, Speaker Conolly. Any pleasure Alan might have taken in his own nomination was spoiled by the presence of the man he would only refer to as 'my colleague'. It was the first time a commons Speaker had been appointed and marked a belated acknowledgment of the importance of the political management of the lower House. Henceforth the nomination of the Speaker alongside the lord chancellor and primate (for whom King was standing in, since it was clearly impossible for the whig administration to appoint such a violent tory as Archbishop Lindsay of Armagh) became a regular pattern.

Alan's outrage was ostensibly directed at what he considered to be Conolly's low social origins, as a former attorney whose father was widely (if incorrectly) assumed to have been in trade. Nor was he alone in finding such an advancement inappropriate.[23] But behind the social snobbery lay a seething resentment at the way in which the man he now perceived to be his principal political rival had exploited an intimacy with the outgoing justices and their secretaries to place himself on the same level as the chancellor. It can have been no coincidence that in the same month that Townshend was appointed as viceroy Alan secured for himself a seat in the Westminster house of commons, coming in at a by-election for Midhurst in Sussex on the interest of an independent whig peer, the duke of Somerset. The brothers probably reasoned that a presence at the heart of English politics would provide them with leverage to counter Conolly's influence at Dublin Castle.

Townshend never came to Ireland. He had been unhappy at his removal from the English secretaryship of state to a position which, while 'not quite equivalent to disgrace', certainly 'indicated a loss of face'.[24] It had been hard for his fellow secretary, and *de facto* chief minister, James Stanhope, to persuade him to accept the viceroyalty, and Townshend's discontent soon issued in a refusal to follow the court line in the house of lords. On 31 March 1717 he was dismissed. His cousin Robert Walpole followed him into opposition, splitting the whig party at Westminster and leaving Stanhope and Sunderland at the head of the administration. Previous experience inclined Alan towards suspicion of Sunderland, partly because of Sunderland's long association with Charles Delafaye, who had served as Grafton's chief secretary and was considered to be in Conolly's pocket. Alan may also have been suspicious of Stanhope; at any rate he had reason to be, for one of Stanhope's friends and regular correspondents was Henry Maxwell, an intimate of Conolly whom Alan would later christen 'the Speaker's echo'.[25] Nevertheless, the choice of Townshend's successor could not have been more to his liking. Charles Powlett, second duke of Bolton, had, like Galway before him, served as lord justice in Ireland in the latter part of William III's reign. Unlike Galway,

---

[22] See for example, Raynham Hall, Norfolk, Townshend MSS: Alan I to Townshend, 20 Sept. 1715.

[23] BL, Stowe MS 750, f. 244: Sir John St Leger to Lord Parker, 21 Feb. 1716/17.

[24] J.H. Plumb, *Sir Robert Walpole: The Making of a Statesman* (1956), 235–6.

[25] D.W. Hayton, *The Anglo-Irish Experience: Religion, Identity and Patriotism* (Woodbridge, 2012), 105–6.

he had then enjoyed a cordial relationship with Alan and Thomas, to whom he was distantly connected. He was now the brothers' preferred candidate for the viceroyalty; indeed, it had been reported in 1715 that Alan had been actively intriguing to secure his appointment on Sunderland's resignation.[26]

Bolton's first Irish parliamentary session, in August to December 1717, promised to restore Alan's authority over the Irish whig party. He was able to plume himself on his intimacy with the new lord lieutenant, and before the session opened had the gratification of being promoted in the peerage to the title of Viscount Midleton, which was presumably some compensation for the social embarrassment of having to sit alongside Conolly on the board of lords justices. Through Bolton's influence he was also able to obtain for his younger son, Alan II, and his stepson Trevor Hill the joint reversion of the office of register of the memorials of deeds, after the death of the current holder, Benjamin Parry.[27]

Suitably gratified, Alan worked hard in the Lords to smooth the path for the viceroy. It was not as easy a task as he had perhaps envisaged. In the second half of the previous session the tory interest in the upper house had temporarily revived when presbyterian sympathisers raised the question of a partial repeal of the test. Tories were handed another opportunity in 1717. This time the bone of contention was different. The British house of lords had heard an appeal against a ruling of the upper house in Ireland in favour of a widow, Hester Sherlock, in a lawsuit against Maurice Annesley, the guardian of her brother's orphan children, and had overturned the decision. Hester now brought a petition to the Lords in Dublin seeking redress. The possible ramifications were extremely dangerous, threatening a constitutional conflict between the two parliaments. Bolton himself was at a high pitch of anxiety and Alan, who genuinely felt that claims being made on behalf of the jurisdiction of the Irish house of lords were too extravagant, strove to the best of his abilities to smooth matters over.[28] Although isolated in the Lords, he battled on against a phalanx of enraged 'patriot' orators numbering whigs like Archbishop King alongside the tories Primate Lindsay and Lord Abercorn. Even though he made himself unpopular and was ultimately unsuccessful in preventing the Lords from granting a decree which reasserted their original decision, he could at least congratulate himself on having done as much as possible to deserve the continuance of viceregal favour.[29]

Alan was not alone in assuming that he had re-established his personal ascendancy. In separate letters to the duke of Grafton and Charles Delafaye, Conolly admitted his own conviction that he would himself be dropped from the commission of lords justices; that the lord chancellor would be appointed to govern on his own, which would have been an unheard-of distinction; and even that Alan would go over to England for the parliamentary session there to become 'one of the managers in your house of commons'.[30] Not only had Alan distinguished himself in the debates in the upper house, it was noticeable that St

[26] NAI, M 3036, ff. 31–3: —— to Lord Nottingham, 24 Dec. 1715.

[27] Kent Archives, U1590/O145/33: 'Memorandum for Lord Stanhope' [1717].

[28] HALS, DE/P/F56/9–10, 11: Bolton to Earl Cowper, 30 Aug., 8, 13 Sept. 1717; Wake, Epist. xii: Bishop Godwin to [Archbishop Wake], 10 Sept. 1717; Isolde Victory, 'The Making of the 1720 Declaratory Act', in *Parliament, Politics and People: Essays in Eighteenth-century Irish History*, ed. Gerard O'Brien (Dublin, 1989), 14–16.

[29] HALS, DE/P/F56/11, 12, 14: Bolton to Cowper 13, 19, 23 Sept. 1717; Wake, Epist. xii: Bishop Godwin to [Archbishop Wake], 24 Sept., 12 Oct. 1717, to Delafaye, 9 Oct. 1717; TNA, SP 63/375/194–6: William Caulfield to Delafaye, 11 Oct. 1717.

[30] TNA, SP 63/375/212, 266: Conolly to Delafaye, 18 Oct. 1717, to Grafton, 9 Oct. 1717.

John, although not receiving any preferment himself, had behaved himself in the Commons, thus providing circumstantial evidence to substantiate the notion that he acted as his father's instrument.[31] Conolly could also congratulate himself on his own performance in the chair: supply had been voted for two years, and a potential revolt over rumours of a land tax had been averted. He had established a superficially amiable relationship with the viceroy – who, he reported, was 'very civil' to him – and with the new chief secretary, Edward Webster. But as the session drew to a close, he could not help but observe that Bolton's manner towards him, though affable, remained distant. By contrast, viceroy and lord chancellor were often in each other's company, and perfectly at ease. Conolly assumed that their long evening conferences would determine, among other things, Bolton's recommendation of lords justices.[32]

If so, it was a further unpleasant surprise for Alan Brodrick to discover that the new commission of lords justices was the same as the last, even to the extent of including Archbishop King alongside the lord chancellor and Speaker, despite the vehemence with which King had argued for the rights of the Irish house of lords during the debates on *Annesley* v. *Sherlock*. To the Brodricks' intense frustration, Lord Sunderland's influence had secured Conolly his place.[33] The Speaker was surprised and quietly gratified, both by his own recognition and the evident discomfiture of his rival.[34] This was the second time that Sunderland had intervened in his favour: during the preceding summer Sunderland had ensured that the lucrative office of chancellor of the Irish exchequer had gone to Conolly's henchman, Sir Ralph Gore, rather than the Brodrick candidate, provoking Alan to such an extent that he apparently contemplated refusing to pass the patent.[35]

For the time being Alan kept his resentment private. When he came to London in the winter of 1717/18, he seems to have given no indication of his feelings. Bolton presented him to the king, and he soon made his maiden speech in the British house of commons, on the court side.[36] Ministers were sufficiently unaware of his true state of mind to contemplate including him in a batch of new English peerage creations designed to bolster their position in the Lords.[37] Later that year came William Brodrick's appointment as second serjeant in Ireland. At the same time, Sunderland made Thomas vague offers of employment.[38] However, these came to nothing, and by the autumn Alan was becoming increasingly nervous about his own position and was condoling with Thomas about 'the undeserved treatment you have hitherto met with'.

3

The turning-point came in March 1719. In a document prepared some years later, Alan provided 'a narrative of the manner, in which I have been treated by Lord Sunderland',

[31] TNA, 63/375/204–5: Conolly to Delafaye, 3 Oct. 1717.

[32] TNA, SP 63/376/214, 220: Conolly to Delafaye, 3, 30 Nov. 1717.

[33] TNA, SP 63/376/216: Conolly to Delafaye, 17 Nov. 1717.

[34] TNA, SP 63/376/216: Conolly to Delafaye, 17 Nov. 1717.

[35] BL, Add. MS 47028, f. 197: Charles Dering to Lord Perceval, 12 Aug. 1717.

[36] BL, Add. MS 47028, f. 220: Lord Perceval to Philip Perceval, 16 Jan. 1717/18; *Historical Register*, 1718, p. 54; *A History of the Last Session of the Present Parliament* … (1718), 78.

[37] Huntington Library, LO8325: [Sir David Dalrymple] to [earl of Loudoun], 11 Feb. 1718.

[38] TNA, SP 63/376/11: Conolly to Charles Delafaye, 8 Mar. 1717[/18].

laying the blame for the final breakdown in their relations firmly at Sunderland's door.[39] In doing so he took as his model Archbishop Abbot of Canterbury, who had fallen foul of King Charles I's favourite, Buckingham, and similarly 'drew up a declaration … of the manner of his treatment', to which he might have recourse 'if question should be made about his conduct'. Sunderland, Alan wrote, had once 'entertained a good opinion of me', and had been responsible for Alan's appointment as lord chancellor, but they had quarrelled irrevocably over Alan's principled objection to one of Sunderland's pet projects, the Peerage Bill introduced into the Westminster parliament in the 1718–19 session, which would have curtailed the royal prerogative in the creation of peers, and was designed to preserve the short- and medium-term security of the Stanhope–Sunderland ministry.[40] Having informed Bolton that 'I thought the bill was a very dangerous and pernicious one to the constitution, and that it would not pass, at least that it would not have my concurrence',[41] Alan then found himself pressed several times in personal interviews with Sunderland himself. Where Bolton merely expressed surprise and disappointment, Sunderland, whose own character was as volcanic as Alan's, lost patience completely. According to Alan, Sunderland's 'nose burst out a bleeding when I could not be either wheedled or bullied'.[42]

Alan presented his refusal to assist the ministry on this occasion as decisive in confirming Sunderland's hostility to him, and also as beginning his estrangement from Bolton. Certainly, Sunderland allowed his anger to become obvious. Reporting to Bolton on the outcome of a meeting of pro-government MPs which agreed to defer the Peerage Bill until the next session, Secretary James Craggs made it clear that there was 'a great indignation' in both the king and 'his servants' against Alan Brodrick in particular, whose conduct had been 'very remarkable of late'. There was even talk of him being replaced.[43] Bolton's response seems to have been more measured. Alan subsequently declared that on arrival in Ireland Bolton immediately '[took] other people entirely into his bosom', meaning Conolly. But that after all this seems to have meant in practice is that the viceroy ceased to rely solely on his old friend the chancellor and was now open to other influences.

It was the 1719 session of the Irish parliament which proved critical. Bolton came to Ireland fearing the worst. His principal concern was the likely reaction of the Irish house of lords to the refusal of the barons of the Irish exchequer, two of whom were Englishmen (Jeffray Gilbert and John Pocklington), to comply with the decree ordering Hester Sherlock to be restored to possession of her property. But he had also been saddled by Sunderland and Stanhope with the politically impossible task of securing a repeal of the sacramental test. Earlier, while he held the viceroyalty himself, Sunderland had discreetly ignored the representations of Irish presbyterians. In 1719, however, repeal was politically desirable in a British context. It followed on from the ministry's initiative to repeal the Occasional Conformity and Schism Acts at Westminster, which was designed to identify Stanhope and

---

[39] Printed in Coxe, *Walpole*, ii, 178–80.

[40] Clyve Jones, '"Venice Preserv'd; or A Plot Discovered": The Political and Social Context of the Peerage Bill of 1719', in *A Pillar of the Constitution: The House of Lords in British Politics, 1640–1784*, ed. Clyve Jones (1989), 79–112.

[41] Coxe, *Walpole*, ii, 178.

[42] Coxe, *Walpole*, ii, 171–4, 176.

[43] N. Yorks RO, Bolton MSS, ZBO VIII, D/54: Craggs to Bolton, 14 Apr. 1719.

Sunderland with traditional whig principles and undermine the standing of Townshend and Walpole with their followers.[44]

The Brodricks seem to have seized on the issue of the test as a means of giving themselves political leverage. Before leaving England, Bolton warned his cabinet colleagues that there was little likelihood of persuading a majority of both Houses in Dublin to vote for repeal, especially the bishops in the upper house. Having consulted his parliamentary managers and other interested parties, including both the lord chancellor and the Speaker, he reiterated this view. He took Conolly's advice to abandon the English ministers' notion of a simple repeal, and instead allow a group of sympathetic MPs to prepare a more qualified measure that might be acceptable. This was interpreted by Alan Brodrick as a devious attempt by the Speaker to promote repeal without having to commit himself publicly, and indeed there may have been something in this interpretation, for even the viceroy conceded in letters to England that Conolly 'strongly espouses the dissenters' interest', and was the man 'in whom they entirely rely'.[45] The upshot was heads of a bill prepared by one of Conolly's allies, Marmaduke Coghill. Though much more restrained, it was still perceived as going too far in exempting jp(s) from the test. After leave was given to allow Sir Ralph Gore to bring it in, under the title of a bill 'For rendering the protestant dissenters more useful and capable of supporting the protestant interest of this kingdom', nothing more was heard of it.[46] Instead another set of heads was introduced which merely provided an indemnity from prosecution for those who had accepted commissions in the militia without having taken the test, together with a statutory toleration, as nonconformists in England enjoyed, a concession to which Ulster presbyterians were indifferent. This bill did eventually reach the statute book, after further struggles at the Irish privy council and in parliament, with Archbishop King and his fellow spiritual lords to the fore.[47]

Informing Secretary Craggs of the loss of Gore's bill, the principal spokesman for the dissenting interest in Ireland, Colonel Clotworthy Upton, a presbyterian himself and one of the knights of the shire for County Antrim, noted sardonically that although the lord chancellor 'at last seemed pretty warm for us' his efforts were 'too late' and he failed to persuade any member of his family (including St John and William) to take the same line.[48] Other reports suggested that while the heads were being prepared 'the Br[odric]ks met the country party and many of those whom they had formerly ill used, assuring them no old sores should be ripped, or railings for past things, but that they should unanimously join in this matter.'[49] Alan himself seems to admit as much in one of his letters, without being specific: he had, he said, observed a 'resentment taken up by members' against Conolly for having 'undertaken' to obtain a repeal bill, and so

---

[44] D.W. Hayton, 'Ulster Presbyterians and the Confessional State: The Sacramental Test as an Issue in Irish Politics, 1704–34', *Bulletin of the Presbyterian Historical Society of Ireland*, xxvi (1997), 224–5; G.M. Townend, 'Religious Radicalism and Conservatism in the Whig Party under George I: The Repeal of the Occasional Conformity and Schism Acts', *Parliamentary History*, vii (1988), 24–33.

[45] Burns, *Politics*, i, 85–6; Hayton, *Ruling Ireland*, 225.

[46] Burns, *Politics*, i, 86; ILD.

[47] J.C. Beckett, *Protestant Dissent in Ireland 1687–1780* (1948), 75–80.

[48] N. Yorks. RO, ZBO VIII, D/73: Upton to Craggs, 30 July 1719.

[49] Wake, Epist. xiii: 'A brief account of proceedings in the parliament of Ireland', 16 July 1719.

I endeavoured to show them that it was not our business to have parties, and that the forming and increasing them in smaller matters might in consequence influence the greater, people who once have got into the way of doing it being apt to oppose those in everything from whom they differ in some things. Their answer was they would as a man assist the crown and government and join with the others in granting the supply, or doing it without them if they showed any backwardness. And in this manner they did, tho' their meetings were represented as designed to obstruct the public affairs, by the Sp[*eaker*] and his friends.

The issue had clearly given the Brodricks an opportunity to make common cause again with other discontented whigs, and even with tories. And so, St John reverted to the oppositionist line he had taken in 1715–16, with the result that, according to the chief secretary, the Commons became embroiled in conflict on a daily basis.[50]

Once more Alan seems to have tried to cover his tracks by blaming his son's wilfulness. He himself could not be faulted for his conduct in the upper house. When the *Annesley* v. *Sherlock* case blew up again, in an explosion of patriotic enthusiasm, he continued to do all he could to pacify emotions and dissuade the lords from precipitate action. The exchequer barons bore the brunt of the House's anger. They were examined by a committee of inquiry, which concluded that they had violated their oaths of office. The terms of the committee's resolutions were modified at the report stage on 29 July 1719, but the barons were still declared to have acted 'improperly' and 'contrary to law' and ordered into custody in Dublin Castle, where they remained for the rest of the session. Then in early October the Lords drew up an address to the king justifying their actions, in the form of a representation of their grievances.[51] In all this time Alan 'bore up bravely against the prevailing humour', arguing against the imprisonment of the barons, and even more vehemently against the representation: he 'wished them to consider the precipice they were upon and to look before they made the fatal leap'.[52] He was particularly concerned at the expression of sentiments which recalled William Molyneux's notorious argument for legislative independence, *The Case of Ireland Being Bound by Acts of Parliament in England Stated*, published in 1698 and condemned at the time by the English house of commons. This was not necessarily an attitude assumed in order to serve a political purpose, namely to ingratiate himself with the viceroy. For one thing, such a very public stance risked unpopularity; for another, observers like Bishop Nicolson of Derry, who listened to these speeches, certainly considered their sentiments genuine.[53] If the English came to believe that Irish protestants were pressing for some form of legislative independence, as some had done in the previous constitutional crisis of 1697–1703, the consequences could be disastrous.

Despite these displays of loyalty, relations with the viceroy took a downward path. Already, by the time of the parliamentary debates over repeal of the test, the Brodricks' behaviour was being explained by jealousy of the viceroy's favour: 'what seems to have contributed to this unexpected turn is said to have arisen from my lord lieutenant making use of Mr

---

[50] TNA, SP 63/377/59: Edward Webster to Charles Delafaye, 6 Aug. 1719.

[51] Victory, 'Declaratory Act', 17–21; Burns, *Politics*, i, 93–8.

[52] BL, Add. MS 6116, ff. 89–91: Bishop Nicolson to Archbishop Wake, 2, 31 Oct. 1719.

[53] BL, Add. MS 6116, f. 91: Nicolson to Wake, 31 Oct. 1719.

C[*onoll*]y whereas in the first year of his government he was wholly ruled by lord chancellor'.[54] Conolly's quiet reliability, and the success of his management of supply business, was bound to make a favourable impression, in contrast to Alan's more demanding personality and outbursts of petulance. Despite Alan's valiant efforts to restrain the anger of the house of lords over *Annesley* v. *Sherlock*, he was inexorably losing the viceroy's trust, as Bolton came to realise that it was really not worth defending his former ally against the settled antipathy of the chief ministers. There may even have been a suspicion that the Brodricks were intriguing with Townshend and Walpole, with whom they had a long-standing association.

The last straw for Bolton was Alan's surprising opposition to the bill 'to prevent the further growth of popery'. All penal legislation was assured of popularity with protestant public opinion, and, given the apparent resurgence of 'patriotic' feeling in Ireland, Bolton was anxious to have something positive to show from the parliamentary session. Alan had supported this bill at the Irish privy council, even with its most notorious clause, imposing the penalty of castration on all unregistered catholic priests found in the country, which the British privy council eventually removed. But when the bill returned from England, he joined other peers – tories and discontented whigs, including Archbishop King – in voting it down.[55]

Alan's unexpected opposition to the Popery Bill, coming on top of the imbroglio over the appellate jurisdiction, which promised further trouble when the British house of lords came to consider the Irish response to their judgment, seems also to have been a decisive moment for Sunderland and Stanhope. It was compounded in November when Thomas Brodrick divided against the Peerage Bill in the British house of commons, confirming his position as an 'independent' whig, even if he was not aligned formally or permanently with the Townshend–Walpole faction.[56] Rumours immediately began to circulate of changes to be made in Ireland. Edward Southwell, a former tory chief secretary, told a correspondent in mid-November 1719 that 'There seems to be a resolution to employ more Englishmen in the high offices of state [*in Ireland*] since they grow headstrong in that country and forget their mother.'[57] What this meant in practice was soon clear. Alan had kept his position on the commission of lords justices when Bolton departed in November 1719, in tandem with Conolly (as Archbishop King, not unexpectedly, lost his place). But in February 1720 an unsuccessful attempt was made to interest an English lawyer, John Willes, in taking over as lord chancellor of Ireland, and from this point on Alan began to consider his dismissal as inevitable.

4

Sunderland and Stanhope now embarked upon a radical overhaul of their Irish policy. The key element was the passage through the British parliament in April 1720 of the

[54] Wake, Epist. xiii: 'A brief account of proceedings in the parliament of Ireland', 16 July 1719.
[55] Wake, Epist. xiii: Bishop Evans to Archbishop Wake, 23 Oct. 1719, Bishop Godwin to Wake, 7 Nov. 1719; BL, Add. 6116, f. 92: Bishop Nicolson to Wake, 30 Nov. 1719.
[56] *HC 1715–54*, i, 491.
[57] Leicester and Leicestershire RO, DG7 Bundle 26/42: Southwell to Lord Nottingham, 17 Nov. 1719.

so-called 'Declaratory Act' asserting Westminster's authority over Ireland. There were only two clauses: the first, and ostensibly the occasion of the act, confirmed the right of the British house of lords to act as the final court of appeal in Irish cases; the second declared the competency of the British parliament to legislate in Irish matters. The motive for adding the second clause was not clear at the time. Alarmist reports from English-born bishops and office-holders in Ireland that 'patriots' were aiming at 'independency' may have frightened ministers into a conviction that some clear legislative statement of political realities would be salutary. On the other hand, there was enough evidence from recent history to encourage scepticism of this analysis, for in the controversy which had followed the publication of Molyneux's tract many prominent Irish protestants had gone out of their way to deny that they had any such aspirations. The muted protests in the Irish press and parliament after the passage of the Declaratory Act would bear this out. More cynically, the addition of the second clause may have been an attempt to address a problem that Thomas Brodrick identified: how to ease the passage, through the British house of commons, of a bill which might otherwise arouse 'jealousies' of the authority of the Lords. The ministry was appealing to the prejudices of backbenchers, for English MPs of all stripes agreed that Ireland was a conquered country and its parliament a subordinate legislature.

It is equally possible that ministers were actively considering legislating for Ireland. This power had always been assumed, but since the Glorious Revolution had been used sparingly. While the Westminster parliament was happy to pass laws regulating Anglo-Irish trade, there had only been two occasions when internal Irish affairs had been made the subject of English/British statutes, excluding the transfer of the crown in 1689 and the establishment of the Hanoverian succession in 1701, both of which occurred at times of crisis when no Irish parliament was sitting. In 1700 the Act of Resumption had taken back royal grants of Irish forfeited estates, and in 1714 English tories had extended the Schism Act to Ireland, enforcing a prohibition of dissenting educational institutions.

The Schism Act had been repealed at Westminster in 1718, and it may have been in the mind of Lord Sunderland, in particular, that further relief to Irish nonconformists, including perhaps a repeal of the test, could be achieved directly by a Westminster statute. This would have been of a piece with the ministry's general political strategy of appealing to whig party traditions; it would also have been typical of the audacity, not to say recklessness, characteristic of Sunderland. The fact that the MP chosen to pilot the Declaratory Bill through the Commons was a presbyterian, Grey Neville, offers some supporting evidence for this hypothesis.

There was also another, even more dangerous, prospect; that rather than calling another parliament in Dublin, Ireland could be taxed from Westminster.[58] This was a step no English ministry had yet dared to take, but the fury of the Irish house of lords over *Annesley* v. *Sherlock*, and the evident intractability of both Houses over the test, seemed to show the fragility of parliamentary management in Ireland. Something would have to be done. In October 1720, after Bolton had been replaced as lord lieutenant by the duke of Grafton, various proposals were circulated among cabinet ministers as to how the calling of a new Irish parliament might be avoided. They included sweeping cuts to the Irish establishment,

---

[58] This was Lord Perceval's fear (BL, Add. MS 46971, f. 31: Perceval to Berkeley Taylor, 15 Mar. 1719/20).

and even a return to the Restoration practice of tax-farming. None of this was discussed with the servants of the crown in Ireland.[59]

Left to his own devices, Sunderland could well have taken such radical measures, but in the spring of 1720 the context of British politics changed. The defeat of the reintroduced Peerage Bill in November 1719 brought about a political crisis during the following winter, which culminated in April 1720 in a reconciliation between the king and the prince of Wales, whose court at Leicester House had been a centre for opposition politicians. Soon afterwards Townshend and Walpole were readmitted into the ministry. It was almost certainly Walpole's moderating influence which held back the cabinet from taking extreme measures to deal with what Sunderland perceived as a political impasse in Ireland. This included the retention of Alan Brodrick in the lord chancellorship, against Sunderland's determination that the seals should be given instead to Jeffray Gilbert – perhaps the least tactful choice of any as a replacement.[60] Possibly a connection had been established between Walpole and the Brodricks which induced Walpole to protect a political ally – or at least a potential ally – or he may simply have considered it wiser to avoid the prospect of the ex-chancellor putting himself at the head of the 'Irish interest' in the house of lords.[61]

Walpole's position within the British ministry was strengthened immeasurably by the way he had handled the South Sea crisis. The previous year the South Sea Company had taken over part of the national debt, in return for a loan of £750,000 to government. Annuities from the 1710 lottery were to be converted into South Sea stock. In early 1720, after an approach from government, a scheme was concocted for the company to take over the remainder of the debt, in exchange for shares. The chancellor of the exchequer, John Aislabie, announced the scheme to parliament in January 1720, whereupon the Commons, following a decisive intervention from Thomas Brodrick, demanded that the Bank of England be permitted to make an alternative offer.[62] The company then increased its original bid, beyond its capacity to deliver, and once this was accepted began to talk up the value of its stock, creating a classic 'bubble', a frenzied market in stock, which was followed by an almost inevitable collapse. By September 1720 the value of shares had crashed to a tenth of the price prevailing at the height of the boom.

The disastrous effects of the failure of the South Sea Company were felt across society, as individual investors, banks and finance houses, faced bankruptcy. Ireland was also affected, where many among the propertied classes had fallen victim to the mania.[63] Despite Thomas Brodrick's intense and undying scepticism of the project, several members of his family lost money, including Martha Courthope, the maiden aunt of Alan's first wife, whom the brothers treated as a 'sister'. Even Alan himself gave way to the temptation of quick returns, and contemplated investment in order to provide for his younger children. Fortunately, he made his decision too late to act upon it.[64]

[59]D.W. Hayton, 'The Stanhope/Sunderland Ministry and the Repudiation of Irish Parliamentary Independence', *EHR*, cxiii (1998), 610–36; Hayton, *Ruling Ireland*, 229–30.

[60]Hayton, *Ruling Ireland*, 230.

[61]Wake, Epist. xiii: Bishop Evans to [Archbishop Wake], 21 July 1720.

[62]*HC 1715–54*, i, 491.

[63]Patrick Walsh, *The South Sea Bubble and Ireland: Money, Banking and Investment, 1690–1721* (Woodbridge, 2014), ch. 4.

[64]Walsh, *South Sea Bubble*, 106.

By the time the British parliament resumed sitting in December 1720, after several proro-
gations, the hue and cry was up for those responsible. Public anger focused on the directors
and officials of the company, though there were strong suspicions of corruption in government: Aislabie was the centre of this unwelcome attention, alongside Secretary Craggs and
his father James Craggs sr, the postmaster-general. Rumours were even circulating about
Stanhope and Sunderland, which put Sunderland in an even more vulnerable position. All
these men had in fact benefited from the company's largess, being given the opportunity to
purchase stock at an artificially low price before the announcement of the extension of the
scheme to take over the national debt resulted in an inflation of the value. The only saving
grace for Sunderland was that the king's mistress and several Hanoverian courtiers were
also involved, which meant that his rivals within the cabinet would have an interest in suppressing investigations. It was also vital for government to find a means to rescue the public
credit, through involving the other two great joint-stock companies, the Bank of England
and the East India Company. Robert Jacomb, Walpole's banker, and deputy as paymaster of
the forces, devised a plan and Walpole took the lead in piloting the rescue package through
the Commons, thereby earning the gratitude of the king and, paradoxically, increasing the
enmity of those ministerial colleagues whose skins he had saved.[65]

It was at this point that Thomas Brodrick stepped into the political limelight. At a pre-
sessional meeting of government supporters to discuss the king's speech and the loyal address, which Thomas attended despite his previous display of independence over the Peerage
Bill, he demanded that the address should contain some mention of an investigation into
the conduct of the South Sea Company's business, threatening a rebellion against party discipline if ministers did not agree.[66] He got his way, and eventually, on 4 January 1721, the
Commons ordered a 'secret committee' of inquiry, to be chosen by a ballot of MPs. When
the results were announced, Thomas found himself in first place, and thus the committee's
chairman.[67] The next four to five months, during which the committee reported four times
(on 16 and 25 February, 21 April, and lastly on 22 May[68]) were a whirlwind of activity;
demanding and scrutinizing documents, examining witnesses and preparing conclusions.

While determined to get to the bottom of any skulduggery that might have occurred in
the South Sea affair, Thomas was not interested in a witch-hunt for its own sake (in contrast
to some of his fellow committee-members). He felt strongly about the destructive effects
that unregulated financial speculation would have on the national economy, and thus to
society at large, and his performance as chairman of the secret committee has earned the
praise of historians of the Bubble, even if he sometimes showed himself unduly 'punctilious',
and even 'narrow-minded' with regard to some practices in the world of City finance that
were in fact perfectly legal.[69]

The committee's inquiries brought mixed results. Aislabie, who was found to have accepted bribes from the company, was declared guilty of 'most notorious, dangerous, and
infamous corruption', expelled the House, and sent to the Tower, with Thomas speaking

[65] Carswell, 203–6.
[66] Carswell, 209.
[67] *CJ*, xix, 395, 399.
[68] Cobbett, *Parl. Hist.*, vii, cols. 711, 743, 783, 797.
[69] Carswell, 221–2.

against him in debate.[70] Sir George Caswall, one of the directors of the Hollow Sword Blades Company, the South Sea Company's bankers, suffered the same fate. James Craggs, jr, died of smallpox on the day the committee's report was made, and a month later his father committed suicide. But Treasury secretary Charles Stanhope was acquitted by the Commons on a vote in which two members of the secret committee, Sir Joseph Jekyll and Robert, Viscount Molesworth, deserted.[71] Even more of a blow was the abscondment of Robert Knight, the South Sea cashier, after his interrogation. Knight took with him the 'green book' which contained proof of the bribery of many prominent individuals. He was apprehended at Brussels, and the British government went through a charade of publicly requesting his extradition while privately encouraging the Austrian authorities to permit his departure for France.[72] The loss of the 'green book' effectively prevented the committee landing its largest fish: Sunderland himself. After a long debate in the Commons on 15 March Sunderland was cleared of the charge of corruption by 51 votes, the written evidence against him being adjudged too flimsy.[73]

The consequences of the South Sea crisis brought some political benefit to the Brodricks, at least in the short term. The ministry had disintegrated in a series of personal disasters. Stanhope had died suddenly of a stroke on 5 February, having been taken ill the previous day after an over-strenuous performance in a Lords debate. The Craggses were both dead, and Aislabie's political career was finished. Most important, Sunderland, who had been Alan's principal enemy within the British cabinet, was driven to resign as first lord of the treasury for the much less prestigious office of groom of the stole. Robert Walpole replaced him at the treasury, with Townshend as secretary of state. These two cousins were now arguably at the head of affairs, though Sunderland still had the king's ear, and several of his allies remained in positions of power and influence.[74] Walpole's own position was also not quite as secure as it might have been: his role in the recovery of public credit may have earned him a degree of popularity, but against this had to be set the odium incurred through his defence of some of the greatest culprits in the South Sea affair, reflected in a newly acquired nickname of 'Screen-master general' or simply 'The Screen'.

The exact state of relations between the Brodrick brothers and Walpole and Townshend at this point is hard to gauge: the appointment of Grafton to the viceroyalty in 1720 was not a promising development, given Grafton's previous closeness to Conolly.[75] But Walpole and Townshend themselves were at least not openly hostile. And they had good reason to tread carefully. For one thing, Thomas had become a figure of consequence in the house of commons through his chairmanship of the secret committee. He could prove a useful ally. He had spoken against the court in key debates on the South Sea, but was not committed to opposition. Instead, as he explained to a friend in Ireland, 'I am one of those affected

---

[70] *Historical Register*, 1721, p.120.

[71] *HC 1715–54*, ii, 434.

[72] *Oxf. DNB* (*s.v.* Knight, Robert).

[73] Carswell, 243.

[74] Plumb, *Making of a Statesman*, 347–58.

[75] Some over-excited commentators in Ireland reported that Conolly was to receive an earldom under the new chief governor, an advancement which was wholly out of the question (NLI, MS 50545/3/1: Henry Rose to Sir Maurice Crosbie, 25 June 1720).

animals, who call themselves independent, and this I resolve always to be'.[76] Alan and St
John were equally unpredictable: it remained to be seen whether Grafton could persuade
them to work with him in spite of their rivalry with Speaker Conolly.

The situation in Ireland was still potentially dangerous. For one thing, it was unclear how
the Irish parliament, especially the Lords, would react to the passage of the Declaratory Act;
for another, the Irish economy, like the English, was suffering an acute depression in the
wake of the bursting of the South Sea Bubble. The anonymous publication in 1720 of
Swift's incendiary pamphlet, *A Proposal for the Universal Use of Irish Manufacture*, caught the
public mood. In this situation, to relieve Alan of the seals would be too much of a risk.
Nor was there an obvious replacement. Jeffray Gilbert's reputation in Ireland was as toxic
as ever, if not more so; and the other candidate whose claims were being canvassed, Lord
Chief Justice Whitshed, had made himself unpopular by his high-handed treatment of the
case against Edward Waters, who had printed Swift's pamphlet.[77] In May 1721 Grafton
met Walpole and Townshend to discuss the situation and reported to Conolly a decision to
retain Alan Brodrick in office for the time being, 'grounded on the difficulty of finding a
successor'. According to Conolly, this had already become obvious to both Alan and St John,
who attributed Alan's continuance in office to Thomas's solicitations, and the assistance of
powerful friends, including the other secretary of state, Lord Carteret. All that Conolly
could suggest was that Grafton speak to St John, whom he had got to know well during
his time in Dublin, and try to extract some sort of promise of good behaviour.[78]

5

Whether or not promises were asked for and made, Grafton's first session of parliament in
Dublin, from September 1721 to January 1722, went better than he or his cabinet colleagues
could have foreseen. Whatever might have been published in the press, parliament did not
express itself forcibly against the Declaratory Act. In the debate in the house of lords on the
loyal address Archbishop King attempted to raise the issue, demanding to know why the
king had not replied to the representation sent over by the House in the previous session.
But his was a lone voice. He was called to order for this 'reflection', and when the Lords
voted instead to thank his majesty for his 'gracious acceptance of the expressions of duty
and loyalty of the Lords in former sessions' King's was the only negative vote.[79] In the
Commons there were irritations, but St John Brodrick did not set himself up as the head
of a 'patriot' opposition. This was partly because government wisely avoided a repetition
of the controversy raised by proposals to repeal the test, and partly because Grafton had
prepared his ground well. Before setting off for Dublin he met Thomas Brodrick in London
and did what he could to conciliate the family, arranging for one of Alan's younger Barry
connections to be given an army commission. He also wrote a conciliatory letter to Alan,

[76]NLI, MS 41580/2: Thomas Brodrick to Jane Bonnell, n.d.

[77]Irvin Ehrenpreis, *Swift: The Man, His Works and the Age* (3 vols, 1962–83), iii, 128–9; Irish Architectural
Archive, Conolly MSS, A/3/17: Conolly to Grafton, 3 Dec. 1720.

[78]Irish Architectural Archive, Conolly MSS, A/3/29: Conolly to Grafton, 11 May 1721.

[79]Philip O'Regan, *Archbishop William King of Dublin (1650–1729) and the Constitution in Church and State*
(Dublin, 2000), 296.

requesting his co-operation. And when the session began it was noted that the two men seemed to be 'on good terms'.[80]

Grafton was helped by the fact that the issue which dominated this session – 'the only affair of consequence'[81] – was one that cut across party lines: proposals to establish a national bank. Although the financial sector in Ireland was seriously undeveloped, with banking still the preserve of small, private firms, resulting in the lack of capital formation sufficient to kick-start a struggling economy, this was an unpropitious time to launch grandiose financial schemes, in the wake of the South Sea crisis in England and the Mississippi Bubble in France. The idea of extending into Ireland the same kind of financial institutions which had recently been discredited in England awakened old-fashioned 'country' antagonism towards the 'moneyed interest', which animated both the discussions in parliament and the surrounding pamphlet debate.

The scheme had been initiated in May 1720, in response to a pamphlet by John Irwin, who had argued that a system of paper credit based on a banking institution was the only way to deal with one of the recurrent problems of the Irish economy, the chronic shortage of specie. Subscriptions were opened, and a draft charter of incorporation agreed, under which a number of managers were elected. A petition for a royal charter was then submitted to the king. The managers included politicians of all sorts: the tory Lord Abercorn was one of the most prominent; there were ex-tories like Thomas Medlycott; some cronies of Speaker Conolly, notably the chancellor of the exchequer Sir Ralph Gore and Thomas Marlay; and also St John Brodrick, together with another of the Brodricks' connections, Michael Ward. Various sympathetic individuals in England, including Thomas Brodrick, approached Grafton for assistance. In the meantime, however, another syndicate produced a counter-proposal. Grafton referred both to the lords justices, Conolly and Alan Brodrick, who gave their opinion in favour of the original scheme. All seemed to be going well, with Grafton looking forward to 'some particular advantage or offer' of a financial kind from the 'undertakers' for 'the service of the crown in Ireland', until an opinion came from the British treasury that the project ought to be established by Irish statute, in order to prevent the kind of abuses that the inquiry into the South Sea Company had exposed. So, in July 1721 a charter was granted on the condition that an Irish act of parliament be obtained within a year.[82]

Grafton's speech from the throne at the beginning of the 1721–2 session of the Irish parliament recommended the establishment of a national bank, and leave was given to bring in heads of a bill to this effect, which were referred to a committee of the whole House.[83] However, the committee was adjourned on 14 October 1721 for two months, after a vote in which Michael Ward and Sir Ralph Gore were tellers together for the minority. St John was also against a long postponement and, according to a division list in the Brodrick papers, MPs from all factions could be found on either side.[84] Opponents of the bill were convinced that this vote effectively marked the end of the matter, but the 'undertakers' went

---

[80] Sir Richard G.A. Levinge, *Jottings of the Levinge Family* (1877), 61.

[81] BL, Add. MS 47029, ff. 87–8: Philip Perceval to Lord Perceval, 14 Nov. 1721.

[82] Michael Ryder, 'The Bank of Ireland, 1721: Land, Credit and Dependency', *HJ*, xxv (1982), 559–64.

[83] For what follows, unless otherwise stated, see Burns, *Politics*, i, 127–9; Ryder, 'Bank of Ireland', 564–9.

[84] *CJI*, iv, 780. The accounts given by both Burns and Ryder are misleading on the nature of the division. The division list is printed below, Appendix 1.

ahead with subscriptions, and on 7 November, seizing the opportunity of a thin House, secured votes thanking the former lords justices for their favourable report and declaring that the continued taking of subscriptions was legal. The Lords then decided to consider the materials relating to the project, and on 8 November passed a resolution condemning the bank. In order to avoid a quarrel between the two Houses, which would disrupt other business, Grafton hurriedly brought forward the mid-sessional adjournment, dissuading the Lords from drawing up an address to the king by promising to report their resolutions personally, and that the charter would not be sealed until the king had been consulted. When parliament reassembled both Commons and Lords declared forcibly against a bank: the Commons rejected the heads at the report stage, and for good measure made an address condemning the project as 'pernicious', while the Lords followed this up with similar resolutions of their own. The scheme was finally dead.

Although Alan had reported favourably on the original proposal (albeit principally in relation to its superiority over the alternative scheme), he took a strong line in the Lords against establishing a bank. This was even more surprising given that St John had been one of the strongest supporters of the scheme from the very outset, and both Alan's wife and his stepson Arthur Hill subscribed on a significant scale.[85] He may have been genuinely concerned at the implications for the Irish economy and for social stability more generally, as laid out in the 'paper war' which erupted during the adjournment, though his opposition predated the appearance of much of this literature. Martha Courthope's experiences in the South Sea crash, and his own narrow escape, may also have preyed on his mind. But there was also a political context: it had become clear early on in the session that there was a strong movement of opinion in both Houses against the scheme, which Conolly would not join, because the potential profit to government from establishing a bank made it highly desirable from the viewpoint of the viceroy and the ministry in England. Conolly's acolyte Henry Maxwell was also one of the bank's most prominent advocates, writing two pamphlets to justify its creation.[86] Alan could thus hope to embarrass his rival, and, having spent two sessions as a lone spokesman for government in the matter of the appellate jurisdiction, could for once stand shoulder to shoulder with the 'patriots' in the Lords, whose leading spokesman, Archbishop King, was also the bitterest enemy of the bank.[87]

Whatever Alan's stance over the bank may have done to his political reputation in Ireland, it does seem to have signalled the fracture of the fragile relationship which had existed between himself and Grafton. Alan's letters to Thomas during the recess show an increasing impatience with what he perceived to be the viceroy's prevarications, and a growing suspicion that Grafton was resolved to do whatever he could to force through the scheme, irrespective of the views expressed by the majority in both houses of the Irish parliament. And Grafton, for his part, seems to have come to realise that Alan was simply too mercurial to be trusted. The viceroy was more at ease in the company of the Speaker, on whose loyalty he could rely. Already during the session, even though giving the lord chancellor 'visible favour and credit', Grafton was making himself dependent on the advice of a small group from whom the Brodricks were excluded, a 'secret council' said to comprise the chief secretary, Speaker, Lord Chief Justice Whitshed (who had now become another of Alan's mortal

[85] Walsh, *South Sea Bubble*, 154.
[86] Hayton, *Anglo-Irish Experience*, 114.
[87] Burns, *Politics*, i, 129–30.

enemies), Lords Fitzwilliam, Shannon, Shelburne and Tullamore, and Benjamin Parry, MP.[88] When the session was over, and Grafton returned to England, this situation was given formal recognition in the appointment of lords justices. The commission comprised Conolly, Shannon and, surprisingly, Archbishop King. Alan's name did not appear. Naturally, he did not take this well. Conolly, by contrast, with a characteristic show of modesty, accepted the honour with ostentatious reluctance.[89]

In the years that had passed since the elation of the whig triumph in 1714, the Brodricks had seen their leading position in Irish politics at first challenged and then subverted, by the rise of a rival with a greater 'interest' in the Irish house of commons who made himself indispensable to the government in Dublin Castle while they made themselves difficult. The party battles of Queen Anne's reign had given way to a duel between 'two great men', and the factions they were able to command. In contrast to Alan and Thomas, William Conolly had not attempted to cut a figure on the English political scene, but had concentrated on building up his political strength in Ireland. It was a sign of the changing context of Irish politics that this strategy seems to have been the more effective. For all the powerful friends the two brothers were cultivating at Westminster, in 1722 the advantage lay clearly with the Speaker.

[88] Levinge, *Jottings*, 65–8.
[89] BL, Add. MS 47029, f. 95: Charles Dering to Lord Perceval, 20 Feb. 1721/2.

Note on Editorial Principles

The bound volumes of Brodrick papers contain a variety of materials: letters to and from various correspondents belonging to or connected with the Brodrick family, together with assorted papers. In order to give some system to the selection of letters and to reduce as far as possible the element of subjectivity, we have chosen to print only the correspondence between Alan Brodrick I and his siblings and offspring: his brothers St John II, Thomas and William, his sons St John III and Alan II and his daughter Alice. There is one exception to this rule: sometimes, in order to evade the prying eyes of political and personal enemies, Alan I addressed letters to his wife's aunt Martha Courthope in England, who was clearly expected to pass them on to his brothers or his son. Such letters have therefore been included in the edition. We have also exercised a limited discretion in omitting material of an entirely domestic nature, including references to the management of property and the pursuance of cases at law, where these have no discernible relevance to the political and public lives of the principals. We have indicated such abridgments by ellipses.

In presenting the text, we have generally sought to preserve the original spelling and punctuation, including underlinings. We have silently modernised thorns, extended standard contractions (including ampersands), and lowered superior letters. (Contemporary material quoted in footnotes and in the introduction, has, however, been modernised throughout.) Words or short phrases repeated by the writer in error have also been deleted. A full point has been added at the end of each sentence where the writer has omitted to do this (usually when the sentence ends with a closing bracket). We have not reproduced subscriptions, superscriptions and signatures to the letters. Square brackets have been used to indicate editorial interpolations: doubtful readings are printed in roman type, editorial extensions in italics. Dates are given, in letter-headings and in footnotes, in the customary fashion, that is to say in Old Style (the Julian calendar) but with the year beginning not on 25 March but on 1 January (which was the case with New Style, under the Gregorian calendar). Where a letter is dated using both year-dates, as for example 1 Mar. 1712/13, this has been preserved; where the year-date given is only in Old Style, the New Style year-date has been added in square brackets.

Every effort has been made to identify persons who figure in the letters, but not always successfully, since the Brodricks often wrote allusively or elliptically, in the hope of mystifying those in the Irish post office (in particular the postmaster-general Isaac Manley) whom they suspected of attempting to intercept their correspondence. To prevent repetition in the footnotes, biographical information relating to family members and connections, and to members of the Irish parliament, has been gathered into appendices. On occasions where the letter-writer provides a full name, and the context makes it clear that the person concerned was an Irish MP or a member of the Irish house of lords, no footnote reference is given. Similarly, in order to conserve space, an individual mentioned by his or her full name in the text is fully identified in a footnote only on first appearance. An index to introductions and text will appear at the end of the third and last volume in the edition. Unless otherwise stated, basic biographical details (dates of birth and death, place of residence, offices held, constituencies represented) have been drawn from standard sources, such as the *Complete Peerage* and *Complete Baronetage*; the relevant volumes produced by the History of Parliament Trust; Edith Mary Johnston-Liik's *History of the Irish Parliament*; the *Dictionary of Irish Biography*; and the *Oxford Dictionary of National Biography*.

Correspondence 1714–1722

225. *Alan I, Dublin, to Thomas, 16 Oct. 1714*

(1248/3/193–4)

It would be a very great satisfaction to me to hear of your being recovered of that ill fit of the stone under which you laboured since my coming away as well as when I left London. I have the letter you wrote since we parted, and will very well weigh what you mention in relation to Senny's standing for the County of Corke: that (like other things) hath two handles, and the skill will be to take it by the right: he must not disoblige the City where he is secure, to stand for any other place where, after a greater expence, there may be some hazard; beside if he should decline standing att Corke it would occasion wonderful divisions in the City, and there would be five or six competitors, which would create partyes and factions in a town very unanimous att present, which may not be easily allayed again: but there is time enough to think more maturely and resolve more prudently in this important point then we can at present doe. I am sensible I ought to doe every thing in my power for the honour and ease of my Lord Lieutenants governement, and am as sensible that it is absolutely necessary to act with all caution, least the opposition which will certainly be given him here create him more uneasinesse then is apprehended. To write plainly and directly about matters that are not properly part of ones province is not advisable; on the other hand I am sensible it is necessary that such hints and informations be given my Lord, from which he may form a judgement and take proper resolutions. You may from time to time see him, and give such notices as occur to your own observation or which you receive from me; it will be an acceptable service to my Lord, it will convince him of the honor and regard you have for him and his administration, and will be a means of my transmitting my thoughts without having letters lye out, which may hereafter fall into other hands then those to whom they were designed: And that consideration alone would be sufficient to caution a prudent man in being too free in giving just accounts of things and characters of particular men: but hints by word will be sufficient, and not liable to those objections.

Upon these considerations I will venture to write that to you which I am not so willing to leave under my hand in any other mans power; not that I have the least apprehension of anything but the most honourable and candid treatment imaginable from my Lord, and the worthy man who is his Secretary;[1] but papers fall into Clerks hand, in whom the same confidence ought not to be reposed. I apprehend application will be made for leave to be

---

[1]Joseph Addison (1672–1719), of Sandy End, Fulham, Mdx., St Margaret's, Westminster, and Bilton Hall, Warws., MP [GB], chief sec. [I] 1714–15, lord of trade [GB] 1715–17, sec. of state [GB] 1717–18.

given to the top man of the other party to sell etc.[2] You will know whom I mean by calling him (as he really is) the cheif man of the party in the house of Commons: but when I tell you he is a very near relation to a freind of yours and mine now in London, you cannot possibly be to seek. I love one brother too well to doe the other an ill office; yet methinks if the sale be designed to enable him to give opposition with the better grace and without endangering anything, care should be taken in that particular: he came not in by purchase, soe hath not (what hath now obtained to be called) a right to sell; and a Governement would not willingly with eyes open putt a man into the condition he desires to be in to oppose it. How this matter is to be managed I leave to be considered on your side; but it seems to me to admit of no great difficultye. Before I left town I thought Mr Pennyfather had fixed himself in his employment;[3] I hope he hath given or will give my Lord the satisfaction of not lying under some influences which I cannot but say prevailed very far over him heretofore; and sure something of the kind will be expected. Mr Theophilus Butler[4] spoke to me in favor of his brother Brinsley Butler, who is now Captain of the Battleaxes;[5] he was made Lieutenant of them by the Duke of Ormond when they were raised,[6] and Captain by the Duke of Shrewsbury on the death of Colonel Harman.[7] You know how steddily and worthily his brother acted all along, and as he hath spoke to preserve his brother he hath assured me he will be very far from doing any that may deserve my Lords displeasure. I promised I would give an account of what he said, and do beleive his brother will make good what he hath undertaken on his behalf; and to say truth I think him a Whig in principle, but can say little as to his late behavior.[8] Probably there may be no design to remove him; if there be, sure care will be taken to put in a better and more unexceptionable man: and I confesse I think some allowance ought to be made at the intercession of a very deserving brother. These hints I give because I beleive they may be of service in a certain place, not to serve or prejudice any particular person. Our accounts now are that Justice Coote is to be removed;[9] and if what I hear be true, he seems to me to act as one who was certain of losing his Cushion[10] or resolved to provoke his being turned out: In short I am informed

---

[2] Probably Philip Savage (1644–1717), of Dublin, MP [I] 1692–1714; in his case the office to be sold would be the chancellorship of the exchequer [I], which he held 'during good behaviour'.

[3] Matthew Pennefather, MP [I].

[4] MP [I] 1703–14, cr. Baron Newtownbutler 1715.

[5] Brinsley Butler, MP [I].

[6] James Butler (1665–1745), 2nd duke of Ormond, lord lieutenant of Ireland when the Battle-axe Guards (the equivalent in Ireland of the English Yeomen of the Guard) had been raised in 1704 (HMC, *Ormonde MSS*, n.s., viii, 73, 74).

[7] Wentworth Harman (bef. 1655–1714), of Bawn, Moyle, Co. Longford, MP [I] 1695–9, 1703–13.

[8] Unlike his whig brother Theophilus, Brinsley Butler had voted with the tories in the Irish parliament in Queen Anne's reign, and more particularly had divided against Alan I in the contest over the Speakership in 1713. Archbishop King also sought to intercede on his behalf, telling the lord lieutenant that Butler's personal circumstances were pitiable (as a younger son and the father of eight or nine children), and his character unexceptionable: Butler had taken no part in parliamentary business in 1713 except to vote, as he was obliged to by virtue of his office (TCD, MS 750 (13), p. 11: King to Sunderland, 29 Oct. 1714). Nonetheless, Butler was dismissed from the Battle-axe Guards in Nov. 1714 (*Hist. Ir. Parl.* ii, 338–9).

[9] Thomas Coote (c.1663–1741), of Cootehill, Co. Cavan, 2nd justice of king's bench [I] since 1699. He was indeed dismissed, for his supposedly partisan conduct in the controversy over the Irish lord mayoralty in 1711–14 (Ball, *Judges*, ii, 60–2; *Hist. Ir. Parl.*, iii, 502–3; see *Anglo-Irish Politics, vol. 1*, 30–1).

[10] The seat of a judge or senior legal officer.

he uses all the interest in his power in two Countyes[11] to bring not only Toryes in, but men who have gone under a worse character.[12] If the interposition of his freinds on the other side of the water have been prevalent, may it not be reasonably expected that he act for the service and not in opposicion of etc. He made me a visit, and I returned it; the same to my Lord Cheif Baron Deane;[13] but he was very politickly silent, and never opened his mouth about publick affairs, or in enquiryes about my Lord Lieutenant etc. When you give these or any hints you may hereafter receive from me, gett them to be written down where you give them for fear of being forgotten. Sir Ri: Levinge[14] is either not come to town or I have not seen him yet: hath not he made application of some kind or other? Perhaps the D[*uke*] of Shrewsbury make think his behavior toward him may deserve some favor,[15] and I am sure he told me the last term his ambition was to be made a puisne Judge:[16] and I confesse I think he will doe lesse harm in such a Station then he may be capable of doing elsewhere: This is a nice subject to write upon: for I own that I am very unwilling to recommend any man to the Bench of whose behavior I have not at all times had very good thoughts. I shal write more letters of this kind if you will allow it, but then pray let the contents be timely communicated in the proper place … I will soon write something about the Upper house, and more about the house of Commons …

226. *Alan I, Dublin, to Thomas, 30 Oct. 1714*

(1248/3/195–6)

When you see the date of this, you will conclude that your letter of the fourteenth came late to my hand, as it did yesterday, when five pacquets came in together. The subject of it hath given me a good deal of thought: I consider the thing proposed by you, in the first place, as an eminent instance of the continuance of that goodnesse and favor which my Lord Lieutenant hath been pleased to shew toward me, and am sure I ought not to question but that he conceives it proper to have the thing done: The maner of your writing plainly lets me into your thoughts about it, and you go farther and say that all for whom men of our principles have the greatest esteem are unanimously of opinion I ought not to decline it.[17] I ever was and will be guided in what personally concerns me by my freinds, and since this is beleived to be of some use in publick affairs I doe entirely resign my self to be disposed of in what maner may be of most service to the publick. I consider that with a good deal of pains I have soe encreased the estate which came to me from my father, that there will be

---

[11] Counties Cavan and Monaghan. Coote regained his seat in the Irish house of commons at a by-election for Co. Monaghan in 1723.

[12] Reputed jacobites.

[13] Joseph Deane (1674–1715), of Castlemartyr, Co. Cork, MP [I] 1703–14, chief baron of the exchequer [I] 1714–15 (*Hist. Ir. Parl.*, iii, 36; Ball, *Judges*, ii, 190–1).

[14] Sir Richard Levinge (1656–1724), 1st Bt, of High Park, Mullalea, Co. Westmeath and Parwich, Derbys., MP [I] 1692–3, 1698–1714, and MP [E & GB] 1690–5, 1710–11, solicitor-general [I] 1690–5, 1704–9, Speaker, house of commons [I]1692–3, attorney-general [I] 1711–14. Appointed chief justice of common pleas [I] in 1720.

[15] Levinge had been the duke's recommended candidate in the Speakership election of 1713.

[16] An ordinary, or junior judge, as distinct from a chief justice (or, in the case of the exchequer, the chief baron).

[17] The offer of a peerage.

after my death an estate in my elder son capable of supporting the dignity of a Peer of this Kingdome handsomly and with reputation, and yet I shal be able to leave my younger son in possession of an estate after my death worth between fourteen and fifteen hundred pounds a year; not incumbred with one penny debt, or porcion; nor probably with a jointure. I consider how fond some people will be of using me in an other maner in the house of Lords when I am restrained from speaking or debating then they will otherwise;[18] and have fancied that my condition there in the chair would be like that which I have some where read; that the way of treating prisoners is to bind them naked and defencelesse to trees and sett on their children to kill them, and that the greater cruelty may be exercised upon them, every child is armed with a very blunt weapon without point or edge: But I think I have spirit enough to contemn such treatment, and should find freinds enough to support me in doing my duty, which shal ever be my aim. There is one reason which you urge for my going readily into what is proposed, that ought immediately to determine me: but in the first place I shal not be able to doe that service which I find it is thought I am capable of doing by way of debate; my talents and abilityes are thought better of then I am sensible they ought: in the next place I assure you, by making Dr Synge a Bishop there is a man of as sound an head, as honest an heart, and as good a maner of arguing putt into the house as this Kingdome affords:[19] and tho I know the wonderfull sufficiency, and learning of many English Bishops and their admirable way of discoursing, yet I confesse I think him as close as convincing a reasoner as any one of those bright, those excellent Prelates. But since it is thought I may be of serviceable this way I will not despair being soe: for I remember when I was of the house of Commons, we all thought the Peers were not as much above us in reasoning as in Station.

But I entreat you to consider, if this matter be thought advisable, whether considering the post his Majestye hath been pleased to put me in, and that I am not descended from a mean familye, whether it will not be so ordered that I may be the eldest of the new creation: for your letter imports that there will be other Peers created. It will be under my Lord Lieutenants consideracion I beleive on what Bench in the house they will be placed; if on that of the Viscounts it is the highest that I think should be: I am unwilling to give occasion of resentment or envy. And now brother having spoken to you with all this freedome I must tell you I have a good deal to object to what I have already given up: but your telling me what is thought proper by them to whose judgement and commands I must alway defer, I chuse to delay telling you what my difficultyes are till I write to you next. But one I ought not to delay mentioning: what reason have I to carry a title while you are living and have none? But neither Station nor any other accession can ever make me other then …

227. *Alan I, Dublin, to Thomas, 1 Nov. 1714*

(1248/3/197–8)

I have your last letter which by mistake you date on the 27th instead of the 26th of October, and one from Mr Addison which I desire you to acknowledge to him when

---

[18] As lord chancellor, Alan would be *ex officio* Speaker of the upper House.
[19] Edward Synge, consecrated bishop of Raphoe in Nov. 1714.

you see him: for I have not time to answer it before the boat goes off this night about ten. I have said soe much in my last to Mr Addison in relation to Captain Butlers affair, that I will add little; only speak my thoughts plainly, that if Sir Ch. Feilding had been removed to make way for Colonel Southwell (which I apprehend was Southwells original view, and in effect he said as much while I was in London) a man had lost an employment which he hath long enjoyed, and made a good fortune out of, that would not have been pityed by any body that I know:[20] I am well satisfyed no one man would have been disobliged who is not as heartily an an enemy already as he can be: but the case is otherwise with Mr Butler, he hath a good many hearty freinds among us, and a brother who hath deserved very well, and takes it extremely to heart; not to mention a very compassionate circumstance in his unfortunate case, his having no fewer then nine children.

As soon as I received yours, I went to his brother and shewed that part of it which relates to the Battleaxes; this I did because it must convince him that I had been sincere in my interposition to preserve his brother, that you had acted a freindly part; but my cheif motive was that it let him plainly see my Lord Lieutenants goodnesse and gave him just reason to conclude, if the thing had not been out of my Lords power and the order past, he had not lost his employ. I then advised him to consider with his brother what to propose for him and took on me to say my Lord Lieutenant had too much goodnesse in his nature not to goe into any reasonable thing. Mr Theo[*philus*] Butlers behavior in this whole affair hath been soe gentlemanlike that it must make a great impression in favor of his brother, if it were as well represented by me as it appeared handsome in him. I am sure since you tell me you are directed to give him this encouragement, he cannot fail to succeed in any modest request, and I will not transmit any that I doe not apprehend to be such. Pray let me know who named Mr Butler as a person to be turned; we say here somebody had no hand in it, and I own I think if it was on a publick account, it was ill judged. My meaning is that it will not contribute any way to make affairs easier; several who will be in the house of commons I am sensible are concerned at it; but I cannot be positive that as many would have been uneasy if he had kept his employment. Since you know of the offer to be made Sir R[*ichard*] L[*evinge*] I can tell you that it passed through the hands of a freind of yours, but the result is too long to tell you: he is (as ever) tricking. They tell me my Lord Cheif Justice Parker passes his word for him:[21] he ought to know him better then I doe when he undertakes that task; or perhaps I should say not so well. But can his Lordship create a confidence of him in other freinds, or carry on businesse with him without one? I will on Tuesday write at large to my Lord Lieutenant: you cannot imagine the difficultyes we lye under by Mr

[20]Sir Charles Feilding (1644–1722), of Dublin, MP [I] 1692–9, was master of the Royal Hospital at Kilmainham until removed in 1715 (*Hist. Ir. Parl.*, iv, 134–5). William Southwell, MP [I] was made captain of the Battle-axe Guards in Nov. 1714.

[21]Sir Thomas Parker (1667–1732), of Derby, a judge of king's bench [GB] and one of the lords justices appointed to take charge of the government of Great Britain on the death of Queen Anne. Parker recommended Levinge to Sunderland on 10 May 1715, but a week later conceded that if he could not persuade Sunderland he would 'give … up' Levinge and instead support the appointment of an English whig lawyer, Jeffray Gilbert (1674–1726) (BL, Add. MS 61639, ff. 151, 159, Parker to [Sunderland], 10, 17 May 1715; *Oxf. DNB*). Parker was raised to the woolsack as lord chancellor [GB] in 1718. The Derbyshire connection may account for his favour to Levinge.

Whitsheds not being yet landed:[22] I deferred meeting other Gentlemen in expectation of his arrival and being of the number: but resolve to have a meeting to morrow. Justice Coote is to be out; suppose he should refuse to goe to Court the first day of term, and the wind not just serve to bring Whitshed and MacCartney[23] from Holyhead in a day or two after their arrival there, what confusion would this create? I speak of a day or two, because they were not att the Head last night, and our full term or time of sitting is on next Saturday. In the mean time intreat my Lord not to resolve of mentioning the time of issuing writs for a Parliament till I write by next post; I goe farther to tell you that Mr Gore[24] pretends want of strength of constitution to undertake the chair; soe that till our meeting tomorrow I cannot say what is advisable to be done in that case. I cannot but with regret repeat that the Cheif Judges staying in London hath putt things under much confusion. Particularly it will be very mischeivous in the pricking of Sherifs,[25] If Whitshed and MacCartney be not here on Wednesday morning. My humble duty to my Lord Lieutenant: my thoughts are he should be on the spot before the writs issue. Pray tell me what Irish Gentlemen interposed soe warmly to make Sir John St Leger a Judge.[26] I doe not find Lord M[27] hath done any thing yet about the Countyes of Tyrone and Cavan: his own brother, Justice Coote (who is marryed to his Aunt)[28] and Lord Abercorne are very busy in those Countyes, and unless my Lord doe in time bestir himself may do mischeif. Sure he does not lye by till the Ordinance is disposed of.

228. *Alan I, Dublin, to Thomas, 4 Nov. 1714*

(1248/3/199–200)

By the petulancy of some men, whose unreasonable expectations are not gratifyed, and the perversenesse of others, I foresee my Lord Lieutenant will meet difficultyes in his Governement; but that is no more then every prudent man must expect: However it is the businesse of every person who is in the service of the Crown or pretends to be my Lord Lieutenants freind to doe all in their power to prevent or remove any dissatisfaction as far as possible; and to weaken the hands of those who design to be troublesome. When I left London

[22] William Whitshed (1679–1727), of Dublin and Killincarrig, Co. Wicklow, MP [I] 1703–14, solicitor-general [I] 1710–11; appointed chief justice of king's bench [I] and a privy councillor [I] in 1714 (*Hist. Ir. Parl.*, vi, 538–40; Ball, *Judges*, ii, 103–5).
[23] James Macartney (c.1651–1727), of Belfast, Co. Antrim, MP [I]1692–9, judge of king's bench [I] 1701–11; reappointed to king's bench in Oct. 1714 and transferred to common pleas [I] in Dec. (*Hist. Ir. Parl.*, v, 156–8; Ball, *Judges*, ii, 65).
[24] George Gore, MP [I]. He had been Alan's preferred candidate for the Commons Speakership before crying off (BL, Add. MS 61636, f. 114: Alan I to [Sunderland], Oct. 1714).
[25] In response to a request from Alan concerning the shrievalty of Co. Cork, Archbishop King had written in September that he was uncertain how far Sunderland would leave the choice to the lords justices (TCD, MS 2536, p. 72: King to Alan I, 23 Sept. 1714). On 21 Nov. 1714 King reported to Sunderland, 'All the sheriffs are now settled. We have fixed I think on honest gentlemen … and we hope for a fair and equal election' (BL, Add. MS 61635, f. 147).
[26] Sir John St Leger (1674–1743), of Capel St., Dublin and Grangemellon, Co. Kildare, MP [I] 1713–14; appointed a baron of exchequer [I] in 1714 (Ball, *Judges*, ii, 192–3).
[27] Charles Coote (c.1680–1715), 4th earl of Mountrath.
[28] Thomas Coote's second wife Elinor, or Eleanor (née St George), was his distant cousin.

I apprehended there was no intent or thought of removing more then six of the Judges: The three cheif Judges had taken effectual care to make it impracticable that they should be continued by disobeying the commands of the Lords Justices of Great Britain; Mr Nuttley[29] had dispossessed Mr MacCartney formerly and could not reasonably expect not to see him on the same Cushion again: these removes were made before I left London, and I find Sir John St Leger is to be putt on one of the Benches here, tho I know not which; and it is also discoursed that one Mr Gilbert[30] is to be a Judge here. If these two Gentlemen succeed those whom the town names to be removed, I mean Justice Coote and Justice Upton[31] I will not say but that if I had been consulted, which two of the Judges should have been superseded, that I could not have found out any where in my opinion that misfortune could have fallen better. But sure it is time to think of stopping, unlesse it be resolved to remove all the Judges, which I suppose is not intended; nor doe I think it politick or advisable; and if that be intended to make room for men who are perfectly strangers to the constitution and people of the countrey, it will create uneasinesse. If to answer any particular scheme, one person must be removed I should humbly offer it as my sense that for more reasons then one the two puisne Barons might be continued: Lord Kildare was extremely uneasy att receiving my Lord Lieutenants letter for constituting Lord Thomond Lord Lieutenant of the County of Clare in the stead of his father in Law the Earle of Insiquin and I beleive will leave the warrant for making out a fiant for that place to be signed by the other two Justices. This place is honourary only, and I told my Lord Kildare that I apprehended that County had usually been governed by Lord Thomonds ancestors and that my Lord Insiquin (being related to Lord Thomond)[32] had been only made Lord Lieutenant of Clare in the minority of the now Earle of Thomond: His Lordship assured me the contrary, that the family of Insiquin had been generally Lords Lieutenants of that County: how that matter is I have not yet had time to inform myself: but if what I hear be true that a certain person is solliciting for Lord Insiquins Governement of the fort of Kinsale, and should succeed; nothing can be thought of, soe disobliging to my Lord Kildare; for beside the relation between Lord Kildare and Lord Insiquin there is a strict tye of freindship between them and Lord Mountcashel; who generally go together in the house of Lords.[33] Beside, the unfortunate scituation of Lord Insiquins affair make that Governement necessary for his support, and that of an un-married fine young Lady, and three sons grown almost to mens estate. And truly it seems to me to be worth consideration what the merit or interest is of the person who pretends to it: If the man mentioned to me be the person, he is and alway hath been very honest and hearty, and hath been very ill treated: but a little discretion would have secured him from a good deal of the usage he hath mett with: and in obliging or disobling him you oblige or disoblige a man of very little interest; I think I may almost venture to say one man. May it

---

[29] Richard Nutley (1673–1729), of Dublin, MP [I] 1703–11, judge of queen's bench [I] 1711–14.

[30] Jeffray Gilbert had been promoted to chief baron of the Irish exchequer in July 1715.

[31] The English tory lawyer Anthony Upton (1656–1718), judge of common pleas [I] until 1714 (Ball, *Judges*, ii, 66–7).

[32] The Thomond and Inchiquin titles, both held by the O'Brien family from Co. Clare, had been separated in 1551 on the death of Murrough O'Brien, 1st earl of Thomond and 1st baron Inchiquin: Murrough's son inherited the barony while the earldom passed by a special remainder to a nephew, the son of Murrough's elder brother.

[33] Kildare was duly gratified by Sunderland's 'kindness' to Inchiquin (TCD, MS 750 (13), p. 16: Archbishop King to Sunderland, 27 Nov. 1714).

not be worth considering whether my Lord Lieutenant ought not to keep some things in his power and disposal when he lands, and not part with every thing before. We all know of what consequence it is to have it in ones power to gratifye such as may deserve it; and expectations of being considered according to their merit and behavior will putt many on doing all in their power to deserve the favor of the Governement, nay more will expect and hope and endeavour to deserve favor then can be provided for. I make no doubt but that his Excellencye will bring over with him a new establishment. He will on looking over the present establishment find the Earle of Granard and his sister the Countesse of Donegal on the establishment each of them for £500 a year as I remember.[34] My Lords unfortunate circumstances are such, that tho I am sorry his Lordships sentiments have been hitherto otherwise then I could wish, yet I should be troubled to have his Majestyes bounty to him struck off. Lady Donegall hath a very good jointure, and there is a great estate in the family: yet her Lords being killed in the service att Barcelona seems a reason for continuing her Ladyship also on the establishment. But may it not be reasonably expected that the interest of his Lordship in the boroughs of Mulingar and St Johnstowne,[35] and of Lady Donegal att Belfast and Carickfergus will not be made use of to send up members whose businesse it will be to distresse the Governement and obstruct the Kings affairs in Parliament. I doe not say, that either of the interests will be soe used: but if those pensions instead of being put actually on the establishment were left a little to be considered till my Lord Lieutenant landed, I cannot see but it would have a good effect. Lord Monjoy is nearly related to both,[36] and hath great intimacy with the Lady, and probably will act the part of a freind in getting both continued on the establishment: may not my Lord Lieutenant in confidence tell his Lordship that the Kings favor intitles him to a better return, then chusing members perfectly disaffected to the present ministry. I formerly wrote my mind that tho it might be hard on Lord Montjoyes brother[37] to deny him liberty to sell,[38] yet if he sought it only to be the more free to obstruct all publick affairs and to be warm and zealous at the head of a party in Parliament, that I did not see any cause for enabling him to do mischeif. Why may not he be asked whether he designs to serve in Parliament or not: he never will be with my Lord Lieutenant, and is the most considerable man of the adverse party. When you mention these things, which I intend only for the service of the publick you will tell his Excellencye that it is my humble request that he make such use of these hints as he seeth proper without bringing your name or mine in question: for the persons concerned are of resenting tempers and will in the warmest maner expresse their dissatisfaction against any body that thwarts their interests or designs. Mr Addison is a most honest and prudent man, to whom I give you free liberty to communicate this or any thing I shal hereafter write touching our Irish affairs. Tho Lady Burlington was very well disposed in recommending to her

---

[34] Lord Granard's pension of £500 p.a. on the Irish civil list dated from Apr. 1703; Catherine (née Forbes) (d.1743), dowager countess of Donegall, had been awarded her pension in Nov. 1708, in recognition of her late husband's military services in Spain (CTB, xviii, 226; xxii, 440).

[35] St Johnstown (otherwise known as Ballinalee), Co. Longford.

[36] Mountjoy's grandmother, Catherine (née Newcomen), had married, as her second husband, the 1st earl of Granard: the 2nd earl of Granard and Lady Donegall were half-brother and half-sister to Mountjoy's father.

[37] Hon. Richard Stewart, MP [I].

[38] His army commission.

boroughs,[39] yet she had not finally determined in some of them. It is high time she should finally conclude. Sir Arthur Shaen and General Meredyth at Lismore[40] and Mr Maynard[41] for one at Tallough[42] are extreme well: she hath absolute power to bring another in that borough. I wish she may recommend Mr Luther and Mr Hyde to Youghal.[43] My services to my Lord Lieutenant, and to my freinds att Whitehall and Bond Street. Pray let her be pressed to name whom she intends every where and let me know the names; and what can be done at Mulingar, St Johntown, Belfast and Caricfergus. Mr Whitshed is not yet landed.

I acquainted Col. Theoph[*ilus*] Butler what you wrote in relation to the providing for his brother in lieu of the battleaxes: he received it very well, told me he could not propose to have any one displaced to make room for his brother, soe could pitch on nothing; but desired you would lay before my Lord Lieutenant his humble request, that the first thing which fell, that was worth acceptance as an equivalent might be given him. Pray stir in it, and since I have on your letter assured him successe gett Mr Addison to enable me to keep my word, or rather yours and my Lords.

229. Alan I, Dublin, to Thomas, 16 Nov. 1714

(1248/3/201–2)

In a former letter I desired you to find out Mr Edwin[44] and inform him I had obeyed his commands and I hope did it effectually; the particulars I had not then time to mention, but will doe it in some measure now. Know then that I find by letters from Corke that as Mr Edwin wrote to me and I wrote to Mr Brown the Mayor[45] to manage for me; Mr Milner[46] had also wrote to Alderman Hoare[47] on the same errand, and he acted very heartily in the businesse: but not soe ingenuously in one respect, for Ned Brown having applyed to and been promised letters from Jo Pike[48] and others, Hoare called for them next morning and

---

[39]Juliana, dowager countess of Cork and Burlington, had been managing the electoral interest of her young son Richard (1694–1753), who had succeeded to the earldom as a minor (Rachel Wilson, *Elite Women in Ascendancy Ireland, 1690–1745: Imitation and Innovation* (Woodbridge, 2015), 136–9).

[40]Thomas Meredyth, MP [I].

[41]Samuel Maynard, MP [I].

[42]Tallow, Co. Waterford.

[43]Henry Luther (1667–1714) of Ballyboy, King's Co., MP Youghal 1703–*d.*; Arthur Hyde, MP [I]. After Luther's death the Burlington interest was given to Hyde and Francis Palmes, MP [I], who were duly returned (NLI, MS 13254/4: Anthony Spurret to Foulke and Joseph Walker, 24 Sept. 1715).

[44]Samuel Edwin (1671–1722) of Llanmihangel Plas, Glamorgan, a defeated whig candidate at Minehead in the British general election of 1715, and briefly MP for that borough in 1717 (*HC 1715–54*, i, 316).

[45]Edward Brown (*d.* c.1724), mayor of Cork (Phillimore, *Indexes*, ii, 14).

[46]James Milner (aft.1658–1721), of Weston Green, Thames Ditton, Surrey; a defeated whig candidate at Minehead in 1713, and again in 1715 when he partnered Edwin. Served as MP for that borough 1717–*d.* (*HC 1690–1715*, ii, 524–5; *HC 1715–54*, ii, 259).

[47]Edward Hoare, MP [I].

[48]Joseph Pike (1657–1729), a merchant in Cork, and a prominent member of the quaker community in the city (R.S. Harrison, *A Biographical Dictionary of Irish Quakers* (Dublin, 1997), 80–1). A quaker, Joseph Alloway, overseer of the poor, had played an important role on the tory side in the 1713 election in Minehead (*HC 1690–1715*, ii, 525).

sent them away as part of the fruit of his industry: but since the work is done (which is what I have in view) let him please himself with making merit of it. But beside these letters some of which went by shipping and some by post Mr Brown sent by the post which left Corke the 7th instant two letters to Mr Blake[49] one from Mr Hare[50] and one from Mr Kirkpatrick.[51] he also sent two letters from Mr Boyle[52] one to Mark Goddard[53] the other to Nathaniel Wroxal of Bristol,[54] who have good interest in Minehead. Mr Devonshire[55] a very honest knowing man assures me my freinds will assuredly carry it, as he hath the account from very good hands in Minehead: and Mr Kirkpatrick and Mr Hare assure Mr Brown all their freinds (who I suppose are dissenters) are intirely in Mr Edwins and Mr Milners interest. So much for that matter. I have this pacquett a letter from Mr Pocklington[56] and another from Sir John St Leger acquainting me of their being Barons of the Exchequer and intending to come over before next term: since Sir John is made a Judge, he should give assurances to use his interest (if he has any) with Lord Donerayle for that borough;[57] and pray feel his pulse as to buying my Judges robes which are very good. My recommendations for the preservation of people have been hitherto very unsuccessful: your last letter and two which this mail brought, one from Sir John St Leger the other from Mr Pocklington convince me, the two puisne Barons (for whom I interposed) are out: a former letter from Mr Addison and two from you convince me that Brin[sley] Butler hath had no better fortune or successe from my endeavours to serve his brother by preserving him. By my receiving no letter either from Lord Lieutenant or Mr Addison in reference to Lord Insiquins governement of Kinsale and that of Charlemont[58] I give up them also as condemned: I wish those who push and advise things to be carryed so far (particularly in the house of Peers) may be able to answer for

---

[49] Henry Blaake (c.1659–1731), of Bristol, MP [GB] 1695–1702; steward of the sheriff's court in Bristol, and later town clerk (*HC 1690–1715*, iii, 220–1).

[50] John Hare (*d*.1732), a merchant in Cork (*The Letterbook of Richard Hare Merchant of Cork 1771–1772*, ed. James O'Shea (Dublin, 2013), pp. xiv, 253).

[51] William Kirkpatrick (*d*. c.1742), merchant, of Cork (Reg. Deeds, 10/77/3099, 90/78/62958; Vicars, *Index*, 271).

[52] Probably Henry Boyle, MP [I].

[53] Mark Goddard, haberdasher, merchant and shipowner of Bristol, who had been accused of organising attacks on tory voters in the Bristol parliamentary election of 1713 (Jonathan Barry, 'The Society for the Reformation of Manners, 1700–5', in *Reform and Revival in Eighteenth-century Bristol*, ed. Jonathan Barry and Kenneth Morgan (Bristol Rec. Soc., xlv, 1994), 59).

[54] Nathaniel Wraxall (1687–1731), of Mays Hill, Gloucs., a merchant of Bristol (*Debrett's Baronetage of England* (6th edn, 2 vols, 1828), ii, 667).

[55] Jonas Devonsh(i)er (*d*. c.1756), a Cork merchant and probably a quaker (Vicars, *Index*, 132; *Hist. Ir. Parl.*, 53–4; Reg. Deeds, 33/510/21079).

[56] John Pocklington (c.1658–1731), MP [GB] 1695–8, 1705–13, appointed baron of the exchequer [I] in 1715 (*HC 1690–1715*, v,163–5; Ball, *Judges*, ii, 192).

[57] Doneraile, Co. Cork, for which Sir John had been elected, on his half-brother Lord Donereaile's interest, in 1713.

[58] Charlemont had appealed to Alan for help in retaining the governorship of the fort of Charlemont, in Co. Armagh, near to his principal seat and thus crucial to the maintenance of his position in the locality. In response, Alan had assured Lord Sunderland that, although a tory, Charlemont was not one of the hotter sort, and might be kept in line by retention in his post (BL, Add. MS 61636, f. 114: Alan I to [Sunderland], Oct. 1714). Alan inquired about Inchiquin and Charlemont in a letter to Chief Secretary Addison, dated 16 Nov., stating that he was not personally obliged to either but feared the consequences of certain persons persuading the viceroy into making unnecessary dismissals which would imperil the government's position in the Irish house of lords (BL, Add. MS 61636, ff. 119–20).

the consequences there. When you have given this hint leave it to their conduct who give such warm advice; one of the Lords is in great want, the other really hath that which seems to me to create a very good pretension to his Governement, unlesse he hath been greatly faulty. Soe that I think I must give off all hopes of supporting those who are in danger of tumbling, and give an helping hand to putt in an honest Gentleman in the Collection of the Port of Dublin: Mr Sandford[59] is the Gentleman I heartily wish in that employ if the present possessor be removed; which he never will be, if he hath the tenth part of the interest with the present ministry which he had with the last,[60] and indeed I think he very well deserved their favor and countenance for no man was ever more attached to a party, or more avowedly justifyed all their actions then he alway did.

The Archbishop,[61] Lord Kildare, Lord Cheif Justice Forster[62] and othe[rs] write this post in Mr Sandfords favor,[63] pray let me cast in my mite, and give him such assistance as I am able. Perhaps a word to Sir Wm St Quintin[64] would be of use, and I confesse I am sollicitous not to have this Gentleman disappointed for his own sake and because Lord Kildare (whose sister he is marryed to) espouses his interests with warmth.[65] Tell this to Lord Lieutenant. The inclosed paper you may shew to Mr Addison and will be able by comparing the columns and seeing the names to tell him what his thoughts of the men should be: I will give you liberty to suppose the third column to contain doubtful persons: for I hardly know which way men will goe whose principles are very violently one way, and of whom you have no other hold then a small pension: this I say as to some of them.[66] There is one indeed of whom I doubt because he is uncertain in his conduct and judgement of things. Another of them is I know related to Lord Lieutenant and owes him a good deal: I mean the last.[67] I wish all that may keep or rather bring him right. I putt your collegue in the second column nottwithstanding his having a regiment and your good thoughts of him.[68] As to those in the first column I judge of them from what they have been and are

[59] Henry Sandford, MP [I].

[60] The previous incumbent was Martin Tucker (*d.* c.1719) of Dublin (Vicars, *Index*, 462), one of the tory candidates in the notoriously partisan parliamentary election for Dublin city in 1713. Instead Sunderland recommended Sandford to succeed another strong tory, Charles Melville (or Melvyn) (b. c.1671), MP [I], 1692–1714, as collector of excise in Dublin. The Irish revenue commissioners replied in Jan. 1715 that they would concur with this recommendation if pressed, though the collection was, in their view, too important to be given to someone like Sandford, who, however worthy personally, had not been 'bred up in the revenue' (NLI, MS 16007, pp. 6–7: revenue commrs to Sunderland, 13 Jan. 1714[/15]).

[61] King of Dublin.

[62] John Forster (1668–1720) of Dublin, MP [I] 1703–14; appointed chief justice of common pleas [I] in 1714.

[63] Sandford was married to Lord Kildare's sister.

[64] Sir William St Quintin (c.1662–1723), 3rd Bt, of Harpham, Yorks, MP [GB] 1695–*d.*; formerly a revenue commr [I] and now a lord of the treasury [GB].

[65] Kildare was Sandford's most prominent supporter (NLI, MS 16007, pp 26–7: revenue commrs [I] to treasury commrs [GB], 16 Sept. 1717).

[66] This document has not survived, though it may have formed one source for the several analyses of membership of the Irish house of lords in 1713–15 prepared for Lord Sunderland, which are to be found in the Blenheim papers in the British Library (see Hayton, 'Party and Management in the Irish House of Lords 1713–1715', 106, 109–11, 119–25).

[67] The 1st Viscount Mountcashell: Sunderland's sister, Lady Elizabeth, was Mountcashell's aunt by marriage.

[68] The 4th earl of Barrymore, who had been elected to the British house of commons for Stockbridge alongside Thomas, in a by-election in 1714.

in principle; but perhaps some of them may be disobliged and be absent. I have wrote my self blind. Good night.

230. *Alan I, Dublin to Thomas, 28 Nov, 1714*

(1248/3/203–4)

Inclosed I send you the Copy of the oath of a Privy Councellor here, attested by me as Chancellor to be a true Copy; which will be sufficient for one of the Barons of the Exchequer to administer the oath to you as a Privy Councellor; which I would have you forthwith take and transmit hither to intitle you as a Privy Councellor to your wine warrant.[69] I doe not know whether there will come over any orders from the Lords of the Treasury in England to the Commissioners of the revenue here for continuing or removing Collectors, Surveyors, or other Officers of the revenue but this I have good ground to beleive that Mr Steele Collector of Kinsale,[70] and Mr Badham Collector of Youghal[71] are gone over to secure themselves; I know not by whose means the former hopes to make his peace, but the later gives out he will stand his ground in spite of all his enemyes by the countenance of Lord Orrery[72] and Lord Hallyfax:[73] I know not what their successe will be, or how they will gett themselves represented to the great men on your side the water; but of this I am certain, that their behavior hath been such in the County of Corke on grand Juryes, and other publick occasions, that of my own knowledge I resolve to strike them out of the Commission of peace as men who shewed such affection to the late vile proceedings that in my opinion they cannot be very well affected to the present administration. Badham was one of Sir Con[*stantine*]s great undertakers in our countrey, and both thought it the greatest sedition to expresse any fears of the Protestant succession being in any sort of danger in the late reign. They and Walker the Collector of Mallow[74] were constant Grand Jurors att the Assises of Corke when any dirty work was to be sett on foot or good to be prevented. Steele was one who signed the address at Bandon Sessions last January, against the proceedings of the house of Commons, in which they magnify Phips; and tell the Queen they are against her Majestyes being uneasy in possession of the Crown by the

---

[69]By the terms of an Irish statute of 1569 (11 Eliz. I, sess. 4, c. 1), privy councillors were allowed to import wine free of customs duty. By the 18th century this privilege had been converted into a standard annual cash payment (BL, Add. MS 46972, f. 88: Berkeley Taylor to Lord Perceval, 25 Aug. 1721; f. 93: Perceval to Taylor, 5 Oct. 1721).

[70]John Steele. He was replaced in due course by John Elsmere (TNA, CUST 20/83: revenue establishment 1716).

[71]Brettridge Badham (c.1678–1744), of Ballyheen, Co. Cork, MP [I] 1713–14, 1743–*d*., collector of customs and excise for Youghal and Dungarvan. He secured Sunderland's recommendation to be continued in office, which the Irish revenue commissioners accepted with a bad grace (NLI, MS 16007, p. 8: revenue commrs to Sunderland, 13 Jan. 1714[/15]).

[72]Charles Boyle (1674–1731), 4th earl of Orrery. Badham acted as agent for the absentee Orrery's Cork estates and had already been recommended by Orrery for promotion in the revenue in 1712 (Toby Barnard, *A New Anatomy of Ireland: The Irish Protestants, 1649–1770* (New Haven, CT, 2003), 165–6, 218).

[73]Charles Montagu (1661–1715), 1st earl of Halifax, 1st lord of the treasury [GB].

[74]Joseph Walker. He was replaced by Richard Southwell (TNA, CUST 20/83: revenue establishment, 1716).

Popish or any other Pretender;[75] they are on the Spot and can explain whom they meant by the later words. Badham seldome spends two dayes in a month att his collection, and is as violent a Tory as lives on earth: but if Sir Con[*stantine*] or his freinds have any interest he will continue. For Gods sake speak to Sir W[*illia*]m St Quintin, and Southwell[76] and if possible, either by yourself or some other person to Lord Hallyfax: I am sure if it were known how great a support to the Tory interest in our Countrey it will be to have these men continued, or how violent they are in their inclinations against the present ministry, not to go farther, they will not be continued: and I cannot but beleive Mr Addison, nay my Lord Lieutenant will take a time to speak to Lord Hallyfax on this subject: on my word it deserves it. Doe not lay this letter by but doe something in it out of hand for fear of coming too late. If being personally an enemy to our family would have any weight with either of us, Badham hath without provocation expressed as much malice to it as any one man that breathes upon earth. Nothing would more please me then to have these two insolent Toryes humbled. Pray let me know how the election is like to goe att Haslemere,[77] and generally in England. I can not write to my sister or Ally; indeed my time is so taken up that I have only Sundayes to write upon: if those who have gone before me had not a better way of dispatching businesse, or were not lesse sollicitous how it was done then I am, their time had full emploiment. I wish I could hear what Lady Burlingtons final result is as to her boroughs. Tell General Meredyth[78] he is a little remisse in the matter of the County of Meath by which not only his but his Colleagues interests may suffer; I fear he depends so much on Lismore as to be regardlesse of the other, which is not right: but certainly nothing can be more wrong then not to lett Mr Preston[79] know he is not very sollicitous in the thing, if that be the truth, that he may take care of him self ...

231. *Alan I, Dublin, to Thomas, 14 Dec. 1714*

(1248/3/205–6)

You will more readily excuse my taking soe much time to answer your letter of the sixteenth of November when you have considered the importance and difficultye of the subject upon which that letter was written, and that it was necessary to converse with other men and find what their sentiments would be before I could give you such an answer as would in any measure satisfye you. Some time since I desired Mr Addison in a postscript to a letter to tell me in confidence whether a great man in England did not endeavour to embarasse affairs etc[80] to which he gave me a full answer by writing nothing one way or other. Before

[75] See *Anglo-Irish Politics, Vol. 1*, 306–8. The exact wording of the address was: 'we hope that neither Popery nor schism can prevail with any of your Majestyes subjects to abett or assist any Pretender to the Crown and Kingdomes'.

[76] Sir Thomas Southwell, MP [I], a revenue commr [I].

[77] Eventually, on 1 Feb. 1715, after a scrutiny, two whig candidates, Sir Nicholas Carew, 1st Bt, and Sir Montague Blundell, 4th Bt, scored a notable victory over the tories John Walter and George Vernon (*HC 1715–54*, i, 329).

[78] Thomas Meredyth, MP [I].

[79] John Preston, MP [I], re-elected for Co. Meath in 1715.

[80] A subsequent reference in the letter would suggest that Alan is alluding to the former lord lieutenant Thomas Wharton (1648–1715), 1st earl (and later 1st marquess) of Wharton.

I left London I foresaw that in all probabilitye something of that kind would be attempted, and soon after landing here found that there was a settled correspondence; Mr Harrison the banker[81] is att the head of the malecontents, and fancies they will make a formidable body; young Mr Allen[82] and I beleive all that family and their freinds are of the party: the pretence is that there are undertakers for a Land tax, an augmentation of forces, and indeed for every thing: You know how invidious a term that is, and that nothing is soe likely to disappoint a reasonable thing as possessing men with an opinion that it is stipulated for. Whether Mr Harrison be sowre because he could not gett Feildings Lodge,[83] or on another score (which I will not name it is so very foolish) I will not take on me to say: but this I am sure of, that he takes great delight in giving himself airs of a man att the head of a discontented people under the name of freinds to their countrey. Mr Allen[84] I beleive would have Lord Sunderland think he and his sons are as considerable, and deserving, as Mr Molesworth[85] and his sons,[86] to be taken notice of; and this I take to be the true meaning of his setting up against Molesworth in the County of Dublin. No man hath fewer freinds in it then Colonel Allen,[87] yet such hath been his industry, and soe remisse hath Mr Molesworth been that a man would fancy he were in combination to have himself thrown out, as he certainly will: and indeed no man can blame Gentlemen for saying they will not reserve votes for those who think it below them to desire them. Yet it is said here that Mr Molesworth apprehends that his declaring he will serve if chosen is all that he hath thought fit to doe as yet; and indeed if there were not one other honest man who would serve, he might reasonably hope to be chosen, but I think not otherwise. When Colonel Allen is chosen for the County of Dublin, his son Robin for the County of Wicklow,[88] his son Josuah for the County of Kildare, his son Dick for MacReddin[89] and his namesake Frank Allen for some other borough,[90] he will perswade himself (or to say more truly his son Jos. will perswade him) that he is very considerable, and worth seeking to: This I think is the view of that family, who in conjunction with the Banker will oppose the undertakers as they are called: I must add that Mr Harrison vaunts himself not a little on having Lord W[*harton*]s interest in Carlow and Dublin att his disposal: But I am sure you join with me in opinion that any opposition from this quarter will be insignificant if it shal be attempted: as you also will in thinking any thing of this kind is no farther to be communicated then by such hints as may putt Lord Lieutenant on his guard and apprise him from what quarter discontents

[81] Francis Harrison, MP [I].

[82] Joshua Allen, MP [I].

[83] The mastership of the Royal Hospital at Kilmainham (see above, p. 28).

[84] John Allen (see below, Appendix 3 (Viscount Allen)).

[85] Robert Molesworth (see below, Appendix 3 (Viscount Molesworth)).

[86] John, 2nd Viscount Molesworth (1679–1726), formerly a commissioner of the stamp office [E] and envoy to Tuscany, would in due course succeed his father as a lord of trade [GB] in Jan. 1716; Richard Molesworth, MP [I] and later 3rd viscount, was made lieutenant of the ordnance [I] in 1714; and William, MP [I], was appointed surveyor-gen. [I], also in 1714.

[87] John Allen.

[88] Robert Allen, MP [I].

[89] Richard Allen, MP [I] was elected for Athy in 1715, not the borough of Carysfort, Co. Wicklow, the alternative name of which was Macreddin.

[90] Francis Allen (bef.1682–1741), of St Wolstans, Co. Kildare, son of Patrick Allen of St Wolstans, was a former catholic who had conformed to the established church in 1709. He was not elected to the Irish parliament until 1725 (*Hist. Ir. Parl.*, iii, 82–3).

arise. I would not have wrote soe largely upon this matter, but to introduce that which I mean for the subject of my letter viz. the danger of being an undertaker. I agree entirely with you in what passed between Mr Molesworth and you before my Lord Lieutenant. I am convinced that the next Parliament will not fall short (in shewing their affection for and loyalty to his Majestye) of what any preceding Parliament hath done; I mean they will heartily give effective funds to answer whatever they pretend to give the Crown; and I think they will give whatever they find necessary to pay the debts of the Nation and to support the establishment. Whether the nation will appear to be in debt and if soe how much, I cannot take on me to say, but I am sensible that the additional dutyes will not now yeild near as much as they did formerly; soe that if it be found necessary to give as much money as heretofore, I cannot think the Commons will beleive they have made good their word to the Crown by giving the additional dutyes for the same time as formerly, when they plainly see it is impossible they should produce as much money as heretofore. The consequence of which I think must be their thinking on some other farther fund: but what that will be is very hard to foresee: Yet this I think may be reasonably hoped and consequently depended upon, that it will be such as will produce the summe it is given for. And if I am right in this, methinks people need not be sollicitous to know in what way the money will be given, or whether a land tax will passe: Nothing is more affrighting to countrey Gentlemen, and it is the story spread industriously about the Countrey, that fowre shillings in the pound[91] and a repeal of the test Act[92] are to be the master strokes of the next Session of Parliament. As to the augmenting the forces beyond twelve thousand men, I doe not think any thing but an absolute necessity will ever bring Gentlemen into it, since we have been so unkindly treated as after giving the additional dutyes to support 12000 upon assurances from the throne of having the money spent in our own countrey[93] we have seldome had half of them with us and have not now above 5000 effective men in Ireland.[94] The treatment we have mett on this foot hath been so severe, and the assurances given to incline us to raise money soe much neglected and constantly violated that he will be heard with a very ill grace that proposeth encreasing our expence. Yet after all I doe beleive what is found necessary for his Majestyes service will be gone into by an affectionate people to the utmost of their power. I have just received yours of 7 Dec. and will conclude after telling you that Lord Blaney was lately with me, and told me the Duke of Shrewsbury had spoken to my Lord Lieutenant for an augmentacion of his pencion of 10s to 20s a day as it was in his fathers time.[95] He is no

[91] A land tax.

[92] Strictly speaking, the 'test clause', a provision in the 1704 Popery Act (2 Anne, c. 6 [I]), which imposed on all holders of office under the crown in Ireland the necessity of taking the sacrament once a year in the established church.

[93] The number of troops on the Irish military establishment had been fixed at 12,000 by the English Disbanding Act of 1699 (10 Will. III, c. 1). On 28 Aug. 1710 the lord lieutenant, Lord Wharton, informed the Irish parliament that he had 'power and directions' to give assurances that supplies voted would be put to 'purposes, for which they were intended' (*CJI*, ii, 809).

[94] For the reductions made in the army in Ireland after the conclusion of the peace of Utrecht see C.I. McGrath, *Ireland and Empire, 1692–1770* (2012), 127.

[95] William, 6th Baron Blayney had been appointed in 1693 as governor of Sligo at a rate of 20s. per day. After the appointment came to an end in 1699 he was allowed to retain half his salary as a pension on the Irish military establishment, and following his death in 1705 the pension was continued in the name of his son and heir Cadwallader, ostensibly in trust for the dowager Lady Blayney and her children. Despite various attempts on her part to secure the restoration of the deducted half, payment was continued at this level until 1720, when it

freind of mine, so that I doe not interpose for him as such, but his condition is low, which forced him to go into measures with the late Governement here; but I am convinced he will act with the greatest duty to the Crown and deference to my Lord Lieutenant: and if his pencion be encreased he will entirely owe it to my Lord, and know he lyes under the strictest obligations to doe the Crown and his Excellency all service in his power.

232. *Alan I, Dublin, to Thomas, at his lodgings in Whitehall, 30 Dec. 1714*

(1248/3/207–8)

By a letter from my Lord Lieutenant dated the 22th instant I find it is determined to call up Lords Brabazons and Paisley by writt to the house of Peers,[96] and to create six new Barons by patent, whom my Lord names in this order, and desires my thoughts of the maner of precedence. The Chancellor,[97] Sir Jn Percival,[98] Sir George St George,[99] Mr FitzPatrick,[100] Colonel Allen, Mr Evans.[101] My son (and I beleive) he speaks the sense of Mrs Hill and his wife, but this only is conjecture) would have me insist on being distinguished from the rest by being placed on the Viscounts Bench; I wish it could have been soe, because it is their sense as well as desire that the King should shew a thought of merit appearing in me more then in some of the others: but as I was passive in the beginning and left the whole to be settled as my Lord Lieutenant saw most easy and for the publick service I continue of that mind, and will never recede from what I said to you on your first mentioning the thing to me. My Lord desired me to say what title I proposed to be called by; I wrote to him that without advising with you I cannot resolve; and must therefore refer it to you to wait on him and agree that matter. I have no part of my estate which can give me a title with a tolerable sound or English name: Glanor[102] is part of Colonel Courthopes estate,[103] but beside that it will go to my younger son and and not to my elder, which may create heartburnings between them; I say beside that if it ever come to either of them it must be to the youngest, that part of the estate on a division made between my brother Clayton and me fell to his wives share:[104] and to have a title from another mans estate is not right. This is as strong an objection against taking it from your estate: for I would not be supposed

---

[95] *(continued)* was increased to £300 p.a. (*CTB*, xvi, 274, 396; xx, 81; xxi, 489–90; xxvi, 256; *CTP*, 1708–14, pp. 133, 379, 429; *CTBP*, 1720–8, pp. 12, 315.)

[96] Brabazon succeeded his father as earl of Meath before the parliament sat. James Hamilton (1686–1776), the eldest surviving son of Lord Abercorn, and styled Lord Paisley in 1701, was not called up to the Lords. For the process by which the eldest son of a duke, marquess or earl could be called to the upper House of parliament in his father's barony – by a 'writ in acceleration'– see *HL 1660–1715*, i, 22–3.

[97] Alan himself.

[98] See Appendix 3 (1st Viscount Perceval).

[99] See Appendix 3 (1st Baron St George).

[100] Richard Fitzpatrick (see Appendix 3 (1st Baron Gowran)).

[101] George Evans (see Appendix 3 (1st Baron Carbery)).

[102] Glanure, Co. Cork (SHC, G145/box 102, 1, Alan I's account of his title to properties, n.d.).

[103] John Courthope of Little Island, Co. Cork, only brother of Alan I's first wife, Lucy. John died without issue in 1695.

[104] By the will of Sir Peter Courthope, John's father, the family estates were divided on John's death between Lucy and her sister Ann, the wife of Laurence Clayton (for whom see Appendix 2).

fond of having the title of being Lord of that town which really you are true Lord and owner of. Consider of it with my sister and doe in it just as you please ... The living of the rectory of Croome and vicarige of Adare in the Diocese of Limrick are void by the death of the last incumbent Mr Engram, and the livings are in the gift of Lord Kildare:[105] his Lordship on my instance hath given a presentacion to both to Barry Hartwel a son of my sister Jephsons by a former husband, an honest Whig, and as such not at all preferred tho of unblamable conversation and a good scholar: He hath six children and not more then thirty pounds a year.[106] Perhaps application will be made by the Bishop of Limrick[107] or somebody else for some other person to the Duke of Richmond:[108] It is not my businesse to say what my opinion is (upon what I knew when Councel) of his Grace having or not having a title; but I beg you not to loose any time in laying this matter before his Grace, and if need be in getting his concurrence to the establishing poor Hartwell: for if there should be a suit he will be grounded to powder between the contesting Lords. Sure if any notice be taken of this to Dean Jephson[109] he will try to doe his best for his wifes son. There is a place called the Chamberlain of the Exchequer; it was given to George Rotchfort son of the late Cheif Baron during pleasure; it hath a pretty good salary on the establishment:[110] If you could gett this for Will Smith,[111] it would be a wonderful support to a declining family. Thomas Thorn[112] (nephew to the Primate[113]) is also keeper of the great Beam in Dublin:[114] he came over with Lord Capel, but is the most furious party man in the City;[115] this place would be a pretty support for some young man: I beleive it to be worth about £40 a year. Since you resolve not to stand but have devolved your interest at Stockbridge on two good men[116] I see no reason why now you should not lodge the memorial you formerly mentioned. I think you served as well and have been treated as ill as many who have succeeded in their pretensions. I am sorry Lord Sunderland hath been prevailed upon

[105] Edward Ingram (c.1654–1714), prebend and vicar choral of Limerick since 1695 (Cotton, *Fasti*, i, 350).

[106] Barry Hartwell (c.1685–1741), Alan's nephew by his first marriage (*Al. Dub.*, 377; Cotton, *Fasti*, i, 80; Brady, *Records*, ii, 371). One of his sons was given the forename Brodrick.

[107] Thomas Smyth.

[108] Charles Lennox (1672–1723), 1st duke of Richmond.

[109] William Jephson (c.1658–1720), dean of Lismore (*Al. Dub.*, 439; Cotton, *Fasti*, i, 47). Hartwell's mother Anne (née Barry), had married Jephson as her second husband; hence, presumably, Hartwell's preferment in the cathedral at Lismore.

[110] George Rochfort, MP [I] had been appointed chief chamberlain of the exchequer [I] in 1708: his patent was renewed in Jan.1715 (*Lib. Mun.*, pt 2, p. 61).

[111] Possibly William Smith of Ballymore, Co. Cork (Phillimore, *Indexes*, ii, 150).

[112] Thomas Thorn(e), a Dublin merchant. In 1729 he was elected steward of the Blue Coat School. (TNA, SP 63/372/15: examination of ThomasThorne, 8 Mar. 1714[/15]; Reg. Deeds, 57/34/37054; 57/49/39257; *Daily Courant*, 20 Sept. 1729.)

[113] Thomas Lindsay. Thorn had married Lindsay's niece.

[114] Thorn had been weighmaster-general for Dublin since 1695, but his would be the last royal patent for the office, since by a clause in the Irish Act of 1705 for the regulation of weights (4 Anne, c. 14) the office of weighmaster-general in each town or city was henceforth vested in the chief magistrate of the borough corporation.

[115] Thorn had been listed among the tory common councilmen of Dublin in *A Station List for the City of Dublin, for the Year Commencing 1711* ... [Dublin, 1711], as one of the 'sheriffs' peers' from the merchants'guild. Lindsay himself had originally come over to Ireland as chaplain to the lord deputy, Henry, 1st Baron Capell (*DIB*).

[116] In the event, Thomas did stand for election at Stockbridge, and was returned on 26 Jan. 1715 together with Martin Bladen, MP [I], in a contest with two tories (HC *1715–54*, i, 254–5).

to beleive Mr Stern equal to the collection of Corke.[117] With what indignation will many Gentlemen of the house of commons of course receive the news that one of their under Clerks is thought worthy of an employment which would have been a reward to many of them for long and faithful services.

233. *Alan I, Dublin, to Thomas, at his lodgings in Whitehall, 17 Jan. 1714[/15]*

(1248/3/211–12)

I have yours of the third in which you tell what passed in relation to Badham and Steele att Lord Sunderlands: If the language of the Toryes, that a man who went in with the other party may yet be and have been all along a freind of and have intended no prejudice to the succession, come to be our language too at Court, assure your self it will soon spread over the countrey. I will send over the Copyes of those addresses in which those Gentlemen had an hand, and if after that they have freinds among us who will say or beleive that the framers or promoters of them had no intention to prejudice the Session, I shal begin to doubt whether my ill understanding the tendency of things hath not made me uncharitable in my opinion of them: for I did verily beleive they were among those who made direct strokes att the root of the tree. This I write only for your own information; for assure your self that I know it to be true, that Badham instead of being left to the consideration of the Commissioners (as you were told) stands recommended by name by the person with whom you discoursed to be continued in the Collection of Youghal, upon promising to behave better for the future. This must not be made use of, for the letter was to be kept a great secret; and indeed I could almost wish I had not seen it, since it convinces me that some body is capable of doing what looks in my opinion inconsistent with what you were told. I find the letter for continuing Lord Charlemont in his Governement is come over; that matter stood thus: It seems Mr Budgell[118] was entrusted to find out in what places several Gentlemen depending on Lord Lieutenant might be chosen in our Parliament. Charlemont[119] and the Colledge[120] first occurred to him; but by the insincerritye of the Provost[121] and the general corruption of the Colledge in their principles with reference to the present administration; I beleive it was very doubtful how far the honest well affected part would be able to prevail for a man of Mr Addisons sentiments and merit. Somebody had told Budgel that the borough of Charlemont entirely depended on the Governor, and that the same person alway commanded both; and I found he had insisted on my Lord Lieutenants naming two for that place, and for ought

---

[117] Enoch Ste(a)rne (*d.* c.1751), of Waterstown, Co. Westmeath (Jonathan Swift, *Journal to Stella* …, ed. Abigail Williams (Cambridge, 2013), 677; *Report of the Deputy Keeper of the Public Records … in Ireland* (Dublin, 1936), 294); committee clerk in house of commons [I], and from 1715 clerk of the parliaments [I] (Glenn McKee, 'The Operation, Practices and Procedures of the Irish House of Commons from 1692 to 1730', King's College London PhD, 2017, 43, 169, 272). He was not appointed to the collectorship (*Lib. Mun*, pt 2, p. 149).

[118] Eustace Budgell, MP [I].

[119] Lord Charlemont had the predominant interest in the borough of Charlemont, Co. Armagh. He assured Alan that 'what person soever my lord lieutenant named should be chosen one of the members' (BL, Add. MS 61636: Alan I to Joseph Addison, 18 Mar. 1714[/15]).

[120] Trinity College Dublin returned two MPs to the Irish parliament.

[121] Benjamin Pratt (1669–1721), provost of Trinity since 1710 and later dean of Down; a great friend of Jonathan Swift (*DIB*).

I know it might be done so inadvertently (by that I mean soe openly) as to be proposed in nature of a previous condition to the renewing the patent. By your letter I apprehend he hath wrote into England as if there had been a fair intimation of my Lords consenting to Lord Lieutenants recommending two: he spoke something leaning that way to me, but rather as a thing to be desired then expected: But when Lord Charlemont came to me about renewing his Commission he talked wholly in another strain: expressed his readinesse to complement my Lord with one, and that he intended his son for the other; and this I intimated either to you or to Mr Addison, which ever of you it was to whom I wrote about Lord Charlemont. His Lordship desired me to write in his favor; I neither have acquaintance with him nor obligation to him; but I thought (as I stil do) that it was not advisable to disoblige him or other Peers, who had not shewn any open disaffection to his Majesty or the succession; but I find that it is thought by those who represent things from hence that it is the more desirable to disoblige a member of that house where you know freinds are most likely to be thin, then leave a man out of the house who may fear he shal not be able to gett in but by insisting on what Lord Charlemont I think would not have consented to, and consequently making a breach between Lord Lieutenant and him. For Mr Addison expresseth it in this maner, that I should consider whether it would be advisable to continue one who might make use of the power he had by his office to influence an election against the Crown. I doe not use his words, nor must my letter be shewn to Lord Lieutenant or Mr Addison. But I have in a late letter wrote very fully on this subject. I have been ill, my stomach was entirely gone, my sleep broken and I had some fitts of my feaver; proceeding cheifly from being tired to death and not having time once to gett an [*sic*] horseback, or take the air. But by taking some Physick and a bitter draught which I stil am in, I am much better and can eat tolerably: but how the next term will leave me God only knows … I hope your Commission of the revenue will be better purged then ours is like to be. This morning I have signed recepi's for abundance of fiant[*s*][122] for continuing thorough Toryes…

234. *Alan I, Dublin, to Thomas, at his lodgings in Whitehall, 24 Feb. 1714[/15]*

(1248/3/217–18)

It is a very great time since I last heard from you, but possibly when the five pacquets arrive which are now due they may bring letters from you or some others of my freinds. Yesterday I finished all my businesse in Court, not leaving one cause or motion unheard that was ready: and I doe assure you considering how prodigiously businesse increaseth I cannot but look upon it to be a very happy thing that I have been able to goe through with so much, in addicion to what I am obliged to undergoe at the Councel board and committees, enquiring into the affairs of the hospital, meeting the Governors of the baracks, trustees of the first fruits, publick schools etc but God be thanked I have had such health as hath enabled me to attend the Court without being obliged to go late or to be absent one hour during the whole term or sittings after it.

[122]Receipts for writs to the Irish chancery to mandate the issue of letters patent under the Great Seal.

The increase of businesse is proportionable in the other Courts, which some people attribute to an opinion people have that every body may find equal justice in every Court against any person: I am unwilling to beleive that is the cause, since such an insinuation carryes an heavy reflection on those who sate formerly on the Benches here; but I think no body will deny that people for some time past were soe sollicitous about the event of publick affairs, and soe apprehensive of what was designed by the late Court and ministry, that they were very unwilling to part with ready money; but people begin again to improve, plant etc as expecting they are now doing it for themselves and their own posterity, and not for those to whom the Lands would certainly have come, if the grand design had taken place. I depend upon your giving me light into the proceedings of your Parliament from the beginning to the end of the Session; but it would be a very great pleasure to me to know before hand what the schemes are at present, who is like to be Speaker, how the house will be constituted, whether the Whigs have (as we say) a fair majorityе, how the elections and returns have been, and which side it is that complains with justice of unfair proceedings, whether maleadministration is only to be hardly spoken of, or to receive its due reward, and such other matters as you know must gratifye a man sollicitous for the Kings service and the good of his countrey. Particularly whether any of the late great men are inclined to save themselves by laying mismanagements at the door of their brethren in iniquity. Our pulpits run very high here, and there are abundance of Toryes in several parts of the countrey, no doubt in some measure to shew a dissatisfaction at the present administration of affairs:[123] but these things will vanish, nor can those who foment fewds and encourage sedition doe much harm; there will be a good house of commons as ever sate in the Kingdome, if I guesse right. I hear nothing about making the new Peers once spoken of; but let me intreat you to take care (if I be one of them) that the honour be not limited to me and my heirs in fee; for then if Senny should survive me, my second son (being by a second wife) will never be inheritable to it; but it will for want of Sennyes issue male go to his daughters, nay to my younger brothers, and not to my younger son and his sons: soe as I desire it may be limited to me and the heirs males of my body; and if it be thought proper a remainder may be limited over in such maner as shal seem fit. When our Parliament meets I am sure the peevish B[*ishop*] of Corke,[124] and the no lesse malicious tho more plausible B[*ishop*] of another place,[125] will endeavour to raise clamor about Middleton school:[126] and indeed I am afraid they have too fair an handle for being malapert. There was no care taken that I could ever hear of, to have a deed or conveyance of the ground on which the school is built executed to the trustees: and considering the settlements now in the familye I doe not see how it can be effectually done without an act of Parliament, tho in my fathers lifetime and some time before Senny was married it might have been done with more facility. It will be said the money allotted to a publick charity hath bee[*n*] laid out on a private persons estate, therefore it may be insis[*ted*] on that

---

[123] Archbishop King reported bodies of tories active 'in seven or eight counties', and especially in the vicinity of Dublin (TCD, MS 2536, p. 192: King to Arthur Charlett, 19 Feb. 1714[/15]; MS 750 (13), p. 31, King to Sunderland, 3 Mar. 1714[/15]).

[124] Peter Browne.

[125] Charles Crowe, bishop of Cloyne.

[126] The school founded in 1696 by Lady Orkney at Midleton, of which Alan I and Thomas were both governors (Trevor West, *Midleton College 1696–1996: A Tercentenary History* (Midleton, 1996), 9).

an account of the money be given without regard to the laying it out in that building. God knows how far such a clamor might have obtained here, if things had stood as they were just before the first of August last. Pray consider whether it will not be most advisable to have an act passe this Session in England to make good the title of that ground on which the school is built and which is to be allotted for gardens a play feild etc to the trustees, and advise with freinds there; you cant imagine what clamor a sett of men will raise here if any doubt be made of the title on which the building is not being conveyed to the trustees. In order to such an act, a conveyance should be now made without losse suppose of fowre acres of ground on and contiguous to which the school is built. Let me hear soon from you and know where Lady Orkneys original deed is, for I have it not, among my papers here …

[PS] Every body is putting in for one of the eight horse baracks to be built here; Mr Molineux among the rest, who writes to me and tells me he hath spoken to and hath the promise of my Lord Lieutenant.[127] Pray speak to my Lord in favor of Middleton and gett his promise: I shal order matters so with Lord Tirawly Brigadier Morris[128] and others here as to gett their good word. Loose no time, nor speak about it to Molineux.

235. *Alan I to Thomas, 9 Mar. 1714[/15]*

(BL, Add. MS 61636, ff. 137–40)[129]

Since a matter which hapned lately here, and hath been the occasion of a good deal of discourse, may create in you the curiositye of knowing the truth, without addition or diminution; I will inform you of it in the best maner my memory will serve me: What I write you may depend upon to be the truth, which you may let my Lord Lieutenant know; but I doe not doubt his Excellencye hath a much better account of the thing from the Lords Justices, soe that tho the subject is worth his notice it would appear improper in me to send his Excellencye an account of it addressed directly to him.

On Monday last about noon the Lords Justices in the Closett told me they had ordered the Councel to be summoned to meet that day to impart to them a discoverye of the importation of a parcel of libels intituled English advice to the freeholders of England,[130] and soon afterward in the Councel chamber spoke to the Lords of the Councel to the same

[127] Samuel Molyneux (1689–1728), of Dublin and St Martin-in-the-Fields, London, MP [GB] and secretary to George, prince of Wales. For the enthusiasm of Irish landowners to have these new barracks situated in or near their estates, see Edward McParland, *Public Architecture in Ireland 1680–1760* (New Haven, CT, 2001), 125–6; McGrath, *Ireland and Empire*, 89.

[128] Richard Morris (d. c.1720), quarter-master gen. and barrack-master gen. [I]; a colonel rather than a brigadier (Dalton, *Army Lists*, v, 240; vi, 229; *Lib. Mun*, i, pt. 2, p. 113. Vicars, *Index*, 336).

[129] The presence of this original letter in the Blenheim papers must indicate that it was forwarded by Thomas to Lord Sunderland: this may well have been Alan's intention.

[130] [Francis Atterbury,] *English Advice, to the Freeholders of England* (1714). Described by Atterbury's 20th-century biographer as 'a bombshell, designed to shock the country supporters and impel them into realising what a whig single-party regime could mean', this contained a powerful – and at times scurrilous – personal attack on King George I. The government immediately issued a proclamation condemning the pamphlet and offering a reward of £1,000 for information leading to the apprehernsion of the author. (G.V. Bennett, *The Tory Crisis in Church and State 1688–1730: The Career of Francis Atterbury, Bishop of Rochester* (Oxford, 1975), 192–4.)

effect: The Lord Primate it seems had about one of the Clock on Saturday gone to the Archbishop of Tuam[131] and discovered to him that a parcel had been brought to his house from the Custom house, on opening of which he found it to contain a great many of those libels, and the Archbishop of Tuam imparted the matter to the other two Lords Justices on Saturday. The Lord Primate was called in who being examined said that he had recd a letter from James Kenna of Chester[132] importing that he observing a parcel directed to the Lord Primate of Ireland to lye in Paines warehouse att Chester had taken it out and sent it to the Park Gate[133] to be shipped in the Ormond Galley,[134] which was the first ship which was to sail for Dublin; that he recd that letter on or about 4 February and ordered one Perry a servant of his[135] to write to Kenna that he thanked him for his care in any thing that related to him, but wondred that there should be a parcel sent him and yet he should have no notice of any such being sent, which letter was wrote the fourth of February. That Perry told him as he was going to the Castle on Saturday last about eleven of the clock that Tho: Thorne had brought a small bundle or parcel for his Grace from the Custom house, which he ordered him to keep till his return from the Castle; when he directed Perry to bring the parcel up stairs where it was opened in his Graces and Mr Whaleys (his Chaplains)[136] presence, and upon seeing the title page of the pamphlets the bundle was tyed up and carryed by the Primate to the Archbishop of Tuam etc. The Councel ordered a Committee immediately to sit and examine into the whole matter,[137] and the Primate being examined upon oath delivered himself much to the above effect, and added that he carryed all the pamphlets which were in the bundle when it was opened before him and his Chaplain to the Archbishop of Tuam, and that none were taken out: Perry said he recd them from Thomas Thorne on Saturday morning who went away immediately after delivering them to him; that he locked them up on the Primates going to the castle and that none of the books had been taken out while in his custody. Thorne said that being on Saturday morning at the Custom house one Edwards the storekeeper[138] told him there was a small parcel[139] for the Lord Primate in the storehouse and that he went for it and when Mr Roberts the controuler of stores had opened it and found it to be only unbound papers that paid no duty the same was delivered into his hands, who gave it to Christopher Carne his Apprentice who was then shipping goods for him on the Key with directions to carry it to his

---

[131]John Vesey.

[132]James Kenna (*d.* c.1716), an innkeeper in Chester (*Rolls of the Freemen of Chester: Part II, 1706–1805*, ed. J.H.E. Bennett (Lancs. and Cheshire Rec. Soc., lv, 1908), 207; *An Index to the Wills and Inventories Now Preserved in the Court of Probate at Chester, from A.D. 1701 to 1720 …*, ed. J.P. Earwaker (Lancs. and Cheshire Rec. Soc., xxv, 1892), 121).

[133]Parkgate in Cheshire, a port on the western side of the Wirral peninsula, was a principal point of embarkation for travel to Ireland.

[134]A 230-ton vessel, previously owned by English merchants, which by Queen Anne's reign had come to be based in Dublin conducting trade to the European continent (TNA, HCA 26/3/23; *CSP Dom.* 1704–5, p. 502).

[135]John Perry (TNA, SP 63/372/35: report of committee of privy council [I], 14 Mar. 1714/15).

[136]Nathaniel Whaley (c.1677–1738), rector of Loughgilly, Co. Armagh; formerly a fellow of Wadham College, Oxford (Lindsay's old college) (J.B. Leslie, *Armagh Clergy and Parishes* (Dundalk, 1911), 114; *Swift Corr.*, ii, 117, 333–5).

[137]Including Alan (TNA, SP 63/372/38: report of committee of privy council [I], 14 Mar. 1714/15).

[138]John Edwards (TNA, SP 63/372/17: examination of John Edwards, 8 Mar. 1714[/15]).

[139]'in his closet' erased. Roberts was surveyor and comptroller of stores in the custom house (TNA, SP63/372/36: report of committee of privy council [I], 14 Mar. 1714/15).

house: that he went from the Custom house to his own house in half a quarter of an hour, and found the bundle in his parlour and carryed it to the Lord Primates, but that none of the books were taken out to his knowledge; nay he believed that the cover of brown paper was so little broken that none could have been taken out. But the Committee finding the bundle to contain an odd number of books viz. forty three and apprehending some might have been taken out and dispersed asked him whether he had not seen any other of those pamphlets intituled etc. beside those which were carryed to the Primates house and lay then before the Committee, to which he answered that he had seen one; being asked where the book was he said he had lent it and that either John Anderson[140] or Richard Gratton had it;[141] but (intending I suppose to convince us that he had not forsworn himself in saying none of the books were taken out of the bundle) added that he had lent it about eight or ten days agoe. The Committee then finding that the book had been in Thornes and other peoples hands before the parcel was taken out or brought to the Custom house asked him from whom he had the book which he lent to Anderson or Gratton; he owned it came under a cover, in which nothing was written; but the superscription he believed was the handwriting of Augustine Woodward a merchant in Liverpoole, with whose handwriting he is very well acquainted being his correspondent.[142] Edwards spoke to what passed at the custom house much to the same effect with Thorne; only being asked how it came to passe that he called to Tho: Thorne to take away a parcel directed to the Primate he said Mr Thorne usually received what was directed to the Primate being his nephew. Mr Roberts the controuler of stores spoke to the same purpose, as to what passed about delivering the bundle to Thorne, after he had viewed it and saw it contained only unbound paper: being asked if it was so far opened as that he read the title page of the pamphlet, saith it was not. I am apt to thinke if such a bundle had lately come directed to a Whig, it might have been more strictly examined. Christopher Carbe said he carryed the bundle by his Masters orders to his house and laid it down in the parlour where his mistrisse was and went out of the room leaving his Mistrisse there; owned one Croker an Apothecary[143] seeing him with a parcel under his arm as he was going from the Custom house to his Masters house called him in to his shop, asked him what that was which he had under his arm, and that they opened it and took out two of the books, read the title and put them in again; and that all the books that were in the bundle when he recd it att the custom house were in the bundle when he laid it down in his masters parlour, and that his master came home from the Custom house half a quarter of an hour after him. Richard Gratton owned that he had seen a book of the same title and import (as he believed) with the book then shewn, which was one of the libels etc that he had it from a person whom he refused to name, and at the time of his first examination was doubtful whether it was lent him on Fryday or Saturday last, but in hearing his examination read over on Tuesday morning recollected

---

[140]John Anderson (d. c.1743), an apothecary of Dublin (Reg. Deeds, 4/440/1144; Vicars, *Index*, 201).

[141]Richard Grattan (d.1736), a merchant of Dublin, later alderman and lord mayor of the city; son of a former fellow of Trinity College (Patrick Grattan, d.1703), and himself a friend of Swift (*Calendar of the Ancient Records of Dublin*, ed. J.T. Gilbert and R.M. Gilbert (17 vols, Dublin, 1889–1921), vii, 217; *Swift Corr.*, iv, 91–2, 314; Irvin Ehrenpreis, *Swift: The Man, His Works, and the Age* (3 vols, 1962–83), iii, 337, 821).

[142]Augustine Woodward (d. aft. 1739), of Water Street, Liverpool (*The Registers of Our Lady and St Nicholas, Liverpool, Part II: 1705–1725*, ed. Robert Dickinson (Lancs. Parish Register Soc., 1963), 41; *CTBP*, 1739–41, p. 97).

[143]Edward Croker (1685–1759), of Capel St., Dublin (Nick Reddan, 'The Irish Crokers', 111 (http://www.members.iinet.net.au: accessed 4 June 2018)).

himself and said it was either on Wednesday or Thursday; could not charge his memory whether he asked the person from whom he had the book for it, or that he gave it him without being desir'd but he believes he desired to borrow it having heard much of it and being very desirous to see it: being asked how he came to enquire for that book from the person from whom he afterward had it and whether he knew or believed he could help him to it said he enquired for it of that person among several others of his acquaintance from whom he hoped to have a sight of it; Owned he had it at his chamber, and being sent for it in company of Mr Budgel returned without it, pretending not to be able to find it among his papers, but being asked whether he could have found it if he had used his best endeavours, owned he could and being sent back again for the book brought it and owned that to be the book he borrowed or had from the person he declined to name; but being asked whether Tho: Thorne was the person, finding the thing was known, owned he was; But refused to answer to his having heard any person read, or disperse the pamphlet, excluding himself out of the question and answer. John Anderson being examined as to his having borrowed or seen the book, or as to his knowing of its being dispersed or published by any other person (excepting himself) would give no answer to any of those questions. On the examination of these two persons it appeared to the Committee that this libel was printing here, and sixteen pages of it printed, when news came of the proclamation promising a reward to the discoverer of the Author or printer: The Committee apprehending one waters to be the printer[144] and some of the Councel having heard he was concerned sent for him, who frankly owned it, swore he had the Copy from John Hyde a bookseller[145] who told him it would sell; came to his house in some short time after to know how forward the work was; Dr Stone[146] also called at the door to know whether it was printed: some of sheets that were printed off were delivered out to one Shaw the Colledge baker, and to one Bexton;[147] and three Gentlemen (whose names we cannot yet learn) came at different times to encourage and propose the printing: men well clad, with swords and long Wigs.

Thorne and Hyde are bound over to answer next term, and the others to prosecute: we meet this evening again and shal I think find out more people concerned. Ill affected men take advantage That Thorne is the Primates nephew, Dr Stone his Vicar General I think, Shaw Anderson Gratton people much concerned in the riot of Dublin,[148] and as they say not wholly strangers to his Grace, But sure his having made the first discoverye to the Government, his being surprised at his having such a packet coming over so as to expresse it on 4 February in Perrys letter to Kenna before the libels came, or he could know what

---

[144]Edward Waters (*d.*1751), printer and bookseller, of Essex Street, Dublin (Mary Pollard, *A Dictionary of Members of the Dublin Book Trade 1550–1800* … (2000), 589).

[145]John Hyde (*d.*1728), of Dame Street, Dublin, eventually indicted (on Waters' information) for printing this pamphlet (Pollard, *Dictionary of … the Dublin Book Trade*, 304–5).

[146]Richard Stone (1674–1735), of Dublin, MP [I] 1695–9, a master in chancery [I] 1694–*d.* (*Hist. Ir. Parl.*, vi, 355–6; *Lib. Mun.*, pt. 2, p. 22; *Swift Corr.*, ii, 334–5); a political associate of the high tory earl of Anglesey (TCD, MS 1995–2008/1572: Frederick Hamilton to Archbishop King, 27 Jan. 1714/15).

[147]TNA, SP 63/372/36: report of committee of privy council [I], 14 Mar.1714/15, identifies these two men as Nathaniel Shaw (*d.* c.1743) (Vicars, *Index*, 421) and Moses Beckston or Bexton, a member of the tailors' guild and a Dublin common councilman (*A Station List for the City of Dublin, for the Year Commencing, 1711*…, 2; *Cal. Ancient Records of Dublin*, ed. Gilbert and Gilbert, vi, 396).

[148]During the parliamentary election for the city in 1713 (*Anglo-Irish Politics*, Vol. 1, 281–3).

was coming, his opening them before his Chaplain and servant shew his innocence as well as prudence and great caution.

Under the same cover with this you will find a paper which contains something in answer to what your last mentions: You know how invidious as well as dangerous a task it is that is put upon me: I have done something and will soon doe as much as comes to my province; but I desire for more reasons then one that the paper may be transcribed in a fair hand and delivered; which as it will be more respectful, soe will it also be lesse liable to future inconveniencyes then to let such a paper under my hand lye out which may fall into a Secretaryes or Executors hand. I find all applications for a patent to coyne small money have been reported against from this side, and would not have any friend of mine take up with it, being an invidious a dangerous and I believe in the end no very profitable undertaking. ... The Toryes here are outragious to the last degree, and I suppose the spirit of the Doctor[149] is in double measure diffused among some of his brethren here. By a letter dated 19 June 1714 now remaining in the Book of letters written by the Comissioners of the revenue at the Custom and signed by Mr Keightley,[150] Mr Ogle,[151] Mr Ludlow[152] and Mr Walpoole,[153] and directed to their Surveyor[s] General, they are required among other things to make diligent enquiry into the behavior of all officers whether they constantly attend on the service and worship of the Church or go to meetings with any sect of dissenters or to masse with papists, or any way interest themselves with persons[154] factions or enemyes to the established Church and Queen, and to make an exact return with all convenient speed. You know who the factions, the enemyes of the Church and Queen were in the language of June last; and to give you an hint what the words interesting themselves meant, and how understood by the Surveyors, one of the Surveyors returns thus from[155] Wicklow, that one Hamilton was an Officer there, with this remark that he voted with the faction the last election.[156] The question was about a Soveraign,[157] whether a Whig or Tory and he voted for the Whig; but this is but one of abundance of instances of returns as well grounded. But to put the matter out of all maner of dispute what the intention of men in power on this side the water was just before the late Queens death as to continuing or removing out of the revenue (which I suppose was to be done likewise in all other Cases) persons of Whiggish principles I send you the Copy of a paragraph of a letter written by John Loyde

---

[149]Dr Sacheverell, the high church preacher impeached before the house of lords at Westminster in 1710. For the impact of the Sacheverell affair in Ireland, see D.W. Hayton, 'Irish Tories and Victims of Whig Persecution: Sacheverell Fever by Proxy', in *Faction Displayed: Reconsidering the Impeachment of Dr Henry Sacheverell*, ed. Mark Knights (Oxford, 2012), 80–4, 96–8.

[150]Thomas Keightley (c.1650–1719), of Castlemartin, Co. Kildare, MP [I] 1695–1714; revenue commr [I] 1692–1714.

[151]Samuel Ogle (1659–1719), of Bowsden, Northumb., MP [I]1707–13 and [E & GB] 1690–1710; revenue commr [I] 1699–1714.

[152]Stephen Ludlow, MP [I].

[153]Horatio Walpole (1663–1717), of Beckhall, Norfolk, MP [GB] 1702–10, 1710–13; revenue commr [I] 1712–16.

[154]'with persons' repeated.

[155]'Hamilton' erased.

[156]That is to say, with the tories.

[157]The chief magistrate. Wicklow was a corporation borough, with the sovereign its returning officer.

(an Officer in the revenue)[158] to Mr Cust Collector of Ardmagh.[159] The letter bears date the 30th of July 1714 at Monaghan. The paragraph is in these words.

Likewise I am to return a report the Commissioners of each Officers principles as to Church and State, signed under the Collector of each districts hand, with my observations thereon per order of my Lords Treasurers of Ireland etc (These Lords Treasurers I presume must be Rochester and Anglesey[160]) Therefore must desire you will write me one forthwith, without any partiality for your own sake and send it etc. There is a postscript in These words: Also mention who have certificates of their having qualifyed themselves and who not; pray be very exact.

The Commissioners letter was to know who had interested themselves with persons factions etc that is who had any converse with or kindnesse for or appeared at any time a friend to any Whig: for doing that was as good and sure a ground for removing a man out of the revenue as conversing with an excommunicate person is to bring the party so audacious under the same sentence. But least the Commissioners letter might not make a clean sweep or find due compliance the Treasurers (as they are called) dive into heart; principles are evince enough.

Loyde hath not yet shewn his orders from the Lords Treasurers for doing what he did: I suppose when he doth, he will only be able to shew some letters from the late Commissioners, which is founded upon or mentions such an order to them, but that the original rests with their late Honors.

236. Alan I, Dublin, to Thomas, 15 Mar. 1714[/15]

(1248/3/219–20)

This minute I have received yours of the tenth, and must beg you to wait on my Lord Lieutenant and excuse my not owning the honour of his Excellencyes of the eighth; resolving by Saturday nights post at farthest without fail to send over whatever is within my knowledge or power in relation to mismanagements here in the time of the late people: and after all more will fall to my share then ought, or then I can well bear or go through with: My Lord Cheif Justice Whitshed is this day gone the Circuit and hath done no part of it; the Cheif Baron[161] is ill of the gout; the cheif Justice of the Common pleas[162] hath taken a good deal of pains and I think hath done the part (which he took on him) with care. It is not possible for those who were not in the secret of affairs to give such proofs of

---

[158]John Lloyd, surveyor-general since 1710. A tory, who had been recommended to the revenue commissioners by Robert Harley, after a 'violent prosecution' by Lord Wharton and the whig party in Ireland. Lloyd defined the duty of his office as to 'inspect the transactions and qualifications of all the inferior officers of the revenue' and 'to report … neglects and miscarriages' (BL, Add. MS 70201: Lloyd to Harley, 19 Oct. 1710, 23 May 1713; Add. MS 70247: Lloyd to Harley, 17 Mar. 1710/11, 2 Nov. 1714). The revenue commissioners' minutes record four dismissals in Aug. 1714 on account of reports submitted by Lloyd (TNA, CUST1/11, pp. 334, 338, 349).

[159]Jones Cust (*d*.1754), of Armagh (L.A. Clarkson and E.M. Crawford, *Ways to Wealth: The Cust Family of Eighteenth-century Armagh* (Belfast, 1985), 25–6, 34–9; Barnard, *New Anatomy*, 166–7).

[160]Henry Hyde (1672–1753), 2nd earl of Rochester, and Arthur Annesley, 7th earl of Anglesey (see Appendix 3), who held the office of vice-treasurer and paymaster-general [I] jointly since 1710.

[161]Joseph Deane.

[162]John Forster.

matters of fact as might be had if any of the parties concerned were willing to speak what they know: nor is it practicable to produce witnesses even of facts capable of proof. Who will take upon him the charge or expence of soe difficult a task: What man is so mad to take on him to prove matters transacted in Ireland, at London? Therefore nothing of that kind can be expected: but such lights may be given as will shew what was doing here and what they aimed at, if men will not shut their eyes for fear of being convinced: but to descend to proof is what nobody will undertake. Let me while it is in my memory correct a mistake in my last, Dr Stone is not (yet) the Primates Vicar general, but his secretary. I hope you have been careful not to name me for any thing my former carried in relation to the Primate or the bundle of Libels called English advice etc. By this pacquett the Lords Justices att the desire of the Council transmit to my Lord Lieutenant the report of the Committee of Councel upon that affair together with the examinations taken upon it;[163] Perhaps what I am about to say will not be intelligible to you without you can gett a sight of the report and examinations; but if you can I doe not know but that it may give you some light into the matter. The Primates discovering that the pamphlets came to his house must either be out of a detestation of the vile libel and to shew his abhorrence of the designs for which it was wrote, or to secure himself from being called in question for receiving and not discovering it. Charity obliges us to beleive the best, as far as the matter will admit. He came of his own accord, immediately after he knew what the bundle contained, to one of the Lords Justices; the books came to him unexpected, he had no account of them, wrote to Kenna to tell his surprize at his not having any notice of the parcel being sent him, took none of them out etc. Now all this looks well enough; but then I consider at the same time that his Grace told the Councel last night that he suspected some ill design against him when he heard of such a bundle coming by Kennas letter; he took care to have a witnesse of his writing to Kenna that he knew of no such bundle coming; and to have two witnesses present when it was opened att his house: the bundle had been opened at the Custom house, his Nephew Thorne knew it, so did Thornes apprentice Can, and Croker brother in Law to Can: nay the two later read the title pages of two of the libels, and this was after the proclamation promising a great reward to the discoverers of the Author or Printer had been the town talk and made a great noise all over the town.

The bundle untyed had been left in Thornes parlour with Thornes wife the Primates neice: And truly after so many people had seen what it contained, not to mention the Custom house officers, I should have thought a man of lesse prudence then the Primate would for his own sake have made the discoverye for fear somebody else should discover that such a parcel of treasonable books were brought to his house and soe might be traced into his hands. But when I find his Nephew Thorne to have received one of the same libels before, when I find Dr Stone enquire att Waters the Printers house to know if it was printed off; when not only they, but Anderson and Gratton to whom Thorne had lent the book refuse to answer as to their knowledge of the publishing or printing of that libel here; when Shaw and Beckston own to have had the sheets from Waters as they were printed off, but will not answer what they know as to its being read to company or published by others: Nay when his Grace refuses to be sworn or without being sworn to declare what he knows touching the printing or publishing that libel here as being against the liberty of the

---

[163] TNA, SP 63/372/35–8: report of committee of privy council [I], 14 Mar. 1714/15. Sent by the lords justices to the lord lieutenant, 16 Mar. 1714/15 (TNA, SP 63/372/45).

subject, and therefore will make no answer to that matter, I know not what to think. Tho it be not contained in the Primates written examination he insisted that the oath tendred viz. True answer to make to such questions as should be proposed relating to the printing or publishing that libel, was the oath ex officio, that as a Peer he was not bound to answer on oath, at least in the first instance (as he expressed himself) and that he would answer only as to the bundle brought to his house on Saturday the 5th of this month: soe that it looks as if he only misliked the English advice etc which came in that pacquet; but would not let the Councel know whether he knew any thing of any of them except those which came in that bundle: and it is plain the book was here and reprinting before the Ormond Galley came in. He might and one would think should have answered, if he could with a good conscience.

237. *Alan I, Dublin, to Thomas, at his lodgings in Whitehall, 17 Mar. 1714 [/15]*

(1248/3/221–2)

Since Postage now costs you nothing[164] I may venture to trouble you the oftner with my letters. I have formerly hinted that it is beleived it may be of considerable advantage in carrying things easy here, if the original addresses that were sent over hence during the later part of the Queens reign could be gott and brought over for Ireland: there men have said what they now would be very unwilling to have remembred; and unlesse it be proved against them by such authentick testimonyes as their own hand writing, they will not only deny that ever they went those lengths and were inclined to the measures which at that time prevailed; but sett up again for persons as zealously affected to the house of Hanover as any in the Kingdome. But the Bandon addresse att the Sessions held there the 12th of January 1713 which commends the peace, and Sir Con Phips,[165] concurs with the most loyal Lords and faithful Clergy in recommending Phips (whom the Commons had addressed to be removed) to be continued, will shew that the Addressers did not think the remembrance of King W[illia]m or the prospect of the Hanover succession ought to abate the duty and allegeance which was only due to the Queen; and were sorry any thing or practice should be observed which may have any other views; that is, that all respect shewn to the memory of King W[illia]m, and all satisfaction and hope expressed on the prospect of the Hanover succession were inconsistent with the duty they owed the late Queen: The next paragraph is an home one in these words We hope that neither Popery nor schism can prevail with any of your Majestyes subjects to abett or assist any Pretender to the Crown and Kingdomes, or to disturb or elude your royal successors.[166] Here they who are very fond of the Hanover succession have brought in more Pretenders then one, and it is pretty easy to tell what person was understood in the languge of those dayes to be the Pretender whom the schismaticks were said to design to sett up: nay the Jacobites

---

[164] Letters sent by MPs at Westminster were carried free of charge within Britain and Ireland: Kenneth Ellis, *The Post Office in the Eighteenth Century* … (1958), 39.

[165] Sir Constantine Phipps (1656–1723), lord chancellor [I] 1710–14.

[166] See *Anglo-Irish Politics, Vol. 1*, 306–8. The address is printed in D.W. Hayton, 'Tories and Whigs in County Cork, 1714', *Journal of the Cork Historical and Archaeological Society*, lxxx (1975), 84–8.

and Papists would then readily drink confusion to the Pretender. There are other more extraordinary addresses, particularly one from the County of Downe, in which I hear even his Majesty is very freely treated. These if brought over will at least keep the signers within bounds and in awe, and may be made good use of when some of the promoters insist on being received well, and continuing in emploiment or perhaps getting better. I am told they lye as wast parchment in the Secretaryes office:[167] They are worth being carefully read over, and the most flagrant may be brought over, and the rest laid up. But this is an invidious task and it will be enough for you to give the hint to my Lord Lieutenant. And just as I had closed this paragraph Captain Hedges came in to pay me a visit, told me he was just landed and was going into the County of Corke: by his coming to me I suppose he hath had the fortune to be established in his Governement of Rosse Castle:[168] If that be soe I am sure high Church cannot say all their freinds are removed: You will find he was one of the foremost in the Bandon addresse, and upon my word he hath not been behind hand, but kept pace with the foremost in their applauding the late ministry and all their measures. But so much for him. Mr Addison tells me my letter for being a Baron was signed; that I am to have the precedency over the Gentlemen of Ireland who are to be created at the same time: This seems to import that Mr Cholmondley is not (as you told me) to be a Viscount but only a baron:[169] this is a little hard on me: but I will be easy in that and in every thing. My sister will order money to passe the offices, and I hope no delay in that will give others the start of me. Mr Addison tells me that truly Mr St George was forced to be once or twice conferred with before the precedency could be adjusted.

238. Alan I, Dublin, Thomas, 26 Mar. 1715

(1248/3/338–40)

In another letter which goes by this pacquet under Mr Addisons cover I send you such an account as I have been able to form of the behavior and inclinations of our great men when the matter of listing men for the Pretender came to be made more publick then some of them did I beleive desire.[170] You must know that it cost me a good deal of pains to extract the substance of the several examinations, which I thought to be absolutely necessary to make the thing understood: I have to the best of my power abstracted them fairly and truly,

---

[167] Eleven Irish county addresses made in early 1714 in vindication of Lord Chancellor Phipps from the attacks of whigs in the Irish house of commons (together with one from the borough of Galway) were the subject of an inquiry carried out by the Commons in Dublin in Nov. 1715. They included one from Co. Down, dated 19 Mar. 1714, but not the Co. Cork address (*CJI*, iii, 46–51).

[168] Richard Hedges (c.1670–1737), of Macroom Castle, Co. Cork, governor of Ross Castle, Co. Kerry (Marc Caball, *Kerry, 1600–1730: The Emergence of a British Atlantic County* (Dublin, 2017), 37–9; Reg. Deeds, 89/19/61880). He was eventually replaced in Oct. 1715 (*London Gazette*, 18–22 Oct. 1715).

[169] Hon. George Cholmondeley (1666–1733), of Cholmondeley, Cheshire, MP [GB] 1690–5, was raised to the Irish peerage as Baron Newborough on 12 Apr. 1715, and to the British peerage as Baron Newburgh the following year.

[170] SHC, 1248/3/324–31: 'Account [*by Alan I*] of the examinations of persons enlisting in the Pretender's service'; relating to information taken in Dublin, Cork and Waterford in Jan. and Feb. 1714 of Irish catholics being recruited for the French armies with promises that they would serve the cause of the jacobite Pretender (for which see *Anglo-Irish Politics, Vol. 1*, 312–14).

and am confident the Copyes out of which I did it were true Copyes: Those which were taken at Corke and that of Lehye were sent up to me or to Senny by the Mayor of Corke at the time the matter was transacting; and the other copyes I had from one in the Crown office in whom I can confide. I have sent you the Copy of Wm Lehyes examination,[171] thinking it to be very necessary to shew you what he swore at Waterford; I have not that of Michael Lehy, but am assured that it perfectly agrees with Williams; and soe the proclamation of the second of February seems to shew, when it couples them as having sworn the same thing.[172] One thing however I must observe upon perusal of that proclamation that it imports only that Butler had told the Lehyes that he had listed fourteen men (beside them) for the service of the Pretender; whereas in truth the examination expressely saith that the men were inlisted, and every part of it, as Butlers telling them the necessity there was for more men, his cautioning them not to appear openly together, directing them to go to Passage[173] when the wind presented etc shew they were listed: nay some of them were found guilty of being listed, but it was forsooth in servitio cuiusdam Principi ignoti:[174] The late Chief Justice[175] best knows by what Law that fact barely, as laid in the Indictment, is punishable by indictment. The Prelate mentioned in the Paper[176] is the A[rchbishop] of D[ublin][177] and the Privy Councellor is that person who told my Lord Lieutenant that Sir Con[stantine Phipps] never removed a Justice of peace but by direction of the Privy Councel, whereas another turns men out without rhime or reason.[178] If you knew how little assistance I have had in these matters especially from him who I beleive was in great measure the cause of giving me all this trouble you would pity me. My Lord Cheif Justice Whitshed when he came over told me something of this kind was expected from this side the water, and every now and then on receiving letters from Lord Lieutenant repeated the same thing. I gave little regard to it, my Lord never having spoken one word to me on the subject while in England, nor wrote a line about it to me in several months after all I landed; soe that I thought it a proposal and undertaking which arose from the Cheif Justice, Mr Molesworth and others:[179] and truly at first he did not vouchsafe to let us see any letter he had: but at length he shewed a paragraph of one letter, and soon after my Lord wrote to me, and seemed to think he had spoken about it in London; but he really never did to me. The three cheif Judges and I then undertook each to doe something toward it: Lord Cheif Justice Forster took the Case of the Mayor and Sherifs of D[ublin] as his province[180] and hath done it very fully but a little too much at

---

[171] SHC, 1248/3/59: deposition of William Lehy, of Three Mile Bridge, Co. Waterford, made on 26 Jan. 1714.

[172] The depositions of William and Michael Lehy, both given at Waterford, had resulted in a proclamation by the Irish privy council on 2 Feb. 1714 for the arrest of the recruiting officer, and all those who had enlisted (see *Anglo-Irish Politics*, Vol. 1, 312–14).

[173] Passage East, Co. Waterford.

[174] In the service of an unknown prince.

[175] Sir Richard Cox (1650–1733), 1st Bt., of Clonakilty, Co. Cork, lord chief justice of queen's bench [I] (1711–14).

[176] Alan's 'account'.

[177] William King.

[178] Presumably a reference to Alan himself.

[179] An inquiry into the misdeeds of the previous tory administration in Ireland, 1711–14.

[180] The long-drawn-out conflict between the corporation of Dublin and the Irish privy council over the election of a lord mayor, for which see *Anglo-Irish Politics*, Vol. 1, 30–1.

large; the Cheif Baron had formed and digested heads to goe upon, but falling into the Gout and now being gone the Circuit could doe no more: Lord Cheif Justice Whitshed acted the part of a trumpeter, sounded a charge, but resolved not to engage in person. The length and nature of the thing hath created me great trouble and uneasinesse; I could not use a good Clerk whom I have, because he will understand more of the matter then I would willingly intrust him with; soe that writing and altering and transcribing hath been a tedious task. It is a task I would not undertake but under the last necessity, and not having time to gett these sheets transcribed I send them in my own hand; but intreat you not to part with the originals: if my Lord thinks them worth it they may be copyed. I repeat what I said formerly that I will not be called upon to prove matters; I am no informer nor witnesse, and I am sure my Lord knows me better then to beleive I can be capable of being made use of in that capacity: but what lights are given in what I have wrote may serve to let his Lordship know something of the late management here. I think I have shewn that the succession was struck at in reflecting on the revolution, in dividing Protestants, supporting and countenancing the Papists and new converts;[181] in encouraging or not punishing Loydes attempt to reprint a book calculated to facilitate the Pretenders coming in and to reconcile mens minds to the receiving him:[182] by the not putting in execution the Acts against Toryes and raparees,[183] by their attempts on corporations in order to form a Parliament of sentiments opposite to those of the last house of Commons:[184] and to go the last step, in acting so remissely in stopping and discovering the listing men for the service of the Pretender, and taking so little care when the news came of the Queens death. These seem to me instances and flagrant ones of maleadministration; and I hope my well meant zeal and multiplicity of other businesse will attone for the meanesse of the performance. Let me again enjoin you that I may not be made the single butt of the partyes malice; it is enough that I have had the whole or much greatest part of the trouble. Now as to Sir Con[*stantine*]s maner of removing Justices.[185] First

[181] Catholics who had only recently conformed to the established church. Whigs like the Brodricks were deeply sceptical of this new-found commitment to the 'protestant interest', considering it to be opportunistic and fundamentally insincere, and believing furthermore that these 'new converts' were infiltrating the political establishment in order to undermine it: see, for example, *The Conduct of the Purse of Ireland* …(1714), 13–14; *The Resolutions of the House of Commons in Ireland, Relating to the Lord-Chancellor Phipps, Examined* … (1714), 20–3.

[182] SHC, 1248/3/341–4: note, in an unidentified hand, on the prosecution of Edward Lloyd; SHC, 1248/3/183–4: transcript by Alan I of 'The papers relating to Loyde's affair'. Edward Lloyd was a Dublin bookseller who in 1712 published proposals for reprinting the *Abridgment of the Life of James II* from a London edition. He was prosecuted for treasonable libel, but the prosecution was stopped on the advice of Phipps and Archbishop Vesey, the Irish lords justices. The case was investigated by the Irish house of commons in Nov. 1713 as part of the whig campaign against Phipps (see *Anglo-Irish Politics, Vol. 1*, 33, 257, 292–3).

[183] Generic terms for Irish rural bandits. Whig allegations that the tory ministry in general and Phipps in particular had been lax in enforcing these laws, presumably as part of a strategy of encouraging the catholic and jacobite interest in Ireland, prompted Archbishop King to search for proclamations against tories and rapparees issued during Phipps's tenure of office. He claimed he could find none (TCD, MS 2536, p. 207: King to Frederick Hamilton, 12 Mar. 1714[/*15*]). The judges on the Lent circuits were then instructed to inquire what presentments had been made by grand juries against 'tories' during the previous six years (PRONI, DIO/4/5/3/60).

[184] Through the systematic use of the power afforded the Irish privy council (by the 'new rules' of 1672) to ratify the elections of chief magistrates in 21 named corporations.

[185] Like his English equivalent, the Irish lord chancellor was responsible for issuing commissions of the peace. Politically-motivated purges of ps were regarded as the norm in contemporary England (L.K.J. Glassey, *Politics and the Appointment of Justices of the Peace 1675–1720* (Oxford, 1979), 6). The situation in Ireland was complicated by the scarcity of suitable candidates in some counties (Barnard, *New Anatomy*, 50–2), but for one supposed example of Phipps dismissing a whig justice on political grounds, see TCD, MS 2536, p. 262: Archbishop King to Alan Brodrick I, 3 May 1715.

I intend not to make him the pattern which I propose to copy after; but the fact is not as represented; he did not advise with the Councel in removing every Justice of peace: I think he took up a resolution not to put any man into Commission who was not recommended by some one or more of the Privy Councel, and as the Councel then was it was mighty possible for a very ill man to g[et] into Commission without breaking that rule. But I have not taken this resolution when the Councel is I think much better formed; I shal alway have great respect for the recommendation of a Privy Councellor; but know there are a great many not of the Councel on whose understanding and sincerity I can entirely depend in a greater matter then recommending a man to the Commission of peace: nor will I lessen the power of the Chancellor by giving way to the Councels prescribing to me who are fit only to be in Commission; they have by Law sufficient power already and I intend to maintain the dignity of the Seal while I carry it.[186] But the truth is this, when the Grand Jury of the County of Dublin addressed or rather presented Higgins as a disturber of the peace and laid it before Phipps in order to put him out of Commission: he to secure himself laid the presentment before the Councel board, who in the most extraordinary maner made a formal hearing of the thing before them selves, and gravely determined that Higgins was a very pretty fellow and ought not to be turned out;[187] and if I am not mistaken Sir Con either by order of the board or on his own head superseded Mr Carter[188] and Mr Hill[189] who appeared against him. Sir Con[*stantine*] also had an order or application of Councel to turn one Disney out of Commission in the County of Waterford; the thing was this. A servant of General Stewart[190] was destroying game on Disneys estate; he challenged him for the thing and was going to take away the fellows gun who I think was a Stewart too: The man thinking to carry things off by naming the General as his Master, Disney was soe sawcy as to speak lesse respectfully of General Stewart then the other beleived he ought, and sent the fellow packing from off his Land. This was improved into a complaint of Disneys speaking contemptuously of the Stewarts, of the whole family of the Stewarts;[191] he was sent for to answer it at Councel board, bound over by order of the board to the Kings Bench, and then dismissed his farther attendance at the Councel table, which with the other charge he was put to by means of this complaint amounted as I have been informed

[186] Alan's pious professions would not have convinced his political opponents, one of whom accused him of turning out 70 tory justices (BL, Add. MS 38157, f.145: Sir Richard Cox to Edward Southwell, 23 Dec. 1714; see also NLI, MS 50549/2/19: Henry Rose to David Crosbie, 8 Jan. 1714/15).

[187] Francis Higgins (1669–1728), rector of Balrothery, Co. Dublin, and a high church firebrand who earned himself the reputation as 'the Irish Sacheverell', attending the assize dinner in Kilmainham on 4 Oct. 1711 in his capacity as a justice of the peace, behaved in so provocative a fashion that a number of whig justices persuaded the grand jury to present him as 'a common disturber of her majesty's peace'. The case was raised before the Irish privy council, which decided to take no action (*A Full and Impartial Account of the Tryal of the Reverend Mr. Francis Higgins, Prebendary of Christ-Church in Dublin; Before His Grace the Lord Lieutenant and Council of Ireland ...* (1712); Hayton, 'Sacheverell Fever by Proxy', 90–1).

[188] Identified in *A Full and Impartial Account of the Tryal of ... Francis Higgins*, 21, as Thomas Carter (c.1650–1726), of Robertstown, Co. Meath and Hollybrook, Co. Dublin, MP [I] 1695–1713 (*Hist. Ir. Parl.*, iii, 376–7).

[189] Samuel Hill (*d.* by 1724), of Kilmainham, Co. Dublin (Reg. Deeds, 1/240/146; NLI, MS 36623/1: conveyance, 11/12 June 1724).

[190] William Steuart (1652–1726), of Hanover Sq., London, MP [I] 1703–14, c.-in-c. [I] 1696–1701, 1712–14.

[191] William Disney of Churchtown, Co. Waterford. Information against Disney was given in an affidavit by one Edward Stewart, sworn on 21 Feb. 1712/13, who reported that Disney had explicitly included General Steuart in his general condemnation of the whole tribe of Stewarts (M. Butler, 'Crotty the Robber', *Journal of the Waterford and South-East of Ireland Archaeological Society*, xviii (1915), 123).

to £150. Beside this there was an order or intimation from the Councel that Disney should be turned out of Commission and he was soe. In an instance of this nature I doe not wonder att his having the countenance of the board; but in [oth]er Cases he removed Justices when he saw proper and too well knew his own authoritye and that it was the right of the Seal to displace Justices of peace when he saw reason without their order. Disney was never farther proceeded against in the Kings Bench: and indeed the thing was a scandalous oppression of a man to whom his Highnesse the General was pleased to shew marks of displeasure.

239. *Alan I, Dublin, to Thomas, 31 Mar. 1714 [recte 1715]*

(1248/3/225–6)

… The King hath determined to give the Precedence to Lord Brabazon, next to Mr Cholmondley under the title of Newborough, and then to me: Now Lord Brabazon being to be called up by writ I doe not see how a writ can passe the Great Seal to summon him to appear and sit as a Baron in Parliament till a Parliament is summoned; the writ mencions the day and place of holding the Parliament at which he is summoned to attend and give the King his advice with the Prelates, Great men and other Peers of the realm: And if it be impracticable to call a Baron by writ till there is a Parliament either actually in being or summoned to meet at a day and place certain, in which we are much strangers on this side of the water, and must be governed by the nature of the thing and from the form of the writ of summons: I say if that be impracticable, then the Barons patents must stop, or else by their bearing date prior to Lord Brabazons writ, they will have precedency of him contrary to his Majestyes intentions. The Lords Justices have wrote about this matter into England: for my part I am not in pain about the delay, but very desirous every thing should be done in that maner which may fully answer his Majestyes intentions, and give a worthy young Gentleman that precedency which I think he very well deserves on every account. I am to own the favor of your three letters of 22th, 24th, and 26th of this month, and to expresse my satisfaction for the steps already taken, and the hopes they give that such matters will be brought to light as will open the eyes of all who are not determined to continue obstinately blind. If what follows had been within my knowledge when I closed the last paper relating to the management of affairs in this Kingdome of late, I should have thought it an instance of maleadministration worth taking notice of. On Tuesday morning I went into the Closett to the Lords Justices where my Lord Archbishop of Dublin said their Excellencyes would take my advice in a matter which just then came to the knowledge of his Grace and my Lord Kildare as I understood. The Archbishop of Tuam it seems had shewn them a paper found in the house of one Duffy an Irish Popish Preist[192] by one Robert Miller a Justice of peace in the County of Mayo:[193] the paper was signed by several Irish Papists, particularly

---

[192]Patrick Duffy (b.1658), parish priest of Ballinrobe, Co. Mayo since 1696 and rural dean of the district. Although he had taken the oaths and registered according to law, he was arrested in 1712 on suspicion of exercising ecclesiastical jurisdiction, in breach of the Bishops' Banishment Act of 1697 (9 Will. III, c. 1 [I]), and found in possession of a number of incriminating documents (W.P. Burke, *The Irish Priests in the Penal Times (1660–1760)* (Waterford, 1914), 239–40, 427).

[193]Robert Miller, MP [I].

by one W[*illia*]m Brabazon a Gentleman well born,[194] and imported to be a confession of the greatnesse of the sin they had committed in taking the oath of abjuration,[195] which they owned to have done rashly and thereby to have given great and just offence to the Church: they ask pardon for the sin which they had confessed and obliged themselves to perform such penance as should be enjoined them by the Church for that great sin. I found this paper had been delivered to the Archbishop of Tuam two or three years agoe and his Grace has shewn it as well as given notice of it to former Governements. When it was admired that nothing had in all this time been done upon it his Grace said, that truly Duffy was not to be caught; and I think he added that he doubted whether Miller could at this distance of time swear to the paper. All that we could then think of which was fit to be done was to cause the paper to be sent down by Mr Budgell to the Judges of Assise then sitting att Galway, who would have an oportunitye to discourse Mr Miller about it, who is a very honest man and present Sherif of the County of Galway, with directions to have a warrant issued to apprehend Duffy and bring him before the Judges at Ballinrobe which is the town in which the Assises for the County of Mayo are to be held, and the next place where the Judges of that Circuit sit after their leaving Galway. Upon his Grace of Tuams saying that Duffy could not be caught, it was observed that he being a parish Preist registred must of recourse have given security by recognisance with good suretyes to be forthcoming and to surrender himself whenever ordered soe to doe by the Governement,[196] but I did not find that he had been called upon his recognisance: and indeed if any steps were made to call Duffy to account for this behavior I could not learn what they were. The Judges were also directed to have Duffy called upon his recognisance and that his suretyes should have notice to bring him in at the Assises, if he should not be taken on the warrant. The notice is very short, to prepare witnesses against him this Assises; but Justice MacCartney and Mr Serjeant Caulfeild[197] who go that circuit will do what becomes honest men in a matter which so much imports the safety of the Governement and of the Protestant interest of the Kingdome. I will conclude with this remark; that we have very little reason to depend on some peoples swallowing the Oath of abjuration, and that great care was taken not too much to expose or discourage those who endeavoured to make it not only not obligatory, but to represent the taking it as a damnable sin: this is one instance of some peoples care of and affection to the Protestant Succession. Whether this paper was left in his Grace of Tuams hand on the removal of the two late Lords Justices[198] I cannot tell: perhaps it was not thought by the Governement to which he shewed it first (for Mr Miller sent or gave it to him) fit to be lodged with the Secretary, but returned to be kept by his Grace: the time it came to his hands I could not particularly learn; but I fancy he then was one of the Lords Justices. The paper is gone to Galway soe that I cannot send you a Copy; but you shal have one in ten dayes.

[194] William Brabazon (1650–1731), of Lough Mask, Co. Galway.

[195] The oath abjuring the jacobite Pretender (whose right to succeed to the throne had already been recognised by the pope) had been imposed on Ireland by an English act of 1703 (1 Anne, c.17).

[196] According to the 1704 Registration Act (2 Anne, c. 7 [I]).

[197] William Caulfeild (1665–1737), of Donamon, Co. Galway, MP [I] 1692–1714, prime serjeant [I] 1714–15, and judge of king's bench [I] 1715–34.

[198] In Sept. 1714 the previous commission of lords justices [I], comprising Vesey, Sir Constantine Phipps and Archbishop Thomas Lindsay was replaced by a new commission, for Vesey, Archbishop King and the earl of Kildare.

240. *Alan I to Thomas, at his lodgings in Whitehall, 3 Apr. 1715*

(1248/3/227)

I am in great hast, and not very well: you I beleive know where Mr Hart[199] is; I know not how to direct to him, therefore desire you will send this by a porter whom he will pay; for the speedy delivery of it imports him. It is an answer to a letter of his dated 29 March about the Deanry of Connor if Dr Loyde[200] be preferred when the Bishop of Meath dyes who probably cannot hold out long.[201] … By yours, Mr Addisons, Mr Harts and Mr Temples[202] letters I perswade my self some of the late villanyes will be detected: the infatuation of the people is no otherwise to be cured.

241. *Alan I, Dublin, to Thomas, 12 Apr. 1715*

(1248/3/228–31)

I have your letter of the seventh; and from it as well as the observations I make from other occurrences doe apprehend that there is a sett of men in the world that would put all things into the last degree of confusion. Pray inform me whether it be true that the mob frequently huzzaes and attends the D[uke] of O[rmond's][203] Coach: This day I heard a story, that his Coach coming after that of the Prince,[204] and some of the Princes guard being behind or about it, that a rabble of people assembled as apprehending him to be in confinement under a Guard: the number was mentioned to have increased prodigiously in a short time. For my part I beleive it all to be invention; but I ought not to be too rash in my censure, when I consider that he who told the story said it came from an house near St Maryes, by which I understood that of a great man who ought not to be suspected of divulging things that are not true, and is supposed to have the best intelligence that one sort of people send over hither. I find the Attorney Generals[205] letter went not to the Post office till the pacquet went off, so that this will come as soon to your hand as that. I am in some pain for fear I may be thought not to have acted consistently with my self in the matter of the Cushion which is now to be filled, since it is at length determined Levinge shal not be the man. The thing stands thus. Before I left England Mr Luther[206] was the first named by those of Ireland who were in London as fit to be put on the Bench after the three Cheif

---

[199] Probably Josiah Hort (c.1674–1751), formerly chaplain to Lord Wharton as lord lieutenant, then rector of Kilskyre, Co Meath. He became dean of Cloyne in 1718 and eventually archbishop of Tuam (*Oxf. DNB*).

[200] Owen Lloyd (c.1664–1738), fellow of TCD, and dean of Connor 1710–d. (*Al. Dub.*, 506; Cotton, *Fasti*, iii, 254).

[201] William Moreton (1640–1715) died on 21 Nov. 1715.

[202] Henry Temple (c.1673–1757), of East Sheen, Surrey, later 1st Viscount Palmerston.

[203] James Butler (1665–1745), 2nd duke of Ormond. For his popularity among tory and jacobite mobs, see P.K. Monod, *Jacobitism and the English People 1688–1788* (Cambridge, 1989), 180–2.

[204] George (1683–1760), prince of Wales, later King George II.

[205] George Gore, MP [I] had been appointed attorney-general [I] in Dec. 1714.

[206] Henry Luther. Sunderland had sent him a message in Nov. 1714 that, although he had not been raised to the bench in the recent round of appointments, he would be the first provided for on any new opportunity (BL, Add. MS 61639, f. 63: William Whitshed to Sunderland, 17 Nov. 1714).

Judges and McCartney: Mr Pocklington Mr Gilbert and Sir John St Leger were named in England, and Sir Gilbert Dolben[207] continued; so as there was only one place to be filled; and Levinge was thought the proper person. His letter came over long before Christmas and he refused it early in December; Luthers freinds then thought he stood fair: and for ought I know he would have then succeeded but that some application was made for Mr Boate.[208] Levinge all the while gave himself such airs that I thought were not for the Kings honour or my Lord Lieutenants, and I did represent him and his behavior as I think he deserved with intent to oblige him to accept or finally to relinquish: for the letter lay here stil, and it seemed a mighty desirable thing in England that he would vouchsafe to accept. At length I wrote soe warmly that I had this answer, that it was thought fit he should be the man, for reasons that I should be told when Lord S[*underlan*]d came over. Upon this I desisted till after Mr Luthers death,[209] and one reason was that I might not seem to have my freinds interest in view only, as I should seem to have had if I should again write after being told this by a person who best knew how far honour was concerned in it. When Luther dyed I thought I could not be then suspected of being influenced by my freindship to him in what I wrote, and again shewed how much too great a value had been putt upon him; and with how little respect he had acted toward the Governement. On 29th March Mr Addison wrote to me, that Mr Luther being dead Lord Wharton and Mr Denton[210] made interest for Boate; told me he did not know how the matter of Levinge stood, and seemed to ask from me what character Mr Boate bears. I who beleived by Lord Sunderlands letter that some reasons had been given for continuing the tendernesse to Levinge which nothing from this side could prevail against,[211] in answer to Mr Addisons letter told him at large how Levinges affair stood: and I doe confesse I think him to have acted such a part in this matter, that if there were no other objection he ought to be the last man living now putt on the Bench: how far he merited such a post before in my opinion, is very well known. I told Mr Addison I beleived Levinge was so fixed as not to be shaken; and at the same time reminded him how Levinge had behaved toward Lord Wharton in Ireland, and hinted that his Lordship owed him a good turn.[212] I also gave Mr Boate the character of an honest Gentleman, but did not recommend him to the Bench: tho I must own I could not expect Lord Wharton would endeavour to remove Levinge to make way for any body but his own freind; and when I wrote that letter I did not foresee that anything lesse then a very

[207] Sir Gilbert Dolben (c.1659–1722), of Finedon, Northants., MP [E & GB] 1685–98, 1701–15, judge of common pleas [I] 1701–20 (*HC 1690–1715*, iii, 890–6).

[208] Godfrey Boate (1673–1721), of Dawson St., Dublin, made prime serjeant [I] in 1715, and promoted the following year to become a justice of king's bench [I] (Ball, *Judges*, ii, 194).

[209] Luther died on 19 Mar. 1714 (*Hist. Ir. Parl.*, v, 140).

[210] Alexander Denton (1679–1740), of Hillersden, Bucks., and the Middle Temple, MP [GB] 1708–10, 1715–22, formerly private secretary to Lord Wharton as lord lieutenant of Ireland, and MP [I] 1709–13 (*HC 1690–1715*, iii, 871–2; *Hist. Ir. Parl.*, iv, 50–1).

[211] According to Joseph Addison, 'our great men' in England were 'studying … to gratify' Levinge, an intention which Sunderland strenuously (and successfully) opposed (*The Letters of Joseph Addison*, ed. Walter Graham (Oxford, 1941), 323–4).

[212] Although holding the office of solicitor-general in Ireland, Levinge defied Wharton in Aug. 1709 by speaking and voting against the money bill, for which he was summarily dismissed (NLI, MS 38369/18: Charles Robins to Hugh Howard, 13 Aug. 1709; *The Prose Writings of Jonathan Swift*, ed. Herbert Davis et al. (16 vols, Oxford, 1939–74), iii, 239). He continued in opposition in 1710 (*Addison Letters*, ed. Graham, 222) and in Dec. 1710 was reported to be in London, promoting a proposal for Wharton's impeachment (*Swift Corr.*, i, 323).

powerful enemy could shake Levinges interest. On 31th March Denton writes to me in behalf of Boate, tells me Lord Wharton would also have done it, but thought it unnecessary after having wrote to me on his behalf before. As to what Denton said about Lord Wharton I took that to be only Dentons own words, and answered that it would alway be a great pleasure to me to obey Lord Whartons commands; but neither on his former letter nor now recommended Boate; only in answer to Dentons letter told him I was not Mr Boates enemy, which he might know by what I had written the post before to Mr Addison, who could (I beleived) tell him how the matter stood as to Levinge. After all this comes a letter from Mr Delafoy[213] of 5 April that it was at length resolved Levinge should not be the man; names Caulfeild,[214] but then starts the objection of his being wanted in the house of commons; and points at Boate under the description of a person against whom no such objection lay. I now perceiving that Levinge was not laid aside upon Lord Whartons application, but really because it was understood to be very wrong to let him act longer toward the Governement as he had done, gave my thoughts freely for Serjeant Caulfeild: and the Attorney General and Will Conelye[215] were of the same mind: and I hope he will be considered as having served in every Parliament very well, and being related to a very great part of the honest Gentlemen in one part of the Kingdome. I hope I have made this matter so intelligible that my letters to Addison or Denton may not be used to prejudice Caulfeild; nor my letter to Delafoy to be thought any way inconsistent with the letters I wrote to Mr Addison and Mr Denton: Of this I would have you spoke to Lord Lieutenant and Mr Addison. And at the same time pray take an oportunitye to tell my Lord Lieutenant, that when the three Cheif Judges Mr Conelye and I mett to consider whether the revenue stood soe that probably there would be sufficient to provide for the seven regiments his Majesty had resolved to send over and put on the Irish establishment on 25th March 1715 that we considered the debt and credit of the nation as it appeared to us at that time; but that if the regiments continue stil in England, and are paid while there according to the English establishment and this charge shal in the end fall on this Kingdome, if money be sent over to them by way of advance for their subsistance, and we are to pay the exchange, if new demands are made on our treasury (for example to reimburse Officers of regiments which were put on our establishment before they came into the Kingdome, and the Officers consequently had paid more men and a greater pay then our establishment allows) as in the case of Colonel Chudleigh,[216] who hath a letter which if it be not otherwise ordered by the King, will draw about £2000 out of the Treasury, and be a precedent to half a dozen more regiments to make the same demand: I say if things of this sort (which we could not foresee at that time) shal fall on the Kingdome it will mightily alter the case. When I call Colonel Chudleighs case a precedent I would not be thought to fancy the like was never done before; I know the contrary: but as it was alway wrong it was hoped a representation made by the Lords Justices in a letter wrote by them to Lord Lieutenant in February last had and would put a stop to every thing of that nature for the future. But his Majestyes letter in favor of Colonel Chudleigh dated in December is now produced and an order from the Lords Justices on the

---

[213] Charles Delafaye, MP [I].

[214] William Caulfeild.

[215] William Conolly, MP [I].

[216] Thomas Chudleigh (c.1688–1726), col. of the 34th regiment of foot and later lieutenant governor of the Royal Hospital, Chelsea (Dalton, *Geo. I's Army*, i, 170).

Treasury for the money is immediately expected. You may also remind my Lord that none of the seven regiments are landed, and that it will be very greivous to have so much of the little money we have drawn off on that score. Not to mention three other regiments putt upon our establishment as from Lady day,[217] whose pay is to go to the raising the regiment and consequently to be remitted into England with exchange att our expence; but when we are to have the men God only knows; but in all probabilitye not till our Parliament is over. It is better to mention these things before hand then hear of them hereafter: Some of them may be prevented; as the regiments may be sent over, and by what we were given to understand they were on their march long before 25 March and some if not all of them it was beleived would have been on the spot by that time. As to the money to make the pay of regiments on our establishment before they come hither, equal to the English or Flemish, I protest I know not where a fund will be found for it, and hope this blow will be warded by my Lord Lieutenants care and goodnesse. I know how unacceptable an emploiment I am now desiring you to undertake, and that it were better to come from another hand then mine: but the Judges are out of town who were spoken to and advised with by my Lord Lieutenants direction; and it is not unlikely things may have gone too far in England to be recalled if I should be silent till their coming to town. Mr Conelye sent over to my Lord the state of the debt and credit of the Nation; by the establishment and an estimate of the revenue a pretty near guesse may be made what condition we shal be in at the opening of a Parliament; and when such a thing is done, it must be upon a supposition that great summes will not be drawn off by letters, which will much alter the case; and yet be no reason for taxing any body with having miscalculated, or said the revenue would go farther then it doth, when a considerable part is diverted into a chanel not thought of. I wish to God these matters may be well considered and that there may not new difficultyes be laid in the way of my Lord Lieutenants having every thing easy in Parliament. I wonder Sir Thomas Hanmer is become soe inconsiderable as not to be thought worth notice in any private letter how he manages.[218] Our freind in Ormond Street I doubt is the same dead vote as ever … Pray what was the particular behavior of our freind on Chelsea Commons which intitled him to be one of the six: I doe not doubt he deserved the treatment he mett with.[219] Is it true that when Sir W[illia]m Windham[220] was ordered to withdraw one hundred and thirty members went out with him.[221] Such behavior we are not used to here.

[217] The feast of the annunciation (25 Mar.), a quarter-day and the beginning of the New Year in the Julian calendar (Old Style).

[218] Sir Thomas Hanmer (1677–1746), 4th Bt, of Mildenhall, Suffolk; MP [GB] Suffolk. Speaker of the British house of commons, and a prominent 'Hanoverian tory', he had been offered the chancellorship of the exchequer [GB] by George I in 1714 but had declined it (Linda Colley, *In Defiance of Oligarchy: The Tory Party 1714–60* (Cambridge, 1982), 181).

[219] The friend in Ormond Street may be William Ashe (*c.*1675–bef.1732), MP [GB] Heytesbury (*HC 1715–54*, i, 422–3). The inhabitant of Chelsea Common may be Sir John Perceval, who as Viscount Perceval was one of six new Irish peers ennobled in Mar. 1715 alongside Alan I. Besides being the only tory on the list, Perceval was a political rival of the Brodricks in Co. Cork.

[220] Sir William Wyndham (c.1688–1740), 3rd Bt, of Orchard Wyndham, Somerset, MP [GB] for Somerset and a leading tory.

[221] On 6 Apr. 1715 after Wyndham had denounced the king's proclamation for a new parliament as 'unprecedented and unwarrantable', and even as 'of dangerous consequence to the very being of parliaments' the Commons voted on a division by 208 to 129 that he withdraw from the House. He was accompanied by all those who had voted in the minority. (John Oldmixon, *The History of England …* (1735), 592).

242. *Alan I, Dublin, to Thomas, 14 Apr. 1715*

(1248/3/232–3)

I goe within two hours with Mr Conelye to spend a week att Castletowne[222] but before I goe, will own the receit of yours and my sister Martha's letters of the ninth instant. I doe not know what resolutions are taken by Lady Burlington in relation to a representative at Youghal now Mr Luther is dead; but I could be very well contented her Ladyship were spoken to and would not too readily engage her interest, for fear her good disposition may be wrought upon to make a promise where she would not have given her interest, if she had throughly known the person recommended: beside a good deal of care ought to be taken that in soe populous an election the person pitched upon be one whom some of the people know and think well of. I write to Senny this night, to know what the thoughts of the town are, and who are making interest.

The paper following is a true Copy of that which I formerly mentioned.[223]

We the undernamed do hereby acknowledge and declare our error, and fault in taking the oath of abjuration most rashly, against the visible rules of our holy mother the Church, who condemned it as invented in odium fidei Catholicae[224] and of dangerous consequence to it; of truth uncertain, scandalous and unjust: for which we ask God and his Churches pardon: And do promise to perform any penance, at our rulers discretion to be at any time imposed as satisfaction thought necessary for our sin on the account of this Oath; which, as unlawful, we beleive does no ways bind our consciences to stand by it. Witnesse our hands this [bank] day of March. 1711.

This paper is signed with the following names. W[illia]m Brabazon. David Bourke. W[illia]m Towlfer. Christopher French. James Garvey. Mathias Gata. Richard Bourke. Richard Bourke. John Merish. Anthony Garvey.

Some of these ten persons are men of note: particularly Mr Brabazon. I formerly told you when and in what maner I came to the knowledge of this matter, and what care was now taken to enquire into it, whatever remissenesse there may have been formerly. The truth is, it seems to me that some people were willing enough to have it beleived not to be a paper signed by the persons whose names are written under it as having signed it: for the person who produced that paper produced also another at the same time in the following words.

Whereas a paper was found in the custody of Patrick Duffy, Popish Preist of the parish of Ballinrobe signed with my name, and the names of several others containing a recantation of, and expressing our sorrow for having taken the oath of abjuration, acknowledging our error and fault in taking it, begging Gods and his Churches pardon for it, as a thing unlawful; promising to perform any penance that should be imposed by way of satisfaction; and farther

---

[222]Castletown in Co. Kildare, where Conolly would build his principal country seat from 1722 onwards.
[223]See above, p. 57.
[224]In hatred of the catholic faith.

declaring that we beleive the said Oath does not bind our Consciences to stand by it. Now I William Brabazon of Loghmaske Esq doe hereby declare that I did not sign the said paper, nor any other paper to that effect; nor did I ever make any such acknowledgement, promise or declaration as is therein expressed, either by word or writing to any person whatsoever; and that my name is putt to the same paper, without my direction knowledge or consent. And I doe farther declare that I did not rashly (as in the said paper is falsely expressed) but on due consideration take the said oath, which I do beleive to be imposed by lawful authority, and to contain nothing in itself unlawful, and that therefore it does bind my conscience. Witnesse my hand William Brabazon.[225] This paper is witnessed thus: Present Martin Blake[226] Henry Bingham.[227] I am yet to learn at what time, to what end, and at whose instance this paper of recantation was signed, or by what means it came into the hands of his Grace the Archbishop of Tuam; but it is pretty observable that Sir Henry Byngham (who was his Graces son in Law and a most zealous Tory) is one of the witnesses to it.[228] Perhaps it might be thought reasonable to make enquiry into the matter soe far, as to see whether Brabazon would confesse it; and upon his denying it, his word was of so much weight as to supersede all farther enquiry: but beside that his Grace said, at the time of his producing this paper, that the countrey beleived it to be the subscription of Brabazon, notwithstanding the paper which disowns it; why was it not enquired whether the other nine names were the handwriting of the persons who carry those names? Why was it not enquired how and for what end the Preist gott or counterfeited such a paper? For the paper was found by Mr Miller a Justice of Peace among the Preists other papers, which he seised upon some occasion not necessary to insert. I confesse I think the politicks that then prevailed did not allow of making any discoveryes that might shew, we were not certain of those people being through enemyes to the Pretender who had abjured him: any thing of this kind might have been a reason to shew lesse countenance to the Papists, and to place lesse confidence in new converts then it was judged reasonable about that time to shew. In short while the scheme was carryed on to bring the grand affair about nothing could be more uneasy then to shew or discover that there was any prospect or danger of the matter being effected: They were the best subjects who could not be perswaded to beleive he had any party in the Kingdome; and those who were of another opinion, were termed factious, and disaffected to her Majestyes governement and to the Administration. I hope soon to be able to tell you what the new Judges have been able to doe in it.

This matter coming to my knowledge in the maner I mention, you will not have me vouched as the Author; but it will be publick enough when the Judges return to town and give an account of this affair, and what they have done in it at Ballinrobe Assises.

[225] Printed in the *Dublin Gazette*, 29 July 1712 (John Brady, 'Catholics and Catholicism in the Eighteenth-century Press', *Archivium Hibernicum*, xvi (1951), Appendix, 17–18).

[226] Martin Blake (*d*.1744), of Moyne, Coolcon Castle, and Ballintober, Co. Mayo, a recent convert to the church of Ireland (Eileen O'Byrne and Anne Chamney, *The Convert Rolls...* (Dublin, 2005), 13, 299; M.J. Blake, *Blake Family Records ...* (ser. 2, 1905), 191. Blake's name is not included in a list of jps for Co. Mayo in Feb. 1714 (NAI, M 6236/7).

[227] Either Sir Henry Bingham (1654–1714), 3rd Bt, of Castlebar, Co. Mayo, MP Co. Mayo 1692–*d*.; or his cousin and brother-in-law Henry Bingham MP [I] Co. Mayo in 1712 and Castlebar from 1715.

[228] It was Henry Bingham of Foxford who married Archbishop Vesey's daughter Anne.

243. *Alan I, Dublin, to Thomas, at his lodgings in Whitehall, 21 Apr. 1715*

(1248/3/234–5)

I am just returned from Mr Conelyes where I spent the last week and mett yours of the sixteenth just on my alighting out of the Coach. You may be sure I foresaw and sorely regretted the losse the publick had in my Lord Marquesse of Whartons death, whose fiant for passing a patent to create him Marquesse of Carlow was brought to me and signed by me as then received on the very day of his death: but his patent was not sealed in his lifetime. The Toryes have it that our Lord Lieutenants ilnesse is such as will certainly kill him, and give out that it hath already soe far affected him as to make him wholly unfit for businesse. I know it to be natural, to give an easy beleif to what you wish should be true, and I know also that they are such vile lyars that not one word they say is to be depended upon because they report it; especially when it is in favor of their villainous Jacobite cause. Pray tell me hath his intermitting feaver soe far laid hold on him as to affect his head, for so they report. We are also told that it is among them that the Archbishop of Canterbury,[229] the Duke of Marleborough[230] and Mr Walpole[231] are irrecoverably ill; and it comes from several hands, and particularly from one between whom and a near relation of yours there once was a very near prospect of a match, that a new Lord Lieutenant is talked of, and particularly that Lord Pembroke is named:[232] pray tell me whether Lord Sunderlands ilnesse hath not in great measure proceeded from being insufferably teazed with perpetual sollicitation.[233] A later letter about Serjeant Caulfeild hath shewn you that tho I could have been content Lord Wharton should have been able to set Levinge aside, which I had reason to beleive nothing from hence could doe; yet when that was resolved in without being Lord Whartons act in favor of Mr Boate, I was and am of opinion the Serjeant hath much the better pretensions to the Cushion: and I hope my last letter hath prevented your doing any thing pursuant to my first in favor of Mr Boate to the prejudice of the Serjeant. I find my self better for the little air and exercise I have had in the countrey, but far from being well: my stomach to flesh is very much gone, which I attribute in great measure to the Tea and Coffee I usually breakfast on. Beside I am frequently troubled with sicknesse at stomach, which is succeeded presently by giddinesse. According to my sisters advice I let bloud and took much stuffe given me by Dr Cumin,[234] but find my self very little the better for it. Pray tell me doe the people without door follow the example of those within whom you mention to own that they have been imposed upon by the cry of the

---

[229] Thomas Tenison (1636–1715) had been seriously unwell since Sept. 1714. He died on 14 Dec. 1715 (*HL 1660–1715*, v, 512).

[230] John Churchill (1650–1722), 1st duke of Marlborough.

[231] Robert Walpole (1676–1745), of Houghton, Norfolk, MP [GB] King's Lynn and paymaster of the forces [GB].

[232] Thomas Herbert (c.1656–1733), 8th earl of Pembroke.

[233] Sunderland had been 'much out of order' since the middle of March and for a time had been confined to his rooms unable to see anyone. He had recovered by the middle of April, after taking himself into the country (TCD, MS 1995–2008/1613–14, 1623: Charles Delafaye to Archbishop King, 5, 16 Apr. 1715; Frederick Hamilton to [King], 5 Apr. 1715).

[234] Duncan Cumyng (*d.*1724), of Dublin, a noted presbyterian physician (Barnard, *New Anatomy*, 129, 381–2; Robert Whan, *The Presbyterians of Ulster, 1680–1730* (Woodbridge, 2013), 152–3).

danger of the Church. By the chearfulnesse or rather sawcynesse of the Toryes one would think they were uppermost; especially the French Kings answer to Lord Stairs memorial,[235] and the new[s] of Mr Cadogans negotiation not having heard [*sic*] the desired effect[236] have arrived.

244. *Alan I, Dublin, to Thomas, 26 Apr. 1715*

(1248/3/236–7)

I wonder since yours of the sixteenth mentions the secret Committees[237] having sate and acted that day as well as the day before, that you should take no notice of Mr Walpooles ilnesse, which Mr Israel Feilding[238] gave such an account of to Mr Manley[239] as made us fear the next post would have told us he was dead: but we are eased of that painful apprehension by later letters which mention his having been at the Committee on the 21th and that his ilnesse had in some sort retarded the proceedings and inquiry of that Committee. Is it true that Dr Brett who some time since spoke in plain terms what I perswade my self some more of our Clergy would fain be at, that auricular confession was necessary etc hath laid down all his livings, in order to declare himself of that Church which hath made it a sacrament:[240] If he hath quitted his preferment in our Church I shal not be much to seek for the inducement to his so doing. I neither have authority from Major General Pearce[241] to name him, nor doe I know whether the thing be true or not, so desire not to be named on the occasion, if what I write be thought worth the notice of those who seem to be desirous of getting true informacion by what steps our late ministry proceeded in quitting the Allyes and striking up that peace that Europe owes so much to. But I heard an odd story of orders being sent by a certain Ambassador to Lord P who at that time (I mean when the orders were sent

---

[235] Louis XIV's response to a memorial delivered by the newly appointed ambassador extraordinary from King George I, John Dalrymple (1673–1747), 2nd earl of Stair, complaining at the failure of the French to comply with the terms of the peace of Utrecht in relation to the port of Dunkirk. Although couched in conciliatory terms, the regent's response refuted British allegations (Boyer, *Political State*, ix, 251–60).

[236] William Cadogan (c.1671–1726), of Caversham, Berks., MP [GB] New Woodstock and envoy to the United Provinces, and entrusted with negotiations for a revised barrier treaty, which were eventually completed in Nov. 1715.

[237] The secret committee, or 'committee of secrecy', comprising 21 members, under the chairmanship of Robert Walpole, appointed by the house of commons in Apr. 1715 to inquire into the making of the peace of Utrecht and the management of the previous ministry.

[238] Israel Feilding (b.c.1655), of Denmark Street, Westminster, sometime commissary-gen. of stores [E], and a near-contemporary of the Brodrick brothers at the Middle Temple, having been admitted in 1676 (*VCH Yorks., North Riding*, i, 134–8; HMC, *Portland MSS*, v, 497; *CTBP*, 1742–5, p. 510; *M. Temple Adm.*, i, 193).

[239] Isaac Manley, MP [I].

[240] Thomas Brett (1677–1744), rector of Ruckinge in Kent, had published in 1711 a sermon which landed him in a controversy because of its 'high view of sacerdotal absolution'. He refused to take the oaths to George I and resigned his livings, being received into the nonjuring church of England. He strenuously denied the kind of accusation Alan I is making in *Dr. Brett's Vindication of Himself from the Calumnies Thrown upon Him in Some Late News-papers, Wherein He is Falsly Charged with Turning Papist … (1715)*. (*Oxf. DNB*).

[241] Thomas Pearce (c.1667–1739), of Ballyhearsy, Co. Wicklow, MP [I] 1703–13, 1727– *d*., and [GB] 1710–13; major-gen. and governor of Limerick.

away by the Ambassador) either was or was supposed to be in Portugal:[242] but it seems before they came to Lisbon, he was gone for England, and they[243] followed him; by which means our men were drawn into the feild by Major General Pearce, to the great surprize of the Spaniard who depended on our not joining the Portugueze.[244] If this was the Case, there was a cessation also to be in Portugal, and that confederate was to have been at the mercy of the French just as the Imperialists and Dutch were to have been in Flanders, if all the foreign troops in the pay of great Britain had followed the orders and example of the Pacifick General.[245] If this be thought worth enquiring into, I should think by the maner I heard the story related that Major General Pearce must be able to give a full account of it; I heard that the orders were sent back again from England to him, but that it was soe ordered that our troops continued that campaigne with the Portugueze and probably were the means of their enemyes not having the greatest advantage possible of them. I formerly told you something of a paper found among the papers of one Duffy a Popish Preist importing an acknowledgement of the great sin some papists confessed themselves to have been guilty of in abjuring the Pretender, and obliging themselves to undergoe any penance that should be enjoined them for that wicked act: Justice McCartney is come to town, and tells me that Duffy the Preist is not to be caught, at least was not while he was in the Circuit. But by an account he brings up of that matter from one Mr Miller the Justice of peace who seized the Papers, there were several papers delivered by him to his Grace the Archbishop of Tuam, and among the rest one signed Albani and entred in several Offices, which Miller saith he took to be a bull empowring some here to absolve those who had taken the oath of abjuration, upon confessing their sin and engaging to perform penance for it.[246] This, and other papers I suppose remain stil with his Grace, he having only produced the two of which I sent you Copyes to the Lords Justices; I was by when Justice MacCartney reported to the Justices how he found this matter, and expressed my self pretty freely upon the occasion, that I thought lesse notice had been taken by the Governement that then was of this matter then it deserved: and desired the bull might be produced: his Grace with some warmth said Miller was mistaken (he put it in worse language) in saying there was any bull: I desired to see the writing signed Albani and entred in so many offices: I mean I expressed my sense that that and the other papers should be laid before the new Lords Justices: and will before they meet next speak to the Archbishop of Dublin and Lord Kildare on that subject: by a certain persons behavior I perceive an enquiry into it will not be very

---

[242] Charles Mordaunt (c.1658–1735), 3rd earl of Peterborough, c.-in-c. of forces in the Peninsula, had returned to England in 1707, and though there were rumours in Nov. 1710 that he would return, he did not do so (*HL 1660–90*, iii, 935).

[243] The orders.

[244] Pearce had fought in the Peninsula campaigns in Anne's reign, and served as deputy c.-in-c. in Portugal 1711–13. In Oct. 1712 he mistakenly brought his forces into action after the cessation of arms between Britain and France and Spain had been agreed, which led to complaints from the French (*HC 1690–1715*, v, 119; *Evening Post*, 4–7 Oct. 1712; *London Gazette*, 15–18 Nov. 1712; *Letters and Correspondence, Public and Private, of … Henry St John, Lord Visc. Bolingbroke …*, ed. Gilbert Parke (4 vols, 1798), iii, 185).

[245] The 2nd duke of Ormond, appointed in Feb. 1712 c.-in-c. of the army in Flanders but in the following May issued with orders not to engage with the enemy (the so-called 'restraining orders'). These were debated in parliament in 1712 and may well have formed part of the case behind Ormond's abortive impeachment, begun in June 1715 but forestalled by his flight to France in August.

[246] Confirmed in 'a letter written from Castlebar', 23 Sept. 1712, printed in Burke, *Irish Priests in Penal Times*, 240. Annibale Albani (1682–1751), a nephew of Pope Clement XI, was cardinal-archbishop of Sabina.

agreeable; but I hope things of this sort will be fit for the view of the new Governement, which perhaps may think them worth being taken notice of in a letter to the ministry in England I mean to my Lord Lieutenant. I was so bold to desire to be informed by his Grace of Tuam whether the then Justices had written about this matter into England, to which I doe not remember he gave any answer, yet cannot take his silence for a consent that the Justices had written over. Two of the Pretenders men was convicted of high treason on full evidence this Assises for listing for the Pretender in May last att the Assises at Wexford. It was proved that it was declared at the time of their listing that it was in the service of King James the 3d as they called him, that they were to come back with him into England before the harvest was over etc and it is remarkable that the indictment was found and the witnesses were ready last Assises, on whose testimony they were now convicted, yet the then Judges did not think fit to try them. I think Sir Ri[chard] Cox was one of them. Do not vouch me of the matter of the Bull but you shal soon hear more of it.

245. *Alan I, Dublin, to Thomas, 28 Apr. 1715*

(1248/3/238–9)

I have just received yours of the 23d with an account of your having had a severe fit of the stone which creates me a great deal of anxiety and trouble; for beside the danger of that distemper, it renders a mans life extremely miserable for a great time before it puts an end to it: but I hope yours is not more then gravel, in which case moderate exercise often doth wonders; but that is what you too much disuse.

The two battalions of Lord Orkney[247] are landed at Corke and are on their march to Limrick; and the sooner the others come you know it will be the better for the reasons I gave formerly. I am sorry that you have ground to hint to me those causes of their not being yet on their march which you mention: it is most true, that it greatly imports this poor countrey to have those men in Ireland which we are to maintain: for as no countrey that I know beside this payes very near its whole current Cash into the Treasury once every year, it is impossible but we must be utterly undone if we continue to have what little ready money we have carryed out of the Kingdome by paying troops abroad; for if they are in England, we are as fully ruined by paying them there as if they were in the West Indies.[248] I gave my Lord Lieutenant an account which letter I delivered, and sent the other back the day I delivered that; I have also told him that a Councel was held, and intimation given of such a letter, but that nothing farther was then done; the reason offered for not doing any thing then was the thinnesse of the Councel, most of the Councellors being out of town, and all the Judges in their Circuits. It was also thought that the letter was not very pressing nor seemed to require much dispatch; and from that time to this no Councel hath been held. The Councel may now be called, for the Judges are all returned; but I hear of no step toward it yet; but will make bold to remind the Justices of my Lord Lieutenants

---

[247] George Hamilton (1666–1737), 1st earl of Orkney, general of foot and col. of the Royal Scots.

[248] Irish whig politicians repeatedly urged on English whig ministers the political necessity of retaining in Ireland troops on the Irish establishment who were subsisted from the Irish public revenue. The issue had become of greater importance since the Hanoverian succession, as troops were moved more often (McGrath, *Ireland and Empire*, 155).

letter, and the mischeif that will attend the establishment so much exceeding the revenue, if it continue soe long. You will guesse at some of the reasons why all people may not be equally sollicitous to have the Parliament meet soon, and cannot fail of one which hinders me from being too ready to note any thing that seems to me to be an omission or fault in those who govern: but I wish my Lord Lieutenants health and his Majestyes service in England may admit of his being soon among us[249] ... I have no account from my Lord Lieutenant since sending him the accounts of what seemed to me to have been done very irregularly here; nor what is thought of the report of the privy Councel in relation to the bundle of pamphlets called English advice etc nor is there any letter come to the castle relating to making Serjeant Caulfeild a Judge; but perhaps these things depend upon my Lord Lieutenants return to town, which I hope will be soon, and in good health. I doe assure you I hear and doe observe great industry is used by some men to gett themselves well with high Church; and if I am not mistaken that humor will spread, if some little care be not taken to convince people that they must not make their court to those who expresse no great respect for such as are no higher Church men then my Lord Lieutenant etc. Some of our own sett are mighty well pleased to have gained the character of being misunderstood as not so good Church men as they now appear to be: and you know a good deal of zeal must be shewn to gain the good word of the Tory party: this to your self only. ... Now Lord Wharton is dead, I observe some people not lesse respectful in their expressions toward Lord Sunderland: I know there was a very strict correspondence between two persons here and his Lordship: My sister will tell you whom I mean: one is he whom we used to banter Ally with as being very handsome; the other she used to put out of countenance by calling him by a nickname out of the Bath. I will tell you an observation I have made since my landing. I doe not hear of one man preferred in the Church by a certain A[*rchbisho*]p who would be thought a State Whig,[250] but who are very high Church men; and as to a certain person now in London, his letters are very frequent in favor of rank Toryes to preserve them in their places in the custom house; but what step he hath made in favor of any one Whig I am not yet to learn. I mention these things, that if possible things may not too entirely be in their disposition. What I wrote lately about the bull, and the little successe I had in getting some people to call for it, startles me much: Are the mismanagements of the late people in so very flagrant an instance to be covered, and no endeavour used to disclose them by those who only have power to doe it. I will not give that matter over; and resolve if I cannot gett that paper to be called by the Lords Justices, to move to have it brought before the Councel, as a paper of which they were once possessed of, and greatly importing the State. I think you mean Mr Stephens in one part of your letter by the description you give him of a man who spoke to you about a certain affair:[251] I wrote my mind very honestly to Mr Delafay,

---

[249]Lady Bristol reported from London on 30 Apr., 'Lord Sun[*derland*] is going in a few days to the Bath; he is in town, but sees no body, he is so extream ill, and vomits every thing he takes' (*Letter-books of John Hervey, First Earl of Bristol* ... (3 vols, Wells, 1894), ii, 3). Sunderland did receive some benefit from the waters, staying in Bath for well over a month, but even when he returned to London was easily tired and avoided public occasions (TCD, MS 1995–2008/1643, 1659, 1678: Charles Delafaye to Archbishop King, 21 May, 9 June, 21 July 1715).

[250]A letter-writer announcing William King's death in 1729 commented, 'His general character was this – a state whig, a church tory' (Sir C.S. King, *A Great Archbishop of Dublin William King, D.D.* ... (1906), 275).

[251]A 'Counsellor Stephens' had been employed as an agent by the General Synod of Ulster since 1705. This is most likely to have been Walter Stephens, a master in chancery [I]. (See *Anglo-Irish Politics, Vol. 1*, 229.)

of how ill consequence it would be to hearken to Sir Alexander Cairnes[252] or Mr Shute[253] in an affair of that kind: And indeed it seems odd to me that men of that sort should at all interpose in things of such a nature with which they ought not to concern themselves, nor are any way qualifyed to give an opinion in.

246. *Alan I to Thomas, 3 May 1715*

(BL, Add. MS 61636, ff. 155–6)

You will easily beleive I write to you under a good deal of disorder and melancholy, when I am to tell you that my Lord Cheif Baron dyed about two of the clock this morning of a feaver;[254] not a burning raging one; on the contrary he was outwardly cool; but very much oppressed in his spirits, his distemper lying cheifly in his head: the methods taken with him were those constantly used by the Physitians here, bleeding, vomiting, and purging him to a great degree.

He went into his Coach from his own house on his circuit in a very violent fit of the Gout, which I confesse gave me very much pain: but he undertook the journey in that very ill condition of health upon this worthy principle, that since his colleage (Baron Pocklington) was a gentleman perfectly a stranger to the course of our Courts, as much to several of our Laws (I mean those Statutes which are of force here and not in England) it was his duty to undergoe a great deal of uneasinesse rather then leave the Baron (whom he very truly valued) under the whole trouble of any one part of the Circit. For you may believe I ordered it soe, as to divide the three new Judges and Serjeant Caulfeild who had not gone any circuit in Ireland before, and to join each of them with a man well versed in the Statute Laws and practice of the Courts here. But little foresaw what the event would be in relation to this very valuable man, of whom I may most truly say (without derogating from any one wom he hath left behind) that no one man on any of the Benches exceeded him in the qualifications which constitute and justly intitle a man to the character of a very able and a very good Judge. Possibly my conjecture may have little in it; but I am apt to think his journey and fatigue in the Circuit might strike the gent into his head and hasten his death that way. No doubt the place will be sollicited for by more then would be able to fill it with reputation after him; all my care is that my Lord Lieutenant may be apprised of what consequence it will be to have that Cushion well supplyed: his Excellencye will consider that Mr Baron Pocklington and Sr John St Leger, tho very deserving Gentlemen, yet are both of them very new in the businesse here; and particularly that neither of them attended the Exchequer in England, tho if they had, the course of that Court and this are intirely different: soe that I hope his Excellencye will consider whether his Successor ought not to be a man conversant in the businesse and well versed in the course of the Exchequer of Ireland. Nor doe I say this with a view to keep out any English Lawyer as such, or in

[252]Sir Alexander Cairnes, MP [I].

[253]John Barrington Shute (1678–1734), of Beckett, Berks., MP [GB] Berwick-upon-Tweed; a presbyterian himself and a spokesman for protestant dissenting interests in the British house of commons (*HC 1715–54*, i, 437–9).

[254]Joseph Deane died of a fever, having caught cold during an eclipse of the sun while riding back to Dublin from his assize circuit (*Hist. Ir. Parl.*, iii, 36).

prejudice to Mr Justice Gilbert or Mr Baron Pocklington, for both of them I have great respect; or of Sir John St Leger, between whose family and ours you know there hath been a long freindship, But really I think no body will at this time make a good Cheif Baron who hath not been before very well versed in the practice and course of the Court: At this time I say, because the other two Barons are not fully masters of it yet: and the case is widely different from what it was when Mr Freeman was made Cheif Baron,[255] there being at that time two other Barons in the Court who had long sate on the Bench: and yet Mr Freeman tho a very good Judge, was a good deal at a losse in the beginning.

Having now given my thoughts that it will be (I humbly apprehend) very proper to have some person already acquainted with the Court made Cheif Baron, I own my self pretty much at a losse to find out a person here against whom there may not be objection. Very probably Sr Ri[chard] Levinges freinds will now presse that he may be the man, and no doubt he will greedily embrace it if it can be compassed: but beside that this will exalt him to the greatest degree and make people who think not well of him in point of character beleive him to be a necessary man, and to be courted and taken in at any rate; it must be considered that he will at the same time be of the Councel: and I am very much mistaken, if his freind on this side the water is not already endeavouring to form a party and create an interest, which he may at some time or other make use of peevishly enough. I suppose there will be no thoughts of the late Sollicitor General Mr Bernard; the only person whom I can think fit on all accounts for the place is Mr Gore his Majestyes Attorney General. I foresee the objction of his not being to be parted with out of the house of Commons; and it hath right in it: but not soe much as I think ought to prevail against his being the man; the difficultyes are greater, if any other person be pitched upon, in my opinion. I have not yet spoke with the Cheif Justices and Mr Conelye, which I resolve to doe: the former as men who must have great regard to the dignity and honour of the Courts and the due administration of justice; the latter as Speaker. If he be thought proper Mr Rogerson hath the fairest pretensions to be made Attorney, and as to the Sollicitorship I will not pretend to mention any body for it:[256] most of our top men are preferred, so as the young ones muct be taken in; but between you and me no one of them deserves or would fill it better then a relation of your own.

Since writing this I find Sr Ri[chard] Levinge is come to town, and hath applyed to his freind here for a recommendation, but without successe, which I am very much pleased with. I also beleive Justice Gilbert will endeavour at it, but the objections I have made before seem to me very strong,[257] and the two Cheif Justices are of my mind in this whole affair, soe is Justice McCartney who might much better pretend (I think) by his long experience in our Courts, tho his being so long a Judge of the Kings Bench hath made him lesse

---

[255] Richard Freeman (1646–1710), an English barrister appointed lord chief baron of the exchequer [I] in 1706.

[256] John Rogerson, MP [I].

[257] According to Sir John St Leger, when the vacancy in the exchequer occurred Alan and the other Irish judges first argued that the country could not afford the delay to the court's business resulting from an external appointment, then took a diametrically opposed line, that it was in the king's interest to keep Gilbert in England, where he was needed, and there was no hurry to name a chief baron in Ireland (BL, Stowe MS 750, f. 104: St Leger to Sir Thomas Parker, 15 June 1715). Meanwhile, the English lord chancellor, Cowper, nominated Gilbert. Sunderland was happy to agree, but urged strongly that Gilbert's successor be an Irishman, to placate 'our friends' in Ireland (HALS, DE/P/F56/55: Sunderland to Cowper, 14 May 1715).

conversant in the Exchequer then formerly, and I beleive his sense of that is one cause of his modestly waving all his pretensions. Pray lay this matter early before my Lord Lieutenant; it is of mighty consequence not to have an ill man; nay not to have one a stranger to the Court, and truly we have already foure Judges now on the Benches from England, Dolben, Gilbert, Pocklington and St Leger: which is more then was ever known before; and Mr Gore hath a numerous relation among our freinds. That of being out of the house may be thus answered: suppose a fiant were passed on the Kings letter, but the patent not sealed till after the Session: or suppose the letter kept dormant for that time as in the Case of Levinge: The two terms will be over in two weeks and one of them will probably be spent before a Cheif Baron can be appointed and sit whoever the man is.

247. Alan I, Dublin, to Thomas, 9 May 1715

(1248/3/242–3)

I write this in the morning to give you an account of the intercourse the Toryes on your side keep with some here as far as it appears in a letter which by accident fell into another hand then that for which it was designed. Among other letters which came in by the pacquet on Saturday night, one Whaley an Almanack maker, who also deals in news writing[258] had (as usual) some letters; and the letter carryer by mistake left among other letters at his house one which was directed to George Horton Esqr in York Street[259] Whaley opening it found it to contain a copy of verses perswading the people of England to send King George home to his Germans whom he ruled with mercy and justice, whereas saith the Poet he uses neither in England[260] and to call in the Hero of the martyrs line, to mount the throne in which he hath a divine right; it also contains a scoundrel doggrel libel on the Bishop of Salisbury and Lord Wharton supposed to be in Hell and there conspiring to putt that place into rebellion against the Devil[261] and also an Epilogue to the Tragedy Jane Grey[262] In which the Author mentions Nassaus Iron hands, Gods punishing a mutinous and rebellious people by laying aside the father, but that his wrath being appeased, the son may be restored[263] Saith King George is what King William was, and the Pretender what Queen Anne was and will put all things into the same state they were in her time: and is written in favor of the Pretender against the King and plainly tends to create disaffection to

---

[258] John Whaley (1653-1724), printer and almanac compiler, of Arundel Court, Dublin (Pollard, *Dictionary of … the Dublin Book Trade*, 603–4). Archbishop King called him 'a coffee-man' (TCD, MS 2536, p. 276: King to Bishop Nicolson, 13 May 1715).

[259] George Houghton, MP [I].

[260] The original is at TNA, SP 63/372/50. This first verse is quoted in Éamonn Ó Ciardha, *Ireland and the Jacobite Cause, 1685–1766: A Fatal Attachment* (Dublin, 2002),175–6.

[261] Original at TNA, SP 63/372/50. Another copy of 'The Devil and Dr Burnett' can be found in the commonplace book of the Cambridge don Henry Docker (St John's College, Cambridge, MS Aa. 3 (pt), (James 503), 92).

[262] Original at TNA, SP 63/372/51. This was interpreted as a jacobite declaration (TCD, MS 2536, pp. 284–6: Archbishop King to Francis Annesley, 24 May 1715).

[263] Quoted in part in Ó Ciardha, *Ireland and the Jacobite Cause*, 176.

and rebellion against him and his Governement. I beleive I may in telling you the import of the first copy of verses have (by mistake) borrowed something of the last; but probably you may be able to see them in England, at least Mr Addison or Lord Lieutenant can shew them to whom the original goes. The main name for whom the letter is intended is mispelled by Sir Henry Bunbury who superscribes the letter, and doth not only frank it by writing his name;[264] they who know Sir Henrys hand say it is his: and it is the more probable if the inside be all the handwriting of one William Wight a Captain now in half pay of the late regiment of horse commanded by Lord Windsor,[265] as Mr Houghton for whom the letter was intended informs us; as I beleive he doth him no injury in saying he beleives it to be his handwriting. In the same sheet after the three copyes of verses there is also a letter dated 3 May 1715 owning the receit of a letter from Houghton dated 28 April importing that there would be near 100 to dine together on the Duke of Ormonds birthday (which was the day following) and rejoicing at it; the letter also saith that there were several meetings on that occasion in London, particularly that 55 mett at the Devil tavern.[266] But before I tell you more of the letter give me leave here to say that Houghtons papers being searched other letters from Wight were found with his name to some of them; and one particularly saith that Ox[for]d,[267] S[traffor]d[268] H[arcour]t[269] and O[rmon]d were talked of as likely to be impeached, but that they stood their ground and resolved to doe soe: the greater part of the people being on their side, and particularly soe as to the last of them. How far these meetings are intended to countenance the mobs (which I take to be what the letter writer calls the greater part of the people) I leave any one to guesse: The letter of the third of May goes on to say Mr Vicars (one of the Captains of our pacquet boats)[270] went suddenly out of town soe that he could not send things by him not having then gott much, but that he soon should have something from him; which I take to be a promise to send over out of hand some of those papers, which Wight in a former letter writes came out very well written and with a great deal of spirit: He then saith you are much imbarassed in England, your secret committee divided, and that it is thought the intended impeachments will dwindle into a representation of both houses. I beleive care will be taken to seise and examine Mr Houghtons[271] letters for some time to come: Way hath been given to this Gentleman to deal with one Hamilton for his employ, but the thing is not done nor the money paid: Wight is an half pay officer, Vicars in the service and of the same kidney and

---

[264]Sir Henry Bunbury (1676–1733), 3rd Bt, of Bunbury, Cheshire, MP [GB] and revenue commr [I] 1711–15. As a member of the British house of commons Bunbury was able to send a letter free of charge by 'franking' it with his name (see above, n. 164).

[265]An army captain since 1705 (Dalton, *Army Lists*, v, 43), and a half-pay officer in Lord Windsor's regiment (TNA, SP 63/372/47); he 'had the reputation of a man of wit and letters and was said to act as a sort of private secretary to the earl of Anglesey' (BL, Add. MS 61635, f. 119: lords justices to Secretary Stanhope, 10 May 1715). 'A 'Captain Wight' was actively working for the jacobite interest by Oct. 1715 (HMC, *Stuart MSS*, i, 533).

[266]'The Devil and St Dunstan', in Fleet Street, close by Temple Bar (H.C. Chelley, *Inns and Taverns of Old London* (1899), 93–101).

[267]Robert Harley (1661–1724), 1st earl of Oxford, lord treasurer [GB] 1711–14.

[268]Thomas Wentworth (1672–1739), 1st earl of Strafford, ambassador plenipotentiary to the congress of Utrecht 1711–14.

[269]Simon Harcourt (1661–1727), 1st Baron Harcourt, lord chancellor [GB] 1713–14.

[270]James Vickers was manager of the packet-boats between Ireland and Britain between 1689 and 1715 (Edward Watson, *The Royal Mail to Ireland* … (1917), 63, 69).

[271]George Houghton, MP [I].

perfectly well acquainted with Wight, as also is our Commissioner Sir Harry. All Wights letters will be sent over, there you will find great intimacy between Wight, Houghton, Dick Stewart[272] and some more of our Countrey; and Lord Kildare assured me Wight and Sir Harry were very great here. One of Wights letters hath a peice cutt out which contained another seditious copy of verses, which Houghton saith he cutt out and burnt but never told any magistrate of them nor cautioned Wight not to send more of the kind. We also found a Copy of the Pretenders declaration[273] all in Houghtons own hand writing, and abundance of rascally pamphlets but have not gone through examining his papers; the truth is great part of his converse is with Frank Anesley,[274] who I beleive writes cautiously; they were viewed cheifly if not wholly by the Archbishop of D[*ublin*] only Lord Kildare perused a letter here and there and his Grace hath alway had better thoughts of A[*nnesley*] then he deserved; but I have not seen a line of his, nor almost any one of the letters. To add to this you know how well inclined a third person is to have matters of this kind laid open. Be not too free in naming me or shewing this letter. Soon I shal be able to tell you the whole of the paper found att Kinsale …

[*PS*] This letter is very confused, being written in hast just before my going to Court; upon the Justices having the letter shewn they ordered Mr Houghtons papers to be seised and himself to be brought before them where he was examined by the Chief Justice, none being by but the Lords Justices, the Cheif Justice Mr Budgel and I.

248. *Alan I, Dublin, to Thomas, 14–19 May 1715*

(1248/3/244–5)

[14 May] I write this to you under a great deal of concern, when I consider that almost every day discovers the names of persons who by their actions appear plainly to be disaffected to his Majestye and his Governement, and some appear to be avowed and professed Jacobites; if there can be any difference made between the former and the later: for since every body must be sensible that it is desirable to live under some Governement or other, what or whose governement doe they affect or desire who shew disaffection to the present? I pass by the pacquet of English advices; and the defence of the King in answer to a paper called his Majestyes most gracious Speech etc[275] of which I have formerly given you an account:

---

[272] Hon. Richard Stewart, MP [I].

[273] The declaration issued by James Francis Edward Stuart at Plombières-les-Bains in Lorraine in Aug. 1714, setting out his claim to the throne and a manifesto for his reign; printed in Perth in 1715 as *His Majesty's Most Gracious Declaration…*, and reprinted there in two further editions. There is a MS copy in Parliamentary Archives, HL/PO/RO/1/42.

[274] Francis Annesley (1663–1750), of Castlewellan, Co. Down, Lincoln's Inn Fields, Mdx., and Thorganby, Yorks, MP [I] 1695–1703, 1713–14, and [E & GB] 1705–15, 1722–34. Houghton was a relation of Annesley's (TCD, MS 2536, pp. 294–6: Archbishop King to Annesley, 24 May 1715).

[275] *A Defence of the King, in Answer to What Is Commonly Called His Majesty's Speech* ([?1715]), a tory pamphlet attacking the king's speech at the opening of the British parliament, under the cloak of seeking to 'vindicate his majesty from the falsehoods, the blunders, the rancour, the unreasonable and indecent insinuations, which the contrivers of this speech labour to make him patronise' (p. 1).

but will add that in Councel last Fryday Mr Dennis the Soveraigne of Kinsale,[276] John Doran, and John Woolcock[277] were examined; the two later being brought up in custody of a messenger. The Cheif Justice[278] not being at the Councel and Mr Budgell not being very expert or ready in taking examinations, I reduced them to writing; and in them it appears plainly that Woolcock and Doran dispersed that vile paper, or I should rather say they published it by handing it about and reading it aloud in company; for but one of the papers was seised. I think the Governement will order them to be prosecuted by the Atturney General. Doran is employed under the patent Officer of Kinsale who is a freind of Sir Richard Onslow[279] one Shepheard.[280] It is a miserable case, that in this and other matters of this kind two of the Lords Justices are forced to meet and resolve what to doe before the third is sent to or thought proper to be advised with by them. It is also remarkable that the libel was sent by one Dan. Mills a Clerk in the Navy Office in England,[281] and that one Lake who is an half pay Lieutenant[282] was one of the persons in whose company Doran read it publickly, but I doe not find he gave any account of it to a magistrate or discouraged the reading of it. People who eat the Kings bread should not send or publish seditious pamphlets, or hear his Majesty abused. But soe it is that there are many who scruple not doing this at the same time they are in his service. An Officer in Wades regiment is charged with being concerned in singing a seditious song with several young Collegians, the burthen this. I never shal rejoice Till I hear the heav'nly voice That the King shal enjoy his own again.[283]

Dublin 19 May.

This hath lain by till yours and my sisters of the 14th are come to hand, for which I thank both of you. The same pacquet brought in one Mr Jefferyes (an English barrister and a person recommended heretofore to my knowledge by the Doctor)[284] who pretends to come over on some private affairs of the Bishop of Derry.[285] Among his goods an Officer of the

[276] James Dennis (*d.* aft.1738) of Kinsale, sovereign of Kinsale 1710–15, 1724 (Reg. Deeds, 92/165/64241; *The Council Book of the Corporation of Kinsale* …, ed. Richard Caulfield (Guildford, 1879), 201, 212–15, 433).

[277] John Woolcock (*d.* aft. 1731), merchant of Kinsale (*Council Book of … Kinsale*, ed. Caulfield, 198, 212, 218, 223, 225, 236).

[278] Either John Forster (common pleas) or William Whitshed (king's bench).

[279] Sir Richard Onslow (1654–1717), 3rd Bt, of West Clandon, Surrey, MP Surrey; *cr.* Baron Onslow, 19 June 1716.

[280] John Shephard (*d.* aft.1725) customer of Kinsale since 1708 (*Lib. Mun.*, pt 2, p. 149).

[281] Daniel Mills, clerk to the clerk of acts in the Navy Board from 1697 until discharged in Feb. 1722 (J.M. Collinge, *Navy Board Officials 1660–1832* (1978), 123).

[282] William Leake, a lieutenant in Townshend's foot, was placed on half-pay in 1713. He was still drawing half-pay in 1722 (Dalton, *Army Lists*, vi, 110–11, 174).

[283] 'The King Shall Enjoy His Own Again', a cavalier ballad originally published in 1643, which had been adopted by jacobites. Several undergraduates at Trinity College were arrested for drinking the Pretender's health during celebrations of the duke of Ormond's birthday on 29 Apr. (*Weekly Journal* …, 4 June 1715; Éamonn Ó Ciardha, '"The Unkinde Deserter" and "The Bright Duke": Contrasting Views of the Dukes of Ormonde in the Irish Royalist Tradition', in *The Dukes of Ormonde, 1610–1745*, ed. Toby Barnard and Jane Fenlon (Woodbridge, 2000), 185).

[284] Possibly Edward Jeffreys (formerly Winnington) (1669–1725), of Ham Castle, near Droitwich, Worcs., MP [GB] and a judge on the Welsh circuit. Jeffreys was at this time a strong tory. Archbishop King reported that Jeffreys was the bishop of Derry's 'agent', and further that some considered him to be 'an agent sent over to manage for the [tory] party here', though King himself was doubtful of this (TCD, MS 2536, pp. 291–2: King to Bishop Ashe, 23 May 1715; pp. 292–3: King to Edward Southwell, 23 May 1715).

[285] John Hartstonge.

Custom house seised a pacquet directed to Dean Swift, in which among other things were contained English Advice etc A Defence of the King etc An half sheet relating to the proceedings of the house of Commons against Sir W[illia]m Windham and some other papers and letters:[286] He swears he received them from Mr Charleton the Dutchesse of Ormonds Chaplain[287] with directions to deliver them into the Deans own hand: Among the letters one tells the Dean their party is in great heart all over the Kingdome, assures him things will doe well and wishes he might speak plainly. Saith Onslow[288] Jekyll[289] Hampden[290] and Vernon[291] disagree from the rest of the secret Committee;[292] that Jekyll hath left them and the other three will not sign the report. This letter, and one from the Bishop of Ossory (that was) and now of Derry[293] to the Primate tells him the bearer will communicate the arcana imperii[294] to him, and that it may be done more safely that way then writing; he hath the like credentials from the Bishop to Sir Standish Hartstonge;[295] and from Mr Ezechiel Hamilton[296] to one Scot a schoolmaster here,[297] which saith he will let him know the temper and sentiments of the people. The Bishop saith the Pretenders freinds increase by the treatment honest men meet; and in a letter to somebody calls these iniquous times. Saith the honest party will appear with great solemnitye the 29th of May,[298] and then saith the Kings birthday is the 28th.[299] By his maner I think they expect something very considerable that day, and I am glad to find care is taken to prevent mischeif from mobs by having the Guards and Train bands ready on that day. Assure yourself the enemyes of the present administration hope for something very extraordinary in their favor soon. Scott is not at home, so hath not been examined: the Dean is at young Rotchforts in Westmeath.[300] It is not worth your notice that a letter dated the seventh from London written by an unknown

[286] For this incident, see *Swift Corr.*, ii, 122.

[287] Arthur Charleton (b. c.1685) (*Al. Dub.*, 147; *Swift Corr.*, i, 603–5).

[288] Sir Richard Onslow sat in the Commons until 7 Nov. 1715. He had been granted a peerage in Nov. 1715, but because of his membership of the secret committee delayed taking out his patent 'until the impeachments were out of the way, so that "they who had been accusers might not sit as judges in the same cause"' (*HC 1715–54*, ii, 310).

[289] Sir Joseph Jekyll (1662–1738), of Westminster; MP [GB] Lymington.

[290] Richard Hampden (aft.1674–1728), of Great Hampden, Bucks., MP [GB] Bucks.; chairman, committee of privileges and elections.

[291] Thomas Vernon (1666–1726), of Twickenham Park, Mdx.

[292] Confirmed in *Swift Corr.*, ii, 123.

[293] Hartstonge had been translated from Ossory to Derry in Mar. 1714.

[294] The secrets of state.

[295] Sir Standish Hartstonge, 2nd Bt, MP [I].

[296] Rev. Ezekiel Hamilton (c.1681–1750) originally from Co. Donegal and a graduate of TCD (*Al. Dub.*, 361). A jacobite agent, he had been sent to London by Bolingbroke in Oct. 1715 (HMC, *Stuart MSS*, i, 434, 436, 443, 451).

[297] For evidence that a clergyman called 'Scot' was keeping a school in Dublin at about this time, see Whan, *Presbyterians of Ulster, 1680–1730*, 76. He may have been the John Scott who subsequently appeared as a friend and correspondent of Swift (*Swift Corr.*, iv, 590).

[298] Restoration Day, commemorating the restoration of the monarchy in 1660.

[299] George I's birthday.

[300] George Rochfort, MP [I]. Swift was Rochfort's guest at Gaulstown in Co. Westmeath from 16 to 20 May, before travelling on with his friend Knightley Chetwode to Chetwode's house at Woodbrook, King's Co. (*Swift Corr.*, ii, 127).

hand gives me vile language, tells me the writer neither loves my person nor principles; assureth there is a design against my life, bids me repent and prepare for death, and beware of a lean black man on 29th May att the Castle, and pretends to doe this later part for conscience sake: I beleive it to be wrote by some rascal to see if I can be frightned from being there on that day, which will be made use of as a sign of disaffection to the occasion of making that an holy day. I resolve to act as at other times and under the protection of God to attend my duty in all places. You tell me the bull about absolving people who took the oath of abjuration will be of use: first the Archbishop of Tuam denyes it was a bull, but hath not yet produced the papers: but I must not be named in these things. By the Bishop of Derryes letters we find the Primate hath summoned his posse, and really the losse of Lord Bellew,[301] Roscommon, and from my sisters letter I fear of Lord Montrath will much weaken us. This is to be considered very well The Archbishop of Tuam did not come to examine the papers which came over by Mr Jefferyes …

[PS] One letter saith it was Atterbury[302] wrote Lord Bolenbrookes letter.[303]

249. *Alan I, Dublin, to Thomas, 24 May 1715*

(1248/3/246–7)

I have received yours and my sisters of the nineteenth, fraught as all letters of that date were with the most melancholy tydings of Lord Halyfax death,[304] tho the letters which came by the former mail gave us very little reason to expect we should hear of his recoverye. The losse of this and other great men hath strangely dispirited us, and exalted other people: but I beleive something else contributes to the one and the other. I intend what follows for your own perusal only, but I fear the observations which people make from these and some other proceedings here a little contribute to animate our enemyes and give our freinds disorder. People are concerned that Captain Wight (whom I mentioned formerly) is gott away, as our publick prints inform us; but then they reflect that tho his letter to Mr Houghton was discovered on the eighth of May in the morning, and Houghtons papers were seised and himself examined that night, yet our expresse went hence either on the tenth at night, or rather in truth on the eleventh in [th]e morning; if this be so, as I am apt to think it is every[bod]y will know he might have had earlier notices from his freinds here then the Secretary of State had from the Governement. I doe not find that any bill of indictment hath yet been offered to the Grand Jury against any who were concerned in dispersing and publishing the English advice etc the reason of which some say is because the Lords Justices sent over the examinations and have received no directions in the matter from thence. No doubt my Lord Lieutenants indisposition hath delayed businesse a good deal: but why there should need orders from your side of the water for prosecuting the publishers of so seditious

---

[301] Richard Bellew, 3rd Baron Bellew, died on 22 Mar. 1715.

[302] Francis Atterbury (1663–1732), bishop of Rochester.

[303] *A Genuine Letter of Advice and Consolation, Written from Paris by the Lord Viscount Bolingbroke, to the Earl of Oxford* … (1715).

[304] Charles Montagu (1662–1715), 1st earl of Halifax, died at his home in Westminster on 19 May 1715.

and treasonable a libel I confesse I am yet to learn. Others impute it to the time of the Judges of the Kings Bench, Kings Councel, and for ought I know the Lords Justices time being so employed in examining into some seditious pranks played by several of the College here. It is certain much examination there hath been, and I hear a libel called Nero the second hath been traced to the hands of one of the fellows,[305] and from his table another took it and gave a Copy of it afterward; we also hear that a good deal of seditious discourse hath been used by some young men there; [bu]t you will excuse me for telling you any of the particulars; for they are made as great a secret to me as to any one man in the Kingdome; neither the Lords Justices nor Cheif Justice having vouchsafed me the sight of any one of the examinations about the College. They have been taking them I beleive a full fortnight; but no one of them was returned into the Crown Office last Saturday; whether at this time I cannot say; but I hear that indictments are drawing against one Bingley,[306] Gunning[307] and Mallorye:[308] Gunning was in custody but found means to gett out of the Constables hands: and beside the share he had in dispersing that libel he was the man who had it from Mr Kearneys table, who is one of the fellows of the Colledge, and I am told the Pr[ima]tes Chaplain,[309] but I am not sure of this. Some say these slow proceedings are in order to a full detection, others think that there being so many young men concerned some tendernesse is to be shewn toward them; and that it may bring an imputation upon a society etc and we seem very desirous to trace it to some on whom I doubt it never will be effectually fixed. But people grumble that no body is brought yet to trial, and on the other hand I beleive those who are principally concerned beleive they are only to be censured by the provost and fellows, and that the civil magistrates intermeddling is an infringement of the rights and libertyes of the College. This afternoon Harry Purdon[310] brought a Gentleman to me who told me a fellow of the College in his hearing began an health in these words in a numerous company of Collegians. viz. To all those honest men who make no other distinction between Oliver Cromwell and King William then that the former killed a King and the later dethroned one.

I gave an account of this to the Lords Justices this evening and the Gentleman is ordered to give his Examinacions before my Lord Cheif Justice: when this matter comes to be

---

[305] There is a copy in Henry Docker's commonplace book (St John's Coll., Cambridge, MS Aa. 3 (pt), (James 503), 94).

[306] Edmund Bingley (b. c. 1692 (*Al. Dub.*, 67)): in 1722–3 taken into custody for suspected involvement in the Atterbury Plot; later worked for the jacobite tory newswriter Nathaniel Mist, was briefly secretary to the duke of Wharton in exile, and in 1729 was serving in a similar capacity to the duke of Ormond (P.M. Chapman, 'Jacobite Political Argument in England, 1714–1766', Cambridge PhD, 1983, 164–5). Bingley was convicted of publishing this squib and was sent to the pillory (*Whalley's News-Letter*, 1 July 1715).

[307] John Gunning, who took his BA at Trinity in 1710 and his MA in 1713 (*Al. Dub.*, 352). Having been committed to gaol on a charge of publishing a seditious libel and 'uttering … treasonable and seditious words' impugning King George's title to the throne, he absconded, and on 21 May a proclamation was issued for his arrest (*The Proclamations of Ireland, 1660–1820*, ed. James Kelly and Mary Ann Lyons (5 vols, Dublin, 2014), iii, 26–7).

[308] George Mallory (c.1695–by 1740), subsequently rector of Mobberley, Cheshire (*Al. Dub.*, 550; J.P. Earwaker, *An Index to the Wills and Inventories Now Preserved in the Court of Probate at Chester, from A.D.1721 to 1740* (Lancs and Cheshire Rec. Soc., xxii, 1890), 728). For this incident, see James Kelly, 'Regulating Print: The State and the Control of Print in Eighteenth-century Ireland', *ECI*, xxiii (2008), 159.

[309] John Kearney (c.1687–1771), fellow of Trinity since 1712 (*Al. Dub.*, 453; Leslie, *Armagh Clergy* …, 34–5; *Gentleman's Magazine*, July 1771, 448).

[310] Henry Purdon, MP [I].

prosecuted and I hear more of it you shal know as much as I doe. I had almost forgott to tell you, that after the papers brought over by Mr Jefferyes and directed to the Dean of St Patricks were examined it was not thought fit to search the Deans closet for papers; for my part I saw no difference between doing it in that case and in Mr Houghtons, but that the later was not a Clergyman. But a Gentleman said it would make a great deal of noise. A certain great man was saying he thought it might be fit to send for the Provost and fellows on the Kings birthday and give them intimation what ill principles and practices obtained etc and I suppose this was proposed as a method to put that matter at an end: but it seemed to be only one mans opinion.

I again desire and caution you not to name me; but I will add that we have gott into a method which will I think make my Lords administration very uneasy if he stayes in England much longer. I have formerly hinted at somebody who is laying a foundation of such a power as may be troublesome.

250. *Alan I, Dublin, to Thomas, 30 May 1715*

(1248/3/248–9)

I am to own yours of the 24th, in which you tell me great interest was made that Levinge should be Cheif Baron, but omit saying by what hands; I am not soe desirous to know who in England could appear for him, as to be certain whether one man in a great station here did: for by it I should have been able to form a more certain judgement of that persons views, who seems to me to design to put himself at the head of a party who shal act with great temper and tendernesse toward those who have hitherto opposed every thing. If I have not been mistaken a great while, many of us are too much whigs, or too little Toryes to bear a part in the scheme; and I cannot but observe that those that have most publickly owned themselves at all times to be Whigs and for the succession have not been distinguished to their advantage, when Church preferments have fallen in his disposal: and now that soe many vile practices are detected in the College, the matter is carryed in soe secret a maner, that I am kept as much a stranger to them as if I had not the honour to be in the Kings service at all; a treatment my predecessors have not been used to. But if the design be, not to punish the faulty, but only thence to take an handle to shew the necessity of visiting the College, and because the present Visitors are the Chancellor of the University (the Duke of Ormond), the Vice Chancellor (the Bishop of Limrick) and the Archbishop of Dublin; that it may be thought advisable for his Majesty (if the Statutes allow it) to appoint more in conjunction with them; without mentioning what my thoughts are of the later part of the project, I confesse I do not approve of such palliating methods; it short it seems to me that we are very unwilling to disclose the nakednesse of our freinds, and to let the world see how far we are gone in principles of sedition and disaffection to the present constitution. And where as the source of all our evils arises from the Gown, we are very tender of discovering any spot or stain in it, tho till that be done it is impossible to wash and make it clean again. I told you that Dean Swifts closet was not to be opened, nor his papers seised, nor he himself summoned notwithstanding the pacquet brought for him by Jefferyes; whereas Mr Houghton was taken into custody and his papers examined on Captain Wights letter to him being intercepted. I saw no distinction but the Gown; but was told since, that indeed the Deans correspondent in his letter taxed him with not writing or answering letters, as the ground for not examining his papers: now I own I was of opinion and am that the Deans not writing is none of his faults: But depend on it the Dean (tho he is allowed to have faults) is in good esteem and favor somewhere. If my Lord Lieutenant be not aware of the recommendations to livings in the Kings gift he will in time find they will all fall into hands who will know they owe them to the favor of one man and will immediately depend on him, which I think is not a desirable thing; he is as likely to ride resty[311] on occasion, as another man. There is one Mr Whitingham[312] who hath alway appeared and acted the part of an honest man and he beleives he shal be recommended to the living or Union of Navan in the Diocese of Meath now in the gift of the Crown by the death of Archdeacon Benson the last incumbent.[313] However he also presses me to speak for him, tho I hope that will be unnecessary if he be heartily espoused by the Archbishop of Dublin. He is the man that under the title of a Country Curate hath wrote answers to our Bishop of Corkes two very odd books against drinking the healths of those who love and honour the memory of King William.[314] He is a vertuous and modest man, a good scholar, an hearty Whig, and sure I have said enough to shew that I think him worth being preferred; but if he stayes till he is preferred on this side of the water, he may wait till he is gray in my opinion; but that will not be long, for he is no young man.

Pray speak to Mr Addison for him in my name, and tell him if he knew him he would assist a man of his vertue. His Christian name is Charles, the united parish consists of these livings The Vicarage of Donnamore,[315] which payes £24 a year Crown rent, the rectory of Navan payes £12; Arsillagh[316] Balsoon and Athsie. This Union hath its parish Church in Navan, great part of which is blown down in the late storm. By reading the paper which comes inclosed under the same Cover with this you well see what papers Miller saith he gave to the Archbishop; but he denies there ever came such paper or bull with Seals, or subscribed Albani to his hand; but hath given in a parcel of scrub old letters and scraps of papers little to the purpose, as all he had from Miller. Do not name me but the paper is certainly a true Copy.[317]

---

[311] Of a horse: refractory, resisting control (*OED*).

[312] Charles Whittingham (c.1664–1724), subsequently archdeacon of Dublin (*Al. Dub.*, 877; Cotton, *Fasti*, ii, 130–1). Described in 1717 by a whig bishop as 'a person of very good learning and seems honest, bold, and active at all times' (Wake, Epist. xii: Bishop Evans to [Archbishop Wake], 31 Mar. [1717]).

[313] Thomas Benson (c.1654–1715), archdeacon of Kildare 1681–*d.* (*Al. Dub.*, 60; Cotton, *Fasti*, ii, 246–7). Bishop Ashe of Clogher recommended Whittingham to the rectory of Navan in Jan. 1716 (BL, Add. MS 61639, f. 189: Ashe to Joseph Addison, 13 Jan. 1715[/16]).

[314] By demonstrating the theological impropriety of toasts to the 'glorious and immortal memory' of King William, Peter Browne's published address to the clergy of his diocese, *Of Drinking in Remembrance of the Dead …* (Dublin, 1713), had provoked responses from several whig clergymen. *A Brief Examination of the Bishop of Cork's Discourse, of Drinking to the Memory of the Dead* (Dublin, 1714), which was advertised as having been written 'by a country-curate', may well have been Whittingham's work. Another version, with a slightly amended title, *A Brief Examination of Drinking to the Memory of the Dead* [1714], was published by a different Dublin printer.

[315] Donoughmore.

[316] Ardsallagh.

[317] See above, p. 66.

251. *Alan I, Ballyannan, to Thomas, Westminster, 31 July 1715*

(1248/3/252–3)

I am obliged to you for the very particular account you give of the precautions taken to prevent the designed invasion;[318] and the zeal and wisdome of the Parliament, together with the affection the City hath expressed to his Majesty and the publick service. I am of your opinion that either the matter will be for this time disappointed, or else end in the confusion of the undertakers and their accomplices, and in the establishment of his Majestyes throne and Governement by rendring it safe and easy. This is what of all things on earth I most wish, because I really think it the most general good that can befall these nations; and people are apt readily to beleive what they heartily desire. But I own I am not altogether so sanguine as you, in thinking if matters come to an actual invasion that there will be so little difficulty in quelling them: I wish that in some parts of England, and Scotland, as well as in all the Papists here there be not too great a disaffection to the present establishment: But after saying this I declare I am not at all in doubt of the event. We have certainly, (what we should have thought ourselves happy a year since to have had but hope of) an oportunity of drawing our swords and venturing our lives in the feild like men, in vindication and support of our religion, our King, our countrey; and men who fight upon these motives will not be beaten ...

252. *Alan I, Dublin, to Thomas, 5 Aug. 1715*

(1248/3/254–5)

Yours of the 21th of July I received on Saturday night (the 30th) at Ballyanan, and the next day had a letter from the Secretary to tell me the Lords Justices required my immediate attendance in town; where I gott about nine on Thursday morning, and waited on the Archbishop of Dublin and Lord Kildare; but his Grace of Tuam was not in town, but att his sons att Lucan within five miles of town;[319] where I was told by his servants he had been for some dayes past. Unlesse he be detained by indisposition, it seems to me to be pretty odd not to think his attendance on the Kings service att so critical a juncture of absolute necessitye: for I can hardly beleive he is of opinion with some others that it really is not. How can this be accounted for? Must not people beleive there is nothing in all the noise that is made about an invasion, when one of the Lords Justices lets the world see it is not in his opinion of weight enough to put him to the trouble of coming five miles: I wish this affair may blow off as easily as some people are willing to flatter themselves, from the timely discovery of it, the zealous resolutions of the Lords and Commons against the Pretender and his abettors, and the affection the City hath expressed on the occasion.[320] When so

---

[318] The rumoured jacobite invasion of England. The future English chief justice Dudley Ryder, then studying at the Middle Temple, recorded in his diary on 23 July visiting the army camp in Hyde Park (*The Diary of Dudley Ryder 1715–1716*, ed. William Matthews (1939), 60–1).

[319] Agmondisham Vesey, MP [I].

[320] On 20 July both Lords and commons had agreed loyal addresses promising to stand by the king against his enemies (*LJ*, xx, 123; *CJ*, xviii, 232). The corporation of the City of London, having assured the king in person of

many of the common people are poisoned in their principles, when the Pretender hath an armed force of the Kings own subjects to attend him, sufficient to make a stand till they can be joined by evil disposed persons, of which there is too great a number in every one of the Kingdomes, what may not be apprehended? The giddy people will be told that this is no invasion by a foreign enemy, and have the doctrines, which have been broached on purpose to facilitate this very undertaking, strongly inculcated; and what encouragement the least stand they may be able at first to make may give a foreign Prince to powre in forces upon us, God only knows: And tho you seem to be of opinion that there is no danger of any thing of that kind I very much doubt there are others whom nothing but the danger of their estates contains within their duty: and if by any prospect of successe they can propose to themselves impunitye, no man can tell how far party rage and resentment may carry them.

Doe not fancy that I am under fear, or any way dejected; but I cannot deny that it creates me a good deal of anxiety that we may be forced to the hazard of laying our religion, libertyes and estates (for I will not think of lives after the other are gone) against nothing: for what better condition will the nation be in after the design is disappointed then now; unlesse as in case of a feaver well gott over, you will say the malignant humor is spent; but then you must allow the man generally is more weak after, and that some remains of the distempers usually lurk about him. The Protestants are full of heart and resolution; but to say truth there are several things which I wish were otherwise. I doe not find that there are above six thousand of the ten thousand arms (for which we gave money to be ready to arm our militia) in the stores; who took or ordered them out we cannot learn; neither the Master nor Lieutenant of the Ordinance (Lord Montjoy or Mr Molesworth[321]) being here; and I heard the Archbishop of Dublin say the Justices could have no satisfaction about these arms from any officer of the Ordnance now here. We had lately thirty regiments here, and but two Colonels or them in all the Kingdome; this I heard from Lord Kildare; and that 270 Officers are absent by licence; that the Justices had represented this to his Excellencye, but stil new orders for licence of absence came; and when the Justices refused to give some Officers leave to be absent, that letters immediately from the King have been obtained; three I think of the later kind was the number named: Speak to my Lord earnestly how much it imports the Kings service, his Excellencyes honour, and the safety of the Kingdome to have things otherwise, at least while matters stand as they doe at present. Our forces are also drawing off every day, by which means our money will be spent out of the Kingdome to the very great impoverishment of it, but what is much worse we shal be left very naked and exposed. If you say the militia will be raised and armed, that is true; but when this affair blows over, as I hope and beleive it will in time, will it not be suggested that we are able when we have arms in our hands to defend ourselves with a much lesse standing force in the Kingdome then our present establishment consists of; and that therefore they may be employed elsewhere, yet stil continue on our establishment and be paid by us: Our wise men who find fault with the Privy Councel for transmitting a bill of recognition will when they take time to consider the matter be sensible their notions of that matter are very ill

---

[320] *(continued)* their 'fidelity', at an audience at St James's, quickly followed this up with loyal addresses (*Weekly Journal*, 23 July 1715; *London Gazette*, 26–30 July 1715; *Flying Post*, 28–30 July 1715).

[321] Richard Molesworth, MP [I].

grounded:[322] Will they claim a sole and undoubted right to form bills of recognition?[323] I beleive no one of that kind ever arose in the house of Commons; I am sure some did not, and I beleive they cannot shew that any ever did: but when the Councel is to certifye causes for holding a Parliament, I think the doing this alone to be a sufficient, as I think it the most weighty cause of calling one now; and I hope those considerations may be certifyed by the Councel in the form of a bill. I have ordered Jemmy Barryes eldest son to wait on you; he is an officer formerly on half pay and now on full pay of Whitrouges regiment, and goes to attend the service.[324] He is very honest in his principles and very brave; but hath the misfortune to be a little deaf by means of a cold he took in the feild. his fathers circumstances are such as not to allow him to make such provision for him as he ought which hath almost broke the young fellows heart. I have furnished him with money out of my own pockett to carry him, and desire you will let him wait on you to be presented to my Lord Lieutenant; If he could be put into immediate service it would be a great pleasure to me, and ease me of the danger and trouble of being again obliged to supply his occasions at my own proper expence. Sir Edward Crofton[325] was with me yesterday, and tells me that my Lord Sunderland hath given his son[326] assurances from time to time of giving him what he went over about, the reversion of his brother in Law Mr Nixons office of Clerk of the Pleas in the Exchequer here;[327] but that the thing remains yet in suspence. You know Sir Edward very well, and will much oblige him if you can facilitate or expedite this matter. Really he is a very deserving honest Gentleman; and my Lord may doe it with the greatest ease imaginable …

[*PS*] My Lord Corke[328] is Lord Lieutenant of our County, and consquently will be to appoint Deputy Lieutenants; Colonel Harry Boyle,[329] Mr Maynard[330] and I, were three of the Deputy Governors during last war;[331] and I think our sons Mr Henry Boyle[332] Mr Maynard[333] and Senny will well fill our places; Jemmy Barry was another and well deserves

---

[322] The bill for recognising George I's title to the throne of Britain, France and Ireland, which was prepared by the Irish privy council and transmitted to the privy council in Westminster in advance of the parliamentary session. The objection was presumably on constitutional grounds but the procedure – the Irish privy council preparing a bill in advance of the beginning of a parliament – was legitimate and, indeed, essential, as the privy council sought to demonstrate the necessity of calling the parliament. The constitutional importance of this bill may have heightened 'patriot' sensibilities, especially among MPs who were anxious to demonstrate their loyalty to the new dynasty. The bill eventually passed into law as 2 Geo. I, c. 2 [I].

[323] A reference to the supposed 'sole right' of the Irish house of commons to initiate money bills, for which see *Anglo-Irish Politics, Vol. 1*, 13, 15.

[324] James Barry, for whom see below, Appendix 2, eldest son of James Barry, MP [I], had been a captain in Stanwix's regiment of foot 1706–12 before being placed on half-pay in 1712 (Dalton, *Army Lists*, v, 195). In Feb. 1716 he was commissioned as a captain in Tyrawley's foot (Dalton, *Geo. I's Army*, ii, 135).

[325] 2nd Bt, MP [I].

[326] Edward Crofton, MP [I].

[327] David Nixon (c.1692–c.1759), an attorney, of Dublin (*Al. Dub.*, 620; *K. Inns Adm.*, 364; Vicars, *Index*, 351). The reversion was given to Martin Bladen, MP [I] in Apr. 1716 (*Lib. Mun.*, pt 2, p. 63).

[328] Richard Boyle, 3rd earl of Burlington in the English peerage, was also 4th earl of Cork in the peerage of Ireland.

[329] Henry Boyle (c.1648–93), of Castlemartyr, Co. Cork (*Hist. Ir. Parl.*, iii, 239–40).

[330] Samuel Maynard (1656–1712), of Curryglass, Co. Cork (*Hist. Ir. Parl.*, v, 232–3).

[331] The jacobite war in Ireland, 1689–91.

[332] MP [I].

[333] William Maynard, MP [I].

to be continued; Sir Ralph Freake[334] and Colonel Bryan Townesend[335] seem to me also very fit, and Batt Purdon.[336]

253. *Alan I, Dublin, to Thomas, 9 Aug. 1715*

(1248/3/256–7)

I am confirmed by the letter which you sent me by Captain Brady, and by one of a later date under my Lord Sunderlands own hand, that he is determined to remain in England, and that of consequence we are like to have another cheif Governor: nothing can more disconcert our measures here then such a turn; and if we are to goe into new schemes, I wish they may succeed as well as those which were formed must in all probabilitye have done. Whether it proceed from this or any other ground I cannot tell; but I resolve to let you know that yesterday morning I had a letter from a County of Corke freind, in which he assures me that at this time I am struck att in England, and that you are thought a grum there. I doe not give much heed to the information he hath from London, being sensible that probably enough some of this countrey, whose merits are not sufficiently considered may envy me among those of whom his Majesty hath been pleased to take notice; or perhaps some men may be at the bottom of it, whom I could not bring my self to recommend in the maner they fancy they deserve. I am sensible I have no way disserved the King, but to the best of my power have endeavoured to serve him in every instance before and since his accession to the Crown: I know I have acted honestly and incorruptly, and I think unblamably on the Bench: but if a new Lord Lieutenant must have a new Chancellor, or if (as the Toryes here flatter themselves) people will be frightned into a coalition, and I am to be sacrificed to make room for a man more agreeable to their palates, I cannot help it; nor will I repine and grow peevish or complain. Only I have made an ill voyage of it. The Chancellors place I sought, and am not to impute the impossibility of my resorting to the bar to any body but myself: but indeed my fortune was such then that when I had been removed I might have sate down in very good circumstances for a Commoner, tho I had not encreased my fortune one penny after the Seal was put into my hand; and so had no difficulty in taking it, let the time be never so short of my holding it. But it hath been thought fit, nay necessary to create Peers and me in the number; this was not of my seeking, nay you know I objected to it on account of my fortune not being such as ought to be to support such an honor. This objection you know I made, and made it in earnest; and in the matter of the Peerage declined instead of seeking it; and was purely passive and left it to the determination of my freinds, meerly because I was told it was of absolute necessity. Now tho I needed no increase of fortune for a Commoner, I am not of the same opinion as to my estate being such as I ought to leave to my son, whom I have necessitated to be a peer after my death: and consequently to quit his profession which is now sufficiently beneficial to him and will very soon be considerably more soe; for he really doth very well at the bar. What is left me is; if I am displaced, by prudent management of that fortune I already have to endeavour to

---

[334]Sir Ralph Freke, 1st Bt, MP [I].

[335]Bryan Townsend (bef. 1660–1726), of Castle Townsend, Co. Cork (*Hist. Ir. Parl.*, vi, 428–9).

[336]Bartholomew Purdon, MP [I].

leave it better at my death then it now is; and on that I am determined. Pray let me know from whence I am to apprehend danger, and from whom I may expect support, that I may make fit application, if there be anything in the matter; which I confesse to you I do not think there is. You will ask me then, why I have given you so long a trouble; the answer is because the thing is possible, tho I doe not beleive it to be true. Pray tell me whether there be any and what grounds for your being thought a grum: Sure people cannot expect servile compliances from a man of your known steddinesse in what you think right; and therefore neither your dividing in the contested election of Shaftsbury,[337] nor your not liking all the managers or the way of settling and appointing them by concert among a few, nor your silence in the matter moved by Lord Coningsbye[338] relating to the dissenters here, when the alteration in the wording of the oath as to be taken by the presbyterians in North Britain can be any foundation for it.[339] Who is or are the Cheif Minister or ministers? In what credit doth my Lord President[340] stand; and what part in civil affairs doth the Duke of M[arlborough] take? If we should have troubles here, is it right to have Lords Justices; nay two of them Clergymen? If the militia of the whole Kingdome is to be arrayed and consequently the great body of Protestant[s] that is in the North, who are resolved to serve, and their Gentry to take Commissions in the militia and risque their being within the penalty of the Act to prevent the farther growth of Popery,[341] ought not their being or not being made Commissioners of array or Officers be very well weighed before it be determined to put or not to put them in such commissions? And do Clergymen come perfectly unbiassed in this particular. This to yourself only. If I judge right the wishes and hopes of that part of the high Church here which is not at all hazards for bringing in the Pretender, is very far from being displeased with the riots that have been lately; they whisper that they do not see the mob proceeds to do no other outrages then pulling down meeting houses, which may sufficiently shew how the bent and inclination of the body of the people stands; and that the right way to quiet the minds of the people is to employ those whose zeal for and concern that the Church by Law established should alway flourish endears them to the people that is that the late ministry or just such another should be employed: And I perswade myself they think they have gone a great way toward bringing their party into a share of the administration: They instance in the Bishop of Bristols being continued among other Officers of the household,[342] and are in a good deal of expectation. Sure it will be considered that a party so ungovernable out of power will be intolerable when clothed with power …

[337] The election petition of the defeated whig candidates for Shaftesbury in the 1715 general election, William Benson and Henry Andrews, was heard at the Bar of the House on 3 May. After a series of divisions the tories Edward Nicholas and Samuel Rush were declared not duly elected, and Benson (though not Andrews) was seated in their place (*CJ*, xviii, 72; *HC 1715–54*, i, 236).

[338] Thomas Coningsby (1656–1729), Baron Coningsby [I], MP [GB] Leominster; created Baron Coningsby in the English peerage in 1716, and earl of Coningsby [E] in 1719.

[339] An amended version of the abjuration oath was enacted in 1715 (1 Geo I, st. 2, c. 15 [GB]), in order to facilitate compliance by presbyterian non-jurors (Colin Kidd, 'Conditional Britons: The Scots Covenanting Tradition and the Eighteenth-century British State', *EHR*, cxvii (2002), 1152).

[340] The Hanoverian tory Daniel Finch (1647–1730), 2nd earl of Nottingham.

[341] The 'test clause' in the Irish act of 1704 'to prevent the further growth of popery' (2 Anne, c. 6).

[342] The high churchman George Smalridge (1662–1719), appointed bishop of Bristol and as lord almoner by the tory ministry in 1714, would lose his almoner's place by the end of the year (*HL 1660–1715*, v, 451–3).

254. *Alan I, Dublin, to Thomas, Westminster, 30 Aug. 1715*

(1248/3/260–1)

The pacquet which came in this morning brought me no letter from you, but Mr Hutchinson[343] explains that matter to me by telling me he hath sent one from you to me by a private hand, who is not yet arrived.

Your proceedings confound me; is Lord Oxford after all never to be tryed; or if he is to be brought to the stake, when is the day to be? If you had resolved to disconcert matters which I think could not have failed of the desired successe, a more effectual method could not have been taken then by removing Lord Sunderland, or (which is the truth) by his quitting the Governement at the time he hath done it. If it had been done earlier it would not have had half the ill consequences that must in my opinion attend his doing it now. This pacquet contradicts what the last gave us an account of, that Lord Derby would be one of our Justices;[344] and puts the Duke of Grafton in his room in conjunction with Lord Galwey, who is named with great positivenesse in every letter.[345] I will wait a post longer before I complement Lord Galwey upon the occasion, and then perhaps there may come such certainty of the Duke of Grafton that I may pay him the same respect at the same time; for I would not be too early with one, which would be to be too late with the other. If the Duke be one I wish you would (before he is engaged) gett his promise for some handsome preferment for Mr Charles Carre, a Gentleman born, perfectly honest, alway a whig, of a most unblamable life, and against whom no exception lies but his being openly at all times an avowed champion for the Hanover succession.[346] Pray doe this.

255. *Alan I, Dublin, to Thomas, 13 Sept. 1715*

(1248/3/262–3)

… I wish to God our Cheif Governors were here; this is a time when we ought not to have too many in the Governement, for the reason given by the black in a certain play, that two keep a secret better then three.[347] I think I ought to complement the Duke of Grafton on his accession to the Governement; for tho our acquaintance be not great, yet that with my post may make it not only excusable but expected. If it be not proper burn the inclosed,

---

[343]Possibly Archibald Hutcheson (c.1660–1740), of the Middle Temple, MP [GB] and currently a lord of trade. Hutcheson was strongly pro-Hanoverian with some whiggish credentials, but as a former client of the duke of Ormond his political opinions and allegiances did not fully align with those of the Brodricks (*HC 1690–1715*, iv, 449–52; *HC 1715–54*, ii, 163–4).

[344]James Stanley (1664–1736), 10th earl of Derby.

[345]Charles Fitzroy (1683–1757), 2nd duke of Grafton; Henri de Massue (1648–1720), 2nd Marquis de Ruvigny, and 1st earl of Galway. They were appointed on 6 Sept. 1715.

[346]Charles Carr, made bishop of Killaloe in 1716 (see Appendix 2).

[347]Aaron the Moor, in Shakespeare's *Titus Andronicus*, IV, ii, 144: 'Two may keep counsel when the third's away'.

or deliver it as you see fit. We have been very unwilling here to beleive there is any thing in the Highlanders meeting:[348] truth is, it shews too plainly that none but Presbyterians in Scotland are in a certain interest.

256. *Thomas to Alan I, 6 Oct. 1715*

(1248/3/266–7)

… I came to town last night, and thinke of returning in three or four dayes. Collonel Bladen[349] tells mee care is taken for your having the Act of attainder of the late D[*uke*] of O[*rmond*][350] sent you, the necessity of which hee sayes they are oblidged to you for the notice of, the justices having made nott any mention of itt; the reason given for nott corresponding with the Lords Justices here, may (for ought I know) bee justifiable according to the usuall methods, butt att soe critical a conjuncture, I thinke formes ought to give way to substance, which may prove of such consequence. I wrote a long letter to you att my going out of town which Mr Whitshed assures mee hee sent by a safe hand. Lord Berclay the latter end of last weeke by expresse signifyed his apprehension of a rising in Somersetshire and supposed an intention of attacking Bristol, where hee commands,[351] since which wee have an account of a very great meeting (to the number of 300) on pretence of a hunting match, yesterday sennight, att which itt is sayd some spoake very despondingly, others were silent, the result (as we apprehend) was, laying aside their former intentions, which appears more then probable from Sir W[*illia*]m Windhams having surrendred himselfe.[352]

Hee[353] lay this day sennight in Winchester, on fryday rode through Guilford, having sent a servant before him to Ned Nicholas[354] with a letter, which Mrs Nicholas (in her husbands absence) refused to open, butt carryed both messenger and letter to Lord Ailsford,[355] the fellow was committed to Guilford gaol, and the letter sent unopened to Lord Townsend.[356]

---

[348]The mustering of clansmen in Sept. 1715 which signalled the beginning of the jacobite uprising (Daniel Szechi, *1715: The Great Jacobite Rebellion* (2006), 110–11).

[349]Martin Bladen, MP [I].

[350]The British act of 1715 (1 Geo. I, st. 2, c. 17). In November heads of a bill were introduced into the Irish house of commons (eventually enacted as 2 Geo. I, c. 8) 'For … vesting in his majesty the estate of James Butler, commonly called James, duke of Ormond, and for giving a reward of £10,000 to any person who shall seize or secure him, in case he shall attempt to land in this kingdom'.

[351]James Berkeley (c.1680–1736), 3rd earl of Berkeley, lord lieutenant of Somerset.

[352]Sir William Wyndham's arrest was ordered on the outbreak of the rebellion. Having tricked the arresting officer and made his escape he subsequently surrendered himself into the custody of his brother-in-law, Lord Hertford (Sir Charles Petrie, *The Jacobite Movement* (1959), 224–5; *HC 1715–54*, ii, 562).

[353]Wyndham.

[354]Edward Nicholas (c.1662–1726), of West Horsley, Surrey, tory MP [GB] Shaftesbury.

[355]Heneage Finch (1649–1719), 1st earl of Aylesford, chancellor of the duchy of Lancaster and PC [GB].

[356]Charles Townshend (1675–1738), 2nd Viscount Townshend, secretary of state for the northern department [GB].

Itt plainely I thinke appears by calculating time, that this motion of his was immediately after the meeting from whence I thinke may reasonably bee inferrd what I sayd before of their having given over the intended rising, att least for this time. I am told Sir W[*illia*]m is very sturdy, pleading perfect innocence, and being taxt with the treasonable papers taken by Collonel Hunt upon him,[357] none of which are subscribed, gives for answer that any man may att his pleasure write to another, without the knowledge of the person receiving, and for which hee cannott in justice bee answerable, butt I fancy hee will alter his note ere long.

The parson of Kingston[358] (whoe administred the sacrament to Ned Harvey[359] and has always been his creature) dined with us on Tuesday; by what hee told Mr Onslow[360] in confidence, I apprehend his Patron had discovered to Lords Townsend and Nottingham[361] (whoe examined him) a great deale, perticulars I know nothing of, butt must observe that the parson makes meritt of this, and indeed after a manner bespeaking more of the Jesuite, then that honest simplicity which becomes his function.

Sir W[*illia*]m is to bee examined this evening, nott having hitherto been soe; Sir J Packinton[362] appeard in the house to the astonishment of some, tis sayd hee has given his parole of honour. Letters from Lord Argyll[363] come in this morning sayes hee has nothing to feare; upon a rumer spread of his marching towards Perth halfe my Lord Mars men left him,[364] butt upon better information to the contrary they returned againe.[365] Wee are by the kings direction adjourned to this day fortnight.[366]

This morning I acquainted the Duke of Grafton with your having wrote to Lord G[*alway*], as you desired, with the reason why twas nott jointly, I dare say you will bee throughly well satisfyed with his Graces conduct in publique matters. Hee begins his journey next Munday, Lord Galwey went hence the last in order to bee att the same time att Hollyhead, which I beleive may bee on Wensday sennight ...

[357]John Huske (*d.*1761), lieutenant colonel of the Coldstream Guards (Dalton, *Army Lists*, vi, 320), who had made the original arrest, at Wyndham's house in Somerset, finding in the process 'a bundle of papers' in Wyndham's pockets (Boyer, *Political State*, x, 331–4).

[358]John Broughton (c.1674–1720): W.D. Biden, *The History and Antiquities of the Ancient and Royal Town of Kingston-upon-Thames* (Kingston, 1852), 55; *Biographical Register of Christ's College* ... (2 vols, Cambridge, 1910–13), ii, 116–17. Broughton was a former chaplain to the duke of Marlborough.

[359]Edward Harvey (1658–1736), of Coombe, Surrey, tory MP for Clitheroe, arrested as a jacobite in 1716 (*HC 1715–54*, ii, 114–15).

[360]Either Denzil Onslow (c.1642–1721), MP [GB] Guildford, or Thomas Onslow (1679–1740), MP [GB] Surrey.

[361]Harvey's cousin (*HC 1690–1715*, iv, 291).

[362]Sir John Pakington (1671–1727), 4th Bt, tory MP for Worcs. and a known jacobite sympathiser, whose arrest had been ordered in Sept. 1715 alongside Wyndham. Since then Pakington had surrendered himself and proved his innocence before the British privy council (*HC 1715–54*, ii, 321).

[363]John Campbell (1680–1743), 2nd duke of Argyll (and earl of Greenwich in the English peerage), c.-in-c. Scotland.

[364]John Erskine (1675–1732), 22nd earl of Mar, the jacobite commander.

[365]At this point the jacobite forces in Scotland were based at Perth, which they had captured the month before (Szechi, *1715*, 113–14, 120–1).

[366]From 6 to 20 Oct. (*CJ*, xviii, 327).

257. *Thomas, Peper Harow, to Alan I, 23 Oct. 1715*

(1248/3/270–1)

I have just now yours of the 15th and 17th before I came out of towne I ownd the receipt of your long letter … You little know my condition when you thinke of my being able to undertake an Irish journey; I alwayes make two dayes journey hither, and yett am ill able to bear itt, I came hither from Cobbam[367] on Wensday, I never went one step faster then a walke, notwithstanding which I am nott yett able to goe upright; butt were nott this the case I should nott easily bring my selfe to what some people would call a submission, and which others perhaps expect, butt will never have. I wrote to you when I came out of towne, since when you may bee sure I know nothing more then what wee have in the publique prints.

You forgett that in former letters I told you my Brother St John had Lady Orkenyes deed,[368] and I am as confident as I can bee uppon memory hee sent itt to you on notice that the Trustees would nott execute theirs, pursuant to the Act of parliament, without a sight of itt, because itt made referrences to that deed; I know Mr Lamb[369] was the man I employed when I was in Ireland, and I beleive after my coming away (when the Trustees had nott conveighed[370]) hee pursued the businesse till you gott itt done, which you wrote mee word you had gott done with great difficulty …

258. *Alan I, Dublin, to Thomas, 15 Nov. 1715*

(1248/3/274–5)

Sure brother you are too sanguine on your side the water, I mean at Court and where you converse to make light of this rebellion, which seems to me to spread and gain greater head every post: you know that I apprehended it to be very dangerous from the very beginning, and I confesse it gives me more uneasinesse then it creates in wiser people, but I cannot by any arguments I have yet heard be soe unconcerned and secure of the issue as some seem to be: not but that I firmly beleive it will at long run end in the destruction of the rebells. We shal I doubt have a warm Session in the upper house; I cant but think some people will be very well content to have it soe: and others seem not much sollicitous to prevent it. I cannot but observe a sullennesse and dissatisfaction in some where I did not expect it: you will easily guesse what makes some men lesse concerned at the successe of the Session then were to be desired. On Saturday when I was to be introduced as a baron, after having been introduced as Chancellor, I left the woolsack and went below the bar to put off my robe of Chancellor and put on that of a Baron; I then was brought and introduced within the bar to be sworn; when his Grace the Lord Primate was of opinion the house was dissolved or fallen or something, by my leaving the woolsack; that the Speaker was the cement of the

---

[367] Cobham, Surrey.

[368] Establishing the school at Midleton. St John Brodrick II had died in 1707.

[369] William Lamb(e), an attorney in the court of exchequer (see *Anglo-Irish Politics, Vol. 1*, 127).

[370] The trustees for forfeited estates in Ireland, established by act of the English parliament in 1700.

parts together which constituted an house (he would not call him the principle of unity, that is proper to another function) that when he was gone the house was fallen, nothing could be done, unlesse the house were resumed: that the Baron had carryed away the Chancellor and much to this purpose. Nobody seconded and I think few understood him, but I think his intent was to have prevented my being sworn as a Baron, at least in that method, but he proposed no other; he was told this was the course in England, that a Chancellor goes from the woolsack to debate, to receive a message from the Commons, to communicate the pleasure of the Governement when the Justices are in the house without all these consequences of the houses falling or being dissolved; but nothing was satisfactory, he was up again and again, as often as the Clerk began to read my patent; but at length his Grace not being seconded by any one Peer withdrew in some heat to take a turn in the robing room and then I was sworn without opposicion or interruption. By this you may guesse what may be expected hereafter. Yesterday Lord Anglesey moved the house on a breach of privilege;[371] the Case was this: The Popery act empowers two Justices of peace to tender the oath of abjuration to any person by them suspected etc. Three Justices tendered the oath to the Lord Montgarrett after he received a writ of summons to Parliament, he refused to take the oath (and it is said he did so as not liable to be summoned or have the oath imposed on him by Justices of peace) they demanded 40s on his refusal, which he refused to pay; and there upon they signed a mittimus[372] to send him to Gaol; but the Constable did not carry him to gaol. The words of the Act are general that the oath may be tendred to any person, but when the bill was before the house of Lords and under their consideration whether fit to be passed into a Law, an objection was made whether those general words would not include Peers: for if they would the Lords seemed determined not to passe the bill and you know we cannot mend it. The Judges opinions were asked and they were pleased to give it as their opinion that those general words would not comprehend the Peers. This opinion and the sense of the Lords in this matter is entred in their journal previous to their assent to the bill, and the matter was also stirred in the house of Commons and they were of the same opinion and declared it was not their intention to have the Peers liable to be summoned to take the oaths etc but I doe not find any entry is made of this in their journal. After these steps taken and upon these opinions and declarations the Lords passed the bill.[373] And now the Justices are to be questioned for a breach of privilege: They give out they were mislead by the general words of the Act; the Lord Montgarrets freinds say it was not done in service of the Governement or because he was really suspected but as a designed affront: but be that as it will, it is now looked on as the case of every Lord of Parliament. I wish this had not hapned, for I foresee it will be carryed as far as possible by the Lord Mongarrett and I could wish the offence complained of had hapned in any other act rather then tendring the

---

[371] On 14 Nov. 1715 Anglesey (as Viscount Valentia in the Irish peerage) presented a complaint for breach of privilege in relation to an order for commitment made against Edmund Butler (1663–1735), 6th earl of Mountgarrett, for refusing to take the oath of abjuration as required by the Irish Popery Act of 1709 (8 Anne, c. 3): *LJI*, ii, 461.

[372] An order directing an officer of the law to conduct an offender to prison.

[373] After the committee-stage of the Popery Bill was completed on 22 Aug. 1709 the Irish house of lords requested to hear the opinion of the judges as to whether this clause applied to peers. The opinion was given on 24 Aug. 1709, the details not being recorded in the Lords' *Journals*, after which the bill was passed (*LJI*, ii, 301, 303.). In the meantime, on 23 Aug., the Commons declared that it had not been their intention in passing the bill that this clause should apply to the lords spiritual or temporal (*CJI*, iii, 685–7).

oath of abjuration at this time. Pray let me know on which Bench Lord Cowper sits when he leaves the woolsack in order to speak in a debate.[374] Do not mention me in any of these matters which happen in the house. You must take notice that Lord Mongarrett is an Irish Papist who I beleive never did take the oath of abjuration, God knows what he may do hereafter; and the Justices pretend to be informed that the outlawry of his ancestor for the rebellion in 1641 is not reversed;[375] I beleive they are mistaken; but you will wonder how he could have a writ of Summons if the outlawry be of force; the answer is this; the return of the names of the Peerage by the King att Arms is the ground of preparing the writs of Summons; and it is possible there might be a certificate from the Crown Office that the outlawry is reversed; for I am told there was a rule for reversing it in King James time, but whether the judgement of reversal be entred up I cannot tell; and if it be not the Lords will then consider whether the judgement now stand reversed; I remember the Kings Bench in Lord Fingales case refused to order the judgement to be entred in a few years after the revolution upon such a rule in the Case of Lord Fingall.[376] This to yourself, or not from me.

259. *Alan I, Dublin, to Thomas, 18 Dec. 1715*

(1248/3/280–5)

I borrow an hour from this day of rest to give you a short account of the transactions of a busy part of last week in the house of Peers, where nothing remarkable passed since the opening the Parliament except the behavior of the Primate on my being sworn, and on the Committal of the bill of recognition (of which I gave you formerly a full account); except the complaint of the breach of privilege brought into the house by Lord Anglesey on the second day of the Parliaments sitting viz. 14 November, which hath been the foundation of two very warm dayes work in the house of Lords on Friday and yesterday, of which I will now give you a full account; by which you will find how some men stand affected; and how far he, who pretends to have come over hither to make matters easy, and to be a man of great interest, hath contributed to the quiet of the Session, or is able to doe what he thinks fit to undertake. By an act made in the eighth of Queen Anne just after the intended invasion of Scotland Justices of peace are empowred to tender the oath of abjuration to any suspected person, and on their refusing to take it they are to demand 40s and on non payment they are empowred to commit etc. When the present Parliament was summoned a writ went to Lord Viscount Mongarrett to attend in Parliament as a Peer; after the delivery of the writ and within forty dayes before the meeting of the Parliament three Justices of peace having too good reason to apprehend he was very ill affected to the present establishment,

---

[374]William Cowper (1665–1723), 1st Earl Cowper, lord chancellor [GB].

[375]Mountgarrett's great-grandfather, Richard Butler (c.1578–1651), the 3rd earl, a general in the confederate forces in the 1640s. The Irish house of lords had resolved in Dec. 1697 that his outlawry had indeed been reversed (*LJI*, i, 675).

[376]Luke Plunkett (1639–81), 3rd earl of Fingall, was outlawed posthumously in 1691, but the outlawry was reversed by special warrant in 1692 on the grounds that he had died before the Glorious Revolution and his son Peter (1678–1718) the 4th earl, was 'a minor, and never in Ireland' (HMC, *Lords MSS*, n.s., iv, 30).

in the heighth of the hopes of the rebells of the North[377] summoned him to take the oath of abjuration, thinking that the word person included Peers as well as Commoners and committed him etc: now you must know that at the time that bill was before the Lords (having already passed the house of Commons), they were apprehensive that a Lord might be summoned by Justices of peace and obliged to attend them, and in default of obeying the summons that they might be subjected to the penalty of 40s or to be committed; and such slavish attendance (as they termed it) they seemed determined not to subject the Peerage to; as on the other hand the majority was against losing the bill if they could be convinced that as it stood it would not subject the Peers to attend on the Summons of two Justices etc for you know we cannot alter but must passe the bill as transmitted under the Great Seal or reject the whole. The then Judges were advised with and, as several Lords (who were then in the house) affirmed on Fryday, gave their opinion unanimously that the bill did not extend to Peers (A strange opinion in my sense) and upon that confidence the Lords passed the bill; and entred a resolution or declaratory vote in their journal previous to their passing the bill and subsequent to the opinion of the Judges that the bill did not in that part extend to Lords: The journal saith that the Judges gave their opinion, but what that opinion was doth not appear on the journal: but no doubt it was as the Lords affirmed. Lord Anglesey said that the opinions of the Judges never appear on the journals in England: pray inform me whether that be so, for I have no reason to give entire credit with implicite faith to his Lordships memory. When Lord Mongarrett was committed he applyed to the Lords Justices and to me; the former procured or (I may say) ordered his enlargement; and I summoned the Justices to appear before me to answer Lord Mongarretts complaint against them for misbehavior in their office; but before the time came when both partyes were to be heard Lord Anglesey eased me of the trouble by making a complaint of what the Justices had done in summoning and committing Lord Mongarrett as a breach of the privileges of the house and moving it might be referred to the Committee of privileges. I foresaw that if that motion took place the matter would end in this question whether two Justices of peace had power to summon a Peer to take the oath, and to commit him even in Parliament time or time of privilege for not appearing: or not paying 40s. I thought that as things then stood in Great Britain it might be of very ill consequence for the house of Lords to do anything which might without doors look like discountenancing Justices of peace for tendring the oath of abjuration to any person of any degree, or like supporting an Irish Papist whose ancestor was guilty of the rebellion of 1641 and who had been guilty himself of that in eighty eight (tho by being within the articles of Limrick he was intitled to reverse that outlawry and actually had done soe[378]) in his obstinate and undutiful refusal of taking the oath of abjuration now in a time of such danger. I therefore told them there was no necessity of engagin the house in the question whether a Peer may have the oath tendered to him and be committed for refusal, unless they were satisfyed something of that kind had been done; that the matter having been opened to me on the complaint against the Justices as Chancellor, they insisted his ancestor was outlawed for the rebellion in 1641 and that outlawry remained stil of force; which fact if true would ease the house of the complaint and enquiry; and upon this the house ordered the Committee to enquire whether the Lord

---

[377] In Scotland.

[378] Mountgarrett, a cavalry officer in James II's army, had been taken prisoner by Williamite forces in 1689.

Mongarrett had been allowed a Peer of the realm, and whether any of his Ancestors under whom he derives his honor were oulawed for high treason and whether such outlawry or outlawryes remain of force. My Lord Abercorne was put into the chair of the Committee,[379] which was attended with unusual diligence and zeal by very many Lords of very different sentiments; and if I may give credit to the affirmacion of some Lords which constantly attended the Committee nothing was omitted which could be done for the service of the Lord Mongarrett; which Justice since one of the Lords who voted against him hath done to the Committee I think I may venture to say those Lords who were of opinion against Lord Mongarrett did also endeavour to have every thing laid as plain as possible before the house to convince it that the outlawry remained stil of force: but if I may judge from the maner of the wording the report (which I hear Lord Anglesey had the drawing or supervising of) the Lords who thought the outlawry was reversed have put the evidence in as strong light as it will bear; but by looking on the journals I apprehend somethings might have been added from them which would have done Lord Mongarrets cause some disservice. On Thursday last the report was agreed to and signed by the Committee and brought into the house and ordered to be made the following day;[380] After it was made great endeavours were used to put off the consideration of it till Monday; but the house having the day before ordered all the Peers in town to be summoned to attend and all the Lords attending in their places great opposition was made to the putting it off till Monday, so that the house came to divide on that matter; and on the division were equal till my vote was demanded and I gave it against putting off the debate, which therefore was to have been immediately entred upon;[381] but instead of it the Lord Primate said there was something which he conceived was previous to our debate viz. the taking the three Justices into custody,[382] which he moved might be done and was seconded by the Bishop of Limrick[383] Lord Altham and others; I shewed the house that when the complaint was first made Lord Anglesey only moved to have it referred to the Committee of privileges, but the house would not do that till they were ascertained whether the person who made the complaint was within privilege; and that when a report was brought in which laid that matter before the house, it would be extraordinary to commit the Justices when from that report as it seemed to me, and I beleived to many other Lords the person committed was no peer but a Commoner. Upon this the general sense of the house being to proceed first on the report the Bishop of Limrick began the debate and with great zeal argued for Lord Mongarrets being a Peer; I say with zeal; he was answered with great clearnesse and

---

[379] As Viscount Strabane in the Irish peerage: confirmed in *LJI*, ii, 481. Abercorn entered a lengthy protest against the final decision of the House (*LJI*, ii, 486–7).

[380] Confirmed in *LJI*, ii, 481.

[381] In the British house of lords the Speaker did not have a casting vote: divisions resulting in a tie were automatically resolved in the negative (J.C. Sainty and David Dewar, *Divisions in the House of Lords: An Analytical List 1685 to 1857* (House of Lords RO Occasional Publications, no. 2 (1976), 10–11; *British Parliamentary Lists, 1660–1800: A Register*, ed. G.M. Ditchfield et al. (1995), 10). This rule did not apply in the British house of commons, where the Speaker did exercise a casting vote and was not bound by precedent or standing order in the way he should give it (*HC 1690–1715*, i, 362). The section on voting in *The Standing Orders of the House of Lords of Ireland…* (1795), 16, makes no reference to procedure in the event of a division being equal, though it is possible that in this case Brodrick was simply being called upon to exercise his vote as a peer, having not already done so at the division (13).

[382] Best, Fitzgerald and Browne, jps in Queen's Co. (*LJI*, ii, 461).

[383] Thomas Smyth.

strength by the Bishop of Rapho (Dr Synge)[384] Lord Santry spoke on the same side with Bishop of Rapho and was followed by Lord Abercorne who concluded with the Bishop of Limrick. The Bishop of Down[385] spoke for Lord Mongarrett with much concern, yet a good deal of art: whom the Bishop of Clogher[386] answered with great ingenuity, modesty, and a becoming warmth when he came to speak of Lord Mongarrets behavior formerly, which intitles him to no more then strict justice some of the Lords particularly Bishop [of] Down and the Primate having expressed a pretty deal of tendernesse toward him and seeming to compassionate his being like to be dispeered (as they termed it). The Bishop of Waterford[387] with warmth (and I think rancor) expressed himself against the Bishop of Rapho, taxing him with having used sophistry and laid down the most fallacious principles in the world in debating; the house resented it and would for ought I know have censured him and he was called down to orders; I then spoke and fearing the house might fall into warmth or at least spend so much time in this thing as would of course put off the debate to a farther day, which was the aim of Lord Mongarretts freinds, I endeavoured to soften and explain the words; that the Bishop having had an University educacion and lead a retired life retained stil the language of the schools; which had led him to use language not so well suiting that house and desired he might explain himself, which he did in a slovenly maner, and soe as would not have been accepted at another time: but this accident eased us of a long speech he intended to have made, if I may judge by the bulks of the papers and notes he held in his hand when he stood up and spoke out of: but I verily think Lord Mongarretts cause suffered nothing by his not saying all he intended; all that could be said for him being offered by other Lords. The Bishop of Clonfert[388] spoke after him very shortly but very honestly, and said he was against admitting that which the Bishop of Waterford owned not to be a legal proof of a record of the reversal of Lord Mongarrets outlawry in 1641, but an equitable proof; to wit circumstances and presumptions to induce the house to beleive there once had been such a record; he thought legal proof was required and was not for going out of the way to vote a man to be a Peer who plainly appeared disaffected to the present establishment. I should have told you that Lord Castlecomer spoke next after the Bishop of Waterford and before the Bishop of Clonfert against Lord Mongarrett very modestly, very handsomly, very sensibly. Lord Charlemont then stood up and with a good deal of confusion talked very sillily for Lord Mongarrett, and by his behavior during this matter, and particularly yesterday hath given me great uneasinesse at having done him the best service I could with Lord Sunderland to keep his Governement of Charlemont; for which I resolve to ask my Lords pardon and withdraw any security I may seem to lye under for his future good behavior; for tho I think the man not ill enclined, yet I see him so much under influence of people who are of sentiments perfectly opposite to ours that I shal never hereafter expect good of him.

After Lord Charlemont the Bishop of Downe stood up again and made a long whining discourse, full of seeming conviction of his being in the right and therefore pressing his sentiments with more earnestnesse on others. Lord Anglesey then spoke who had waited

[384] Edward Synge.
[385] Edward Smyth.
[386] St George Ashe.
[387] Thomas Milles.
[388] William Fitzgerald.

hitherto in expectation my warmth would have called me up, but I resolved (as you horse-men call it) to wait on him; the cheif part of his harangue was that the farther consideration of the report might go off to another day: but as to the Case before the house he spoke very little that had weight in it in my apprehension: and indeed at the time of his speaking I observed a want of that vivacity and presence of mind which at other times appears in him: but I since find that while this matter was under debate the Commons were applying the six pence per pound which would have become due to the Vice Treasurers Lord Rochester and Lord Anglesey out of the new aids given by this parliament to the building the Castle; which will amount to above £5000.[389] This proceeding of the Commons shews how great his interest is in the lower house, as the event of the present debate on so popular a question as privilege demonstrates what his power (added to that of his fast freinds) is in the upper.[390] I closed the debate, and took some pains in it, thinking the carrying the question to be of very great consequence: and my freinds flatter me, if I did not doe some service upon this occasion and the next day on the debate of Lord Barrymores question which was the work of Saturday.[391] I would not be understood by saying I closed the debate as if no body spoke after me, for the Bishops of Down Waterford and Limrick did speak: but it was only to make little remarks on and objections to somethings which I had said, which seemed to me of so little weight as not to need an answer. During the debates I had spoke to Lord Cavan to move this question That the outlawry for the rebellion in 1641 of the Ancestor of the Lord Viscount Mongarrett under whom he derives title to his honor is reversed. The Primate again insisted on the question by him moved and seconded by the Bishop of Limrick for taking the Justices into custody, after Lord Cavan had moved that question and been seconded, but the house disliking the Primates question which had been so long waved and another matter debated; Lord Barrymore proposed another question that Lord Mongarrett had been allowed a Peer: I shewed the house that the reason of that inquiry was to enable the Committee to bring the matter before the house how far he had been looked on as a Peer to the intent that might give Lords the best light into the probability of his Ancestors having reversed his outlawry; but not to foreclose or prejudice that enquiry; for if the son of a person outlawed for treason should have sate in the house (which this Lord however never did) yet on the outlawry appearing to be stil of force he would no longer be permitted to sit in the house. And Lord Cavans question being put (after the

[389] An order made by the Commons on 17 Dec., after hearing the report from the committee of ways and means, that the committee drafting the supply bill should insert a clause to this effect (*CJI*, iv, 136). The purpose of the appropriation was the completion of the 'public buildings and offices' in Dublin Castle, which were being repaired after the fire in the privy council chamber and treasury offices in 1711 (David Dickson, *Dublin: The Making of a Capital City* (2014), 123–4).

[390] According to Charles Delafaye, no one spoke in Anglesey's favour in the Commons debate on the vice-treasurers' fees (TNA, SP 63/373/336–7: Delafaye to [Robert Pringle], 17 Dec. 1715). Delafaye thought him 'universally hated' (TNA, SP 63/374/57: Delafaye to [Pringle], 24 Jan. 1715/16), and that the resolutions against him had been orchestrated by 'Brodrick's friends' (BL, Add. MS 61640, f. 81: Delafaye to [Sunderland], 24 Jan. 1715/16).

[391] A motion made on 17 Dec. that for the future, in relation to the 1709 Popery Act (and the proposed bill to explain the various popery acts, for which leave had been given in the Commons on 24 Nov., but which never reached the statute book), a justice of the peace tendering the oath of abjuration to any peer would be guilty of a breach of the privilege of the House (*LJI*, ii, 488).

previous question demanded and carried in the affirmative 26 against 21) It was carried in the negative by the same number against the same number.[392]

Lords for the negative

Kildare, Mount Alexander, Cavan, Loftus, Shanon, Strangford, Castlecomer, Donerayle, Bishop of Clogher, Bishop of Clonfert, Bishop Dromore, Bishop Rapho, Bishop Kilaloo,[393] Bishop Kilmore,[394] Blaney, Santry, Tirawly, St George, Shelburn, Ranelagh, Carbery, Farrard, Newtown,[395] Stackallen, Moor, Lord Chancellor

Lords in the affirmative

Lord Primate, Barrymore, Bellomont, Mayo, Valentia, Strabane, Charlemont, FitzWilliam, Bishop Kildare,[396] Bishop Down, Bishop Limrick, Bishop Waterford, Bishop Cloyne, Bishop Cork, Bishop Ossory,[397] Athenry, Kerry, Kingston, Gowran, Altham.[398]

The mortification which some people shewed on this occasion is inexpressible; Lord A[*nglesey*] was in the utmost confusion, in which rage had a great share: Our neighbour[399] looked paler then his Cravat and in the agony of his mind immediately after the division of the house, and the question of striking Mongarrett out of the roll of Peers being carried in the affirmative without division moved another question upon which a debate arose which was adjourned till next morning,[400] and so much passed then as will be an ample subject of another letter. In the mean time let me assure you that I am credibly informed while I am spending my lungs and impairing my health in endeavouring nothing may go wrong in the house where I sitt, some people (and I think the triumvirate is your freind,[401] the Speaker,[402] and one who fancyes he could well fill the Seat on which the King hath placed me[403]) are endeavouring to possesse the Justices as if I had an intention to distresse or break their Governement: and I am told one of the Justices was so frank to say it must not be wondred at if they endeavoured to break him who aimed at breaking them. You long have known my inclinations to retire, and know my want of health; but to be represented or thought disaffected to or backward in serving the King, to whom I stand obliged by the strongest bonds of duty gratitude and inclination, and for whom I so often exposed my self to the rage of malicious and cruel men when I never had seen or received the greatest or any favors from him is what affects me deeply; and I am sure I shal either here or in England

---

[392] The sequence is confirmed in *LJI*, ii, 486, but without any record of the numbers voting. The numbers are confirmed in Wake, Epist. xii: Bishop Godwin to Bishop Wake, 20 Dec. [1715], and the voting record of the bishops confirmed in Wake, Epist. xii: Bishop Synge to [Wake], 17 Dec. 1715.

[393] Nicholas Forster.

[394] Timothy Godwin.

[395] Lord Newtownbutler.

[396] Welbore Ellis.

[397] Sir Thomas Vesey, 1st Bt.

[398] All protested except Lords Fitzwilliam and Gowran, and the bishop of Kildare. In addition, Lord Massereene also signed the protest (*LJI*, ii, 481).

[399] Probably Lord Kingston.

[400] On a motion to resolve that any peer obeying a summons from justices of the peace to take the oath of abjuration was breaking the privilege of the House (*LJI*, ii, 487–8).

[401] Galway's secretary, Martin Bladen, MP [I], who was Thomas's (British) parliamentary colleague at Stockbridge.

[402] William Conolly, MP [I].

[403] Chief Justice William Whitshed.

know who accuses me and for what, and as sure I shal be able to answer and silence the calumny: but Mr Bladens ill treatment of your nephew,[404] added to some things being done in the house in a maner wholly unnecessary and carryed on by a junto, who having little merit to found their pretensions upon, are forced to represent a necessity of going into methods, to attain ends which might be otherwise obtained with a general consent, which methods many Gentlemen scorn and detest because they seem calculated to create merit to particular from what not their schemes but the good inclinacion of the people bring to passe, hath made him speak his mind freely and mention undertakers in the matter of the dutyes on wine brandy which is now added to the former dutyes on those liquors:[405] and indeed he and some others expresse great dissatisfaction at the maner our Secretary manages (beyond anything we ever saw here) in so much that really our men who desire to be well at the Castle pay him the most entire submission I ever heard of, if it be such as I hear from several Gentlemen. Yesterday there was a motion about heads of a bill to qualify the dissenters to serve in the militia, Bladen seconded it, and I hear spoke largely on their being incapacitated etc but Upton spoke directly for repealing the sacramental test: but the house fired at the mention of it;[406] and I beleive the motion made will a good deal imbarrasse the Governement if things be not carryed with great conduct and prudence: which can hardly be wanting while the Cheif Justice, the Speaker and secretary are intirely and solely confided in. I have not for this fortnight been spoken to about any thing in the house of Commons.

260. Alan I, Dublin, to Thomas, Westminster 27 Dec. 1715

(1248/3/289–90)

I am to own the favor of two letters from you dated the 17th and 20th instant, but cannot expresse the concern the later (which gives me an account of your being fallen into another fit of the stone) hath created me: the nature of the distemper and the consideration that it is fallen on the man whom I have the most reason to love of any freind living makes the thought of it very greivous to me. The Easterly winds I find have kept a letter I wrote to you more then a week since on this side of the water stil, and I would make this letter a supplement to that but that I apprehend your letter of the 17th needs an immediate answer. As soon as I had received it I went to the Castle and desired to know from the Lords Justices whether they had any directions from England about a bill to be framed on this side of the water in relation to the late Duke of Ormond; for you must know there were heads of a bill brought into the house of Commons by Mr Tigh upon that businesse and they passed the house and were laid before the Justices in order to be transmitted in form into England,[407]

---

[404] St John III: during an altercation in the Commons over St John's opposition to the Militia Bill (BL, Add. MS 47028, ff. 109–11: Charles Dering to Lord Perceval, 10 Dec. 1715).

[405] On 17 Dec. the committee of ways and means reported. All its resolutions were adopted, including the imposition of a duty of 8*d.* per gallon on spirit and fortified wines made in Ireland (on top of the continued 'additional duty' of 3*d.* per gallon) and another of £4 per tun on imported wine (*CJI*, iv, 183–6).

[406] Upton's motion was reported in BL, Add. MS 47028, f. 112: Philip Perceval to Lord Perceval, 24 Dec. 1715, along with the fact that it received no support.

[407] Heads of a bill 'For extinguishing the regalities and liberties of the … county palatine of Tipperary, and for vesting in his majesty the estate of James Butler, commonly called James, duke of Ormond, and for giving a reward

and these heads being read at the board and referred to a Committee gave me oportunity to take notice of the nature of them. At my first asking the question I apprehended there had been nothing wrote from the other side, but immediately after it was said that indeed the intimation from England was no more then that an act was desired to put the County of Tiperary, where justice formerly had been administred by Commission from the Duke of Ormond upon the same foot with the rest of the Kingdome.[408] I could not omit taking notice that Mr Tighs bill had quite another tendency, in answer to which Mr Bladen said that indeed the Sollicitor general had prepared a clause which would answer the end, but that the bill was carryed with that dispatch through the house that there was not time to add it to the heads of the bill in the house, but that it would be offered at the Committee of Councel. One would think that a thing of this nature should have been so taken care of that the drawing the bill should have been put into the hands of the Attorney or Sollicitor General or at least of some knowing Lawyer, and not left to the care of a man no way conversant in affairs of this sort; but it was otherwise, and the thing was so much a secret to me, that any directions in that matter had been sent over, that your letter gave me the first intimation of it. Whether this proceeded from a resolution taken up by the Secretary to communicate nothing to me since my son hath not gone into all his schemes in the house of commons I know not; perhaps that may be the case, but I rather beleive it was a thing not so much minded as it required; the truth is nothing of late hath taken up the thoughts of three or fowre who sett the matter on foot, but the getting the additional dutyes on wine and brandy;[409] after Gentlemen had reason to give their freinds assurance no more then the dutyes on beer ale tobacco etc would be expected: but the farther encrease of the supply was schemed or gone into by Gentlemen who resolved to create to themselves peculiar merit by going greater lengths then others thought necessary; building on this assurance, that tho men did not think them necessary, yet they would not willingly refuse any thing proposed under our good and gracious King: but there was a farther view in it, by necessitating those who had said nothing farther then the former addicional dutyes would be expected either to forfeit their character in their countrey by pressing their freinds farther after making that declaration, or by not going roundly into it to lye them open to the censure of men who have no other way to render themselves considered but by lessening and misrepresenting other Gentlemen. And indeed the conduct of the Session in the lower house hath fallen much to the share of the Speaker and Secretary, to whom the honour of all that is well done will I think be wholly imputed. I beleive we shal be in a few dayes in a Committee to consider Tighs bill, but methinks the scheme you mention as expected to be gone into by those in London is impraticable: In the first place you expect we should attaint him, but the houses will expect evidence of particular treasons committed before they will go into such an act of attainder; for as I understand you, it [is] expected we should attaint him so

---

[407] *(continued)* of £10,000 to any person who shall seize or secure him, in case he shall attempt to land in this kingdom', brought in by Richard Tighe on 7 Dec. and sent to the lords justices on the 21st (ILD). The resultant bill eventually passed into law as 2 Geo. I, c. 8 [I].

[408] For the history of the palatine jurisdiction of Tipperary, see V.T.H. Delany, 'The Palatinate Court of the Liberty of Tipperary', *American Journal of Legal History*, v (1961), 95–117.

[409] The annual income of the Irish treasury consisted of the crown's hereditary revenues, supplemented by short-term parliamentary grants of taxation, the so-called 'additional duties'.

as his forfeiture may r[each][410] higher[411] then 10 September last: to what time must that [—[412]] Certainly you mean to the time when he committed his treason: will it not then be asked what act of treason did he commit before 10 September and when was that treason committed. The truth is I doe not apprehend it was an oversight but done on consideration that the English Act doth not make his forfeiture reach higher then 10 September; for in Law he was on 9 September an innocent man and would stil have been so notwithstanding that Act if he had surrendred himself before or on 10 September.[413] Then as to settlements or conveyances for paiment of debts; those which were made for valuable consideration and bona fide are good in Law if made before he was attainted, and no subsequent Act ought to invalidate them, nor will or ought such an Act to passe; on the other hand all voluntary or fraudulent conveyances made to skreen the estate from forfeiture will be avoided by the Crown as the Law now stands: but depend on it all that I think ought to be done shal be done to bring this affair into order.

261. *Alan I, Dublin, to Thomas, 30 Dec. 1715*

(1248/3/291–3)

The wind is at length come to the Westward so that we may send off one of our pacquet boats; on board of which I think eight pacquetts will goe. I formerly told you that after Lord Mongarrets businesse was over in the house of Lords, the Earle of Barrymore moved a question which occasioned a debate which was adjourned till next morning, when his Lordship brought in two questions in writing, which differed very little in substance from that proposed by him the night before.[414] He no sooner proposed his questions but he was seconded and the house called on me to put the question: I took his Lordships written paper and repeated his first question and asked whether that was what the house expected I should put, and finding no body to stand up to debate tho I saw a good deal of dissatisfaction in a great many Lords I stood up and told the house that as the question was framed it was too general and sought to involve in indefinite terms a thing which perhaps Lords would not so readily go into if, when things which were meant should be called by their proper names; he moved it thus, that for any justice of peace to summon a Peer to tender the oaths was a breach of the privilege etc. I said the oath meant was the oath of abjuration as was plain from the occasion of the question and time of moving it, and desired it might be explained what oaths were or could be intended unlesse that of abjuring the Pretender. Lord Anglesey very freely told them I had sett the matter right and proposed the question should be altered by mentioning the oath mentioned in the Act to explain and amend the Act to prevent the farther growth of Popery: I pressed him to reduce his question to writing, but he would not, but insisted on my doing it: I cannot say positively that he named the oath of abjuration,

---

[410]Gap in original manuscript.

[411]Longer.

[412]Gap in original manuscript.

[413]A reference to the Act of Attainder passed against Ormond at Westminster (1 Geo. 1, st. 2, c. 16).

[414]The difference was that now it was the justices, in offering the oath of abjuration to a peer, who were to be guilty of a breach of privilege (*LJI*, ii, 488).

tho I think he did: but the Bishop of Dromore[415] who sate near him tells me he did not: but that is not of any consequence; for beside that no oath is contained or mentioned in that Act but that of abjuration, the altering Lord Barrymores question consisted in changing the indefinite word (oaths) to one particular oath the tendring of which to Lord Mongarrett had been complained of. At length the question was stated in these words That for any justice or justices of peace to summon any Peer of this Kingdome to take the oath of abjuration mentioned etc is a breach of the Privilege of the Peerage of this realm. Several Lords moved against the putting this question at that time, there being no complaint then before the house of any Peer being summoned to take that oath; it was said this would be understood without doors as if the Lords not being able to punish the Justices who summoned Mongarrett (a Commoner) were resolved to go out of the way to tell people the Peerage were not obliged to take that oath at a time when there is an actual rebellion in Great Britain and that such magistrates who endeavoured to lay suspected Lords under the tye of an oath not to assist the Pretender would fall under the displeasure and censure of the Lords: it was therefore insisted that the previous question should be put, which was done accordingly and twenty six were against the main question being put, fifteen for it viz. Primate Barrymore Bellamont Anglesey Abercorn Charlemont Mazareen Bishop Down Bishop Limrick Bishop Cloyne Bishop Ossory Lord Kerry Athenry Kingston Altham. You must know the Judges gave their opinions when the bill to amend the Act to prevent the farther growth of Popery was under the consideration of the house to be passed or rejected that the Lords were not liable to be summoned to take the oath: and many well meaning Lords chose rather to come into the previous question, then to carry the main question that Lords might be summoned etc tho it is as certain they may as that they are persons: for the words are Justices may summon any suspected person or persons. Lord FitzWilliams and Gowran were with us in the previous question, tho against us in Lord Mongarrets vote. There go with this boat three bills, one to attaint the Pretender;[416] When the heads as brought from the Commons were before the Councel board I objected to that part of the bill which attaints him, because he is actually attainted already in England: so as that part of the bill seemed to me to be unnecessary, and I thought it might give offence on your side, as if the Act which attaints him in England were not sufficient here: but the nature of the bill carryed it through the Councel; where nobody would leave out even an unnecessary clause which related to expresse our aversion to and detestation of the Pretender: the bill also gives £50000 to any person who shal take or kill him in Ireland; but our managers in the house of Commons might and I think should have added a clause to make good that money to the Treasury which by the bill the Treasury is obliged to make it good to the person who by doing the service shal intitle himself to it: but I beleive there is no great prospect of our paying that money, so as their omission may be thought of lesse concern. The bill to encourage tillage is the same in effect with a former bill,[417] except that it gives liberty to transport when wheat doth not exceed 25s barlye 10s etc whereas the former bill

[415]John Stearne.

[416]A bill to attaint the jacobite Pretender and to offer a reward of £50,000 to anyone apprehending him should he attempt to land in Ireland. The heads of bills process in the Irish house of commons had been completed within eight days of leave being given on 21 Nov. The resultant bill would eventually pass into law as 2 Geo. I, c .4 [I] (ILD).

[417]Heads of bills for the encouragement of tillage had been introduced into the Commons in the sessions of 1710, 1711 and 1713, but had failed either at the British privy council (1710) or in the Irish parliament (1711 and

left the same latitude to the Councel board as they had by Law to prohibit transportation when they thought fit; and they pretended to have power by an old Statute to doe it at any time; for that Act gives them power to hinder exportation when corn is of a price therein mentioned, and corn never is of so low a price now as that Act speaks of: but the truth is the measures and prices in that Act we are now very much in the dark about: this Act also gives a praemium for exporting corn when it is of such prices viz. wheat 12s barley 6s etc or under. Our Countrey Esquires are willing to think this a very useful bill, and therefore I hope it will come over; but I think it is not of such importance, yet wish it may come back, for truly it is all that our great men have yet done for the Countrey this Session. The third is a money bill, which layes £4 per tun on wines and 8d per gallon on brandy imported: this bill gives the Vice treasurers 6d in the pound for the aids given this Session to build the Castle and was put in to let the world see how well our Vice Treasurer was loved and what interest he had in an Irish house of Commons; the tax laid of 4s in the pound on pensions and salaryes to people residing in England was moved by Anderson Sanders and seconded by Trevor Hill. I think it was a little warm and unneccessary; and sure with the least addresse might have been prevented, but it was either not thought of in time, or looked upon as not worth endeavouring.

Our Lords Justices are now at the Speakers who is the man in the good graces of those at helm; the truth is the court he payes your collegue and his brother[418] entitle him to a double porcion of their good offices and freindship. You cannot imagine the uneasinesse people expresse at our late conduct here: I have done all in my power to keep people in humour, but there appears more dissatisfaction then I ever expected to see among men of the same principles; and all occasioned by mens contriving to bring that to passe by management, which might have been attained openly and with a good grace, if Gentlemen had been at first told what was expected or desired. But I hope all this will be gott over and that freinds will again come to look upon and treat one another as formerly: there are two things which require Gentlemens being lesse opposite to one another then they have been in some instances: I mean the farther consideration of the establishment, which will give angry men oportunity of being uneasy; the other is the bill about indemnifying dissenters from the penaltyes they have incurred by taking Commissions in the militia: this I think no honest man would scruple as to the time past, but nothing would serve Upton but a virulent declamation against the test as to all civil emploiments, whose behavior with that of one Gentleman more put the Commons into such warmth that in my opinion they will find it very difficult to gett a clause to enable them to be Officers in the militia for the future; or at least I think there will be strong endeavours used to restrain them to Commissions of the lower sort and not to extend to feild Officers. And perhaps Mr Uptons behavior in this and some other matters may be one great motive to the house to deny them to be made feild Officers, when they know his haughty temper will not stoop, but will expect to command in cheif in the County of Antrim.[419] You will say it is very unfortunate the King should at a time of this difficulty not have the assistance of all who would fight heartily

---

417 *(continued)* 1713). This particular set of heads, presented by the Brodricks' brother-in-law James Barry, would be rejected by the British privy council (ILD).

418 Martin Bladen and his fellow secretary, Charles Delafaye, MP [I].

419 Clotworthy Upton's estate lay at Templepatrick, Co. Antrim, and he was MP for the county. He had also served as high sheriff in 1695.

for him; and I confesse I think soe too: But this matter was concerted (as I hear) between the Secretary or secretaryes, the Speaker, Sir Gustavus Hume and a very few more: I am told Lord Montjoy was let into it the night before it was moved by Sir Gustavus Hume; in very undigested terms, That a bill might be brought in to enable Protestant dissenters to take arms in defence of his Majesty (or to that effect). Your Nephew added to the question words which restrained it to their doing soe when commissioned by the Crown so to do. If this matter had been communicated to and considered by more it might have stood upon a better foot then it seems now to doe, and would have been supported so as not to have the matter rufled as it was in the house; but it was made a secret till moved by Sir Gustavus and seconded by the Secretary.[420] I wish it may be better digested against our next meeting; but under the management of our present few I fear it will come to another issue then seems to me to be desired.

262. *Thomas to Alan I, Dublin, 15 Jan. 1715[/16]*

(1248/3/294–5)

The Commons[421] this day agreed to a very dutifull Addresse, in answer to each paragraph of the speech.

Gave leave to bring in a bill for the farther suspension of the Habeas corpus Act.

Expelld Forster and ordered a new writt[425] and

Ordered the house to bee calld over this day fortnight;

Mr Shippin[422] was the onely man (as hee was before) whoe opposd the motion for leave to bring in the Bill, and sayd all uppon itt that soe ill a cause would beare.

In the debates of both dayes the late ministry, and the Sacheverel parliament[423] were layd on very thick.

The seven Lords (impeacht yesterday)[424] were this day brought to the Lords Bar, where their Articles being read to them, they desired Councill might bee assigned them, and being calld on to name such as they desired, in answer to itt, they sayd (and probably with truth) that they knew the names of none, upon which some Lords are ordered to goe to them this night to the Tower, there to receive from them the names of such as they desired to advise with, for which an order will bee made uppon the report tomorrow. They are ordered to putt in their answer on Saturday, and will I beleive bee tryed next weeke, if they stand itt, which generally twas thought they would nott, till this demand made, some of their freinds

---

[420] Martin Bladen.

[421] At Westminster.

[425] Thomas Forster (1683–1738), of Adderstone, Northumberland, MP [GB] Northumb. from 1708 until his expulsion from the house of commons for participating in the jacobite rebellion.

[422] William Shippen (1673–1743), of Norfolk Street, London, MP [GB] Newton. Shippen's speech is summarised in Cobbett, *Parl. Hist.*, vii, col. 276.

[423] The British parliament of 1710–13, elected after the impeachment of Dr Henry Sacheverell in Mar. 1710, the popular reaction to which helped produce a tory landslide: Geoffrey Holmes, *The Trial of Doctor Sacheverell* (1973), ch. 10.

[424] Lords Derwentwater, Widdrington, Nithsdale, Winton, Carnwath, Kenmure and Nairne. Articles of impeachment had been engrossed by the Commons on 9 Jan. (*CJ*, xviii, 333–4) and the impeached lords were brought to the Bar of the upper House the following day (*LJ*, xx, 256).

(as I heare) have given outt that they would insist on the Pretenders declaration, and disown the Jurisdiction, butt what they will doe herein a little time will determine, till when I take the matter to bee uncertaine.

A point is stirrd which I take to bee very plaine, whither the words and intendment of that clause in the Bill of Rights against the power of pardoning[425] shall be construed to bee in bar of pleading a pardon graunted before the impeachment, or of doing soe after conviction. The Commons will nott (as I beleive) bee easily brought to part with their hold.

I have seen a very sensible letter out of Scotland, to a member here, giving the following accountt. That a ship had att Peter Head[426] (agreeable to former accountts) sett on shoare five or six persons, one of whom was sayd to bee the Pretender, butt that (if soe) they still kept him incognito, and the writer says hee beleives they will doe soe till they can ship him of againe, that hee is there seems now lesse doubtfull then hitherto, for there is a certaine account come of his embarking att Dunkirke from one whoe saw him on board, butt cannott say whither bound.

Tis generally agreed that the late D[*uke*] of Ormond is att Morlaise.[427] Here has been a flying report this evening that wee had taken Perth, if there bee truth in itt, I presume they must have quitted itt, for I am told that uppon their receiving notice of a detachment from Sterling being ordered thither, the Highlanders were for shifting for themselves, butt were prevaild uppon by Echlin[428] to send to Lord Mar, whose answer I am told was that having had a fall from his horse hee was nott able then to come to them, butt would doe itt soone, desiring them to continue their steddinesse and loyalty, which tis sayd they tooke to bee a trick in order to facilitate his getting of, soe that tis I thinke probable they may have thought fitt to provide for themselves as well as they can.

Things here are very quiett, and I thinke like to continue soe, thanks to a good body of Troopes and those soe posted as to give noe opurtunity for any risings, every day will make us more secure then other. Butt that the Pretender has some great encouragement to which wee are strangers surely is beyond question, or those about him must bee changelings, butt their courage will be coold when they see the fate of those wee have taken, and shall consider the likelyhood of its being theirs. All the 7 Lords are putt into the same Articles together.

263. *Alan I, Dublin, to Thomas, 20 Jan. 1715[/16]*

(1248/3/300–1)

I have waited some dayes in hopes of English letters arriving, which hath occasioned my having been longer silent of late then I ought to have been; but I resolve to continue no

---

[425] Presumably the clauses declaring the dispensing power to be illegal (in the English act of 1689 declaring the rights and liberties of the subject (1 Will. and Mary sess. 2, c. 2).

[426] Peterhead, Aberdeenshire.

[427] Morlaix, Brittany.

[428] Robert Echlin (1657–1724), of Monaghan and Purfleet, Essex, MP [I] Monaghan 1695–9, Co. Monaghan 1703–13 and MP [GB] 1710–15. A professional soldier who by the end of Queen Anne's reign had risen to become a lieutenant-general and colonel of a regiment of dragoons, he was 'turned out' of his regiment early in 1715 and promptly went over to the Pretender (*HC 1690–1715*, iii, 954–5).

longer so, and will take this day of leisure when the house of Lords doth not sit and before term comes in. The inclosed are copyes of the association of the house of Lords[429] and of their addresse to the Lords Justices on the news of the Pretenders being landed in Scotland; the former was moved for and prepared by my Lord Moore, and shewn me before he offered it to the Committee where it underwent some small alterations; particularly in the later part the words (of a just indignation till they are brought to punishment) were offered by the Bishops as an amendment in the room of a just revenge; which last word they desired the Committee not to put them under a necessity of coming into, revenge being usually taken in an ill sense, tho just revenge never is: but they declared if the Committee would not gratifye them in it that they would not refuse to sign it for that reason. And indeed all the Bishops in town (who were not sick) but two, viz the Primate and Bishop of Corke signed it the first day:[430] as also did all the temporal Lords in town who were able to come to the house but Barrymore Kerry and Anglesey: and the first fowre of them did it yesterday morning: but Lord Anglesey was it seems preparing to go on ship board the day it was moved for, and went aboard that evening; but the wind being crosse he landed again and was on shore the day it was brought in by the Committee and agreed to by the house, as he was also yesterday morning; but came not to the house, tho Anglesey street where he lyes is just at the back of the Parliament house.[431] Whether he went away last night or this morning I know not, but I presume it will terminate in Lord Abercornes signing for him after he is gone, he having left that Lord his proxy. As I have very good ground to be satisfyed if any ill was designed me by little people, their schemes were not such as could have weight with the Governement; so all professions are made every where by the persons whom I had most reason to beleive a little tricking, that nothing was farther from their wishes then to have a misunderstanding with, or to do a prejudice to me: and indeed the behavior of some people hath lessened their character, but depend on it neither your Nephew nor I have suffered in ours: who have taken care without little servile compliances with little men to shew the Kings service and interest to be at least as much in our wishes as other people would have it understood to be in theirs: and yet have not thought a slavish submission to the sentiments of a Secretary or two to be necessary as some of your acquaintance have had the meanesse to doe … The disturbances with you make our markets here very dead and low; we are doing all in our power to prepare for a storm if such a thing should happen. I hope the zeal of our house of commons in promising to make good the charge the King should be at in raising new troops (if there shal be occasion) will be taken in the right sense as the result of our fidelity and affection to his Majesty and the succession in his Royal house, not as an argument of our wealth or being able (but with the last difficulty) to give more money or other funds then are already given: but I am so sensible of some people beleiving and representing us to be able to bear more then we doe already, that I cannot but apprehend some consequence from the indefinite wording of that vote beyond what the Commons ever intended or foresaw: that would be an ill return of so hearty an assurance

---

[429] An association 'to defend and assist his most sacred majesty King George, and the protestant succession, in his royal house, with our lives and fortunes, against the Pretender and all his adherents' (*LJI*, ii, 4).

[430] Confirmed in Wake, Epist. xii: Bishop Godwin to [Archbishop Wake], 14 Jan. 1715[/16]. According to Charles Delafaye, Primate Lindsay signed 'with a very bad grace, two or three days after everybody else' (TNA, SP 63/374/57: Delafaye to [Robert Pringle], 24 Jan. 1715/16).

[431] Anglesea Street, running between Dame Street and Fleet Street. Anglesey's failure to sign is confirmed in Wake, Epist. xii: Bishop Synge to [Wake], 23 Jan. 1715[/16].

and effort made by a poor but very Loyal people. Senny I depend on it hath sent you the Commons addresse; if he hath not I will take Care he shal doe it. Our Toryes in a certain house[432] are so humbled, that as I told you formerly no danger need be apprehended from that quarter: and indeed you may be sure little remains to be done when Lord Barrymore and Anglesey have leave to go for England.

[PS] I drew the Addresse to the Lords Justices …

264. *Thomas to Alan I, Dublin, 21 Jan. 1715[/16]*

(1248/3/302–3)

Six of the seven impeacht Lords pleaded guilty on Thursday; further time was then given Lord Winton[433] (on suggestion that hee had nott been able to gett either sollicitor or Councill) till Monday.[434]

Wee were this day to have demanded judgment; butt were employd in considering the kings speech, which Lord Chancellor read after the royal assent to the Act for suspending the Habeas Corpus Bill till the 24th of May. The king in general termes takes notice of advice from abroad giving reason to suspect connivance att least (if nott more) at the imbarcation of Troops to assist the Pretender, this was explaind by Mr Secretary[435] whoe told the house that by last nights letters an accountt came of the late D[uke] of O[rmond] passing thro Burdeaux in his way to Bayonne, where hee was to embarque with a body of Irish Troops; peoples conjectures are different as to the place they designe, butt from what the Secretary likewise sayd, of three hundred officers some already saild, others ready to doe soe, from Dunkirke, all Irish and Scots, I should thinke this country (nott Ireland) the place intended, unlesse the consideration of so many men drawn from thence might encline them that way, nor doe I thinke there attempting both there and here att the same time impossible for tis inconceivable that they would entertaine thoughts of this kind after knowing of their ill successe both att Dunblaine and Preston,[436] from any other motive, then the greatest encouragement from hence. The house of Commons have voted (as is usuall) thankes etc and pray his Majesty that hee will augment his Troops (indefinitely) as hee sees occasion, and assure him in strong termes of supplyes etc.

265. *Thomas to Alan I, Dublin, 7 Feb. 1715[/16]*

(1248/3/304–5)

By an expresse which this day arrivd from Scotland wee are informed that the kings forces were divided into two bodyes, the one under the Duke of Argyle marcht towards

---

[432] The Lords.

[433] George Seton (c.1678–1749), 5th earl of Winton.

[434] The two lawyers he had originally approached to act as his counsel having declined, Winton asked the Lords on Thursday, 19 Nov., to appoint two other counsel and two other solicitors (*LJ*, xviii, 266).

[435] James Stanhope (1673–1721), later 1st Earl Stanhope, MP [GB] and secretary of state [GB] for the southern department.

[436] The inconclusive engagement on 13 Nov. 1715 at Sheriffmuir near Dunblane, between the earl of Mar's jacobite army and the government forces commanded by the duke of Argyll, which effectively halted Mar's advance in Scotland; and the surrender of jacobite forces at Preston, Lancs., on 9 Nov.

Aberdeen, the other under Mr Cadogan[437] towards Dundee; that the former were within eight miles of a party of the Rebels whoe kept together, though nott many in number; whither the like were done by them in any other place is nott sayd, butt I thinke itt may bee reasonably supposed some of them might doe soe, and take the way toward Dundee, I beleive wee shall soone hear (att least I hope soe) that some of the most considerable of them are taken, and indeed I thinke if due care bee taken (which I doe nott in the least doubt) the Pretender may bee soe too. The Jacobites say the Duke of Savoy will insist on his right if the Pretender were out of the way,[438] and may possibly prove a more dangerous Rival, butt whither all those whoe I doubt would have gone into the former will assist the latter I know nott, butt doe heartily wish that were their onely game. The accountt which came on Sunday of our march, and their quitting Perth you have in the prints, wherfore twas unnecessary to mention any thing of that. You will in the post boy of this day see a memorial of Lord Stairs to the Regent which I take to bee genuine.[439] Lord Angleseys freinds say that his appearing warmly with his interest for the additional duty on wine had soe irritated the Brodrick party, that they resolved on revenge, and had therefore carryd the Addresse against him, from whence (were the fact true) people would bee induct to thinke our interest very considerable. I suppose I need nott tell you Lord Sunderland has his place, which I am glad of, bee the occasion what itt will.[440]

266. *Thomas to Alan I, 7 Feb. 1715[/16]*

(1248/3/306–7)

I omitted owning[441] yours of the 20th of last month two posts, there being nothing which required a speedy answer, and I hoped by this time I might bee able to say something considerable of the Scotch affair.

I am glad to find that people with you are nott to bee imposd uppon, and doe assure you that neither yourselfe nor your sonne have lost any creditt in the opinion of the generality of people, butt the contrary; what some may thinke whoe expect hunting under a pole[442] I know nott; when the storme which as yett hangs over our heads is blowne of,

---

[437] William Cadogan (c.1671–1726), later 1st Earl Cadogan, MP [GB]; col., Coldstream Guards and lieut.-gen.; subsequently c.-in-c. Scotland Feb.–May 1716.

[438] Victor Amadeus II (1666–1732), duke of Savoy since 1675, and king of Sardinia from 1720. His wife, Anne-Marie of Orléans, was a granddaughter of Charles I, which gave her and her children a claim to the English throne, and in 1701 the Savoyard ambassador formally protested against the passing of the English Act of Settlement (Christopher Storrs, *War, Diplomacy and the Rise of Savoy 1690–1720* (Cambridge, 2004), 151–3)).

[439] Reprinted from the *Dutch Courant* of 12 Feb. N.S. 1716, and said to have been presented by Stair on 31 Jan. N.S., this brought to attention the activities of jacobites on French soil, and the involvement of French army officers in the preparations for the invasion, contrary to the assurances previously given by the Regent that he would 'faithfully and punctually observe' the terms of the peace of Utrecht (*Post Boy*, 7–9 Feb. 1716).

[440] As joint vice-treasurer [I], with Lord Rochester, replacing Anglesey (*Lib. Mun.*, pt 2, p. 47).

[441] Having received.

[442] Another term for 'stop-hunting', where dogs are so well trained that they will stop their pursuit at the word of command, or a flourish of the hunting-pole, and follow the huntsmen until told to move forward (Thomas Fairfax, *The Complete Sportsman; or Country Gentleman's Recreation* ... (1765), 107–8).

gentlemen will speake their minds with more freedom, and act differently from what they thinke advisable under our present circumstances. There being noe order of the day, nor any material businesse in veiwe for Saturday last, twas supposed nothing would have been movd worth notice, butt itt fell out much otherwise; itt may therefore bee reasonable to give a perticular account of what does in general make a noise here, and probably will with you, where twill be lesse understood then here, though to say the truth, even in this place people are a good deale in the darke. After the message from the Lords of having agreed to the bill for attainting Lord Mar etc without amendment Mr Letchmere[443] movd an addresse for a Proclamation promising a reward for taking any of the attainted Lords, which passed without opposition.[444]

Hee then movd a second Addresse to witt that the house doe humbly offer their advice to his Majesty for issuing a proclamation offering termes of pardon to those in rebellion whoe should lay down their armes, and returne to their due obedience, with such exceptions and under such limitations and restrictions as to his Majesty should seem reasonable; hee introduced the motion with saying that the necessity of affairs had required what otherwise might bee lookt uppon as severity, uppon which consideration the house had with great chearfulnesse and unanimity exerted, and shewed such a spiritt, as had apparently given check to this unnatural and horrid rebellion by despiriting the contrivers and formentors of itt att home, as well as by letting such whoe abroad had entertaind hopes of its successe, plainely see how far they had been imposd on by the false accountts of the kingdoms inclination; That hee thought (which hee modestly referd to gentlemens consideration) itt might now become us to convince the world that prudence and nott blood thirstinesse had been the reason of our acting, butt that hee would nott bee understood to meane any of the first formers, or the most forward and active in these traiterous measures, confining himselfe to such as had been drawne in by them through inadvertency or want of consideration. Noe sooner had hee concluded then the motion was fired att as unseasonable (as most certainely itt was) and what would give creditt to the cause of our enemyes both att home and abroad, for that they would most certainely attribute such an act of lenity (att this time) to a diffidence of our own strenghth, and power to oppose them; several spoake very well and strongly (among them Secretary Stanhope) as to the unseasonablenesse, and did very prudently confine themselves to that topick.

Two gentlemen (Sir John Brownlow[445] and Mr Liddell[446]) spoake hansomly on the side of the question, butt argued in general uppon mixing mercy with judgment uppon the reasonablenesse of putting as speedy an end as possible to the Rebellion on account of the blood which would otherwise bee spilt, especially that of our freinds, many of whom must fall in the prosecution of itt; the debate was hitherto regular, and the house very easy, for the unseasonablenesse of the thing was generally agreed, as far as could possibly be discerned, and I thinke, nay I am sure itt might have gone of quietly on that foote, butt Mr Pultney[447] (whoe came in very late) fell uppon the motion after a most satirrical manner,

---

[443] Nicholas Lechmere (1675–1727), of the Middle Temple, MP [GB] Cockermouth.

[444] On 4 Feb.; recorded as passing nem. con. in *CJ*, xviii, 368.

[445] Sir John Brownlow (1690–1754), 5th Bt, of Arlington Street, London, MP [GB] Lincs.

[446] Thomas Liddell (*d*.1718), of Bedford Row, London, MP [GB] Lostwithiel.

[447] William Pultney (1684–1764), MP [GB] Hedon.

prefacing that hee knew nott whoe made itt, butt that if itt were the effect of pique for having lost an employment or what were worse if from an expectancy of gaine (for that gentlemen were noe strangers to the great sumes offered for a pardon of this nature) itt could nott bee enterteind with too much resentment, and a good deale more of like nature; which soe apparently disgusted the house that I was under very reall concerne, nott knowing what effect itt might have. To putt a stop to itt a motion for adjourning was made, which was like to have been debated, butt by the temper and prudence of a gentleman was prevented, by saying hee hoped the gentleman whoe made the motion would uppon having heard so much sayd of the unseasonablenesse, thinke fitt to wave itt. Mr Letchmere then rose, and after having in the sharpest termes resented the treatment (soe utterly ungentlemanlike) which hee had received, and having sayd a good deale upon the consequence of such practice, as putting an end to all freedom of debate, professed his making the motion to have proceeded from noe other principle then that of conviction that itt would prove of advantage to the nation, and having very strongly insisted uppon his having in every instance gone heartily into the measures concerted, notwithstanding the ill treatment hee had received, hee desired the house would proceed uppon other businesse, for that hee should bee very unwilling to create a difference (by insisting on the question) between gentlemen whoe had hitherto drawn together, for the security and good of the nation; thus hee came of with general applause, and here the matter att present ended, butt I doubt though the embers are rakt over, the fire will burst out att one time or other, for the house seemd wonderfull uneasy; nott a Tory spoake a word; they lay by, and with an apparent pleasure lookt on our dashing against one another. You must know Mr Walpole sayes publiquely that hee was offered three score thousand pounds for obtaining such a like pardon as seemd to bee movd for, exclusive of the persons now impeacht, or under attainder. I choose to say nothing of the Scotch affaires till the very last, resolving to keep open my letter as long as possible, that if any farther accounts come, I may adde them …

I have had a letter or two from Mr Mildmay neare Rosse whoe marryed a neice of my wives,[448] desiring I would recommend him to you, in order to getting some employment in the revenue; hee is well related here, to people of worth and honest principles whoe have spoake to mee on his behalfe; I have in general termes told him I did beleive you would readily doe him any service in your power, butt that I could nott tell how far you did att any time intermeddle in affaires of that nature. I thinke Mr Wylde[449] would on any occasion (if such should offer) assist him on my account, if you shall thinke the mentioning my name to him, reasonable … Pray send mee a list of your Parliament.

[448] Possibly Thomas Mildmay, of Lisburn, Co. Antrim, who married Margaret Adderley of Innishannon, Co. Cork. By 1719 he appears to have held a revenue office in Fethard, Co. Wexford (John Lodge, *The Peerage of Ireland* … (4 vols, 1754), iv, 345; NLI, MS 16007, p. 72: James Forth to Thomas Mildmay, 17 Nov. 1719).

[449] Thomas Wylde (c.1670–1740), of The Commandery, Worcester, MP [GB] Worcester; revenue commr [I] 1715–27.

267. *Thomas to Alan I, Dublin, 9 Feb. 1715[/16]*

(1248/3/308–9)

Judgment was this day pronounct uppon the six Lords whoe had pleaded guilty,[450] uppon the question putt severally what they could say, each of them spoake. Lords Derenwater[451] and Withrington[452] by way of extenuation that they were in noe wise engaged in any formed design, or acquainted with any such, butt that they had through inadvertency been drawn in (even unprovided for such an enterprize) by their relations neighbours and freinds having taken up armes; Lord Canworth[453] spoake very hansomly and movingly, acknowledged his guilt without much extenuation, the other three sayd little more then what all six insisted uppon, that they had surrendred (when some of them might probably have escaped by opposing, and that many of our men must have fallen) uppon an expectation of mercy, which they thought they had reason to hope from what Generall Wills had sayd, of the kings mercy etc.[454] Lord High Steward (Lord Cooper)[455] spoake long and very well, and shed tears plentifully when hee pronounct sentence. This morning an expresse from Mr Cadogan brings advice of the Pretender and Lord Mars having gone on shipboard last Saturday might att Montrose, and sailing thence in a small vessell, they marcht that day six miles in their way to Aberdeen att the head of the Rebells, from whom they gott away undiscerned in the night; this confirmes the account wee had two dayes agoe of a suspition enterteind by the Rebels of their intent to gett of, and resolution taken nott to suffer itt.

268. *Thomas to Alan I, Dublin, 14 Feb. 1715[/16]*

(1248/3/310–11)

I have noe late letter from you, which I ascribe to the load of businesse which now lyes on you. I perceive your advices directly from Scotland are earlyer then what can goe from hence, therefore I presume you long since know of the Pr[etender's] scandalous manner of leaving his freinds in the lurch, surely his auntcient kingdom have their bellyes full of him. Tis sayd from Holland that Hamilton[456] was returning to him from Paris with assurance of 6000 men in a very short time; and on his way towards Scotland att the same time the Prettender was soe towards Paris, They further say that they are very well assured, that by a

---

[450]See above, p. 104.

[451]James Radclyffe (1689–1716), 3rd earl of Derwentwater; executed on 24 Feb. 1716.

[452]William Widdrington (1678–1743), 4th Baron Widdrington; sentenced to death but reprieved.

[453]Robert Dalzell (1697–1737), 5th earl of Carnwath. Although he was sentenced to death, his execution was at first delayed and then remitted by virtue of the Indemnity Act of 1717 (4 Geo. I, c. 15 [GB]).

[454]Charles Wills (1666–1741), lieut.-gen. and col. of the 3rd regiment of foot. He had taken the surrender of the jacobite forces at Preston.

[455]Lord Chancellor Cowper, 'lord high steward on that occasion' (Oldmixon, *History of England*, 626–7).

[456]George Hamilton (aft.1658–aft. 1728), of Reidhouse, Haddingtonshire, MP [GB] 1712–13; major-gen. and lieut.-gen. under Queen Anne. Having lost his regiment in 1714 he joined the jacobite rising in Scotland and became Mar's chief military adviser, but after blundering badly at Sheriffmuir and losing his reputation, was sent away to France, ostensibly to secure supplies but more likely to remove the taint of incompetence (*HC 1660–1715*, iv, 166–7).

Secr[*et*] article, (which wee always suspected) between the late queen and french king, the former was to endeavour his succeeding her by fair meanes, if those faild, the latter was to assist with force; and from hence the Dutch infer a war, beleiving the Regent will urge that treaty (if such there bee) in justiffication of his proceedings; the accountt now come of the Pr[*etender's*] landing on Wensday publiquely att Gravelin[457] seems to confirme this, for if hee bee receivd and owned, there can bee noe doubt of the thing; wee are providing a very considerable sea force, which is in good forwardnesse. Noe Commissions are yett given for our new levyes here, butt those for 8 Regiments of foot and 5 of Dragoons for you, are adjusted, the Colonels onely excepted, att least tis nott yett publique, though probably agreed on … J. Butler[458] is att Paris, and was soe when Hamiltons message of assurance was agreed to, and there to remaine till they should from him hear out of Scotland, soe that I beleive his intended visitt to his Dear joy freinds[459] is adjourned sine die.[460]

269. *Thomas to Alan I, Dublin, 25 Feb. 1715[/16]*[461]

(1248/3/312–13)

Your letter to Mrs C[*ourthope*] under cover to mee came on Wensday, which next night I sent to her … I then forbore writing in order to give you an accountt of the effect of that days debate in each house. The condemnd Lords preferd petitions, I should say offered them, for that to our house was nott receivd, butt the Lords was. The same motion was made in both places, to witt, adjourne, which question was debated above four hours; upon a division in the Lords twas carryed in the negative by ten after which an Addresse was carryed by five that his Majesty would bee pleasd to repreive such of the Lords as should appeare to him to deserve mercy, the words such of was an amendment offerd, and agreed to, the question movd being in general termes;[462] the Bishops whoe were against the question withdrew, that they might nott forsooth have their hands in blood, those for itt (which were three) stayd,[463] and had two proxeyes; Incredible has been the sollicitation in favour of these Lords, several Ladyes of the first quallity appeard att each doore, after having gone (for some dayes before) from member to member; a pretty many Lords gave into itt out of pitty, as supposing the storme blowne over, whoe on all occasions have shewne an unshaken steddinesse for our present establishment. You must know that on Sunday a peticion was delivered to the king by Lady Derentwater, whoe answered that hee pittyed the condition into which her

[457] Gravelines, a small port in northern France, 15 miles south-west of Dunkirk.
[458] James Butler, 2nd duke of Ormond, whose attainder in Aug. 1715 meant that his honours were extinguished.
[459] 'Dear joy' was a derisive term for a native Irishman, in common usage.
[460] For an indefinite period.
[461] Endorsed by Alan I: 'Brother Brodrick … seems to approve the matter of Lord Gowran'.
[462] After a division to adjourn, which was lost 51–41, two amendments were passed, by 58–52 and 56–51 respectively, and the amended address carried 57–52. Proxy votes were included in all divisions (J.C. Sainty and D. Dewar, *Divisions*, microfiche).
[463] *LJ*, xx, 298–9 records that the bishops present on 22 Feb. were Chester, Hereford, Lichfield, Lincoln, London, Oxford, Peterborough, St Asaph, and Winchester.

Lord had brought her.[464] Thursday the Lords of the white staf[465] presented the Addresse to which his Majesty gave the following answer, I will on this and all other occasions doe what shall bee for the honour of my Government and safety of my kingdoms. On the question of adjournment in our house (which you know according to order must bee putt before any other motion can bee made) gentlemen lett themselves into the debate of what would have been the main question, (though a little irregularly) offering such their reasons against adjourning; and indeed in my opinion the allowing the peticion to bee brought up, would have been the better way, for I am very confident several negatives to the adjournment would have been for rejecting the Peticion, butt our Leaders (having concerted with the Lords) would nott alter their method; att last the question of adjournment was carryed by seven, Yeas 162 Noes 155.[466] You see how ill our people attend, indeed they are nott in town, for the toryes (within call) attended to a man, and several of them came to town the night before from remote parts. With the minority were att least forty whigs on very different motives; the cause itt selfe you may bee sure was sufficient to engage the Toryes, butt they had farther in veiw, throwing the odium on the king, as having an inclination to blood, and this use you may bee very sure they will make of itt; butt steddinesse in him became absolutely necessary, for even as tis, the Pretenders interest will in forreigne courts be magnifyed, for to that (how falsely soever) will be ascribed their numbers, in order to support a cause which seemd desperate, the ill consequences wherof our good naturd creatures did nott (or would nott) sufficiently consider.

On Thursday in the evening Lord Nidedale[467] made his escape out of the Tower in his Ladyes cloaths, having her behind in his, butt I am perswaded with consent of the Warder.[468]

Yesterday Lords Derentwater and Kenmure[469] were executed, the latter sayd nothing on the scaffold, the former a pretty deale,[470] to my great amazement I confesse, for from the time of his having receivd his sentence nothing ever appeard more terrifyed then hee did;[471] nay, as I am well assured, when hee was in the Tower deliverd to the Sherrif of London, hee

---

[464] Anna Maria (d.1723), daughter of Sir John Webb, 3rd Bt, of Odstock, Wilts., whose sister was married to the 1st Earl Waldegrave. Dudley Ryder's diary confirms that on Sunday 19 Feb. Lady Derwentwater 'fell upon her knees' before the king and presented her petition, but he 'told her in French he was sorry for her misfortune but he never sought the life of her husband, and could not help her' (*Diary of Dudley Ryder*, 186). In her diary entry for 21 Feb., Mary, Lady Cowper (the wife of the lord chancellor) recorded that the duchess of Bolton told Caroline, princess of Wales, that 'Lady Derwentwater came crying to her, when the duke was not at home, and persuaded her to go [*to court*] to plead for her lord' (*Diary of Mary, Countess Cowper … 1714–1720*, ed. Hon. Spencer Cowper (1865), 80–1).

[465] The great officers of state, who carried a white staff as the symbol of office.

[466] Confirmed in *CJ*, xviii, 384. Ryder reported 'a great deal of debating' before the division (*Diary of Dudley Ryder*, 186).

[467] William Maxwell (1676–1744), 5th earl of Nithsdale.

[468] The famous story of Nithsdale's escape is recounted in a letter from his wife to her sister, printed in William Fraser, *The Book of Carlaverock: Memoirs of the Maxwells, Earls of Nithsdale* … (Edinburgh, 1873), 222–34. The warder is not implicated.

[469] William Gordon (c.1672–1716), 6th viscount of Kenmure.

[470] For an account of the executions, including a transcription of Derwentwater's lengthy scaffold speech, see *A Faithful Register of the Late Rebellion* … (1718), 86–93. Kenmure, by contrast, had nothing to say in public, contenting himself with private prayers.

[471] According to Dudley Ryder, on the scaffold Kenmure showed 'all the courage and resolution of an old Roman' (*Diary of Dudley Ryder*, 188).

trembled like a leafe, I know people doubted whither hee would have been able to stand or speake on the scaffold, butt this provd quite otherwise, hee spoake distinctly, and with an audible voice, appearing as little concernd as could bee expected; Great are the charmes of Preists surely, for to nothing else was this change due. You will see what hee sayd in print to which I refer you.

As to the substance of your letter I can say little more then that I agree entirely with you, in the general notion people have of the person you mention, and one would thinke hee has livd too long, and too publiquely to bee mistaken; therfore for what appears to mee att present, his circumstances are the material things, to bee considered, you say when the question was askt, twas introduc't with supposing this unexceptionable, that expression is very full, butt still depends on the opinion which the proposer might have of what would bee soe, surely hee can bee noe stranger to an offer in a former case, I must therefore beleive this must att least equall itt, and indeed I thinke itt ought to bee soe for some reasons you give, which neverthelesse I could gett over, if fully satisfyd in this perticular. You say in the close of your letter that I shall hear from you uppon a clause offerd in the house to a certaine bill,[472] which I long to doe, butt I thinke itt very improbable that you should satisfie my curiosity in one point, without putting the question directly, because I am confident the fact is false, though I am very sure tis wrote hither as an undeniable truth, and this I beleive (though I am nott sure of itt) by the gentleman whoe already has, and will in the end bee found to have created a great deale of trouble, more out of vanity then any thing else. Tis sayd that the Bill from the Lords movd for by Lord A[*nglesey*] was done in concert with you, to lay the other aside,[473] pray lett mee know this matter very plainely; tis sayd that both bills will come over, and that from the Commons bee returned …

[*PS*] The other Lords are repreivd to Wensday sennight.

270. *Alan I, Dublin, to Thomas, 1 Mar. 1715[/16]*

(1248/3/316–17)

Sometime past I mentioned the matter in the house of commons relating to the giving some ease to the dissenters here; the thing was as I hear concerted only between fowre or five and not communicated to other Gentlemen. Sir Gustavus Hume moved it first in general terms and concluded without proposing any regular question; I think Mr Bladen seconded it: and then Mr Upton[474] stood up and made one of his tedious, incoherent, disgustful harangues; and concluded in repealing the test in all respects, as well in relation to Civil as military emploiments. What he said and some other mens behavior on this occasion so exasperated the house that the question was loudly called for by a great number with resolution to have thrown it out wholly, as it certainly would have hapned if it had been then put. This was plainly perceived and many Gentlemen who know the dissenters to be well affected to his

[472] The bill 'for the security of the king's person and government': the addition was to exempt dissenters from the penalties of the test clause for taking commissions in the militia and regular army.

[473] The Lords' bill 'for the security of the king's person and government', identical to that of the Commons but omitting the clauses in favour of dissenters.

[474] Clotworthy Upton, MP [I].

Majestyes service and sincerely enemyes to the Pretender and foresaw the ill consequence
of the question being carryed in that maner; and at length the house came to a temper to
give them some ease, and gave leave to prepare heads of a bill to that purpose: It was very
surprising that a thing of such consequence should be concerted between no more then
the Speaker, Sir Gustavus, Mr Bladen and (as I hear) one Commoner more, and one very
honest Lord of your acquaintance who hapned to be by. Mr Upton was so ill pleased with
the disposition of the house that he gave his negative to the question for bringing in heads
of a bill, the same not being in the latitude he wished. And on this foot matters stood till
the day the Lords Justices declared they had reason to beleive an invasion of Ireland might
be immediately expected; for those who were ordered to bring in those heads of a bill had
either not prepared them or at least nothing was done on them in the house: but the Speaker
upon this intimation from the Governement to the Parliament took hold of that oportunity
when the house was in a Committee on heads of a bill for farther securing the Kings person
and Governement, to propose a clause to be added to that bill for indemnifying dissenters
for acting in the militia, and also all such as should be commissioned or employed in the
army within ten years: This point was debated warmly in the house of commons, and three
years, afterward seven, at length ten proposed and agreeed to; and the clause was added to
those heads of a bill; which however were kept so long in the house of commons, as to
give the Lords oportunity to bring in and go through heads of a bill with the same title,
and to lay them before the Governement the same day the Commons laid theirs. The truth
is the Lords bill (as brought in) was the same and a Copy of the Commons bill omitting
only that clause and a clause to excuse Quakers from taking the oaths on their making a
declaration etc but some few addicions and alterations were made in the Committee of
Lords. When the heads were agreed on Lord Abercorn proposed a question that if any
clause were added or tacked to any heads of bills framed by the Lords that their Lordships
would come to a resolution to reject such bill: but that foolish matter fell. Both bills were
laid before the Councel together and referred at the same time to a Committee, and the
bill from the Lords was first proceeded upon and some amendments made to it, and then
that from the Commons was taken into consideration which in most parts was the same
with that from the Lords. The Quakers clause was carried by a great majority, Archbishop
Dublin, Lord Abercorn, Bishop Clogher and Bishop Dromore dissenting: on another day
the clause brought in by the Speaker was under debate; people were of different sentiments,
and a good deal was said with a good deal of warmth and some bitternesse against the
dissenters; nay we were told all the rebells at Preston (except 400) were of that stamp. The
clause was carried by a considerable majority in the Councel without division; and is not
yet reported. It is to me pretty unaccountable that the Governement hath not (as far as I can
learn) either on this or your side the water explained their intentions in this matter. The
thing seems to me of greater consequence then is apprehended: others are more sanguine,
but I think it cannot be carried in the upper house, and it will passe with difficulty (if at all)
in the lower: I think the majority of both houses would come into their being indemnifyed
for acting as Officers in the militia for ever, but I must doubt the successe if it be carryed to
the Army: the clamor raised and industry used on this occasion is incredible, and I doubt
this matter if pushed farther will reunite an high Church party here to the great disservice
of publick affairs. I found by what was said by some Lords on the Tory side that they would
go into a toleration, which nothing but distraction can (I think) prevent the others from
accepting; but Upton and some of their hott men spurn att it, while others seem fond of

it provided it might be on the terms that the Episcopal men in Scotland have it, not as the dissenters have it in England. Lord Castlecomer warm against their being in the Army.[475] I wish you would without shewing this discourse the honest and wise men and let me hear soon.

271. *Thomas to Alan I, Dublin, 6 Mar. 1715[/16]*

(1248/3/318–19)

I received last night from Pepper Hara your letter of the 23d of last month to Mrs C[*ourthope*] and went this morning to my Cosen Clayton,[476] whoe some time since did on a letter telling her of W[*illia*]m J[*ephson's*] desperate condition, wrote to Tom Ruby,[477] that having promised A[*nthony*] J[*ephson*][478] to give noe opposition to such as that family should recommend,[479] on their having assured her of her sonnes being chosen when of age, she resolved to keep strictly to her word, and therefore ordered him to act accordingly.

Shee will write to you this night, (which I desired least I should nott have time) and will tell you what I doe, soe that matter being settled by Mr J[*ephson*] will bee safe; Shee told mee shee has had two letters from H[*enry*] P[*urdon*] whoe pretends to have made a great interest, butt that weighs very little with mee, knowing his temper.

You will from all hands heare of the probabillity of our going into a new war, on the Pretenders being received in france; the latter part is gratis dictum;[480] that hee landed there is certaine, butt that hee remains there, or indeed that the Regent was acquainted with his landing is nott onely uncertaine, butt both the one and the other contradicted, butt I thinke little depends thereon, for that France would bee glad to embarasse us is past dispute, butt whither they bee in a condition (their present circumstances considered) to make a new war their choice I doe question; however itt serves a turne, and indeed this far good use may bee made of itt; The better wee are prepared for our defence, the lesse probabillity will bee, of their attacking; I write this before the sitting of the house, and possibly may bee to adde to itt, the King being to come to passe the Bill for tryals of traytors in any County hee shall thinke fitt,[481] if any fresh advice bee come, wee shall probably have a speech, if wee have none I shall continue to thinke as now I doe. Noe speech nor forreigne news of any kind.

The condemned Lords are farther repreivd.

---

[475] He took the same line subsequently in a committee of the Irish privy council (see below, p. 120; and TNA, SP 634/374/105–6: Grafton and Galway to James Stanhope, 24 Feb. 1715/16).

[476] Randal Clayton (see Appendix 2).

[477] A servant of Randal Clayton (1248/4/169A–B: [Alan I] to Thomas, 5 Nov. 171[?19]).

[478] MP [I].

[479] To succeed William Jephson as MP [I] for Mallow.

[480] A legal term, meaning a statement made voluntarily, without any necessity.

[481] The royal assent was indeed given to this bill on 6 Mar. (*CJ*, xviii, 390).

272. *Thomas to Alan I, 10 Mar. 1715[/16]*

(1248/3/3/320–1)

Your letter of the first came late on Thursday night, since when I have endeavourd (as far as I could) to apprize my selfe of what is desired in relation to the Bill for ease of Protestant dissenters; wherin If I doe nott mistake people here are nott generally agreed, nott butt that all are for making itt as extensive as possible, butt the difference of opinion arises from the different notions how far the point can be carryed, for attempting what cannott bee soe, will prove more disadvantagious then att first appears. I have as my owne sence of the matter mentioned the difficultyes which probably will arise att the Councill board; after which (supposing them surmounted) twill bee to undergoe opposition in each house; that of yours is supposed the most considerable objection, for I find they doe nott lay an equall stresse on itt with the Commons.

As to the first (that of the Councill) tis sayd what shall bee defective, may bee supplyed here, as far as shall bee advisable with respect to the two latter. What seems mostly to bee expected, is that itt extend to the militia, Justices of the peace, and Corporations, these being of a publique nature, and in the maine offices of trouble and expence without gaine, tis thought may and ought to bee agreed to; Thus itt stands (in my opinion) with the moderatest; others would carry itt much farther even [?Mr. U.] lenghth.[482] Consider this matter very well, and lett mee have such a letter (taking notice that tis att my desire and for my own information) as I may shew, for I know I shall bee calld uppon when the bills come over. I have very fully explain'd the nottable management in relation to Lord O[rmond's] bill, which is utterly disapprovd of. Having to doe in matters of this nature, where itt is impossible to determine before hand the successe, is you may be sure a part a man would nott choose, however since the good of the countrey as well as the service of the crowne makes itt necessary that all due helpe should bee given, I am the better reconciled to itt, nott butt that I foresee a possibillity, nay a very great probabillity of undergoing censure, and that without the least prospect of having itt thought more then duty, even in case of successe, butt tis nott from these motives of either kind that I shall act. Ile doe what I thinke my duty, by saying what I thinke right, and leave the issue to him whoe will approve the integrity and sincerity of the intention.

You see by the repeated advices from France, that I did nott misjudge the issue of that affaire, in beleiving those whoe seemd extremely frightned, nott in such imminent danger as they beleivd, or att least affected being thought to doe soe. I can say nothing perticular of what the condemned Lords doe confesse, butt in the main doe beleive that they really own all they know; people talke very variously (and I beleive very uncertainly) of that matter; some soe sanguine as to expect mighty discoveries, others doubtfull whither they can make such. I am perswaded Lord Derentwater knew as much if nott more then any of them, butt his Preist had certainly seald up his mouth, and indeed I thinke that paragraph of his speech uppon the point of honour, calculated purely that the others might follow his example. I am told Lord Winton will endeavour farther time, butt without successe, for that hee will bee tryd next Thursday. Lord Bullingbrookes disgrace is very certaine, our Toryes say

---

[482]'Mr U,', if a correct reading, would refer to Clotworthy Upton.

for suppressing a letter wrote by Lord Mar to the Pretender, advising (that since hee had stayd soe long) his deferring coming till spring, when he might bring forces with him, till when hee could keep life in his affairs in Scotland by retiring to the mountains, which (say the toryes) Lord B[*olingbroke*] conceald having given soe very many repeated assurances of success, of which noe other hopes remaind then the expectation of numbers appearing uppon his arrival, whoe (till he did soe) would lye by.[483] I begin to doubt whither our two impeacht Lords will be tryd this session, if itt should prove soe, my cold water will bee thought an argument of some foresight.

273. *Alan I, Dublin, to Thomas, 20 Mar. 1715[/16]*

(1248/3/322–3)

In a letter which I received from you near a month since you told me that it was given out by some good freinds of mine that the heads of a bill brought into the house of Lords by Lord Abercorne for the farther security of his Majestyes person and governement, were so brought in by him with my privity and by concert with me: any body may see the malicious tendency of that insinuation: for what Lord Abercorne brought in under that title was the same which the Commons had before agreed upon, excepting the two clauses, one for qualifying the dissenters to be in the militia and army, the other for exempting the quakers from the penaltyes of the Act for refusing the oath of abjuration, provided they made a declaration testifying their renouncing the Pretender and fully acknowledging the Kings title: soe that if I was consulted with and privy to Lord Abercornes project I must be averse to those clauses. You may remember I formerly told you when I gave an account of this bill and the steps it took in the upper house, that Lord Abercorne pressed the house to come to a resolution that if any thing should be added or tacked (as he termed it) to any bill sent from the Lords, the house would not passe such bill to which such addition should be made; and that I exposed his mocion so far as even to satisfye him, by shewing that he did not know what that is which now hath obtained the name of a tack,[484] and letting him see that his mocion was in other words to this effect: To desire that tho Councel board either here or in England had right by Poynings Law to alter heads of bill framed in either house of Parliament, by adding to or taking from them such clauses as they saw reasonable or by altering what they judged proper;[485] and tho the case should be that one or both Councel should add clauses so reasonable and necessary in themselves as the house

---

[483] The circumstances surrounding Bolingbroke's dismissal as the Pretender's secretary of state in Mar. 1716, for 'culpable negligence' (as his rivals argued), or (from his own standpoint) as a scapegoat for the failure of the Fifteen, are surveyed from different perspectives in Sir Charles Petrie, *The Jacobite Movement* (1959), 281–2; George Hilton Jones, *The Mainstream of Jacobitism* (Cambridge, MA, 1954), 116–21; and H.T. Dickinson, *Bolingbroke* (1970), 140–2.

[484] The addition of an extraneous clause to an otherwise uncontroversial bill, in order to secure the passage of the clause.

[485] The Irish statute of 1494 requiring that acts of parliament in Ireland must have the prior approval of both councils. The 'heads of bills' procedure modified this practice: most legislation now began as 'heads' in one or other House before being transmitted to the chief governor or governors. These 'heads' would then be engrossed as bills by the Irish privy council and sent over to Whitehall for approval and possible amendment. When returned they could only be passed or rejected.

would have gone into them if they had been thought of while the heads were framing, yet
that we should by a previous resolution determine against having our bill amended or even
considering whether the alteration made it unfit to be passed into a Law. I reminded the
house that the Commons had heads of a bill before them much to the same purpose with
our heads, only that they contained something more; that they might as well resolve not
to passe the bill if any thing contained in their heads were omitted when they came back
in the form of a bill; and if both houses should make and hold to such resolutions neither
bill could passe. I told his Lordship that the little time between moving for leave to bring
in the heads and his bringing them in shewed they had not been long nor consequently
well considered; even by him; but the house in general had hardly time to read them; for
there were not above two full dayes between the mocion and their being brought in, and
gone through in a Committee, soe as they would need farther consideration. Every body
must see what I said was in direct opposition to what he intended, which was to throw the
bill out if the dissenters or Quakers clause should be added. But since receit of your letter I
took oportunity at the Councel to say I heard it was given out in England that I was privy
to bringing in these heads, and expressed my self in such a maner as not only to declare
the thing to be untrue, but gave his Lordship occasion to clear me there of that imputation;
and this I am sure the Duke of Grafton will do me the right to justifye. This together with
talking this matter over with the Lords Justices, who affirmed they never heard or beleived
any thing of the kind, had I thought put that matter at peace. But I lately received a letter
from my son from the Countrey and in it there came inclosed a letter from Trevor Hill
without date, in which he tells Senny I am to be soon out, and that a freind of his was
offered the Seal, who refused it; but some body from England will be soon sent over in my
place: He goes farther and saith that the King expressed himself publickly in this maner
in the drawing room; that the Brodricks had been represented to him as Whigs, but that
he found them clear otherwise. I shal not be greatly surprised if I should be removed and
some body of great merit and interest on your side of the water should be put into my
place: I have never made it my businesse to make personal interests with the ministry, nor
have I ever troubled them with letters, or made great professions; soe that if I have been
misrepresented, it may probably obtain credit, especially when the weight of all the Toryes
will be thrown into the scale to bear me down: but I cannot with patience think of lying
under the vile character of not being a Whig, or which I think means the same thing, not
sincere in the interests and from the bottom of my heart devoted to the Kings service: No
man living can shew one action of mine that had the least tendency to the prejudice of
his Majestyes affairs; and I verily beleive the Lords Justices and every man in the Kings
service here (if the question were publickly asked) would doe me the justice to own it, and
perhaps some might add that it had been in my power as well as inclination to doe him
service; I owe so much to Lord Sunderland, as well as to my own character, not to let a
man recommended by him to so high a Station sink under the infamy of not loving and
serving the King; of being ungrateful as well as a mad man in opposing that Prince under
whose Governement only we can ever expect to be happy; and this at a time when I had
received the most distinguishing marks of his favor and had nothing to ask or desire but
to shew my duty and gratitude to the Crown. If I am not a whig what am I? I am sure as
I disown high Church and Toryism and have opposed both on every occasion, they will
justly disown me: Is there one great tory in the Kingdome with whom I have intimacy or
freindship? But perhaps Mr Hill may speak at random; perhaps what he heard was about

the time when your Nephew indiscreetly enough (tho too much provoked) thwarted in the house of Commons our Secretarye[486] in some instances; if I am told truth, what he did (tho not intirely justifyable) was not any way with intention to oppose measures here, but to the maner of carrying things by particular persons and in cabal, and some time with an air not becoming the freedome of Parliaments: but I think his indiscretions neither ought to be nor will be fairly imported to me: beside (tho he is now his own Master[487]) I have wrought on his warm temper so that he will not (I think) act so much on his own strength and judgement for the future in relation to publick matters …

274. *Alan I, Dublin, to Thomas, 23 Mar. 1715[/16]*

(1248/3/332–7)

I have now time to write to you, having yesterday finished and gone through with the heads of bills from both houses of Parliament in the Committee of Councel; perhaps you may be surprised at our not being able to doe it sooner; but when you consider how ill digested heads of bills generally come from the houses, and are told that lesse care hath been taken in the lower house then ever I remember in any former Session in framing their bills, you will charitably beleive we made all possible dispatch: for my share of the businesse I can assure you I have brought my self into a very ill state of health by the pains and constant attendance I have been obliged to, and perswade my self that I shal be justifyed as having done every thing in my power to expedite them. The transmisse will I beleive be very soon, several of the bills being already ingrossed and the others are to be reported to the Councel which meets at six this evening. I am sensible there are many things in the bills (as they are agreed to) which will be thought on your side of the water not to have been well weighed here: but it ought to be remembred that when the wording of our bills depends on the opinion of the majority of a Committee of Councel, many of which are not great masters of parliamentary style and expressions, no one man can be accountable for what may seem to be incorrect or perhaps to carry some impropriety. If I can find leisure I will give you some light into the nature of the bills which are to be sent over, as well for your own satisfaction, as to enable you to make any of the ministry and particularly my Lord Sunderland (if he desire it) entirely masters of their tendency: but for the present will content my self with telling you all I know relating to the bill which is entitled An Act for the farther security of his Majestyes person and governement, which by your letter of the tenth you seem very desirous of. It would save me some pains to refer you to such hints as I have given you in former letters from time to time, and to take the thing up where I gave off: but you express your self fond of being told the whole story together, in which I cannot deny to gratifye you, having in the beginning of my letter owned that I now have leisure. The bill for farther securitye of the Kings person and governement was brought in by Mr Jephson (as I remember)[488] but there was no clause in the heads of the bill as offered

---

[486] Martin Bladen.

[487] Either a reference to St John III having attained his majority (which had occurred in about 1706), or having married an heiress (in 1710).

[488] Presented by Mr Jephson on 21 Nov. 1715. *CJI*, iv, 204 records that John Jephson reported from the committee on the bill on 1 Feb. 1716.

by him in ease of the dissenters: some little time before the house was to resolve itself into a Committee to consider these heads, fowre or five Gentlemen mett together (probably by accident) and fell into a discourse of offering some clause to be added to that bill in ease of the dissenters: You may be sure I have this only by hearsay, and therefore can not answer for the thing being just as I relate it; but I heard that the Speaker, Sir Gustavus Hume (and I think Sir Raph Gore) were of the company: I cannot tell whether Colonel Bladen was there or not; but what then passed had this effect that when the house was in a Committee on that bill, Sir Gust[*avus*] Hume moved to add a clause in favour of the dissenters and to repeal the sacramental test; the words I could not be informed of, for his discourse was loose and ended in no formed question: Mr Upton afterward stood up and in a very long and indigested harangue so magnifyed the service of the dissenters and the obligations which the Kingdome lay under to them, as to distast the greater part of the house, who thought the comparison as he had framed it to be very invidious; and concluded in a mocion for a repeal of the test in general as well in respect to civil emploiments, as to the army and militia. The Secretary also spoke on the side of the question in favor of the dissenters, but I cannot hear that he did it in the same latitude with Mr Upton, but handsomly shewed they had been useful formerly, that they were well affected to the Kings governement and might now be of use to secure our religion libertyes and propertyes and ought not in policy to be continued under the same discouragements and incapacityes as hitherto.

One would have thought a matter of such consequence should have been communicated to the Governement here before it was moved in the house of commons; and the rather, since the Speaker Sir Gust[*avus*] Hume and others could not but be sensible that great opposition would be given to it by the Tory high Church party, and a thousand rumors would be raised of designs to ruine the Church, so as the Governement seemed to be interested so far in the event, that it ought to have been previously consulted: and indeed when news was brought to me in the upper house of the motion, I could not but apprehend it was done with the privity of the Lords Justices and had been resolved on by a much greater number then I afterward heard were present when it was first thought of. But I cannot find that the thing was communicated to the Governement here, much lesse that they had any directions about it from England: however considering the persons who first stirred in it, there is no doubt but that it obtains among the Toryes that the Governement here was in the secret: But I doe firmly beleive the contrary, having good reasons to doe soe from what I heard one of the Lords Justices say, and having no cause to think the contrary from any thing I could ever observe or hear from the other. The Commons at length came to a resolution to have a clause brought in to qualifye them for the militia; but as matters were managed would certainly have put a negative on the question if more had at that time been insisted on: and in this scituation the affair stood till the day when the Lords Justices intimated to the Parliament that by late accounts they had reason to beleive this Kingdome would be soon invaded: Among many others one effect of this speech was that upon the motion of the Speaker in a committee leave was given to bring in a clause to qualifye dissenters to serve in the militia or army for ten years: I need not trouble you with the debates nor can I now repeat particulars; but there was a good deal of warmth in the house (at that time, and under all those apprehensions which they then had upon them) about this matter: some were for three years, some for seven; and when those who were for being most easy to the dissenters saw a prospect of successe they mentioned making it perpetual: but at length it terminated in ten years, and so the heads of the bill came from the Commons. The High

Church Lords took the alarm; and I hear there was a meeting at the Pr[*imate'*]s about it, but I cant learn who were present: but soon after Lord Abercorne moved for leave to bring in heads of a bill with the same title as that of the Commons; and soon after brought in the Commons heads in haec verba,[489] omitting only the clause about qualifying men to serve in the Army and militia for ten years without taking the sacramental test, and the other clause to exempt Quakers from the penaltyes (contained in the Act) for refusing the oath of abjuration, upon making such declaration of their fidelitye to King George and such renuntiation of the Pretender (without oath) as in the Commons heads was contained. These heads were brought in, read, committed and gone through in two dayes, which was I think with the utmost precipitation. I gave the Lords Justices notices from time to time of all that passed with my best thoughts upon every emergency: and so expeditious were the Lords and so dilatory the Commons that the Lords were ready to present and did in a body present their heads of a bill on the same day the Commons presented theirs. I need not repeat Lord Abercornes motion to reject the bill when it came back if any thing should be added to it, which was exposed abundantly in the house and of which I gave you an account at large in a former letter.

The Lords Justices laid the heads from the Lords and those from the Commons on the same day before the Councel and after some time those from the Lords had the preference to be first read; and then those from the Commons, and both were referred to a Committee of the whole board. It was attempted that the Committee should have been directed to have first gone through the heads of the Lords and have agreed thereto, and then to have considered those which came from the commons: but I foresaw that this use would have been made of that method of proceeding: when the Committee had gone through, amended, or approved the bill drawn on the heads which came from the Lords, that bill must have passed the Committee without the two Clauses, or they must have arisen by mocion at the Committee without the weight of the house of Commons having recommended them, if they had been added to the bill drawn on the heads which came from the upper house: If that course had not been taken, the bill drawn on the heads agreed to by the Commons must have been taken next into consideration, the much greater part of which would have appeared unnecessary because it was already contained in that drawn on the heads from the Lords, and it would then have stood a bill with a title for securitye etc but (as Lord Abercorne called it) for the ease of Dissenters and Quakers, there being nothing in it to any other purpose. To prevent this the Councel intimated to the Committee[490] that they should consider both bills and out of them form one bill as they saw fit. The heads which came from the Lords took up one whole day in the Committee and on 23 February those from the Commons came under consideration: The Archbishop[491] and Lord Abercorne objected against the recital of the dissenters being well affected, and said they refused to take arms when the Pretender first attempted to land in Scotland and Lord A[*bercorn*] undertook to prove that some of them said since the Church men will have all the places let them draw the sword and keep them: the Archbishop said they were no otherwise affected to the King then because they expected favor from him. They were told the expressions

---

[489] In these words.

[490] The committee of the Irish privy council entrusted with examining the various 'heads'.

[491] Lindsay of Armagh.

supposed to be used proceeded from the opinion they had of being severely treated by means of the test and seemed to be one reason to give them ease.

Lord Cheif Justice Forster, Mr St George,[492] Lord Newtown,[493] Lord Montjoy Sir Gust[*avus*] Hume Lord Cheif Baron[494] and others gave them their due characters of being zealously in the Kings interest, nay Lord Mount Alexander owned they had shewed a readinesse to oppose the Pretender when he attempted to land formerly; but could not part with them without wondering why they would not now serve without repealing the test as they did then: Whereas they have now taken Commissions and subjected themselves thereby to penaltyes and there then was no Parliament sitting which could give them ease, as now there is. The first question was whether they should be qualifyed for officers in the militia for the future, for every body was for indemnifying them for what they have now done. Lord Abercorne spoke against it,[495] Lord Moore was for qualifying them as officers in the militia, not in the Army or Civil emploiments but toward the end of his discourse seemed to conclude for sending over the clause as it came from the Commons. Lord Castlecomer in a formed harangue[496] was for giving them a toleration and letting them into the militia, that the now rebellion proceeded from clamors of the danger of the Church; the passing this bill would strengthen the argument in the mouths of disaffected men who would call this a forerunner of what would soon follow in Great Britain. He thought it against the Act of Union and all the Acts made for establishing the Church, and that it would make room for Scotts presbyterians. The Bishop of Dromore inclined to let them into the militia, if they would renounce the solemn League and covenant particularly that part of it against Episcopacy.

Lord Mount Alexander in answer to Lord Montjoy who mentioned their services and numbers in Londonderry and Iniskillin[497] said if they were so numerous, they were the more dangerous.

The Bishop of Clogher said the King was obliged to maintain not only the Act of Uniformity but all other Acts for preservation of the Church. The Archbishop of Dublin was for allowing so many in the militia as had now taken Commissions and no more.[498] It is worth your notice that he was one of the Justices when the Commissions of array issued, and hardly any dissenters were put into that Commission and consequently very few dissenters were returned for Officers or had Commissions. I proposed the excluding all those who had refused accepting Commissions in the room of his Graces limitation. Lord Cheif Justice Forster, the Cheif Baron, Mr Bladen and others spoke fully to this matter and very well:

[492] Probably Oliver St George, MP [I].

[493] Lord Newtownbutler.

[494] Jeffray Gilbert.

[495] The only person to do so (TNA, SP 63/374/105–6: Grafton and Galway to Stanhope, 24 Feb. 1715/16).

[496] A prepared speech.

[497] Key engagements during the Williamite war: The siege of Derry, Apr.–July 1689, and the Battle of Newtownbutler, near Enniskillen, on 31 July 1689.

[498] According to the report sent by the lords justices to the secretary of state, the Commons' clause permitting dissenters to hold army commissions during the next ten years, was opposed in the committee by the archbishop of Dublin, the bishops of Clogher and Dromore, Lords Abercorn, Castlecomer, 'and others' (TNA, SP 63/374/105–6: Grafton and Galway to Stanhope, 24 Feb. 1715/16).

My Lord Cheif Justice Whitshed spoke but in a maner peculiar to himself;[499] differed from every body, thought dissenters had served well formerly, that they were well affected, should be sorry to see any but of the established religion general Officers; we were raising 13 regiments, men not to be had here without the North supplyed them; and common men would not come in without Officers: And I think he meant they might be any thing but general Officers for ten years and who were during that time employed to be alway capable. The Archbishop was up again, told us King Charles the first and King James employed Papists and lost the hearts of ten times as many Protestants (you see the threat contained in this innuendo) and that the ease given the Quakers etc in King Williams time was the cause of all the disquiets he mett during his reign. You see he owns from what quarters those and the present disorders arise; I told him every body knew to what sett of men the misfortunes of both reigns were due, but that he forgott that the principles inculcated of unlimited passive obedience and indefeasible hereditary right were the engines made use of by them who can never be easy but while they have every thing of profit or power in the hands they recommend to them. He said not above 400 of the present rebellion but were dissenters, and gave himself airs of threatning what the consequences would be if Dissenters were let into emploiments. At length the indemnifying clause passed, and one for qualifying them for the militia; and at last another to qualifye such as should have Commissions in the army during the present rebellion and to the end of the succeeding Session of Parliament. Soon after this the Duke of Grafton dined at Chappel Izod[500] where the prospect of successe in the Parliament of the clause relating to the Army was under consideration: Lord Montjoy, Mr St George and I were of opinion it would not passe, the person in whose favor I lately drew on my sister for £500 gave other hopes both of himself and some of his freinds but when the bill was reported on 15 March he was the first man who spoke against the Clause, so did Bishop Dromore, Dublin, Abercorne and Lord Mount Alexander with wondrous warmth, but nothing new; others spoke for it: the Cheif Justice[501] spoke last but whether for or against it I could not tell till he voted for it. He owned that the number of those who spoke against it had great weight with him; that when the clause came in, Scotland was in rebellion, so as there was a necessity to bring in foreign forces, which he beleived was one inducement to the Regent to assist [*the*] Pretender: that he thought subjects of any sort fitter to be employed then foreigners. Expressed a concern that men who professed passive obedience had shewn great indifference during the rebellion; this inclined him to go into the clause formerly; thought if the regent would dismisse the Pretender there was no occasion for the dissenters being employed; but could wish there were farther time given to consider a thing of such weight. Mr Bladen said the reasons for the clause subsisted stil and without our repeating as others had done the clause was carryed in the Councel by ten

---

[499] According to the lords justices, Alan Brodrick and Whitshed were both working to find a 'temperament' (compromise). Whitshed proposed to reduce the period during which dissenters could hold army commissions without taking the test from ten years to the duration of the present rebellion or the end of the next session of parliament. However, the wording he proposed seemed to permit those who had been commissioned during the rebellion to continue to hold their commissions for life, and the bishops opposed it. Thus, although his amendment passed the committee it seemed unlikely that it would be carried in the house of lords. (TNA, SP 63/374/105–6: Grafton and Galway to Stanhope, 24 Feb. 1715/16.)

[500] On the outskirts of the Phoenix Park. The country residence of the chief governors.

[501] John Forster or, more probably, William Whitshed.

against nine. For it The Chancellor, Montjoy, Whitshed, Forster, St George,[502] Southwell,[503] Parry,[504] Bladen, Allen[505] and one more: Against it Archbishop Dublin, Lord Kildare, Mount Alexander, Abercorne, Donerayle, Bishop Clogher, Dromore, Shelburn, Gowran.

My tale is told; my thoughts are this matter was ill judged at first to stir in it without leave of the Governement and apprising others of what was intended; and worse judged when moved in the Committee by the Speaker, who might by what he had observed before foresee it would find great opposition: and indeed it is unaccountable that between the first and second stirring of it no method was taken to know the sense of the Governement; yet for any thing I can find that was the case: tho I must beleive one man must have communicated and known the sentiments of him to whom he ought to communicate it. The truth is this is one of those matters which particular persons resolved to have the conduct and honour of, which measures I am sorry were taken because I see they have laid us under great difficultyes. It will be very well worth considering what ill consequences sending back the bill with this clause may have, if it shal not passe; as I am too well convinced it never will: A victory of this nature will cement a party and sett them at open defiance. I have often said a certain Archbishop[506] would be found very hard to be dealt with; the dispute between him and the Pr[imate] is which of the two shal be at the head of the Church men; but both aim at a new Model of things which formerly was termed a coalition, but I think they now aim at more. If you let me be vouched for any thing in this our correspondence of this kind is for ever at an end. Depend on it a certain Cheif Justice[507] and a certain Archbishop have an entire good understanding in all points.

275. *Alan I, Dublin, to Thomas, 27 Mar. 1716*

(1248/3/414–15)

In a former letter I took notice to you of what Mr Hill[508] wrote to Senny; which together with the hint you gave me that some of my good freinds had given out that I was in the secret of Lord Abercornes bringing in the bill into the house of Lords for farther securitye of the Kings person and Governement without the clause which was in the Commons bill for qualifying the dissenters to serve in the militia and army, convinced me that I have enemyes who scruple nothing that may doe me a disservice: Very lately my Lord Gowran shewed me a letter from Lord FitzWilliam, in which there is a paragraph in these words. The ministry here are a good deal angry with my Lord Chancellor; I think him much wronged and endeavoured to doe him all the service in my power. By his letter it is plain he wrote upon what had passed in discourse between him and some one of the ministry: This makes me give more credit and weight to what Mr Hill wrote then I thought it

---

[502] Either Baron St George, or Oliver St George, MP [I].
[503] Baron Southwell.
[504] Benjamin Parry, MP [I].
[505] John Allen, MP [I].
[506] Archbishop King of Dublin.
[507] William Whitshed.
[508] Trevor Hill.

deserved before; tho I alway beleived there must be some foundation for it by his maner of expressing himself. I carryed and read that part of the letter to Lord Galway (the Duke being then and stil at Kilkenny) in the presence of Mr Bladen, and said what I really do think, that if I had not done the King much service, I had however had his service soe much at heart in every instance, that I could not beleive I had upon any occasion given cause to any of the ministry to be angry with me; that the Lords Justices were the constant witnesses and the best Judges of my actions, which I thought had ever been such as would secure me against his Majestyes displeasure and the ill opinion of the ministry, if my behavior had been or should be fairly represented. That I appealed to Lord Galway whether I had done any thing to obstruct the Kings service, or omitted any thing in my power to promote it; he gave me the pleasure to assure me I had served well and that he had upon occasion wrote to that effect, and that he had never represented any action of mine as tending to his Majestyes disservice; and indeed said more in my favour then I ought in modesty to repeat. Mr Bladen spoke to the same purpose. I then said it was plain that I had ill offices done me with the ministry tho I could not tell by whom, or who the minister was who had received evil impressions of me, or on what foot I was accused; and that I thought of writing to Lord Sunderland on this subject being the person who recommended me to his Majestye for Chancellor; soe that I ought on many accounts justifye my self to him, least he might be uneasy in having recommended me under a better character then my subsequent behavior intitled me to. Lord Galway advised me to inform my self from Lord FitzWilliam by some freind who the minister was who had expressed himself toward me as having not answered the expectations of the Governement; and wherein it was supposed I had been faulty: and added he beleived this might arise from the part Senny took in some matters debated in the house of Commons, which officious men might write over to my prejudice, and added that he would at all times be ready to do me right, in representing me as having faithfully and zealously served the King. I think the method he proposed may be a very reasonable one, and desire you will from me thank Lord FitzWilliam and make him my complements on this occasion; and if the minister he means be one whom you know, it may not be amisse in you to take notice of what Lord FitzWilliam saith (but stil by his permission) to that minister, and tell him what I have now wrote; I think too that you may speak to and discourse this whole matter over with Lord Sunderland; for I had rather dye then create him the least uneasinesse as having recommended a man to his Majestyes service capable of obstructing or acting remissely in any thing that is for the ease honour and happinesse of his Governement. I am sensible that the Cheif Governors here are the persons from whom his Majestye and the ministry will take the characters of men, and am in no pain about the final result of this affair: for I am certain the justice and honour of our Lord Justices is such that I shal not be misrepresented by them, and I think they have so much goodnesse to give me an obliging character; I have served faithfully, with indefatigable pains, and (to you I will venture to add) well: Any indiscretion of my son will not be imputed to me, supposing him to have been faulty: and perhaps he was, but I wish others were not more so by unnecessary provocations given, and methods taken which might have better been omitted. I doe not think it is my businesse to make this any way publick; If the minister who entertained worse thoughts of me then I hope I deserved doe not shew he stil is of the same mind and beleives ill of me, I think no more need now be said of or done in it; but if he doth, and will let you know in what my fault consists I hope to clear my innocence to him in such a maner as will intitle me to the honor of his good opinion. In the mean time I am convinced the

Lords Justices will doe me the justice to say I have neither been an unfaithful, slothful, or unuseful servant. My health is so much impaired that I shal be obliged to presse for leave to go into England in the long vacation, when I hope my attendance here may be spared for three months. Into how low and vile a creature is he dwindled who formerly pretended so much zeal for his Majestyes person and interest and such an irreconcileable enmity to all the enemyes of the Hanover succession. If the letter handed about here as his, was written by Sir R.S.[509] I must own I think him as malicious and ill a man as ever was born, and the very reverse of what he hath endeavoured to passe upon the world for … I perswade my self that My Lord Galway and Mr Bladen are both hearty in this matter, and by the behavior of the later for some time past I beleive he could be content some things had not passed which are now past recall, but I beleive pretty much worn out of peoples mind on both sides; which is the best thing the matter is capable of.

276. *Thomas to Alan I, 29 Mar. 1716*[510]

(1248/3/346–7)

Last night I receivd yours of the 20th before which I had very throughly been satisfyed of the falsity of the insinuation relating to the bill, butt yours is soe perticular, that I will againe take up that matter, notwithstanding those whom I formerly talkt with, uppon the subject, ownd entire conviction, for I am very sure twas wrote from Ireland, nottwithstanding I could nott gett that ownd, much lesse whoe was the honest intelligencer.

I verily beleive what Mr H[*ill*] wrote to Senny an utter mistake, for though I doe nott goe to Court, that could nott have happened without my having itt from some hand or other, butt thus much I know, some gentlemen talkt pretty much after the same manner both in relation to Ireland, and affairs here, whoe have nothing to doe with either, and whose intermedling will in the end bee found disservisable, as well as impertinent, itt begins to give great offence, and will daily doe soe. Our Reverend Doctor[511] has given very just grounds for asserting what Mr H[*ill*] wrote, by being the man whoe turnd the matter of Lord Arans[512] being chosen steward of Westminster in opposition to the Duke of Newcastle,[513] for without his vote the thing could nott have been effected; butt twas matter of conscience, as hee pretends, in returne of which I suppose hee is to bee a Bishop when his late Grace[514] comes over Generall with the Pretender, and can subdue our kings freinds.

---

[509] Possibly the Irish whig writer and British MP Sir Richard Steele (1672–1729).

[510] Endorsed by Alan I: 'Brother Brodrick 29 March 1716 that I have had ill offices done me, yet have convinced the people in England of my innocence. That the Doctor gave a casting voice for Lord Arran against the Duke of Newcastle.'

[511] Possibly Robert Friend (1667–1751), headmaster of Westminster School.

[512] Charles Butler (1671–1758), 1st earl of Arran, younger brother of the 2nd duke of Ormond.

[513] Thomas Pelham-Holles (1693–1768), 1st duke of Newcastle-upon-Tyne. Arran was elected high steward of Westminster on 18 Feb. 1716.

[514] The duke of Ormond.

Both houses are adjourned to Munday sennight,[515] when I beleive wee shall endeavour as fast as possible to gett through the necessary businesse of the session, the turning the triennial act into a septenniall will bee the first attempt, and will (I thinke) bee carryd. I beleive a Bill will bee sent from the Lords for the banishing and inflicting other censures on Lord Oxford, after the president of that against Lord Clarendon, whose case however had this difference, that hee was gon, when the other being in custody might bee brought to tryall,[516] however I beleive thus itt will bee; for if I am rightly informd, the king resolves going to Hanover, for which there cannott bee time, in case the summer bee taken up in tryals; you see my former conjectures were butt too well grounded, I am one of those unfortunate men whoe judge of things as they appeare to them, without having itt in my power to give entire assent uppon implicit faith; Wee are therefore criminal on the same foote; as to my part I am out of every bodyes power, having nothing to aske, nor any thing that can bee taken from mee, your case is in some measure different, butt the reasonable part holds equally as to us and all honest men, When integrity and the candor of a mans actions prove insufficient against the underhand practices and schemes of little designing fellowes tis time to leave the feild of action to the bold undertakers whoe will in a little time expose themselves, and disappoint those whoe build on such a foundation.

Doe nott refine uppon what I have sayd soe far as to beleive I doe in any way prepare you for what I may apprehend likely to happen, for uppon my word I have nott any reason to doe soe, other then that from a general observation of the practice of all courts and att all times such things have happened, I see noe reason against their doing soe againe, for I thinke wee tread in the steps of our Predecessors.

I have now leisure to write to you, which really I had nott whilst the house remaind sittizing, the fatigue of which was more then I could well beare, therefore you may expect another letter of next weeke.

277. Alan I, Dublin, to Thomas, 30 Mar. 1716

(1248/3/416–17)

I have wrote so long and many letters to you of late that I beleive you little expected that another would have followed them soe soon. Notwithstanding my postscript you may if you please shew any one or more of the ministry whom you know my long letter about the bill for securing the Kings person and Governement, the postscript being added that it might not seem calculated for any bodyes view but yours; but do not leave the letter with any body soe as a copy may be taken of it, since it is so very particular, and names people and gives my thoughts of their conduct with a good deal of freedome. You know Mr Pulteney who is Clerk of the Councel here?[517] Mrs Hill hath a great mind to buy that

---

[515]On Wednesday, 27 Mar. the Lords adjourned until Monday, 9 Apr. (*LJ*, xx, 323); the following day the Commons also adjourned until 9 Apr. (*CJ*, xviii, 416).

[516]Edward Hyde (1609–74), 1st earl of Clarendon. In Nov. 1667, following Clarendon's flight to France to escape impeachment proceedings, a bill of banishment had been passed against him.

[517]John Pulteney (c.1661–1726), of St James', Westminster, and Harefield, Mdx., previously MP [I] 1692–3 and [E & GB] 1695–1710.

place for her younger son[518] and desires me to gett somebody to treat with him about it: I beleive Mr Dawson who is now in London[519] will make it one of his businesses thither to gett footing again in that office, which would be great cause of triumph to a certain party here and of very ill consequence to the publick. Beside the relation between our familyes I lye under a great many particular personal obligations to Mrs Hill and should be glad to serve her, beside that I think it would be of great use to the young Gentleman to be bred up to businesse in a genteel and beneficial emploiment; and that my now being at the head of the Councel gives me oportunitye to instruct and assist him while he is young and unexperienced in the method of things. Pray try to gett him to fix a price if you can without mentioning for whom you treat, and on return of a letter you shal be qualifyed to make offers or close with him. I doe not know whether you often see General Sankey;[520] if you doe give him my service and tell him tho he hath not yet answered my letter, yet I hope when it comes it will be such as I wish to see it. I cannot beleive it miscarryed, and can hardly think the disagreeable subject would hinder him from giving it some kind of answer since it was written in the way of freindship: It is about his daughters having marryed without his consent (which I confesse to be a great fault) but the Gentleman is well spoken of by those who know him.[521] Perhaps he may keep at Blackheath or have discontinued St James Coffee house[522] where it was to be left by the direction …

278. *Thomas to Alan I, Dublin, 2 Apr. 1716*[523]

(1248/3/350–1)

I write this a day before hand, designing to goe out of towne this evening, or very early tomorrow, butt am layd under a very firme promise of returning by Sunday night att farthest, in expectation of your bills.

　　I spent an hour yesterday in company where I must have learnt the truth of what you mentioned in your last, if there were any thing in itt, which I am confident there is nott, I am nott sure that itt might nott bee driven att from your side, butt pretty confident itt neither has nor will take place; the pitt dug for others often falls to the share of the projectors, and I thinke itt more then probable this will doe soe; for I am very sure some peoples actions are nott soe well thought of as they may imagine.

　　The Bill which I mentioned in my last[524] will I thinke have a different turne from what was att first intended, by beginning with the Lords, bee that as twill, twill bee carryed through.

---

[518]Arthur Hill, MP [I].

[519]Joshua Dawson (c.1660–1725), of Castle Dawson, Co. Londonderry and Dublin, tory MP [I] 1705–14; formerly under-sec. [I] 1699–1714.

[520]Nicholas Sankey (1657–1722), MP [I] 1703–13; col. 39th foot 1703, lieut.-gen. 1710.

[521]Anne Sankey married Solomon Whyte (*d.*1747), a captain in Kane's regiment of foot; and great-uncle of Richard Brinsley Sheridan (https://www.findagrave.com/memorial/167677398/solomon-whyte).

[522]Near St James's Palace.

[523]Endorsed by Alan I: 'Brother Brodrick 2 April 1716. that any designs laid to my prejudice will be disappointed.'

[524]The bill 'for securing the King's person and government'.

The Regent[525] gives fair words, butt wee have too sensibly found what french bona fide[526] amounts to.

279. *Alan I, Dublin, to Thomas, Westminster, 5 Apr. 1716*

(1248/3/352–5)

I have your letter of 29th of March and will trouble you no farther about what I have mentioned heretofore, relating to my carrying myself in Parliament affairs; viz the farther demand made after the two years were proposed, agreed to and accepted: and the bill for securitye of the Kings person: for I am satisfyed whatever was done or aimed at, the actors are sorry for and ashamed of as far as the thing related to me. I told you formerly that the Speaker, Lord Chief Justice Whitshed, Mr Manly,[527] Mr Bladen, together with Sir Ralph Gore and Mr Maxwell (the Speakers two confidents)[528] were deep in the first matter; and under hand Mr Vesey[529] and a good many nay most of the Toryes: The maner of attempting this was not very reputable, nor could it be carryed if any body had in earnest opposed: but nothing more was done by some then to let the world see they were not in the secret, but would not thwart the measures of the Governement. By this means the projectors attained one thing they aimed at, I mean the credit at the Castle of being the men to whom the encrease of the addicional dutyes on wine and brandyes was owing: but they were obliged to leave to other Gentlemen, who would not cooperate in what must end in their breaking their word with their freinds (to whom they had declared no more would be expected then the addicional dutyes for two years) the character one would be fond of that they were true to their professions, and not capable of leaping over a stick when they were bid. This galled you may be sure, and it is very possible some of the persons who formed the scheme might at the first represent to their freinds that they who would not go into it were opposite to the Kings interest: Sir W[illia]m St Q[uintin] keeps a constant correspondence with the Speaker, of whom I am unwilling to entertain hard thoughts; but if the Knight was one of those who talked in the maner you mencion, depend on it you know from whom the intimation comes: and perhaps your Nephews sometimes shewing him how ill he observed and indeed is instructed in the orders of the house may be another provocation; for by every bodyes confession the Chair is filled in the maner the Speakers enemyes would have it, very insufficiently. Mr Manly too is like enough to give his sense of persons and things, at least as far as it comes to his share; but I am backward in beleiving one who professes so much kindnesse and freindship should unprovoked do an ill office, much more an injustice to me. But perhaps Mr Delafay may have taken oportunity of writing to Lord S[underland] and indeed I have more than once expressed indignation when he hath pretended to take more to himself in publick and parliamentary affairs (when the Lords Justices have called several of us together) than came to his share, as Secretary: or became a man who hath no interest

---

[525] Philippe, duke of Orléans (1674–1723), regent of France during the minority of Louis XV.
[526] In good faith.
[527] Isaac Manley, MP [I].
[528] Sir Ralph Gore, MP [I]; Henry Maxwell, MP [I].
[529] Agmondisham Vesey, MP [I].

in the Kingdome, particularly in relation to giving money and charging the Nation: and I apprehend Mr M[530] on your side the water to be likely enough to give me his ill word: for I frequently am lett into his sentiments, by my Lord Moore, Lord Cheif Justice Forster and others (who correspond with him) shewing me his letters: but I confesse I cannot go into all his warm notions, and unfortunately am of opinion that his passion, or you may call it zeal, very often if not generally runs away with his judgement: to which may be added that he hath a very high conceit of his own abilityes, and merit; and an insatiable thirst after preferment and places of profit; which are motives to me not too readily to go into what a self designing man setts on foot or proposes, till I have well weighed the reasons and grounds for doing it. The nature of this part of my letter will be sufficient hints to you not to shew it. I come now to another affair, which you perhaps may think worth your notice. The Bishop of Down about the 16th of March left with the Lords Justices a paper of which the following is a Copy word for word.[531] To their Excellencyes the Lords Justices of Ireland: The memorial of Thomas Lord Archbishop of Armagh Primate and Metropolitan of all Ireland and Edward Lord Bishop of Down and Connor Humbley sheweth That the Clergy and others who are members of the Church as by Law established in the Diocese of Connor and Province of Ulster have of late suffered great hardships, by having their houses searched as disaffected persons, and those arms which they kept for their necessary defence taken from them, and in some Cases by some who seem not to have had any lawful authority so to do; And that the dissenters who have alway been treated with much tendernesse by us, have been very active in carrying on and cheifly concerned in these practices, in which they have been assisted by one Mr Porter, a Presbyterian Teacher.[532] By these means many of the Clergy in those parts who have behaved them selves loyally to his Majesty King George, and given all the security to the Governement to be true to the Protestant succession in the house of Hanover which the Law requires, have been much discouraged in the performance of their religious offices and dutyes; and their people have been terrifyed from coming to the publick prayers and service, as may more evidently appear to your Lordships by the annexed depositions. We thought it our duty to lay these matters before your Excellencyes, whose affection to the established Church we question not incline you to take Care of those in her Communion, providing proper remedyes for the evils complained of and preventing the like for the future.

This paper had been delivered some time before I heard any thing of it, and the first notice I had that there was such an affair on the anvil was from Lord Cheif Justice Forster about 20th March, to whom a Copy of it together with a Copy of the examinations to which it refers was delivered by the Justices about that time, he intending soon to go out of town to meet Justice McCartney who was on the Circuit: but I found reason to beleive Forster intended not to go farther then Down, so as the whole businesse of Antrim must have fallen to the share of Justice MacCartney, who being of that countrey, and endeavoured by some to be unjustly represented as a great favourer of the dissenters, I thought it was

[530] Robert Molesworth, created Viscount Molesworth in July 1716 (see Appendix 3).

[531] The memorial, together with various depositions, is printed in *The Report of the Judges of Assize, for the North-East Circuit of Ulster; upon a Memorial Given in to the Lords Justices of Ireland* ... ([Dublin,] 1716). See also PRONI, T2310/1: copies of depositions, 1716.

[532] John Porter (c.1680–1738), minister of the presbyterian congregation at Dunluce, Co. Antrim (W.D. Killen, *History of the Congregations of the Presbyterian Church in Ireland*... (Belfast, 1886), 68).

very proper Forster should also go to Carickfergus and intimated as much to him: but to put that point out of dispute I went to the Lords Justices and gave them my sense of the necessity of his being present at the examination into this matter, and either on what was spoken to him by the Justices pursuant to this hint, and from his own inclinations he left town time enough to be at Carickfergus Assises. You might reasonably expect that I should send you a Copy of the examinations referred to, but I cannot doe it; for soon after the delivery of the memorial I find Mɪ Bladen by order of the Lords Justices wrote a letter to the Sherif of the County of Antrim, containing the great care which ought to be taken to preserve Church men in the free enjoiment etc a copy of which I could not get, but as it was reported to me it seemed to give more credit to the facts contained in the memorial then was necessary, or indeed proper till the thing had been farther enquired into. I found that the original memorial and examinations were sent down inclosed to the Sherif, and that the Memorial had been received without being signed by either of the Memorialists. The Cheif Justice also told me that the Lords Justices had directed him that the matter should be very narrowly searched and enquired into, but had not given directions to him in writing.

Next morning I waited on the Lord Galway (the Duke[533] being at Kilkenny) and advised a letter to be written to both Judges on this occasion and a draught of one was prepared by Mr Bladen in general terms, which was sent to me to be perused; but I thought it ought to be very particular and went to Mr Bladens chamber (who was then sick) and drew a draught of a letter, which he seemed to like, and was (I beleive) the letter which was sent, because I find the Judges have by their maner of proceeding answered the import of it in the method the letter directed; which told the Judges the Lords Justices sent them the memorial and examinations; and that several parts of the memorial contained facts of great consequence if true, viz. hardships suffered by Clergy and others of the established Church, by searching houses as disaffected, taking away their arms necessary for their defence, and sometimes by persons having no lawful autority: the dissenters cheifly concerned in the practice, assisted by one of their teachers. Clergy men discouraged in performance of religious dutyes and the people terrifyed from coming to Prayers. And they were desired to enquire what hardships, search, seising of arms had been and by whom, and whether dissenting ministers had been busy, whether Clergy men or their people had been discouraged etc and to enquire whether there was cause of suspecting the persons for disaffection whose houses had been searched. I also advised a letter should be wrote to the Bishop of Down to acquaint him such enquiry would be made, and to desire the Primate and he would take care the witnesses who could prove the allegacions of the memorial should attend. Thus you see matters were like fairly to be brought on the Stage and after dining I will add the rest of my tale, which will contain what birth the mountain brought forth. But let me first observe to you that at this time the heads of the bills for farther security of the Kings person were depending before the Council in which the Commons had inserted a Clause to allow their coming into the militia and army; and that the memorialists were two of the Lords who once were but now are not of the Privy Councel; and I do assure you in debating those heads we heard at the Committee of Councel more then once of the insupportable difficultyes and oppressions the Church men lay under in the County of Antrim. Let me also remind you

---

[533]Grafton.

that Lord Antrim is marryed to one of Lord Massareenes sisters[534] and the Bishop of Down to another;[535] and that Lord Antrim was at this time a prisoner in the Castle as suspected to be too far concerned with some of his neighbours in North Britain;[536] and that several applications had been privately but unsuccessfully made to the Justices for his enlargement by one who went a great way in beleiving well of his loyalty and affection to his Majesty: but freindship and relation, neighbourhood and strict intimacy incline people to judge favourably; and indeed I once heard and was inclined to hope Lord Antrim a little before his marriage had thoughts of becoming a Protestant; but every thing of that kind seems to have long been over. As soon as the Countrey was called over and before the Grand Jury was sworn the Cheif Justice acquainted the Court that the Lords Justices had received information of several enormous and illegal Acts committed in the County of Antrim to the disturbance of the peace and discouragement of the Clergy and others of the Church by law established, and (I think) caused the memorial to be read over, or at least ennumerated the particulars it contained, which they as Judges of Assise were by vertue of their office to cause enquiry to be into in order to punishment, but had received particular directions from the Lords Justices to inform themselves so fully of the facts as to be able to lay a true state of it before them at their return, as well as to execute the Law against such as should be found offenders. He told the Sherif it was his duty to return a good and sufficient grand Jury and acquainted those who were witnesses of the facts set forth in the memorial or attended to justifye the truth of the matters laid to the charge of those who are complained against in it, that if any men were returned on the Grand Jury concerned in the matters alleged in the memorial or against whom any cause of exception to be on the Grand Jury should be offered, the Court was ready to hear what should be objected: and indeed the Court went far enough of all conscience herein, setting aside some at the instance of Mr Stewart a Clergyman[537] and others who appeared to countenance this complaint, without any Legal challenge or objection to them that I could hear; tho perhaps the objections might have weight in them, but I hear no more then that they were objected against and sett aside. It is certain Mr Upton and one or two more of the leading dissenters at their own request were excused, and I think this to be an unusual act of temper and prudence in our freind Clotty. The Jury sworn consisted of seventeen, of whom I hear nine were Churchmen and the other eight dissenters.[538] You must know that the County of Antrim consists of eight

---

[534] Although a catholic, Randal MacDonnell (1680–1721), 4th earl of Antrim, had married Rachel, daughter of Clotworthy Skeffington (1660–1714), 3rd Viscount Massereene, and sister to Clotworthy Skeffington (*d*.1738), the 4th viscount.

[535] Edward Smyth was married to Mary Skeffington, Rachel's youngest sister.

[536] Antrim was one of a number of catholic peers and gentlemen taken into preventive custody in Jan. 1716 as a suspected jacobite. He was said to have sent 'blankets and tenting' to the rebels in Scotland (TNA, SP 63/374/57: Charles Delafaye to [Robert Pringle], 24 Jan. 1715/16; *Evening Post*, 31 Jan.–2 Feb., 7–9 Feb. 1716).

[537] Archibald Stewart (c.1677–1760), vicar of Ramoan, Co. Antrim, who resided with his brother Alexander, the earl of Antrim's seneschal, at Ballentoy (George Hill, 'The Stewarts of Ballintoy…', *Ulster Journal of Archaeology*, vi (1900), 160–1; *Clergy of Connor … Based on the Unpublished Succession Lists Compiled by Canon J. B. Leslie…* (Belfast, 1993), 609–9; *Report of the Judges of Assize … upon a Memorial*, 30). Archibald was himself a tenant of the earl of Antrim (PRONI, Antrim papers, D/2977/3A/2/1/24, 26: leases, 12 Mar. 1711, 22 Mar. 1715). He had married a daughter of Archbishop Vesey of Tuam.

[538] The jury is listed in PRONI, ANT4/1/1: Co. Antrim grand jury presentment book, 1711–21. In fact, ten out of the 17 jurors are identifiable as presbyterians and the seven churchmen included Clotworthy Upton's brother Hercules, who had recently conformed. The detailed evidence for this calculation is set out in D.W.

Baronyes, fowre of which belong in great part to the Lord Antrim; and the other great estates in that County are that of Lord Donegall,[539] Lord Massareene, Lord Conway,[540] and the Bishop of Downe; all which you know are very far from being dissenters, as are all those who depend on them and whom they can influence: on the other hand it is most certain that the body of the freeholders as well as many Gentlemen are Presbyterians: and such is the warmth between the Church men and dissenters in the North particularly, that one would wonder that seventeen men, divided as equally as an odd number can be, who were to enquire of a matter in which party seems so much concerned, could be brought to be unanimous: but so it hapned as you will see by the following copy of what they delivered to the Judge as the result of their enquiry: which I beleive proceeded from the due sense they had of their oath of Grand Jurors, and the evident truth of things. The paper is in the following words.[541] To the right honourable the Lords Justices of Assise for the North East Circuit of Ulster: The report of the Grand Jury of the County of Antrim at an Assises and general Goal deliverye held at Carickfergus in and for the said County on Wednesday 28 March 1716. Your Lordships by the command of the Governement having directed us to enquire into the facts contained in the memorial of the Lord Primate and of the Lord Bishop of Downe and Conor, We the Grand Jury who are here from all parts of this County were surprized to find that matters of so publick a nature could happen in this County without the knowledge of any of us, before the said memorial with the examinations thereunto annexed were laid before us by your Lordships.

We think ourselves obliged to pay that regard to truth as to present, and on the oaths we have taken to declare that on the most solemn and strict enquiry we are capable of making, no one Clergyman of the established Church in our County has since his Majestyes happy accession to the Crown been discouraged from the performance of his religious dutyes, neither have any of the Laity of the Church been terrifyed from coming to the service thereof as in the memorial is sett forth. We farther find that no search for Arms or suspected persons has been made in any part of this County but on or near the Sea Coast, where part of the Earle of Antrims estate lyes over against Scotland: and not until one Andrew MacCooke had appeared in rebellion,[542] and committed a murther in those parts, who with several other persons afterwards fled into Scotland, and that several persons were preparing to goe off to the Lord Marre then in Scotland.

That in the places searched there were not over two Clergymens houses searched on that account; which searches were made by persons empowred by the Sherif, Subsherif, Justices of the peace or high Constables, who made it appear on oath before us that they had reasonable ground to make such searches.

That in the aforesaid searches there was no disorder or rudenesse committed, and but one muskett taken; neither doth it appear to us that Mr John Porter complained of in

---

538 *(continued)* Hayton, 'Presbyterians and Jacobites in County Antrim in 1716: The Interplay of Local and National Politics in Early Eighteenth-century Ireland' (forthcoming).

539 Arthur Chichester (1695–1757), 4th earl of Donegall.

540 Francis Seymour Conway (1679–1732), 1st Baron Conway.

541 Printed in *Report of the Judges of Assize ... upon a Memorial*, 31–2.

542 Or MacCook. Evidently a local criminal, possibly a smuggler, who had fled to Scotland in 'Mr Stewart of Ballentoy's boat' after murdering a man. He was said to be a presbyterian. (*Report of the Judges of Assize ... upon a Memorial*, 21, 23, 26, 28).

the said memorial, nor any other of the dissenting teachers were active or concerned in any of the searches. This affair being out of our Common way of proceeding we hope the informality of this our return will be excused and that this our representation together with the examinations taken this day in open Court before your Lordships and in our presence may be laid before the Governement to convince the world that the established Church in this County and Diocese is in a safe, peaceable, and flourishing condition, under the just and equal administration of our Sovereign Lord King George, who has our daily prayers that he may overcome the spight, malice, and dark designs of his secret, as he has those of his open enemyes. It was signed by seventeen whose names I cannot yet send you, but Mr Chichester Uncle to the Earle of Donegal[543] was the foreman.

I must now tell you that before this search the Lords Justices had too much reason to beleive the rebellion which raged in North Britain was to be carryed on here; and tho I had not the sight of the papers yet I was assured by those who must know best that there was just ground to think a regiment was to be commanded by a certain great man in favor of the Pretender and the names of most if not all the Captains were mentioned; the Lords Justices sent down the Duke of Roxboroughs Uncle Lord Marke Kerre to Carickfergus;[544] his instructions I know not but make no doubt they were to doe every thing in his power to keep the countrey in its obedience to the King, and to prevent and suppresse all rebellious meetings: and in this he acted with great care and spirit; and I hear employed among other officers one Boyde to search for horses and Arms:[545] And I am told it is at him the memorial points under the term of men who seem not to have lawful authority so to doe. I presume the Memorialists councel Mr Nuttley[546] (for that I beleive to be the Case) gave it as his opinion that in time of an intended nay an actually begun rebellion, none but Constables and civil Officers were to be employed against the rebells: How unfortunate was it for his Preston friends that this Gentleman hapned not to have established that point of Law before General Wills and his brave men interposed,[547] for they seem to me to have acted without lawful authorite upon the Memorialists Councels notion. The discouraging Clergymen to perform religious dutyes, and terrifying people from attending divine service, as it seems to be very much the most reasonable motive to induce the [*sic*] and justifye the Memorialists intermeddling at all in this affair, so it not only might but ought to have been so far enquired into by them as that they might have certainly known whether there was foundation for such complaint: If the fact was true I think the Metropolitan and Bishop of the Diocese might very reasonably lay it before the Lords Justices as an insupportable insult and of the last ill consequence: as on the contrary if it happen to have no maner of foundation I can hardly tell what other term to give it but that of a wicked Libel; Their laying down that such things had been, and then referring to annexed examinations will not I think excuse them: since

---

[543] Hon. John Itchingham Chichester, MP [I].

[544] Lord Mark Kerr (1676–1752), 4th son of the 1st marquess of Lothian, brig.-gen. 1711, col. 29th Foot, 1712, appointed in 1716 governor of Carrickfergus Castle and commander of forces in Counties Antrim and Down (Dalton, *Geo. I's Army*, 356).

[545] Hugh Boyd (1690–1765) of Ballycastle, Co. Antrim (*DIB*).

[546] Though protesting his innocence, Richard Nutley had also been arrested as a suspected jacobite and imprisoned for a time in Dublin Castle (TNA, SP 63/374/59: Nutley to [?James Stanhope], 5 Feb. 1715[/16]; *Evening Post*, 7–9 Feb. 1716).

[547] General Charles Wills (1666–1751), the commander of the government forces at the Battle of Preston in Nov. 1715.

they were as proper Judges whether those examinations justifyed that affirmation of theirs, and ought to have only laid the examinacions before the Justices, without their tragical representation of the miserable estate of the Church in that Diocese, which required other then the ordinary methods to be used in laying the pressures and greifs the Church lyes under there, and other then the ordinary remedyes for what was past, and great care to be taken for prevention of the like for the future. I say such an extraordinary application ought I think to have been founded on a certainty of the truth of the facts which were represented, and their Lordships wanted no oportunityes of finding out the truth: for probably some or most of those who applyed to them were Clergymen. Now the proof of this part of the memorial was this: One Mr Martin a Clergyman[548] was examined and said a noise had been made about twelve of clock one night by the watch about his house, for not sending out a man to be on the watch (I suppose that is one of the many exemptions claimed in that Diocese) and truly he beleived this discouraged people from coming to Church: he was urged to name any one whom he thought to have been terrifyed from coming to divine service by that behavior; but could name none, and confessed he had no other offence or interruption given, but added that he would not have appeared in this matter but that the Bishop of Downe wrote to him to be at the Assises in order to testifye it. The two Clergymens houses that were searched were that of this Mr Martin, and one Mr Stewarts of Ballintoy as I hear; the Jury hath left you in the dark for the reasons of those houses being searched but they say there was good cause to make the search. This may seem done to conceal the weaknesse of the grounds of suspition, but I think proceeded from their tendernesse toward the Gentlemen concerned: but I have reason to beleive that it was proved upon oath in Court, that after McCooke had rose in rebellion (as the Grand Jury mention) and done a murther, a party being in that part of the Countrey near which Mr Martin dwells, the Cheif or commander of them was informed that Mr Martins son was to the last degree disaffected to the Kings Governement and as fit to be secured as any man in the County;[549] and particularly drank an health to the late Duke of Ormond about Christmas last etc and the search was made only for this son it no way related to the father nor any body else. As to Mr Stewart, his house lyes on the Sea Coast near the Island of Rachlin,[550] and it appeared that not only MacCooke had after his rebellion and murther gone of in Mr Stewarts boat (tho probably without his privity) but several of his goods were found in Mr Stewarts house: and perhaps one reason of not assigning the just causes for making search there might be least their assigning it might prejudice him in his Chaplainship to Lord Montjoyes regiment. I have tyred you, as the Court was, with raking into this sink of calumny, which seems to me levelled higher then the dissenters: God forgive the contrivers and formenters of these wicked practices. I ought not to dignifye this subject without assuring you Dr Tisdal attended on the Bench during the whole examination;[551] tho I suppose uncovered, I having at the first renewing of the Commission of peace left

[548]John Martin (1660–1740), curate of Ballentoy and, from 1723, rector of Rathlin (*Clergy of Connor*, 488; *Report of the Judges of Assize … upon a Memorial*, 7–8).

[549]George Martin (*d*. aft.1770), of Artimacormick, Ballentoy (*Report of the Judges of Assize … upon a Memorial*, 8; *Clergy of Connor*, 488; Reg. Deeds, 277/553/179784).

[550]Rathlin Island.

[551]William Tisdall (1669–1735), vicar of Belfast and rector of Drumcree, Co. Armagh; a noted high church controversialist (see *DIB*).

him out of Commission, as more fit to put a County into a flame then keep it in quiet and peace. I am not surprised at the Doctors behavior; shew me one prudent or good action of his, and you will inform me of what I am hitherto a stranger to. Our family is very little beholding to that part of it which wears or is related to the Cassock … It is a very melancholy consideration that the people of England continue stil under the influences of a sett of men who alway are for putting things into a flame except they may be the arbitrary managers and disposers of every thing: Will this infatuation never have an end? And yet I am sensible nothing but this could put you under a necessity of doing so unpopular [a] thing as the repealing, or rather enlarging and amending the triennial Act:[552] this was one of those Laws which had a very plausible title and promised good consequences: but sure are considerate men must see that it hath already in a great [part] ruined England, and will not fail to finish the utter destruction [of][553] the Gentry of it if it continue much longer. Yet so popular is that [will] have a great struggle from those who will endeavour to secure their [?own] freinds election in a future Parliament; which end they will I doubt [in a] great measure attain; as I little doubt they will obtain theirs who are for altering that Act. Nothing but an absolute necessity would I think induce our great men to attempt doing it at this time; tho the late rebellion and disaffection may be made use of as grounds for doing it in this juncture: all I can add is to pray and wish you successe in it: for a disappointment after attempting it must be fatal to the last degree. Lord Gowrans horse (as he is called) but that is to blind me who am not to know he belongs to your Nephew) won the great plate and beat the horse of Sir Donogh O'Bryen[554] of whom Mr Hill hath so very great an opinion …

280. *Alan I, Dublin, to Thomas, 10 Apr. 1716*

(1248/3/356–7)

I forbore to trouble you with any account of the import of the last twelve bills which went over, because very few of them need any kind of explanation; the militia bill is a very indigested thing,[555] tho I ought not to say so, since I have no share in the preparing of it: for I was sick and not able to attend when it was gone through and agreed unto by the Committee: soe it will be supposed I am the more inclined to censure where no part of the blame falls to my own share. But the truth is I think it would have been very difficult for a lesse number of the best heads in the Kingdome then attend the Councel or Committees to have brought a thing of that import into such a form that very strong and perhaps just

---

[552]Under the English Triennial Act of 1694 (6 & 7 Will. & Mary, c. 2), the Westminster parliament met annually, with a general election at least every three years. The Septennial Act passed in May 1716 (1 Geo. 1, st. 2, c. 38) extended the maximum period of the life of a parliament to seven years.

[553]Side of MS torn.

[554]Sir Donough O'Brien (1642–1717), 1st Bt, of Dromoland, Co. Clare, MP [I] 1692–1714.

[555]A bill 'to make the militia of this kingdom more useful', prepared in the Irish house of commons and transmitted to the British privy council in April (ILD). Controversial because it allowed a degree of exemption to protestant dissenters from the penalties of the sacramental test, it was the subject of considerable debate in parliament and privy council in Dublin, but eventually passed into law as 2 Geo. I, c. 9 [I]. For the debates over the bill, see Neal Garnham, *The Militia in Eighteenth-century Ireland: In Defence of the Protestant Ascendancy* (Woodbridge, 2012), 26–31.

objections would not have been made against it: and to tell you the truth, I observe the number of Cooks with us generally spoil the broth. When it comes back, as I beleive it will, there will be a good deal of struggle about the passing it as I apprehend: for I am certain a very great majority of both houses are for a militia bill, yet when they hear such objections as I fear will be against it I mightily doubt what the fate of the bill will be. No doubt it is a very desirable thing to have the Protestants armed and regimented so as to be able to do service in case of intestine commotions or foreign invasions: but then say those who are not fond of having a militia, where will your charge end: Your establishment as it now stands is $£408707=19=1\frac{3}{4}$ a year. There have been several regiments raised since which encreases the charge; but they do not say nor can I tell how much; but I think the addicional regiments are six and then computing the yearly pay of a regiment at $7868=15=10$ which is the rate they are computed at in the establishment, the addicion will be more then $£46000$ per annum: if then our hereditary revenue and addicional dutyes will not support the establishment, how shal we make paiment of the $£50000$ which our Lords Justices, upon the vote of credit and clause in our last money bill have taken up as necessary to carry on the publick affairs? Must we not of necessity fall into a Land tax? And how great the additional charge may be to support our militia, if the bill passes which empowers our Deputy Governors and Commissioners of array to levy money on the countrey for that occasion no body can tell. Do not imagine I am now arguing against the bill: the Commons seem inclined to delegate their inherent right of levying money, with very little limitation or restriction; it is true the Act is to be only temporary, but really I almost dread the consequences of it. I wish some of our Commons had either more knowledge or lesse opinion of their own sufficiency; but such precipitate steps as have been taken by them in some instances I do not remember to have observed before: and I do confesse I think there are people in the world who care not what becomes of this poor Kingdome, if the present end be answered. If you or any body else appears warm against this bill, it will be construed disaffection; but in troth as the bill is framed, our militia may with a little addresse be turned so far into an Army that what we maintain as such may hereafter be drawn out of the Kingdome and be maintained out of our revenue. The bill for easing the subject in paying their quitrents takes nothing from the Crown which it ought to have,[556] but gives a more easy and lesse chargeable way to the subject to prevent the Crowns receiving the quitrent of the same denomination of Land twice, by reason it hath been twice granted or decreed to different persons. The bill to prevent abuses in his Majestyes revenue was drawn by the Sollicitor General who as Recorder of Dublin is very much under the direction of his voters,[557] great part of which are men who make or deal in Irish stuffs and half silks: now these people promise to themselves great advantages in their manufacture if they can obstruct the importation of Calicoes and East India goods and those made in Persia or China: and beleive (what is most true) that the running the dutyes of those fine goods occasions the importation of greater quantityes of them then would come otherwise into

---

[556] The bill 'For the ease of his majesty's subjects in their paying of quit rents, crown rents and composition rents' was rejected in the British privy council (ILD).

[557] The bill 'for preventing abuses and deceits in his majesty's revenue by the fraudulent importing of Indian goods and wrought silks', which also dealt with importing brandy, and reached the statute book as 2 Geo. I, c. 18 [I] (ILD). John Rogerson, MP [I], had been appointed solicitor-general [I] in Dec. 1714, having been elected as recorder earlier in the year.

the Kingdome: and this bill they think will make the running the duty of such goods impracticable. The Commissioners of the revenue will never be backward in promoting what may increase their power and the revenue; and Mr Sollicitor at the same time made his Court at the Custom house and on the Combe.[558]

It will not be worth your notice if I should subjoin what the other bills import; yet the clause of credit in the bill for continuing the additional dutyes from 21 May 1716 to 21 Nov. 1717 is considerable: It takes notice of a vote of credit, and enacts that an interest of £8 per Cent shal be paid out of the funds given this Parliament to such persons as shal advance money for the necessary uses of the Governement. I formerly told you I had the subscription paper handed to me, and subscribed £1000; but had the mortification to be able to write only a fifth part of Mr Speakers offering: And the Duke of Grafton tendred the paper to your Nephew who also wrote for £1000 but I have been forced to pay the money. It was an odd ill natured thing in Jos[hua] Allen on a day of adjournment to move the house to sit and pay the debt already contracted, for fear of farther use being made of the vote of credit, which I think he needed not to apprehend: but he added that they were in the right who borrowed at £6 per Cent and lent at £8. I must tell you that I beleive the forming a new establishment is now under consideration, with a view I suppose to lay aside some few unnecessary branches; those of Lord Ormonds pencion and prisage will I hope fall of course,[559] but I think there are others for which nothing can be said. I wish no new ones come on: for the late addicion of 4d a day to a trooper and 2d to a dragoon will be a whipping new load upon us.

281. *Thomas to Alan I, 10 Apr. 1716*

(1248/3/358–9)

I have yours of the 30th of March, and the others of older dates, the last came on Saturday, the others the middle of the weeke; I take the opurtunity of writing this before my going to the house, and may probably bee to adde to itt in the evening, the Secretary[560] having yesterday told mee hee would this day appoint a time when hee might agree upon a leisure hour or two for talking over the matter of the bills, which now lye before a Committee of Councill, butt are none of them (as yett) referrd to the Attorney.[561] Tis very possible (perhaps probable) the offer might have been made to the person you mention, if soe, youl easily beleive with intent to gett rid of him, since hee proves very intractable; by the measures hee has taken tis evident hee has veiwes of a higher nature, wherein I thinke hee will faile, for there is very ill blood between them. I will take the first convenient opurtunity

---

[558] The Coombe, in the Dublin Liberties, the centre of the city's weaving manufacture.

[559] Edward III had granted the Ormond Butlers the right to a tenth of all wines imported into Ireland (the prisage), which the 2nd duke had leased back to the crown for an annual rent of £3,500, an arrangement due to expire in 1732 (*CTB*, ix, 708; xvi, 44, 1005; BL, Add. MS 61637E). On 10 July 1713 Ormond had also been granted a pension of £5,000 a year for 15 years on the Irish civil list, in recognition of his military service (*CTB*, xxvii, 281).

[560] James Stanhope.

[561] The practice in the British privy council, as established by an order of 9 Sept. 1715, was for Irish bills to be referred to a committee which received reports from the British attorney- and solicitor-general recommending action to be taken (James Kelly, *Poynings Law and the Making of Law in Ireland, 1660–1800* (Dublin, 2007), 177–8).

uppon the subject of your long letter, chiefly for that itt is soe perticular, for in the maine that businesse is understood; I am sorry you gave into the writing that which you inclosed to mee, which I shall make noe other use of, then to lay by, against any time when the writer may change his note, for notwithstanding the opinion you have of his sincerity, I can by noe means bee of that mind; to speake plainly, I attribute his present complaisance to the sence hee has of his late way of managing being disapproved. An enemy would nott wish his character lower, or other then tis. Last night I waited on Lord — whoe seemd a little surprizd att your having seen his letter, butt recovered himselfe soone, soe far, as to tell mee I might name him if I found itt necessary, which hee beleivd I should nott, for that the person hee spoake of (whom hee named to mee) would certainly open himselfe to mee, in case any thing stuck; hee told mee all (I beleive) which passed between them, from whence I infer his manner of writing stronger then well grounded; of this I shall bee able to give you a better accountt in a little time: I have likewise talkt with Mr P[ulteney] whoe has nott the least inclination to part with what you mention, butt on the contrary is determined against itt.[562]

The Bill for altering the Triennial act into continuance for seven years will (as I told you) begin with the Lords where twill bee movd on Thursday.

I thinke our session will nott bee soe long as was expected, the king (as I hear) determining to goe to Hannover, and tis now sayd the Prince will accompany him. Some doubts have arisen uppon the words of nott going into forreigne parts without consent of parliament whither any thing lesse then an act is such consent or nott,[563] this sitts hard and is nott easily digested; indeed I doe nott see the force of the affirmative part of the question which is founded on this maxim, that nothing can bee sayd to bee done by parliament butt what is reduced into an Act with the consent of all three estates.

The Secretary[564] delivered some papers this morning, and left the house immediately after itt, which a little surprizd mee, till I found that the Bill which was intended (as I told you before) for Thursday was last night agreed to bee offered this day.

Twas soe by the D[uke] of Devonsheer,[565] after itts being received and a motion for reading, a debate arose wherein none spoake to the Bill itt selfe, butt argued that a Bill of such consequence ought to lye on the table to bee perused, for that possibly itt might bee of such a nature as nott to bee fitt to give a second reading to, butt after several speeches made twas without division read, and ordered a second on Saturday, gaining time (in order to peticions against itt) I take to have been the drift of the opposition.

A noble Lord (secretary of state when king Will[iam] refused the triennial Bill, and whoe then advisd soe doing) was the first whoe now opposd this.[566]

[562]See above, pp. 125–6.

[563]According to the Act of Settlement of 1701 (12 & 13 Will. III, c. 2), 'no person who shall hereafter come to the possession of this crown, shall go out of the dominions of England, Scotland, or Ireland, without the consent of parliament'.

[564]This occurred on 9 Apr., and the secretary concerned was James Stanhope. The papers related to the palatines (*CJ*, xviii, 416).

[565]William Cavendish (1672–1729), 2nd duke of Devonshire, presented the Septennial Bill to the Lords on 10 Apr. (*LJ*, xx, 325). His speech is given in Cobbett, *Parl. Hist.*, vii, cols 292–5.

[566]Nottingham (Cobbett, *Parl. Hist.*, vii, col. 295). King William had used the royal veto to prevent the passage of the Triennial Bill in 1693. Nottingham, then one of the secretaries of state, had spoken against the

As I satt in the house I overheard (purely by accident) a discourse between two of the long robe, which I hearkened attentively to, one of them saying twould bee before the Chancellor of Ireland, after they had done. I askt him, (being my acquaintance[)] what the case was which hee sayd was before you, hee told mee twas between one o Hara and another whose name I have forgott,[567] that Lord Harcourt[568] had graunted a writ of Ne exeat[569] against O Hara, which Lord Cooper discharged[570] beleiving from his answer that twas a hardship uppon him, butt that uppon hearing the cause such villany and perjury appeard in the answer that hee decreed against him, the benefitt of which the other party has lost by his being gone for Ireland, where the matter must bee all gone over againe, I thought mentioning this necessary, that you may bee the more circumspect, for hee represented the thing soe foule, as that itt had given Lord Cooper some uneasinesse for having acted the compassionate part for one whoe appeard such a villaine …

282. Alan I, Dublin, to Thomas, 12 Apr. 1716

(1248/3/360–1)

I intend to make one particular businesse the subject of this letter, and to send it by the post; notwithstanding I might put it on board the Pembroke[571] which sails this morning with Lord Gowran and other company directly for Chester, who will carry you another of the same date: but his time of being on the road is uncertain, and considering all things do beleive the packett boat and post will be the speedyest conveyance, which is a thing the subject I write upon requires. You must be sensible the death of the Archbishop of Tuam[572] hath put our Preists on making interest who shal succeed him, and in case of a translation, how the other See or Sees which may become vacant shal be filled. No body will be more busy on your side of the water then he of whom I long since gave this caution;[573] not too far to go into his recommendations whose design was to bring the Clergy to depend upon him as being at the head of them; and that use he did, doth, and will make while his recommendations take place: If the King resolves to have the Clergy see he distinguishes between men that were alway for his interests and have appeared and will shew themselves zealous, not indifferent and cool, in supporting him and his ministry; the method seems to me to be this, to consider the persons recommended by the Governement, and not to suffer a private application to one or more Bishops in England take place; which will be alway in favor of high Church men; for such our recommenders are, tho they may wish

[566] *(continued)* bill in the house of lords (Henry Horwitz, *Revolution Politicks: The Career of Daniel Finch, Second Earl of Nottingham, 1647–1730* (Cambridge, 1968), 140; *HL 1660–1715*, ii. 989).

[567] *Charles O'Hara v. Henry Neville* (*The Appellant's Case. Charles O Hara Gent. Appellant. Henry Nevill Esqr; Respondent* … [?1717]).

[568] Lord chancellor [GB] 1713–14.

[569] Restraining an individual from leaving the jurisdiction of the court.

[570] Lord Chancellor Cowper.

[571] One of the Holyhead packet-boats (George Ayres, *History of the Mail Routes to Ireland until 1850* … (n.p., 2017), 20).

[572] John Vesey died on 28 Mar. 1716.

[573] Archbishop King of Dublin.

well to his Majestye: but if it be understood they do so to the present ministry, you are the most imposed upon that can be. Their scheme is to me pretty like Mahomets vision of a beast with two horns, one made of fire, the other of Ice.[574] They would have an high Church ministry, army, and Clergy to support his interests whom the high Church hath been supplanting from the hour the bill of succession took place: they cannot with patience hear of the dissenters having opposed or being inclined to oppose the Pretender; or that his favourers in Britain are the party which seems to be most sollicitous for the Church as we have learned to cant. You will know I cheifly mean the Archbishop of D[*ublin*] whose power is already great enough among the Priests; and you will find by the account I gave you of the proceedings on the bill not long since before us, that we were given to understand some people knew their own power and interest; and as I have already told which way they then used it, your own reason will convince you that it will never fail to be used the same way: to offer one proof of this, I can assure you his Grace was one who thought there was a good deal in the Primates and Bishop of Downes memorial: and after I had shewn him the report of the Grand Jury of Antrim and expressed an abhorrence of the proceedings to lay such an imputation on the administration of affairs here, I could not obtain a word from him owning the complaint groundlesse. Whenever any of the dissenters are named, he is no longer under the conduct of judgement or temper. To come now to the Bishoprick of Tuam: I think Dr Synge Bishop of Rapho[575] is the person recommended by the Justices, and the Bishop of Kilaloo (Forster)[576] to succeed him; and Mr Charles Carre to succeed the Bishop of Kilaloo. It will not be worth the Bishop of Bangors while to take Tuam instead of Meath;[577] for tho I think the wardenship of Galway will appear to be in the gift of the Crown, and I beleive is intended to go with the Archbishoprick, yet I am perswaded the corporation of Galway will contest the right of the Crown, for they pretend to choose whom they think fit by vertue of old Charters and not to be confined to the person nominated by the Crown as their last Charter in King Charles the seconds time runs: beside this it is plain, if the wardenship of Galway be in the gift of the Crown and is to go with the Bishoprick of Tuam as was certainly intended by a patent to that effect in King Charles the seconds time, the same patent shews the consideration of the grant and inducement of the Kings annexing the wardenship etc was the Archbishops conveying or settling the *quarta pars Episcopalii* (as it is called) or fourth part of the tythes of all the livings in that diocese on the ministers, which time out of mind hath been held and enjoyed by the Bishops in right of their See.[578] Now this will be such a lessening of the revenue that Meath will be preferable in point of profit greatly: If the Bishop of Bangor

---

[574]Habib, the angel encountered by the prophet Muhammad during his night journey, a being composed of ice and fire.

[575]Edward Synge.

[576]Nicholas Forster.

[577]John Evans (see below, Appendix 3).

[578]The wardenship was created in the late 15th century, when St Nicholas's church in Galway was raised to collegiate status. The city and some adjacent parishes were then removed from the diocese of Tuam and made into a college of vicars, the head of which was the warden, originally elected at first from among the vicars by the borough corporation but subsequently appointed by the crown. Charles II's charter to the borough corporation, dated 14 Aug. 1677, is printed in James Hardiman, *The History of the Town and County of the Town, of Galway …* (Dublin, 1820), Appendix, xliii–liv. In 1684, on a vacancy in the wardenship, the king united the wardenship to the bishopric *in perpetuo*, but allotted the fourth part of the tithes (the *quarta pars*), normally reserved for the bishop, to the vicars. The warden was still elected annually. John Vesey, who was frequently elected warden while archbishop

shal refuse to come into a scheme to this purpose, he will open the mouths of the Clergy of the Diocese and of abundance more against him: Whereas I think the Bishop of Rapho will be no loser by the exchange tho he should go into the methods proper to settle those portions of tythes on the Clergy, which cannot be done but by act of Parliament; and I find whoever succeeds in that See, an attempt will be made to attain an Act of Parliament to this purpose. These are some of the reasons which make me beleive the Bishop of Bangor will not be fond of the thing; tho I find Mr Manly talked of him, which Gentleman interposes in almost everything which lies in the disposal of the Governement here,[579] and is one of those who think Ireland is to be ruled intirely according to the good liking of those who have no interest in and little regard for the welfare of the Countrey. Upon this intended remove he was very pressing for Dean Loyde[580] to be promoted to Kilaloo: I wish that Gentleman well: but Mr Carre is troubled with no whimsyes; he is a man of good life, hath been twenty years a parish minister, constantly resident, hath a great many children; stands recommended by the house of Commons to which he is Chaplain: In short he is that man who in convocation, Parliament, every where, will support the true Protestant interest and endeavour to influence every man over whom he may have the least power to come to a right mind and to bring us to the temper we were of in eighty eight:[581] and assure your self till men of this sort are preferred, and distinguished; Toryism will not only not be suppressed in Ireland but[582]

283. *Thomas to Alan I, Dublin, 14 Apr. 1716*

(1248/3/362–3)

The Bill for enlarging the time of continuance of this present and future Parliament was this day (according to order) read a second time in the Lords house, and all the Peers summoned.[583]

The debate uppon the question of Committal lasted seven hours; uppon a division Contents seventy seven Nott Contents forty three;[584] I stood during the whole debate which has almost killd mee, butt leave itt, I could nott.[585]

---

[578] (*continued*) of Tuam, had persuaded the vicars to allow him to enjoy the *quarta pars* during his tenure of the diocese (R.J. Kelly, 'The Wardenship of Galway', *Journal of the Galway Archaeological and Historical Society*, vi (1909), 119).

[579] Isaac Manley, MP [I].

[580] Owen Lloyd, dean of Connor. For an example of Manley involving himself in matters of ecclesiastical preferment see Wake, Epist. xii: Manley to [Archbishop Wake], 5 Dec. 1716. In particular, he continued to push Lloyd's claims (Wake, Epist. xii: Manley to [Wake], 1 Feb. 1716/17).

[581] Charles Carr, *A Sermon Preach'd Before the Honourable House of Commons, at St Andrew's-Church, Dublin, January the 30th, 1715/16* (Dublin, 1716) had included a forthright denunciation of the iniquities of the tory administration in Ireland, 1710–14 (pp. 14–16).

[582] Last portion of letter missing.

[583] The Septennial Bill had been brought up from the Commons the previous day and after the first reading, proceedings had been adjourned to the 14th, with an order that all lords in and about London be present (*LJ*, xx, 329; Boyer, *Political State*, xi, 431).

[584] Boyer, *Political State*, xi, 433, listed 24 speakers in the debate. See also Ebenezer Timberland, *The History and Proceedings of the House of Lords from the Restoration in 1660 to the Present Time* … (8 vols, 1742), iii, 29–39, which confirms the figures for the division, as far as concerned those lords present: there were in addition 19 proxies for the contents, and 18 for the not contents.

[585] Before the vote the House was cleared of strangers (*LJ*, xx, 331).

I found att home your long letter of the 5th for which I thanke you, I read itt before I sate, and will answer itt next post.

The Princesse[586] was in the house all the time, twill bee carryed in our house by above 100.

The Irish Bills have nott yett been gon uppon in the Committee of Councill, nor will (as I beleive) till the latter end of next weeke.

Mr Walpole recovers apace, butt I fear Lady Sunderlands condition is very dangerous.[587]

Lord Torrington has given his whole estate of about £5000 per annum to Lord Lincolne, though hee had several near relations, purely on accountt of his steddy adhering to his Principles, notwithstanding the many temptations of the last ministry.[588]

284. *Alan I, Dublin, to Thomas, 16 Apr. 1716*

(1248/3/364–5)

You seem very much to mistake my meaning in your letter of the tenth, when you tell me you are sorry I gave in to the writing of the letter which mine of the 30th of March inclosed: the matter was thus. I expostulated with great resentment the unjust treatment I had mett from some people on this side the water by doing me ill offices and misrepresenting me on the other, and took the freedome to say I had served too faithfully and usefully to meet such a return, as I had mett with: that what had come to the notice of the ministry and had weight with any of them must receive its rise from some in power or confidence here: who could not in justice say that I had ever disserved the King, or declined to serve him with zeal in every instance, and must be obliged to add that my advice had been given with great freedome and readinesse and when it took place proved successeful: as on the other hand, when other measures were judged more proper my respect to the Governement and my modesty told me I ought to acquiesce in their determination with whom his Majesty had intrusted the Governement and to assist them in succeeding in what they judged fit for the publick; yet stil with reserve to my own reputation, who having told my freinds of the house of Commons (after the thing was accepted and agreed to by the Lords Justices) that if they would come roundly into two years addicional dutyes and not publickly find fault with the establishment, I should not presse them to more; which they promised; and when farther demands were made I told the Justices the scituation I was in and added I must be only passive and neuter and those farther demands must be supported by others with their freinds, since not only my judgement was against making them least doing it might put Gentlemen on canvassing and ruffling the establishment; but my word was passed that I would not presse them farther. And indeed it was with a good deal of care and temper that the establishment was defended from being fallen on by some whom this farther demand had much provoked and incensed. This discourse was before the Justices[589] in the presence of the writer of the

---

[586] Caroline, princess of Wales. Her presence at the debate is confirmed in *Diary of Countess Cowper*, 104.

[587] Anne Spencer (née Churchill), countess of Sunderland, died on 15 Apr. 1716.

[588] Arthur Herbert (c.1648–1716), 1st earl of Torrington, died on 14 Apr. 1716, leaving his estate to Henry Clinton (1686–1728), 7th earl of Lincoln, in preference to the heir-at-law, 'whom he hated', because of Lincoln's 'public virtue' and to remedy the earl's relative poverty (*HL 1660–1715*, ii, 627; iii, 302–3).

[589] The lords justices.

letter;[590] the former owned what I said to be true, and expressed readinesse to do me right
when there should be occasion: I told them I knew not to whom the misrepresentation
had been sent, any more then to what person I owed the favor of being traduced; but that
I beleived the ministry conferred with one another and that I thought it a justice due to
me, when I was wounded in the dark, to have right done me; and added that I thought the
part I had acted in the former part of the Session had shewn that any little opposition given
by Senny, which all proceeded from treatment which he had mett and thought injurious
and provoking could not be imputed to me: This also was allowed; I then proceeded to
mention what you had told me that I was represented to have acted in concert with Lord
Abercorne in bringing in the bill for securitye of the Kings person and shewed how I had
exposed as well as opposed his Lordships project, and that the delay the Commons bill mett
at the Committee proceeded not from me, and added that I had a great share in its passing
the Councel when I discovered here that the doing soe was desirable; not that I then did
or now do beleive it will passe into a Law. This part of my conduct was owned and I had
the gratification to be told that as my behavior during the former part of the Session had
been justly represented and with advantage to me, so also should my acting in this if there
should be occasion: I said that it was a peice of justice that I should be indebted for. Then
the writer said a good deal in my favor, made all imaginable protestations of having neither
been privy to or concerned in any character to my disadvantage and expressed a resolution
of doing me justice upon every occasion: I had formerly upon a like declaration said I
should not want his character; and contented my self at this time to say that I expected no
more then to have my actions putt in a true light. From this conversation I suppose it was
that the part of his letter which seems to insinuate that he wrote at my desire arose; and
the only reason I had to send you the letter was to enable you to confront any indirect
practice by him or with his privity to my prejudice. I beleive him now to be in earnest
not to do me ill offices, and I think it proceeds from no other motive but his sense that
attacking me will not be servicable to him, his freinds, or his Master. In short he governs,
and they who are his subordinate powers are the Speaker,[591] Cheif Justice,[592] Mr Manly,[593]
and his brother D—y:[594] people are far from being content, and the countrey in a very ill
way. If I am not much mistaken, land is now in true judgement not worth as much by three
years purchase as it was on the day he landed: this I could explain to you and convince
you of, but the compasse of this letter will not allow it. I am sorry Mr Pulteney hath taken
up the resolution you mention;[595] depend on it I am very circumspect in all things which
come before me and will be particularly so in whatever may relate to the person whom
you expresse to have some uneasinesse for having taken up too good an opinion of O'Hara;
tho by what you write I conceive he did neither more nor lesse then he ought. I find since
the Judges return from the County of Antrim that the houses of the two Clergymen in the

[590] Martin Bladen.
[591] William Conolly.
[592] William Whitshed.
[593] Isaac Manley, MP [I].
[594] Bladen's fellow secretary Charles Delafaye.
[595] See above, p. 125–6.

County of Antrim were those of Mr Martin and of one Faning;[596] but that the house of Ballentoy tho the inheritance of a Clergymen was not looked on [*as*] his but his brothers dwelling house, being set to him.[597]

You will think what follows to be very trivial and impertinent; and indeed I think the dispute to be much so; but since it is come before me in nature of a formal complaint of an injury, and that by writing under the hands of the most considerable Justices of peace of the County of Downe I would not disoblige them in not taking notice of it; nor draw the resentment of them and in consequence of other Justices of peace who are not Clergymen on me on the one hand, or of the Clergy on the other: the doing what is right is in this and all other Cases the best course to be taken. The Complaint is that tho the persons complaining are all Elder Justices of peace then Dean Lambert[598] yet the Clerk of the Hanaper hath put his name before theirs,[599] which they desire may be rectifyed and that they may stand in order according to the seniority of their Commissions; place and precedency being first given to Lords and Privy Councellors: The Clerk pretends Deans have usually had such precedency; perhaps this may have crept in when the Seal was in the Keeping of a Clergymen. I have read somewhere that Doctors of divinity take place after Knights: pray inform me how the course is in England: are not Knights, Deans, or Doctors in Divinity (tho later Justices) put in the Commission before other Justices of peace who are only Esquires.

285. *Thomas to Alan I, Dublin, 17 Apr. 1716*

(1248/3/366–7)

Last post I ownd the receipt of yours of the fifth, this morning came that of the 10th. That the gentleman you mention corresponds constantly with the — I very well know, butt hee is too much on the reserve to have any thing pickt out of him, soe that I have onely to guesse. Butt I thinke you may bee very certaine that another whose thirst after gaine is insatiable has taken (by other hands) every opertunity of prejudicing you as far as hee can, which (if I mistake nott) is of little significancy. Your advising the letter to the judges of Assize being soe perticular as to the facts to bee enquired of, in relation to the memorial of the Pr[*imate*] and Bishop of D[*own*] was certainely right, and the Cheif justice of the Com[*mon*] Pleas being ordered to attend that examination was certainly soe, I beleive this matter will bee of good use hereafter. I must now acquaint you with what you probably know before this time, butt since itt possibly may nott have come to your knowledge, twill be better to overdoe then have you in the darke uppon supposition of your knowing itt. The A[*rch*] B[*isho*]p

---

[596] Geoffrey Fanning (c.1683–1751), of Benvarden, Co. Antrim, subsequently rector of Banagher and vicar of Dungiven in the diocese of Derry (J.B. Leslie, *Derry Clergy and Parishes* … (Enniskillen, 1937), 119; *Report of the Judges of Assize … upon a Memorial*, 5).

[597] Alexander Stewart resided at Ballentoy House, but on a lease from his brother Archibald, the rector of nearby Ramoan parish (*Report of the Judges of Assize … upon a Memorial*, 20).

[598] Ralph Lambert, dean of Down, and later bishop of Meath and Dromore (see Appendix 3).

[599] Sir Thomas Domvile (c.1650–1721), 1st Bt, of Templeogue, Co. Dublin, MP [I] Mullingar 1692–3. As clerk of the crown and hanaper in the Irish chancery his duties included making out and engrossing all commissions of the peace.

of Dublin writes that the A[*rch*]B[*isho*]prick of Tuam would bee what might reasonably bee accepted by any Bishop of Ireland whoe would reside within his Province, and whoe thereby would bee gainer in point of interest, upon which the Bishop of Cloghir (att Mr Molineux's motion as I have heard[600]) was thought on, and accordingly an offer made, and his answer expected, which I am told (by some whoe should know) tis hoped hee will nott accept of; Dr Sterne was intended to succeed him,[601] and a gentleman from hence the latter; whither upon the Bishop of C[*logher's*] refusal (should that bee the case) this scheme will hold I know nott, for perhaps the Lords justices recommendation may have some weight, as indeed (generally speaking) that of a Government ought, butt att present perhaps as little as has been usuall. You may bee sure ile immediately enquire, and doe all in my power for Mr Cars service, whoe deserves soe very well.

Yesterday the Lords in a Committee spent four hours in hearing what had been sayd over and over againe on Saturday against the Bill for prolonging etc which my last mencioned,[602] after which the blanck was filld with the word (seven). Twas this day reported, ordered to bee ingrosed, and to bee read tomorrow, all the Lords to bee summoned; uppon filling the Bla[*n*]ck 74 Contents 39 nott contents.[603]

286. *Thomas to Alan I, Dublin, 19 Apr. 1716*

(1248/3/368–9)

I was very ill whilst I was last writing to you, in an hour I fell into a terrible fitt of the stone and cholick, which necessitated the immediate taking a strong purge, which workt all night, and I thanke God has taken of the exquisite torment, though I cannott say the paine is gon quite of.

The Lords yesterday debated the ingrosed Bill, having resolvd to dispute every inch of ground; upon the question of passing contents 73 Not Con[*tents*] 39.[604] Twas this day brought to us, which carryed mee to the house, though ill able to bear itt.

The Toryes for a little time debated the reading itt, butt gave up that question without division, nott being allowd by the rules of the house to enter into the nature of the Bill (till read) farther then the title.[605] The second reading was strenuously opposd, and a division demanded by Sir W[*illia*]m Whitlock,[606] contrary to the opinion of the leaders of the party. Yeas 276. Noes 156. five Toryes with the majority, twenty four whigs with the minority.[607]

---

[600] Samuel Molyneux.

[601] John Stearne, bishop of Dromore.

[602] The Septennial Bill was discussed in a committee of the whole House, the report from which was ordered to be made the next day (*LJ*, xx, 333).

[603] Confirmed in Timberland, *Lords Proceedings*, iii, 41.

[604] Timberland, *Lords Proceedings*, iii, 4, records the division as 69–36, figures confirmed in Sainty and Dewar, *Divisions*, microfiche.

[605] According to Boyer, *Political State*, xi, 457, Heneage Finch, Lord Guernsey, had moved that the bill be rejected without being read.

[606] Sir William Whit(e)lock(e) (1636–1717), of Phyllis Court, Henley, Oxon.; MP [GB] Oxford University.

[607] Figures confirmed in *CJ*, xviii, 425.

Your Bills are referd to the Attorney and will be dispatcht assoone as possible. I forgott in my last to mention the great rott of sheep, which will raise the price of wool if there bee any demand abroad.

287. *Thomas to Alan I, 26 Apr. 1716*

(1248/3/370–1)

I could nott write by last post, itt being past eleven when I gott home, after a debate of above ten hours on the bill for enlarging the continuance of parliament the house divided on the question of Committal Yeas 284 Noes 162.[608]

The first two hours was spent by those (whoe during that time) spoake against the Bill in saying (almost verbatim) what had been before argued in the Lords house; (where as many of us as could find room were allowd to bee) and the remainder of that long day was spent in repetition on their side, and consequently must bee soe in great measure by those whoe answered them. Mr Hutchisson[609] spoake an hour and ten minutes against the bill, on the popular Topicks of constitution liberty etc. butt such was my dulnesse that I could nott perceive any one proposition provd, or indeed (which was more extraordinary) any one consequence well deduced. Sir Thomas Hanmer spoake long on the same side, his oratory very good, his manner very civill, and entirely void of offence, except in one perticular which might bee construed an oblique reflection on the kings designe by the longer continuance etc. butt his whole speech was in a manner declamatory, tickled the ears, without convincing the understanding, Twas observable that the Prince whoe till hee had begun speaking (att past eight) satt with great attention from the beginning of the debate, rose up, and left the house. Mr Letchmere spoake long, butt void of that spiritt, and that method which hee usually debates with, in short I thought him under great confusion all the time.[610]

The last long speech was Generall Rosse,[611] whoe began att near ten, and was hardly treated by a perpetual noise of calling for the question, and that the house bee cleard, butt hee was quits with them, by going on, and taking as little notice of what they sayd, as they of what hee did.

Those for the Bill had this certaine advantage, that they spoake short, and really (if I am nott very partial) with much greater strenghth of reason then the others. Mr Letchmore did indeed give up the point which all the others had with the greatest vehemency contended for, to witt subversion of the constitution, which they explain to bee, that by vertue thereof

---

[608] Figures confirmed in *CJ*, xviii, 429. Boyer, *Political State*, xi, 459, reported that the debate lasted from about 2 p.m. until nearly 11 p.m., and listed 21 speakers in favour and 19 against.

[609] Archibald Hutcheson (c.1660–1740), of Golden Square, Westminster; MP [GB] Hastings.

[610] Lechmere proposed an instruction for 'the disabling all peers who had pensions from sitting in parliament', which the House rejected (Huntington Library, Stowe MS 57, vol. xiv, 24: James Brydges to Mr Hammond, 26 Apr. 1716).

[611] Hon. Charles Rosse (1667–1732), of Balnagown, Ross-shire, MP [GB] Ross-shire. For his military career, see *HC 1690–1715*, v, 307.

this Triennial Act[612] was as the law of the Medes and Persians nott to bee altered,[613] whereas soone after its being enacted, by a subsequent act the parliament in being att the time of the queens demise was to have continuance six months, although such demise might happen nott above a day or weeke before the expiration of the three years, and in case noe parliament in being the last was to convene, sitt and act as if noe such demise had happened.[614] Twas agreed that this was to bee done onely on a very extraordinary emergency, and the argument carryd noe farther then to prove that on reasons as strong and cogent as the former the like thing might well bee done againe, butt twas certainly a very full answer to several gentleman [*sic*] whoe had wonderfully harangued (and mightily pleased themselves) uppon the notion that whoever satt beyond the three years for which they were elected, became both electors and elected, sitting there by a law of their owne making, which in effect was choosing themselves, and soe far did they goe (as some had done in the Lords house) as to make itt att least a reasonable doubt whither what should bee enacted after the three years expired would nott require confirmation. I have as well as I can recollect told you the utmost strenghth of the argument and cannott possibly have time (nor is itt material) to mention the answers, which I thinke are obvious, much lesse the persons, butt cannott omitt saying that in my opinion, (and I find the Toryes have little to say to the contrary) Sir Jos. Jekill[615] did fully and clearly answer all the objections against the Bill uppon the foote of constitution, grounded on the old custom of annual parliaments with as much learning as clearnesse, after which I thinke hee shewd the necessity of passing this Act from the present scituation of affairs even to demonstration, and concluded with wishing those gent whoe had during the whole debate harp't uppon the word constitution had the same a little more att heart etc.

The Bill was yesterday agreed to in the Com[mons] without amendment reported, and ordered a third reading this morning, soe that I cannott defer going to the house because I thinke itt very probable wee may bee againe enterteind with long harangues. After about three hours debate, wherein noe new argument against the Bill, wee divided; Yeas 264 Noes 121.[616]

I forgott in my last telling you that I had accidentally mett General Sankey in the street, whoe told mee hee had receivd noe letter from you, I had nott then opertunity of talking uppon the subject you wrote, which I did yesterday when hee came to tell mee, hee had sent to every place hee could thinke of, butt found noe letter. When I acquainted him with the substance of what yours told mee you had wrote to him uppon, hee appeard under wonderfull concerne of mind, after having talkt the matter sedately, I cannott say I saw any sufficient reasons against what hee sayd, to witt that time alone could obliterate that sence of his daughters unditifulnesse which now sticks close to him, hee told mee a great many circumstances nott necessary to bee mentioned adding weight to his resentment hee sayd hee had received a letter from Collonel Bladen on the subject which hee had nott answered, butt would certainly have ownd yours had itt come to hand. I beleive when you come over

---

[612]The Triennial Act of 1694 (6 and 7, Will. & Mary, c. 2) limited the life of any parliament to three years.

[613]'The law of the Medes and Persians, which altereth not' (Daniel, 6: 8, 12): the rule that no edict issued by the king of Persia could be subsequently changed.

[614]The Succession to the Crown Act of 1707 (6 Anne, c. 41).

[615]Sir Joseph Jekyll.

[616]Figures confirmed in *CJ*, xviii, 432. According to Boyer, *Political State*, xi, 476, this debate lasted two hours.

you will bee able to doe att least as much in the matter as any other whosoever. After several fruitlesse attempts I gott an oportunity of throughly discoursing uppon the subject of one of your late letters; after having fully spoake to the apparent (already) ill consequences of submitting (as hitherto) to the recommendations of a certaine person, I had the satisfaction of being told with some vehemence, all you have sayd is right, Tis right and must nott bee given into. I thinke likewise I have been able to doe some service to the perticular persons, att least I have done my best. I will in a post or two informe you of the practice in relation to the ridiculous dispute about the precedency of Justices of the peace, and shall then (I thinke) have done every thing you desire, which affords mee a good deal of pleasure, for I am really soe despirited by constant fatigue, that if I doe nott by a little ease of mind and body regaine some strengkth, I must inevitably sinke under the load. I have your letter by Lord Gowran whoe calld this morning to see mee, though I have nott been able to wait on him.

288. *Thomas to Alan I, Dublin, 1 May 1716*

(1248/3/372–3)

I have talkt with my Lord Chancellor[*'s*] secretary[617] whoe tells mee that uppon a renewall of a Commission of the peace, a knight added thereto, is always placed after the Knights whoe were in the preceding commission, and that the like rule is observd with respect to Deans, whoe follow the knts immediately. Nothing material has happend in parliament since my last. The Regent of France makes great professions, and gives Lord Stairs very ample assurances, which a very knowing man (in Holland) ascribes to the vigour of our Parliament. The question (says hee) was whither hee or you should bully best, wherein you have outdon him. You have heard of a tripple alliance on foot between the emperor our king and the states generall.[618] His Imperial Majesty hesitated as to some parts insisted on by us, and seemd pretty stif, wherof the french having notice have proposd one to the Dutch and us, with an overture that the emperor may come in if hee thinks fitt, which will bring the former to a speedyer conclusion, for I am pretty confident that with france will nott bee gon into, beside the war with the Port[619] (now certaine) will very much contribute therto. Your mony bill and five others are ready, the others will follow in a weeke. I beleive our session will end in about a fortnight.

289. *Thomas to Alan I, Dublin, 8 May 1716*

(1248/3/374–5)

I take this opertunity in the speakers chamber of writing because twill bee past the time of sending to the post house before I gett home. I am told that honest Charles Carr's integrity and indisputable charector has carryed him through against a very strong interest.

---

[617] Richard Wollaston (c.1669–1728), of Wormley, Herts., and Whitchurch, Hants, MP [E & GB] 1698–1710 (*HC 1690–1715*, v, 914–16).

[618] The States-General of the United Provinces.

[619] The Sublime Porte, i.e. the Ottoman empire.

The consequence of this must bee the choice of a new Chaplaine for the house of Commons,[620] which tis sayd will lye between Mr Gore[621] and Mr Hort.[622] I was one of those whoe did the best services in my power to the former in Lord Whartons time, how far hee answered what was (I beleive) generally expected you are a better judge then my selfe, having constantly been on the place, whereas I was absent.

This I know that I have mightely been misinformd if hee did soe, butt very much the contrary; for my own part I thinke this is a time when wee are to looke forward in order to putt itt out of the power of mens hurting us, whoe have espoused that interest (when fashionable) which I am sure could have noe other end in veiw (if they considered att all) then what must have provd utterly destructive.

I hope the house of Commons will effectually preserve that reputation, which they have deservedly gaind, I need say noe more, and should nott have wrote in such hast, if I did nott thinke the thing of consequence, for itt will have a very different turne given to itt here, then what gentlemen may att first apprehend, there will bee more inferd from itt then the benefitt which shall accrue to the person chosen.

290. Alan I, Dublin, to Thomas, 8 May 1716

(1248/3/376–7)

I had the favor of yours of the first on Sunday morning, since which time another boat is come in with letters of the third and six of our bills, soe as we shal certainly sit to do businesse on Thursday:[623] in all probability there will happen more warmth in this later part of our Session then the Gentlemen foresaw who at the beginning of it paved the way to peoples being uneasy by very unnecessary and I think impolitick steps. If I considered nothing farther then the treatment I have mett with from some people I should sit down unconcerned if not please my self at the buffets which some Gentlemen may meet with: but when I consider how unfit it is that personal miscarriages of little people should prejudice our publick affairs, and that it will neither be for the honour of the King nor service of the countrey to have any thing fall out which without doors may be looked on as proceeding from distrust of the Governement I resolve to contribute all that lyes in my power to prevent those heats to the raising of which I no way contributed …

291. Thomas to Alan I, Dublin, 10 May 1716

(1248/3/378–9)

… I thinke too many bills are on the anvill to allow our rising before the Hollidays, this day a Bill cheifly taken out of our Popery Act, was read a first time,[624] butt many material

---

[620] The Irish house of commons.

[621] William Gore (1679–1732), archdeacon of Clogher in 1716 and subsequently dean of Clogher and of Down (J.B. Leslie and H.B. Swanzy, *Biographiucal Succession Lists of the Clergy of the Diocese of Down* (Enniskillen, 1936), 21).

[622] Josiah Hort.

[623] Both houses resumed sitting on Thursday, 10 May (*LJI*, ii, 510; *CJI*, iv, 224).

[624] A bill 'for strengthening the protestant interest of this kingdom, by enforcing the laws now in being against papists', presented by Samuel Molyneux (*CJ*, xviii, 440).

parts of ours is left out of this, on supposition that more cannott bee carryd, wherein I differ in opinion. And likewise a Bill to appoint Commissioners of forfeitures, wherein I thinke sufficient powers are given, though nott such as the Trustees had.

On Saturday wee shall have the Bill brought in for farther abridging Priviledge of Parliament youl easily judge these must take up time.[625]

Tis sayd the king is disswaded from going abroad this year ...

292. *Thomas to Alan I, Dublin, 31 May 1716*

(1248/3/382–3)

I returned late this evening from Pepper Hara, where this morning I left all well.

The occasion of my coming to towne was that by letter I was told the king had positively determined going to Hanover, and that in a very few dayes hee would leave us, butt I am just now assured that att present every thing tending to itt is att a full stand, and that this matter appears att least very doubtfull, my freind is of opinion hee will nott goe; I wish itt prove as hee expects, for I really thinke his absence may bee attended with unforeseen consequences, for surely tis from hence that the Jacobites and Papists seem to gather fresh life. I thought itt necessary to tell you thus much, a little time will determine the matter.

293. *Alan I, Dublin, to Thomas, Westminster, 8 June 1716*

(1248/3/384–5)

... If I can gett them time enough from the Clerk I will under this cover send you the votes of the Commons relating to the affair of the City of Dublin, in which ample justice is done to Sir Con.[626] and the late Privy Councel and late Judges, and the Primate very justly comes in for his share; justly I say; for as he was one of the Lords Justices who refused to obey the order of the Lords Regents,[627] so he was at the bottom of the whole management of affairs here toward the end of the late reign, and carryed matters more haughtily and farther then Phipps, if possible; nay I am assured the Duke of Shrewsbury had perswaded the later to some temper, but he took time to advise with his freinds, and the next day the Primate, Phipps and Lord Anglesey would not acquiesce in what even Phipps was content with the night before. Our bill for security of the Kings person is lost in the house of commons; but they have taken a more decent way then to throw it out, by ordering it a second reading

---

[625] A bill to amend the act for preventing inconveniences that may happen because of parliamentary privilege (12 & 13 Will. III, c. 3) (*CJ*, xviii, 445).

[626] Sir Constantine Phipps.

[627] At a meeting of the Irish privy council on 23 Sept. 1714 the lords justices asked the council whether they would comply with the directions of the regents in Westminster to approve a person elected as lord mayor of Dublin by a majority of the aldermen, irrespective of whether that person had been nominated by the sitting lord mayor. However, the privy councillors present, all tories, refused to commit themselves in advance as required (BL, Add. MS 61635, f. 27: council minute, 23 Sept. 1714).

at such a distance of time that it will not passe the houses while the Session continues.[628] The truth is, the whole management of that affair hath been unaccountable: it was thus: Sir Gustavus Hume the Speaker Sir Ralph Gore (I think) Mr Upton[629] and Mr Henry[630] mett at Mr Henrys house and discoursed of altering the bill to prevent the farther growth of Popery in favor of the dissenters: some were for advising with their freinds and considering; but Sir Gustavus was resolved to move it the next day, and did so; very crudely as I have formerly told you: Beside that he is not a rash or precipitate man, you know him to be far from enterprising or fond of framing bills, so that it is looked upon here that he acted by expresse advice or directions: and yet if I may beleive some people, the thing was not communicated to the Governement, at least to one part of it. The steps that affair took in both houses and at the Councel I have in several letters fully informed you; while the heads were under consideration in the house of Commons a clause to oblige people to take an oath that the Pope hath no power Eclesiastical or spiritual etc was on debate thrown out, as obliging the Papists to renounce one principle of their religion; for so it was called and really now is, in so much that whoever will affirm that, can never be owned or received as a member of that Church.[631] The Councel sent the bill hence without it, but so it was ordered on your side of the water that it returned as part of the bill: how this hapned one would willingly know; for I can hardly think it was oversight in the person who caused it to be inserted, who must know it would certainly throw the bill out in the house of Commons where the clause was unanimously rejected when the heads were under the consideration of the Committee of the whole house, if he ever heard what steps it took here. It seems to me very probable that some from this side who were entirely sett against the bill, gave an hint to some freind with you, that putting that clause in the bill, as one great security to the Governement against Irish Papists and consequently likely to passe in England, would infallibly loose the bill: and indeed beside the reason of the thing, such a procedure looks like cramming a thing down mens throats, whether their stomachs will digest it or not. This I say was the handle for laying the bill aside; and indeed that clause was disagreeable to the house in general, as well for the matter of it, as the maner of its coming into the bill: nor were the dissenters fond of the bill, since it gave them much lesse then they desired nay expected: others were as little fond of giving them any thing. Mr Upton speeched at the beginning, and voted against the heads agreed to by the Commons, because it did not repeal the test clause with respect to civil emploiments, and declared nothing would content him but an absolute repeal of the whole: the time also by which people were to qualifye themselves was by the bills being so long kept in England so short that great objection would have been made to it, as I found from several: To say the truth, there would have been a good deal of weight in the objection: and so industrious was the Archbishop of Dublin and some others, that no stone was left unturned to prevent its coming up to the Lords, where my opinion is it would have run a great risque of not passing: When any thing of this or the like nature

---

[628] On 4 June the Commons ordered that the committee of the whole on the bill would stand adjourned for a week, but there was no sitting of the House on the designated day and the committee never resumed its work (*CJI*, iv, 252).

[629] Clotworthy Upton, MP [I].

[630] Hugh Henry, MP [I]. A presbyterian, and a Dublin banker, with offices on Upper Ormond Quay.

[631] The bill 'for the further explaining and amending of several acts of parliament to prevent the further growth of popery' was read and committed on 27 Jan. 1716 but no report was ever made.

comes again under consideration, it ought to be better weighed, and managed in another maner. The Session is near over, and there will be no thing of warmth or uneasinesse; on the 30th of May there was an intent to fall on the establishment of Pensions by way of direct addresse to the King, which would indeed have looked like a representation or rather a remonstrance: but it was prevented; and the vote introductive of it viz. that the hereditary revenue, additional dutyes etc were not sufficient to support the present establishment was laid aside by a question for leaving the Chair.[632] and tho some people who had pretended all along to answer for the house were too stiff to desire it in expresse terms, yet they shewed by their pensivenesse and confusion that they were very uneasy and desirous to have the assistance of those whom they had treated with much distance and little regard before: But I assured <u>one man</u> that people needed be in no pain, for that every thing would be carryed with all duty to the King and respect to the Governement: and tho Gentlemen were angry at some transactions and managements yet they would not go into what would seem to proceed from distrust of the Governement; and I assure you, a good deal of pains was taken to make men a little easy, for there had been wayes taken very unacceptable and disagreeable, which had sowred some very honest men; but they being brought to temper, the matter fell cheifly to the managment of a few little peevish men. The report of the Judges of the North East Circuit relating to the memorial of the Primate and Bishop of Down is now printed here; if it be possible they will bring it into the house of Lords, tho I do not see that they can do themselves any good, or any one else harm by it: but I confesse I am unwilling any thing that may tend to warmth should arise during this very peaceable Session in the Upper house: as for the lower, tho it consists of very honest men generally; the ill order kept there, and want of prudence in those who should foresee the consequences of some of their proceedings, render the house lesse considerable then I could wish. In the City Case you will see some odd resolutions, as naming little people for not having been knaves and not acting dishonestly and contrary to their duty.[633] Add to this their frequent recommendations to pensions, halfpay, and Ecclesiastical preferments, which makes them cheap, and are in my opinion a good deal unparliamentary. The Primate and Bishop of Downe seem to be much humbled. Tell Ally we drank her health on 31 May.[634] I mean Lord Montjoy, Charles Stewart,[635] Bishop Clogher and his son; Mrs Hill and her son, Lady Dun,[636] Mr St George and his wife …

294. *Alan I, Dublin, to Thomas, Westminster, 10 June 1716*

(1248/3/386–7)

I wrote you a long letter by last pacquet and now send you the resolutions of house of Commons on the City Case, which were as well digested as the shortnesse of the time

[632] Not recorded in *CJI*.

[633] The Commons resolutions on 6 June in relation to the Dublin mayoral dispute commended the aldermen and sheriffs (*CJI*, iv, 261–2).

[634] Her birthday.

[635] Charles Stewart, MP [I].

[636] Mary (c.1653–1748), daughter of John Jephson and sister of John Jephson, MP [I]; widow of Sir Patrick Dun (1642–1713), physician and MP [I] (T.W. Belcher, *Memoir of Sir Patrick Dun* … (Dublin, 1866), 38–9).

allowed to those who had a sight of the draught of the report from the Committee before it was made to the house would admit of: for you must know Mr Rogerson our Sollicitor General was in the chair,[637] and tho he is very hearty in the interests of the City and the Protestant interest in opposition to the measures lately taken here; yet he is a very good natured man and hardly brought to doe a severe thing to any body tho never so well deserved: beside he and the late Sollicitor Mr Bernard are marryed to two sisters, the daughters of Stephen Ludlow,[638] and the wife is a furious Tory if not a degree beyond it: and this inclined people to mutter that he delayed making the report in favor of his brother Bernard and other Toryes, to the end things might cool and be forgotten toward the end of the Session. The nature of the Case made the report very long, as you will find when it is printed, being now in the presse: which added to the multiplicity of his businesse as a Lawyer (a matter attended by what he loves extremely money) occasioned the report lying several months before him unfinished, and not any view to lett so great injuryes done the City passe uncensured: tho I cannot but say the order warranted the Committee to report the Case of the City of Dublin, which includes the proceedings against the Sherifs, as well as what relates singly to the Mayoralty; and proof was made of most exorbitant proceedings against the Sherifs, but these are so slightly touched in the report that the Committee came to no resolutions with reference to that matter; in which Frank Bernard was concerned knuckle deep: and here indeed I know not how to say that I doe not beleive he leaned a little. The draught of the report was left with me by Lord Cheif Justice Forster about ten at night under a promise to return it to him the next day by noon, which I accordingly did; but took such notes out of it that furnished me with materials sufficient to point out to a select number which mett in a day or two after what were the most flagrant facts in the report to ground resolutions upon: and accordingly at the first meeting (at which there were present the Speaker the Cheif Justice of the Common Pleas the Attorney and Sollicitor General Mr St George Sir Ralph Gore and I) the six or seven first resolutions were framed to be proposed to the Committee; and at a second meeting (at which the same persons were present except Mr St George and at which the Cheif Justice of the Kings Bench and Cheif Baron were also present) the other resolutions were agreed on. I would not be understood as if there were not a word in any of them altered either in the house or Committee; for I beleive it to be otherwise, but the additions or alterations were I am sure very few and inconsiderable: and it is possible my memory hath not served me to be infallibly certain I have named all the persons who were at either of the meetings right: but I have not designedly omitted any body. We spent fowre or five hours each night when we mett, so that they left not my house till about one in the morning. There were about sixteen negatives to the resolutions in a very full house; the Primate was brought into the vote in the house, so were the Aldermen.[639] Charles Carre was this day consecrated.[640] I

---

[637] The committee inquiring into the proceedings concerning the Dublin mayoral dispute, 1711–14. The solicitor-general [I] (and recorder of Dublin) John Rogerson, MP [I], reported (*CJI*, iv, 256).

[638] Stephen Ludlow, MP [I]. His daughter Elizabeth married John Rogerson; her sister Alice married Francis Bernard, MP [I].

[639] The crucial vote on 6 June took place on the first resolution, condemning Lord Chief Justice Sir Richard Cox for having acted 'partially and corruptly', which passed 133–16. Thereafter successive resolutions against individuals passed without division (*CJI*, iv, 260). A subsequent resolution commended the removal from government of Sir Constantine Phipps and Primate Lindsay (*CJI*, iv, 261).

[640] As bishop of Killaloe.

will soon write at large an account of two votes passed yesterday in each house, and let you into the management on one side and the deep politicks and foresight of our top Politicians in the lower house on the other.

But having I suppose raised your expectations a little by what I have said already I think I ought at least to send you the words of the Votes in both houses. That of the Commons runs thus. Resolved nemine contradicente that communicating heads of bills prepared in this house to the house of Lords for their consideration and concurrence, before they are laid before the Governement in order to their being transmitted to Great Britain will very much facilitate the passing of bills.[641]

That in the Upper house was in the words following

Resolved That communicating heads of bills prepared in this house to the house of Commons for their consideration and concurrence before they are laid before the Governement in order to their being transmitted to Great Britain will very much facilitate the passing of bills.[642]

Do not now apprehend by the nem. con. in the Commons Votes that no body spoke against going into the vote, for both the Attorney Sollicitor and Mr St George did; but when the question was put nobody gave a negative to it; for which I can no otherwise account then that it proceeded from that entire submission which some men pay to the sentiments of a certain Gentleman, who came roundly into it; applauded Mr Ward who moved it, and I think Mr Vesey who seconded it etc nay Mr Maxwel (whom some call the Speakers Eccho) made a long discourse on the side of the question: and to me it seems plain that it was contrived by Ward Vesey and some other Toryes, and by them communicated to your Colleague in the house[643] before the motion was made; who swallowed the bait without discerning the hook under it; the consequences this procedure will occasion are not yet foreseen: how far England will understand this to be aimed at as the foundation of future attempts to alter the maner of our passing bills time must try: but the Commons have already expressed themselves in their discourses and debates, that the Councel boards on each side the water altering the heads of bills sent over (which is an exercising a power the Law hath entrusted them with) is imposing shackles and fetters on them: so saith Mr Singleton another Tory. I beleive your Colleague is sensible he hath overshot himself and regrets his forwardnesse; but thus it will be when men will be at all, tho it relate to matters they know nothing of. Do not you too readily communicate this; for we are so wise to beleive it may be kept a secret; tho the Vote be printed; and that the tendency of it will not be perceived unlesse attended with some farther resolutions which they say they shal be able to prevent: The first part of this is ridiculous, and I think the later part is impossible considering the lengths they have gone along with them already: but your publishing this will look like complaining of, or insulting the management of the persons entirely confided in in the lower house.

A letter (of which this is a duplicate which I send inclosed) goes by this pacquet to Mr Stanhope, but the names of the Commissioners of the seal I do not yet know; as you forward this affair I shal be able to be sooner or later with you; but pray dispatch it, for do what you can it will not be back in lesse then three weeks from this day: Get this alteration in the

---

[641] On 9 June (wording confirmed in *CJI*, iv, 266).

[642] On 9 June (wording confirmed in *LJI*, ii, 529).

[643] Martin Bladen.

letter, (which you find in my hand in the duplicate which I send you, by adding the words which are in my handwriting).

295. *Thomas to Alan I, Dublin, 19 June 1716*

(1248/3/388–9)

Att eight on Saturday night came yours of the 8th and tenth. I overtooke Mr Pringle (under secretary) att the office, by which I hope to bee able to send your order of licence[644] this night, if I can gett itt entred att the Signett Office, Mr Secretary[645] having promised mee yesterday, that hee would this morning lay itt before the king; you ommitted a usuall part of formallity, that of writing to the secretary, which you must excuse by letter, as I have already done on your behalfe.

You will observe a difference in the preamble of the order, from the president which you sent, taken (as I suppose) from Mr Methuens,[646] this nott being any wise material, I should nott mention itt, were itt nott to lett you know that notice is taken by the Lords Justices letter thereof, which I thinke they might have been pleasd rather to have acquainted you with, in order to have had the forme (which they say you layd before them) amended, then to have left that to bee done here, butt I suppose this due to their secretary. I write this in the morning in order to have time to run over your letters, and answer the perticulars.

With what intent the clause enacting the oath to bee taken against the Popes power either Ecclesiasticall or civill, was here added to the Bill, I cannott say, butt am told twas soe, by a noble Lord whoe pretends to a superintendency over the affairs of Ireland, as most knowing (in his own opinion) therein; when the first account came of the Commons refusing that bill, a letter was reade from your side (in my hearing) to our speaker importing that the Commons had unanimously declared they would never passe any bill to which a clause should bee added which had before (on debate) been rejected by them.

The use that might bee made hereof was very obvious, whither the writer had that in veiwe I know nott, nor can I tell whoe hee was; however I thought advisable to say, I beleivd hee either misapprehended the thing, or had ill expressed itt, for that the Commons never did, or ever would reject any bill purely for an addition or alteration made here, as is most evident from their daily passing such, butt that if the reasons subsisted uppon which they had refused admitting such clause, those would probably bee thought sufficient for disapproving the Bill, which I tooke to bee the present case. I doubt whither those whoe went soe roundly into the vote of communicating heads of bills to the Lords will bee able soe well to account for the consequences of itt.

You cannott forgett how often this thing has been attempted by those whoe have had inclination to make the Government uneasy, and with what application twas always defeated.

---

[644] To come to England. The lords justices had written to Secretary Stanhope on 12 June to ask him to move for leave of absence for Alan (TNA, SP 63/374/262: Grafton and Galway to Stanhope, 12 June 1716).

[645] James Stanhope.

[646] John Methuen (c.1649–1706), lord chancellor [I] 1697–1703.

Lord Sunderlands Chaplaine (whoe was like to have provd a very untoward Rival with Car) will bee Bishop, butt nott of Elphin to which Drummore will bee removd; I know him nott personally, butt his charecter is very good.[647]

Wee are just concluding our session, and the kings going fixt for next weeke …

296. *Thomas to Alan I, 23 June 1716*

(1248/3/390–1)

I have att last gott the inclosed letters, I doe nott thinke what you hinted in yours of the 15th very improbable, when you come (which I hope will bee soone) ile tell you whereon I ground my opinion.

Wee shall rise the beginning of the weeke, butt which day, is as yett uncertaine.[648] If I had left your affair to the management of a freind (as I thought I might) I doubt twould have oblidged my returne to towne; tomorrow morning (God willing) I intend for Pepper Hara.

297. *Alan I, Dublin, to Thomas, at his lodgings in Whitehall, 26 Oct. 1716*

(1248/3/392–3)

When you have perused the inclosed you will in a good measure see upon what foot it was that Senny acted in the matter of the sixpences being taken away from the Vice Treasurers.[649] You see he saith he never promised Colonel Moreton[650] and Mr Pratt[651] to vote for the Vice Treasurers, but the later assured me the contrary, which was in great measure the occasion of my writing the letter to Senny to which the inclosed is an answer: and I am apt to beleive he gave farther encouragements to them then he now calls to mind; and the rather because upon my speaking to him upon that head he told me he never could bring himself to speak on their side of the question having been the person who in the last Session proposed and moved the question for taking away the sixpences from the Vice Treasurer; by which I understood him determined to vote with them, and gave Colonel Moreton hopes that he would be so and not hurt him: And I now find by his letter that some popularity and the reproaches of some back freinds[652] during the Session altered his resolutions in that particular; but I must aver he never told me a sillable to that effect (for then I would immediately have acquainted Colonel Moreton of it) tho he now appeals in his letter to his having declared to several Gentlemen that he was early determined to vote

---

[647] Nicolas Clagett (1685/6–1746), later bishop of St David's (Clyve Jones, 'Whigs, Jacobites and Charles Spencer, Third Earl of Sunderland', *EHR*, cix (1994), 65; *Oxf. DNB*).

[648] The session ended on Tuesday, the 26th.

[649] See above, p. 94.

[650] Matthew Ducie Moreton (c.1662–1735), of Moreton, Staffs., MP [GB], appointed vice-treasurer of Ireland in Apr. 1717 (*Lib. Mun.*, pt 2, p. 47).

[651] John Pratt, MP [I], deputy vice-treasurer [I].

[652] False friends.

against the Vice Treasurers having the sixpences: If he had altered his mind and declared it to me, to Colonel Moreton and Captain Pratt, I think he had been very much at liberty notwithstanding his having formerly intended to act otherwise: but for want of his doing so I doubt he hath given too just cause of resentment to two Gentlemen, whom I could have been very glad to have served upon their own account, as well as the freindship that is between them and you: But I perswade my self he hath by this Act subjected me to these Gentlemens displeasure this Session, as he did by another peice of ill conduct in the last to that of the then Governement. Be not too free in shewing the letter for his sake, yet for mine endeavour a little to undeceive them.

298. *Alan I, Chester, to Thomas, at his lodgings in the Privy Garden, Whitehall, 29 Oct. 1716, 11 o'clock a.m.*

(1248/3/394–5)

I am just lighted out of the Coach, after having performed the journey very well, with great ease, and no ill accident: the wind is fresh at East and the Yatch at Parkgate, but under what orders I know not, but hear the Captains orders were to go hence to Bristol for Lady Droghedah,[653] and that he hath wrote to Dublin to gett those orders countermanded. I hear too that there are two letters in town from Ireland for Captain Lawson[654]: and it is possible one of them may be from the Governement to take me in at the Head[655] on Wednesday next: for I wrote to that purpose, but have had no answer. If I were sure that were the case I would go directly to Parkgate and not go to the Head; but since the Captain is at Parkgate and I doe not know whether Mr Allen who hath his letter will open it I must resolve to go forward to Holyhead, and design to lye at Rithland[656] this night, at Bangor tomorrow and on Wednesday to the Head. A lady in mans clothes lay three nights in the Inns I did, viz at Meridon,[657] fowre Crosses[658] and Whitchurch;[659] but my senseless servants never told me of it till I left Whitchurch; She had but one servant, either went out very late, or came in very early, admitted no body to see her undresse etc spoke French etc. I am confident this is the Canterbury Lady; they say she is young and handsome.

299. *Alan I, Dublin, to Thomas, at his lodgings in the Privy Garden, Whitehall, 10 Nov. 1716*

(1248/3/396–7)

I am to acknowledge the favor of yours of the third instant which came to my hands yesterday; that part of it which relates to Arthur Hill I read to his mother, who hath desired

[653] Mary, née Cole (*d*.1726), dowager countess of Drogheda.

[654] Henry Lawson (*d*.1734), captain of the yacht *Dublin* (G.W. Place, 'Parkgate and the Royal Yachts: Passenger Traffic between the North-West and Dublin in the Eighteenth Century', *Transactions of the Historic Society of Lancashire and Cheshire*, cxxxviii (1988), 75).

[655] Holyhead.

[656] Rhuddlan, Denbighs.

[657] Meriden, Warwickshire.

[658] Near Cannock, Staffordshire.

[659] In Shropshire.

me to give you all the acknowledgements of an obliged and grateful woman: I cannot doe it in so good and handsome a maner as she expressed her self: but this I may venture to say, that she receives the favor with as much gratitude, as it was meant by you with kindnesse and freindship. That of Mr Hills travailing I find rather to have been a scheme framed and thought to be advisable by Senny, then any resolution of hers: on the contrary she seemed to me averse to it, as fearing he might by being out of her sight fall into hands which it is not proper for me to name, considering their near relation to her and him: but probably you will soon guesse who the persons are whom I mean. Nor indeed can I say that making the grand Toure (as we have learned to call it) will much conduce to his being an useful man at home: Sennyes reasons seem to me to have been these; that he is now of that age and spirit which must be employed otherwise then staying at home; and unlesse something of that kind be done, he apprehends the young fellow may out of an inclination of putting himself into the way of businesse go into a part of the world where he may and in all likelyhood will be soon undone. Mrs Hill thinks an employment on this side of the water would answer every difficultye and fix him soe as that there would be no apprehension of his being ruined by any body: and indeed he is worth preserving. If Mr Pulteney can be brought by any method to part with the Clerkship of the Councel, it is what his soul is bent upon, what would be a very genteel and handsome entertainment of his time, and an office which he will be able to discharge with sufficiency and ease. I am sensible she will lay out more money to buy it then the thing can possibly be worth; I wish therefore you would either your self or by some other hand sound Mr Pulteney to the bottom in this matter, whether he will on any and what terms part with it: but methinks there is no necessity he should know to whom it is to be till terms are made. He had once actually agreed with Sir Donogh O'Bryens second son[660] for it, and the price was to be (as I have heard) fowre thousand pounds: but the Queens death dashed that project in the head. I would not be so urgent with you but that I find the poor Ladyes heart is so sett upon his getting some place here fit for him to accept, that she can have no peace of mind, till she is free from her fears of his being carryed away from her by reason of his having nothing to do here: and I confesse I could be extremely pleased she owed her successe in it to your kindnesse and endeavours on her behalf. As to that of getting something in England by the way you once hinted to me, Mrs Hill makes this just objection that it takes him from her and puts him into the hands of some from whom she apprehends she hath cause to be very careful and fearful on his behalf: you will guesse [*my*] meaning, and it is possible your Nephew and his children may be sufferers at the same time. In a letter to the Duke of Grafton I tell him I decline writing a little story that is about town directly to him; but that you will tell it to him if he puts you in mind of it. It is this. Some of the intelligencers came very officiously and told a certain person here, that in such a company consisting of about fifteen Gentlemen of figure this health was drunk The Duke of Grafton solus.[661] The old Gentleman would not take the hint but expressed himself with great concern that the Dutchesse was so ill beloved as to occasion so many Gentlemen publickly to express their wishes that she might be left behind. This to the Duke and you only.

---

[660] Henry O'Brien (*d*.1724), of Stonehall, Co. Clare.
[661] The duke of Grafton alone, omitting his fellow lord justice, Galway.

300. *Alan I, Dublin, to Thomas, at his lodgings in Whitehall, 20 Dec. 1716*

(1248/3/398–9)

I am to own the favor of your letters of the 11th and 13th to me, and of that to my wife; for all which I am obliged to you, but in a very particular maner for the handsome and affectionate way in which you treat your sister: she is very sensible of the favor, and I am fully convinced will deserve the esteem and kindnesse of every relation that loves me. The alterations at Court have already given new life to our Grums; for nothing can be more their aversion then the ministry which the King first chose after his accession to the throne; and every alteration, tho for good men, delights them as it is an alteration and certainly removes some whom they zealously hate: but I hope the consequences they hope from this step will not answer their expectations. I doe not very well recollect the discourse which you mention to have passed between a Nobleman and you, unlesse it relate personally to yourself, as I hope it doth. Neither my sister nor you take any notice to me what your thoughts are as to the prudence and advisablenesse of my match with respect to my self and family in general; which I did hope to have had your thoughts upon: for I think it is likely to be of general good to my family and I am sure adds to my reputation as well as increases my happinesse.

301. *Alan I, Dublin, to Thomas, 17 Jan. 1716[/17]*

(1248/3/400–1)

… You will perceive one of the inclosed letters is for the Duke of Grafton, which you will put under a cover and deliver; I am unwilling to beleive him in the matter, yet can hardly beleive it could be done without his privity: and if that be so I must also beleive he was passive at least in wounding me in the dark; yet I am unwilling to beleive so dishonourably of him as to think him capable of doing me wrong by misrepresenting me, or not doing me that right which I have his promises repeatedly to do, and an assurance under his hand of his having done.[662] See and speak freely to him. The other letter is intended for Mr Methuen;[663] I have omitted his title on the top, not knowing the maner of addresse which you will supply. Plainly this is the Act of our managers here, and no doubt of it your colleague[664] is at the bottom of it. I will not say it in expresse terms, but I think I ought to lay down if thus used: This no doubt is an introduction and step to a title for Mr C[onolly]. How far gratifying his pride and ambition will be serviceable to the Crown time will best shew. If I had time I would write by this maile to Lord Townesend and Lord Sunderland, but it will be very difficult how to act toward the former considering the uncertainty whether he will be our Cheif Governor or not: And the misunderstandings between those two great men makes the thing yet more difficult: next boat shal carry letters to them. Advise me whether it may

---

[662] Alan is referring to (unfounded) rumours that he was to be omitted from the commission of lords justices appointed to govern Ireland in the absence of Grafton and Galway. See below, p. 214.

[663] Paul Methuen (c.1672–1757), of Bishops Cannings, Wilts., MP [GB] and sec. of state [GB].

[664] Martin Bladen.

not be proper to gett a licence of absence to wait on the King. If I lay down[665] my late marriage will enable me to live in an handsomer maner than I otherwise should have done, which is but one of the many advantages I have by it, yet I cannot but with greif observe that what is so entirely for my satisfaction and benefit finds not the approbation of those whom I love and who I did beleive wish me well which I apprehend proceeds from their apprehending it may prove prejudicial to my younger children: this I think it will not; but I must at the same time remark that my disconsolate way of life and the melancholy which was the consequence of it seems to have had little consideration in their thoughts which wished the continuance of it rather then an imaginary lessening my childrens fortunes.

302. *Alan I, Dublin, to Thomas, 29 Jan. 1716[/17]*

(1248/3/402–3)

I am to thank you for yours of the 24th: Inclosed I send two letters, either of which you may deliver to my Lord Lieutenant[666] as you see most convenient and burn the other. Your letter which I received this morning gives another date to the letter in the Secretaryes office viz 14 November, whereas your former letter told me it was dated 28 December. Taking your last letter to be right the matter seems capable of being thus accounted for; that about the end of October Lord Galway being ill (as he then was) some notice was sent from this side of the necessity of orders being ready for sealing a Commission to Justices, and probably some pressed it the more then in hopes those persons who should be named in that letter might on another occasion (as for example such as hath now hapned) be the men.[667] Now I not being in Ireland then they may say they did not intend a slight to me, but because I was not on the spot they named others to answer the emergency: and I make no doubt your colleague in the Duke of Graftons absence at Levermere[668] was instrumental in procuring that letter to be signed: for you must know just before I left London I was invited to dine at his house, which I looked on as intended to countenance what would be given out immediately upon it that we were perfectly freinds, or to speak plainer that I had wholly forgott the ill treatment I had met with from the Cabal. Now methinks this use may be made of it to say that when the other three were recommended from this side (as no doubt they were) it proceeded from my being in England and the uncertainty of my time of returning: but that reason now was no longer of force. I would not have a slight put on me, nor throw up in picque: on the other hand I foresee a very troublesome Session, I mean a very difficult one to answer all that may be expected, nay that will be necessary as matters have been managed here of late. When you deliver my Letter to Lord Townesend you will let yourself a little into the affairs of Ireland. I will be very wary in the matter of the proposal of which I will write at large by next post …

---

[665] Resign as lord chancellor [I].

[666] Lord Townshend was officially appointed lord lieutenant on 13 Feb. 1717, but was replaced on 27 Apr. by Charles Powlett (c.1661–1722), 2nd duke of Bolton.

[667] Galway had recovered by early Nov. 1716, by which time the king had decided that no alteration in the government of Ireland was needed (BL, Eg. MS 3124, f. 237: James Stanhope to Lord Townshend, 21 Nov. N.S. 1716).

[668] Livermere Park in Suffolk, not far from Grafton's principal country seat of Euston Hall.

[PS] Since writing this I am told by Mr Campbel[669] that he saw a letter from a certain person intimating that Lord Townesend had been pleased to continue him in the affairs of Ireland; but Senny who went to return the Speaker a visit last night tells me that the Speaker read that part of the letter to him, which implyed no more then that he had hopes of being continued: As for my own part I can only say that I have little prospect of seeing things carryed with that ease to Gentlemen here as were to be wished if the sole author (in effect) of all the misunderstandings be again brought over to act the same part he acted formerly and to triumph over those whom he hath formerly injured and insulted,[670] beside that I must be convinced from such a resolution that I have very little credit with a certain person, if after what I said on this subject to him and Mr Methuen he shal be the person thought most fit to be again brought over. The Speaker was very civil to Senny, said I was to be one of the Justices, and was very busy in writing great numbers of letters; he certainly intends to be made a Peer and cannot bear the thoughts of another time going into the Chair, which will require better and more steady conduct now then it needed last Session. I hope the gratifying his ambition (if that be resolved on) will not be done by placing him in such a degree of nobility as may give offence to other Lords, who may be picqued at seeing one of his birth and condition put over their heads. Upon second thoughts I send only one letter for Lord T[ownshend], and instead of it send you the Copy of the paper which was the result of the Cheif Justices[671] the Speakers and of my meeting at the Castle to advise what was fit to be wrote to England preparatory to the sitting of the Parliament there in relation to this Kingdome. You may shew it to Lord T[ownshend] and it will also give you light into matters; but by it you will find nothing contained in it but what I told you I had before hinted to Lord Townesend and Mr Methuen …

303. *Alan I, Dublin, to Thomas, at his lodgings in the Privy Garden, Whitehall, 3 Feb. 1716[/17]*

(1248/3/404–5)

I send the enclosed to you rather then under Bladens cover, which I desire may be delivered without delay. Sure since Conelye is to be one of the Justices, it is intended to make him a Lord too: but if that be the scheme I hope his vanity will not push at being put over other mens heads by being created more then a Baron. A step of this nature will I doubt give great disgust, and loose three freinds by creating one. As to my particular I cannot but think it will make such a distinction between the services he and I have done in the two houses of Parliament as will be little for my honour; if he be more then a Baron I desire you will in the proper place say it is hoped he shal not be put over my head: At the beginning it was intirely with submission to the Kings pleasure I was made a Peer, and did think I might have then insisted that I ought to have been placed in a distinct rank from some who were then created; but am much more of opinion he ought not to pretend to an higher seat from the chair of the house of Commons during one poor Session then I might who had so long filled that Chair in more difficult times, when he knows he could not have born

[669] Possibly Charles Campbell, MP [I].
[670] Martin Bladen.
[671] William Whitshed.

the burthen: and I will be bold to say I did the Crown more service last Session then he ever will be or ever was capable of doing in the instances of the imposing or tendring the abjuration oath to Peers, the communicating heads of bills between the houses, in order to lessen the power of the Councel and in consequence the prerogative, Lord Mongarrets Case and others: sure he will not aim at being an Earle, and I shal not desire to be more then a Viscount.

304. *Alan I, Dublin, to Thomas, at his lodgings in the Privy Garden, Whitehall, 1 Mar. 1716[/17]*

(1248/3/406–7)

I have yours of the one and twentieth, and fear it was not considered that I am like to be soon one of the Justices here and that the patent is not yet passed nor will be in some time: soe as by the writ being moved for soe early and your going out of town on the occasion of the election I doubt the election will be over before the patent is passed: in which case I doubt there will be a necessity of a reelection: you know the Act better then I doe, for I have it not by me: if soe I doubt it may not be practicable nor worth while to be chosen again.[672] Sure you must have had this in your thoughts, and consequently must have provided against it unlesse you have been misled by beleiving the Commission for Justices to be already passed the great Seal. It was impossible for me to have given you notice time enough to have cautioned you of it tho I had wrote to this purpose upon the first intimation of the likelyhood of my being chosen, as you will see by the date of my letter to you which carryed mine to the Duke of Somersett[673] inclosed, and the time of its coming to London: but indeed I did not think of this till I received yours in which you tell me of the day the writ would be moved for and the election held … I wish our vacant Bishoprick may be well disposed of; Bishops should owe their preferment to the King, not to one another.

305. *Alan I, Dublin, to Thomas, 7 Mar. 1716 [/17]*

(1248/3/408–9)

I have your letter of the 27th of February from Midhurst and resolve to make my farther complement to the Duke of Somersett by next maile under your cover; which you will deliver or dispose of as you shal see most proper; in the mean time I cannot but be sensible of your kindnesse in the pains you have taken in working this matter with his Grace, and in taking a journey to the election; which is in its own nature a thing of trouble, but very much more soe to you to whom riding is become soe uneasy. Pray let me know how the Duke stands now at Court; for if he be not well there, perhaps the ministry may look on me as one

---

[672] Alan had been elected to the Westminster parliament for the borough of Midhurst in a by-election on 27 Feb. 1717 (*HC 1715–54*, i, 336). By the terms of the English Regency Act of 1706 (4 Anne, c. 8), any MP accepting an office of profit under the crown was obliged to vacate his seat, though he could seek re-election. Since this did not happen in Alan's case, we must assume that the legal advice was that the lord justiceship did not qualify under the terms of the act.

[673] Charles Seymour (1662–1748), 6th duke of Somerset, patron of Midhurst borough (*HC 1715–54*, i, 336).

that comes in upon an interest opposite to theirs, and from thence have me in suspition as one inclined to give into peevish measures, which is the farthest thing from my heart. And after all this trouble I doubt by the late coming of the letter for appointing Justices and the early moving for the writ I shal be necessitated to be reelected; for till yesterday morning the letter came not to Lord Galweys hand, as he told me upon his shewing it to me then at the Castle, tho it bears date on 22 February: and the Commission for Justices cannot be ready for the Seal till Saturday morning, when Lord Galwey saith he will call a Councel to swear the Justices and deliver the Sword,[674] and after dining with me resolves to set sail that evening. Upon reading over the letter I found lesse care had been taken in the drawing or wording of it then might and ought to have been: It directs the Chancellor Archbishop of Dublin and Mr Conelye to be appointed Justices, without saying or any two of them in the sicknesse or absence of the third; soe as this being a joint authority to three, two could not have executed it, and yet it was known not only that the Archbishop was in England when the letter was signed but that he resolved to stay there for three months longer. It comes out of Mr Secretary Methuens office,[675] but sure your colleague either in person followed it or appointed somebody to doe it, and lesse care was taken in it then ought to have been: but there being a general clause in the letter to insert in our patent all powers clauses etc which are contained in the present Justices Commission, and there being a clause in that which empowers one of the Justices to act in the sicknesse or absence of the other, Mr Attorney conceives himself sufficiently warranted by those general words in the Kings and my Lord Galweys letter to supply this defect by inserting an expresse clause in our Commission empowring a lesser number to act in the absence or sicknesse of one or more of the three: I beleive this to be the Kings intent and that Mr Attorney will not be blamed as having gone farther then he ought; but certainly it had been as well to have had the letter more particular in this point: As for us who are to be Justices when the powers are in our Commission, we may act; which I would not have done without such a clause and so I told Lord Galwey to prevent his causing a Commission to be put under the Seal which would have determined his own power and yet not empowred others to take the administration of the Governement upon them till his Graces arrival. There are also other defects in the letter; for it contains no direction for inserting an expresse clause that the passing this Commission shal not determine Lord Townesends patent of Lord Lieutenant: I think the direction being that we are to continue Justices only during the Kings pleasure or till Lord Townesend shal arrive and take on him the Governement, the Kings intention will sufficiently appear; however I should have thought a clause directing my Lord Galwey to have taken care to give expresse directions for a clause or proviso in our Commission that it should not in any sort extend to annul or revoke Lord Townesends Commission ought to have been inserted in the letter in cautelam.[676] Beside as this letter is, if it be strictly pursued there must be a clause in our Commission to receive all salaryes perquisites etc of cheif Governors; for the general words of the Kings letter being that all clauses powers etc be inserted in our Commission which are contained in that of the present Lords Justices, and the Lords Justices Commission having that clause, and by it receiving the Salary of Cheif Governors even since the passing of Lord Townesends patent, the Attorney (if he strictly pursues his warrant) will I think

[674] The sword of state, emblem of executive authority.

[675] Methuen was secretary of state for the southern department.

[676] For security.

insert a clause in our patent to intitle us to the salary; and yet I much doubt whether Lord Townesend expects we shal receive the full salarye and perquisites as Cheif Governors: The Attorney was with me about this last night, at which time I told him I doubted whether it were expected that we should receive the full entertainment; that for my part I should be perfectly easy and doe in it intirely to the satisfaction of Lord Townesend, which ever way the Commission should be drawn; but added that I was but one of three whom this matter concerned; for which reason and because it was not proper for me to direct the drawing the Commission in any other maner then as he apprehended the warrant from the Cheif Governor to the Atturney required, I told Mr Atturney I could say no more in the matter; and advised him to speak to Mr Conelye about it. He seemed determined upon considering the thing to draw the Commission without the clause granting the Salary perquisites etc to the Justices: I shal be easy if it be so resolving to be determined wholly as to our appointment by my Lord Lieutenants pleasure: but this also should have been a little better taken care of. If it be true that Lord Towneshend hath not yet taken his equipage money[677] I know not what his resolutions may be in other matters; to you I may speak plain I mean whether he be yet resolved to come into this Kingdome; and if he hath not received his equipage money for that reason, and should happen hereafter to be detained in the Kings service in England and give up this Governement, I see no reason why the salary and perquisites (if not taken by him) should go to any but the Justices. I write this post to Lord Towneshend and take notice in general of some defects in the letter, but doe not descend to particulars; as well because your colleague will of course have the sight of it, who is the person to blame, as because this later part is more fit to be discoursed by word of mouth, which I must intreat you to doe without losse of time. I leave my letter to Lord Towneshend unsealed for your perusal, and write the affair of Sir John Packinton in a distinct paper because perhaps you may shew it to make freinds laugh if no farther use can be made of it.[678] as I wish there may.

306. Alan I, Dublin, to [Thomas], 13 Mar. 1716[/17]

(1248/3/410–11)

The wind is now fair for Lord Galway, but he seems to me not yet determined to goe till the weather be settled: nor hath he yet signed the fiant for the new Justices Commission; resolving I suppose not to stay a moment after he ceaseth to be Cheif Governor. Whether this will go before he sails or not I cannot tell; but hope that you have not soe far depended on his passing our Commission on Saturday last as to beleive it is done; for that may lead you into the same inconvenience as to a new election as the writs being moved for before passing our Commission hath done: soe as I hope if there be occasion for a new election it will not be till our patent is sealed; and when that will be is uncertain: the Easterly winds usually hold pretty long at this Season of the year; and his countrymen are soe unwilling to part with him that I think he is not desirous to leave them before he lies under a necessity

---

[677] A once-off payment made to each lord lieutenant for the expenses of his retinue.

[678] Tories in various counties were said to be promoting complimentary addresses to the prince of Wales in the king's absence, including Sir John Pakington in Worcestershire.

of doing it.[679] By what I see already the Kingdome is left vastly in debt, and I hear he hath since last time I was at the Castle signed warrants for more money, so as we shal find an empty treasury; I mean only about £12000 in it, which is the summe usually left there to answer any emergency. You will see which of the enclosed is to be wrapped for Duke of Somersett, and which for Lord Thomond; and inclose and deliver them accordingly. I have read and considered your letter relating to the proposal, which is I think unanswerable; nothing will be a greater mortification then a flat denial will be. Pray let me know what the King of Swedens answer is when it comes.[680] ...

307. *Alan I, Dublin, to Thomas, 21 Mar. 1716[/17]*

(1248/3/412–13)

The letter I wrote yesterday morning will have in great measure told you what I should otherwise have filled this with; it told you a Councel was summoned to meet yesterday at eleven when the sword would (it was beleived) have been delivered up; but soon after I had sealed and sent that letter to the post office notice was sent to all the Privy Councellors that they need not attend, for that there would be no Councel: this will oblige me to go a little farther back. The Kings letter dated 22 February which appoints Mr Conelye and me to be made Justices either did not come hither till the fifth of March or at least it was not sooner owned to be come over: On Wednesday the sixth Lord Galway told me he would deliver the sword on Saturday the ninth, then dine with me and go from my house directly on board: accordingly summons were left for the meeting of a Councel on Saturday, but they were countermanded that morning and no Councel mett; this was done because (as it was thought) wind and weather were not so favourable as might be wished. I will not say that they were very inviting, but I am sure they were not bad at that time; but for the week after and the beginning of this week (I mean Sunday and Monday morning) it was very stormy weather; and no Councel called, nor thoughts of our patents being sealed till Lord Galway saw he might sail immediately after: but before noon on Monday last the weather and wind proved very fair, and then all the talk was of Lord Galways sailing the next day; but that was not intended, as appeared by what hapned, and indeed the servants of the Castle owned that a pacquet was expected before my Lord would stir: nay Mr Villiers one of his Lordships Gentlemen, said at my Lady Kildares (to whom you know he is related)[681] on Monday night that they should not sail the next day, or till the pacquets came in. However a Councel was summoned to meet on Tuesday morning, and many Lords mett at the Castle; when I came into the Closett my Lord Galway told me that the Captain of the Yatch told him it had

---

[679] The Huguenot community in Ireland.

[680] The arrest of the Swedish ambassador Gyllenborg in Jan. 1717 and the discovery of his correspondence with the jacobites had precipitated a diplomatic crisis, with the prospect that Britain would join with Russia in making war on Sweden.

[681] Mary Fitzgerald (1692–1780) (née O'Brien), wife of the 19th earl of Kildare, was the daughter of Hon. Mary Villiers, sister of the 1st earl of Jersey. The 'Mr Villiers' mentioned could well be Henry (*d*.1753), Jersey's second son, a lieutenant in the Royal Irish Dragoons in 1715 and later lieutenant governor of Tynemouth Castle (Dalton, *Geo. I's Army*, i, 332; ii, 333; John Brand, *The History and Antiquities of the Town ... of Newcastle upon Tyne* (2 vols, 1789), ii, 123; TNA, PROB 11/802/238).

333

33

blown very hard about two of Clock in the morning; and that altho the wind was indeed then fair and the weather very calm, yet there would be a great head sea; but that the next day they might expect a fine passage, and all should be done then. I should have told you that tho the fiant was prepared by the Attorney General to be ready on Fryday the eighth, yet I never had the sight of it till Monday the eighteenth, when I told my Lord Galway I ought to have a view of it; for that I could not put a recepi[682] and seal a Commission of such Consequence on implicite faith in the care of Mr Attorney in preparing the fiant and of the Clerk of the Hanaper[683] in engrossing the patent: he seemed to have beleived it had been shewn me; but indeed it was in Mr Delafayes hand; and then order was given to shew it to me which was done by leaving it at my house that afternoon: I perused the draught and found and corrected some mistakes on Tuesday, and sent it again to the Clerk of the Hanaper, who brought it to me; without signing the recepi that day: Next morning Lord Galways private Secretary Mr Badenup[684] brought me the fiant and told me he was ordered to have it signed; there being a Councel summoned to meet at eleven (as the truth was) in order to seal the patent; I asked whether it was Lord Galways order I should then sign the recepi, he told me it was, and I accordingly did it. The reason of my question was because I was sensible when I had soe done, that the Commission must be of the same date, which would render all acts done by Lord Galway afterward null and void; and yet I saw my Lord thought it well consisted with the Kings letter, and seemed determined not to lay down the Sword till he was just ready to sail; and indeed I told him on Tuesday that after the day of the date of the recepi he could not act, if ever a Commission passed on that fiant. In lesse then an hour the Councel was discharged by reason of the stormy weather; and indeed the day was by that time become very stormy; tho sixteen ships sailed the day before and I little doubt made a very good passage. I immediately went to the Castle and before the Speaker told Galway that the recepi being signed he could not act beyond that day, of which I had acquainted him the day before; he seemed surprised but owned I had said soe the day before, then talked of calling a Councel in the evening, and afterward of doing it this day: It was not fit for me who was to succeed, to presse proceeding immediately, but repeated that he could not do any act as cheif Governor the next day and so we left his Lordship. Holding a Councel is certainly one act of a Cheif Governor, and that he could not doe the next day yet we were to be sworn in Councel: upon considering the matter farther I found very great difficultyes would arise from putting off the sealing the patent that night; and sent for the Atturny General to whom I stated the matter and gave him my thoughts that it might well become him to give my Lord his sense of the matter; he seemed not pleased at being employed on the errand (but at last undertook it) and expressed the reason to be that he did not think the discourse would be very acceptable; and to say truth

[682] A receipt.

[683] Sir Thomas Domvile.

[684] A Robert Badenhop, described as a merchant, was among the French Huguenot exiles in London in the 1700s (D.C.A. Agnew, *Protestant Exiles from France, Chiefly in the Reign of Louis XIV* ... (2nd edn, 3 vols, 1871–4), i, 44; *The Registers of the French Church, Threadneedle Street, London, Volume II* (Huguenot Society of London Publications, xvi, 1906), 54, 96; TNA, C6/377/30: chancery pleading, *Badenhope v. Jempelin*, 1701). Jesse Badenhop, described as esquire, who may well have been related, was listed among the subscribers to *Christiana Religionis* ... (1720), x). He emigrated to America and became clerk to the council of South Carolina, where he died in 1739 (*Statutes at Large of South Carolina*, ed. Thomas Cooper and D.J. McCourt (10 vols, Columbia, SC, 1836–98), iii, 392; *Register of St Philip's Parish Charleston, South Carolina, 1720–1758*, ed. A.S. Salley (Charleston, SC, 1904), 258).

Lord Galway speaking with Mr Conelye and me talked something that if the patent passed that day, he should remain here a private man. But after the Attorney had been at the Castle and Lord Galway had advised and considered on it, a Councel was summoned in an hurry and we sworn about ten last night. Whether he resolved not to passe the patent till he could get away, or had a mind to see the pacquets of yesterday, which might bring news of another Lord Lieutenant, or (which is a little thing but talked of) that the letters for the Bishops were expected then, and his servants would be intitled to the fees of honour by his stay I cannot tell; but certainly there appeared a backwardnesse etc. I write this to you, that you may be able to answer all objections, not to shew it: for some will have it (but very unjustly) that I by signing the recepi put him under a necessity of quitting the Governement last night in all events. Mr Conelye may act as Commissioner tho in the Governement,[685] I mean legally, but how consistent with the character I will not determine. Three Commissioners either of Customs or excise may act.

My Lord is sailed about one of Clock with fair wind and weather.[686] We parted in all appearance well: but I have reason to doubt his being freindly to me: nor will any body who can be influenced by one whom you cannot fail to guesse.

308. *Alan I, Dublin, to Thomas, 25 Mar. 1717*

(1248/4/116–17)

I see no reason why we should not wish our freinds many happy new years on this day rather then on the first of January, since our year begins on this day; unless we shal in time grow soe wise as not to differ in our computation from the rest of the world.[687] but be that as it will, I now and at all times wish you all happinesse imaginable and a long life … I was in hopes to have had a particular account from you of what passed in the house on Tuesday upon so critical an affair as that of taxing the funds; but I suppose you had too much fatigue in the house that day, to enter on so wearisome a businesse after leaving it. Not only private letters, but the publick prints, mention the Duke of B[olton] as likely to be our Lord Lieutenant;[688] if that be the case I hope he will consider he comes into the Governement under the disadvantage of an heavy load of debt, and when Gentlemen who were formerly freinds are very cool toward one another. Both these difficultyes are in my opinion in a good measure owing to one and the same person; and I doubt whether he (having found the sweet of it formerly) may not desire to come over in the same emploiment as formerly: we look on it that the Duke of B[olto]ns pretensions are cheifly supported by my Lord Sunderland, with whom the person I mean[689] hath taken care to create an interest; which probably may incline his Lordship to recommend his being continued: but if things doe not take that turn I perswade my self the game will be endeavoured to be played in this maner; his counterpart, who is now with us (and much in the good graces of Lord

---

[685] May continued to act as a revenue commr while a lord justice.

[686] Galway's arrival in London was reported on 13 Apr. (*Weekly Journal*, 13 Apr. 1717).

[687] 25 Mar. (Lady Day) was accounted the first day of the year under the Julian calendar.

[688] Bolton was appointed on 27 Apr.

[689] Martin Bladen.

S[*underland*]) to be the man named,[690] for the joint benefit of both. Either of these persons will be very disagreeable to a great many honest Gentlemen here, and I for my own part shal expect to find the same scurvy underhand treatment in the dark as hitherto. It is true the former, on Lord Townesends being declared, and his being continued, wrote to me and expressed a desire of being my humble servant for the future; and in answer I told him I was (upon that declaration of his) willing for the future to be his humble servant; and upon this foot we are, which is no very great intimacy; however I think I should not directly oppose him: but I confesse I wish his Grace may bring a fresh man and one as little attached as possible to these two Gentlemen. It will be for his service and the ease of his Governement and I could be very well pleased you would tell him so (but not from me) without any delay. Pray let me know a little who and who are together. We have no directions from England to correspond and transmit all businesse to my Lord Lieutenant directly, and regularly the Chief Governors are to doe it to the Secretary of State unlesse there be such a letter; so did Lord Galwey since Lord Sunderlands patent was passed, so did the Archbishop of Dublin and Lord Kildare after the Duke of Grafton and Lord Galweys patent was passed; and our patent is the same words with the Duke of Grafton and Lord Galways patent: It was otherwise in the Justiceship of the Primate Sir Con[*stantine*] Phipps and Archbishop of Tuam when Duke of Shrewsbury was Lord Lieutenant, it might and I beleive did proceed from a Clause in their Commission by which they were to govern themselves according to such instructions as the Duke should leave with them; now if one of the instructions were to that effect (as I beleive) they could not do otherwise, but we are to act by the instructions given by his Majestye to the Duke of Grafton and Lord Galway, in which nothing of the kind is contained; but in many instances we are commanded to acquaint or certifye the King of matters. This was a rub at our first entry, and I saw a great propensity in Mr Delafay to transmit every thing to Lord Lieutenant, and not to the Secretary, unlesse he meant to doe it to both; my Colleague was ready to doe as the other said in my apprehension, but we took time to consider in what maner to transmit things: You see plainly how much the influence of your colleague must take place, especially if the former method shal be taken; and indeed this is to make us only cyphers and to doe nothing by the Kings Commission without allowance and direction from Lord Lieutenant; and no doubt people will soon find the way to make their application (especially for Church preferments) directly to Mr Secretary, without regarding us. If you know and go to Lord Townesend discourse this matter coolly with him, and prevent my behavior or opinion in this matter to be so represented as to take place to my prejudice. If he hath a mind to have all things passe through his hands without transmitting matters to the Secretarye, the Kings letter to that purpose should be sent.

309. *Alan I, Dublin, to Thomas, 31 Mar. 1717*

(1248/4/1–4)

I am at present in such a scituation that I must necessarily have recourse to your freindship, the constant good effects of which I have ever found and hope ever to retain a grateful sense of. The matter stands thus: I am now in a station that necessitates me not only to

---

[690]Charles Delafaye. In fact Edward Webster, MP [I] was appointed Bolton's chief secretary.

discourse and transact businesse with some persons on whose freindship I have no reason to rely, but what is more difficult, I must write by the hands of one who I verily beleive hath underhand done me ill offices, and my letters must come to the view of and be answered by another, whose good inclinations toward me commence from no earlier a time then his letter bears date in which my Lord Towneshends commands he intimates to me that I am to be one of the Lords Justices, which he did on the 26th of January last: All he desires in the end of that letter is that for the future I would do him the justice to beleive he is my humble servant. I understand that paragraph in this maner, that what ever he had done toward me or to my prejudice heretofore, he desired for time to come we might live well together: I answered his letter by making the same request in his own words; but I suppose this is no very sure foot of freindship between me and so courtlike a man as your colleague; who (with Mr D[*elafaye*]) hath been the means to insinuate things to my prejudice with those persons whose ill opinion of me must create the same with the King; these are the men who have taken care to have all the marks of favor and respect placed on some men and that I should be treated with neglect and made a stranger to every thing; insomuch that while I was in England, the Duke of Grafton, who expresseth and I beleive hath some kindnesse for and opinion of me, never communicated any part of the affairs of Ireland to me, to which no Chancellor before me was ever made a stranger, while at the same time a Cheif Justice (who hath brought himself to be able to make court to little people)[691] was in every instance consulted if you beleive his freinds: and they give this shrewd ground that they have reason for what they say, that he from time to time communicated to them matters while they were only in agitation and in the breast of the Cheif Governor and Secretary or those to whom only one of them could impart them: the great cause of these two Secretaryes resentment to me is really this, that I expressed myself with a good deal of freedome in the presence of one of the Lords Justices and several others at a meeting of Gentlemen about the beginning of the Parliament, that they interposed too much and were too enterprizing in parliament affairs, and that it would be found in the event that the Kings service would be as effectually done and more to the satisfaction of the countrey if Gentlemen were permitted to do the businesse their own way, without being driven or drawn by skill into matters which they would of their own accord do if they were found necessary and for the publick good. Some of your freinds and mine took another course, endeavoured to insinuate themselves into favor by flattering your colleague and have found their account in it hitherto, but I think there will be need of other measures next Session, when the Nation will be found in a miserable condition of debt incurred in a short time. I will not suspect him who is now in the Governement with me[692] of acting insincerely with me; his Station should put him above it now, if he were formerly capable of it, and his professions of desiring to live freindly and well with me gain a good deal upon my good nature, which hardly allows me to beleive unkindly of one who professeth kindnesse; however the part he hath lately taken shews me that either his freindship was never so warm toward me as I once apprehended, and I think deserved from him, or that he is capable of cooling in his freindships; for tho his declarations should be true that he never would go into measures to my prejudice, it is plain by his saying soe he knew of and was advised with

---

[691] William Whitshed.
[692] William Conolly, MP [I].

by some about such measures. If therefore any thing happen which I would willingly have known by my Lord Lieutenant only, I know you have such accesse to him to be admitted on such occasions alone, and that you will discourse him on such subjects as I shal write upon.

I told you formerly how ill the letter for constituting us Justices was drawn; but am in doubt with myself whether the leaving out of it a clause that hath of late years crept into the letter for appointing Lords Justices after a Lord Lieutenant hath passed his Commission and taken on him the Governement was left out of this by oversight or design: To tell you my thoughts freely; however reasonable it may be for a Lord Lieutenant who hath been sworn and taken on him the Governement and goes afterward over to England for a time, to leave Justices who by their Commission shal be tyed to act according to such instructions as he shal leave with them or transmit from time to time (against which I will not speak since it hath once obtained and will not I beleive by parted with) yet I cannot but think it a very different thing for Justices to act under instructions to be given them by a Lord Lieutenant who never was in the Kingdome or was sworn: nor hath this ever been practiced that I know, the case of the Archbishops of Dublin and Tuam and Lord Kildare is very different, for tho they acted toward Lord Sunderland in the same maner their predecessors did toward the Duke of Shrewsbury, that is granted nothing, but only recommended; transmitted all things directly to Lord Sunderland and not to the Secretaryes, yet this proceeded not from any instructions Lord Sunderland sent them, but from their own Commission which referred them to the same instructions by which their immediate predecessors were to govern themselves, and they by expresse instructions from Lord Shrewsbury dated 1 June 1714 were directed to inform <u>him</u> from time to time of every mans care to the end <u>he</u> might lay the same before the Queen and by the tenth instruction as well all propositions moving from them as all accounts of matters relating to the Governement are ordered to be directed <u>immediately to him,</u> to the end <u>he</u> may lay them before the Queen, and that they may receive again <u>from him</u> the signification of her Majestyes pleasure etc.

Their Commission required them to conform themselves to the instructions to be left with them by the Duke of Shrewsbury, which therefore as to the maner of execution were a part of the Commission; but ours refers us to the same instructions the Duke of Grafton and my Lord Galway had, which require us to inform the King etc to transmit an account of the state of the Kingdome, and of what is amisse therein and how the same may be best provided for in writing to the King to the end he may receive a perfect knowledge of it.

It will be improved to our prejudice if we should do this directly to the Secretary of State, and Lord T[*ownshend*] will be told it was otherwise in Lord Sunderlands and other Lieutenants time, and the whole will be laid at my door, as fond of power, acting disrespectfully and ungratefully toward that man to whom I owe very great obligations, and as if out of a turbulent temper I were for altering the course of things; and I apprehend your Colleague will imagine his own influence on the affairs of Ireland will be much lessened by such a procedure, which he will ill bear and consequently will resent. On the other things of the like kind to be transmitted by us directly as recommending Bishops, Officers etc I have not time to enlarge, but we are under the same instructions as to them: Now it is a most tender point to mention these things to Lord Townesend, and will be done best by word of mouth: convince him therefore what our duty requires of us, as to representing matters to the King, and find by him how far we are justifiable in not doing it directly as our Commission and instructions direct:; It is not a thing we are fond of, nay we beleive matters transmitted by us and coming recommended by him will more likely succeed that way then any other; but stil our Commission and instructions are to be followed; and I think cannot be altered without a new Commission or instructions, which whether necessary for so short a time his Excellencye will consider; for to me it will be no mortification but a great ease; and it will be worth weighing whether he will care to bring in a precedent of a Lord Lieutenant signing instructions before he is sworn. Our Case is the same as to granting livings Offices etc we may do it directly by our Commission and are not restrained by our instructions; the late Justices viz Dublin Tuam and Kildare were restrained from doing it by both: yet so careful have we been of giving offence, that we have at the same time shewn my Lord what our right is and assured his Lordship we will not use it without transmitting the persons names to him, by the signification of whose pleasure we will be determined: so as what is in us a power of disposing, we have voluntarily turned into a recommendation; and I am certain this will create me no uneasinesse; for I will recommend good men, and if other good men prevail, I shal be blamelesse: without merit I will join in no recommendation, and when the person is one for whom I lye under an obligation to provide, I will say so in plain words; and hope your Colleagues being at my Lord elbow at all times will not render a few modest recommendations unsuccesseful: I empower you to speak frankly to my Lord on these matters …

[PS] No doubt Lord Galway will lay a state of the Kingdome before his Majestye as we must doe; but I doubt he will say (as he beleives it to be true, for he told me as much) that the Army is cleared to Christmas 1715; but it is otherwise, and only to Michaelmas. Tho I think the Duke of Grafton now wishes well to and thinks well of me, I have too much ground to suspect he was once drawn in to write unkindly of me to the King or ministry.

We have recommended or named Dr Loyde to the Deanry of Rapho if Trench be dead, which I doubt,[693] and Mr Valentine French to that of Rosse,[694] by this my Lord will see we have no thoughts of recommending directly to Bishopricks (if any should fall void) before we have wrote to and received his Excellencyes directions.

Tho I sometimes write in this letter in the plural number, it is my own, and written without my Colleagues privity.

310. *Alan I, Dublin, to Thomas, 3 Apr. 1717*

(1248/4/5–6)

I shal tyre you by writing soe often on the same subject: my last was a very long letter, relating to our power of giving Deaneryes and other Ecclesiastical preferments below Bishopricks, and secular offices not excepted in our Commission; and to the maner of our recommending to Bishopricks, offices reserved to the gift of the Crown, and commissions in the Army, which his Majestye hath kept in his own disposal; You cannot but know that the power of a Secretary, conversant in the affairs of Ireland (and who will pretend to a Lieutenant who is a stranger here to know better then any other every mans merit) will be very great and his interest continue or increase according to the power he hath had and

---

[693]John Trench was dean of Raphoe from 1692 until his death in 1725.

[694]Valentine French (c.1669–1732), rector of Kilcoan, Co. Cork and prebendary of Killaspugmallane, was made dean of Ross in 1717 (Brady, *Records*, i, 154; ii, 428).

will have in these matters; soe as all he can do will be exerted against our granting or rather stil keeping in us the right to grant, tho by what we have already wrote we have in effect said we would exercise it no otherwise then as if our right were only to recommend. My Colleague[695] hath been pretty cool in this matter, tho he agreeth that the right is in us, but hath added that he beleives it was by a mistake in the Kings letter, which he thinks would otherwise have tyed us down to have a clause in our Commission to act by instructions to be received from Lord Townesend. By this kind of behavior he intends no doubt to make the fairest weather with Lord Townesend, to whom I make no question is transmitted either directly or through the hands of Mr B[*laden*] all that either he or I have said or thought of this matter: and among other things that it arose from me whether we should not directly give livings and offices and transmitt accounts of matters to and receive orders directly from the Secretary of State: for it is true that I did first deliver my sense of this matter, that our Commission empowred us to doe the one and required us to doe the other. He must be sensible that he hath alway at my Lords elbow one who will promote the recommendations which are agreeable to him, in which I shal join: as he also will be busy in frustrating such as move from me in which he will join: in short that a certain person will continue to act as formerly (particularly in joining me to such a partner) I mean to doe every act tending to support the interest of one and lessen the other. Since my last letter I have perused all the fiants which are in the rolls office since Lord Rochester was here,[696] and do find that the Earle of Mount Alexander,[697] General Erle[698] and Mr Keightley[699] were on the 11 April 1702 made Lords Justices in the room of the then Archbishop of Dublin[700] and Earle of Droghedah,[701] till Lord Rochesters return into the Kingdome and were by their Commission to conform themselves to such instructions as they should receive from my Lord Rochester. I never saw Lord Rochesters Commission which being passed in England, the fiant is not in the Rolls Office here, nor doe I know whether the patent be inrolled with us; so can only say it is my conjecture that Lord Rochester had by his patent power to appoint Justices, and to leave them instructions to govern themselves by: but I have this reason to make this conjecture, that I am certain the Duke of Ormond had power by his patent to appoint Justices,[702] as appears to me by the Commission dated 15 February 1706 for appointing the Lord Primate Marsh[703] Cox[704] and Cutts[705] Justices, which recites the Duke to have such power by his Commission. Soe that the way by which Justices were to have instructions from Lord Lieutenants came in as I conceive as a natural consequence of the Lietenants having power to name Justices; but in processe of time, it obtained that Lords

[695] Alan's fellow lord justice, William Conolly.
[696] Laurence Hyde (1642–1711), 1st earl of Rochester, lord lieutenant [I] 1700–3.
[697] Hugh Montgomery, 2nd earl of Mount-Alexander (see Appendix 3).
[698] Thomas Erle (c.1650–1720), of Charborough, Dorset, MP [I] 1703–13, [E & GB] 1679–81, 1685–7, 1689–1718; c.-in-c. [I] 1701–5, lord justice [I] 1702–3.
[699] Thomas Keightley (c.1650–1719), of Castlemartin, Co. Kildare, MP [I] 1695–1714; revenue commr [I] 1692–1714, lord justice [I] 1702–3.
[700] Narcissus Marsh (1638–1713), lord justice [I] 1701–2, 1707, 1707–9, 1710–11.
[701] Henry Moore (d.1714), 3rd earl of Drogheda, lord justice [I] 1696–7, 1701–2.
[702] As lord lieutenant.
[703] Marsh had been translated from Dublin to Armagh in 1703.
[704] Sir Richard Cox, at that time lord chancellor [I].
[705] John Cutts (c.1661–1707), 1st Baron Cutts, lieut.-gen. of the forces in Ireland and a lord justice [I] 1705–d.

Lieutenants who perhaps had not that clause in their Commission to appoint Justices, yet ordered matters soe as to have it inserted in the Queens letter requiring them to grant a commission to Justices during their absence, that such Justices should govern themselves by instructions to be left with or sent to them by the Lord Lieutenant: And the following Justices were under instructions.

Mount Alexander Erle and Keightley by Commission 11 April 1702 of Lord Rochester.

Cox Mount Alexander and Erle by Commission 13 April. 1704 [*recte 1703*] of Duke of Ormond.

The same by Commission 4 March 1703[*/4*] of Duke of Ormond.

Lord Primate Marsh and Cox 15 Febr. 1706[*/7*] of Lord Ormond.

Lord Primate and Lord Chancellor Freeman[706] 27 Nov. 1707 of Lord Pembroke.

Lord Chancellor Freeman and Indgolsby[707] 29 Aug. 1710. of Lord Wharton.

Lord Chancellor Phipps and Indgolsbye 19 Nov. 1711 of Lord Ormond.

Lord Chancellor Phipps and Tuam[708] 10 March 1711 of Lord Ormond.

Lord Primate Phipps and Tuam 17 April 1714 of Shrewsbury.

It is to be remembered that in all the above Cases the Lords Lieutenants had first been acting Cheif Governors, had been sworn and been in Ireland before they made such Justices and gave such instructions: and I am pretty well convinced no one instance can be given of the contrary; and that which much confirms me in this opinion is from the contrary course taken when Lords Lieutenants have been appointed and Justices made till their arrival in Ireland.

Lord Chancellor Freeman and Mr Indgolsbye were made Justices of Ireland by Commission dated 28 Nov. 1710. which recites that Freeman and Indgolsby were made Justices during Lord Whartons Governement, and that the Queen had determined Lord Whartons Commission and made the Duke of Ormond Lord Lieutenant, and they are by this Commission made Justices till Lord Ormonds arrival; but to act by instructions to be received from the Queen or Secretary of State (not from the Lord Lieutenant). And when upon Freemans death Sir Con[*stantine*] Phipps was made Chancellor and Justice, he and Indgolsbye by Commission dated 22 Jan. 1710. are to conform themselves to instructions to be received from the Queen or Secretarye of State (not of the Duke who was not then arrived.) But the Duke of Ormond arriving in June 1711 held a Parliament and went into England; and then by Commission dated 19 Nov. 1711 made Phipps and Indgolsby Justices under instructions given then by him. You see here the same Lord Lieutenant who had power by his patent to appoint Justices gives them instructions to act by after he had been sworn Lord Lieutenant and taken on him the Governement in Ireland, but doth not doe so between the time of his being made Lieutenant and his coming over.

The Case of the Bishops of Dublin Tuam and Lord Kildare while Lord Sunderland was Lord Lieutenant turns upon this, as you may see by a former Letter; The Primate

---

[706] Richard Freeman (1646–1710), lord chancellor [I] 1707–*d*.

[707] Richard Ingoldsby (bef. 1651–1712), of Ballybricken, Co. Limerick, MP [I] 1703–*d*.; c.-in-c. [I] 1706–*d*., lord justice [I] 1709–10, 1710–11, 1711–*d*.

[708] John Vesey, archbishop of Tuam.

Tuam and Phipps were by their Commission to govern themselves by instructions left with them by the Duke of Shrewsbury, one of which was not to grant any thing but only to recommend; not to transmit matters to any body but the Lord Lieutenant; their Successors are by their Commission to govern themselves by those very instructions; so that they did not act under instructions sent over by Lord Sunderland who never was in Ireland nor sworn Lord Lieutenant, but forbore to grant, or write by particular instructions referred to in their commission; so as those were instructions given them by the King. These facts are all true, and such as I hope will enable you to shew Lord T[*ownshend*] the reason of our doing what we have done, and that we have been very respectful in not doing things directly, so as our recommendations will deserve some weight; and that there is no reason for his introducing a new method of receiving instructions from a Lord Lieutenant before he is sworn, since we resolve to act to his satisfaction in those things which by our Commission are in our power.

311. *Alan I, Dublin, to Thomas, 9 Apr. 1717*

(1248/4/9–10)

I am very much obliged to you for your letter of the second instant, particularly that part which explains the nature of the debate on the question moved on Fryday the 29th of March in relation to the Munster and Saxe Gotha troops,[709] and the figure your colleague[710] made upon the occasion.

It is unhappy for him to have sate among men, some of which supported him in reflections of like nature on men otherwise affected to his Majestyes service and interests then the world beleives that Gentleman to be on whom he designed his first reflection, that he was not so much concerned to know the maner of the treatyes being made, as that the design for prevention of which the treatyes were made had not taken effect: If freedome of debate without being subject to personal reflections be once taken away, such enterprizing and aspiring sparks will in time endeavour to make a parliament in these dominions as insignificant as the convention at Mosco.[711] It was of a peice, to sett up for a patron of this problem, that where foreigners are appointed to transact matters in behalf of Britain a British parliament shal not enquire into the proceedings of such ministers, because they are foreigners: nothing could be said lesse for his Majestyes service, or more void of reason. But it is his peculiar talent to instil this notion, that every thing done by any minister, which he likes, is to be screened under a pretence of their meaning ill to the Kings interests who are not entirely of his sentiments with relation to that particular person, action or advice on which the debate arises. The Toryes injoined Phil Savage silence, because he did them harm as often as he spoke;[712] and it was a peice of Parliament craft which a certain speaker[713]

---

[709] Before the house of commons resolved itself, according to order, into the committee of supply, several further orders were made, including one that the treaties with the bishop of Münster and the duke of Saxe-Gotha (for the acquisition of troops) be laid before the House. A motion to go into committee was then defeated (*CJ*, xviii, 521).

[710] Martin Bladen.

[711] The council of boyars, which advised the tsar.

[712] Philip Savage.

[713] Possibly an arch reference to Alan himself.

alway used, to call him and Charles Dering[714] up as often as possible; and it turned to ac-count. It would be a great mortification and penance to enjoin so polite an Orator silence: but methinks he should be cautioned against committing the same fault twice in one day. I hope this disaster may humble and amend him. I alway expected (as you will find by my letters) that the discourse which passed in the Closet here in relation to the matter of our transmitting accounts of matters and receiving directions would be sent over; your letter tells me you found it had been done by the maner in which Lord Townesend discoursed on that subject; and the same appears by an expression in his last letter in which he saith he promiseth himself we shal treat him in the maner preceding Justices have treated preceding Lieutenants. I mention this because we shal very soon lye under a necessity of writing into England our reasons why we doe not forthwith comply with the Kings letter to grant Mr Dodington[715] a patent of the Office of Clerk of the Pells (which my Lord Newtown[716] hath for life) for the lives of his Nephew Bub[717] and one Kiligrew.[718] The case is this, Lord Newtown hath the office for life; Mr Dodington passed a patent of it to himself (I think in Lord Pembrokes time) for Mr Bubs life, to take place after Lord Newtowns interest was determined: since his Majestyes accession to the throne, he surrendred that patent and took out a new one to him and his assigns during Bubs and Kiligrews lives and the life of the survivor; to commence after Butlers patent determined.[719] You must be sensible of how ill consequence these patents in Reversion are; but to have two lives is to give oportunity on the death of one to insert a new life, and make it an office renewable for ever. In this later patent Mr Dodingtons council supposes there may be such a flaw as makes it advisable to surrender it and obtain a new patent, and a letter is come from the King to us to accept a surrender of the patent and to grant such new one for Bubs and Kiligrews life in reversion. We are required by our instructions not to grant any confirmation of a reversion of any office or emploiment, nor suffer any grant of a reversion to passe hereafter; and are autho-rised by another instruction to forbear the execution of any warrant letter or order from the King which requires the performance of any thing contrary to the Kings directions in his establishments, or to our instructions: My Colleague could not deny that it would be reasonably done by us to stop our hand till his Majestyes farther pleasure should be known, if this were the first grant of this reversion to Mr Dodington, but seemed to think the case

[714] Charles Dering (1656–1719), of Dublin, MP [I] 1692–1713; deputy auditor-gen. [I] c.1692–1708, jt auditor-gen. [I] 1708–*d.*

[715] George Dodington (c.1662–1720), of Dodington, Som., and Eastbury, Dorset, MP [GB] 1705–*d.*, MP [I] 1707–13; chief sec. [I] 1707–8.

[716] Theophilus, Lord Butler of Newtownbutler (see Appendix 3).

[717] George Bubb (c.1691–1762), of Eastbury, Dorset, MP [GB] 1715–61; envoy to Spain 1715–17, and subse-quently a lord of the treasury [GB] 1724–40.

[718] Guildford Killegrew (c.1700–51), eldest son of Charles Killegrew, master of the revels (for whom see *Oxf. DNB*) was commissioned as an ensign in a regiment of foot raised in Ireland in 1708 and disbanded in 1712, became a page of honour in the royal household in 1718, and subsequently a lieutenant of dragoons (Dalton, *Army Lists*, vi, 256; Guy Miège, *The Present State of Great Britain and Ireland* … (4th edn, 1718), pt 1, p. 358; Dalton, *Geo. I's Army*, ii, 221–2).

[719] Theophilus Butler held the office according to a patent issued in 1678. In 1708 Dodington, then chief secretary to Lord Pembroke, received a grant of the reversion of the office during the life of his nephew Bubb. In 1715 that was superseded by another, adding the life of Killigrew to that of Bubb. A privy seal warrant was issued on 19 Feb. 1716 for a reissue of the patent, which eventually passed in Dublin on 17 Aug. 1717 (*Lib. Mun.*, pt 2, p. 64).

different where it was only to make valid a former grant: but certainly it must either be the confirmation of a former grant, or a new one: both which equally go in contradiction to our instructions: he perceiving how reasonable the objection was, went into a resolution of laying the instruction and case before the King; but no doubt both he and Mr D[*elafa*]y have said (as the truth is) that if I had made no difficultye in signing a warrant for a new fiant, nobody else would. My Secretary Mr Lake[720] is concerned to follow this matter for Mr Dodington, and I have ordered him to lay the thing before Mr Dodington in the best maner and to assure him that it proceeds not from any inclination in me to disserve him that I act in this maner, but from a sense that we ought to observe and not act against our instructions without the Kings expresse pleasure signifyed, after we have taken notice that something formerly commanded interferes with the instructions given us, which are the measure by which our Commission requires us to act and govern ourselves. A like case will be that of Mr Barington (Shute) who hath a letter for a patent in reversion of the Mastership of the Rolls (excepting only the judicial part of the Office)[721] Is not this Gentleman a great freind of Lord Sunderlands? We certainly shal lay his case also before the King, as contrary to our instructions: Pray find by Lord Townesend whether he could not be content these matters should be sent directly to the Secretary of State, from whom we received the warrant under the Kings sign manual. Will his Lordship be fond of being interested in affairs of this kind? ...

312. Alan I, Dublin, to Thomas, 26 Apr. 1717

(1248/4/13–14)

By a letter last pacquet I promised my Lord Lieutenant my thoughts of some matters which I apprehend may create uneasinesse in the approaching Session if not timely prevented: I send inclosed something on that subject, no way perfect nor particular, for my leisure is not such to allow my doing it well: but I hope I have made it understood that care ought to be taken least his Grace and the Kings servants and freinds here be laid under insuperable difficultyes by means of the dissenters panting after what can not I think be attained here,[722] and that the establishment ought to be eased as much as possible instead of being overloaded. If something of this kind be not done, the freinds of the late Justices will impute all to his Grace, and say if the former Governement had stood they would have had credit enough to make good the assurances given and would have employed all their credit to that end. Every new pension will be a means of sowring people, and I doubt may tend to incline some to quarrel with the establishment in more instances then otherwise they would offer to doe. I beleive the late Justices had the Kings order to direct the addicional payment of 4d per diem to the horse and 2d to the Dragoons; they would not have ventured on any thing of the kind without it; and in all probabilitye they told the King that the Commons

---

[720] Francis Lake (*d.*1721), secretary to successive lord chancellors [I] (See *Anglo-Irish Politics, Vol. 1*, 123).

[721] A privy seal warrant was issued on 28 Feb. 1716 for a patent giving Shute the reversion of the office after the then holder, Lord Berkeley. The patent was passed in Dublin on 5 July 1717 (*Lib. Mun.*, pt 2, p. 20).

[722] Repeal of the sacramental test clause. For reports of Irish presbyterian agitation, including a mission to England by Clotworthy Upton, MP [I], see Wake, Epist. xii: Bishop Evans to [Archbishop Wake], 27 Apr. 1717; Bishop Godwin to [Wake], 27, 30 Apr. 1717.

had so far countenanced the thing as to committ the petition; but I very much doubt whether they ever told him that the report of the Committee upon it was recommitted, being distastful to almost every man in the house except the Souldiers: and this being done on 20th December, they had time enough to have laid the thing nakedly before the King between that and the tenth of March; but the truth is the matter was to be done some way or other; and it hath been so ordered that I hardly see how it can be undone without creating a mutiny; yet I am very sensible the house of Commons will think themselves ill used, and say so aloud, and with great difficultye (if at all) go into the thing. By my plain and open maner the Duke may see I act toward him without reserve, and with the confidence in him which the freindship he hath been pleased to renew the professions of requires. The caution I desired may be taken to prevent difficultyes is an argument of my resolving to do every[*thing*] in my power for the honour of his Governement, and that I will discharge the part of a faithful and affectionate freind to him, as well as my duty to the Crown, by giving him all the assistance I am able in whatever is for the publick service: and I flatter my self that the experience he hath had in two former Sessions[723] will convince him I am not capable of acting otherwise toward him. This you may say to him from me, and at the same time conjure him not to make me the object of the rage and indignation of the dissenters, and pensioners; especially of one person who I am sensible is far from being my freind; on no other real ground but the desire I have alway expressed that we may some time or other gett rid of that superfaetation[724] of pensioners with which he from time to time heavily loads a poor Kingdome ... I have considered where to bring in Mr Webster;[725] there are no more then fowre vacancies by death since the prorogation of the parliament: one of them is by the death of Mr Joseph Henry, whereby Mr Conellye will have an oportunity of obliging by bringing in the Secretary at his own town of Newtown Limovaddy, unlesse he lies under any promise; but he will find a way of being released or releasing him self of any engagement, where so doing will turn to the advantage of his interest, especially at this very critical juncture. You must know his freinds give out he will lay down his Commissioners place and goe out in good company: this is one of his peices of skill, to have it thought his own act, if there should be any danger of his being removed with his great freinds St Quintin, Strickland[726] etc whereas I am sensible there is none. But he hath yet a farther fetch, to have this discoursed to the intent if those who are gone out should appear to have such an interest as must in time bring them in again, he may perswade them he is so entirely in with them as to resolve to stand and fall together with them; which however he never will doe, nor regard any thing but himself. But I desire you to go to the Duke of Bolton or Mr Webster (if you know him) without losse of time, and acquaint them from me that Reddy Barry (my nephew by my first wife) is to come in at Dungarvan in the room of his deceased father,[727] upon the recommendation and promise of my Lord Burlington; whose

---

[723]Bolton had been a lord justice [I] in 1697–1700 and in that capacity had presided over the sessions of 1697 and 1698–9.

[724]Superfetation: 'A superfluous or excessive addition' (*OED*).

[725]Webster was eventually returned for the borough of Carysfort, Co. Wicklow, on the interest of John Allen, MP [I] (*Hist. Ir. Parl.*, vi, 510).

[726]Sir William Strickland (c.1686–1735), 4th Bt, of Boynton, Yorks, MP [GB] 1708–*d.*; revenue commr [I] 1709–11, 1714–25.

[727]Redmond Barry, MP [I] (see Appendix 2).

interest in that borough Jemmy Barry not only asserted but recovered, and on that foot Lord Burlington hath recommended Redmond Barry, and he hath fixed the matter with the electors. If the Duke or Mr Webster can prevail on Lord Burlington to recommend Mr Webster I am certain I have that influence on my relation that he will be pleased to resign his pretensions in complement to my Lord Lieutenant, altho I have not yet wrote to him; and I think there will be little difficulty to bring the electors to transfer the promise of their votes from Mr Barry to Mr Webster. This is the only election I know on which I have any sort of influence. I am extremely sorry to hear you continue your complaints of ill health and wish from the bottom of my heart that I had an oportunity to spend a little time with you. Pray write your sense of matters freely; for the stories we have here of misunderstandings where they must have the worst consequences are of that nature, that I should be terribly frightned if I could give credit to half of what is said. Tell me particularly what Mr Pulteney said when the matter of the £250000 was in debate[728] …

[PS] What comes inclosed is not my own writing, soe that it may with more freedome be left with the Duke; and indeed it consists of so many particulars that he will not be able to carry them in his head; especially the summes and computations. If you doe leave the papers with him let it be under a promise never to name me, nor to shew the papers, at least not to any one who may suspect from what hand it comes, and let him also engage to return it in two or three dayes. Tell him I doe not pretend that it is correct and perfectly right in every article.

313. *Alan I, Dublin, to Thomas, 30 Apr. 1717*

(1248/4/15–16)

I am now to own your two letters of the 20th and 23d instant: before this comes to hand my Lord Duke of Bolton will have received a letter from me owning the honour of his private letter of the 13th instant; which I wrote immediately after receit of his; and if it went not off by the pacquett which sailed first from the time of its coming to my hand, I have had wrong done me: of which I intreat you to inform his Grace, who will not think me so senselesse and stupid to omit acknowledging so particular a favor, altho the letter should have miscarryed. My last told you the enclosed papers give a very imperfect account of our charge and debt; nor can you beleive it possible for me to be very certain or particular, if you consider what people are concerned not to have every thing known which may be necessary to sett that matter in a fair light: to which if you add that I must trust no body, but do every thing my self, and then compute how much other businesse I have to employ my time, you will with more readinesse be able to excuse my inaccuracy to my Lord Lieutenant. To give an instance or two; I made the charge of the Nation annually to be but fowre hundred and one thousand odd hundred pounds; but indeed the summes payable by the military and Civil lists amount to that summe; but I omitted to take notice of the annual charge of baracks, and military contingencyes, which amount to about £16000 per annum: Of this you should

---

[728] In the debate on 12 Apr. in the committee of supply, when Secretary Stanhope moved to grant the king £250,000 'to enable him to concert measures against Sweden'. There ensued a long silence, which was eventually broken by Pulteney. His speech is reported in Cobbett, *Parl. Hist.*, vii, col. 443.

give early intimation, and say withal that I doubt it will appear that our charge as it now stands is very little if any thing short of £430000 per annum. I speak from one who can best tell me but could not give me the particulars in figures. I am in the greatest pain till I shal hear whether my Lord Lieutenant hath been able to stem the current of loading the new establishment with fresh pensions, and how far he hath been able to gett it eased of some that were on the former. His Case seems to me to be this. There were assurances given in the house and out of it (if Gentlemen would not doe it in a disrespectful maner, but by private intimations or hints to the Governement) they should find themselves eased of what gave offence, before their next meeting: the particular assurances given, or the maner and terms on which they were given I will not take on me to sett down; but hopes next to assurances were given that the establishment would be discharged of those things which seemed very distastful, provided no representation, addresse, or vote were come to in that matter, or to this effect. My Lord Townesend in his letter to us of the second of April mentions his having represented to his Majestye that the establishment is overloaded in almost every branch of it, especially the pensions; and that the King is resolved to use the utmost frugality in a new establishment etc.[729] I beleive his Lordship was assured that the new establishment should be such as he said the King intended; Mr Bladens freinds say he indeed was not fond of coming over, not seeing a likelyhood of the establishment being eased as was promised: here then were assurances given in one Governement, which it will be said, they would have made good: the intended frugalitye recommended by Lord Townesend was laid aside with him, and instead of taking off old, new pensions are added and all will be imputed to the Duke of Bolton by the freinds of those who are cheifly instrumental in continuing us under our load or laying us under new pressures. The consequence may be a representation to the King of the inability of the Kingdome to pay such an establishment, especially when perhaps some articles of it are in favor of men hateful to the Kingdome and in no sort well affected to his Majestyes interests or service. This will be most unacceptable to the King, and little for my Lord Lieutenants honour; and his predecessors will smile at its falling in his time, whereas they prevented it in theirs. It will therefore extremely import the Duke to endeavour the preventing new charges, and lightning the nation of some of the old. At the beginning of the last Session the talk without doors was cheifly against the weight the nation lay under from the French Pensioners,[730] to divert which storm some people went pretty roundly into the finding fault with other pensions and gave hopes and assurances of taking off such as were unreasonable, if the house would not come into a representation etc soe that the Committee which had the Pensions under consideration only made objections or remarks on some other pensions, a Copy of which report we shal send to the Duke of Bolton, which people were made beleive would be in a great measure omitted in the next establishment; and these were cheifly on the civil, and some of the military pensions; for care was taken that nothing more should be said of the French Pensioners then that the Committee found the expence of them was reduced from a greater to a lesser summe; but little did the house expect an encrease of such would be endeavoured by the same man who

---

[729] Martin Bladen wrote to Charles Delafaye on 28 Mar. 1717 that the lord lieutenant 'is resolved to use the utmost economy in framing the new establishment' and would be writing to the lords justices to that effect (TNA, SP 63/375/66–7).

[730] The lengthy list of French Huguenot army officers awarded pensions on the Irish military establishment, as delivered in to the Irish house of commons, can be found at *CJI*, iv, 101–9.

used so many endeavours to screen those pensions which he had in great measure been the means of laying on the countrey.[731] I hear from a good hand that he gave the Duke a list of names, or a paper for his Majestye to sign as what should be the new establishment with an addicion of great numbers of his freinds, without telling him of the added pensioners: sure this cannot be so, tho the person who writes it is a knowing man: his Grace would not bear such usage. The same Gentleman tells me he at the same time gave characters of the men whom he thought deserving in this Kingdome: I wish I had the list of his new Pensioners, with his freind St Simon[732] at the head of them. His men of merit I know were those who truckled and by mean subserviencyes gott into the good graces of Bladen and Delafay, which I scorned to do; for which and my being more sollicitous to save the Nation money then some others were I am sensible I am far from being in his good Graces. My services to my Lord Lieutenant.

[PS] The way we are directed to inquire into the French and other pensions, and the difficultyes we meet to find out truth after such a tract of time (especially since the Muster Rolls are burnt) is a difficulty we shal be hardly able to surmount: Our Cheif care must be against increasing the load. We are preparing a letter in answer to my Lord Townesends letter of the second instant, which I once thought we might have ready to go by this pacquet, but it is impossible. Pray give me a character of Mr Webster; your Colleagues freinds make him a very little man.

You must know Mr Manly and some others had letters from London intimating you were to be first Secretary. The Letter for passing Colonel Moretons patent is directed right; viz to the D[*uke*] of Bolton, or to the Deputy, or other Cheif Governor or Governors for the time being; but there is a fault in it, for it doth order the office to be granted exercisable by Deputy, only saith the [*sic*] may receive the fees by himself or deputy; but the general words of all such beneficial clauses as his predecessors may for ought I know warrant the Atturney General to draw a fiant with an expresse clause empowring him to act by deputy.

314. *Alan I, Dublin, to Thomas, at his lodgings in the Privy Garden, Whitehall, 5 May 1717*

(1248/4/17–18)

The postage of the inclosed papers will cost you nothing, and Mr Wogans Clerk will call on you for them and passe them through the offices as his master assures me; Mr Wogan is a Clerk under Mr Southwell[733] who hath undertaken this matter in favor of the eldest son of Mr Phaire who married Batt Purdons daughter,[734] from whom and my sister Clayton on her behalf I have letters without number. The young fellow had wrong done him, and his Mother was a great acquaintance of my brother Claytons who by many letters in her favor to me in his lifetime hath intailed her a correspondent on me that will not fail attaining

[731] The 1st earl of Galway, himself a Huguenot refugee.

[732] Not listed in *CJI*, iv, 101–9.

[733] William Wogan (1678–1758), clerk to Edward Southwell, MP [I], sec. of state [I] (*Oxf. DNB*).

[734] Thomas Phaire (*d.*1716), of Mount Pleasant, Co. Cork, married in 1692 Elizabeth, sis. of Bartholomew Purdon, MP [I]. They had three sons, Robert (*d.*1742) of Dunmaine, Co. Wexford, Herbert (*d.* aft. 1760) of Cork and Dublin, and Thomas, (*d.*1748) of Enniscorthy. (Brady, *Records*, ii, 273; T.G.H. Green, *Index to the Marriage License Bonds of the Diocese of Cloyne* (Cork, 1899–1900), 75; W.H. Welply, 'Colonel Robert Phaire, "Regicide": His Ancestry, History, and Descendants', *Journal of the Cork Historical and Archaeological Society*, xxxi (1926), 81–2.)

her end if importunitye will be of any use. If the Clerk be in disburse[735] in getting the matter effected I am content to be out of the money till I can gett it again from the young man or his mother, which I doubt will not be soon: however I desire you to shew this letter to my sister and she will reimburse Mr Wogans Clerke taking his receit and place the paiment to my account. I have reason to think that the discontented resolve never to come to a temper and that they beleive this will make it impossible for those who are now in to carry on matters without the Toryes; and that they also think those who are in, if they can find no other method are resolved to take even that worst method rather then not support themselves; yet I think from what the discontented peoples freinds say, they will rather see that come to passe then cement or come to any agreement. If this be so, who are most to blame? Or what can be said for either? Truly only this, that there is a fate hangs over us, and that the time of our ruine is accomplished ...

315. *Alan I, Dublin, to Thomas, 8 May 1717*

(1248/4/21–2)

... I write this post to my Lord Lieutenant who will shew you my letter; I had a very kind one from him of the second instant; pray continue to see him, and to explain what may be written darkly by me; you know my maner of expression better then he doth. I do not know how far it will be proper for me to write directly to Lord Sunderland on the subject; perhaps it may be as well done by you by word of mouth and doe you no disservice, since I think it will be (as it is meant) a service to him. He qualified him self as joint Vice Treasurer with Lord Rochester by taking the oath in England pursuant to an Act of Parliament there in that behalf: but I doubt he had no act, nor took no oath, on his being made sole Vice Treasurer by a new patent:[736] now his accounts are soon to passe us who are Commissioners of the publick accounts.[737] In whose name will the account be brought before us? If in his, will not this be acting before he was qualifyed subject him to penaltyes? If in the name of Captain Pratt, hath my Lord already received from Captain Pratt the perquisites of that office?[738] I do not suspect any thing amisse, but my Lord should be told of the difficultye he lyes under by not having taken the oath on the new Patent.

316. *Alan I, Dublin, to Thomas, 14 May 1717*

(1248/4/25–8)

We are now in some forwardnesse for making a report concerning the pensions on our establishment, and tho I am perswaded my Lord Townesend wrote the letter to us from whence we take arise to send over remarks on the pensions, with the honest view the

---

[735] Out of pocket (*OED*).

[736] The patent granting Sunderland sole possession of the office was dated 16 July 1716 (*Lib. Mun.*, pt 2, p. 47).

[737] According to the Irish act of 10 Hen. VII, c. 1, the vice-treasurer's accounts were audited by a board of treasury commissioners (the 'ancient board of accounts') comprising, *ex officio*, the Irish lord chancellor, chancellor of the exchequer, three chief justices, secretary of state, auditor-general and muster-master general (T.J. Kiernan, *History of the Financial Administration of Ireland to 1817* (1930), 244, 271).

[738] John Pratt, MP [I], deputy vice-treasurer.

beginning of the letter imports, to ease us of such as shal be found unreasonable, yet when I consider that the same man was Secretary to Lord Townesend who was secretary to Lord Galway,[739] and when I consider the maner of the wording of that letter and the maner it would put the enquiry into the pretensions of the French Pensioners into, I cannot but think that a certain person was willing enough to leave the English pensioners (I mean those who are not French) at large, but to make it not practicable to give the Kingdome ease as to the French Pensioners; on the contrary I think it to be most plain that the cheif view with reference to them was to draw an additional charge on the Nation. To prevent this and to make myself the better understood I must begin this matter a little higher then at the first sight may appear necessary; and desire you to look upon and make use of this letter as a comment on the report which the Lords Justices will sign concerning the pensions on our establishment; in which you will find and lay before the proper person such remarks, as I did not think prudent to communicate to my colleague, whose attachments to a late Governor and Secretary were such that I should be very imprudent too easily to beleive him capable now to desert measures into which he went soe far: not but that I think he and a good many other people are heartily sorry they went soe far; and find now that their behavior hath exposed them to the world for men more capable of being imposed upon then they are willing to passe for.

The Prince in the Kings absence directed the Lords Justices of Ireland to cause a strict examination to be made into the merits and pretensions of all persons residing in Ireland who claim or enjoy the several allowances of half pay on the establishment of great Britain or Ireland as reduced officers formerly serving in any of his Majestyes Land forces or marines, to the end any persons who are not duly intitled to the said provision may be discovered and the publick no longer burthened with them, and his Royal highnesse gave instructions in what maner the enquiry should be made. My Lord Galway in pursuance of this order did on the 31th [*sic*] day of December last authorize constitute and appoint my Lord Tyrawly and several other Officers together with Mr Delafay to be a board to enquire and examine into the merits etc. And so diligent were they in the enquiry that on the fifth day of February 1716 they sign'd and delivered to Lord Galway A Paper intitled A list of the reduced Officers on the establishment of Ireland,[740] whose merits and pretensions were examined into at the Castle of Dublin by a board constituted for that purpose by their Excellencyes the Lords Justices of Ireland. It is not my businesse to remark farther on this paper then to say, that it hath hapned very luckily for this Kingdome, that there is not one unqualifyed person on the establishment of half pay, for any thing appearing in it: but this is a matter I should not have taken any notice of now, if it had not given some handle for the enquiry into the pretensions of the French Pensioners; or perhaps I may with as great truth conjecture that this enquiry was ordered to be made on the 31th of December to make way for another which might turn to the advantage of the French Pensioners. To make this matter the more intelligible I must observe to you that a matter was sett on foot to increase the half pay of the broken Officers on this establishment, which tho much opposed by those who foresaw the heavy charge it would bring on the Kingdome, yet found such

---

[739] Martin Bladen (see above, p. 167).

[740] Grafton and Galway had been asked by Secretary Stanhope to select officers from the half-pay list in order to complete the new regiments being raised in the emergency of the jacobite invasion (TNA, SP 63/374/80–1: lords justices to Stanhope, 6 Feb. 1715/16).

encouragement at the Castle that the Duke of Grafton could not stem the peticions being brought in, tho he opposed it very strongly in all appearance, and on my conscience I think really: Nay so warmly was this pushed that he could hardly obtain the respite of a day from Lord Santry, Colonel Morris[741] etc who acted for the rest of the half pay Officers: Now let any one consider whether half pay Officers, especially whether Colonel Morris (who is quartermaster General now in pay) would have ventured to push a matter against the sense of the Castle; but they very well knew how far from ungrateful this would be on one side of the Castle, which resolved to benefit his Country men, by going into this affair; in which many of the house of Commons (he knew) would be very easy on the account of several freinds and relations which many of the members had on the list of half pay Officers. The Parliament mett on the 12th of November and on the eighteenth the peticion of the half pay Officers for an encrease of their half pay was brought into the house and was referred to the Committee of Supply:[742] On the thirteenth of December the report was made from that Committee, and one of the resolutions was that the Committee directed the Chairman to move the house that an humble addresse be presented to his Majestye that he will be graciously pleased to put the half pay Officers upon full half pay for themselves and servants from the first of August preceding, and upon full pay whenever they shal be commanded upon duty; and an addresse was made accordingly,[743] which had its full effect and the half pay Officers have received their full half pay ever since. I am not yet entirely apprised what the annual expence of the encrease of half pay (as the list of half pay Officers now stands) will amount to, but ought to take notice that the Committee of Supply, previous to their resolution to addresse for an encrease of half pay, came to a vote in these words Resolved That it is the opinion of this Committee, That by the death and promotion of several half pay Officers upon the establishment there will be a summe sufficient to make up the pay of the half pay Officers now remaining on the establishment full half pay for themselves and their servants. Having said this I proceed to shew you the reasons why I do apprehend the letter directing us to enquire into the pretensions of the French pensioners was calculated to load the establishment, and that it was rather a dart out of a certain persons quiver to wound us yet deeper then we are already, tho intended by my Lord Townesend as a plaister to heal the sore.

The letter intimates that Lord Townesend had represented to his Majesty how much the establishment of Ireland is overloaden almost in every article of the Civil and military list, particularly in that of pensions; and that his Majestye out of his tender regard to his subjects of this Kingdome being determined to use the utmost frugality in framing of a new establishment, in order thereto had commanded him to signifye his Royal pleasure to us to make the best enquiry we can into the several pretensions of the pensioners on the Civil and military lists as well English as French, distinguishing the time when and the reasons why such pensions were granted to them:

Hitherto our enquiry is to be carryed in the same maner as to the French and other pensioners, and we seem to be left at large to examine into their pretensions as shal seem

---

[741]Richard Morris (*d.*1720), col., Ikerrin's dragoons 1711 and on half-pay 1712; raised his own regiment of dragoons in 1715; quarter-master gen. by 1716 (Dalton, *Army Lists*, v, 246; vi, 229; Vicars, *Index*, 33; *Lib. Mun.*, pt 2, p. 113).

[742]Confirmed in *CJI*, iv, 127.

[743]Confirmed in *CJI*, iv, 120–1. The committee named to prepare the address included St John III.

most likely to attain the end aimed at viz the easing of the establishment. But the letter goes on and tells us that the French pensioners will require a different consideration in regard that many of them were placed upon the establishment for their military service, and that it is his Majestyes pleasure that we should examine their pretensions as they are distinguished under the following heads.

1. The Officers reduced in the five regiments of Galway, Miremont,[744] Meloniere,[745] Lifford[746] and Belcastel[747] that served in the war of Ireland at the revolution, and likewise in Flanders afterward, and should have been put at the peace on half pay but that great part of them were not naturalized.
2. Officers who did not belong to the said five Regiments, but did notwithstanding serve in the reduction of Ireland, and were put upon the list of pensions for that service.
3. Officers sent from England and placed upon the establishment by warrant for their services abroad in the year 1704.
4. Officers who served in Piemont[748] with King Williams Commission.
5. Officers who were under the command of my Lord Rivers and served in that expedition designed for a descent upon France.[749]
6. Troopers and Gentlemen who served in the five disbanded regiments aforesaid.
7. Widows and other pensioners upon the foot of charity only.

The letter proceeds to tell us that the pensions in the 1st 2d 3d 4th and 5th articles, being all of them granted to foreigners in lieu of half pay, it is necessary his Majestye should be informed whether the Pretensions of the several persons therein comprized be such as would have intitled them to half pay, had they been naturalized; for that his Majestye doth not think it reasonable that they should be on a better foot then his own natural born subjects, however a charitable regard will be had to those whose circumstances shal move us to represent favourably.

The scope of this paper (as drawn) seems to me to be this; to gett the French Officers to be transferred to the military list and intermixed with the half pay Officers and then to encrease their pensions (where they were given in lieu of half pay) to full half pay, as our own half pay Officers are now paid pursuant to the addresse of the house of Commons.

It is most certain and appears by his Majestyes letter of 9 Febr.1715[750] that the Lords Justices had proposed to his Majestye the transferring the French Officers from the Civil to the military list; and whether that proposal was not made with that view, considering

---

[744] Armand de Bourbon (1655–1732), marquis de Miremont (*Oxf. DNB*).

[745] Isaac de Monceau de La Melonière (*d.*1715) (John Childs, 'Huguenots and Huguenot Regiments in the British Army, 1660–1702: "Cometh the Moment, Cometh the Men"', in *War, Religion and Service: Huguenot Soldiering, 1685–1713*, ed. Matthew Glozier and David Onnekink (Aldershot, 2007), 37–8).

[746] Fredéric-Guillaume de la Rochefoucauld, Comte de Marton (*d.*1749), whose promise of the earldom of Lifford from William III was never confirmed by patent and remained a courtesy title (Grace Lawless Lee, *The Huguenot Settlements in Ireland* (1936), 166–7).

[747] Pierre de Belcastel (*d.* c.1711) (C.E. Lart, *Huguenot Pedigrees* (2 vols, 1924–8), i, 6–7).

[748] Piedmont.

[749] Richard Savage (c.1654–1712), 4th Earl Rivers, commander of an expedition in 1707 intended for the coast of France but diverted to Spain.

[750] George I to the lords justices, 9 Feb. 1715/16 (TNA, SP 63/374/92–3), approving this proposal.

how near it followed on the heels of the addresse for encreasing the half pay I leave to any mans consideration: The framing a new establishment was then also under consideration, and probably arose from this side of the water, and as I have been told there was a draught of one formed but the Justices could not agree in it, several charges seeming more reasonable to one of the Justices then to the other, who could not come into all that was expected by his colleague; but this is conjecture, or if I have better grounds for it, I am not at liberty to say how far these matters went: this disagreement or something else having prevented the signing a new establishment till the Governement was resolved to be altered, other methods were to be taken to make it practicable to change the French pensioners into half pay Officers with an encrease to their pensions: and Lord Galway on the first day of February 1716/7 conceived an order to the following effect reciting that among other instructions he hath it in command from his Majesty to examine into the pretensions and circumstances of the French Pensioners on the civil establishment here and that there are many of them who obtained their pensions in lieu of half pay when the Regiments of Galway Miremont La Meloniere Lifford and Belcastle in which they served were broke here soon after the peace of Reswick,[751] and others upon their being reduced after having served in Spain Portugal Savoy and elsewhere with Commissions from the late King W[illia]m or Queen Anne or the Generals by them respectively empowred to grant such Commissions or from the Duke of Savoy and therefore authorizes the Lord Tyrawly and the rest of the board appointed to examine into the merits and pretensions of the half pay Officers receiving pensions of his Majestyes bounty, and to summon the Officers to appear before them or if they cannot to send their Commissions or vouchers of their respective services, and to report unto him the whole together with their observations thereon.

Whether Lord Galway had any late direction to direct this enquiry I cannot tell, but beleive the contrary; if he had not I presume he acted upon the addicional instruction given the Duke of Grafton and him on 24th Sept. 1715 whereby the King dispenses with the French pensioners taking an oath to intitle them to the receit of their pensions, which his Majestyes establishment required them to take; this oath (among other things) was to be that they had no other means to maintain themselves or family etc which would not have gone down with a good many of them: and it appears by that instruction that it had been represented by the Lords Justices to the King that many inconveniences may arise upon exacting that oath and that the K[ing]s bounty may be managed with as much frugality by some other method: and that they had proposed an enquiry to be made into the circumstances of the pensioners, that those who have no need of them or are undeserving the Kings favor may be struck off and in lieu of the oath the Justices are directed to enquire into Pensioners circumstances, and if they find any who have no need of them, or are undeserving they are to transmit an exact account of them.

Perhaps the words which mention an enquiry who deserve the K[ing]s favor may be supposed a sufficient foundation for this warrant dated 1 Febr. 1716 in which I cannot but observe there is not the least mention of any enquiry to be made as to their circumstances whether they need the Kings favor or not, which seems the primary intention of the direction that each enquiry should be made; but whatever ground or motive Lord Galway had to direct this enquiry, the board proceeded on it and made a report dated under the following heads.

---

[751] The Treaty of Ryswick in 1697.

1. A List of the French Officers receiving Pensions of his Majestyes bounty in lieu of half pay whose pretensions were examined into at the Castle of Dublin by a board constituted for that purpose by their Excellencyes the Lords Justices of Ireland. They proceed in this order 1 The Officers of the 5 Regiments of Galway Miremont La Meloniere Lifford and Belcastle.
2. The[y] go on next to the Officers from Piemont recommended [by] Mr Hill.
3. Then to the Officers which were under the command of the Earle of Rivers.
4. Next to Officers put on the establishment by warrants or on the establishment in the [year] 1704. A Copy of which return Lord Galway delivered to me with his own hand on the ninth of March last.

Compare now this return with the heads under which we are ordered to consider the French Pensioners and see whether the instructions contained in the letter of the second of April be not calculated to make it almost impossible for us to doe any thing more then take up that report as a foundation for us to do the same thing.

The return of the board saith that the several French Officers receiving pensions etc receive it in lieu of half pay; for so it is admitted in the title.

The letter of the second of April hath these words in it; the pensions in the 1st 2d 3d 4th and 5th articles being granted all of them to foreigners in lieu of half pay etc soe as we are only directed to enquire whether the persons in those articles were officers who would have been intitled to half pay if naturalized, and to take a thing for granted which we know to be otherwise in some instances viz. that all their pensions were given in lieu of half pay. I say I think it was intended to restrain us from enquiring into that, and then it would be readily said, all these had half pay under the name pensions, put them now on the establishment of half pay Officers, and it would follow of course that they should receive the like half pay with other Officers.

There is another matter of fact or two taken for granted which really are otherwise: the letter in the first article mentions the five Regiments of Galway Miremont La Meloniere Lifford and Belcastle that served in the war of Ireland at the revolution and likewise in Flanders: now we are not directed to enquire whether all these regiments served in the reduction of Ireland and in fact Miremonts never did, but was sent over after the peace of Reswyck and broken; and whatever pretensions to half pay their being broken here may give them, yet they cannot pretend to stand on the same foot with those who were concerned in the war of Ireland. The pretence also which is given for the Officers of those regiments not being put on the half pay when they were broken is I doubt a mistake; for in the first place there was a Statute in force long before and some time after the forming the establishment in 1699 by which all Protestant strangers were naturalized upon taking the oath of fidelity to King William and that whereby we swear we do not beleive that Princes excommunicated by the Pope may be murdered by their Subjects: and indeed the truth is that our gratitude to King William and the resentment we had to the attemt made to endeavour to force King William to break the French regiments after he had been so ill treated in England[752] made this Kingdome willing to pay those pensions in nature of charity, but not as a debt the Crown owed. However I think those who did so serve (I mean

---

[752] By the English parliamentary campaign in 1697–9 to reduce drastically the size of the army after the conclusion of the Nine Years' War (the War of the League of Augsburg) and in particular to disband the regiment of Dutch Foot Guards.

in the Irish war) will not be thought burthensome if they do not (as hitherto) produce new ones when the former fall.

This long paper may be reduced to these short heads.

1. The addresse of the Commons to increase the half pay was meant only of those Officers who were on the establishment of half pay at that time, as appears plainly from the vote which saith that by the death or provision of half pay Officers there will be a summe sufficient to make up the pay of the half pay Officers now on the establishment etc Neither the reason of the thing nor the sense of the house extended to those Officers who should be afterward broke, much lesse to those who were then on the list of Pensioners; and would now be turned into half pay Officers.
2. It is commonly beleived the house intended only that increase of half pay to the Officers then on half pay during the then emergency and as an encouragement in that time of danger; not to be a measure to those officers or much lesse to future regiments or pensioners.
3. It may I think endanger the bringing the whole matter of French pensions into consideration (and nobody knows where such an enquiry may end) if the Commons shal see an addresse of theirs (I must not call an hasty one) made use of to load the Nation in favor of those for whom they never intended to addresse: nay on my conscience if it had been surmised it would have had this consequence, the whole application for encrease of half pay would have ceased.
4. In forming a new establishment great care must be taken to prevent an encrease of half pay to any Officers who are not now on half pay, or to any French pensioner under the notion of half pay; whatever shal be done with the Officers now on the List of half pay: I shal not propose reducing them to their former half pay; but if the necessity of affairs should encline the King to it I beleive many of the Commons would think his Majestye had taken better care of them then they did of themselves.
5. If the French Officers who would have been entitled to half pay and are now on the list of pensions desire to be transferred to the military list of half pay because they think that not so precarious as pensions, and will rest content with the same summe for half pay which they now receive as pensions, I doe not see any harm in it; unlesse this use may be made of it, that when thereby the total summe given in pensions to the French will receive soe visible a diminution it may be a means of adding other pensions on the foot of charity: whereas this poor countrey hopes at some time or other to see an establishment in which the title of French Pensioners shal be wholly omitted. New ones we have no reason to expect or provide for; and as for the French who came over with King William or soon after they are in as good a condition as most people in the Kingdome, and in a much better then the much greater part of it: and are better able to give then they are fit to receive charity.

[PS] I have your letter by Mr Synge for which I thank you. The difficulty which I foresaw would fall soon on us by the encrease of pay to the horse and Dragoons is now at hand: look on my letter of 26 April about the later end, and you will find what the matter is.

Carry that letter to Dover Street[753] when you do this; and probably a letter I write now about it will be shewn you …

I wonder I should not have one line from any body by the two last pacquets, considering the nature of the letter I wrote you on the 26 April and of another since to another hand of as great length. I doe not know whether the Secretary[754] is any way consulted in framing our establishment; if he be and you from me apprise Mr Addison of what I have wrote to you, I verily think he will from the justice of the thing endeavour to ease us of unreasonable loads. Tell me did you write since 4 May.

317. *Alan I, Dublin, to Thomas, at his lodgings in the Privy Garden, Whitehall, 23 May 1717*

(1248/4/29–30)

The pacquet boat which came in yesterday morning brought your three letters of the eleventh, fourteenth, and sixteenth; in the former you give me hopes of knowing the successe the Duke of Bolton hath had with Lord Burlington as to the borough of Dungarvan; yet neither of the two later mention any thing of it.

You must know that as Jemmy Barry recovered that borough to the Burlington family, my Lord hath given a promise to young Redmond Barry to succeed his father in it; and I think he is pretty secure of succeeding. Now I have that reason to beleive he will be directed by me in this matter that I hardly doubt being able to bring him to make a ready complement of it to my Lord Duke; and with Lord Burlingtons concurrence I doe not apprehend a disappointment in the election: but till I hear what his Grace hath done I will not break the thing to the young fellow. By the death of Sir Ralph Freake there is also another vacancye at the borough of Cloghnekilty, where Mr Webster may come in (supposing Lord Burlington should stand off) if the Duke can gett him recommended by my Lord Carleton,[755] who hath a very good estate and consequently a very good interest there; care hath been taken to write down to some freinds there; particularly to Lieutenant Colonel George Freake (nephew to General Erle)[756] to secure an interest, and if Lord Carletons letter can be procured, there will be no great difficultye in the thing; but no time is to be lost, least Sir Richard Cox should interpose in behalf of his worthy son.[757] You would not wonder at the refusal given the Duke by a certain person, if you knew how warmly both he and all his freinds are attached to the late in opposition to the present sett of men in place. I am no stranger to the scandalous report you mention of the ground of Mr W[ebster]s interest; that hath been (as lyes usually are) very much cultivated and spread about here: It is not my businesse to advise in other mens affairs, and perhaps what occurs to me will be entirely improper by his being wholly a stranger to the rumor; which if he be, he must be a good freind indeed that will take on him the nice office of breaking it to

---

[753] The duke of Bolton's residence.

[754] Joseph Addison replaced Paul Methuen as secretary of state for the southern department (with responsibility for Irish affairs) in Apr. 1717.

[755] Henry Boyle (1669–1725), 1st Baron Carleton.

[756] George Freke, MP [I].

[757] Richard Cox, MP [I] was elected for Clonakilty at the by-election.

him: but if the scandal hath reached his ears, he hath a very easy way to remove it by not bringing over a certain person with him: This certainly is the reasonable part if it occur to him. I am much pleased at the character you give him. However Senny may represent the state of Sir John Whitronges[758] health I doe not hear of his being any way out of order, and do beleive him as well as usual; you know he is an intemperate man and by being soe risques a feaver sometimes, but beyond this I beleive nothing; nor is he, I am confident, sick at this time. The Chancellor of the Exchequer[759] is indeed so far recovered as not to be dead, but never can be of other use in Parliament then as a single Yea or Nay. I have wrote to the Duke in favor of Mr Ward,[760] who will be a man of use; he hath parts, and interest, and by bringing him in there will be a blow and mortification given to a certain person and party here, on whom Sir Ralph Gore builds;[761] as they represent his merit and interest very much beyond the just size of either … I see discontent can make men who pretend much to be Whigs to join the Toryes in a very ugly instance; for my part I think it of more consequence then you doe. This will be thought an espousing the interests of those who are very angry at the prorogation of a certain number of men; and will I think encourage those, who are too ready to doe it, to talk and write in such a maner as will not much contribute to the allaying the heats of the Nation: nay I expect to hear very soon with both ears that something is again in the utmost danger. It will certainly be expected that something extraordinary should be brought on the carpett by a Gentleman of Sir W[illiam] W[yndham']s choice; and it will be very difficult to stem the current that will be for thanking the Author for so ingenious and learned a discourse, especially upon so good an oportunitye; the printing it at the desire of the Auditors naturally follows.[762] Mays letter to my Lord Duke was intended to try whether during the absence of Mr Webster all the businesse should not go through his hands;[763] because when Prior was first secretary and he the second, he officiated wholly;[764] but we thought it reasonable to continue Mr Budgel, who was in before, and doth businesse very well:[765] beside tho I think May an honest man

---

[758] Sir John Wittewronge, 3rd Bt (1673–1722), of Stantonbury, Bucks., MP [GB] 1705–10.

[759] Philip Savage, chancellor of the exchequer [I], was buried on 13 July 1717 (*Hist. Ir. Parl.*, vi, 249).

[760] Michael Ward, MP [I].

[761] Speaker Conolly's faction. Conolly wrote to Charles Delafaye in July to ask for his assistance in promoting Gore's candidature for the chancellorship, with an eye particularly on Ward, who was himself currently in England (TNA, SP 63/375/137: Conolly to Delafaye, 10 July 1717).

[762] On 13 May 1717 the British house of commons agreed on a division to ask Andrew Snape, the high church headmaster of Eton College, to preach the Restoration Day sermon. The motion was made by Sir William Wyndham, and seconded by William Shippen (Cobbett, *Parl. Hist.*, vii, col. 452). After the division, in which tories were joined by dissident whigs, Shippen and Wyndham were ordered to acquaint Snape of the House's decision (*CJ*, xviii, 547; Colley, *In Defiance of Oligarchy*, 55, 193). The resultant sermon was printed as Andrew Snape, *A Sermon Preach'd before the Honourable House of Commons, at S. Margaret's Westminster, On Wednesday the 29th of May 1717* … (1717). Later that year, Snape's role in the so-called 'Bangorian controversy', arising from the notorious sermon delivered on 31 Mar. by Bishop Hoadly of Bangor, resulted in him being stripped of his place as a royal chaplain (J.C.D. Clark, *English Society 1688–1832: Ideology, Social Structure and Political Practice during the Ancien Regime* (Cambridge, 1985), 151–2, 160, 289).

[763] Humphrey May, MP [I].

[764] Matthew Prior (1664–1721), MP [E] 1701, had been chief secretary to the lords justices [I] 1697–9, with May as 2nd secretary. In June 1697 May was authorised to act as chief secretary in Prior's absence (J.C. Sainty, 'The Secretariat of the Chief Governors of Ireland, 1690–1800', *Proceedings of the Royal Irish Academy*, lxxii (1977), sect. C, 27, 29–30).

[765] Eustace Budgell, MP [I].

I know his attachments to my Lord Galway to be such, as to have very great weight with him: I do not blame him for gratitude to his old Master.

318. *Alan I, Dublin, to Thomas, at his lodgings in the Privy Garden, Whitehall, 25 May 1717*

(1248/4/31–2)

I have not had a line from my Lord Lieutenant since his dated the second of this month, in which he promised me one by the next post; I know how very busy every body is; and probably the difficultyes he meets with in what he intends to prevent the overloading the establishment of this Kingdome, may occasion his silence. I wish they may not be such as will be too hard for him to overcome. But this pacquet the Justices in very plain words lay down the impossibilitye there is for the Kingdome to support the number of troops and pensions now on the establishment without addition; and much more will it be insupportable to have new Pensions or halfpay Officers charged on us: they who act thus sincerely in order to prevent the difficultyes we shal be under at the meeting of a Parliament, if under a great debt we are to provide for a greater establishment then we are able to support, supposing we were not in debt, ought not I think to be thought to have any other view but to hinder our being reduced to such circumstances as to be under a necessity of quarreling with or not providing for part of the establishment. For my own particular I have determined with myself to do every thing in my power to prevail on those who can lay it before the King to shew his Majestye how much it will be for his service, and how much the condition of the Kingdome requires that the present establishment should be eased instead of being made heavier; on the other hand I have also resolved to take all the methods in my power to incline people to give the largest supplyes and with the best grace; because I am sensible his Majestyes occasions require as much as we can give; and that it will be of importance in these wayward difficult times to have things done with a good grace and with chearfulnesse.

It will be matter of triumph to some people to see things miscarry or goe on heavily in this Kingdome under a Lord Lieutenant who is known to wish well to the present administration: It will be said that the promises made by the late Justices (or one of them) and the hopes given by my Lord Townesends letter that the charge of our establishment would be lessened, would have been performed and made good if things had stil stood on the same foot and not received a turn since; and they who dislike the present sett of ministers will be sure to lay the not easing our establishment at his door who desires it should be done as much as the Kingdome wants it. It is in its own nature unaccountable, that the whole Tory interest here look on the reversal of Nugents decree as a matter of great and publick consequence to them;[766] and on this foot as if it would be a mortification or prejudice to me. If those who were of opinion for reversing the decree slept as well as I did the night I pronounced it and after I heard it was reversed, their minds were very easy; they did what their consciences told them was right: and so did I, when I decreed otherwise; as to the reputation of the thing I happened to have all the Judges of the Kingdome of the

---

[766] An appeal brought by the former lord chief baron of the exchequer [I] Robert Rochfort (1652–1727) against a decision of chancery in Ireland in May 1716 in favour of Ridgely Nugent. The case was heard in the British house of lords on 14 May 1717 and decided in favour of Rochfort (Josiah Brown, *Reports of Cases Upon Appeals and Writs of Error in the High Court of Parliament* … (7 vols, Dublin, 1784), i, 586–91).

same opinion with me in what I decreed: but I have seen some accounts which make the reversal as intended an humiliation to me: I am sorry for it, if the poor man hath suffered on my account; but this I cannot think considering such a judicature cannot be supposed to act on any other motives but those of equity and conscience. None of you will tell me in what maner it was; but I am told my predecessor treated me in a very frank (not to call it scurrilous) way;[767] I think him capable of doing any thing, but beside that I have acted toward him in another maner, when it lay fairly in my way to say very disagreeable things of some of his proceedings very justifiably, I did think the Court where he was would not allow another Court to be ill treated; pray tell me the truth, I mean what he said, for I am sure he lyed if he said any thing to the prejudice of my integritye or impartiality in that or any other matter; I am much unconcerned whether my opinion was well grounded; since I am sure I took the best means I could to inform my self, and (bating[768] the authority of the Court which reversed the decree) have not seen any reason beside offered to incline me to alter my opinion; and I am sure I gave my decree with my judgement supported by the concurring opinion of every one Judge in Ireland. I wish with all my heart I could get a sight of a paper which I hear is in town, I mean the new intended establishment; I mean as it is projected by Lord G[alway] and his Secretary,[769] who I find was a strenuous [ad]vocate for the Appellant; whom I hear the Parton[770] introduce[d][771] to his M[ajesty] as a person once in the service of the Crown and w[ho] served it well, and is now well affected etc. If such recommendati[ons] take place, and no more care be taken by people who can recommen[d] then seems to me to have been taken here, things may soon be in as good hands as the Kings enemyes wish … I doe assure you the Toryes expect some great honour will be done the Appellant: By what hath passed I shal not be at all surprized if Lord Ang[lesey] carry every thing before him which comes by way of complaint from this side: I know the relation a certain person hath to one who is marryed into R[ochfort']s familye, and they make no scruple to say here that a good deal is owing to his interesting him self a good deal in that affair. If he knew how well Mr R[ochfort] and all his freinds wish to that person, and his interests, I perswade my self he would have very little credit or interest with him. Farewell.

Upon enquiry I find that there were letters came over in favor of St Hippolite[772] Sousein[773] Bouget[774] Durand[775] Vivans[776] and Bodens[777] to have pensions;[778] but they were not proceeded upon so far as to bring the Lords Justices orders thereupon to the proper

---

[767] Sir Constantine Phipps.

[768] Leaving out of account (*OED*).

[769] Martin Bladen.

[770] Presumably 'Patron' is intended.

[771] Edge of MS torn here.

[772] Louis de Montolieu (1669–1738), baron de St Hippolyte, a major-general in the Prussian forces until 1716, when he rejoined the Savoyard army (*CTB*, xxxi, 513).

[773] Antoine de Saussin (1681–1723), a brigadier in the Dutch service.

[774] Major Henry Bouguet.

[775] Jean de Durand (c.1665–1743), minister to a Huguenot congregation in Dublin since 1704.

[776] Joseph, Comte de Vivans (Lart, *Huguenot Pedigrees*, i, 7).

[777] Abraham Boden or Bowden (*d.* by 1718) (*CTB*, xxxii, 21).

[778] On 14 Nov. 1715 the Irish lords justices had informed the British treasury that they had no objection to placing St Hippolyte, de Saussin, Bouguet, de Durand, the Count de Vivans and Bowden on the Irish establishment

Office; and I hear there were some other letters and the Lords Justices orders thereupon, which however were never brought to the Auditor nor were the persons put on the establishment; but the Lords Justices letters were vacated, the thing having taken air soe far as to reach the house of Commons; which created such a ferment in several members that all things were hushed. I know nothing of any of these or any other French going off with the Duke of Ormond: and beleived the disgust taken at the procuring these letters was the occasion of the matters falling.

319. *Alan I, Dublin, to Thomas, at his lodgings in the Privy Garden,*
Whitehall, 10 June 1717, '9 at night'

(1248/4/33–4)

This letter will be given you by a messenger whom I have ordered to goe expresse with two letters to the Duke of Bolton and Mr Secretary Addison, upon my Lord Tirawlyes regiment mutinying in Limrick, when men were to be drafted out of it to be sent to Port Mahon.[779] We had orders to have three hundred men and 24 Drummers drafted out of Tirawlyes Wittronges and Veseys[780] regiments before they were broke; to recruit the Regiments at Port Mahon:[781] The men are averse to going thither, but the truth is (I think) they consider if they be broken that they may enter service again as new men and have the usual encouragement to take on in a new regiment, which they loose by being drafted. And tho the drafts for Portmahon are to be made only out of Tirawlyes Veseys and Wittronges regiments, yet there being orders for other regiments to pick out such of the men in the regiments that are to be broken as are to be best liked in room of others, whether of a lesse size, or (for other reasons) not so good men; I doubt that the men of the other regiments may think their being culled out to serve in other regiments here a great hardship on them; for by so doing they loose the money they might otherwise have gott by going into new regiments. The doing this might have been a means to have purged out a good many Papists;[782] but I doubt the men may take this in their head, and if they should follow Tirawlys regiments example, the consequence will be very dangerous; what force have we to reduce such a body, if that should be designed to be effected by force, which is the last thing one would wish to see occasion for. I doubt there is such a disposition in some of them that they will not be quiet without assurance of not being drafted for Minorca or transferred into other regiments here; on the other hand our orders are positive in both those points. These are my private thoughts: When Mr Conelye comes to town we will

[778] *(continued)* (*CTP*, 1714–19, p. 141). Warrants were issued in Aug. 1717 for payment to be made to de Durand and de Vivans (*CTB*, xxxi, 545, 562).

[779] TNA, SP 63/375/117: Alan I to [Joseph Addison], 10 June 1717, enclosing a letter from Thomas Pearce, governor of Limerick, 8 June 1717, giving an account of the mutiny (TNA, SP 63/375/118–19).

[780] Theodore Vesey (*d.*1736) subsequently governor of the Royal Hospital at Kilmainham (Dalton, *Army Lists*, v, 236; *Memoirs of Laetitia Pilkington*, ed. A.C. Elias (2 vols, Athens, GA, 1997), i, 571).

[781] The garrison at Port Mahon on Minorca.

[782] By law no catholic could serve in the army in Ireland, but in practice catholics were enlisted, by lazy or corrupt recruiting officers, in order to bring regiments to a complement (A.J. Guy, 'The Irish Military Establishment, 1660–1776', in *A Military History of Ireland*, ed. Thomas Bartlett and Keith Jeffery (Cambridge, 1996), 217–19).

advise with the Privy Councel and General Officers, who perhaps will be of opinion that we should promise these things: In what a condition shal we then put ourselves?[783] I wish you would without losse of time see my Lord Lieutenant and Mr Addison, to whom you may intimate my thoughts and that perhaps it may be necessary to leave us at a little more liberty in these matters then we now are. If orders should be sent to proceed with severity and to reduce them by force, I cannot say what consequences such directions may have. I have no personal apprehension, but dread the consequences if any general disaffection should take place, if the other troops should think the draughting these men an hardship. Pray talk this matter over; I do not expresse these fears in my letters to the Duke or Secretary; it will be time enough when Mr Conelye joins in it, and the Councel and Officers have given us their advice.

320. *Alan I, Dublin, to [Thomas], 14 June 1717*

(1248/4/35–6)

Yours of the eighth continues me under the greatest uneasinesse of mind, when I find by it the continuance, or frequent returns, of the most acute and dangerous distemper human nature is capable of, upon you: For Gods sake use all medicines and advise with all persons from whom you may reasonably expect any ease or relaxation of your torture, to make the remainder of your life supportable. As the D[*uke*] of B[*olton*] might intend not to let you see my letter about the Deanry of Kilalla, he certainly did not tell you all he knew concerning the additional pay of 4d to each horseman and 2d to each dragoon; for comparing the date of your letter with that of one I had from him I find he was willing to give you hopes of altering that matter, when he told me it certainly would be continued: but there is nothing unkind in either of these things. I am not much troubled tho he should resolve to bestow this Deanry on his Chaplain Mr Cob;[784] it is but a small thing and will be found hardly worth his acceptance when he arrives.[785] The Gentleman I named was Mr John Mathews, a man of a very good character and related to my wife:[786] I wish you would speak to the Duke for his being put early on the list of his Chaplains, and Mr Barry Hartwel to be another next to him: the later is my first wives Nephew, an honest man at all times tho a Clergyman and in the Diocese of Limrick; by honest I mean soe in political matters as well as civil. Mr Conely and I write this post about Dr Leslyes[787] and Dean Roland Davies[788] resigning

---

[783] Conolly was staying at his country seat in Castletown, Co. Kildare (TNA, SP 63/375/117: Alan I to [Addison], 10 June 1717), though he returned to Dublin by the following day and was sending to England his own account of the Limerick mutiny (TNA, SP 63/375/121–2: Conolly to Delafaye, 11 June 1717).

[784] Charles Cobbe (c.1687–1765). He was not given the deanery of Killala on this occasion, but became dean of Ardagh in 1719, then bishop of Killala in 1720. Eventually (in 1743) he was made archbishop of Dublin.

[785] Said to be worth around £200 a year (Lambeth Palace Library, MS 2168, f. 128: list of bishoprics and cathedral dignities).

[786] John Matthews (1683–1733), subsequently rector of Kilkeel, Co. Down and treasurer of Down 1724–d. (H.B. Swanzy, *Succession Lists of the Diocese of Dromore*, ed. J.B. Leslie (Belfast, 1933), 181, 221).

[787] Henry Leslie (1651–1733), archdeacon of Down.

[788] Rowland Davies (1649–1721), dean of Cork.

two livings in the Kings gift:[789] they are both healthy and like to live; and tho the nature of the thing will not admit of its being part of the agreement to know their successors, yet possibly they might not be so much disposed to resign at another time as now when they hope their own and their sons behavior hath been such as may give them hopes that their Successors will be men whom they could gladly see in their livings.[790] Explain this matter a little to his Grace, which will convince him we are not recommending to vacant livings, but countenancing men who have done well. If the matter of the appeal shal be stirred in the house of Lords here I suppose we shal be able to ward every blow made in that place.

Mr Campbel having so far acted in the matter of the Master of the Rolls I write to him to continue to act in it, and wish such a letter of Attorney ready ingrossed on stamped paper were sent over for my wife and me to sign as shal be found necessary there, to attain the desirable thing of ending all matters amicably; and in order to it of agreeing on one or more to administer, and to whom differences shal be referred finally to determine in an amicable way: You and Mr Campbel jointly, and in the absence of one of you the other must be the persons my wife and I must rely on: the kindnesse with which you constantly take notice of her have made a very great impression on her; for she finds not the same kindnesse from most of her own, nor from some of my relations. You may be sure I will cultivate a freindship with Colonel Moreton; and as you have some acquaintance with Mr Webster, and know others who have more, I hope you will take some method to have him laid under a conviction that tho I shal not make him half the professions which I fancy some others will, that however I will upon every occasion as effectually shew him that I am very desirous to be on a good foot with him and doe him all service in my power as any body. The mutinyes we have had have postponed our sending our remarks on the late establishment; the truth is our hands have been so full with receiving expresses, and sending them; writing letters orders, roots etc that the Clerks in the Office have been employed night and day since Monday in that work only … The mutinyes will be all suppressed entirely very soon, and I hope we shal find who they were who first set the matter on foot: I am perswaded some of better figure then common Souldiers had an hand in it; but I would not have you beleive I mean Officers, for I do not suspect that: but some who love to embarasse the Kings affair every way may have encouraged this; our Jacobites say drafting men was hard etc and seem to pity the poor men.

I cannot close this without intreating you as far as is possible to farther the pretensions of Mr Ward[791] to the Chancellorship of the Exchequer: the Duke tells you (and I am truly sensible of his sincerity in the professions he makes and the obligations I lye under to him for making them) that my recommendations have greater weight with him then those made by a certain person whom I need not name to you. There is no one instance in the earth in which I should with more pleasure succeed then in this; the competitor is a creature of and hath a spirit low enough not to disdain being thought a dependant on the other;[790] I

---

[789] In 1717 Davies resigned the rectory of Carrigaline, Co. Cork (Cotton, *Fasti*, i, 241). Ahoghill, Co. Antrim, one of Leslie's many livings, was given to his son Peter (c.1686–1759) in 1717 (*Clergy of Connor …* (Belfast 1993), 441–2).

[790] Davies's eldest son Richard was vicar of Kilcaskan, Co. Cork (*Journal of the Very Rev. Rowland Davies, LL.D., Dean of Ross …* ed. Richard Caulfield (Camden Soc., ser 1, lxviii, 1857), x; C.A. Webster, *The Diocese of Ross: Its Bishops, Clergy and Parishes* (Cork, 1936), 84).

[791] Michael Ward, MP [I].

[790] Sir Ralph Gore, 4th Bt, MP [I] was appointed to the vacancy.

know the interest he hath by his late father in Law[792] and other freinds on one side of the Court; and doe assure you that in my opinion both he and his patron and all his supporters are at least as well affected to late people as to the present. His pretensions are the slightest in the world, if you regard personal qualifications or even interest; unlesse you will call ten persons all men of interest, because every one of them have an interest in or freindship for the other nine. It will be a triumph, if this Gentleman succeeds by the recommendations of a particular man,[793] supported by those who lately went hence; and your colleague will be much elevated if their scheme take place: and its doing soe will be aggrandized soe as to make him be esteemed here as great in his interests now as twelve months since. I cannot write more pressingly; but I doe it as well to serve a Gentleman who I think will very well fill the place as to lower the pride of people who really need to be taken a little down.

321. *Alan I, Dublin, to Thomas, 17 June 1717*

(1248/4/37–8)

Having formerly given you some account of the mutinyes here, I think I ought to put your mind a little at ease, who will certainly have heard that beside that of Tirawlys regiment at Limrick (which was the occasion of my first letter) fowre companyes at Athlone of Montandres[794] Regiment did the same and carryed matters to a prodigious height; a company att Banagher followed the example, hoping to be able to extort the same terms from Brigadier Bor[795] as those att Athlone had done, who made prisoners of all the Officers with the Brigadier and threatned to murther them and fire the town if the condicions proposed were not complyed with.[796] But we had ordered troops to march to enable all the breaking officers to do what they had in orders; and the Banagher men were reduced by force, having shut themselves up in the baracks which they defended and made many shots; fowre of them are wounded, and two of them as is beleived mortally: only one man of the Kings forces was hurt. There have also been mutinyes at Belturbet, Ardee, Caperquin[797] Corke and Kinsale; but all suppressed: the pretences were not to be drafted to Minorca (which the King by expresse orders under his own hand had directed) the Dragoons who had not served a year would have their horses, which by the Kings expresse order were in that case to be left with the Officer, as where the men had served a year the Officer was to leave the horse with the Dragoon or pay him three pounds: and the other regiments would

---

[792] Gore's first wife was the daughter of Sir Robert Colvill (1625–97), of Mount Colvill, Co. Antrim, MP [I] 1661–6, 1692–*d.*; his second wife was the daughter of St George Ashe, bishop of Clogher.

[793] Speaker Conolly.

[794] Francois de la Rochefoucauld (1672–1739), Marquis de Montandre.

[795] Jacob Borr or Burr (*d.*1723), brig-gen. and col. of marines (Dalton, *Geo. I's Army*, i, 360).

[796] Borr had been ordered to disband seven companies of Montandre's regiment quartered at Athlone, Co. Westmeath, Banagher, King's Co., and Portumna, Co. Galway, but the companies at Athlone and Banagher mutinied, held Bor and their own commanding officers captive, and extorted concessions. On 13 June 1717 the Irish privy council issued a proclamation for the apprehension of the mutineers, noting also that there had also been a mutiny at Ardee in Co. Louth, occasioned by the same grievance (*Proclamations*, ed. Kelly and Lyons, ii, 68–70). Alan was not among the signatories.

[797] Cappoquin, Co. Waterford.

not allow their being transferred into the regiments which are to stand, tho the Duke of Bolton told us he was to inform us that such was his Majestyes pleasure: beside these they insisted on half mounting[798] and some demands which the Souldiers say are unjust. We sent money down and general Officers to state allow and pay all their just demands. A general disinclination to being broken (incident to all Armies) and more to being draughted for Minorca; and an aversion to being transferred to other regiments without new listing money were I think among the cheif occasions of these disorders; but whether the absence of several Officers might not give them a better oportunity I leave any body to judge; we shal do ourselves right in laying the musters before his Majesty. Too many are in England, but some here were not on the spot; and in one or two places the mens money lay in their Captains hands, and one of them (Le Brun) tho his Commission is by the name of Captain Brown is dead: he was lately put in having been a Gentleman under the Duke of Grafton.[799] Another Captain (a Frenchman too as I hear) was absent, for he had £24 of the troops money in his hand and could not pay it. But the mutinye of Tirawly's regiment is thus far quashed, that 150 of the 280 mutineers are come in and have laid down their Arms; that at Belturbet and Caperquin are suppressed; the regiment of Wittronges who mutinyed at Kinsale are reduced, and so will that of Vesey at Corke soon be. We shal have more news of disturbances but they will be all soon over; and it is our opinion there must be some severity used for example. A letter from Charles Campbell tells me that Trevor Hill mentions mine, his, and Jack Allens[800] being to be created Viscounts; that he yeilds precedence to me, but expects it from Mr Allen. I hear nothing of the thing from any other hand and suppose it to be the act of my Lord Lieutenant: if so pray make my complements to him, and have an eye that no trick be plaid me in point of precedence: our freind Jack is very full of them …

[PS] Since closing this the Duke of Richmonds[801] messenger hath delivered me yours of the ninth; I did from the beginning think the report of my being made – was with design to prejudice me the way you mention, but I did not think it could have made any impression.

322. *Alan I, Dublin, to Thomas, at his lodgings in the Privy Garden, Whitehall, 19 June 1717*

(1248/4/39–40)

… I formerly told you that the regiment of Wittronge and Vesey had mutinyed; that the former was come to a temper and the disturbance suppressed, and the men drafted; but the later was not returned to its duty when our last letters came from Corke: but by this mornings post we have notice that Dubourgays[802] regiment arriving at Corke harbour just after the mutinye, was marched directly thither; the mutiny began on Thursday last

[798] Minor articles of soldiers' clothing (*OED*): presumably the stoppage in pay made for this.

[799] Brown (no forename given) was commissioned as an ensign in Stanwix's foot in Apr. 1716 (Dalton, *Geo. I's Army*, i, 314).

[800] John Allen (see Appendix 3).

[801] Charles Lennox (1672–1723), 1st duke of Richmond.

[802] Charles Dubourgay (d.1732), subsequently brig.-gen. and British envoy to Berlin (Dalton, *Geo. I's Army*, i, 168).

by the men; without one Corporal or Serjeant they marched out of the baracks (which are near the fort) on the Southside of the river; crossed it early on Fryday morning and incamped in the North Suburbs. The same day Dubourgays regiment landed and came to town upon notice given Major Williams the commanding Officer of it[803] of the posture of affairs by the Mayor of Corke.[804] Next morning Brigadier Stern[805] came accidentally to town and it was agreed to march and suppresse the mutiny or rebellion in its infancy. They overtook them at upper Glanmire bridge, the Granadiers of Dubourgay marched and received the fire of about thirty of the rebells and returned it, and killed fowre or five of them upon which the rest betook themselves to their heels: the regiment brought in about 78 prisoners that night; this account comes to Senny from Mr Rose a gentleman of the bar at Corke.[806] He mentions nothing of any of the Kings Souldiers being killed or wounded, nor have I yet seen the letters sent to the Governement on this occasion: tho I am as much surprised at our not having any account sent us (if that should be the case) as I ought to be at our letters not being come to the Castle (if there be any) at the time that other people have theirs. Mr Manley will let us know how this has hapned.

Since writing this I have seen another account, which saith that some of Pococks[807] as well as a detachment of Dubourgayes were concerned in this action; that some of the Kings men are wounded, and one killed; that near 100 rebels are brought in prisoners, and a good many who run away lye wounded and some dead in the countrey; but it is allowed from every quarter that the rogues are entirely dispersed; soe that the countrey must take care of themselves when these fellows turn Toryes,[808] which I think they will better do by bringing them in before they gett to the mountains. Tirawlyes regiment is also entirely suppressed, and Brigadier Pearce[809] hath above 300 of them Prisoners at discretion: his Majestyes orders what examples to make we must expect with extreme impatience. If his Majestyes general amnesty should reach the leaders of these Villains, I should think it one of the most unhappy effects of Grace and mercy that ever I heard of.

I can now tell you that yesterday we had a letter to make Mr Chetwind a Viscount and Baron;[810] Molesworth was so before.[811] If it be intended to make me one I hope no more will get the start of me; for I really think putting me just in the crowd, and afterward putting others over my head shews me to be of little consideration, or to be forgotten.

[803] Charles Williams, formerly major in Wills's marines (Dalton, *Army Lists*, v, 136; Dalton, *Geo. I's Army*, i, 194).

[804] William Lambley (*d*.1721) (*Cork Council Bk*, 391–2; Phillimore, *Indexes*, ii, 65).

[805] Robert Stearne (*d*.1732), brig.-gen. and col. of the Royal Irish Regiment (Dalton, *Geo. I's Army*, i, 158–9). He was made honorary freeman of Cork on 3 June 1717 (*Cork Council Bk*, 391).

[806] Presumably Henry Rose, MP [I]. No other Rose is listed in *K. Inns Adm.* (429), as having been called to the Bar before 1717.

[807] John Pocock (*d*.1732), of Leicester Fields, London, subsequently a brig.-gen. (Dalton, *Geo. I's Army*, i, 180).

[808] Rural bandits.

[809] Thomas Pearce.

[810] Walter Chetwynd (1678–1736), of Ingestre, Staffs., MP [E & GB] 1702–11, 1712–22, 1725–34; created Viscount Chetwynd of Bearhaven [I] 29 June 1717.

[811] Robert Molesworth, 1st Viscount Molesworth (see Appendix 3).

323. *Alan I, Dublin, to Thomas, 24 June 1717*

(1248/4/41–2)

I cannot but think by the successe which people of worse pretensions find that I have been in some measure wanting to my self in not applying to his Majestye for some thing which may be of use to my familye. Ben Parry by pushing his very little or no pretensions hath gott a patent during good behavior of the office of Register of the Memorials of all deeds and conveyances and of all wills and devises, with all fees allowed by act of Parliament: the patent is dated 18 December in the sixth year of Queen Anne.[812] They tell me it is not now worth above £200 a year, but beside that it will increase, it hath now annexed to it on the establishment £500 upon a former addresse for 11 years; which being now near out, the last Session addressed to continue it to Parry for life;[813] but I do not find that is yet put on the establishment; I mean in nature of a salary among the state Officers, whereas it was on the former establishment among the pencions. You see by the inclosed that I have wrote to the Duke of Bolton about it, which I beg you will deliver when you see a proper season; as little time as possible is to be lost, that if the thing can be effected the letter may be signed and passe the offices before he leaves London. But beside making him, I know others are to be applyed to; and have therefore wrote to Mr Secretary Addison, who will I am confident give it not only dispatch, but support and countenance my pretensions as far as is proper to be done by one in his Station. I leave both letters open for your perusal; but there yet remain my Lord Sunderland and the Commissioners of the Treasury to be applyed to: If Mr Delafay hath not done me injustice, as well as ill offices, I am certain I once had him my freind, and am as certain I never did one act to render him other: as for the Lords of the Treasury I do not so much as know who they are. But there is one thing of most absolute necessity I mean an active and prudent Sollicitor; I think I have taken care by my wifes writing to Charles Campbel how much it is the concern of her own son as well as of mine to engage him affectionately in it; do not you take notice of her letter, but mention my having wrote to you to give your assistance in procuring it for my namesake and Arthur Hill; and tell him in a free way you hope he will exert himself upon such an occasion on behalf of both: and employ his very good talent at passing businesse through offices as effectually here, as he alway doth in other cases. He will I think upon your desiring it take on him the solliciting part, and I will gratifye him to his own content. Pray tell my sister Martha of this and take her advice in it; but speak of it to as few as possible; for no sooner is any thing of the grant of an emploiment talked of in your offices in England, but some Courtier takes the hint and gets the thing; but this being of a reversion and the Office of no great value I hope there will not any thing of that kind happen …

[PS] The first difficultye will be by whose hands to have my application, or memorial laid before the King; if that be the course: I hope the Duke of Bolton will doe it; and

---

[812]Benjamin Parry, MP [I].

[813]Parry had originally been appointed to the office of register of deeds in 1707, the term of the patent being 'during good behaviour' (*Lib. Mun.*, pt 2, p. 80). On 2 June he successfully petitioned the Commons for their recommendation that his salary be continued on the establishment (*CJI*, iv, 250). A privy seal warrant was issued on 26 July 1717 to convert his patent into one for life, the patent being issued at Dublin Castle in the following September (*Lib. Mun.*, pt 2, p. 80).

Mr Secretary Addison should know the time: or for ought I know the Secretary may be inclined to carry it himself; but my Lord Lieutenant I take to be the proper person; yet I have in my letter to Mr Addison left a latitude for your putting it into his hand, if you see proper.[814]

324. *Alan I, Dublin, to Thomas, 24 June 1717*

(1248/4/43–4)

I am sorry to find by Allyes letter of the 18th that you are returned indisposed from Peper-hara, but she tells me you find yourself better since being in town. Last pacquet Mr Conelye and I sent over our remarks on the pensions, which letter perhaps the Duke[815] may give you the trouble of reading over: If so you will perceive that it is written in a maner which shews it was never intended for his Majestyes view, as well by the length of it, as by some expressions in it; but if his Grace shal think fit to lay any part of it before his Majestye in French, I hope his Secretary Mr Guydickens[816] will not be the translator: for tho he bears a better character then almost any body that a certain person employed in the opinion of people here, yet stil he hath a bent toward one for whose view that letter was never calcu-lated. My Lord Lieutenant will not look on that letter as the remarks which might be made on the establishment; since our instructions (I mean Lord Townesends letter) confined us to the pensions; nor indeed is it all we should have remarked on the pensions if we had been at entire liberty: but it cannot be expected we should say any thing to those which his Majesty hath since his accession put on: for example the encrease of Lord G[*alway*]s pension from £1000 to £1500 a year;[817] that of £500 a year to L'Hermitage and others.[818] We have also been very tender in remarking on the pensions on the civil and military lists, which the Commons having had under their consideration, and singling out some of them, we thought might be understood like an approbation of the rest; or that we were very officious and fond of finding fault with that which they did not make objection to: However we have observed on the military pensions of Marquis Miremont and Jansen Teudeboeuf; and should also on the encrease of Lord Liffords half pay as Colonel of foot to £500 a year. It was also my sense to have said that Mr Luttrel having received £500 a year ever since the reduction of Limrick,[819] had been (I thought) paid sufficiently for any service he did or is supposed to have done. Thirteen thousand pounds is a very great summe, yet so much he hath already received of the publick money; and is in no sort of want, having a very great

---

[814]In due course Bolton was able to inform Secretary Stanhope that the king had acquiesced to Alan's request that the reversion of Parry's place be given to Arthur Hill and Alan II (Kent Archives, U1590/O145/33: 'Memorandum for Lord Stanhope' [1717]).

[815]Bolton.

[816]Melchior Guy Dickens (1696–1775), gazetted as a captain in Dubourgay's foot in 1716, subsequently British minister in Berlin and Stockholm, and ambassador to Russia 1755–9 (*British Diplomatic Instructions, 1689–1789*, v: *Sweden, 1727–1789*, ed. J.F. Chance (Camden Soc., ser. 3, xxxix, 1928), 89–129).

[817]Confirmed in *CTB*, xxxi, 536.

[818]Confirmed in *CTB*, xxxi, 520. René de Saumiers, sieur de L'Hermitage, had been the Dutch resident in London since 1692.

[819]Henry Luttrell (c.1654–1717), of Luttrellstown, Co. Dublin. His pension dated from 1692 (*CTB*, ix, 1596).

real estate, and being a very wealthy monyed man without child, and not having any near relation to provide for that I know. But Luttrelstown lyes in the neighbourhood of Castletown[820], and I found a great backwardnesse in somebody as to the maner of expressing our selves on this subject; upon the whole matter you will consider two were to join in making the representations which were to be made. But what we have done is rather calculated to prevent our being laid under additional loads, then that our remarks will very much ease the present establishment: and indeed unlesse his Grace can prevail with his Majestye to reduce the forces from the number they were increased to on the invasion to that which they amounted to formerly, I do not see how the establishment can be supported, altho the half pay officers of the thirteen broken regiments should be provided for elsewhere, which I take for granted, because it is utterly impossible to do it here. Whether his Majestye will think of reducing more regiments, or beleive it may be done another way, by bringing the troops and companyes from being full (as now) to their former numbers, I will not pretend to conjecture: nor am I sure the later way will intirely doe the thing; but sure some way will be found to make things possible to be supported. I write this post to the Duke in behalf of Will Southwell, who commands the battle Axes or Guards as Colonel, yet hath but 10s a day;[821] the Commons among many recommendations of people much lesse worthy addressed to have his pay made equal to that of other Colonels. The addresses in favor of Iniskillin Officers,[822] and others, particularly of Topham for £300 a year salary for an office in the forfeitures (the benefit of which England has)[823] have been laid before the King, and had their effect; the persons being put on by letters; but I find that addresse in behalf of Southwel never was laid before his Majestye; I say this because you give me the title of it as one of the papers left by Lord Galway and delivered over to the Duke. In my letter I doe not take notice that I know this, but only conjecture it: Southwel hath given offence to Lord G[alway] by not paying him and his French all those servile compliances others have gone into; nor was he of the Bladen faction, and I think he fares the worse for not being soe. Pray make his Grace sensible that when he can gett this Gentleman an encrease of pay on the foot of the Commons application without blame, he hath it in his power to make a freind who will be useful, and it will be a mortification to your Colleague and others to see that it is possible for a man not countenanced by them and Mr Sp[eake]r may sometimes have right done him. The inclosed letter from Mrs Ward to her husband I have at her desire sent under your cover, in hopes it may have better luck in coming to his hands, then she thinks some of his have had in coming to hers; for she cannot beleive he would omit writing to her at so critical a juncture as this. If the Duke of Bolton cannot so far support Mr Wards pretensions, as that he may hope to succeed immediately, if the place were void; I should think (but speak first about it to Mr Ward) that it might not be

---

[820] Luttrellstown Castle, Luttrell's estate, was less than ten miles from Speaker Conolly's property at Castletown, in Co. Kildare.

[821] William Southwell, MP [I], captain of the Battle-axe Guards in Dublin Castle, the Irish equivalent of the Yeomen of the Guard.

[822] On 2 Dec. 1715 the Commons resolved to recommend to the lord lieutenant the case of Captain Arnold Cosby and the other officers of the Inniskilling Horse, a regiment originally raised from the Fermanagh militia to defend the town of Enniskillen from the jacobite forces in 1689 (*CJI*, iv, 53, 55–6).

[823] In Feb. 1715 James Topham, MP [I] was appointed register of forfeitures under the Irish revenue commissioners. The following December, not having been paid any salary, he petitioned the Commons to be placed on the Irish establishment (*CJI*, iv, 139).

amisse in my opinion to have the grant attend the end of the Session of the Parliament: this will gett Mr Ward time to work the thing here, and you know hath the face of keeping somebody in awe of being disappointed of his great expectations, which may be of some weight in England to prevent an immediate grant to Sir R.[824] if the thing should become void: but in this I would willingly have you speak to Mr Ward and have his thoughts before you mention it. The letter tells you where he lies, but if it be left at St James Coffee house it will find him.

325. *Alan I, Dublin, to Thomas, 27 June 1717*

(1248/4/45–6)

I doe not know that I ever sate down to write under more confusion then at this time. The Duke of Bolton in a letter I had from him lately mentioned that Redmond Barry had not wrote to Lord Burlington to decline the favor he had promised him of being chosen at Dungarvan; upon which I immediately wrote down to Barry, and in answer to my letter received one yesterday from him in which he tells me that he had not done it, but upon receiving a letter lately from my Lord Burlington (I suppose he means Mr Graham his secretary[825]) had disavowed doing so and craved and insisted on his Lordships promise. You see the circumstances I am in with relation to this affair and must now have the patience to be informed of the maner of my getting into them, and the steps that I am about to take to gett out of them. You know that I mentioned the borough of Dungarvan to be void by Jemmy Barryes death, who indeed had retreived my Lord Burlingtons interest in that corporation and for that reason not only alway had that interest for his own election, but as I was informed since his death my Lord had either promised or intended the thing for his son: I proposed his Graces applying to my Lord in behalf of Mr Webster, and if nothing hindred but the promise made to Mr Barry I thought I had such an interest in Mr Barry, or to expresse it more fully that he had such expectations from me that I never could fail of a compliance in him: and to bring that matter to passe spoke to Mr Coghlan (a servant of my Lord Burlington)[826] about Redmond Barryes being to be elected at Dungarvan, and that I made it my desire he would quit his pretensions in favor of another: I chose to transact this matter by a third hand knowing how jealous not to say troublesome some people are, if they find the Lords (especially one in my Station) too busy in elections: sometime afterward the beginning of last term I saw Mr Coghlan in the Chancery chamber and calling to him to know what he had done, he told me the businesse was settled. After receiving the Duke of Boltons letter in which he mentions Barryes having said nothing to my Lord, I spoke to him again, and he repeated to me that the matter was settled past any dispute; soe as my mind

---

[824] Sir Ralph Gore, 4th Bt, MP [I].

[825] Richard Graham (NLI, MS 43102/1: Burlington to Richard Graham and Jabez Collier, 5 Aug. 1717; George Knox, 'Sebastiano Ricci at Burlington House: A Venetian Decoration "alla Romana"', *Burlington Magazine*, cxxvii (1985), 201; Jane Clark, '"Lord Burlington is Here"', in *Lord Burlington: Architecture, Art and Life*, ed. Toby Barnard and Jane Clark (1995), 287).

[826] Jeremy Coughlan (*d*.1735) of Lismore, Co. Waterford (H.F. Morris, 'The "Principal Inhabitants" of County Waterford in 1746', in *Waterford: History and Society* …, ed. William Nolan and T.P. Power (Dublin, 1992), 324–5).

was perfectly att ease, I imputing Barryes not writing to my Lord to the carelessenesse of a young man: When next morning I received a letter from him in answer to mine (in which I had told him that tho Mr Coghlan had assured me he had waved his pretensions, that yet I found he had not wrote into England to that effect which was absolutely necessary, and pressed him to do it without delay; with all transcribing some few words out of the Duke of Boltons letter in which he promises to be mindful of Mr Barry). In this answer he tells that Mr Coghlan had no authority for what he said, that he had never declined; but had received a letter from my Lord Burlington wherein he shews a resentment upon a supposal of his having relinquished to another, in answer to which he had wrote and disavowed his having relinquished, and had insisted on my Lords promise. Immediately on receit of this letter I expostulated with Mr Coghlan and told him the difficultyes I was brought under by Mr Barryes behavior; he then told me that Mr Barry was not in any sort to blame, for that he understood me to have spoken to him about Mr Barryes being remisse in prosecuting his pretensions to an election at Dungarvan and not to wave them; and indeed I find the truth to be that he had hardly stirred in the thing of late till he heard out of England or till Mr Coghlan spoke to him; soe as I now find my writing into England and speaking here have not occasioned his declining, but had a clear contrary effect. Mr Coghlan is a man of so much sincerity and so much my freind that I cannot entertain a thought of his playing a double part; tho it is amazing to me that he should so far misunderstand me as to imagine I spoke to him to quicken Redmond Barry in prosecuting his own pretensions, when the very motive of my speaking to him was in order to bring the matter to passe for Mr Webster. He affirms that he understood me otherwise, I speaking softly to him in the presence of a good deal of company; and that when he told me that the matter was secure he meant in favor of Barry. In what a scituation am I? The Duke apprehends by my writing Barry hath quitted, hath told Lord Burlington soe; Barry assures him the contrary. My comfort is his Grace must I think be sensible that all this proceeds from a most unhappy mistake: that I spoke twice to Mr Coghlan he will own, and about Dungarvan: now I must be a fool and madman as well as a knave if I should at the same time sett the Duke on seeking my Lord Burlingtons interest upon a supposal of Mr Barryes declining, and should pretend to have some power over Mr Barry to incline him to quit his pretensions; and at the same time should be the instrument and means of his prosecuting and persisting in them, and the person who should quicken him to doe soe when I was endeavouring (in all appearance to the Duke) to act a quite contrary part. Nor was there the least reason for Coghlan to be guilty of a trick, supposing him to be capable of such a thing; which in my soul I think he is not. But when the Duke is convinced of the ground of this misunderstanding I doubt whether my Lord Burlington may not entertain such thoughts of me as I should be very sorry should make any impressions on him to my prejudice. I really am above telling a lye or prevaricating in a greater matter then a seat in our house of Commons. What remains is that I write this night to Mr Barry in such a maner that he will have it in his choice (if he can do it without disobliging Lord Burlington) to relinquish his title to being a member, or all intercourse with me for ever; and as he hath had personal obligations to me and expects more, he knows what his father did and what his brother doth owe me. If Mr Webster knows Mr Graham my Lords Secretary I think a word on this subject to him may be of use: sure my Lord Burlington will not think Barryes consenting to my Lords recommending Mr Webster to be a slight or neglect: and if he doth consent and my Lord recommends him to be supported by his Commissioners I do not think he can loose it. You may remember I told you of another place Cloghnekilty, in the recommendation of Lord Carleton: I thought Cox would put in but hear young Sir Ralph Freke (who is but 17)[827] hath or intends to apply to Lord Carleton. I shal be under the last confusion if the Duke should be under a disappointment …

326. *Alan I, Dublin, to Thomas, at his lodgings in the Privy Garden, Whitehall, 8 July 1717*

(1248/4/47–8)

I am afraid your bill of attainder is not well considered; it cannot I think have any good effect considering the steps already taken: Will they who took soe large ones not to try him at all in a regular way, go into to condemning him without trial?[828] There must be more and greater people in this affair then you seem aware of. Mr Barry[829] hath now answered my letter, and insists on being elected: If he persevere I will look on him as the man who hath most disobliged me of any one living: I am not yet without hopes in that affair, tho I own I can depend little after what I have seen from him: but I will abandon him, I will discharge his brother who is my pursebearer,[830] and throw off all thoughts and concern for that familye which I have hitherto supported in effect. He inherits his fathers pride and ingratitude. I am extremely sorry for what you write of your own ilnesse; I wish to God you could come over hither; the Duke desired me to presse you to it, and indeed such an one we shal extremely want: for you may be sure they who the last Session have laid this load of debt on us will lye by this and see how another sett of men will pay it without prejudice to or forfeiting their interest in and credit with the Countrey. Pray consider whether you can come: Your sister will be glad to see you in her house. I tell the Duke of Bolton I write this post about Barry, speak to him: and at the same time mention the Kings reducing the Army, I mean either Regiments, or the private men (as formerly) to 34 in a company; we shal else not be able to pay them; and hardly then.

327. *Alan I, Dublin, to Thomas, at his lodgings in the Privy Garden, Whitehall, 16 July 1717*

(1248/4/51–2)

By your writing to me in another hand one pacquet and not at all by the other I have too much reason to be in pain, for fear of your being soe in extremity; by that miserable distemper which is of late fallen soe very heavily upon you: if expressing my greif for it,

---

[827] Alan seems to have mistaken Ralph Freke, 2nd son of Sir Ralph, 1st Bt, MP [I], for Freke's elder brother, Sir Percy, who was born in 1700, and inherited the baronetcy in 1717 on their father's death. Sir Percy was eventually returned to the Irish parliament in 1721.

[828] Articles of impeachment had been brought in the Westminster parliament against Robert Harley (1661–1724), 1st earl of Oxford, in 1715, and ever since he had been imprisoned in the Tower. In June 1717 he petitioned to be brought to trial, and in the ensuing debates an argument was made for a bill of attainder (Cobbett, *Parl. Hist.*, vii, cols. 494, 496; HMC, *Portland MSS*, v, 527). Ultimately, however, the articles were dropped and Oxford was released.

[829] Redmond Barry, MP [I].

[830] James Barry, Redmond's elder brother (see Appendix 2).

would ease your pain I could be as profuse in my expressions as others; but that is not the way you desire your freinds to shew their concern for you. I have made the best enquiry I can after young Mr Renault[831] about whom my Lord Duke of Somerset wrote to you; and have been the more sollicitous in it because I should be concerned his Grace (to whom I owe so very many and very great obligations) should suffer through my not getting the best information possible about him. He is on all hands agreed to be a very good horseman and to understand that businesse; the occasion of his leaving his father was (I hear) that he did not give him an allowance suitable to the others desires; and he hoped he might deserve and gett a better livelyhood by seeking his fortune in England: this argues either that he is addicted to expence, or hath a spirit to push him forward in the world; and I am willing to take it in the later. I doe not find that he hath been looked on as given to wine, women or gaming: on the other hand I cannot from the character I have of him advise his Grace to trust him too much with money; of which I fear he is not a good manager. You will oblige me in giving my Lord Duke my humblest services and best wishes; and assuring him I have a very deep and grateful sense of a thousand favors I have received from him since I had the honour and happinesse to be known to him. I had this morning a letter given me by Mr Joddrel[832] from my Lord Thomond which I will answer soon, and in the mean time endeavour to obey the commands contained in it. As soon as I sett my eyes on Justice McCartney I judged him to be in a very ill state of health and indeed a great deal worse then he seemed to me to be when he left Ireland; but this morning by discourse I had with his son I have reason to beleive him worse and in a very dangerous way; he saith he is fallen into a violent loosenesse and inclined to fainting fits. If he should dye soon (as it is not unlikely he may) is there no way for my brother William to make his Court now soe as to gett a promise not of this particular thing, but the first preferment of that kind here; I doe not know whether I am proposing a reasonable thing because I doe not know whether he took the advise I gave him when he went last to Jamaica, to make up by his industry and study the time he lost in his youth which should have been employed in the profession he was designed for, and to qualifye himself for those posts of profit and honour which ought to be the reward of industry and knowledge. Whether this be his case or not I am wholly a stranger; as indeed I have all along been to his affairs, which he never let me into the knowledge of, very seldome writing to me and but once since his coming last into England. Methinks he should have waited on the Duke of Bolton and offered his service in Parliament here by coming over; for we gott him to be chosen for Mallow in his absence, upon his writing word he resolved to leave the Indies and settle in Europe. If this scheme shal appear not feasible probably our Attorney General will be fond of a Cushion, and then the Sollicitorship will (I hope) devolve on Senny; whom I think as fit for it as any one who may be named competitors for it…

---

[831]John Baptist Renoult appeared in a lease dated 14 Mar. 1719 as rector of Drumcliffe and Ahamplish, Co. Sligo (Reg. Deeds, 31/11/17306) but his name does not appear in the published succession lists, where the incumbent's name is given as James Reed (*Clergy of Kilmore, Elphin and Ardagh*, ed. D.W.T. Crooks (Belfast, 2008), 148, 176).

[832]Burdett Jodrell (*d.* c.1718), of Dublin. He originated from Staffs., and having undertaken a legal training, came to Dublin in 1700 as solicitor to the forfeiture trustees. He subsequently set up as a banker, and was one of the commissioners for Thomond's estate (H.A.C. Sturgess, *Register of Admissions to the Honourable Society of the Middle Temple* … (3 vols, 1949), i, 247; NLI, Gen. Office MS 141, p. 22: abstract of Jodrell's will, 1718; Hayton, *Ruling Ireland*, 78; NLI, Inchiquin papers, 45312/3–4: correspondence of Sir Donough O'Brien with Jodrell and Upton, bankers, 1711–15; Reg. Deeds, 9/252/3601).

[*PS*] Mr Barry hath been pleased to persist in his serving for Dungarvan; soe I have done with him for ever. But I hope by the next post to be able to say secured an election another way, which however I would not have you mention to the Duke of Bolton for fear of another disappointment: but I think this will be compassed: yet I wish he may have spoken to Lord Carleton for his recommendation of Mr W[*ebster*] to Cloghnekilty in the room of Sir Ralph Freake; a line to that effect with the care taken already there, would secure it …

328. *Alan I, Dublin, to Thomas, at his lodgings in the Privy Garden, Whitehall, 27 July 1717*

(1248/4/53–4)

… By the time this reaches your hands I think the election time will be at Eaton and consequently my boy will be in better company then his school fellows, from whom he now begins to have thoughts of weaning himself, since Christmas is so very near. I am and shal continue in a great deal of pain till by the advice and assistance of his and my freinds I have determined where and in what maner to dispose of him upon taking him from school. Many here would perswade me to place him in this College, and give for reason that now there is a good Provost and the education and discipline will not be the same as it was of late. This I own to be very true, but beside other reasons this weighs soe with me as not to be capable I think of an answer. Whoever proposes to come to any thing considerable hereafter must make England the theatre he resolves to appear on: and this is so true that I see little fellows of this countrey by only spending some of their time there make them selves thought to be men of consequence, while others of real merit fare like our best Clergymen [and][833] never rise by attending their cures. I think too that I should not rob them of the comfort of his company when he is able to expresse his gratitude to them who have had the care and trouble of his tender years … I find you have not lately seen the Duke of Bolton, who hath not yet heard of Mr Barrys determinate resolution. I cannot approve of any one of the brothers administring exclusive of those who are in equal degree.

329. *Alan I, Dublin, to Thomas, at his lodgings in the Privy Garden, Whitehall, 5 Aug. 1717*

(1248/4/55–6)

I have been more sparing of writing then usual for a fortnight past, have a bile in the fleshy part of my hand which pained and tortured me exceedingly, and would not break kindly; but started up and broke first in one place, then in another with so small orifices that the core or humor which created me so much pain could not come away; and so returned into the flesh and toward the bones: this I attribute partly to the callousnesse of the lower part and inside of my hand, and partly to the heat and angrinesse of the humour, which did not incline at all at first to suppuration. This laid me under the necessity of having my hand laid open by cutting the flesh and skin between the several orifices, to make one at which the purulent matter might vent itself; and after undergoing a good deal of pain I thank God I can now tell you that I think the matter is over, the poisonous humour being in a

---

[833]MS blotted.

great measure drawn away and the swelling and inflammation gone. I keep it stil open as well to draw away as much of the hot humour as I can, as to prevent its rising in another place: of which I confesse I have not now any great apprehension. I suppose the Duke of Bolton brings over with him the letter for creating me a Viscount; as he first mentioned the thing to me as a thing done, and as having the Kings directions to give me the precedency I would not interpose in calling for the letter or doing any thing in it: but I find by the publick prints that Trevor Hills, and by private letters that Sir Tho[*mas*] Southwels and Jack Allens letters are signed; but not one word relating to me; the Duke of Bolton told me in a letter of the 9th of July that he would take care if new Peers were created I should be the first Viscount: the white Hall letter[834] mentions Mr Hill Mr Allen and me and names my title to be Middleton. I suppose the Duke brings over all the letters and mine among the rest; the complement being made by him, and his Grace telling me in his of the sixth of July that the day before he had leave to signifye his Majestyes pleasure to prepare a warrant for making me a Viscount I thought it not proper to intermeddle in carrying on the matter or taking out the letter; sure he will not have left it in the office and by that means give other Gentlemen the start of me. Your being out of town, and Mr Campbels not having wrote to me of late put me in some suspence; tho I have little apprehensions of the letters not being brought over with the rest by his Grace. If it should be otherwise I will find some way to gett the warrants on the others to be soe long delayed that it may be sent over after them and yet come in time: but since I was ordered to have the precedence I will not quit it on any score: nor indeed hath any one of the number any pretence to contest it with me, considering the station I am now in and my being already a Peer, both which put me before them who without those advantages had pretensions equal to them in every other respect …

330. *Alan I, Dublin, to Thomas, at his lodgings in the Privy Garden, Whitehall, 8 Aug. 1717*

(1248/4/57–8)

Yesterday about noone the Duke of Bolton came into the bay, and about fowre he was sworn;[835] they had a very fine passage:[836] the Duke, Dutchesse, Duke of Wharton,[837] Lord and Lady Hillsborough (for so we already call them tho the patent is not yet passed)[838] and Mrs Chamberlain a neice of my Ladyes[839] with Mr Webster supped with us, and are to dine with us again this day, together with my late colleagues. To morrow the Archbishop of Dublin, and on Saturday Mr Conollye entertain them and will be able to doe it in a more magnificent maner (tho perhaps with not more sincere good will) then we can doe; there not being any one large room in the house where we live. The Duke spoke of you with

---

[834]Little is known about this particular newsletter, apart from its longevity, but see BL, Add. MS 69380, f. 3: John, Lord Cutts to [Adam de Cardonnel], 12 Jan. N.S. 1703; *Epistolary Curiosities …*, ed. Rebecca Warner (ser. 2, 1818), 212; Jeremy Black, *The English Press in the Eighteenth Century* (1987), 66.

[835]Confirmed in *London Gazette*, 13–17 Aug. 1717.

[836]The yacht had left Holyhead on the previous day, with a fair wind (*London Gazette*, 6–10 Aug. 1717).

[837]Marquess of Catherlogh in the Irish peerage (see Appendix 3).

[838]Trevor and Mary Hill (the patent was passed on 21 Aug. 1717).

[839]Elizabeth, a sister of Mrs Hill's first husband, Sir Edmund Denton, 1st Bt, of Hillersden, Bucks., married George Chamberlayne of Wardington, Oxon.

great regard and kindnesse, and I am sure would be much more at ease in his mind if your state of health would allow of your travelling and taking a share in the management of this Session; which for want of people of weight, and experience in the house will in a good measure fall into hands one would not wish should have the honour of doing things.

Colonel Moreton spoke to me concerning your state of health with real concern and tendernesse; I have seen him but twice and have taken occasion both times to treat him with all civilitye, particularly this morning I told him I would make it my request that we might live together on a foot of freindship as meaning the same thing and having the same views and interests: he told me nothing could oblige him more, it being the thing he extremely coveted and resolved (if he could) to bring to passe. I wish you would take an oportunitye in a line to him, or if you do not think that proper, to me to recommend our being intimate; for he lies at Pratts[840] and there will be endeavours to bring him into a better opinion of some people then were to be wished. Our establishment is not yet come over; but I find it is reduced from £408000 per annum (which was that signed by the King to take place from 25 March 1715 and by additions made after was increased to above £430000 a year) to £398000 odd hundred pounds a year: which tho a considerable abatement of what we were formerly to pay, and very much more tolerable then that intended by the late Justices, who had framed a plan of a new establishment; yet is in itself a very heavy burthen on the Kingdome; that being more then the hereditary revenue and the addicional dutyes have yet yeilded; tho I am apt to think it is not impossible or improbable that the revenue and addicional dutyes may in some time amount to so much: but then how shal we pay our debt (I mean the £50000 borrowed[841]) and clear the arrears due on our establishment? Perhaps a fund of interest may be found for the £50000, and where is the great prejudice if the Army and pensions should be from time to time six or suppose nine months in arrear: no establishment in Christendome is so well paid, even tho that were the Case. I find that there are only five men in a company (instead of reducing Corps to bring our Army from 15000 to 12000 men) to be broken; which will ease us but of a small part of the expence; which is cheifly occasioned by the General Officers and other Officers; and by our having more horse and Dragoons then usual; for tho they do not consist of so many as foot regiments yet the expence of horse and Dragoons is greater then the other; but this I need not tell you. I beleive Lord G[*alway*] and his freinds are a good deal nettled at our representation of the pretensions of some of the French Pensioners, which I am told hath had some tolerable effect. I am sorry to have too much reason from your letter to be confirmed in my fears that my brother William hath not lived long enough to become a considerate man; and yet he hath spent more then fifty years in the world. You describe him the same wavering man that he hath been all along: and for ought I see you knew not what he intended, whether to go again to the Indies, or remain in England, or sett up his rest here, till you heard of his being gone for Ireland; on the encouragement and invitation of one who wants a good deal of coolnesse and consideration, and can better bear any thing then good advice. If he hath not already made a fortune I doe not see that he is likely ever to doe it. Fifty is an ill time to sett up a trade for a new man, and wor[se] after having tryed unsuccessefully in another place: if he thinks my Station will enable me to give him much assistance he will find himself

---

[840]John Pratt, MP [I].

[841]By an act of 1716 which sanctioned government borrowing of £50,000, thereby creating an Irish national debt (McGrath, *Ireland and Empire*, 184–8).

mistaken: for unreasonable countenance or favor no relation must expect from me, and I doubt what may be fairly shewn will little avail him. I confesse I am something in pain about him, and wish things may succeed: the intimacy between your Nephew and him is wonderful, but those violent freindships are not alway most durable. Tell Ally the Dutchesse of Bolton spoke of her to me yesterday in a great deal of company in the handsomest and most obliging maner in the world …

331. *Alan I, Dublin, to Thomas, at his lodgings in the Privy Garden, Whitehall, 19 Aug. 1717*

(1248/4/59–60)

The pacquet goes off immediately, but I resolve it shal carry a line to you tho of no consequence, farther then to tell you I have not yet seen our establishment, but shal immediately. My brother Will is come to town, and appears to me to be in a very ill state of health and under a deep melancholy: I doubt the later contributes to the former, and is in a great measure occasioned from recollecting the many indiscretions and misconduct of his past life. By his own making the best of his case in point of fortune he represents it but indifferent, and I very much doubt whether it will come out anything near what he tells me it is. Senny is stil in the countrey but will be up by the seven and twentieth. Trevor Hill and my Lady Hillsborough, (for so we call her tho the patent is not yet passed) are in the castle: I think he doth some things which might as well be let alone, because I am sure they will give offence to people of at least as good condition as himself …

332. *Alan I, Dublin, to Thomas, 30 Sept. 1717*

(1248/4/73–4)

I am sensible that it is very long since I wrote to you, as you are that my want of leisure and full employment of my time is the occasion of it. Our recesse draws near and will be either on Saturday next, or on Monday sevennight at the farthest, by which you will understand our businesse is almost over. And considering the coolnesse of some people, and the opposition of others toward the beginning and middle of the time I make no doubt you and all who mean the Kings affairs, and the present administration well, will beleive it is very happily over. The minions of the late Governors and creatures of that ministry could not be expected to be extreamly fond of their Successors; great pains were taken to lessen Mr Webster in the eye and opinion of the people, before he landed and since,[842] in so much that in my hearing the Archbishop of Dublin said (with a flear[843]) he supposed some would think fit to endeavour to bring him into Parliament; I said I hoped so, as well as other Secretaryes: He said Mr Southwel had an estate here[844], I said Mr Dodington, Mr

---

[842] Bishop Evans of Meath had reported in July critical comments in Ireland about Bolton, including the observation that 'his chief secretary (they say) is not equal to his employment and will not be able in any degree to manage our great assembly, as his predecessors used to do' (Wake, Epist. xii: Evans to [Archbishop Wake], 6 July [1717]).

[843] Sneer (*OED*).

[844] Edward Southwell, MP [I], chief sec. to the 2nd duke of Ormond: he owned property at Downpatrick, Co. Down and Kinsale, Co. Cork.

Gwin, Mr Addison, and Bladen had not:[845] he then pretended to allow a good deal to their personal merits but was a stranger to any he had. At the beginning of the Session in the Vote for the foundation of the Commons addresse, the Speaker left out the (present) administration out of the draught as prepared by him tho it was in the resolution the last Session; I observed it, asked if there were any objection to the word or thing, and crammed it down his throat in the Dukes Closett, so as it was moved in the house and carryed with the word present in the resolution, and also in the draught of the addresse; but expunged afterward on Mr Joshua Allens motion, who told people about him he thought leaving that word in might reflect Lord Dorsett who is one of the persons lately removed.[846] Oliver St George also brought in a paragraph relating to the P—[847] in the house in a very odd maner. You see how men of that kidney stood affected at this time. The next thing was to insinuate that the way to prevent overloading the establishment was to take care to keep a good deal in debt; that there was no need to pay off the £50000 borrowed, and that the clearings of the Army might very well be six or nine months in arrear. That a Land tax was aimed at, and under that notion Gentlemen were discoursed in order to bring them to a resolution not to give any new tax of any kind.[848] in so much that when the Archbishop of Dublin applyed to me to countenance the application of the College to the Commons for an addresse for £5000 to finish their Library,[849] and I had promised him to befreind them; and when I in return told him that I hoped he would endeavour to influence his freinds to give such supplyes as might enable the King etc he declared against any new tax, argued so much against one and was so positive the majoritye of the Commons would not come into one that I turned from him with a good deal of resentment. I then saw it was necessary to bring the Kings servants to explain themselves, and my Lord Lieutenant ordered the Speaker, the three Cheif Judges, Chancellor of the Exchequer, Attorney and Sollicitor, Mr Prat and Mr Webster to attend him in the Closet; where after looking over the paper framed by the accountant General[850] relating to the publick accounts and seeing pretty well how our debt would stand, I moved that Gentlemen would declare how they found their freinds inclined: It was the general sense that they did not find them fond of paying the debt, by which I think they meant the whole; Prat said those who lent the £50000 would be well content to have that money continue at interest for some time longer; but Mr Allen[851] was

---

[845] Previous chief secretaries: George Dodington, Francis Gwyn (c.1648–1734), Joseph Addison and Martin Bladen.

[846] Lionel Cranfield Sackville (1688–1705), 7th earl (and subsequently 1st duke) of Dorset, had been removed from his post as gentleman of the bedchamber to George I, following the resignation of Townshend and Walpole.

[847] Probably 'Privilege' is intended.

[848] In August Archbishop King had reported 'the apprehensions of a land tax' (Wake, Epist. xii: King to Archbishop Wake, 19 Aug. 1717). Both a land tax and a poll tax had been under consideration, but Speaker Conolly in particular announced publicly that he would make it a point of principle to oppose a land tax (TNA, SP 63/375/162: Conolly to Charles Delafaye, 13 Aug. 1717; BL, Add. MS 47028, f. 196: Charles Dering to Lord Perceval, 6 Aug. 1717).

[849] Work had begun on the library in 1712. On 21 Sept. 1717 the college drew the attention of the Commons to their need for a further £5,000 to complete the work –'all that was desired', according to Archbishop King – and the House addressed the king, successfully, to recommend the grant as 'royal bounty' (*CJI*, iv, 326–8; McParland, *Public Architecture in Ireland*, 149–50).

[850] William Burgh (1667–1744), MP [I] 1713–14, presented the papers on 3 Sept. (*CJI*, iv, 306–7), even though a privy seal warrant had been issued on 12 Aug. for Eustace Budgell to replace him in the office (*CTB*, xxi, 513).

[851] Joshua or Robert Allen.

intirely for paying that debt, whatever became of the debt due to the establishment (for he was of the company) others said they thought their freinds more inclined to clear the debt of the establishment and to let that continue: but none seemed to have found a disposition at that time to pay both: I said those I conversed with looked on themselves obliged to pay both and seemed resolved to be as good as their words in the last Session and their addresse in this. I then thought it necessary to come [?nearer] and divided the two debts, and asked each of them separately before my Lord Lieutenant what their own thoughts were of paying them; and at length after abundance of circumlocucion every man declared it was his sense both the one and the other ought to be provided for in this Session. My Lord Lieutenant upon this very skilfully took up the matter and told them he had not pressed any body to come into those matters, but since they thought them reasonable, he could not but expect the Kings servants would (as they alway had done) endeavour to dispose their freinds to go into things so very reasonable, and that was promised, and so we parted: The Duke then had another more general meeting where the paying the debt was discoursed of in the presence of 30 or 40 Gentlemen, most of which seemed well disposed; but Mr Vesey and one or two more of the Speakers creatures were very doubtful: however that meeting broke up with very good prospect of carrying things easy. The Kings servant mett several times after, with some other Gentlemen; and by this time Senny was come to town; and stil one difficulty or other occurred; but they said it would facilitate matters if Gentlemen could be apprised what funds were aimed at. This was done I think to see whether there were any private scheme into which they were not admitted; and the papers prepared by the Commissioners of the revenue containing the goods which might admit of additional dutyes, which had been before that time drawn up by my Lord Lieutenants order, was shewn them: the Chief were what they call here party or mixed Gyles;[852] for a smaller quantity of beer very strong is brewed, which being mixed with beer under six shillings price makes strong beer; yet the greater part of it payes duty only as small beer; another was a farther duty on brandy above proof; these were estimated at about £10000 a year and 6d a [?barrel] on beer about £14000. There were also other goods as coals, Coffee Tea, Grocery wares etc but not approved of: there was a reluctance in the same Gentlemen as to these, but stil under the pretence of their freinds not coming in: and the matter whether the debt need be paid was afresh talked of and resolved afresh and all assurances of endeavouring to bring their freinds in: but upon every occasion it was insinuated that people were not inclined to new taxes: and the Speaker in my hearing said he had thirteen or fourteen dined with him, whom he thought he had interest sufficient enough in to have inclined them to any thing, but he found them inflexible; I desired him to name his freinds that other methods might be taken to convince them, but that he declined doing: I then repeated to my Lord Lieutenant that all with whom I conversed were in other sentiments, and that they were a good many: that the majoritye of the house were for continuing all the dutyes of the last Session and granting new ones by clauses to rectifye party Gyles and brandy about proof, and to give an additional duty on beer etc and that a question would soon determine the matter: the Speaker said every thing must end that way at last, but this or some thing else made such an impression on him and the party that a private meeting was appointed to be had at Mr Manlyes on Sunday sevennight among the heads of them, where it was determined

---

[852]A gyle could mean either the quantity of beer in a single brewing, or the wort in process of fermentation (*OED*).

that the advisable thing would be to endeavour to create merit by coming roundly into all measures; and from this time forward the note was altered and their freinds would hearken to reason: and Mr Manly was sent with the joyful news that all things would be well, and go smooth. I told my Lord Lieutenant from the beginning that there would be opposition and rubs laid in the way, but that the Kings businesse could not fail being carryed on; and offered (if those Gentlemen thought fit to give themselves airs and to stand by) to have the thing done with out them, or even against all the opposition could be given; but that the desirable way and most for the Kings service and his honour was to wait and see what they would finally resolve on, well knowing that when they discerned their opposition must prove unsuccesseful they would act the contrary part. At the beginning they seemed averse to new dutyes, or paying the debt; and when they agreed to both, they acted at least cooly with their freinds, but I confesse I think some of them did (under hand) endeavour to influence them against both: by this means things were retarded and protracted by them in the Committee of accounts; but when they saw the matter would be pushed and carryed against them, they withdrew the countenance they had given their freinds to appear restive; and then Mr Manly said it was true all was done, but that it must not be imputed to Lord Ch[*ancellor'*]s freinds; for if Mr Conolly and his freinds had not come into measures, matters might have received another turn. Thus the Toryes brought in King George.

333. *Alan I, Dublin, to Thomas, at his lodgings in Whitehall, 18 Oct. 1717*

(1248/4/79–80)

I hope this will find you returned from Newmarkett in as good a state of health as my sister described you to enjoy when you left Peperhara: but am sorry for your ill successe in your match between my Lord Whartons Chanter and Windham,[853] which he values himself extremely upon; saith he hath won a thousand pounds, most of it your money; the Duke of Somersett inclining to pay of forfeit of fifty pounds: but you opiniated it, gave out Windham was lame for fear of his paying his forfeit, and on the day was the occasion of running the match. You cannot imagine with what pleasure he[854] harps on this string: the ground of it I cannot learn, for no creature hath been used better then he hath been by Senny and me: but this I am sure of, that Conolly by slavish insinuations and ungentlemanlike condescensions hath made him entirely his freind: and I have been told he hath in his Cups began confusion to all the Brodricks. He is very vitious, envious, proud, and expects such mean compliances with his humours and sentiments as no man who is not of a slavish spirit can ever come into: this makes me the lesse concerned for his not being a freind: and if I do not make a wrong judgement, he will not fail to be a very turbulent man in the State, unlesse he can have his will in every thing: And upon my word he will make early, frequent, and very large demands on any ministry which shal endeavour to purchase him.

Mr Boscawen[855] and Mr Moreton are both stil here, detained by contrary winds; the former was at my house to take leave, as I also was at his lodgings; but we missed one

---

[853] The match was to have taken place on 28 Oct., for a prize of £100. Windham belonged to the duke of Somerset (*Weekly Journal*, 28 Sept. 1717).

[854] Wharton.

[855] Hugh Boscawen (c.1680–1734), of Tregothnan, Cornwall, MP [GB] 1702–20, subsequently created Viscount Falmouth. He had been appointed joint vice-treasurer [I] in 1717.

another on Thursday morning: that night we mett at the Castle and each told the other that he had been to wait on him: Mr Boscawen told me he would come again if he did not sail so soon as to prevent it: but two dayes have passed since, which he hath spent in Conollyes company only: whose sneaking behaviour wins extremely on men who think more court ought to be made to them by every body here, then we generally think is their due: But as for Colonel Moreton he never gave himself the trouble to call at my house: so heinously is he pleased to resent my sons voting against the Vice Treasurers having sixpence per pound out of the present aids; and I think it is in his inclination (if it be in his power) to do me ill offices on that foot, tho I did all that an honest man could do to serve him. My Lord Duke is well, and often speaks kindly of you.

334. *St John III, Midleton, to Alan I, 20 Oct. 1717*

(1248/4/81–2)

I would have own'd your Lordships favour by last post, if I had not given you the trouble of a letter the day before. You may be sure tis a more then ordinary satisfaction to me to find that my behaviour in the affair of Mr Addison was not only agreable to your Lordship, but such as deserv'd the least acknowledgment from so truly valuable a man. The share which you have in his freindship added to his great personal merit will always command my little services, and I assure you there is hardly a thing in the world I should more desire or endeavour to deserve then the continuance of his good thoughts of me.

As to the matter of the vice-Treasurers fees my case in short was thus. Collonel Moreton and Mr Pratt gave me a visit one morning, and among other things desir'd my freindship and vote to take of the 6d per pound impos'd on their fees. I told them I was the most improper man alive to be talkt to on that subject having been the person that last session propos'd the laying that on which they now desir'd me to take of; but as to any promise of voting for it, tho I could not speak in it, I utterly deny it, and am of opinion neither Mr Moreton or Pratt will venture to tax me with it. As to Mr Boscawen I protest to you I did not at that time know, tho perhaps I might have heard of his being concern'd in the office; and whatever his resentment may be towards me for my behaviour in that affair, I do assure you I would have gone as great a length as with honour I could to have serv'd him, with whom I have had the honour of a long acquaintance. I will go thus far too as to tell your Lordship that upon what you had said to me of the freindship there was between my uncle and Mr Moreton I had almost brought my self to a resolution to be passive in the matter; but when the business of the officers took the turne it did, and was so warmly oppos'd by a great many of my particular and most intimate freinds, I thought my self under a necessity of joining with them in that of the vicetreasurers, especially when I lookt upon the thing as reasonable in itself, and saw plainly there was a prodigious majority in the house against gratifying the vice-Treasurers. You know very well how much a certain person had the matter of the officers at heart, in which I may without vanity say I did them more service then any man in the house of Commons, and should not have been able to have done so much if I had not the night before promis'd to be for continuing the 6d per pound, upon which a good many whom tis not proper to name readily came into the other, and I will take upon me to say if both had been insisted upon, both had been lost. Your Lordship will likewise consider my particular case, and whither upon the foot I then was twas prudent for me to endeavour to serve Mr Moreton at the expence of my credit in the house and freindship of a great many Gentlemen, and by that means rendred my incapable of serving another Gentleman in the House for whom I own I have infinitely a greater value and honour then for the other. You cannot but be sensible how dangerous a thing it is for freinds to divide even on the most trifling question, and how difficult after such a division to reestablish a confidence in one another without which tis impossible to conduct any affair in the House of Commons. Several of my friends were chagrin enough at my leaving them in the matter of the officers, and I know there wanted not enemys to blow that Coale; and to honour me with the title of a Courtier etc; so that if I had answer'd Mr Moretons expectations, I am perswaded I had forfeited that Interest in a great many Gentlemen; which my vote in that, and taxing the English Parliament men, has I hope regain'd me. Mr Moreton cannot with any justice say I have any way deceiv'd him in this business, or that he had any reason to depend upon my vote in it. About the middle of the session I heard of a list which his freinds had made, and that my name was incerted among several others who were said to be for him. I went immediately to the Gentleman who I was told had the list, and assur'd him if my name were there he was impos'd upon, for that I was so far from being under any promise to vote for his freind, that I was determin'd to vote against him, and from that time acquainted every body that thought it worth their while to ask me with my Resolution to do so. My Uncle Brodrick,[856] Maynard,[857] Ward,[858] Rose[859] Harry Sandford[860] and a great many others, will if you desire it satisfy you of my constant open declaration of myself not to go into this matter. I have taken up too much of your time on this trifle, but have wrote more fully to you that I might as far as I could justify my Conduct to your Lordship, which if I have the good fortune to do, I shall be very little concern'd for Mr Moretons resentment, nor the manner he may take to express it.

I shall now soon have the happiness of seeing your Lordship, and hope to be in Dublin before the returne of the Bills. If the news papers tell truth the English Parliament meets the day our money Bill expires;[861] if so I hope Lord Lieutenant will be over assoon as he desires. We have it all over this Countrey that the Prince[862] is to be one of our Lords justices. If it be not improper, for Gods sake put my mind at peace about this matter, for if it be true, I own him to be a man of Interest and dexterity, as well as fortune …

335. *Alan I, Dublin, to Thomas, at his lodgings in Whitehall, 27 Oct. 1717*

(1248/4/85–6)

This will be delivered you by Mr Tyrrel minister of that parish in which I live; who is called over by reason of a writ of error brought of a judgement given in the Kings Bench at Westminster in affirmance of a judgement given by me when I was cheif Justice of Ireland

---

[856] Thomas.

[857] William Maynard, MP [I].

[858] Michael Ward, MP [I].

[859] Henry Rose, MP [I].

[860] Henry Sandford, MP [I].

[861] The next session at Westminster began on 21 Nov. 1717, parliament having been prorogued to that date on 8 Oct.

[862] George, prince of Wales.

in a cause wherein the Dean and Chapter of Christchurch are concerned against the now Bishop of Kilaloo (then Mr Charles Carre) whom Mr Tyrrel hath succeeded in the living of St Pauls our parish Church.[863] By my giving the judgement you may be sure I thought Mr Carre in the right, and I am confirmed in my opinion by finding the Kings Bench with you concurred in the affirmance of the judgement given by us here. If you can do Mr Tyrrel any service you will oblige me and help to keep in a very learned and well principled Clergy man and at the same time prevent the living falling into the hands of some person to whom Christchurch hath given it or will give it; and you may depend on our Christchurch in Dublin being as like that in Oxford as two eggs are.[864]

336. *Alan I, Dublin, to Thomas, 7 Nov. 1717*

(1248/4/90–1)

… By yours of the eighteenth of October I find that my Lord Duke of Somersett had spoke to my Lord Sunderland about my attending this Session in Parliament, and that my not doing it would tend to the lessening his interest there;[865] and you also tell me Lord Sunderland spoke to you about my coming over. What I am going to tell you must go no farther then yourself, but you will make the proper use of it: Altho my Lord Sunderland might perhaps upon the Duke of Somersetts discourse, and for ought I know out of an opinion that I may be of some use in the house, incline to have me come over by the Kings leave, yet it is possible there was a farther view in the matter. You know that my Lord Lieutenant hath by his patent power to go into England and to appoint one or more Justices during his absence; this our people here very well knew, and I beleive did think those he would have recommended would not have been to their palate, and thus the game hath been played. Mr Secretary Addison in his letter of 29 October tells the Duke that no doubt he hath had it in his thoughts to repair into England as soon as our Session is over, and whom to appoint Justices during his absence: and adds that he hath it in command from his Majestye to suggest to him, that as he by his prudence and temper hath kept tranquillity and peace among those who wish well to his Majestyes service, it were desirable that he should leave the same persons Justices whom he found so at his landing: That no doubt he had the Chancellor first in his thoughts as well for his Majestyes service as etc that from the Dukes own letters the King thought the Speaker had not acted soe this Session as to deserve to be disobliged which might hereafter embarasse the Dukes administration; and that the Archbishop of D[ublin] might be the third unlesse he had given signal proofs of his opposition to his Majestyes measures: that this was written in confidence and a private letter with the import of which no creature but Lord S[underland] was acquainted: that his Grace might to every one of the three make the putting them in as his own act: but adds at the end my being one of the Justices was not meant to debar me from going to London, which I had the Kings leave to do, to take my seat in Parliament where I might be of

---

[863] Duke Tyrrell (c.1681–1722), succeeded Charles Carr as rector of St Paul's, Smithfield, Dublin in 1716. Alan's widow was still recorded as living in the parish in the 1730s. (Brendan Twomey, *Smithfield and the Parish of St Paul, Dublin, 1689–1750* (Dublin, 2005), 39–40, 50–1.)

[864] That is to say, dominated by high churchmen. In the case of Christ Church cathedral, Dublin, this is clear from TCD, MS 2536, pp. 19–20: Archbishop King to Bishop Crowe, 14 Aug. 1714.

[865] In Midhurst.

some use. You know that it hath been the drift of one if not both our late Justices, and
eminently so of both their Secretaryes, in conjunction with the Speaker and others here,
who were wholly confided in by our late politicians, to lessen me in England by breaking
my interest here, and by supporting the little people they were pleased to take in when
they saw fit (without just grounds given) to use me in the unhandsomest maner. With this
view it was that a scheme was formed, at the time my Lord Galway was soe ill in Dublin
that his death was apprehended, to put the Governement into the Archbishop of Dublins
and Conelyes hands, and to leave me out.[866] Of this I acquainted you formerly as soon
as I knew it, and wrote in such a maner on the usage, as well to the then Secretary Mr
Methuen[867] as to my Lord Townesend, that they must see I would not hold a place which
I could not hold with honour; and then this turn was given to it by the projectors, that
truly that was only to be a very short commission till the Duke of Grafton should go back
and resume the Governement, which he would have done without losse of time; but when
Lord Townesend was declared Lord Lieutenant then I was to be one of the Justices, but to
be coupled with the Archbishop and Conelye: Thus tho I was not put under the laters feet,
yet he was made my equal, and an office of the greatest honour and trust in the Kingdome
to be executed in a great measure by one of his birth, and education.[868] This must proceed
on your side the water from impressions given of his vast services and interest; and no doubt
they whom he idolized, and perhaps worshipped in the most acceptable maner by offerings
(I mean the underlings) failed not to trumpet out his services and that he was the useful
and necessary man.

The Duke of Bolton hath not found him so necessary; but hath been able to do the Kings
businesse in the quietest and best maner, without owing it to him, whose part in it you
will know his Graces opinion of by what will follow in this letter. This the party perceived,
and beleiving it might end in his recommending others and not naming him, the method
taken hath been this (in my opinion) Conelyes freinds, and (I suppose) among the rest
Bladen and Delafay have ordered it soe as to anticipate the Dukes nomination by getting
my Lord Sunderland to mention it to his Majestye that the best way will be, when my Lord
Lieutenant leaves Ireland, that he should appoint the same Justices he found. That this is
the act of Lord S[*underland*] I think you cannot doubt, and from whom he hath received his
impressions you need not I think be much to seek: You see he mentioned my having leave
to go over, and the leave is come before I applyed for it; and there hath been an expresse
from my Lord Sunderland to Conelye; not relating to any thing in the revenue, for then
it must have been communicated to the board; but they talk as if it were something about
Delafayes office of taster etc but that is only a blind: where was the occasion of an expresse
and that so relates to the revenue that the other Commissioners must have been acquainted
with it; yet neither they nor my Lord Lieutenant knew one word of his businesse. Add to
this that Whitshed went away all on a suddain, but on what errand no body can say; it is

---

[866] Of the commission of lords justices. See above, p. 158.

[867] Paul Methuen, secretary of state for the southern department between June 1716 and Apr. 1717.

[868] Conolly was popularly supposed to have been the son of an innkeeper (alternatively a miller or blacksmith)
in Ballyshannon, Co. Donegal. The reality was somewhat different, and the evidence shows that Patrick Conolly,
William's father, was a man of some means, though a tenant and not a landlord. William's mother came from
a local merchant family. (Patrick Walsh, *The Making of the Irish Protestant Ascendancy: The Life of William Conolly,
1662–1729* (Woodbridge, 2010), 11–12.) William himself had not attended university, however, nor an inn of
court, and had begun his career as an attorney.

talked he is to make a purchase, or to bring over a wife, yet forsooth he is to be back before the end of term too. He might and probably had other general views to concert measures with his and Speakers freinds; but I am well satisfyed one of his errands was to fix his patron the Archbishop of D[*ublin*] in the Governement; yet perhaps the acres of mountain may also have been another motive; for his proud heart would burst to be found once to have erred. If this scheme should succeed the party have their ends in supporting the interest of C[*onolly*] who even after this Session of Parliament, and the very different parts he and I have taken in that affair can stil be kept on a level with me. Add to this the uneasy game I must play, when I am certain of his going into every thing with the Archbishop against me when ever he and [*I*] should differ, the consequence of which [*would*] in effect be that the Archbishop would direct every thing.[869] It is fit I should now let you know that my Lord Duke in answer to Mr Addisons letter tells him tho he had by his Commission power to go into England and leave Justices, he could not fail so much in his duty or good maners to exercise either without his Majestyes previous approbation (for he thinks and perhaps with some ground that the anticipating his recommendations looks as if it might be thought he would have named Justices and appointed them without sending over for his Majestyes pleasure). He tells him he had it in his thoughts whom to leave Justices, and me in the first place as well with regard to the Kings service as my own deserts: that he must say I had avowedly and heartily gone into the new additional dutyes, which the Speaker etc (by which he means his party) did not till they saw it would be carryed without them; and then indeed they were as hearty as any body; and if after this it was his Majesty[*'s*] pleasure he should be one of the Justices, he was ready to obey, but would add that the Secretary himself must be sensible that his being first made a Justice caused a good deal of wonder. I should have told you that previous to this paragraph he seemed to be under a difficultye whether after such an intimation given him of what seemed agreeable to his Majestye he remained stil at liberty to say what he otherwise would have said: for then he must have shewn the different parts the Chancellor and Speaker had taken etc viz. That I had avowedly and heartily etc.

He then goes on to say that he should not have recommended the Archbishop for reasons which he will give his Majestye at his arrival, which he thinks to be of such weight as to satisfye his Majestye that it will be for his service to have him omitted: and instead of him should have recommended Lord Montjoy as one of good capacity and ever well affected; or in Case his being subject to the Gout should be an objection, he should have proposed Lord Tyrawlye; and mencions it as his sense that there will be an absolute necessity for three Justices if I go over: and that he hath acquainted me with so much of the letter as relates to his Majestyes resolving to make me one of the Justices and yet expecting my going into England. From this whole affair you see my Lord Lieutenant hath done me all the justice in the world and hath told the very truth as to Conelyes power and inclination to serve the present administration: he hankers after the late people and wishes the present as ill as their predecessors doe. He hath a great estate, and while he is at the top of our revenue[870] and

---

[869] Whitshed had gone to England with a warm letter of introduction from Archbishop King to Archbishop Wake, describing Whitshed as a person both 'agreeable and eminent' (Wake, Epist. xii: King to Wake, 19 Oct. 1717).

[870] The patent establishing the revenue commission assigned no precedency, but Conolly was widely recognised as being 'chief' or 'first' commissioner (Walsh, *Making of the Irish Protestant Ascendancy*, 128).

supported in so extraordinary a maner by being put into the Governement must support an interest; but that interest is more then half due to his great Stations; but can never doe any thing to distresse the Governement; from the moment he aims at that he dwindles to nothing. However I doubt stil such methods have been taken that he will be one; and if that must be and that Lord Montjoy shal [*be*] named for the other I shal be more easy; for he is a man of honour and in every thing will do the reasonable part. I cannot but fancy what my Lord Lieutenant hath said as to the Archbishop will be of weight enough to prevent his being one; the particular reasons he hath I must not presume to dive into: but beleive he recollects that no body was earlier or warmer then he in bringing the matter of Mrs Sherlock before the house,[871] or was for carrying it farther without any consideration how far it might imbarrasse his Majestyes affairs by creating a misunderstanding between the house of Lords of both Kingdomes. But beside this I have heard my Lord Lieutenant say his Grace made it his businesse to oppose the new duty on beer ale and strong waters given this Session in addicion to any dutyes formerly at any time given; and that of mixt gyles, which is also another new duty and of very great consequence: and this professedly and at his own table, where he was an advocate in opposition to all new dutyes before a great deal of company, of which the Cheif Baron was one. This I beleive to be true, for he expressed himself in the same maner to me and I suppose you know which of the two contending interests he hath at heart. It comes now to be considered what I must doe; I have wrote the two inclosed letters to my Lord Duke of Somersett and my Lord Thomond that I may be reelected; which will be of absolute necessity on this new Commission as I doe beleive from what you wrote to me lately about Colonel Moreton it would have been before: and if I should now fail of a new election it will turn to my prejudice in point of character and interest that I ever was chosen. All care therefore must be taken with the Duke and borough to secure me. It will not be fit to tell the Duke there is a necessity of my being reelected by reason of my former Commission; for then perhaps a writ may be moved for so early in the Session that the recepi will not be signed here, which cannot be done till the very day the Duke sets sail; and then either another will be chosen or I shal be put to a new reelection: On the other hand it must not be understood at Court that it is my new Commission which will render it necessary that I be chosen again: for then out of pure kindnesse and to secure me against a disappointment upon a new election I may be left out of the new Commission for Justices here: yet I think it will be proper to let them know there will be occasion for my being new chosen, and that it is not impossible I may not succeed: in which case I shal not be obliged to go over.

I confesse I am not very desirous to gett within those walls in a Session which I doubt will prove a very warm and difficult one, foreseeing more will be expected from me then a man perfectly a stranger to the Kingdome and the forms of your house can hope to perform:

---

[871] The notorious case of *Annesley* v. *Sherlock*, arising from a dispute over acquisitions made by Maurice Annesley (*d*.1718) of Little Rath, Co. Kildare, from the forfeited estate of Christopher Sherlock in Co. Kildare, of which he had been appointed receiver by the forfeiture trustees. Annesley had also acted as guardian to Sherlock's children. The family unsuccessfully brought a case against him in exchequer, but when Christopher Sherlock's sister Hester appealed her case to the Irish house of lords in 1716, the decree was reversed. Annesley in turn appealed to the British house of lords, which restored him to possession. Rather than accept this judgment Mrs Sherlock petitioned the Irish house of lords in Sept. 1717. Despite the best efforts of Alan, and the viceroy, Bolton, to try and bring about a settlement, the petition began a constitutional conflict between the two parliaments. (Burns, *Politics*, i, 173–9; Isolde Victory, 'The Making of the 1720 Declaratory Act', in *Parliament, Politics and People: Essays in Eighteenth-century Irish History*, ed. Gerard O'Brien (Blackrock, Co. Dublin, 1989), 14–15.)

On the other hand when I have leave to come over (that is am sent for as a member) I should be sorry to be forced to say I have no businesse there; this would be matter of great triumph to my back friends …. You may be sure I will give you the earliest intimation when the recepi is signed but fancy it will be from the Head or Chester …

337. *Alan I, Dublin, to Thomas, 11 Nov. 1717*

(1248/4/92–3)

I hope my last of the seventh came safe, and desire you to own the receit of it as soon as it comes to your hands, or at least the post after this arrives. I must now tell you that the Duke of Bolton hath given me reason to think I shal be left one of the Lords Justices during his absence: by his Commission he hath power to nominate Justices, but that is a power that never is executed nor indeed ought to be without the Cheif Governors first humbly proposing, to the King, the names of the persons whom he hath in his thoughts as fittest to make Justices, for his Majestyes pleasure therein: but whether he hath already done this or intends to doe it is what he hath not communicated to me, nor is it fit for me to enquire: He told me at the same time that I should have leave to go into England and take my seat in Parliament: this you know must proceed from some intimation thence that my attendance is expected, so as I am almost apt to suspect he may have already recommended and received his Majestyes pleasure about the Justices; but this is kept a very secret. You know how my affair at Midhurst stands, and how far my Lord Galways delaying to lay down the Governement after he had received the Kings pleasure to passe a Commission for new Justices put me under difficultyes whether I must not have been reelected by reason my patent for Justice bore date after the election at Midhurst was over; tho all of you reasonably concluded from the date of the Kings orders to Lord Galway to appoint new Justices that the patent was sealed before the time of my being elected; you were once indeed of opinion I should not have occasion to be chosen again, upon the decision in the case of General Rosse,[872] but Colonel Moretons case in the last Session hath put that matter out of all dispute, and so I find your opinion and that of my other freinds now to be: But if there remained yet any room for doubt, the resolution taken to make me now one of the Justices leaves no possibility for my sitting unlesse I can prevail on my Lord Duke of Somersett to chuse me again. To that end I have wrote the enclosed letters to him and my Lord Thomond, which I hope you will deliver with your own hand. The Toryes here form to themselves hopes of creating great if not unsurmountable difficultyes to the present administration: perhaps I speak improperly by styling all who are opposite to the present ministry Toryes, but I mean all such by that name, whatever they formerly have been, or may pretend now to be. I wish their efforts may be as fruitlesse and their designs as abortive as those of some of their freinds have been here in our Session of Parliament: for you must have perceived by my former letters how averse a certain party of men was from time to time to coming in to new dutyes, particularly the new addicional dutyes on ale, strong waters etc and to that of the mixed or party Gyles: and remember who it was that declared fourteen or 15 of his particular freinds who had dined that day with him, and

---

[872]It is not clear what the case alluded to by Alan might have been (see *HC 1690–1715*, v, 307–10).

with whom he thought he had such an interest that he could have answered for them, were wholly against it. Now this being (as it was) pretty late in the Session, and after promises to do all possible with freinds to bring them into the matter, was really the final result of the juncto: insomuch that I was forced to say my acquaintance were all of different sentiments and that a short question would decide it, of the event of which I ventured to tell my Lord Lieutenant I thought he needed not make much doubt. This had its efect, a meeting was had at Mr M[an]lyes:[873] and it was there found advisable not to give opposition but to come in roundly; and from that time and no sooner a certain party came into the matter in earnest. But why do I trouble you with difficultyes which my Lord Lieutenants prudence and the good affection of the house to his Majestyes service hath so happily and without noise or bustle removed: With what joy should I passe my winter if I could hope to see the same temper and disposition toward his Majestyes service at a certain place as hath appeared here, and ever will while the Parliament meets fair dealing and is not to be managed. You see how sollicitous I am about my spending my time with you in London, but I ought not to be wholly unconcerned at what will be my case when I return again, which must a good deal depend upon my being yoaked with people with whom I may propose to serve the King in the maner I shal alway wish. Probably my Lord Lieutenants recommendacions will go very far in determining who will be fittest to be entrusted in his absence: I know your acquaintance and very professing freind hath it wonderfully att heart to be again in Commission; this he hopes will be a step to some high degree of Peerage which his soul thirsts after; his freinds in England, who were lately here, will push his pretensions: and two late Secretaryes here will do every thing in their power, and they have a good deal of credit with a very great and very good man: but if this Gentlemans designs in the last Session (notwithstanding his dark management) were understood on your side of the water, I think he would not be able to succeed and certainly my Lord Lieutenant knows and hath observed the windings and doubles which have been made to obstruct meaures this Session: If after doing so he hath recommended him I shal be astonished and think him an happy man who by wishing well to and acting for one sett of men renders or keeps himself gratious with the other. That which I am most apprehensive of is the scarcity of fit men; and by what I have within a few dayes past heard fall from my Lord Lieutenant he seems to me to labour under that difficultye. He (as it were by accident) named Lord Montjoy as one very capable of being made a Justice, but then objected his being subject to the Gout: you know my Lord Montjoy as well as I doe, and may be sure I spoke my mind as freely as was proper that there was not in my opinion a fitter man, but endeavoured to find how his Grace thought of the Archbishop of D[ublin] and found he looked on him to be no way proper; his maner of expressing himself shewed that he looked on him to have opposed the Kings measures; and indeed it is certain, and you will find it by my former letters, that no man was warmer in Sherlocks businesse, and that he publickly declared and interested himself in opposition to any new fund or tax. Whatever have been the A[rchbishop']s motives, I beleive he hath no very good wishes to the happy issue of the D[uke] of B[olton']s administration, and I think the D[uke] seeth and knoweth it: but it is plain two certain Bishops since their coming from Britain have spoken more favourably of a certain sett of men then one would expect from such as wish the continuance of another. I take it then for granted that the A[rchbishop]

---

[873] Isaac Manley, MP [I].

hath not been recommended, and therefore hope Lord Montjoy will succeed: I have not gone so far as to tell Lord M[*ountjoy*] so much as I have wrote to you, nor if I should doe I beleive he would make any step on this or the other side to be appointed; but I wish you would take any oportunity of saying it where it may be proper, that it is talked of here who will be left Justices, and that it concurs with the desires of all who stand well inclined to his Majestyes service, if my Lord Montjoy who is talked of on the occasion should be made one. Sure you have sufficient freedome even with my Lord Sunderland to drop a word to this purpose; and it may be of service, especially if my Lord Montjoy stand as well with my Lord Sunderland as I apprehend he sometime since did: You know my freindship for Lord Montjoy, but that doth not byasse me; my concern is least another (whom I will not name) should be thought more proper, in respect of my Lords being gouty: but there is a vast difference in the men, as well with regard to their personal merit as the opinion the Kingdome entertains of them.

I am almost afraid of setting my feet in your house of Commons, where probably I shal make a much lesse figure now then I have formerly done in another place; but I owe the King my best services every where, and will at all adventures and hazards shew my readinesse to serve him …

338. Alan I, Dublin, to Thomas, 11 Nov. 1717

(1248/4/94–5)

I forgott to write last pacquet to my Lord Thomond and have done it now: the other letter to you[874] is wrote on purpose to be shewn (if you see fit) and done in a carelesse way, that it may appear not to have been calculated for that end … You will by comparing it with my former long letter of the seventh see that my design is wholly to conceal my knowledge of the contents of Mr A[*ddison'*]s letter, or of the answer to it; and that I seem to suppose the D[*uke*] of B[*olton*] hath recommended formerly, whereas you do know how that whole affair stands. My design is to let my self into the giving a summary account of the behavior of two persons in this Session: and cannot but think it will lessen my Lord Lieutenant not a little (for I do not mention my self) if they can after their conduct toward him and the Kings service in this Session be upon the same foot with those who took the clean contrary methods in all matters relating to it. You certainly may tell either or both the Secretaryes how valuable a man Lord Montjoy is, and may give an hint to Lord Molesworth that he is talked of for one of the Justices and bid him forward it: for tho I know my Lord looks on him as the most imperious creature alive, and would not be obliged to him, tho marryed to his Aunt;[875] yet a word from him to Lord Sunderland may be of use: and nothing will more incline him to it then to say that Lord Tyrawly is also talked of for one, and that you think he is not so proper a man as the other.

Molesworth looks on Lord T[*yrawley*] to be a Teague[876] and on that foot rather then from freindship to the other will oppose, and indeed Lord Montjoy is the better man in my

---

[874] Letter 337.

[875] Molesworth's wife Letitia (née Coote) was the sister of Mountjoy's mother, Mary.

[876] A derisory name for an Irish catholic.

opinion, nay without exception. You may explain that I mean Lord Tyrawly by the person whom I will not name in my other Letter.

339. *Alan I, Dublin, to Thomas, at his lodgings in the Privy Garden, Whitehall, 17 Nov. 1717*

(1248/4/98–9)

I am glad to find you are come to London: nothing of great consequence hath hapned in Parliament of which I have not already given you an account unlesse you will reckon the opposition given by the Primate on the third reading of the bill to repeal the short oath[877] to be so; which he in a tragical and declamatory style endeavoured to shew to be of most dangerous consequence both to the Crown and Church: but he had so much said in answer to his insinuations as convinced those who heard the debate, that the danger to the possessor of the Crown and to the Protestant Church arose only from those who were fond of that oath and the declaration required by the Act of uniformity that it is not lawful on any pretence whatsoever etc upon which foot cheifly the enemyes to the revolution endeavour to blacken it: and he was told that it was plain the Jacobites alway had that oath and declaration in their mouths, and that the disaffection which was observable in the Universityes and young Clergy could not be so reasonably attributed to any one cause as their taking that oath and making that declaration: he had three Bishops who adhered to him in giving their not content to the passing of the bill: viz Clonfert Kildare and Down; but all the other Bishops and every temporal Lord were content.[878] The next day he signed and put in a very extraordinary protest, in which he said that bill was a breach of the Act of Union, which the King was by his coronation oath obliged to maintain: notice was taken of this reflection on the King, who had already agreed to the bill by signing it with his own hand and ordered my Lord Lieutenant to give the royal assent to it under the great Seal then lying before the house, I mean when the bill was before the house: and the consequences of his protest were shewn to be so manifest and grosse reflections that he was obliged to beg the pardon of the house and to have leave to withdraw it.[879] It was called by more Lords then one a libel, and Lord Newtowns zeal prompted him to have it burnt by the hands of the hangman. My Lord Lieutenant was pleased to say to me that I had spoken to his satisfaction on the occasion and done the King service. My Lord Wharton was a good deal uneasy at my proposing (after laying the matter home on the Primate) that his Grace might be received to ask pardon[880] and withdraw his protest to prevent the judgement and censure of the house upon it: his young Lordship was of opinion we could have committed

---

[877] The oath, forswearing taking up arms against the king, imposed by the 'new rules' of 1672 on members of borough corporations in Ireland, alongside the oaths of allegiance and supremacy. The bill, which had been introduced by the duke of Wharton and reported from committee by Lord Abercorn on 23 Sept., eventually passed into law as 4 Geo. 1, c. 3 [I] (ILD).

[878] The opposition of Lindsay and the other three bishops is confirmed in Wake, Epist. xii: [Bishop Godwin] to [Archbishop Wake], [c. 17 Nov. 1717], which also notes that in a further debate on the bill Clonfert deserted his colleagues. This letter also names the bishop of Down as the principal speaker against the bill, and Alan and Archbishop King as its foremost defenders.

[879] Confirmed in *LJI*, ii, 574.

[880] According to Lord Moore, it was Archbishop King who had proposed allowing Lindsay to withdraw his protest, a motion which Alan seconded. In so doing, according to Moore, Alan had abandoned his friends (BL,

him, not considering how difficult it is to commit an Archbishop where the majority of the Lords then present wear Lawn sleeves.[881] the thing was impracticable, and indeed not desirable: committing him would have raised a noise, with his party. But my Lord is fond of putting me in the wrong in every thing, and indeed my judgement doth not alway suit his, which is a great fault.

340. *Alan I, Dublin, to Thomas, 22 Dec. 1717*

(1248/4/104–5)

… the last letters we had till the arrival of the boat on Thursday (which brought us nine mails) bore date 23d of November; the account all people receive of the unhappy incident at Court fills all honest men with greif.[882] God avert the dismal consequences that may attend such misunderstandings, if not timely made up, and the resentments forgotten; but this is too nice a subject to enlarge upon … I hope to be able to go over with my Lord Lieutenant the beginning of next month: the certain time I cannot yet learn, nor consequently tell you when the Commission for Justices will bear date, who are (as you told me) our former ones: we easily guesse to whom we owe the same mens being honoured with so distinguishing a mark of undeserved favor, I mean some of them. But I must tell you one thing that tho Mr A[*ddison*] used the notice he had of things by your shewing him mine (in confidence) with great tendernesse and prudence, so as a certain person to whom he wrote could not know he had seen it, yet it was obvious from a letter he wrote to that person that he had seen something which he could not have but by the means of one on this side: if you cannot understand me, I must not speak plainer.

But now to the Cheif subject of my letter, I mean that which I think so; for Senny thinks the later part to be more soe then what I write relating to Mr Addison. The last letters from London mention him very ill, some say past hope of recovery, and (I hear) one to Mr Manly saith he is dead.[883] You know how truly I must lament the losse of so valuable a man to the King and Kingdomes, and of so true a freind where he professes: and yet I am not blind enough not to perceive that he knew and perhaps came into the scheme of doing what will contribute to support C[*onolly*]'s pride and the insolence of his few freinds; which such countenance doth in a great measure, and only that can doe it. If he be dead his place of Keeper of the Records in Berminghams tower[884] will fall, and my son (who is eager enough in his own affairs) hath prevailed on me to speak to the Duke and obtain his promise to grant it to him; for it is in the sword, but the grant can only be during his Majestyes pleasure which my Lord Lieutenant can make, and any more durable interest

---

[880] *(continued)* Stowe MS 230, f. 276: Moore to Lord Molesworth, 14 Nov. 1717 (copy, translated into French: 'le chancellier … nous abandonna')).

[881] That is to say, are bishops. On the day of the third reading, 13 Nov., and again on the following day, when Primate Lindsay's protest was withdrawn, the journals recorded the presence of 14 spiritual and 13 temporal lords (including the Speaker). (*LJI*, ii, 573–4.)

[882] The quarrel between George I and the prince of Wales, which resulted in the prince being ordered to quit St James's Palace (Ragnhild Hatton, *George I Elector and King* (1978), 206–9).

[883] Addison did not succumb to this illness, living on until 1719.

[884] In Dublin Castle: a patent office.

must be by direct application to his Majesty which must be made when we land in England … If the next pacquets give us an account of Mr Addisons death the Duke will grant it to Senny immediately which will put him in possession, and give him oportunity of farther application with the advantage which being in possession carryes: and his Grace promises me to send a letter to Lord Sunderland with a flying seal under your Cover, which you are not to make use of unlesse it be true that Mr Addison is dead, which is intended not only in some kind to recommend Senny but to anticipate any recommendations which may come from your side: but if Mr A[ddison] be living, as I sincerely hope he will be many years after your receiving that letter, you must keep it and give it to my Lord Duke when he reaches London. In this you will consult your prudence, and not speak one word upon the occasion, which may cause a breach of freindship which I think very valuable: for I know not by what fate it comes (but it is a certain truth) that few men love to have people use any interest to succeed them in case of death, who never have the least desire of their dying. So much for this point. But now comes another whimsical one: You must know he thinks getting into an English Parliament would be the making his fortune, and that he should be able to make some figure there, because he doth soe here; now he would have me write to Lord Onslow to try if he might by his and your interest succeed at Guilford, where he thinks a vacancy will be by means of my new Lord Onslows becoming a Peer.[885] I am not sure how that will be, but conclude that election is not only settled but actually over before this can come to your hand: beside I have not such acquaintance with my Lord to pretend the freedome of writing to him for such a favor, whatever I should venture to doe by word of mouth if I were on the spot: but if you see the thing any way feasible and will break it to my Lord, you will infinitely oblige one whose ambition leads him to be fond of a seat in a British Parliament almost to madnesse, if I judge the true cause of his uneasinesse; which proceeds only from a fancy of rendring himself very significant if once brought into St Stephens Chappel. You have now his wishes and hopes; and will doe in it what prudence and your kindnesse to him leads you to. My next shal be upon your own affairs: We shal be up to morrow after having passed the Kilkenny bill through both houses since Thursday morning when it arrived here; for I think it will not find such opposicion as may endanger it in our house, none having been made in the house of Commons.[886] The Lords have made an unusual complement to my Lord Lieutenant by thanking him for his good Governement to the entire satisfaction of the whole Kingdome (which is very true) whereas we never did addresse any other Lord Lieutenant at the end of a Session on the successe of his administration: which however I think a better way then to flatter

---

[885] Thomas Onslow (1679–1740), of Clandon Park, Surrey, who held one of the shire seats for Surrey, succeeded his father Sir Richard as 2nd Baron Onslow on 5 Dec. 1717. He promptly gave up his office of out-ranger of Windsor Forest to his uncle Denzil Onslow (1641–1721), of Pyrford, Surrey, in order to disqualify Denzil from continuing to sit in the Commons (where he represented Guildford), and thus enable him to stand for the county vacancy, which Denzil did, successfully, on 25 Dec. 1717. Robert Wroth then took Denzil's seat for Guildford at a by-election six days later. (*HC 1715–54*, i, 327–9; ii, 309–12.)

[886] The bill to impose reforms on the corporation of Kilkenny, which took power away from the previously dominant tory interest. Originating in the Commons, it had passed both privy councils unamended, was presented to the Commons on 19 Dec., went up to the Lords two days later and received the royal assent on the 23rd (as 4 Geo. I, c. 16 [I]) (ILD).

a Governement before we know what it will do, which is our case at the opening of a Parliament.[887]

341. *Alan I, Dublin, to Thomas, 5 Jan. 1717[/18]*

(1248/4/110–11)

The pacquet is just come in and hath brought yours of the 31th of December; the boat sails again this evening and I resolve to write by her to tell you my Lord Lieutenant resolves to go to morrow in the Lively which Captain Charleton commands:[888] but by the best guesse I can make he is not in such forwardnesse to be able to go that day, either with respect to his private affairs or those of the publick. He enquires after you with great respect and affection. A certain person[889] pretends to goe in the same ship; but I heard a bird sing he would goe off privately this evening in the pacquett boat, to avoid some inconvenient applications from people who may ask too importunately to be easily denied for what perhaps can with very great difficulty be found: but this possibly may be only a guesse: tho Mr Manly blurted it out publickly in the Dukes Closett that he was to go this evening in the pacquet boat, and I am sure I heard the same person tell me that we should have a very passage to morrow together if the wind continued as fair then as it was when he was speaking. I will speak to Senny and shew him what you write, which I doe not well understand but fear it is matter of money for rent due. Pray superscribe the enclosed to Mr Wallop in the maner he is to be wrote to, for I know not how to direct to one of your Lords of the Treasury:[890] and seal the letter directed to Mr Jervass who will be heard of at Burlington house[891] …

342. *Alan I, Chester, to Thomas, to be left at Mrs Courthope's, Bond Street, 9 Jan. 1717[/18], 'past three in the afternoon'*

(1248/4/112)

My Lord Lieutenant and the Dutchesse are just come to town; I have only time to say thus much and that we propose to be in town on Wednesday next … If the accounts we have here be true things are in great disorder, or in a tendency to it, with you: but I hope it is Jacobite news which is what is most agreeable to some places.

---

[887] The Lords' address, agreed on 12 Dec., did not use precisely these words, but observed that 'the malice and treachery of ill-designing men' had only served 'to unite all loyal subjects to that becoming zeal, which they have shown for his majesty's interest and your grace's government' (*LJI*, ii, 594).

[888] St John Charlton (*d*.1742), of Apley Castle, Salop, MP [GB] 1725–34, commanded the Royal Navy frigate *Lively*, commissioned in 1715 'for the west coast of Scotland and Irish waters', which during the jacobite rising of 1715–16 had been one of the ships stationed off the west coast of Scotland to intercept supplies intended for the rebels (John Charnock, *Biographia Navalis* … (6 vols, 1794–8), iv, 6–7; *HC 1715–54*, i, 543–4; Rif Winfield, *British Warships in the Age of Sail 1603–1714: Design, Construction, Careers and Fates* (Barnsley, 2009), 206). According to newspaper reports, Alan accompanied Bolton and his duchess (*Original Weekly Journal*, 4–11 Jan. 1718).

[889] William Conolly.

[890] John Wallop (1690–1762), of Farleigh Wallop, Hants, MP [GB] 1715–20, and subsequently earl of Portsmouth, had been appointed a lord of the treasury [GB] in Apr. 1717.

[891] Possibly a reference to the fashionable Irish artist Charles Jervas (1675–1739).

343. *Alan I, London, to Alan II, Clare Hall, Cambridge, 10 Apr. 1718*

(1248/4/150–1)

I found all freinds here very well last night, who enquired kindly after you and remember them to you very affectionately. Do not forget to renew my thanks to Lord Ryalton[892] Mr Cornwallis[893] Dr Laughton[894] and Mr Man[895] for the favours I received from them att Cambridge and the honour they did me there in allowing me the pleasure of so good company: I wish I could promise my self that you might propose to your self to be happy in soe agreeable and vertuous conversation: I should then be a good deal at ease in one of the greatest concernments of my life, your being bred up vertuously according to my best wishes. I told you I carryed you to Newmarkett to convince you that I was satisfyed you would not fall in love with what they call the diversions of the place, and hope you have seen enough of the Cockpitt, Chocolate house, and course to make you hate Cockfighting, gaming and its attendant vices, desperate oathes distraction nay blasphemy; and that you see that horse racing is an introduction to cheating, sharping, hypocrisy, and lying: and ends in the ruine of mens estates as well as the losse of their characters generally.[896] You know by experience how expensive that place is and must begin to consider the value of money better then you yet doe. You are fond of riding, but must not indulge your self in it, nor ever let that tempt you to Newmarkett without my being with you: and must now for a good time apply your self wholly to your study; for that will be necessary in order to recover the time you have spent in recreation while we were together …

344. *Alan I, Dublin, to Thomas, at his lodgings in the Privy Garden, Whitehall, 3 June 1718*

(1248/4/118–19)

I thank you for yours of the twentieth of May, and am very much pleased that the matter of the Curate of Haslemere hath ended in the maner you mention.[897] and beleive a few such examples might have good influence on the people, and bring them a little more to a right mind then some of them seem to be now in.

---

[892] William Godolphin (c.1699–1731), MP [GB] 1720–2, 1727–*d.*, only son of Francis, 2nd earl of Godolphin, and known until 1722 by the courtesy title of Lord Rialton. An undergraduate at Clare Hall.

[893] Hon. Charles Cornwallis (1700–62), son of Charles, 4th Baron Cornwallis, and subsequently 1st Earl Cornwallis. An undergraduate at Clare College.

[894] Richard Laughton (1670– 1723), fellow of Clare College, for whom see *Oxf. DNB*.

[895] Possibly the future diplomat Sir Horatio (Horace) Mann, for whom see *Oxf. DNB*, an undergraduate at Clare College c.1720 but at this point only 13 years old; more likely Horatio's elder brother Edward Louisa Mann (1702–75), himself admitted to Clare College in 1721, having previously attended Eton College (John Venn and J. A. Venn, *Alumni Cantabrigienses* … (10 vols, Cambridge, 1922–52), pt 1, iii, 131).

[896] Among the match-races scheduled to be run at Newmarket in April were two featuring horses owned by Thomas: on 4 Apr. his 'Careless' was pitted against Lord Wharton's 'Snail' for a prize of a thousand guineas; on the 28th his 'Kate' was due to compete with Wharton's 'Chanter' for five hundred (*Post Boy*, 27 Feb.–1 Mar. 1718).

[897] Meredith Jones (c.1693–1727), curate at Haslemere, and later vicar of Westdean, Sussex, had been accused of uttering jacobite sentiments while drinking at a tavern in the town (*Sussex Archaeological Collections*, cvi (1968), 17; J. S. Chamberlain, *Accommodating High Churchmen: The Clergy of Sussex, 1700–1745* (Urbana, IL, 1997), 39–40).

He ought not to be upbraided for his past misbehavior in the countrey, since his Majesty hath been pleased to forgive it; and good usage is the most likely method intirely to alter and bring him over: whereas casting it in his teeth will have the clean contrary effect. It is also some pleasure to me to have been able to gratifye my friends att Midhurst in this affair ... Our weather is now prodigiously hot, yet we have had great rain within these three or fowre dayes. Since the Archbishops[898] going out of town on Fryday to hold a visitacion, and Mr Conelye on Saturday to see his wife at his brother Pearsons near Droghedah,[899] upon notice given me of some Popish fryers, Preists etc being in Dublin I ordered the party to give examinations before Justice Caulfield,[900] for him to ground a warrant upon, directed to the Sherifs of this City, who have taken six; among them the titular Archbishop of Dublin[901] ...

345. *Thomas to Alan I, 11 June 1718*

(1248/4/120–1)

Yours of the 3d came on Munday, I this morning read the paragraph relating to the Preists and fryers to Lord Sunderland; The occasion of my coming to towne was this; the 20th of last month when the Parliament was prorogued, I went up to the house of Lords, where his Lordship told mee hee desired to speake with mee assoone as I conveniently could, I acquainted his Lordship with my intention of going out of town next morning, butt that att my returne I would wait on him; hee began with saying that hee was very sensible of the ill treatment I had receivd, and therefore desired I would pitch on somthing that might bee an equivalent, for that the King was determined nott to remove Mr Bruce;[902] though hee had been told what his principles were, which hee ownd hee knew full well, I told his Lordship that since matters were soe, I could nott thinke of any person soe obnoxious as to desire his removall in order to make way for mee, nor indeed (as things stood) could I thinke such a proceeding fair, if twere to bee effected, butt that since I perceivd my zeale for his Majestys service was outballanced by Mr B[ruce']s interest, I could nott butt conclude any attempt of that kind must prove fruitlesse, that I very well knew by whose meanes hee was supported, and must assure his Lordship I would never create an interest by the same persons, or meanes; that very few things were incompatible with sitting in parliament that such as were nott, must bee probably reservd for members, and that having determined nott to goe to a reelection (which I never would doe) twould bee in vaine to trouble his

---

[898]William King.

[899]Thomas Pearson, MP [I] had married Conolly's sister Jane.

[900]William Caulfeild.

[901]Edmond Byrne (*d.*1724), catholic archbishop of Dublin since 1707, was arrested in 1718 on information supplied by the 'priest-hunter' John Garzia, and charged under the terms of the various laws against catholic bishops and unregistered clergy. The case was eventually dropped. (*Catholic Ireland in the Eighteenth Century: Collected Essays of Maureen Wall*, ed. Gerard O'Brien (Dublin, 1980), 29, 38; Patrick Fagan, *The Second City: Portrait of Dublin 1700–1760* (Dublin, 1986), 110–11.)

[902]Hon. James Bruce (c.1670–c.1732), MP [GB] 1702–5, 1708–10, a younger brother of the jacobite exile Thomas Bruce, 2nd earl of Ailesbury, served as comptroller of army accounts from 1711 until his death, at a salary of £1,500 p.a. He was 'esteemed by all for his integrity and good conduct in the execution of his office' (*HC 1690–1715*, iii, 369–70).

Lordship or my selfe any farther theruppon. I told his Lordship that in addition to what I thought a wrong already done mee, I was layd under a farther load, being very well assured that att a gentlemans table where there was a great deale of company, among other things, the usage I had mett with was mentioned, to which twas replyed that they were mistaken if they thought my case what they seemd to apprehend; for that I had reason to bee very easy, since to his knowledge I had what was much better (meaning a pension) then my former employment; I assured his Lordship I had used my best endeavours to have known the person, in order to have done my selfe right, by exposing him, butt since I could nott any way come att the knowledge of itt, I must and would take all reasonable opertunityes of convincing those, whom this report might have reacht, of the falsehood of itt, for that though I had been able to live without an employment, and could doe soe, I would nott suffer in my reputation, which I thought such a thing as this (were itt true) would deservedly call in question. Hee professed himselfe both willing and desirous to serve mee, on account of our long acquaintance, and desired I would firmly beleive his professions; I returnd my humble thanks, butt told him hee must pardon mee if I consulted what I thought for my honour, and indeed incumbent uppon mee, and uppon my word I will doe itt, to the utmost of my power in every instance as far as is consistent with my duty to his Majesty and the good of my country, from neither of which will I ever depart.

I intend tomorrow morning for Pepper Hara, and will stay there till the worke in hand is finished, after which I may possibly thinke of taking a little tour abroad, this has been in my thoughts some time, the onely obstacle was the expence, which I will make as easy as I can, and I hope to bee able to beare itt.

Lord and Lady Montjoy and Mr Hill begin their journey towards Chester tomorrow; I hear Lord Montrath does soe likewise ....

346. *Thomas to Alan I, Dublin, 2 Aug. 1718*

(1248/4/122–3)

... I hinted in both my last a desire of your coming over assoone as well you could; I am indeed desirous of itt on my own account, butt least you should thinke that the cheife motive, I must acquaint you, there is another of much greater weight, which nearly concernes the future felicity of your life, I beleive I need nott farther explaine myselfe, for you will certainly guesse what I meane; Your coming soe early as to bee master of your time (which you cannott when the parliament is sitting) will bee both advisable and necessary, therfore pray doe itt, and remember that probably the session is nott very distant, for yesterday by an expresse from Lord Stanhope wee have an account of his having (att Bayone) receivd pasports in the manner hee desired, from whence hee was next day going towards Madrid.[903]

Tis very likely hee will soe transact affairs att that Court, as to prevent a rupture; if soe, a generall peace will bee the effect and this leaves little roome for doubting, butt that the Parliament may meet the very beginning of November, att farthest.

---

[903]James Stanhope, created Earl Stanhope in Apr. 1718, was serving as ambassador to Paris and Madrid.

I am nott soe sanguine as some people, whoe promise themselves a very easy time, the good posture which wee hope, in all forreigne affairs, will in great measure contribute to itt, butt I wish wee may find our domestick ones as propitious; for if itt prove otherwise, these may occasion sufficient trouble. I should therefore bee far from pressing your coming, were itt nott for what I have hinted, which leaves noe roome for choice ...

347. *Alan I, Dublin, to Thomas, 10 Aug. 1718*

(1248/4/124–5)

The dark maner of your expressing yourself in your last, in which you tell me that the future felicity of my life will in great measure depend on my going soon into England, doth mightily perplex me. It must have some relation to A[*lice*] but in what regard I am to the greatest degree in doubt: from a letter lately received from her (to which the inclosed is an answer, and to be delivered or not as you and my sister shal judge most proper) and one from my sister, as well as from discourse I had both with you and her in London, and from my own observation, I have no doubt but that A[*lice*] thinks it too great a constraint to be under the eye and direction of etc whereas God knows it is the greatest trouble on earth to take such a trust on one and nobody knows the infinite uneasinesses it creates; nor doth the party most concerned to make returns of gratitude ever think they owe any thing but resentment and neglect, till their age and experience brings them to a better understanding. It is an hard thing for me how to act in such circumstances; I see too well that there is a fault, yet such an one that she who is most concerned never would let me directly mention. I hope this is all; if there be more speak plain and without reserve in your next: My sister no doubt is free with you and you with her in whatever relates to A[*lice*] and I hope both will be so with me. I suppose she hath told you of something which arose at Epsom and of a letter she received from hence; if not, upon shewing this and her seeing I consent to it she will not defer doing it. As to my coming over immediately, I think it impossible; nor can I propose it to the ministry but under the pretence of attending the Session,[904] till which I ought to do my duty here; how shal I quit the office of Justice and Chancellor and neglect the publick to attend my own private affairs? But I will put my matters into the best condition I am able that I may need a very short warning. If I understand you right as to employing some time before the Session in a matter which cannot be so well transacted after it is once begun, I fancy a thing of that sort may be treated and brought to perfection as well during the Session as before: but perhaps I mistake your meaning ... I intend soon to write a letter on the subject which you were upon with Lord Sunderland, when last together.

348. *Alan I, Dublin, to Thomas, at his lodgings in the Privy Garden, Whitehall, 21 Sept. 1718*

(1248/4/128–9)

... I had lately a letter from my Lord Anglesey in which he tells me he was served with a letter missive[905] signed by me within time of priviledge, beleives it was a surprize on me;

---

[904] The British parliamentary session, which opened on 11 Nov. 1718.

[905] 'A letter from a superior authority to a person or persons, conveying a command, recommendation or permission' (*OED*); in this case presumably connected with a Chancery process.

had ordered an appearance in obedience etc looked on it as a breach of priviledge; took this way with me, would produce me another with those who prosecuted the matter; hoped I would take care he should not suffer etc. I ordered the Clerk of the plaintifs six Clerk to give his Master an account of this, and if any thing in breach of my Lord priviledge had been done, to make application to my Lord and stop all proceedings etc. On Thursday last Mr Gering the Six Clerk[906] came to town; I directed him to go to Lord Anglesey; he did so, applyed by freinds but nothing will serve his Lordships turn but a complaint to the Lords: and as I understand it, his aim is at me. In the first place I never examine to whom letters missive are directed but sign them of course; nor are they any processe; he is in town and hath not been to see me, nor as I hear any of the two other Justices. Pray inform yourself whether any thing of this kind is ever looked on in England as a breach of priviledge I mean in the Chancellor; who as he signs all letters missive, so he seals all writs; and consequently must by the same (nay greater) reason be guilty of every breach of priviledge where a suit is commenced against a member of either house. If this should be called a breach of priviledge, what will the consequence be between the two houses; and how do the Commons doe where the Lords vote a Commoner hath broken the priviledge of the house of Peers …

349. *Alan I, Dublin, to Thomas, at his lodgings in the Privy Garden, Whitehall, 3 Oct. 1718*

(1248/4/130–1)

I have yours of 25th and 27th of September: and have wrote a letter to a Gentleman by this mail in answer to a letter from him of 27th of last month who is a good deal the occasion or subject of both those letters from you. I hope you mistake in beleiving him capable of being the means to have that article put into the prints: I have known him long, and never could observe any thing of that sort in his nature. I rather conjecture the thing to be thus from what my sisters letter tells me, that there was a discourse of this affair last Summer in London. Probably upon his return some of his acquaintance might surmise that his errand hither was to attempt effecting this thing; and might ask him what successe he mett with, to which he might return a sprigh[t]ly answer, and they from thence might conclude the thing done: perhaps it might be the act of his — or of our good freind the Duke of W[harton] or perhaps it might take rise from his going to Peperhara immediately after coming to town. I hope and beleive you will have no more trouble on this subject, but shal never be at ease till that can be effected which only can put me out of pain. Pray consider shal I need to be reelected; if so all steps should be made, and the D[uke] of S[omerset] be spoken to; at least so far as to give him my most humble services, and so to Lord Thomond. Till 22 November I cannot leave this place without paying 4s in the pound of my salary which will cost me £400[907] … This probably will overtake you at Newmarkett: Give my services

---

[906]Richard Geering MP [I], one of the six clerks in chancery [I].
[907]In consequence of the tax on absentee office-holders.

to my brother Jockeys: but I will not presume to include the Dukes of Bolton Somersett Devonshire, Lord Godolphin[908] and Lord Bridgewater[909] under so familiar a term.

350. *Alan I, Dublin, to Thomas, at his lodgings in the Privy Garden, Whitehall, 7 Oct. 1718*

(1248/4/132–3)

I have yours of 29th of September, and am glad to find that it hath been thought proper to take again into consideration the undeserved treatment you have hitherto mett with; and cannot conclude as you doe that it will not end in something satisfactory. I am sure I spoke my mind freely on this subject when I was in London and will doe it again when I gett thither, which must now be soon: for by a letter from my Lord Lieutenant I have the intimation of his Majestyes pleasure that I should be over by the eleventh of next month; and he tells me that the next pacquet will bring his Majestyes letter of licence in form, with one to appoint Commissioners for hearing causes and keeping the Seal in my absence, without prejudice to my patent. Upon this subject I write to his Grace by this Post and mention that care should be taken that I may not suffer in my Commission for being Chancellor or in the perquisites of that employ; but take no notice to him that the like care must also be taken that my going out of the Kingdome do not determine my Commission of one of the Justices. This I would not say in expresse words to him out of whose salary the monthly summe of £100 to each Justice for their entertainment issues;[910] but you will hint it to the Duke or Mr Webster that I may not loose the honour of continuing one of the Justices … If there be any difficultye of my coming into the house without being reelected, should not something be done preparative to that …

351. *Alan I, Dublin, to Thomas, 'ten in the morning', 17 Oct. 1718*

(1248/4/134–5)

His Majestyes pleasure for my coming over came to hand in form yesterday, by a letter to me from the Secretary,[911] and by his Majestyes letters to the Justices commanding my immediate attendance on his person and directing the appointing the same persons Commissioners for keeping the Seal and for hearing causes in my absence as were in those Stations when I went over last year. I have put things in a readinesse and resolve to be there by the time I am expected, and have signifyed as much to my Lord Lieutenant and to the Secretary: but the indisposition of the Archbishop,[912] who hath been very ill since yesterday sennight in the night, and continues stil so, must delay my beginning my journey. He is subject to the Gout, was taken with violent pains on Thursday sennight in the night which they call the

---

[908] Francis Godolphin (1678–1766), 2nd earl of Godolphin.

[909] Scroop Egerton (1681–1745), 4th earl of Bridgwater.

[910] The lord lieutenant.

[911] James Craggs (1686–1721), of Jermyn Street, Westminster, MP [GB] 1713–*d.*, had been appointed secretary of state for the southern department in Mar. 1718.

[912] William King.

Cholick; and as such they treated it, by giving him several doses of Physick one after the other, the former not working; they say six in all, but that I cannot beleive to be true; but it is certain he was forced to take several one after another before any would work: At length the Physick made its way, and on Wednesday he was blistred about noon: his blisters were cutt att twelve that night, and he gott a good deal of rest after it; and was better yesterday, and his pain moved from the place it first seised him: but I find by my servant who is just now returned from his house that he rested little or nothing last night: tho his family will not allow him to be in any great danger. But when one considers that he is 70 years old, very subject to the gout, and that in all probability what he labours under is the gout in his stomach; to which if you add the treatment the Physicians here have given him, not only by purging and blistring, but also by blouding him (for so they did tho I forgott to mention it) I cannot think him perfectly out of danger. I wish you and my sister would have an eye where we may have good lodgings against our coming to town; about which I will write more at large by next pacquet. But let not any be actually taken till you hear farther, at least not for any time, for fear of their not pleasing us.

352. *Alan I, Dublin, to Thomas, at his lodgings in the Privy Garden, Whitehall, 26 Oct. 1718*

(1248/4/136–7)

Yesterday I received yours of the fifteenth upon your coming to town from Newmarkett. About Wednesday or Thursday next I beleive we shal set sail; sooner I doe not see how it will be practicable, considering the ill condition the Archbishop is stil in, tho his danger seems to be over for this fit, the gout being gott into his feet with great extremity, whereas it was before in his stomach: for that I take to have been his case, when our Physicians treated him as if his distemper had been the cholick: nor will Captain Stewart[913] (with whom we goe) be ready to sail till then: nor indeed can I settle my own affairs before, and but indifferently then. But I resolve in all events by Gods blessing to be in town on the tenth of November, and hope you will meet my poor wife there; who will in great measure form a judgement how acceptable she is to our family by the reception she finds att her first going to London: but this is a private concern of my own … The matter of my coming over not doing my Commission of Justice a prejudice is done to my satisfaction.

353. *Thomas to Lady Midleton, 15 Nov. 1718*

(1248/4/138–41)

I had last night the inexpressible satisfaction of seeing my brothers letter to Miss, till when I was under more horror then can bee easily concivd. What remains now is that with patience hee waite where hee is, till hee can with the utmost safety begin a journey; this principally

[913] Charles Stewart, MP [I].

occasions my giving your Ladiship this trouble, being well assured of the influence your perswasion must have on soe reasonable a subject. I know his attendance is neither expected or desired till itt may bee given without the least danger; The Duke of Bolton has promised telling him soe, with his desire that hee will nott run a second hazard, which in consequence may prove worse then the first.[914]

Nor doe I thinke his assistance will bee soone wanted, the first (and indeed the greatest) difficulty being gott over by soe vast a majority. You have before now seen the vote for an Addresse, and will easily guesse that the part to which exception was taken, was that which referd to the Alliances made by his Majesty.[915] The debate was in my opinion very loose; several hares on foote att the same time; that according to former usage a day was appointed for taking the speech into consideration before any Addresse voted, though of late years itt had been otherwise, butt that were in such case the Addresses had been meer compliment in generall termes, whereas the motion descended to particulars of the greatest consequence (the approbation of Treatys) before wee were apprizd of the subject matter of them. To this twas answered that they were layd on the table by Mr Secretary[916] pursuant to the kings directions, whoe movd that they might bee read; to which twas objected that being in lattin, and noe translations, reading them would bee of noe use, since probably one half of the house nott understanding lattin would in noe sort bee soe informd as to enable them to make a judgment. This imputation of ignorance to our fellow members was well rallyed, among others Mr H.[917] (whose tallent is better fitted for satyr then argument) (though against the question) sayd hee thought there was little in the objection, for that the noble Lord (Molesworth whoe spoake against the question though hee voted neither way) having wrote a fine Epitaph uppon his dog in that tongue,[918] must certainly bee allowd a great master of itt. That his near neighbour (Bladen) had translated Caesars Commentaryes with such a spiritt as outdid all the author thought of or intended;[919] and must therefore bee allowd an accurate judge of what hee should hear read. Mr W.[920] (with a smile) askt Sir Charles Wager[921] whither hee understood lattin, and receivd for answer that hee did, and could constor tempora mutantur et Nos.[922]

[914]Alan had suffered a chapter of accidents on his journey to London: after a near-miss from 'a ship that fired to salute him', which 'grazed his cheek', he fell from his horse on the road at Nantwich in Cheshire and broke two ribs (NLI, MS 45347/2: James Davoren to Catherine O'Brien, 15 Nov. 1718).

[915]The passage in the address, proposed in these terms on 11 Nov. and agreed the following day, in which the Commons declared, 'we have an entire satisfaction in those measures, which you have already taken, for strengthening the protestant succession to the crown of these realms, in your own family; and for establishing lasting tranquillity in Europe; and particularly in relation to the crown of Spain' (*CJ*, xix, 4, 6). The debate recorded by Thomas occurred in relation to the original motion on the 11th.

[916]James Craggs.

[917]Probably Alan's nephew by marriage, Trevor Hill (see Appendix 2).

[918]In the grounds of his English mansion, at Edlington, Yorks., Molesworth had erected a gravestone to a favourite greyhound, with a Latin inscription (*The Sporting Magazine* (1820), 282).

[919]*C. Julius Cæsar's Commentaries of His Wars in Gaul, and Civil War with Pompey* … , trans. Martin Bladen (1705).

[920]Presumably Robert Walpole.

[921]Sir Charles Wager (c.1666–1743), of Kilmenath, Cornwall, MP Portsmouth; a lord of the admiralty [GB].

[922]'Tempora mutantur nos et mutamur in illis': a saying which may be translated as 'the times change and we change with them'.

This point being given up, they recurd to Mr Freemans[923] first argument, of itts being out of time, wherein the master of the Rolls[924] concur'd, sayd hee beleivd every word and sillable contain in the motion to bee true, and that on a proper occasion hee should give his affirmative, which hee could nott now doe, and voted accordingly.

Mr Smith[925] argued very well the encouragement twould bee to our Enemyes and discouragement to our freinds if what the king had done were nott vigorously maintaind.

The Comptroller that peace or war, in his opinion depended on our resolution, butt concluded differently from those whoe would frighten us with war as the consequence of this question, wheras hee beleivd just the reverse, etc. Mr Letchmere[926] Sir Nath Mead[927] Mr Hambden[928] Collonel Bladen Sir Gilb. Heathcott[929] and many more of inferiour ranke for the question whom twill nott bee necessary to mention after having named our great men.

Mr Snell[930] Mr Horne[931] Mr Hungerford[932] Sir Will[iam] Windham and abundance more against itt. Past eight the question was putt that the words excepted to stand part of the resolution Yeas 215 Noes 155[933] among which latter number there were very honest well meaning men, partly apprehending itt might contribute towards war, and partly thinking itt wrong timed in point of forme.

I thought indeed noe body spoake closer or argued better then Serj. Pingelly,[934] especially to the matter of forme. Hee layd his foundation thus. There is nott a word contain in this motion which is nott expresly asserted in the kings speech, or which does nott naturally and without the least forct construction result from itt, therfore without considering what your Treatyes are, or whither you have them before you or nott is out of the question. Lett any gentleman lay his finger on the particular words hee excepts to, and I undertake to prove what I assert, tis uppon this groundworke that I will farther adde, that I apprehend Gentlemen egregiously mistaken whoe argue that if this vote passe the house has soe far concluded itt selfe, as that twill bee out of their power to censure any thing in these Treatyes stipulated to the prejudice of England, if such should hereafter appeare; Noe Sir I thinke the house att full liberty to censure the thing, and likewise punish the Advisers, and to both these in such case will I readily assent.

Mr Shippen spoake severall times (as many others did especially Mr Secretary[935] and Mr W[alpole] in answer to each other and mostly personally) after his usuall manner, and treated

---

[923]Ralph Freman (1666–1742), of Aspenden, Herts., MP [GB] Herts.

[924]Sir Joseph Jekyll.

[925]John Smith (c.1655–1723), of South Tidworth, Hants, MP [GB] East Looe; teller of the exchequer [GB].

[926]Nicholas Lechmere.

[927]Sir Nathaniel Mead (d.1760), of Goosehays, Essex, MP [GB] Aylesbury; a serjeant-at-law [GB].

[928]Richard Hampden (aft. 1674–1728), of Great Hampden, Bucks., MP [GB] Bucks.; treasurer of the navy [GB].

[929]Sir Gilbert Heathcote (1652–1733), of Low Leyton, Essex, MP [GB] Helston.

[930]John Snell (1682–1726), of Gloucester, MP [GB] Gloucester.

[931]Thomas Horner (1688–1741), of Mells, Som., MP [GB] Wells.

[932]John Hungerford (c.1658–1729), of Lincoln's Inn, MP [GB] Scarborough.

[933]Figures confirmed in *CJ*, xix, 4.

[934]Thomas Pengelly (1675–1730), of Cheshunt, Herts., MP [GB] Cockermouth; knighted in 1719.

[935]James Craggs.

Mr W[*alpole*] with just the same contempt as last sessions, or rather more, for having calld him his worthy freind, hee sayd hee would nott use the terme of new Ally, least hee should sett people laughing, which indeed Mr W[*alpole's*] finishing stroake effectually did. Hee sayd preventing the junction of France and Spaine was alwayes lookt uppon to bee the interest of England in perticular and Europe in generall, That gentlemen ought well to consider whither what wee were doing might nott have a direct tendency thereto, nott indeed by joining France to Spaine, butt Spaine to France by the Regents conquering itt, which might bee a cleane way of setting aside the Renunciation, butt certainly would equally defeate the schemes for preventing itt.

I forgott naming Mr A.[936] among our great men, for really I was soe little affected with what hee sayd, as that I doe nott remember itt, butt nott soe with what Mr Sollicitor[937] sayd, whoe spoake very well, butt in generall termes, as most, if nott all did, on both sides, except Pingelly: With the minority were a sett of people that I could wish judged better.

There was a generall muster of the Toryes, for though some were absent, I dare affirme from my observation of the house, that more then double their number of whigs were soe, this is very visible in the countenances of the former, whoe I thinke appear more dejected then I have ever observd on any occasion whatever, and well they may, for this was their sheet Anchor.

Tis very observable that the apprehension of a war which usually depresses stocks in the citty, has att this time a contrary effect, they rise a little, though indeed they were before higher then their intrinsick vallue, butt what cheifly shewes the opinion of thinking men is, that there are infinitely more buyers then sellers since Tuesday last.

I can make noe other apollogy to your Ladiship for the trouble of soe long and undigested a letter butt that perhaps itt may prove some little amusement in a place where you want itt, and my brother will bee able to explaine what I mention obscurely, and must helpe read those blurs which my ill eyes occasion …

354. *William, Cork, to Alan I, London, 17 Mar. 1718[/19]*

(1248/4/148–9)

I troubled your lordship with a letter on Sunday last, I had not then seen my Nephew[938] or niece,[939] they are both well and in this town. My Lord Chief Baron[940] came in late, nothing done but reading his commission and calling over the county. Mr Maynard received direction this day for providing vessels for the transportation of two Regiments,[941] General

---

[936] Probably Joseph Addison, by now a lord of trade, though another possibility is John Aislabie (1670–1742), of Studley Royal, Yorks, MP [GB] Ripon and chancellor of the exchequer [GB].

[937] Sir William Thompson (c.1676–1739), of the Middle Temple, MP [GB] Ipswich.

[938] St John III.

[939] St John's wife Anne.

[940] Jeffray Gilbert, in Cork to conduct the assizes.

[941] William Maynard, MP [I], revenue collector for the port of Cork.

Sabins[942] from hence and Lord Hinchingbrooks[943] from Kingsale, tis said there are two regiments more to be shipped of for England but whose I cant learn. There are directions likewise come down for the Militia's being put in such a posture as to be in a readyness if occasion Should require, I am told that Nine men of Warr under the command of Sir J: Norris[944] arrivd off Kingsale this morning. The Irish[945] do not show themselves but I am told that Sir Winwood Moyet[946] has taken a house in Wales and is going thither out of hand, upon which some reflections are made …

355. *Thomas to Alan I, 9 Apr. 1719*

(1248/4/234–5)

… The Lords were this day to have read a third time the Peerage Bill, butt have putt of doing soe, to Tuesday next, a pretty plaine indication how (in our great mens opinion) the matter stands; notwithstanding what they give out, of the certainty of successe.[947] My thoughts are, that if in two or three dayes, forcible reasons doe nott take place, wee shall conclude the session without itt. This proceeding gave occasion to Mr Freemans being warme, by way of introduction to a motion for adjourning the call to the same day att the same time declaring against reading the equivalent Bill, however both the one and the other were done, and att Mr Aislebyes motion a second reading ordered tomorrow.[948]

Wee had before this read a third time, and past the South Sea companyes Bill, and ordered itt to the Lords;[949] I see noe other reason to have the least doubt of things standing on the foote you left them, unlesse the C[*ourt*] braging of number of prosilites, att least for obtaining a second reading, butt I thinke the contrary appeard by the temper of the house this day.

A meeting is to bee this evening in the long roome,[950] I cannott butt fancy from the appearance finall resolutions will bee taken, and I very much mistake if the number can

[942]Joseph Sabine (1661–1739), of Kilcullen, Co. Kildare and Tewin, Herts.; major-gen. and col. of prince of Wales's own Royal Welch Fusiliers (Dalton, *Geo. I's Army*, i, 347–8; *Oxf. DNB*).

[943]Edward Richard Montagu (1692–1722), Viscount Hinchingbrooke, 1st son (*d.v.p.*) of the 3rd earl of Sandwich, MP [GB] 1713–*d.*, col., 37th Foot.

[944]Sir John Norris (c.1671–1749), of Benenden, Kent, MP [GB] 1708–*d.*, admiral, c.-in.-c. of the Baltic squadron and lord of the Admiralty.

[945]Irish catholics.

[946]Sir Winwood Mowat (*d.* aft. 1741), 5th Bt, of Inglistoun, and later of Beaumaris, Anglesey; 1st adjutant, Coldstream Guards 1713–15, who had retired from the army on a pension (*Complete Baronetage*, Index and Appendix, 83; Dalton, *Geo. I's Army*, i, 188, 219).

[947]Confirmed in *LJ*, xxi, 123, 'and the lords to be summoned'.

[948]Decisions of the House on 9 Apr. confirmed in *CJ*, xix, 155. The bill concerned related to the terms of the treaty of union with Scotland relating to the public debts and the 'equivalent', the sum paid to the Scots after the Union to offset future liability towards the English national debt.

[949]The bill to raise a fund to redeem the lottery tickets issued for the original subscription to the South Sea Company (*CJ*, xix, 151). The first item of business recorded for 9 Apr.

[950]The 'old committee room' above the lobby (P.D.G. Thomas, *The House of Commons in the Eighteenth Century* (Oxford, 1971), 2–3).

possibly reach two hundred, though I am very well assured there are five hundred and seventeen in towne.

Observe well the seale of this letter …

356. *Alan I, Chester, to Thomas, at the Parliament House, Westminster, 11 Apr. 1719*

(1248/4/236 7)

We are gott hither, but I cannot say well; for my poor wife hath taken very little rest on the road, which you may be sure added to the shaking and fatigue of the Coach hath put her bloud into a ferment; she hath been lett bloud seven ounces since she came hither, and will I hope by lying stil this day and to morrow be able to goe on toward the head on Monday. By a letter dated from Middleton on the 28th of March Senny tells me that the day before the Caldwell Gallye arrived in the harbour of Cork and he hath reason to beleive the master was in Cales when the forces went thence,[951] consisting of no more then about 3000 foot and 500 horse, but they carryed vast quantityes of arms and military stores. They expected to be joined by a squadron from St Sebastians or Bayonne: the master saith he on the seventh of March our style saw two large ships and twenty small ones in the latitude of 40 to the Norward of Cape St Vincent standing due South; and next day eight large ships standing the same course; the former he took to be the Cales fleet, the later that from St Sebastian etc. A ship from the former chaced, the later did not: he judged they stood back for Cales having been rufled by contrary winds. You have all this before now, and will be cautious of doing any thing that may hurt the master of the vessel: I hope and think this armada is destroyed, at least the design disappointed; the man hints that there were several of distinction in one of the vessels from Cales, but the Pretender not of the number.

[PS] Sure some people think they may use others in what maner they please; only slaves who are bought and sold deserve such treatment. Your letter was not opened.

357. *Thomas to Alan I, 14 Apr. 1719*

(1248/4/238–9)

My last, directed to Chester, gave an account of the Lords putting of the Peerage Bill to this day, the consequence wherof, proved, their Lordships thereby having lost, instead of gaining ground; The Commons were extremely irr[*it*]TED threat, insomuch that some whoe had kept themselves in reserve, and seemd a little inclinable to letting the matter fall soft by giving itt a second reading, began from that time to expresse a just indignation against such treatment.

There are now five hundred and nineteen members in towne, of which above Ninety majority against the Bill, from whence twas expected that upon the order of this day

---

[951] A report from Dublin on 1 Apr., printed in the English press, announced that the viceroy had received letters from Cork about the arrival of a ship in Cork on the 28th, whose captain, 'well known to many merchants here and at Cork, and esteemed a very honest and sensible man', gave a detailed account of what he had seen at Calais of French preparations for invasion (*London Gazette*, 4–7 Apr. 1719).

for calling the house, itt would have proved as warme, as full; butt twill I thinke happen otherwise. Last night a very great meeting of gentlemen was in the long roome, (the Ministry present) where after saying that their freinds had nott been acquainted with this designe, purely and onely because itt was thought such as every one would relish, butt that since gentlemen seemd disinclinable to the passing itt, either for want of having duly weighed the consequences, or some other reasons which might bee grounded on different viewes, twas therfore thought proper to lett itt drop att this time, by which meanes itt might bee better weighd before next session, when a Bill of like nature, with this, or perhaps turned into some other shape, would bee offered, and they could nott doubt bee approved; thus ends the matter.

If any thing remarkable should happen in the house I will adde itt att the end … The Lords have adjournd the Bill to this day fortnight, with a declaration of renewing the attempt next session;[952] The call of our house is adjourned to fryday, on Mr Freemans motion,[953] whoe tooke notice that the great appearance having had the good effect of saving to the Commons a materiall part of the constitution, and to the Crowne a necessary branch of the Prerogative, hee hoped Gent would thinke a full house att the opening a succeeding session might save to the Nation a great deale of mony which in a thin house they might be with greater ease loaded with.

Wee then adjourned to fryday, att which time an end will bee putt to the session.

358. *Thomas to Alan I, Dublin, 18 Apr. 1719*

(1248/4/240–1)

The Parliament was this day prorogued to the 19th of next month, the Lords nott having gone through the bills soe early, as to admitt of the kings coming yesterday. I make noe doubt of the speech being sent this night to Lord Lieutenant though I shall nott bee able to send itt to you, being very long twill scarcely be printed by Midnight, if itt come out before I goe to bed, Ile send itt.

Nothing was done in our house either yesterday or this day worth notice …

359. *Alan I, Dublin, to Thomas, 25 Apr. 1719*

(1248/4/242–3)

After considering all I have seen as well before as since the date of my last letter to you I confesse I am apprehensive and almost convinced that there was a design formed of a general rising (and consequently of a massacre) by the Irish: and tho I will not say it amounts to full evidence or to a certain account of such a design, yet I think it such as very well justifyes the Governement and Councels intimating that such an affair was concerted, and their putting the Protestants on exerting themselves and doing every thing in their power for their own

---

[952] On Tuesday, 14 Apr. 1718 (*LJ*, xxi, 130). The adjournment was until the 28th, and the parliament was prorogued on the 18th.

[953] Also on 14 Apr. (*CJ*, xix, 159).

preservation: but possibly the putting this hellish project in execution was to have depended either on the landing some foreign force here, or on some considerable disturbance raised in Britain whereby more of our forces might have been drawn away.[954] It is certain the Irish are very insolent in the remote parts of the Kingdome, and they as little beleive that the designed invasion is in a great measure defeated, as they formerly pretended to beleive any such thing was intended: and indeed the Protestants seem to be a little too secure and not to apprehend as much danger as there certainly was and I doubt stil is from their enemyes. One is in a good deal of difficulty in what maner to write to ones freinds in the countrey on this subject; to represent the matter extreamly formidable will strike a greater damp on trade then there is already, and ruine our markets to that degree that there will not be a penny of mony stirring; and to this may be added that letters of that nature will intimidate our freinds and if known to be written will encourage our enemyes. On the other hand it must be done in such a maner as to awaken them, least they should be undone by being over secure; and I hope the late proclamation hath convinced them of their danger; which I doubt was thought either to be over by dispersion of the fleet, or that nothing was to be attempted here but in great Britain. The accounts agree from several places of general Masses, and prayers for the Catholick Church, and others for the prosperity and successe of a certain design; these are the usual forerunners of rebellion. A letter was intercepted by Arthur Hyde from Mr Cotter (the eldest son of Sir James)[955] to his younger brother Laurance in which he represents the militia of our County not to be so formidable as the Irish apprehend it, being ill armed etc.[956] To what intent, but to encourage them to rebel and not be frighted from prosecuting their design by our militia's meeting, patrouling etc. You know Cotter is indicted for a rape and hath been for more then six months on his guard and as we call it here on his keeping.[957] My Lord Lieutenant is really not only very vigilant but acts with great prudence as well as vigor to prevent and disappoint all the designs of his Majestyes enemyes. You must have full accounts from Scotland of the forces which are landed there; Two ships appeared off Black Sod (in the County of Mayo) on 21 March and stood in toward the Land by day and went to Sea by night till toward the end of the month. On the first of April and for some dayes after sometimes fowre sometimes more ships appeared off the same place; the winds were such that they might have come in or gone off but did neither for about ten dayes: On Wednesday the Lord Justice Clerk

[954] The militia had been arrayed, and in Co. Cork at least nightly patrols were maintained to watch for signs of an invasion (BL, Add. MS 46940, f. 44: Berkeley Taylor to Lord Perceval, 28 Apr. 1719). On 2 May a church of Ireland clergyman, John Leathes, wrote from the north of Ireland that 'for some time past we have been under apprehension of a general insurrection of the jacobites in this kingdom, but since the Spaniards are disappointed in their projects by the dispersion of their fleet, we hope the storm is over' (Suffolk RO, Ipswich, De Mussenden Leathes MSS, HA/403/1/6: to William Leathes).

[955] James Cotter (1689–1720), of Ballinsperry, Co. Cork, son of Sir James Cotter (c.1630–1705), the jacobite governor of Cork city in 1690 and commander of King James's forces in the south-west of Ireland in 1691 (who was included within the articles of Limerick). There are entries for father and son in *Oxf. DNB* and *DIB*.

[956] According to Lord Perceval's agent the intercepted letter declared that the militia would be 'but a breakfast to 'em' (BL, Add. MS 46940, f. 53: Berkeley Taylor to Lord Perceval, 14 May 1719).

[957] James Cotter, who had failed to appear at the summer assizes in Cork in 1718 to answer the charge of having raped a quaker girl, Elizabeth Squibb, subsequently surrendered himself to the Cork sheriff and ever since had been awaiting his trial, which did not take place until the spring of 1720 (Neal Garnham, 'The Trials of James Cotter and Henry, Baron Barry of Santry: Two Case Studies in the Administration of Criminal Justice in Early Eighteenth-century Ireland', *IHS*, xxxi (1998–9), 329–30).

of Scotland[958] gave account in a letter dated at Edinburgh 18 April that they had certain account from the Shire of Rosse that 800 foreigners with some officers and Gentlemen were landed att Garlough[959] in that shire, but mentions not the day when nor the number of ships: the post master at Portpatrick writes to Mr Manley that the talk there is that 1400 and others sayd 2000 were landed at Garlough and Sky: we had informacion from one MacAulay who left the Isle of Lewes on the 14th and came hither the 23d that two ships with 300 foreigners came to Lewes on 30 March staid there till 4 April then sailed South East (toward Garlough and Sky as I find by the map) returned the seventh and sailed again the same way on the eleventh. These I make no doubt are part if not the whole of the 800 men mentioned by the Justice Clerk and of the greater number mentioned by the Postmaster: but I am almost singular in my opinion that they are not the whole: for I cannot but suspect that some other of the ships seen off black Sod in the beginning of April came the same way, and I the rather think this because the Justice Clerk saith they have a <u>certain</u> account from a <u>good</u> hand that 800 men are landed. No diligence is or will be wanting here, and in truth our fault seems rather to be an overconfidence then any fear of our enemyes. God blesse King George and confound all his enemyes … Pray have you had any visit or message from the Great Man?

360. *Thomas to Alan I, Dublin, 14 May 1719*

(1248/4/152–3)

… Wee waite impatiently for an account of the kings landing, and hope hee did soe Tuesday evening, since which time the weather has been exceeedingly tempestuous. There is noe news of any kind, the more though[t]full people among the rich citizens are very jealous of a farther rupture, rather then an approching peace in the North,[960] you will readily guesse what handle one sort of men make of this, I hope what they say will prove groundless …

361. *Alan I, Dublin, to Thomas, 16 Aug. 1719*

(1248/4/156–9)

I suppose by the time this can reach London you will be come back from the North; and hope your riding and exercise hath contributed to your health, as well as seeing so much of the countrey must have done to your diversion. I wish it had been in my power to have done something of the same kind; for I severely feel in the pains I undergoe and in the want of health how ruinous the course of life is in which I have been for some time past; perpetually either at the Court, Castle, Councel, or Parliament house: and in every one of those places I have such a share of the toyl as is sufficient to wear out and destroy a more firm constitution then mine. Your being out of town hindred me from giving you accounts

---

[958] Adam Cockburn (c.1656–1735), of Ormiston, Haddingtons., Lord Ormiston.

[959] Gairloch, Ross-shire.

[960] The several treaties of Stockholm (1719–20), which ended the Great Northern War.

of every thing at the times they hapned; but I will now send you a short view of our Session.

You know how strongly our great men were possessed with an opinion in the Spring that it was very practicable to obtain an entire repeal of the sacramental test here; of this some made little doubt, while others thought that at least the dissenters might be qualifyed for Offices in general, excepting some great ones as being of the Councel, Judges, Commissioners of the revenue, Governors of town and garisons etc. You know also that my Lord Lieutenant thought the sentiments of the Parliament here were not truly represented by those who gave our ministers such accounts of things: I expressed my self to the same purpose, and said I beleived Gentlemen would be content to admit them into the militia, and to carry Commissions in the Army of the lower kind, and perhaps some other little things: but added that they did not know the temper of either house of Parliament who beleived them fond of the dissenters or inclined to do more for them. Upon this a great man said the thing could not fail, if heartily espoused in Britain and supported and countenanced by those in his Majestyes service in Ireland: those words were easy enough to be understood.[961] Mr Upton[962] no doubt represented the interest of the dissenters to be much more considerable in the Parliament and every where else, then it really is:[963] and I am apt to think so did another Gentleman, whose great interest in England is founded on his being at the Head of that party here, which endeavours to gett it beleived that they are the only considerable body of Protestants in this Kingdome.[964] But his cunning I beleive would not permit him to go Mr Uptons lengths, or to give such strong hopes of successe as the other probably did.[965] You know I staid some time in London after my Lord Lieutenant, and found at my landing the greatest aversion possible in the members of Parliament generally against admitting the dissenters into offices; and indeed partyes actually formed in several Countyes to oppose it, and many in this resolution who had formerly shewn a great tendernesse toward them: This proceeded in great measure from the indiscretion of the dissenters and their freinds, who at the beginning would hear of nothing lesse then an entire repeal of the test, at least they talked of it in that manner: There also came letters from Lambeth[966] and other places near London to impresse the necessity of opposing this attempt on the Church (as it was called) and to assure people that doing any thing would be only an inlet to doing every thing; but that which I really think had as great an influence on the house of Commons as any other thing was, an opinion that had obtained with a good many that a certain person[967] had undertaken for the successe of the bill in that house,

---

[961] Lord Sunderland, in a conference in Feb. 1719 at Sunderland's house attended by Alan, the duke of Bolton, and James, Earl Stanhope (TNA, SP 63/377/235–5: Bolton to [James Craggs], 27 June 1719).

[962] Clotworthy Upton, MP [I].

[963] For evidence of Upton's solicitations, see BL, Add. MS 61640, f. 193: Upton to [Sunderland], 15 June 1719.

[964] William Conolly.

[965] Upton reported that Conolly had spoken 'openly' in parliament for the dissenters, but that his influence over the Commons had been lessened by reports from England that he had 'undertaken' to secure a repeal (N. Yorks. RO, ZBO VIII, D/73: Upton to James Craggs, 30 July 1719). Conolly's wife certainly ascribed the difficulties her husband had met with in the house of commons in 1719 to the fact of 'his being for taking off the test' (NLI, MS 41580/4; Jane Bulkeley to Jane Bonnell, 15 July 1719).

[966] That is to say from the archbishop of Canterbury, William Wake.

[967] William Conolly.

which for the reason before mentioned I verily beleive he did not;[968] and am certain he was sensible in a week after the Session began, if not earlier, the thing was impracticable: Others who perhaps did not beleive he had undertaken it, yet very well knew he would greatly magnifye himself at London in case of successe, which his freinds would wholly impute to his interest with the Commons. And they resolved to convince the world and him that he had very little, and failed not to give him frequent mortifications; by carrying some things meerly in opposition to him, which perhaps they could have without difficulty gone into. When I observed this spirit in Gentlemen, and saw it had its foundation from the resentment taken up by members at that Gentleman and his freinds attributing to themselves what was due to the good inclinations of the house in general I endeavoured to shew them that it was not our businesse to have partyes, and that the forming and increasing them in smaller matters might in consequence influence the greater, people who once have gott into the way of doing it being apt to oppose those in every thing from whom they differ in some things. Their answer was they would as a man assist the Crown and Governement and join with the others in granting the Supply, or doe it without them if they shewed any backwardnesse. And in this maner they did, tho their meetings were represented as designed to obstruct the publick affairs, by the Sp[eaker] and his freinds, which indeed were only to keep a body together who would not be rid, and would shew where the interest of the Commons lay: but care was taken to represent these things in the most formidable shapes, which had such effect that I have observed great concern for the successe of things, notwithstanding the assurances I gave from the beginning and all along (which the event hath verifyed) that the addicional dutyes would be given for two years, and no ill natured thing be done in reference to the establishment. The view they seem to have had who scattred these terrors was to possesse some people that they were the people sollicitous for the successe of Session and service of the Governement. I said, if those Gentlemen had the interest they pretended to have, nothing could be carryed against them, and added that they had not, but that the weight was more then double in the other scale; and that therefore I was sure the supply would answer the expectations of the Governement and that I would pawn my life and reputation on the event. This my Lord Lieutenant will not refuse to do me the justice to own I alway said to him, when some about him (at least) seemed to be under great apprehensions how matters would end. I wish the Commons would have gone farther in easing the dissenters then barely granting them a toleration;[969] but so have they and their freinds managed as to make it impracticable; Lord Molesworth at first coming over talking of nothing lesse then an entire repeal of the test, all or none etc but he soon quitted the thoughts of the dissenters and employed his fire in the house of Lords, to blow the difference between the Lords of England and us into such a flame as I fear will not be soon quenched:[970] to him as much as any one Lord (unlesse his Grace of Dublin and Lord

[968] Certainly, by the time parliament met, Conolly was pessimistic about any chance of securing repeal of the test. See TNA, SP 63/377/230: Conolly to [Charles Delafaye], 2 July 1719.

[969] By the bill 'for exempting dissenters of this kingdom from certain penalties to which they are now subject', the heads of which had passed the Irish house of commons on 16 July. The engrossed bill was returned from England, presented to the Irish parliament on 3 Oct., and eventually passed into law as 6 Geo. I, c. 5 (ILD). For the background to the passing of the act, to which the dissenters themselves were 'indifferent', see J.C. Beckett, *Protestant Dissent in Ireland 1687–1780* (1948), ch. 7; Burns, *Politics*, i, 84–90.

[970] On 10 July the Irish house of lords began an inquiry into the case of *Annesley* v. *Sherlock* and the overturning of their own judgment by the British house of lords. After the report the House agreed to draw up a representation

Anglesey may be excepted) we owe it that most of the warmest steps have been taken in that matter. I come now to what particularly relates to my self. The insupportable fatigue of this Session hath almost killed me: but I think the pain [*in*] my breast, of which I lately complained is not any remain of my fall; and I have reason to beleive I have no inward bruise; but I had a rash for three weeks or a month, which I kept constantly out by taking powders etc. At length it struck in at once, and I was seised with a most violent pain in the small of my back and reins, soe that I could not rise from my seat without help; and the house adjourned on my account for fowre dayes.[971] I let blood, took Physick, and am now drinking the Spaw waters; by which my pain is a good deal abated; but far from being entirely removed. I want exercise, and am confined to attend Committees of Councel to draw and form our bills: all the Judges are out of town, and the whole trouble lyes on my shoulders. What thanks I shal have for sacrificing my self in this maner I do not know; perhaps the same I mett with lately. Probably my Lord Lieutenant may propose me and the Sp[*eake*]r to be left in Commission when he goes over; for I take it for granted there will be no thoughts of his Grace after the part he hath taken lately.[972] Deal with me freely and give me your thoughts after considering the thing. Is it not reasonable to decline serving with such a Colleague? There never was a good reason for putting him into a certain station; but to perpetuate him is unaccountable. I never will serve another Session, for it must end in my death: and there is no great difference in laying down a year or two sooner. Beside I foresee a vast difficultye which necessarily will attend my accepting etc for probably the Lords of England may presse and prevail on the King to direct the Cheif Governor here to send the Sherif of Kildare into England in custody;[973] and the obeying or not executing such an order will be sure to put one under great difficultyes at one time or other. On the other hand I have no mind to spend this winter at Westminster; I had little joy in being there last winter and little thanks for undergoing the drudgery. You may depend of it that the matter of restraining the number of Peers will be sett on foot again the next the Session ...[974]

---

[970] (*continued*) to the king. For these proceedings, and Molesworth's role, see Burns, *Politics*, i, 94–7; F.G. James, *Ireland in the Empire 1688–1770: A History of Ireland from the Williamite Wars to the Eve of the American Revolution* (Cambridge, MA, 1973), 104; Victory, 'Declaratory Act', 17–20.

[971] *LJI*, ii, 635, records an adjournment from 6 to 10 Aug., with no reason stated.

[972] In relation to the active role he had played in pushing the inquiry into the proceedings over *Annesley* v. *Sherlock*, and especially his desire to call to account the exchequer barons who had implemented the decree of the British house of lords (Philip O'Regan, *Archbishop William King of Dublin (1650–1729) and the Constitution in Church and State* (Dublin, 2000), 261–72).

[973] Alexander Burrows or Burrowes (*d.* c.1741), of Ardenwood, Co. Kildare (Vicars, *Index*, 65), who as sheriff was charged with restoring Annesley to possession according to the judgment at Westminster, and had been ordered to do so by the Irish exchequer barons. Placed in an impossible position, he had gone into hiding and had then been fined nearly £2,000 for failure to attend to the affairs of his office and not delivering up his accounts. He had petitioned the Irish house of lords for protection (Burns, *Politics*, i, 79).

[974] A reference to the unsuccessful Peerage Bill brought into the Westminster parliament in 1719, which prevented future additions to the English peerage, above the number of six, other than to replace extinct titles, and replaced the 16 Scottish representative peers by 25 hereditary peers.

362. *Thomas, Peper Harow, to Alan I, 30 Aug. 1719*

(1248/4/160–1)

Last Wensday came yours of the 16th which I did nott answer by that post, being of such a nature as required a great deale of thought; what you mention being attended with circumstances, each of which ought to bee duly weighd, as to the first thing (which is noe more then a supposition) that possibly itt may bee intended to leave you and Mr Conely in the Government I thinke admits of little dispute, for though twould have been unreasonable in you to have declined acting with him when the A[rch]B[ishop] did soe the case differs widely when hee onely is joined to you; and I am sure under this circumstance I would nott doe itt.

Beside that hereby your coming into England will become impracticable, unlesse there shall bee a clause in the Commission empowering one to act, which I suppose will nott bee thought of; That your being here this winter will nott bee matter of pleasure, or indeed in any sort satisfactory, I readily agree; notwithstanding which I thinke twill bee both advisable and necessary.

That the Lords of England, will att the very beginning of the session (probably before they enter on other businesse) fall into the consideration of what your Lords have done, I make noe doubt, what may bee the result noe man can foresee, butt supposing them much softer then I expect, itt cannott bee doubted butt that they will take such methods as will putt the Government of Ireland under very great difficultyes, one way or other, which surely you ought (if possible) to avoid; for my own part were I oblidged to say my thoughts, I cannott bee of opinion that the Lords of England have nott a right of receiving Appeals against decrees of the Lords of Ireland, uppon supposition that they have such a right in the case of decrees made by the Courts of equity here, which however you know the Commons have never expresly allowd here, though they acquiesce under itt, and tract of time has, or will give such a right, butt this is out of the case soe that I thinke the onely question will bee, which house will bee best able to enforce their judgment which cannott admit of dispute; I could give you another reason for your coming over, which I omitt, and an undesirable one itt is; you will certainely understand my meaning.

Now if a third person bee putt in Commission twill answer all, butt if that bee refused, I thinke the meaning is plaine, in which case I should advise your dealing as plainly with Lord Lieutenant and that without losse of time, least an opertunity for knowing his Majestys pleasure may bee used to you as an argument; if you agree with mee as to the first part, this last you will certainely thinke right, and consequently will immediately bring the matter to a decission, for though the session here may probably bee later then is generally expected, the time of his Majestys returne being uncertaine, I thinke itt more then probable, that Lord Lieutenant will come away assoone as hee can.

You seeme determinately fixt nott to undergoe the fatigue of another session in the post you are; this deserves consideration, butt if you adhere thereto, the difference of quitting a yeare sooner or later, signifyes little, nay I am of opinion you will have an opertunity for doing itt now with more honour then possibly hereafter, for in addition to that of the Commission (supposing what I have spoake to already insisted uppon) people here, will remember, how you acted last session, by which you left a very valluable charecter behind you; I thinke the Peerage Bill may probably bee resumed, butt I am nott soe confident thereof as you seeme; The attempt has putt the people in every part of the kingdom into such a ferment as may (att least in my opinion should) make our great men consider very well before they adde fuell to a fire already kindled; butt were the thing as certaine as any other whatever, I should rather choose (were I in your station) to confirme the opinion which gentlemen entertaine of you, by acting [?above] board according to my judgment, then leave the matter in suspence by my absence. If a Bill bee pusht I fancy twill bee very different from that of last yeare, butt att the same time I beleive encreasing the number of Scots Peers etc. will bee retaind, which surely if nott the worst, is as bad a part, as any other, and cannott butt appeare soe to those whoe are unwilling to make those of that Nation the perpetuall ballance of power in the house of Lords.

I doe not att all wonder att what has happened in relation to the Dissenters, when I consider with how much warmth and zeale (without knowledge) they push that affair, aiming att what every rationall man must conclude they could nott att this time, attaine, surely reasonable men would have contented themselves with what was att present feazable, expecting another opertunity for gaining more, butt the summer proving soe very hott, has had such effect on them and their Patrons, as I feare will prove a lasting prejudice to them. I make noe doubt butt this and every other disappointment even in the minutest things, will by some people bee imputed to your coolenesse, if itt obtaine soe favourable a name; and that whatever has been attended with success shall bee attributed to the care and interest of those whoe have had the least share therein, for you know by experience that worthlesse sycophants (generally speaking) carry the Bell,[975] butt surely never more then now.

I am unwilling to attribute what I see every day done, to a worse cause (though God knowes this is bad enough) butt mallicious people ascribe many things to another reason, and the misery is, they argue soe plausibly as to obtaine beleife.

I am nott without my fears that you mistake the cause of your illnesse; The striking in of a Rash on the suddaine may bee of ill consequence by mixing that with the Masse of blood, which nature endeavourd to throw of; butt the paine fixing in the manner you describe, in your back and Reines, brings fresh to my memory that the first complaint I had of what afterwards provd the stone seizd mee exactly soe, uppon which (without haesitation) the last Lord Godolphin[976] told mee what I was to expect, and itt provd as hee sayd.

One great (and indeed the cheife) inducement to my late journy, was a notion inculcated by many of my freinds, that gentle and constant motion would probably occasion the coming away of that gravel, which by lodging some time was formd into stones, butt I found itt quite otherwise. From the second day I left the towne, till now, I have never been an hour att any one time free from paine, my water att all times free from the least appearance of gravell, on the contrary very pale, and clear as rock water.

Whilst I was in the North I lay two days in exquisite torment, after which three stones came from mee, one a good deale bigger then any former, butt happily, very smooth. Since my coming hither I am much easyer then whilst on my journy, though I travaild butt from 10 to 15 miles a day, the paine gradually butt very sensibly decreasing, which I attribute to the quiett and rest which I now take.

---

[975] To bear the bell, or carry off the bell, is to take the first place, or take the prize (*OED*).
[976] Sidney Godolphin (1645–1712), 1st earl of Godolphin.

363. Thomas, Peper Harow, to Alan I, 29 Sept. 1719

(1248/4/162–3)

I have nott heard from you of a long time, your last I answered from Pepper Hara, and long to heare what is resolved on the subject of your letter, I see noe reason to alter my opinion on that head, butt am every day more and more confirmed in itt.

I am fully satisfyed from those whoe are in the secret, that the Peerage bill will bee brought in againe, butt after what manner seems as yett uncertaine, this gives great uneasinesse to some considerable men in businesse, whoe thinke carrying it impracticable, and feare the consequence of a failure, butt our furious drivers (whom you may easily guesse) are determined … I … am this morning going toward Newmarkett with Lord G[odolphin] …

364. Thomas, Newmarket, to Alan I, 24 Oct. 1719[977]

(1248/4/168A–B)

I returned hither last night, after spending twelve dayes with Lord Godolphin att Lord Bridgwaters in Hertfordsheer.[978] Here I found yours of the 21st of September and the sixth instant, the former lay long on your side, five or six packets coming togather; before my going hence a certaine Great man read to me a paragraph of a letter to the effect following, I thinke I can remember the words. Viz. The Brodrick faction have been very troublesom, butt Mr C[onolly] provd honest, and is now the great favourite. I am pretty sure this letter was writt from London, and I thinke by one who brought over some of the bills, I am told hee has bought an office with you, if soe you will know whoe I mean.

Yesterday came your latter letter, and att the same time one from Dr H. to the same person, which hee shewes to our great men here, tis dated the eighth, and gives just the same account you doe of what had passed in the Lords house before the sixth, going forward to the conclusion of that matter; hee exceedingly applauds your conduct etc. … I could nott omitt writing by this post, though you know the hurry wee are allwayes in here, especially when wee have somuch good company as att present.

What your first letter concludes with, is surely monstrous, and in my opinion very im-pollitique, notwithstanding which I am inclind to beleive itt may bee intended, and if soe will probably bee done …

365. Alan I, Dublin, to Thomas, Westminster, 5 Nov. 17[19], 'eight at night'

(1248/4/169A–B)

… My obligacions to my Lord Duke of Somersetts generosity and goodnesse are beyond my power of expressing my sense of them and the maner so truly noble and obliging that

---

[977] Letter endorsed by Alan I: 'one of Lord Lieutenants people wrote a letter into England to my disadvantage and in favor of Conelye: I think he means Hoey to Lord Wharton'. See below, p. 246.

[978] Bridgwater's principal seat was at Ashridge, Herts.

I shal want words to cloth my thoughts in when I write to him which shal be the very next mail. In the mean time add this favour to all those you have formerly done me, to go to Yorke house on purpose with my complements and duty to his Grace, and in that plain and honest maner which best expresses the sense of a plain and honest heart give his Grace my humblest services and hearty thanks and assure him that living and dying I must alway continue his most faithful and obliged dutiful servant …

[*PS*] I have recovered the use and motion of my Toes and ankle and have no sort of numbnesse and take all possible [*care*] of my self. I walk up and down stairs without help or the use of a Cane, but am forced to limp a little, through the weaknesse in my sinews. I will follow your advice in respect to my own conduct and thank you for it. Your letter will be of singular service, for your character and credit makes everything you write carry the weight which ought alway to attend the opinion of a prudent and honest man.

366. *Alan I, Dublin, to Thomas, 21 Nov. 1719*

(1248/4/170–1)

I chuse to send my letter to the Duke of Bolton under cover to you, that you peruse it: and by it know upon what foot it is my fortune to stand with his Grace. The pretence is my having voted against and indeed being the means of throwing out the bill for amending the Acts to prevent the growth of Popery;[979] when I shal have transcribed the paper I have drawn on that subject you will see what grounds I had for doing what I did, and how little reason the Duke hath to concern himself in or to be greived at the fate of that bill, supposing it had been a good bill; but alas! when you consider that he went from London without me, nay made the time of his going such a secret that his footmen told mine of it before he imparted it to me, and how he had struck in with Mr C[*onolly*] and his party by means of Webster and Manly before I landed, you will with me know that the part I tooke in a certain bill that was on the carpet last winter at Westminster sticks in his stomach:[980] he hath all the Session shewn great regards to one sort of men, and been weak enough to be perswaded that the Kings, nay his best freinds, laid all the difficultyes they could in his way: the opposition which the majority of the house avowedly shewed to the repealing the test gave C[*onolly*] and his squadron occasion to represent themselves the people who were ready to go into all measures; and the meetings which Gentlemen had about the dissenters

---

[979] The bill 'for securing the protestant interest of this kingdom by further amending the several acts of parliament made against papists and to prevent the further growth of popery', which fell in the Irish house of lords in Oct. 1719 (ILD). Originally the heads of the bill had included the notorious clause providing for the castration of unregistered catholic priests. This had been removed by the British privy council. (Ian McBride, *Eighteenth-century Ireland: The Isle of Slaves* (Dublin, 2009), 201; James Kelly, 'Sustaining a Confessional State: The Irish Parliament and Catholicism', in *The Eighteenth-century Composite State: Representative Institutions in Ireland and Europe, 1689–1800*, ed. D.W. Hayton et al. (Basingstoke, 2010), 57.) Alan's vehement opposition to the returned bill, though he had been reputed one of the promoters of the original heads, is noted in Wake, Epist. xiii: Bishop Godwin to Archbishop Wake, 7 Nov. 1719; Bishop Nicolson to Wake, 30 Nov. 1719. Evans of Meath informed Wake on 26 Nov. 1719 that Bolton had left Ireland 'full of indignation against his friend (the chancellor's) conduct in the popery bill' (Wake, Epist. xiii).
[980] The Peerage Bill.

bill[981] were represented as Cabals where methods were concerted to obstruct his Majestyes affairs: and every step which was taken to shew that it was not the juncto but the Country Gentlemen that could and would carry on the Kings service and therefore opposed the doing of some things and did others contrary to the wishes of those who would have been thought leaders was represented as the result of a concerted design to give opposition to every thing: They who made these remarks and insinuations very well knew nothing was intended but the Kings service, and I from time to time gave assurances and pawned my reputation for the happy issue of the Session just in the maner it ended; but a certain person was frightned, and they who whispered him what terrible designs were on foot had the good fortune to be beleived; and then it is natural for the same person to conclude that the disappointment of those designs was owing to the same persons fidelity and diligence, who had the sagacity to discover them. I desire you to wait on the Duke with the inclosed letter and to tell him that the paper is transcribing which I mention in it; and you may at the same time take notice to him of the letter which you tell me a certain great man shewed at Newmarkett: Was not that great man the Duke of Wharton, and is not Mr. Hoey[982] the person who wrote it? For I cannot find out the person you mean by the description you give me of him, viz. that he is one of those who came over with our bills, and hath lately purchased a place here: The three persons who carryed our bills were Hoey, Bruce, and Carmichael; none of which hath purchased any place that I can hear of. Pray give me some light into the schemes of this winter particularly at what time and in what shape the Peerage bill is expected: My Lord Molesworth is to be as zealous an advocate for that bill in the British house of Commons as he was against the jurisdiction of the British Peers here.[983] Let me also have the earliest notice of what is intended or shal be done by the Lords in relation to our representation, from which I apprehend terrible consequences to Ireland, and possibly great difficultyes to those who are in the actual exercise of the Governement here, if any orders shal come from the British Peers for sending the Sherif of the County of Kildare into England in custody: Such an order did come over in the Marquisse of Winchester and Lord Galways time to send over the Bishop of Derry in custody: but was never executed:[984] and indeed I beleive it will create the best Lawyers here a good deal of difficultye to advise by what person or officer and in what maner such an order is to be executed: sure a military force is not meant, and it will be difficult to find out what civil Officer the Law hath appointed on this occasion; let me hear what people say on this occasion, but mention it not as from me … Loose no time in sending the Dukes letter.

[981] The bill 'for exempting dissenters of this kingdom from certain penalties to which they are now subject', commonly referred to as the Toleration Bill.

[982] 'Hoy', employed as a courier with the Irish bills, was noted as one of Bolton's gentleman ushers (TNA, SP 63/377/17: Edward Webster to [Charles Delafaye], 16 Aug. 1719).

[983] Bishop Nicolson described Molesworth as 'a brisk asserter of the independent rights of this kingdom' (BL, Add. MS 6116, ff. 89–90: Nicolson to Archbishop Wake, 2 Oct. 1719).

[984] In a dispute between the Irish and English parliaments arising from the legal case of *The Honourable the Irish Society* v. *the bishop of Derry*, which William King, then bishop of Derry, had appealed to the Irish house of lords, securing a judgment in his favour, and the Irish Society had in turn appealed to the English house of lords, which overturned the Irish judgment. On 29 Mar. 1699 the English house of lords had ordered that King and some of the officials who had attempted to enforce the judgment of the Irish house of lords be arrested and brought to Westminster to appear before the Bar of the House. After a series of attempts at mediation to prevent the order being enforced, the matter dropped (O'Regan, *Archbishop William King*, 118–21).

367. *Thomas to Alan I, 1 Dec. 1719*

(1248/4/172–3)

Late last night I receivd yours of the 21st of last month, with the inclosed to the D[*uke*] of B[*olton*] when Lord G[*alway*] and other company were with mee, I seald that to his Grace and sent itt immediately, with an excuse for nott carrying itt, butt hee was nott att home. Hee spent an hour with mee on Sunday morning, and then told mee you had never given him to understand your having the least dislike to the Popery bill, that the judges both here and with you were of opinion twas in effect the same with the former, onely explaind some doubts, that your giving itt up in the house gave occasion to people to thinke that what you did was with his approbation;[985] I told his Grace I was entirely a stranger to that whole affair, butt did beleive assoone as you had leisure I should heare from you, and would fairly tell him what you sayd on the subject.

The Person to whom the letter was writt which I mentioned from Newmarkett I tooke for graunted you would understand to bee the D[*uke*] of W[*harton*]. Itt happened thus, Drinking Tea in a morning with Lord H.[986] his Grace told mee hee would read a paragraph of a letter, which was to the effect I mentioned; Lord H sayd this is from Mr H[*oey*] the other answered I doe nott tell you soe, to which Lord H. replyed, Butt I know the hand; I was lead into the mistake of his having lately bought a place by Lord H telling mee hee heard hee had done soe. You may bee sure Ile mention this matter the first opertunity I have, and will speake my thoughts freely.

The Peerage Bill was brought by the Duke of Som[*erset*] into the house of Lords on Wensday, read a second time Thursday comitted for fryday and reported and ordered to bee ingrosed on Saturday, wee rose early yesterday, butt twill bee sent us to day. Tis in substance the very same as last year onely with the addition of two clauses one taking away Scan[*dalum*] M[*agnatum*][987] the other taking away the power of pardoning uppon Impeachments. Some people say they are sure of carrying itt, you may remember they did soe last yeare, Tis true the house is nott full, butt the members are coming up. I write this in the morning and will add what passes this day, butt you may bee pretty sure that letters are lookt into, lett that bee, what I write I care nott whoe knowes.

My spirits are soe sunke with a long dayes debate that I am able to doe noe more then tell you the successe of itt, The Bill being read the question for a second reading went without debate; Sir Willifred Lawson[988] then with a noble spiritt spoake as it its consequences, which must bee exceedingly bad or very good, butt that in a matter where our constitution was to bee entirely altered, unlesse the latter manifestly appeard, gentlemen could never goe into itt, that this required time to consider, besides that in a matter of such moment the house twere to bee wisht might bee full; and therfore the call being ordered for Munday next concluded for a second reading this day sennight, which I seconded.

---

[985] Alan's opposition to the returned Popery Bill surprised Bishop Nicolson (BL, Add. MS 6116, f. 92: Nicolson to Wake, 30 Nov. 1719).

[986] Possibly Algernon Seymour (1684–1750), MP [GB] 1705–22, eldest surviving son of the duke of Somerset and known by his courtesy title of earl of Hertford.

[987] The offence of defamation against a peer, punishable under the terms of the Statute of Westminster of 1275.

[988] Sir Gilfrid Lawson (1675–1749), 6th Bt, of Brayton, Cumberland, MP [GB] Cumberland.

The Secretary[989] movd tomorrow, butt they soone found that exploded, when Mr Letchmere skilfully proposd Fryday or Saturday, att lenghth the question for Tuesday was putt Yeas 203 Noes 158.[990]

The two additionall clauses which I mentioned on the other side are nott in the Bill, butt left to bee askt by the house of Commons as great favours.

368. *Alan I, Dublin, to Thomas, at his lodgings in the Privy Garden, Whitehall, 1 Dec. 1719*

(1248/4/178–9)

I am concerned not to have received a line from you by either pacquet which brought in the letters of the 24th and 26th instant: I see by his Majestyes speech but by the vigorous steps already taken in the house of Lords that it is resolved not only to try but to carry the Peerage bill without losse of time: perhaps you may be now in Surrey about the election for that County,[991] but I desire you will as often as you conveniently can send me notices of what is intended, as well as what is actually doing; together with the reasons of things, and who and who draw together. Our accounts from London among other changes have named the Duke of Argyle to succeed the Duke of Bolton; if that should happen, some who professed great respects for his Grace and had the good fortune to be beleived to be real freinds will not be at all uneasy at a more Northern Lieutenant then out of Hampshire[992] ...You already know my poor sister Newcomen is dead; her death as near as I can compute was much about the same time with My Cousen Ettricks. My services to my Lord Godolphin, to my Lord Aylmer[993] and Mr Gibbon[994] ...

[*PS*] I told Jemmy McCartney[995] I would write to you to do him all the good offices in your power in a certain affair;[996] I desire you to doe soe, as well in freindship to his father, as for the sake of justice: for he hath been extremely delayed and I beleive injured.

369. *Alan I, Dublin, to Thomas, at his lodgings in the Privy Garden, Whitehall, 7 Dec. 1719*

(1248/4/180–1)

I am obliged to you for your letter of the first instant; the account it gives of the proceedings of that day tho short is the best and most full of any which is come over hither: I confesse I cannot foresee that such a judgement can be formed from what hapned that day as some

---

[989] James Craggs.

[990] *CJ*, xix, 177–8, gives the numbers as 203–58. Lawson was one of the tellers in the majority.

[991] Held on 15 Dec. and strongly contested (*HC 1715–54*, i, 327).

[992] Bolton's home county.

[993] Matthew Aylmer (c.1650–1720), MP [GB] 1697–1713, 1715–d., 1st Baron Aylmer in the Irish peerage.

[994] Phillips Gybbon (1678–1762), of Hole Park, Kent, MP [GB] 1707–d., revenue commr [I] 1714–26.

[995] James Macartney, MP [I].

[996] See below, p. 258.

people here think may be made, who are very well inclined to the bills passing:[997] It is certain it hath created some people very great uneasinesse, who (if it shal happen to miscarry) will as publickly then declare themselves against it, as they are now secretly for it in their hearts; and if it succeed will in the most insolent and triumphant maner declare they were alway for its passing, as a thing of the last consequence to the King and his affairs. The last letter which I inclosed under your cover hath made you sufficiently master of the bill on which the Duke discoursed you pray let me know the maner of his talking on that subject; for by his speaking immediately after the bill was rejected, and just before his going away, I plainly discerned that he was nettled, having been made to beleive the losse of it was to his dishonour, or the publick prejudice: he told me at first he knew how ill it would be taken by the ministry. I am apt to beleive his speaking of it so often to me and after to you was with this view: that if it should hereafter come to light he had wrote to my disadvantage on that subject (as I beleive he hath been prevailed on to do) he may be able to say he had expressed his resentment to me and you of that bills being lost. I have taken too much pains, and done too much service to find such returns, and see a flattering Sycophant reap the acknowledgements of services in the doing of which he had the least hand; and am more sorry on the Dukes account then my own; for I did and stil do love him.

370. *Thomas to Alan I, 8 Dec. 1719*

(1248/4/174–5)

You have I beleive before this an account of what passt in the house of Commons this day sennight in relation to the Peerage Bill, and shall at the end of this what this day produces; What is usually called a spiritt in the house, generally shewes itt selfe in what resembles rage, butt twas far otherwise, for instead of venting themselves in that manner, every body whoe spoake for the longer day treated the subject with the utmost contempt, a specimen of which take from Bishop Nevils speech, (whoe by the way is now called Arch=Bishop).[998] Hee in answer to Mr Letchmere professt the utmost astonishment that that Learned gentleman could bee for the shorter day;[999] Hee whoe allwayes argued with the greatest force of reason, Hee whoe allwayes sayd what hee thought, Hee whose Oratory ever charmed his hearers, That such an one could thinke of denying himselfe the just applause of a full house, by throwing itt away upon a thin one was more surprising then any thing hee had mett with etc. Those against the shorter day argued from the weight of the thing, and generally concluded for a full house. They insisted uppon the methods taken last yeare att the close of a session, when every body beleiving all businesse over, were gone into the Country; That now the other extreme was thought by the Lords more feasable, and that what they then

[997] The reintroduced Peerage Bill, which came down from the Lords on Tuesday, 1 Dec. 1719. It was then read the first time. A motion was made that it be read a seond time on Friday the 4th, but this encountered considerable opposition and the House resolved on a division, by 203–58, to adjourn the second reading for a week (*CJ*, xix, 177–8; Cobbett, *Parl. Hist.*, ix, col. 609).

[998] Grey Neville (1681–1723), of Billingbear, Berks., MP [GB] Berwick-upon-Tweed, nicknamed 'Bishop Neville' on account of his religious enthusiasm (*HC 1690–1715*, iv, 1014–15).

[999] Nicholas Lechmere.

faild in might bee obtaind before members were come up; To which the others answered
that there was a very competent house, That if gentlemen would nott come up in reasonable
time after publique notice given when the Parliament should goe uppon businesse, things
must nott stand still till they pleased to attend, on this occasion they were rapt over the
knuckles, by putting them in mind how long last yeare the Parliament were putt of, after
such notice given as they had mentioned. I presume the play this day will bee endeavouring
to bring gentlemen into a Committall by mentioning a great many fine things which the
Commons may insist uppon to their great advantage, by way of amendments which noe
doubt the Lords would agree to, as to the last part I am very throughly convinct they are in
the right, for I thinke their Lordships will swallow any thing for obtaining their end, butt
how far these arguments shall prevaile this day will determine; I thinke they will nott take
place.

I mett the D[*uke*] of B[*olton*] three dayes agoe at Lord Bridgwaters, where hee shewd mee
the letter which came under my cover, I read itt with great attention, and after having soe
done, made a marke with my naile on that paragraph which mentiond what a gentleman
sayd of the glorious session which would have been if the Popery Bill had passed, his Grace
sayd the fact was true, to which I replyed that I hoped if I should forgett itt when I had
next the honour to waite uppon him (and that I would doe assoone as I received the paper
from you) Hee would bee pleasd to remind mee of telling him a story of what happened
att Newmarkett which I beleivd would by setting matters in a true light, unfold somethings
which to those whoe did nott looke throughly into them might nott be soe intelligible,
Hee told mee hee beleivd I should hardly forgett what I had a mind to say, butt if I did, hee
would putt mee in mind of itt, I told him what I desired was by way of caution, for that
probably I should nott forgett what had made soe deep impression on mee.

The Peerage Bill has soe entirely taken up the Lords that I doe nott beleive they have
thought of any thing else, in my conversation I have nott heard once mentioned (of late)
the Lords Representation,[1000] butt att Newmarkett a great man sayd something must bee
done in that matter butt att the same time seemd att a losse how to come att itt, and I fancy
all the care that can bee will bee taken to prevent itts being brought on the stage, though for
my own part I doe nott see how twill bee obviated if any one single Lord whoe has a mind
to trouble the waters, bee inclined to make complaint of what will bee calld an invasion
of their right, you may bee sure I am in noe secrets, however I will bee as allert as I can in
enquiring into every step that shall bee taken, and will give you the earlyest information I
can. The noble Lord you mention acts to the life the part you expected, butt att the same
time protested sollemnly in our debate, his being wholly undetermined, and would govern
himself on the arguments hee should heare.

Passt ten a clock. This long day (and a long one itt has been) is well over.

The house devided uppon the Question of Committall Yeas 177 Noes 269.[1001]

[1000] The representation of the Irish house of lords to King George I on the *Annesley* v. *Sherlock* case, agreed on
17 Oct. 1719 (*LJI*, ii, 654–60).

[1001] *CJ*, xix, 186, confirms the numbers in the vote against committing the Peerage Bill.

371. *Thomas to Alan I, 10 Dec. 1719*

(1248/4/176–7)

By last post, I told you the numbers uppon the devision for the Committall of the Peerage Bill, by which you cannott butt see a more then ordinary firmnesse of mind in those gentlemen whoe opposed itt; to doe the Secretary justice, hee made as much of the cause as itt would beare, spoake extremely well, and with good manners the whole debate was calme to a miracle, butt yett some plaine truths as plainly expresst.

The tenor of Mr Smiths[1002] argument was this, that all those whoe had spoake for the Bill resulted in this, that wee were to suppose the worst of things, Viz That wee might have soe ill a King as might in time to come aime att the destruction of innocent men, and protecting the most guilty, because a weake Queen att the instigation of the most daring ministry that the world ever saw, had made an attempt of like nature once, that hee was far from being unwilling to have ever soe remote a possibillity prevented, which might bee done by much safer and better methods etc. Sir John Packinton enumerated what had been done in every session for the Crowne, and att the end of each sentence concluded, whoe was this done by, why surely by the house of Commons against whom the doore of the house of Peers is to bee now shutt, and why? why truly to screen two noble Dukes, and advance half a dozen of our members, when that was done, all would bee safe.[1003] Mr Letchmere went through the Bill applauding each part, butt sayd nothing being therein contained for benefitt of the Commons, hee hoped they would take care of themselves by adding what was necessary, and then putt us in mind of the many suggar plums wee were to hope for, conluding on his word and honour to bee against the whole, if every part of what hee had mentioned were nott agreed to by the Lords,[1004] uppon which Lord Carleton (in the gallery) made this remarke, that twas to bee now throwne out as a Bill, or afterward as Cowcombers.[1005] The first opertunity I have, Ile write what I doe nott thinke fitt now to say plainely, for a reason youl guesse; One thing I must observe; Gentlemen were tryd (a freind of yours in perticular) how farr they would goe into warme measures after the Bill should bee rejected, from whom the Proposers receivd answers soe little to their mind, that I may for certainty say, they putt an entire stop to that project. This day I sent your letter with the inclosed papers (which came on Tuesday night) to the person to whom twas directed, and will if possible see him tomorrow. I thinke of going in the afternoon or Saturday morning att farthest toward Pepper Hara, our election being appointed for Tuesday. Twill bee a very hard Tug.

[1002] John Smith. A very brief version of his speech is given in Cobbett, *Parl. Hist.*, ix, col. 624.

[1003] See Cobbett, *Parl. Hist.*, ix, cols 617–18.

[1004] See Cobbett, *Parl. Hist.*, ix, col. 618.

[1005] In Act 1, scene 1 of Gay's *The Beggar's Opera* Mrs Peachum sings bitterly of her daughter Polly (Air 7) 'And when she's drest with Care and Cost, all tempting, fine and gay, / As Men should serve a Cucumber, she flings herself away'. According to Boswell, in his *Journal of a Tour to the Hebrides*, s.v. 5 Oct. 1773, 'It has been a common saying of physicians in England, that a cucumber should be well sliced, and dressed with pepper and vinegar, and then thrown out, as good for nothing'.

372. *Alan I, Dublin, to Thomas, 11 Dec. 1719*

(1248/4/182–3)

This letter will be delivered you by Mr Michael Ward, a Gentleman of the house of Commons of good estate and understanding, and for whom I have a personal esteem and value, and that very justly. The occasion of his going over is to endeavour something in favor of our linnen manufacture, which will suffer extremely if they who petition against the wearing stained or printed linen shal be able to carry their point in the house of Commons.[1006] It is true that the taking away our woollen trade was the foundation of Englands going into the encouragement they promised to the linnen;[1007] and that the South part of Ireland suffered by the former, as the North is the gainer by the later: however that which brings money into the Kingdome, is a benefit to the whole; the more immediately so to that part of it where the manufacture is cheifly carryed on. But beside the relation that one part of Ireland hath to the other I must tell you that the linnen manufacture begins to spread Southward, and turns to good advantage to some parts of Munster in which it is settled already; and I beleive will doe more so from time to time. But I could not go their lengths who in preparing of the state of the case agreed on by the Commissioners of the linen manufacture to be transmitted into England,[1008] had ordered matters soe as to make it look like a sort of agreement between England and Ireland that we should entirely part with all maner of woollen manufacture, and have in lieu of it the full use and benefit of the linen trade: I told them that some small part of the woollen manufacture remained stil untouched, and that we were yet at liberty to transport woollen yarn, frizes etc, That some places of England every Session endeavoured to prohibit us from the benefit of exporting those poor manufactures: and that I did hope and suppose the Commissioners had no view toward the taking away from that part of the Kingdome which had suffered so much already in their woollen manufactures the little remains of that trade which they stil enjoyed, and upon which great numbers maintained their familyes. I found that the Commissioners thought (at least they seemed to do so) that no kind of woollen manufacture remained capable to be exported, and they professed they had no such design, and consented to alter the frame of their paper by leaving out what looked that way; but this morning a fair copy of the paper was brought to me with these words in it, that they had the faith of the King Lords and Commons to enjoy the linen manufacture (granted to them on so valuable consideration). The words in the parenthesis were left in, tho I had objected to their mentioning as if Ireland was to relinquish its woollen trade and betake themselves wholly to the linen; and it was told me by the Clerk who engrossed it that they had omitted these words which followed after the words so valuable consideration viz (as the woollen trade of Ireland) which

---

[1006] Lord Perceval reported from Westminster that Ward was 'very diligent in serving' the interests of the Irish linen manufacture (BL, Add. MS 47029, ff. 5–6: Perceval to Lord Abercorn, 9 Jan. 1719/20).

[1007] The English Woollen Act of 1699 (10 Will. III, c. 16) had prevented the export of Irish woollen yarn or cloth to England or its plantations. In compensation, following pressure from Ireland, endorsed by the lord lieutenant, Ormond, the Westminster parliament passed the Linen Act (3 & 4 Anne, c. 8), allowing Irish linens to be exported directly to England's overseas colonies. See James, *Ireland in the Empire*, 62–3.

[1008] The representation to the king from the Linen Board, in response to the introduction into the British house of commons of the Calico Bill, which targeted the wearing of printed or stained linens as well as calicoes. It was laid before the Commons on 26 Jan. 1720 and is printed in *CJ*, xix, 237–8.

he said the Commissioners thought were the words by me objected to: I told him indeed I did object to those words, but little intended the words so valuable consideration should stand, for if they did that which I objected to was so strongly insinuated and implyed that it had as good stand expressed and in words at large; he hath carryed away the paper to write it over fair witha resolution to leave the valuable consideration out; whether Lord A=[1009] and some others will consent to it I cannot yet tell. I will send you the copy as prepared by them and then you will be able to compare it with that which is to be now laid before the King and Parliament ... Our Courtiers seem to apprehend the bill to be lost:[1010] I suspend my faith till Sunday.

373. *Alan I, Dublin, to Thomas, 14 Dec. 1719*[1011]

(1248/4/188–9)

I am obliged to you for the account you give me of the fate of the Peerage bill on Tuesday last: it was what I expected as well as wished; tho I confesse I was and am a good deal confounded how to account for their prudence who after a former unsuccesseful attempt resolved on renewing it so very soon after without having taken a more exact muster of the troops they should be able to bring into the feild on the day of battle. You knew last Spring what my sentiments were on this subject, and I remember to have told you in what a maner my going into the bill was pressed upon me and by whom: For fear of mistakes I wrote down my resolution and read it to a certain Great man,[1012] which was in the words following. I cannot with honour or conscience vote for the Peerage bill, it being perfectly against my judgement: I desire I may without displeasing his Majestye be absent from the house while that bill is under consideration, not thinking it becoming me to give opposition by voting or Debating against a bill introduced and carryed on as this hath been. If this be too great a favor to be allowed me I am ready with the most dutiful submission and with out the least reluctancy to suffer any thing which I may be thought to deserve for not being able to perceive the reasonablenesse or expediency of the bill. This I read on 17th March 1718[*/19*], and desired the person I read it to that he would acquaint the King with it; he seemed much out of humour, said he was sorry nay surprized to find me to have taken this resolution, having formerly thought I would have been for the bill; but promised to acquaint Lord Sunderland with it. On the 19th I went to his house and asked him if he had seen his Majestye; he told me he had not, but should see him that day. About an hour after he called at my lodging, expressed great kindnesse for me, recommended the Old Whig to me,[1013] and hoped I would be convinced: I gave him no reason to expect it and so we

---

[1009] Abercorn.

[1010] The Calico Bill.

[1011] Endorsed by Alan I: 'Contains the grounds and steps of the Duke of Boltons coolnesse to me'. Printed in Coxe, *Walpole*, ii, 172–4, with some emendations to punctuation and capitalisation, and expansion of abbreviated names (as was the case in all instances in which Coxe published letters from the Brodrick papers).

[1012] The duke of Bolton.

[1013] Joseph Addison's *The Old Whig...*, originally published in two parts in 1719 in response to Sir Richard Steele's *The Plebeian*, put the case for the Peerage Bill.

parted. From that time I suppose it was resolved he should leave town without so much as letting me know it, much lesse giving me oportunity of going at the same time he did: and tho I knew that he was preparing for Ireland yet he never mentioned it to me till after his footmen had talked with mine of the day they were to be ready.

I knew the meaning was to try whether I would stand it and resolved not only to have staid in town but to have been at the debate, and to have voted as my judgement lead me: Soon after his going out of town I had a visit from Lord S[*underland*] by whom I was pressed on the same subject, but I continued firm: and after some expressions of concern (with a good deal of warmth) we parted: and soon after I was told I might prepare for Ireland without losse of time etc.

At this time it was not determined to drop the bill in the Lords house without sending it down to the Commons. Hence arose the coolnesse of a certain person toward me,[1014] in so much that when I landed in Ireland I found he had taken other people entirely into his bosome, and I also found that some measures which they had resolved upon about pushing the matter in favor of the dissenters were so unpalatable that they would prevent doing as much for them, as might have been attained, if no wrong steps had been taken at his first landing: but it had obtained (I suppose from the great favour and intimacy a certain person was taken into) that an entire repeal of the test was intended; and this had taken so deep root before I came over that it was impossible to gett people free from engagements they had mutually entred into to go thus far and no farther; and to convince the world they were not under the direction of one man. Notwithstanding the countenance I saw given to one person and the Court paid by all the attendants of a great man to him, I went on in my constant course of carrying on the publick affairs in the easyest and best maner; and by doing every thing that could be done, and assuring him that the imaginary fears with which he had been possessed would come to nothing, and shewing him from time to time that what I said had come to passe, as on the contrary what they had suggested never did, brought him to see that I sincerely wished him well and served him effectually; so that I think he had entirely good wishes toward me till toward the end of the Session, I mean till after he returned from a certain place during the recesse:[1015] when I received your letter from Newmarket which I communicated to him and told him I was sorry to find that every body as well as I observed in him a coolnesse toward me in comparison of the favourite. He said I was ill used by him who wrote the letter, who he beleived must be one of Mr C[*onolly*]s freinds; professed great kindnesse etc but when so sencelesse an objection as my being against the Popery bill is made the foundation of resentment I must think otherwise. In short, I was again urged (by order) whether I should have leave given me to attend the Session of Parliament and told the bill would again come in: I said I had rather remain here, then go over and disoblige (as I certainly should) in that particular. From that time I take it the fixed and grounded distast is taken. This is written for your own satisfaction ...

[1014] Bolton.
[1015] Conolly's country estate at Castletown.

374. *Thomas to Alan I, 22 Dec. 1719*

(1248/4/190–1)

I returnd to towne last night a good deale out of order, butt hope a little rest will sett mee to rights againe; Sir Tho Mullineuxes death[1016] kept mee three or four dayes longer then I intended.

Mr Walters carryed the election by a hundred and seven,[1017] hee pold above three hundred who have noe more freehold in Surry then your footman, butt I thinke Sir Fr. V. will nott bear the expence of a petition.[1018]

The King this day gave the Royall assent to the land tax Bill; Tomorrow wee shall send the mault Bill[1019] to the Lords and then adjourne to the 11th or 12th of next month.[1020] You will before receiving this have heard of the Lords addressing the King for your Representation etc. to bee layd before their house, in order (as I suppose) to passe some law on that subject.

Last night I receivd yours of the 7th and 14th. Assoone as I am able to goe abroad, Ile waite on the person, whose manner of expressing himselfe was intended to lett mee understand that those here were soe very uneasy att the failure that hee feard itt might prejudice a freind of yours, my answer was that acting unrightly would allwayes bee right, bee the consequence what twould.

375. *Alan I to Thomas, n.d. [c. Jan. 1720]*

(1248/4/184–7)

… All here are your humble servants. Pray let me have the earliest notices of the steps taken by the Lords in their affair with our house of Lords; the addresse and order about the papers we have received: Lord M[*oleswor*]th wrote over hither some time agoe, that he had discoursed that matter with a great many British Peers, and (as he never fails to doe) had convinced all with whom he had spoken that the Lords here were intirely in the right, and gave us to understand that the British Peers knew not what to doe in it, and that it must fall and we should hear no more of it. You know I have not the happinesse of that Politicians correspondence; but I was told last Saturday by Mr C[*onoll*]y in the Closett, when we received Mr Craggs letter to send over extracts out of the Lords journals here, that a letter to this purpose had been wrote by him; he did not say to whom, and I am satisfyed it was not to him. Nay it was hinted to me in discourse by Lord A[*bercorn*] that he supposed

---

[1016]Sir Thomas Molyneux of Westhoughton, Lancs., whose wife had inherited the More estate at Loseley in Surrey, died on 13 Dec. 1719 (E.W. Brayley, *The History of Surrey* … (5 vols, 1841–8), i, pt 2, p. 415).

[1017]The tory John Walter (*d.*1736) of Busbridge, Surrey, was elected by a margin of 1,735 votes to 1,629 (*HC 1715–54*, i, 327).

[1018]Sir Francis Vincent (1646–1736), of Stoke d'Abernon, Surrey, MP [GB] 1690–5, 1710–13, the defeated candidate.

[1019]The bill continuing the tax of malt, mum (a flavoured wheaten beer), cider and perry, and to enable the treasury to call in such exchequer bills as were to be cancelled.

[1020]The House adjourned to 12 Jan.

the English Lords would not meddle with us again: and I am confident that letter was the best ground he had for such a conjecture: Indeed it imports that noble Lord (being now on the spot) to employ his great abilityes and interest in the ministry and both houses to make a matter easy as possible to this Kingdome, in the bringing of which upon it he was so instrumental: His declaring here that the dispute was so uneasy to the Lords in great Britain that they were weary of it, that it was an hot Iron which they would be very glad to throw out of their hands and not burn their fingers more with it then they had done greatly spirited up people to doe what they have done; and which it was not in the power of man to prevent, considering the nature of the thing and the maner in which he and others managed it.

376. Alan I, Dublin, to Thomas, 7 Jan. 1719[/20]

(1248/4/192–3)

… His Grace of Bolton hath not given himself the trouble to take notice of any one of three letters which I wrote to him since he left us; he shal be sure to answer my next which I write before I hear from him. I suppose he is under some difficultye in what maner to doe it; to go to particulars will not be for his service; and it will look very odd in him to own his having entertained unkind thoughts of me; and I am apt to beleive having wrote little to my advantage about a certain bill, without being able to shew why he was so fond of it, or wherein it concerned him, or the ministry that that bill should passe: but indeed some people whom he hath taken into his bosom were very angry at its being rejected, and I am satisfyed they had their particular reasons for being soe. I hope and think I laid that matter in soe clear a light that you and every reasonable man must be satisfyed, if that be the occasion of coolnesse in him to me, it is a sought one: but last winters businesse sticks in his stomach, and I beleive in other peoples too: but I am very easy, when I am sensible I am not to blame. Tell me nakedly your thoughts of that bill, and of the part I took in that matter.

My brother William (on the death of Dr Lake[1021]) told me the living of Capagh in the Diocese of Waterford[1022] was become void and in the disposal of the Governement; and pressed me to write to the Duke of Bolton about it in favor of Mr Chinery, who is marryed to Nelly Whitfeld:[1023] I did soe, but have had no answer from his Grace; and doe now find, what I ought to have suspected earlyer, considering what author I had for the thing, that there is no such living in the Governements gift, nor can I learn that Mr Lake ever had any such Living.[1024] Pray when you first see his Grace mention this to him, and make my excuse for troubling him by mistake, that I may not have a complying answer which will be of no avail to Mr Chinery …

[1021] Richard Leake (*d.*1719), prebendary of Killardriffe in the diocese of Cashel (Cotton, *Fasti,* i, 59, 66).

[1022] The rectory of Cappagh, Co. Waterford.

[1023] George Chinnery (c.1679–c.1755), who married Alan's niece Eleanor, the daughter of his sister Katherine Whitfield. One of their sons was named Brodrick (Brady, *Records,* ii, 326).

[1024] There was indeed such a living: it was given in 1719 to Edward Synge (1691–1762), son of the archbishop of Tuam and himself a future bishop, who was at that time a fellow of Trinity (Brady, *Records,* iii, 114–15).

377. *Thomas to Alan I, 16 Jan. 1719[/20]*

(1248/4/194–7)

Last night I receivd yours of the 7th. I have twice since my last to you seen the [*duke of Bolton*] and as often had excuses for his nott calling on mee according to promise with fresh assurances of doing itt soone; I doe apprehend the delay arises from the same cause why none of your three letters have yett been answered.

The case stated to the Judges upon the Popery Bill[1025] proves to a demonstration the unreasonablenesse of the clause which by a law ex post facto[1026] would noe doubt have avoided all leases in Reversion, and indeed I thinke ought to doe soe in all cases where the lease in being and that in Reversion exceeds the number of years allowd by the former Bill to be sett by Papists,[1027] butt surely where the terme demisd comes within the power given by the first Act, supposing the two leases had been in one, the case is otherwaies; the Principle aime of the Act relating to the time, and not the manner of graunting itt … I feare by the sketch of the account you send, you have forgott to call for my wine licence mony, doe nott lett that run further in arreare, least itt bee calld an old debt, nott likely to be retreivd by one whoe neither is, or probably ever will become a favourite; for I cannott bring my selfe up to the termes which are generally the conditions annext.

I formerly told you my opinion of the effect of what your Lords house did, Viz That an Act would passe here, declaring they have noe jurisdiction in case of Appeals; and hitherto I see noe reason to thinke otherwise, for I have nott been soe lucky in all my conversation as to meet with any one of the many whoe have been convinct of the Irish Lords right in that perticular, butt the person whoe gives this account may possibly bee in the right, for hee has many opertunityes of knowing things, which I avoid, however I suspend my judgment a little time will shew whoe guesses best.

I am afraid wee beleive what wee desire uppon too too slight grounds, that expressions may have fallen from some Lords here of the difficulty of the matter, I can easily beleive, butt att the same time am of opinion this difficulty is nott meant on account of determining against the Irish Lords right, butt uppon a nicer point. Itt may perhaps prove hard soe to frame a Bill as nott to create a jealousy in the Commons (through which house you know itt must passe) that in aftertimes use may bee made therof in maintenance of what the Lords here seeme now to lay a claime of right to, which however the Commons have never yett yeilded. I am unhappy in nott thinking (very often) as this Lord does, butt I cannott helpe itt, I judge as well as I can, and in every case after due consideration governe myselfe by what seemes to mee most reasonable, which must allwayes bee my plea, in case I bee mistaken; and soe I may perhaps in a matter now afoote; Mr Ward[1028] gives himselfe sometimes the trouble of calling on mee about the matter of our Linnen; hee desired my thoughts in relation to the method of his proceeding. Wee readily agreed on making application to his Majesty in such manner as the Ministry thought most proper. The next consideration was

[1025] The failed bill of 1719 'to Prevent the Further Growth of Popery'.

[1026] With retrospective force.

[1027] Section 8 of the 1704 act to prevent the further growth of popery (2 Anne, c. 6 [I]) allowed conforming catholics who benefited from the provisions of the act to make leases for 21 years.

[1028] Michael Ward, MP [I].

whither the house of Commons ought to bee applyed to, and how; my thoughts were that private application might bee usefull, butt I much doubted whither publique would bee soe, nay the contrary, and therfore thought lying by (att least for some time) advisable; Lord M[olesworth] (as Mr W[ard] tells mee) was warme for delivering cases to the members att the doore, for that they knew nott what wee had to say for our selves, butt I perceive others whoe have been talkt with incline to my sentiments. In most things (especially where Ireland is concernd) my consideration is nott somuch what ought, as what will doe; for really wee may talke as big as the fly on the Cart wheele, and to as little purpose.[1029] Thus much I can say, that hitherto this method has provd of use, wittnesse the Bill endeavourd against running woole out of Ireland without including England, two years since,[1030] and the soe often repeated attempts of prohibiting barkes being exported, or att least laying a great duty uppon itt,[1031] in neither of which cases I receivd much assistance; were itt worth troubling you with, I could give other instances of like nature, butt lett that passe; I allways have and allways will faithfully discharge my duty ... You will by last post have heard that Plunkets Appeale against mcCartny was dismissed with £40 Costs.[1032] Yesterday that of Lopdell had the same fate, and like Costs.[1033] Lord Stanhope returnd to towne yesterday,[1034] I am nott able to give any account of what hee brings, nor probably shall I, for till things are pretty publique I seldome give creditt to Coffee house surmises.

If before I seale up this, I can learne any thing worth communicating Ile adde itt.

I am sorry that what I have learn't will goe in soe narrow a compasse, Things seeme to bee in the position they were (as far as depends on the Court of Spaine) before Lord Stanhope went over; They scrupling coming into the termes of the Quadruple alliance as the Basis on which a peace shall be treated of; A Gentleman whoe has been conversant in things of this nature (and whoe went over with Lord Stanhope) is certainly gon to Madrid, this was knowne before my Lord came back, butt I am now told nott from us seperately, butt in conjunction and in the name of all the Allyes, whose returne wee are to expect before wee can say more, The word now being every thing will certainly end well.

Being alone, Ile bestow a little more time in relating a passage which happened in the House of Lords.

Last Thursday they had the Duke of Dovers case (as wee yett call him) under consideration, you know the case, tis therefore unnecessary to mention more of itt, than that the

---

[1029] From Aesop's fable, 'The Fly on the Wheel': a fly sat upon the axle of a chariot-wheel and said 'What a lot of dust I raise!'

[1030] In Jan. 1718 the British house of commons had received petitions from a number of west-country clothing towns complaining about the smuggling of Irish woollen yarn to France. On 1 Feb. the report from the investigating committee was referred to the committee of ways and means, but no further action was taken (*CJ*, xviii, 683, 686–8, 692–3, 705).

[1031] Oak bark was an essential ingredient in the process of tanning leather, and in Feb. 1718 the Commons received numerous petitions from leather manufacturers against the unrestricted export of bark to Ireland, which, they argued, disadvantaged them against Irish competition (*CJ*, xviii, 701–4, 722–3). No legislation resulted. There had been a similar co-ordinated campaign the previous session which had also failed to produce a bill (*Failed Legislation 1660–1800 ...*, ed. Julian Hoppit (1997), 288–9).

[1032] An appeal to the British house of lords brought by Stephen Ludlow and Richard Fenner, the surviving executors of Sir Walter Plunkett, and Plunkett Plunkett, in their case against James Macartney, sr and jr, and others (Brown, *Reports of Cases*, ii, 104–10). The case was decided on 13 Jan.

[1033] The case of *Smith et al. v. Evans et al.*, arising from several decisions in the Irish court of chancery in 1717–18. Charles Lopdell was one of the appellants (*LJ*, xxi, 198).

[1034] From Paris (*Daily Courant*, 16 Jan. 1720).

question stated and afterwards putt was That the Duke of Dover has a right to demand his writt of summons to Parliament contents 41 N[ot] C[ontents] 62.[1035]

To make his case (in its nature) the same with Duke Hamiltons[1036] twas insisted that hee was a Peer of Scotland att the time of being created Duke of Dover, by the stile and Title of Lord Sallaway,[1037] which honour his father had nott long before gott conferred on him with viewe of what is nott materiall in this case. To which twas answered That hee was a minor att that time, and consequently by the laws of Scotland (as the Kings Advocate had argued) might demitt, i.e might renounce the honour when hee came of age, for that noe man was obligded to accept against his will, to which twas replyed that by our laws every of his Majestys subjects were by their Allegiance obligded to serve the state etc. especially in such an instance as giving their best advice In arduis negotiis Regni.[1038] The Lord whoe first insisted on the Power of Refusall in a man of Ripe years, and consequently that a minor had the same right when hee should become soe, rose againe. Sayed Hee did nott rise to argue the point with the noble Lord whoe spoake last as a Lawyer (though they were both soe) butt as a Peer to desire their Lordships would please to consider what the consquence of such a notion might bee, if allowd to take place.

For putt the case sayes hee the Crowne should thinke fitt (against the will of the man) to call up one to this house whoe had an excellent tallent in creating difficultyes in the house of Commons, sometimes on one side, sometimes on the other, as his caprice movd him to, or as hee thought might best serve a present turn (Here looking uppon a learned gentleman of our house whoe stood very near him) and that hee should bring this temper with him thither (as perhaps had been done) (looking then uppon a Peer whoe within your memory and mine was created soe) would their Lordships nott bee well satisfyed with the benefitt they would receive from this negative power which hee had been arguing for. I suppose twas generally agreed the satyr was more intended, then argument, for after some smiling the contest between the two Lords ended.

378. *Thomas to Alan I, 19 Jan. 1719[/20]*

(1248/4/198–9)

The King yesterday giving the Royall assent to the Mault and Mutiny Bills, without a speech (as people expected) leaves roome to doubt whether any thing will be mentioned

---

[1035] Charles Douglas (1698–1778), 3rd duke of Queensberry in the Scottish peerage and 2nd duke of Dover in the British peerage. The decision was made on 14 Jan. (*LJ*, xxi, 196). The numbers given here are confirmed in Sainty and Dewar, *Divisions*, microfiche. Cf. HMC, *Portland MSS*, v, 591.

[1036] Having been elected a representative peer in 1710, James Hamilton (1658–1712), 4th duke of Hamilton in the Scottish peerage, was created duke of Brandon in the British peerage in Sept. 1711. There was considerable opposition to his being permitted to sit by virtue of his British title and on 20 Dec. the Lords voted that no Scottish peer could sit by virtue of a British peerage created since the Union (*HL 1660–1715*, v, 695–6). This was despite the fact that James Douglas (1662–1711), 2nd duke of Queensberry, had been admitted to sit in the Lords in Nov. 1708 in his British dukedom of Dover, granted since the passage of the Union. The only difference was that Queensberry was not a representative peer at the time (*HL 1660–1715*, ii, 865).

[1037] Queensberry was the second son of the 2nd duke, and succeeded by a special remainder. In 1706 he had been created, in his own right, earl of Solway.

[1038] Peers were summoned to give counsel 'pro arduis et urgentibus negotiis' (for difficult and pressing business).

this session of the deficiency as tis called of the Civill list;[1039] though att Court that name is nott relished: for say they twould have been brought to answer had the whole been applyd to the payment of itt.

Butt the necessary affairs of the Kingdome requiring an advance of mony (nott provided for by Parliament) what is now wanting is noe more then making good what has been soe payd. Had Lord Stanhope returned with an Ollive Branch I fancy wee had heard of this, butt as things stand perhaps deferring itt is thought advisable. A whisper has some dayes gone about, that the King of Spaine had declared a resolution rather to risque his Crowne then submitt to the Termes of the Quadruple Alliance; which I doubt is better founded then att first I thought, having seen a letter from a good hand, out of Holland, to the same purpose; the sending Monsieur Shobe (as I told you in my last) from Paris to Madrid,[1040] when wee expected nothing like itt, gives ground to question whither Peace bee as near as was given outt, att best, tis plaine new difficultyes are made, soe that tis more then probable those are to bee adjusted att Madrid before any thing will be concluded; I wish itt end well. You will remember what Mr Fuller[1041] sayd last year in the house upon the French declaration of war against Spaine, wherein tis att least fairly insinuated that there might bee hopes of our parting with Gibraltar, for which reason hee was for burning the Paper by the hangman, as a libell upon our good Ally,[1042] this however blew of att that time, butt the thing being a fresh talkt of (thought nott ownd) has produced a sharpe pamphlet (wrote by Mr Trenchard)[1043] shewing the importance of that place; and I am told that a motion will soone bee made for an Addresse to his Majesty praying that in the approaching Peace his Majesty would bee graciously pleasd to use his best endeavours towards procuring some tract of land for the convenience and greater security of that Garison, the manner after which this is handled by the Ministry will in some degree give light into the matter; I own I thinke every precaution necessary in order to obtaining somthing like advantagious conditions (as to trade) for England, Wee beare a great share of the war, without prospect of getting uppon any other head, and twould bee terrible to loose that in case the ministry should now thinke themselves under as pressing necessityes for a Peace, as those in the Queens time did; Tis true twould bee very welcome, butt I hope wee are nott soe hard prest as to foregoe insisting uppon something in favour of England. I beleive some day

[1039] At this time the government was anxious that parliament write off the accumulated deficit of £600,000 on the civil list, something eventually accomplished later in the session through the agency of Robert Walpole (Plumb, *Making of a Statesman*, 287, 291–2).

[1040] Luke Schaub (1690–1758), Stanhope's secretary, and from the British 1721 ambassador to the Spanish court, had left Paris for Madrid when his master returned to England (*Post Boy*, 14–16 Jan. 1720).

[1041] Samuel Pargiter Fuller (c.1690–1722), opposition whig MP for Petersfield (*HC 1715–54*, ii, 324).

[1042] According to a despatch from the French diplomat Philippe Néricault Destouches, Fuller, a 'creature' of Robert Walpole, had brought into the Commons a lampoon entitled 'A manifesto on the causes of the rupture between France and Spain' (probably *Observations and Remarks upon the Declaration of War against Spain, and upon the Manifesto Publish'd in the Name of the King of France* ... (1719), once attributed to Defoe), in which, he said a foreigner had taken it upon himself to dispose of the property of the English crown, boasting that he had assured the restitution of France to Spain. This had produced only a brief and astonished silence, and not the debate Fuller had intended to provoke on rumours of the ministry's willingness to cede Gibraltar. (Wolfgang Michael, *England under George I: The Quadruple Alliance* (1939), 130; Jeremy Black, *Parliament and Foreign Policy in the Eighteenth Century* (Cambridge, 2004), 187.)

[1043] *Considerations Offered upon the Approaching Peace, and upon the Importance of Gibraltar to the British Empire, Being the Second Part of The Independent Whig* (1720). The *Independent Whig* was a periodical produced jointly by John Trenchard (c.1668–1723) and Thomas Gordon (d.1750).

this weeke a Proposall will bee made by the Chancellor of the Exchequer for receiving a scheme towards payment of the National debt; which you may bee very sure is before hand concerted with the S[outh] Sea Company, I heare (though tis kept very close) twill bee in substance that they take uppon themselves the payment of the whole, having all the appropriated funds to doe itt withall; and as an inducement hereto, the Nation shall bee gainer one tenth uppon the whole, in compensation whereof, the company to have some minute advantages (as they are to bee represented) graunted them.

After passing the Bill for that companyes taking in the lottery Tickets of 1710 their stock in a few dayes advanced five per Cent; and well itt might if what I my selfe heard Mr Lowndes[1044] say were true, that we ought and might have made a better bargaine by £200,000. If you ever take notice of the Price of stocks in the Printed papers you will find that run up to neare a hundred and forty, for which the buyer when payd of by the publique shall receive butt a hundred, and in the meane time onely £5 per Cent for that hundred. Every body knowes this late prodigious Rise was occasioned by the expectation of this scheme, this was noe secrett; itt will surely deserve due consideration whither a Job for a perticular sett of men, and such others as beyond question are to find their account in itt, shall bee gone into hand over head as the last was; I beleive this matter will nott bee carryed through as that was, att least the ensnaring question of taking the Proposall in the lump, or rejecting the whole will be avoided, by going into a through discussion of each perticular Article butt this will depend uppon the attendance Gentlemen will please to give; one perticular sett of men will doe their duty, I meane observe the orders they receive and thereby carry their point, if others are negligent. I doe protest solemnly I am greivd att what I every day see, and for that reason heartily wish my selfe out of that place where such things are done, butt whilst I am in the house, I will faithfully doe my part. Lord Onslow has earnestly presst my acceptance of some honorary place whereby my seat may bee vacated, in order to my standing att Guilford upon the death of Generall Wroth, which I feare is neare att hand,[1045] being informd of a certaine designe to sett up a Tory in opposition to his[1046] interest, and beleiving my standing would make the election more secure, or att least lesse troublesome then otherwaies itt may prove, butt this I have absolutely refused; Itt must necessarily bee attended with some expence, besides that I am firmly resolvd nott to come againe into Parliament.

Mr Mollineux is the person to whom I shewed your letter.

379. *Alan I, Dublin, to Thomas, at his lodgings in the Privy Garden, Whitehall, 22 Jan. 1719[/20]*

(1248/4/200–1)

… I have burnt your letter and another from a freind of ours occasioned by a letter sent to my sister under your cover: I am perfectly at ease and am satisfyed it was all mal-

---

[1044] William Lowndes (1652–1724), MP [GB] St Mawes and secretary to the treasury.

[1045] Robert Wroth (1660–1720), MP [GB] Guildford, died on 4 Feb. 1720 (*HC 1715–54*, ii, 559).

[1046] Onslow's.

ice: and for ought I know my sister and you guesse right at the contriver: I am unwilling to give entirely into those sentiments, but rather beleive it the spawn of a relation of that party: but for reasons you cannot but guesse I keep the matter entirely within my own bosome. I think every letter relating to this matter, tho couched in the darkest terms should be destroyed. One part of your letter I cannot well decypher: the Gentleman of the Law etc I took to be the Ch[*ancello*]r of the D[*uch*]y:[1047] One of the Lawyer Lords I take to be Lord I—[1048] but cannot find out the other: nor doth there seem to be much in the satyr ... I know I have not of late called for your wine licence money, but will doe it: I beleive I may have received some for you formerly, but have no entry of it that I can find: but am confident if ever I did, I gave you credit for it or ordered you payment of whatever I received some way or other. Probably you may have some more distinct notion of this then I have. [?In][1049] the Treasury I shal see what I have received and in the Clerk of the Councels office I shal see what warrants remain there for you unissued.

Dean Davies is dying if not dead:[1050] his Deanry of Corke is inconsiderable not worth more then £100 a year,[1051] so not worth my Lord D[*uke's*] favourite Chaplains taking:[1052] His son Mr Richard Davies is a very worthy man and every way qualifyed for that or a more considerable Church preferment. The animositye which hath been shewn by the Bishop of Corke to this familye for some time leaves no room for him to expect any thing from him: for indeed he is as opposite as possible to the Bishops politicks and schemes; and it will be a matter of triumph to his Lordship if another should gett this Deanry: yet I fancy Mr Mawle[1053] will be recommended by a certain person from this side whose recommendation may probably now take place of mine who have not of a considerable time had an equal share of confidence, notwithstanding all outward professions of affection, trust etc. But I am one of those people whose fate it will never be to stand favourable in the opinion of those who surround and beseige great men and alway have their ear. You know that Mr Davies is our relation;[1054] I am unwilling (after a perfect silence to or to give it a juster term a neglect of three letters) to write again; but if it be not uneasy to you I could be content you mentioned the thing as from me, and I doe not care tho you tell him why it is I doe not write a particular letter on the subject.

[1047]The chancellor of the duchy of Lancaster, Nicholas Lechmere.

[1048]Possibly Archibald Campbell (1682–1761), Lord Islay, lord justice gen. and an extraordinary lord of session in Scotland.

[1049]MS torn.

[1050]Rowland Davies made his will on 2 Sept. 1720 but did not die until 11 Dec. 1721 (*Journal of ... Rowland Davies*, ed. Caulfield, ix–xi).

[1051]A list of the values of Irish church dignities, dating from the mid-18th century, estimated the income of the deanery at over £200 p.a. (Lambeth Palace Lib., MS 2168, f. 127).

[1052]See above, p. 192.

[1053]Henry Maule (c.1676–1758), appointed dean of Cloyne in 1720; later bishop successively of Cloyne, Dromore and Meath.

[1054]The connection is unclear.

380. *Thomas to Alan I, 24 Jan. 1719 [/20]*[1055]

(1248/4/202–5)

My Brother W[*illiam*] appointed two severall days to call for a letter, Wensday the last, butt I heard nothing of him till now, when hee tells mee he goes tomorrow, I wish hee may have gott any thing by his stay here, butt make noe doubt his absence in terme is a losse. I have by this means an opertunity of telling you what has since happened, as well as what I have heard. On Thursday came on the businesse of the Callicoes, severall of the Petitioners were heard, and the further consideration adjourned to Tuesday next,[1056] what this matter will end in, I cannott foresee, butt tis plaine the popular side of the question is with the Petitioners and the country gentlemen seeme fixt uppon trying their strenghth uppon the question of prohibiting all painted callicoes and linnen being worne.

Fryday (the day of great expectation) the Chancellor of the Exchequer,[1057] in pretty generall termes opened the South Sea companyes scheme of a proposall for putting the Nationall debt in such a way of payment as might effect itt in the shortest time possible,[1058] this hee gave us to understand would bee 25 yeares, butt Mr Letchmere in the subsequent part of the debate, icked[1059] itt out to 26 years. After Mr Aisleby had spent above an hour in his harangue, the Secretary[1060] gott up, congratulated him uppon the cleare and perfectly intelligible light hee had putt the matter in, and the nation on the prospect they had hereby of finding themselves out of debt sooner then was generally expected, concluding that noe other regular motion could bee made then that the chairman should report our having made some progresse, and desiring leave to sitt againe, for that hee tooke for graunted every gentlemans being very ready and willing to receive a Proposall from the South Sea Company uppon the foote of what had been soe well opened; A profound silence ensued for a full quarter of an hour, every body expecting whoe would first rise, when the Secretary getting up, to make his motion in forme, I rose and was pointed to, I readily agreed with the two gentlemen whoe had spoake, that till the nationall debt was discharged, or att least in a fair way of being soe, wee were nott to expect making that figure wee formerly had, I sayd I could goe farther making use of the expression of a gentleman (Mr Hutchisson[1061]) whoe told us in a former session that till this were done, wee could nott (properly speaking) call our selves a nation, that therefore every scheme or proposal tending therto, ought to bee receivd and considered, butt that the occasion of my now speaking was, that the first gentleman whoe spoake seemd to mee to recommend this scheme nott onely in opposition, butt even excusively of all others, and that the next had chimed in with him, That I hoped in order to make the best bargaine wee could, every other company nay any society of

---

[1055] Partly printed in Coxe, *Walpole*, ii, 181–4.

[1056] The committee on the petition from the Weavers' Company of Worcester against the importation of calicoes, to which a large number of other, similar, petitions had been referred.

[1057] John Aislabie.

[1058] This must refer to a debate in the committee of the whole House on the South Sea Bill on Friday, 25 Jan. (*CJ*, xix, 318–20). On the background, see Carswell, 98–111.

[1059] eked.

[1060] James Craggs (1686–1721), MP [GB] Tregony, secretary of state [GB] for the southern department.

[1061] Archibald Hutcheson.

men might bee att as full liberty to make proposals as the S[outh] S[ea] company, since every gentleman must agree this to bee the likelyest way to make a good bargaine for the publique.

Our great men lookt as if Thunder struck, and one of them in perticular turned as pale as my cravate; Uppon this ensued a debate of above two hours, Our ministers (as they might in a Committee) spoake againe and againe, for their auxiliaryes provd faint hearted. Mr Aisleby in heate used this unguarded expression, Things of this nature must be carryd with a spiritt, to which Sir J[oseph] Jekill with a good deale of warmth tooke very just exception. This spiritt sayes hee is what has undone the nation, our buisnesse is to consider throughly, deliberate calmly, and judge of the whole uppon reason, nott with the spiritt mentioned. Mr Aisleby desird to explaine, sayd hee onely meant that creditt was to bee soe supported, which causd some smiling. Mr Walpole applauded the designe, and agreed in generall to the reasonablenesse of the scheme, wherein however somethings wanted amendment and others (though butt few) were unreasonable, butt concluded strongly for hearing all, as indeed every body did, three or four onely excepted. Mr Letchmere answered him, butt little God wott to the matter in hand, for quitting that hee fell into invectives against W[alpole's] former scheme, giving great preference to this. The towne sayes the bargaine with the S[outh] S[ea] company was agreed att his chambers between Mr A[islabie] Sir G Caswell,[1062] and three or four other S[outh] Sea men, since which they say Mr A[i]sl[abie] has bought £27000 stock.[1063]

Wee often observe how far passion carryes men beyond reason, and certainly interest has generally the same effect; for W[alpole] being irritated rose againe, and began with shewing by papers in his hand how very unfairly L[echmere] had represented facts, then proceeded to shew his fallacious way of reasoning, and concluded with going more perticularly into the Scheme, which in severall materiall parts hee exposd sufficiently. L[echmere] rose up (butt hee tooke time to consider whilst another had spoake) in order to reply, butt this was prevented by the whole Committee rising att once, and going into the floore, the Poore chairman tore his throat with to order, hear your member, butt all to noe purpose, other then to mortifie L[echmere] by the members crying out wee have heard him long enough. If they were nott infatuated the Specimen given them the preceding day might have taught them, when a Bill empowering the Commissioners (in a former act for finding out the longitude) to give £2000 to such person as they should judge to have made a good progresse therein, although reduced to noe certainty[1064] – The resonablenesse whereof was in a very long sett speech presst by Mr Hambden, to which little more was answered then that this was noe time to squander away publique mony uppon projects (butt the truth is twas generally understood to bee a job[1065]) and therfore concluded against passing the Bill, the Ministry marcht out att the head of 86 yeas, and left within 192 Noes.

[1062]Sir George Caswall (*d.*1742), MP [GB] Leominster; a major stockholder in the South Sea Company and a director until 1718.

[1063]Aislabie had bought £22,000 worth of South Sea stock in Dec. 1719 (Carswell, 108).

[1064]During the Commons debates on the act of 1714 (13 Anne, c. 14), 'for providing a public reward for such person or persons as shall discover the longitude at sea', Robert Walpole had successfully proposed that the sum of £2,000 be allotted for 'preparatory trials' (Tessa Mobbs and Robert Unwin, 'The Longitude Act of 1714 and the Last Parliament of Queen Anne', *Parliamentary History*, xxxv (2016), 165).

[1065]A piece of public business undertaken by, or resulting in, private gain.

Whither the Banke will make a proposall (as is generally expected) I know nott, butt am very well satisfyed many a fair pound will bee savd to the publique, even by the very proposal the S[*outh*] S[*ea*] company will make, for this affair is in a very different scituation from what they expected uppon concerting without doores; and consequently a great many will fail in their hopes for when the bargain will nott bear itt, they must bee quiett. The motion for an Addresse relating to Gibraltar which I mention in the former part of this letter, taking wind, has hitherto been delayd, uppon assurances given by the ministry to members, from man to man, that nothing of that kind should bee done, notwithstanding which I have very good reason to beleive that att this very moment itt is under consideration, butt I thinke they will nott bee hardy enough to dare doe the thing, And yett if another whisper bee true noe man can tell what lenghths they may goe.

That the interest of the Roman Catholicks of this kingdom should bee espoused by some of our most considerable Allyes, is nott to bee wondred att butt that they should thinke of obtaining what in humane probabillity must in lesse then an age establish that religion here, is surely monstrous, I will not give my selfe leave to mention the four perticulars sayd to be insisted uppon, much lesse can I bring my selfe to beleive, that any expectation of successe should bee given them, God deliver us if itt bee the case, butt noe more on such a subject. The affair of your Lords will soone come to an issue, for by adding to the first a second wise step of Printing their Representation,[1066] which (in part) has been reprinted in one of our scurvyest newspapers (the daily post)[1067] they have irritated a fresh the house of Lords, one of whom yesterday carryd that paper into the house, butt what was done thereon I know nott – however without a prophetick spiritt I beleive a man may well apply the old saying, That whither the stone hitt the pitcher, or the pitcher the stone twill goe ill with the pitcher.[1068]

I have this evening a message to attend the D[*uke*] of B[*olton*] tomorrow att ten, when I will most certainly take an opertunity of talking on a Subject which I beleive is nott what hee intends, for I thinke tis in relation to your linnen; by what Mr W[*ard*] tells me, I apprehend our great men are now for his petitioning the house of Commons, which I confesse I can nott approve of. You may bee sure some in our house will enquire into his power, supposing him to petition in behalf of the Kingdom, and this would bee a nice and very hazardous point for him to venture, whoe has noe such power. Hee is indeed empowered by the Trustees[1069] to apply to his Majesty butt I doe nott apprehend itt goes farther, and in my opinion if they intend well to Ireland, that end may bee better obtain by the Kings laying before the house of Commons a memoriall, and recommending itt. This might possibly have some weight, because they would then bee obligded to espouse itt, whereas if itt came by petition they may drop us (and probably would) as they find may best comport with what perhaps they have more att heart; I have nott ventured to give Mr W[*ard*] any opinion, butt have fairly stated to him (as far as I am capable) the reasons for and against, and then leaving him to judge, for I am nott the onely man (though I have

---

[1066] On the issue of the appellate jurisdiction; originally printed in Dublin after an order of the Irish house of lords on 2 Nov. 1719 and reprinted in London (*Historical Register*, v (1720), 90–102).

[1067] A popular daily newspaper, with pronounced tory sympathies (C.B. Realey, *The Early Opposition to Sir Robert Walpole, 1720–1727* (Philadelphia, PA, 1931), 147).

[1068] From the proverb, 'Whether the pitcher strike the stone, or the stone the pitcher, woe be to the pitcher'.

[1069] The Irish Linen Board, or more accurately the Trustees of the Linen and Hempen Manufactures of Ireland.

had my share) whoe have been traduced without the least reason, for doing what from the bottom of my heart I thought best for that country, The envy of some and folly of others is such, as ought always to make a prudent man act cautiously, and more especially when (bee the successe never soe great) you are sure of having itt overlookt att best, butt oftner some mallicious turne is given to itt; and if you faile of successe you are sure to bee bayd on by those whoe never putt a finger to the worke.

This long letter may make such hints as I may venture by post more intelligible to you.

381. *Thomas to Alan I, 27 Jan. 1719[/20]*

(1248/4/206–7)

I guesst right in what I told you by my B[*rother*] W[*illiam*]; for his Graces businesse was to consider of the best method for laying the state of your linnen before the house, which was yesterday done by Mr Secretary's laying before the house the Trustees Representation to his Majesty.[1070] After this was agreed uppon, I resolved to enter uppon what I have soe long waited an opertunity to doe, I askt my Lord Duke whither hee had read your letter, and considered the reasons therin contained, hee told mee hee had nott gone through the whole, butt would doe itt, having now receivd from Mr Sterne[1071] the minutes of the Lords house, I sayd I did nott see how they were necessary in this perticular which I thought my self (on your account) more immediately concernd in, and therefore prayed that for my satisfaction hee would tell mee whither uppon the state of the case (as you putt itt) either Lord Chancellor or any other lawyer were of opinion that the rejected Bill containd noe more then the former Bill,[1072] as his Grace had formerly told mee, hee sayd that what hee tooke unkindly (avoiding making answer to my question) was that till fryday night hee knew nothing of your dislike to the retrospective part, or that on that account you objected to itt, I told him I thought you had very fully answered that perticular, by putting itt as strongly against your selfe, as your worst enemy could doe, that itt might bee very reasonably supposed a plainer case then this might passe unobservd considering the load of publique buisnesse which lay on you, butt taking for graunted that you made a wrong judgment could hee thinke (as an honest man) you would persist against the plainest conviction; butt that I was very throughly convinct ill offices had been done, uppon supposition they should never come to your knowledge, and as I beleived by those whoe had personal interest in doing them, a further proofe of which I had very lately received, from one now in towne (a member of Parliament of Ireland) whoe told mee that the clause was calculated for the benefitt of Mr Trotter[1073] and Mr Worthington,[1074] whoe were to have a graunt of the

---

[1070] The Linen Board.

[1071] Enoch Stearne, clerk of the parliaments (i.e. clerk to the house of lords) in Dublin since 1715, and a cousin of Jonathan Swift (McKee, 'Irish House of Commons', 272).

[1072] The engrossed bill 'for securing the protestant interest of this kingdom by further amending the several acts of parliament made against papists and to prevent the further growth of popery' which had been sent to the Irish house of lords on 30 Sept. 1719 after passing the Commons, only to be rejected there (ILD).

[1073] Thomas Trotter, MP [I].

[1074] Bruen Worthington (*d.*1736), of Dublin, clerk of the Irish house of commons, a patent office he had purchased from Trotter in 1715 (Twomey, *Smithfield*, 43–4).

forfeitures by this ex post facto law, that I left him to consider whither noe body else had a finger in this, or were to receive benefitt by itt, for that I had seen a letter from Mr Hoey to Lord W[harton] the contents of which (as to your part) I repeated, telling him I had given you an account of this, though perhaps you might nott have mentioned itt to him, hee then sayd Mr Hoey was att that time in London, I told him I very well knew the letter was wrote thence, which certainly did nott in any wise differ the case; I told him hee would find that upright candid dealing was and ever would bee of more advantage to every great man then what came from selfe interested people, whoe to obtaine indirect and base ends, would alwayes represent those whoe would nott cooperate with them in dirty worke, as acting in prejudice of the person they intended to impose uppon, in short I tooke the liberty of saying freely my thoughts; to which noe reply was made; in a very short space of time when I was taking my leave hee told mee Lord M[olesworth] was a through enemy to our family, I told him I beleivd soe, and could if twere necessary tell the reason, butt that I beleivd he wer nott the onely one.

Yesterday Mr Secretary acquainted the house that a report having obtaind much without doores, and perhaps too much even within that Gibraltar was to bee parted with, hee would take an opertunity in a full house, that gentlemen might nott say they were surprizd (though I thinke wee were about 300) of making a motion for leave to bring in a bill to annex Minorca to the Imperiall crowne of this Realme,[1075] when itt would lye very fair to gentlemen to speake their thoughts in relation to Gibraltar, for that the King would always have great regard for the advice of Parliament especially to that of this house, and would in truth save his Majesty the trouble of sollicitation in case wee should bee against parting with itt, That itt might bee True that when a plan of peace was first concerted itt might have[1076] been sayd in discourse that since that place was of noe great advantage to England, though an eye sore to Spaine, an equivalent of better vallue to England might bee offered, to which itt might possibly bee answered that if such equivalent could bee thought of, itt might bee taken into consideration, butt that the King lay under noe engagement in any wise uppon this matter.

Yesterday Lord Stanhope layd before the house the papers transmitted from Ireland in relation to the Lords affair, the Lords are ordered to bee summoned for tomorrow,[1077] when twill bee gone uppon, and I beleive soone bee over, by ordering a Bill, which method I always thought would bee taken, and formerly told you that as my opinion.

They have taken into custody the <u>author</u> and publisher or more properly the <u>Printer</u>, whoe in a newspaper as I told you in my last had reprinted part of the Lords Representation.[1078] Surely they whoe were with you soe very warme should thinke themselves oblidged in honour to defray these two poore divles expences; The person whoe carrys this is just come for itt, and tis time to goe to the house, to hear what the South Sea and Banke proposals will bee, wherefore I cannott have time to say more.

[1075] Granted to Britain by the peace of Utrecht.

[1076] The word have is repeated in the original.

[1077] On Monday, 25 Jan., in response to an address from the Lords on 18 Dec. 1719, Stanhope presented to the House extracts from the journals of the Irish house of lords relating to the case of *Annesley* v. *Sherlock* and other appeals heard during the last session of parliament in Ireland (*LJ*, xxi, 210).

[1078] The publisher, Hugh Meere (*d.* c.1724) of the Old Bailey (H.R. Plomer, *A Dictionary of … Printers and Booksellers* … (1922), 202–3), and the printer, William Boreham, were ordered into custody on 23 Jan., and examined on 28 Jan. (*LJ*, xxi, 206, 213–14).

382. *Thomas to Alan I, 28 Jan. 1719[/20]*

(1248/4/208–9)

The letter my Brother carryed will shew in what scituation the project for payment of the national debt stood on fryday last, and what share I had therein; according to my expectation (and I am sure according to my wishes) itt has happened, by a proposal from the Bank delivered yesterday att the same time that from the S[*outh*] Sea was. You will observe by Mr Aislebyes opening the scheme three millions benefitt was what the publique was to expect, butt the S[*outh*] S[*ea*] company being apprehensive that their rivall might outbid them, added halfe a million thereto, notwithstanding which the Bank proposal was infinitely more advantagious. The farther consideration is adjournd to Munday, att the instance of the Chancellor of the Exchequer for others were for going uppon itt tomorrow. Being thus hard driven, a motion was this day made (butt without a question) that the S[*outh*] Sea might bee att liberty to mend their proposall; and I am told they will adde another half million, which they hope with the assistance of monosillables may doe, thus however a million is gott to the nation by my motion, and I am nott very sure whither the whole posse will bee able to carry the point, if nott wee shall gett two millions, for somuch I am satisfyed the Banke exceeds the others. This is as earnestly contended for as the Peerage Bill was, butt uppon a larger bottom, which renders the successe more doubtfull; You would have been surprised to have observd with what violence Printing both proposals was opposd, where noe argument founded uppon reason could bee brought, wee were forct to have recourse to order.

The Proposals were delivered to the Committee of the whole house, were never in possession of the house, therefore the house could make noe order for printing; This was assigned for a reason, butt the true one was very different.

The Lords satt late uppon the affair of your house of Lords. I could nott stay itt out, butt from what I heard, may (I thinke) certainely conclude, that they came to a resolution that the Barons of the Exchequer had discharged their duty etc and mention was made of application to the King for a satisfaction being made them for what they had suffered on accountt of the obedience by them payd to the orders of this house. And that the Judges bee ordered to bring in a bill.[1079]

All this I foresaw and I beleive foretold you.

383. *Thomas to [Alan I], 30 Jan. 1719[/20]*

(1248/4/210–11)

I have just now receivd yours of the 22d, which I will answer in order as twas writ ... The two Lords were Cooper and Trever,[1080] though perhaps I might mention butt one, the person you cannott decypher is Lord Conigsby, read therefore the letter againe ... I will if

---

[1079] A bill was ordered on 28 Jan. 'for the better securing the dependency of Ireland upon the crown of Great Britain'. It was far from being the last item of business recorded in the Journals for that day (*LJ*, xxi, 214).

[1080] Thomas Trevor (1658–1730), 1st Baron Trevor.

possible gett att the D[*uke*] of B[*olton*] tomorrow morning, in order to say what you doe for Mr Davies … The satyr I thinke very sharpe considering whoe twas levelld att, true jests cutt to the bone.

384. *Thomas to Alan I, 2 Feb. 1719[/20]*[1081]

(1248/4/212–13)

Yesterday the Committee of the whole house came to a resolution to accept the S[*outh*] Sea proposal, which is to bee reported (and will bee agreed to) this day.[1082]

That you may comprehend how this affair has been managed ile give you a short detaile of the whole. You know by my former letters that Mr A[*islabie*] when hee opened the scheme concluded that they would offer three Millions to the publique towards payment of the nationall debt, applauded their candour in going the greatest lenghth the thing could beare, and concluded with the great benefitt to the nation.

The South Sea company foreseeing that since the house were resolvd to hear every proposall that any other company should make, became sensible that the Banke would bee able to offer a much better, and therefore in that which they delivered in writing advanced half a million, when att the same time the Bank out bid them full two millions, this putt them under a necessity to desire they might amend their proposall, which was easily graunted, the generality of the house being for making the best bargaine for the publique. Yesterday they gave a second proposal in writing, by which they made the three millions and a half (which their [*sic*] formerly bid) four millions, payable by four quarterly payments. This they were to pay in all events, they farther offered that instead of three years purchase which the Banke had prepared to pay out of the long termes (which (for distinction) we call the irredeemable funds) they were willing to pay four year and a halfs purchase, which (uppon supposition the whole should be taken in) does amount to above three millions more, and to shew that they would truly endeavour doing soe, they submitted to pay one years purchase certaine, in the nature of a Nomine Pena,[1083] which one years purchase amounts to above six hundred sixty od thousand pounds; They had by their first proposal demanded a continuance of the present interest of five per Cent for seven years, when the whole was to bee reduced to four, which by this proposal they reduce to four years, the Banke having in their proposal offered the same, the saving uppon this head amounts to three hundred thousand pounds yearly, and lastly they propose to circulate two millions of exchequer Bills for the terme of four years Gratis, the saving uppon this head is fifty thousand pounds, uppon the whole instead of three millions which they first offered, they are now to pay above five certaine to which is to bee added the contingency of two millions and a halfe more, uppon their purchasing in the long termes, which tis their interest to doe, and consequently they will. Whoever had heard how highly the first scheme was applauded, how earnestly recommended for our acceptance and how very neare itt was to bee soe, would stand amazed that ever the publique (in any instance) should bee soe fortunate, as to more then double the summe

---

[1081] Printed in Coxe, *Walpole*, ii, 184–5.

[1082] The committee's report was duly made on 2 Feb. and the company's proposal accepted (*CJ*, xix, 246–8).

[1083] As a fine.

intended for them, butt thus itt has for once happened: Tis nott vanity in mee to say that this is due to my motion, because even those whoe I am sure wish mee ill, are pleasd to congratulate mee (from the teeth outwards) uppon the very vast advantage accruing to the publique thereby.

I will nott say the first scheme was formed in order to any perticular sett of men finding their account in the acceptance of itt, butt am sure tis plaine as the sun there was roome enough for their doing soe.

The calculators shew that by the first scheme the national debt would have been discharged in twenty eight years, and even this prospect pleased people, butt tis now demonstrated twill bee done in lesse then eighteen.

385. *Thomas to Alan I, 6 Feb. 1719[/20]*

(1248/4/214–15)

Writing in great hast by reason of latenesse Tuesday last, I forgott telling you that I had on Sunday morning attended his Grace uppon what you wrote of Mr Davys.[1084] Hee had nott then receivd any notice of his death, nor had application been made to him, though I beleive itt had then been done to another, for by considering the date of a letter, which with the memorial deliverd to you hee shewd mee last night; Lord G[1085] being then with mee, his Grace bid mee read them over, and meet him this day att the house of Lords butt hee came nott, I will therfore bee with him againe tomorrow.

The letter is from Mr Smedley,[1086] and proposes a very pretty scheme, such as in a layman would bee thought extraordinary. After stating the matter of Carigoline, which hee says D[*ean*] Davys stript the Deanery of, to accomodate his sonne, hee desires leave to treat with these two contending gentlemen and Lord Shannon, beleiving that by giving to one the Deanery of Kilalla with the livings annext, and a parish hee has in the Diocesse of Corke to the other, the matter may bee accomodated;[1087] next post ile tell you what farther passes. The Judges this day brought into the house of Lords the Bill against the Judicature of your house of Lords.[1088] I know the coppy of itt will bee sent over this night by the D[*uke*] of W[*harton*] for hee told mee soe, and sayd hee would speake against every clause in itt, and wisht all the Lords of Ireland were to heare him, I sayd I hoped this resolution did nott proceed from a certainty that what hee sayd would take noe place to which hee replyed that hee thought every Lord whoe might have any prospect of being C[*hief*] Governor should consider very well the matter, by which you see one of his inducements, I will nott

---

[1084] Rowland Davies, dean of Cork.

[1085] Probably Lord Galway.

[1086] Jonathan Smedley (1671–1729), rector of Rincurran, Co. Cork, and later dean of Clogher.

[1087] Rowland Davies resigned the rectory of Carrigoline, Co. Cork, in Sept. 1717. His son Boyle Davies (1683–1763) received letters patent for the living, but Lord Shannon disputed the right of presentation and in Jan. 1718 Samuel Webber was inducted, having been presented by Shannon. (Brady, *Records*, i, 61, 205–6.)

[1088] The bill 'for the better securing the dependency of the kingdom of Ireland on the crown of Great Britain', which eventually passed into law as 6 Geo. I, c. 5 [GB], the so-called 'Declaratory Act', regularly excoriated by Irish patriots in the 18th century as 'The Sixth of George the First'.

give my self leave to thinke itt the cheife. Yesterday the Appeale of Trevor etc was heard,[1089] Lord H[arcourt] and Lord T[revor] were warmly for reversing Lord N[ottingham] argued very strongly against itt, after which Lord Chancellor[1090] acquainted the house with his reasons for making the decree, which in a short time was affirmed without division.

I thinke there is noe maner of publique news nor doe I know any home, except that Lord Drogheda makes court to one of the Comptrollers daughters,[1091] which I take to bee pretty far advanced.

I bought yesterday another little thing in Stockbridge after the same manner I did formerly, by giving a moderate price, and setting a lease att the interest of my mony to the vendor, by which method I shall in all probabillity make itt pretty difficult (att least during my life) for any person to carry an election there against my will, though I have noe thoughts of standing my selfe on any future choice … Yesterday in a Committee of wayes and meanes they came to a resolution for taking of the Draw back uppon hops exported for Ireland, against which noe one was pleasd to speake butt my selfe; I told the chair the many difficultyes putt uppon Ireland had been soe far from being advantagious to England, that the direct contrary was very apparent; wittnesse the cattle Bill[1092] and their favourite Bill against exporting woollen manufactures,[1093] the consequence whereof had been sending thousands employd therin into forreigne parts, a wound to England which was irretrivable, that I made noe doubt this would prove of like nature, by putting the people of Ireland under a necessity of doing themselves good by planting hops: Mr Lownds was really staggerd, and willing to withdraw his motion, butt the Committee being possest of itt, would have the question, and soe itt went; The Petioners have dropt the scots linnen, butt intend to presse against Irish next Tuesday.[1094]

386. *Alan I, Dublin, to Thomas, 7 Feb. 1719[/20]*

(1248/4/216–17)

I have two letters of the 28th and 30th of last month by the pacquets which came in on Fryday morning: his Majestyes answer to the addresse of the Lords is what greatly surprizes and greives some people on this side of the water, who were told from the other that the Lords in Great Britain were weary of the businesse; nay I have good reason to beleive that my Lord S[outhwel]l wrote the very pacquet before the letters came in which shewed the ill foundation of his intelligence that nothing would be done in it: but that which is more surprising is this, that we were induced, by our inclinations to have it soe, to beleive that his Majestye would (if it came to any thing in the house of Lords) have shewn himself

---

[1089] *John Trevor et al. v. Edward Trevor, Alan Brodrick, Viscount Midleton and Lady Midleton*, in a case arising from a dispute over the estate of Lady Midleton's father, Sir John Trevor (details are given in Brown, *Reports of Cases*, ii, 122–8): John Trevor's appeal was dismissed (*LJ*, xxi, 221).

[1090] Sir Thomas Parker, now Baron Parker.

[1091] On 11 Feb. Drogheda married Charlotte, daughter of Hugh Boscawen, controller of the household.

[1092] The English act of 1667 prohibiting the importation of Irish cattle (19 & 20 Chas. II, c. 12).

[1093] The Woollen Act of 1699.

[1094] English weaving interests seeking to include Scottish and Irish linen imports in the proposed ban on imported calicoes and printed and dyed linens.

more in favour of the Lords here then his answer to the addresse seems in the opinion of people to import. But now all the discourse among that party is about an union of this Kingdome with Great Britain: methinks what hath hapned of late is a strange introduction to it. Others have determined that the Judges have private directions not to be over hasty in framing the bill, and they say it will fall that way; or else the ministry will not be hearty in it, or if they be that there is a party among the Commons which for that reason of the ministry being for the bill, will oppose it: Others flatter themselves that a bill cannot be so framed as to consist only of denying any jurisdiction in the Lords here without lodging or at least insinuating that it resides in the house of Peers of Great Britain: and that they think the Commons will never come into.

Upon the whole matter many who would not give themselves time to think or to hear-ken to reason, begin now to be of opinion that they were more prudent and more truly served their countrey who endeavoured to prevent the proceedings which lately hapned here, then they who for a short time had the vanity to publish themselves, and to gett themselves to be cryed up by sycophants as the only true Patriots. And now we are talking of Patriots, I cannot but enquire how my very good freind and neighbour in the house of Commons bears this disgrace: they tell me his actions on this occasion savour a little of Bedlam.[1095] I delivered the letter which came under cover; he to whom it was wrote mentioned not a word of its real contents to me, only he read a paragraph relating to Mr George Rogers[1096] to perswade me it contained nothing else.

In a short time I shal take occasion to remind him of what concerns both him and you nearly. I have not yet had one line from – and cannot but think he doth not treat me with common civilitye: by this behavior and from what I have formerly intimated to you I am sensible what the Great ones have determined: they are men of honour, and seldome fail to make good a promise of that nature which was made to me upon a certain occasion so long as since the time that promise was made, which is now near a year …

387. Thomas to Alan I, Dublin, 9 Feb. 1719[/20]

(1248/4/218–19)

Lord Lieutenant dining on Sunday out of towne, I came too late to overtake him, butt hee was soe very good as to sitt two hours with mee last night, I explained soe fully to him the affair of Mr Davys, that hee told mee hee was perfectly master of what hee had been entirely a stranger to, and uppon the whole, told mee Mr D[*avies*] should have the Deanery, hee hopes hee will come recommended, because twill make the matter easyer, butt takes for graunted (should Mr C[*onolly*] refuse to joine) you will nott joine for another, butt will write seperately; the Bishop of Bangor[1097] has been prevaild uppon to espouse Mr S[*medley's*] interest, how or for what reasons neither of us could guesse, his Graces answer was, that hee had promisd mee, for I must acquaint you that I made noe use of your name,

---

[1095]The colloquial name for the Bethlem Hospital in Moorfields, London.

[1096]George Rogers (*d.*1721) of Lota, Co. Cork (Reg. Deeds, 33/228/20162, 35/364/24613; Vicars, *Index*, 405).

[1097]Benjamin Hoadly (1676–1761).

nott knowing how far itt might bee necessary to say the reason why you had nott wrote on the subject; hee desired mee to excuse his nott having answered your letters wherein a great deale of businesse has been the cause, butt that hee would very soone write att large, I thinke I have sett every thing in a right light.

The Lords read yesterday the Bill relating to your house of Lords.[1098] Wee goe this day on the Calicoes, butt I think shall proceed noe farther then hearing the (unheard) Petitioners till Thursday.[1099]

388. *Thomas to Alan I, Dublin, 11 Feb. 1719[/20]*

(1248/4/220–1)

The Committee this day voted that noe painted Callicoes bee used for clothes furniture etc after a day to bee fixt.

The next question movd was that noe painted linnen bee used except the growth and manufacture of Great Brittaine and Ireland, an amendment was movd for leaving out the words and Ireland.

This bore three hours debate. The question you know must bee that the words stand part of the maine question Yeas 149 Noes 138.

They intend to attack us againe tomorrow upon the Report,[1100] I wish our freinds attend as well as the others most certainly will.

The Lords this day read a second time the Bill against the Jurisdiction of the Lords of Ireland and committed itt for Tuesday, the D[*uke*] of Wharton spoake against parts of the Bill, butt was nott seconded.[1101]

389. *Thomas to Alan I, 14 Feb. 1719[/20]*

(1248/4/222–3)

Last night I received yours of the 7th. Your people whoe flatterd themselves with nothing being done in relation to your house of Lords are surely now convinct how ill founded that notion was; those whoe from this side gave such hopes were very sanguine, or kept very

---

[1098] The Declaratory Bill, read the first time (*LJ*, xxi, 224).

[1099] The committee of the whole House appointed to consider the Worcester weavers' petition had already heard other petitions from Colchester, Norwich, and the upholsterers and quilters of London (*CJ*, xix, 259).

[1100] See below, p. 274.

[1101] Lord Perceval reported that Wharton 'was the only advocate for Ireland' (BL, Add. MS 47029, f. 10: Perceval to Philip Perceval, 15 Feb. 1719/20). Wharton made 'three exceptions' against the bill: first, against the assertion in the preamble that 'Ireland in general is endeavouring an independency'; second, that declaring cases already decided in Ireland to be *coram non judice* 'would create great confusion in property'; and third, that if the bill pass it would throw into question the capacity of the Irish house of lords to try any case (Bodleian Library, MS Add. A. 209, p. 89: Bishop Gibson to Bishop Nicolson, 11 Feb. 1719/20).

ill company, for that itt has been determined from the very moment the account of your Representation came over is most certaine; if you recollect you will remember I told you my thoughts that a Bill would bee brought in, and att the same time I thought I foresaw of a good deale of dificulty in framing itt soe, as the Commons here should nott take exception to, this is what has occasioned that false suggestion in the Preamble of a general disposition to an independency, which will bee swallowd here, and more particularly by those from whom some on your side expect assistance, for those whoe cheifly oppose the ministry in other things and whoe were the onely advocates against your linnen will I beleive exert and vallue themselves uppon having such a topick to talke uppon; you cannott surely wonder that the person you mention should act like a madman, did hee ever doe otherwise? I keep out of his way, for feare of becoming such, by a bite; his madnesse now seems sullen; I am told the Irish Peers will make speeches, butt I doubt they will bee ill supported.

What my last told you I apprehended, provd yesterday to bee rightly judged, when (uppon the report) the whole matter of the words <u>and Ireland</u> were againe insisted on, Mr Walpole (whoe had nott spoake in the Committee, and whoe I then thought reservd himselfe for the Report) argued with the utmost skill, and nott lesse ill will, with him joind his slender party, all the Toryes except three, and the North Brittaines except just the same number, uppon a division wee carryd itt to agree with the Committee by a majority of twenty five, Yeas 151.[1102] The house on this occasion was much fuller then the Committee butt the debate being long abundance went away in couples, for noe body of either side left the house without carrying his man with him; I gott Mr Ward[1103] every day into the house, and Mr Doppin[1104] was likewise soe, from whom hereafter you may probably have a more particular accountt then a letter will allow. I beleive the former is throughly convinct that my advice against printing was right, which I thought might give opertunity for artfull plausible answers, and which must of course fall into the hands of the ill judging multitude, especially since the whole substance might and would bee sayd in the debate, as indeed itt was, butt herein I had nott the good fortune to bee of Lord M[ountrath's] sentiments[1105] sentimetnts, which I was sorry for. I was told att the house to day, that an Addresse or rather a Representation (for I know nott the title of itt, translated into French) would next Tuesday bee delivered to the King by the Peers of Ireland against the Bill.

I was likewise told that some of their Lordships have been pleasd to say I should appeare a very zealous advocate for the Bill when itt should come to our house, butt misrepresenting is a little new as misjudging, for were itt nott that a more then ordinary curiousity to hear excellent speeches carryes mee to the house of Common the day when tis debated, I would sitt att home by my fire side, for I intend neither to speake or vote.

[1102]On 12 Feb. the house of commons heard the report from committee of the whole House on the Worcester petition. The first resolution, against the use of imported calicoes, was accepted; the second, to prohibit the use of printed or dyed linens except those produced in Britain and Ireland was challenged, by an amendment to include Irish linens with foreign imports, which was defeated, by 151 to 26 (*CJ*, xix, 263). According to Lord Perceval, Scottish MPs 'pressed very hard the putting out the words <u>and Ireland</u> [*sic*]' (BL, Add. MS 47029, f. 10: Perceval to Philip Perceval, 15 Feb. 1719/20).

[1103]Michael Ward, MP [I].

[1104]Samuel Dopping, MP [I].

[1105]See below, p. 275.

390. *Thomas to Alan I, Dublin, 16 Feb. 1719[/20]*

(1248/4/224–5)

Nothing materiall has happened since my last to you ... The Lords have this day gone through the Irish Bill in a Committee[1106] and have agreed without any other material alteration save that they omitt coram non judice[1107] and all the last clause except declaring the nullity of appeals, and by soe doing have annext noe penalty, ile bee particular as to some things when I find a convenient opertunity.

I hear the Irish Lords whoe mett last night att the D[uke] of W[harton's] did nott then agree uppon their intended representation.

391. *Thomas to Alan I, Dublin, 18 Feb. 1719[/20]*

(1248/4/226–7)

The Irish Lords Petition to his Majesty (signed by twenty, or one and twenty) was shewne mee this morning,[1108] itt is in as modest termes as the subject will admitt; however I am nott voyd of apprehension that if notice bee taken of itt (as probably itt will) in our house, those whoe are members of itt, may possibly fall under censure, the feare of which I take to be Lord Montraths reason against signing itt. Tis very probable a coppy may bee sent over, if soe you will see his Grace of Wharton (by the title of Catherlogh[1109]) in the front, I should thinke hee runs att least as much hazard in the house of Peers, as the others in our house; They intend to read itt to the King, and in course of things, doing soe, should fall to his share; I cannott perswade my self that twill have any effect; if nott, those whoe putt the nation as well as themselves under these difficultyes are answerable. Tis now whispe[re]d among them that I intend to declare in my place that a majority of the Kingdom are for itt. How will these penetrating men looke when they find how much they are mistaken, butt tis nott the first time they have been soe in more particulars.

392. *Alan I to Thomas, at his lodgings in the Privy Garden, Whitehall, 21 Feb. 1719[/20]*

(1248/4/228–9)

... I am glad you have gott the Dukes promise of the Deanry of Corke for Mr Davies: indeed it would have been matter of great triumph if that Deanry in that part of the countrey

---

[1106] The Declaratory Bill.

[1107] Literally 'not before a judge', used here to mean a legal proceeding that is invalid because lacking jurisdiction. The bill declared the right of the British house of lords to hear appeals from the Irish house of lords (and the right of the British parliament to legislate for Ireland).

[1108] The idea of a petition subscribed by Irish peers in London had been proposed by Archbishop King to Lords Perceval, Molesworth and Fitzwilliam, among others (BL, Add. MS 47029, ff. 7–8: King to Perceval, 25 Jan. 1719/20). The petition was presented to George I on 18 Feb., with 22 signatures (BL, Add. MS 47029, ff. 15–16: copy of petition).

[1109] His Irish title of marquess of Catherlogh (Carlow).

should have fallen into other hands, on the recommendation of Mr C[*onoll*]y who I know was applyed to and hath wrote on behalf of Dr Maule: it would really have been looked on as a designed and avowed honour done to one and indignitye placed on those to whom Mr Davies is related, and especially when it is in a countrey where our estate and freinds are, and where the other hath no pretence. As to Mr Smedley, he hath the recommending qualityes of assurance and being alway at London, and very few more, unlesse being a paultry scribbler make a man a fit dignitary of the Church. Pray be circumspect in your conduct when the bill relating to our Peerage comes into your house: You are of Ireland and know how severe and groundlesse the recitals in the bill or some of them are in the latitude they are worded; whatever ground some Lords may have given to say some men have aimed at or attempted to become independant.

Presse the sending over orders for about the Deanry. I do not expect Mr C[*onolly*]s joining in recommending him.

393. *Alan I, Dublin, to Thomas, at his lodgings in the Privy Garden, Whitehall, 5 Mar. 1719[/20]*

(1248/4/230–1)

The repeated accounts I have received of your late indisposition have given me many melancholy reflections; but the late accounts of your fit being over for the present greatly ease my mind: tho I cannot but with horror consider that the nature of your disorder is such as gives too much reason to apprehend a return with the same if not greater violence … Your indisposition I suppose prevented your being in the house when the bill about the jurisdiction of the Lords here was read the second time; and I am not much concerned at your not being in the house, tho I am at the occasion of your absence; for it would be hard for one who knows the contrary to be true to hear it suggested as if the Protestants of this Kingdome in general affected an independancy on the Crown of Great Britain,[1110] whatever handle some late proceedings may have administred to insinuate there are some who wish or mean an independancy. I have a letter from Dover Street, but truly it takes not the least notice of any former letter, and is wholly about the Duke of Ormonds pension:[1111] I answer it this post in the same maner the letter is written, but with an hint that I might reasonably have hoped the common decency between Gentlemen who converse by letter might have been observed: I never was nor will ever be dependant, and indeed I have fully returned by my pains and useful services every obligation I may be supposed to have received: but from my not going into the measures on foot when he left me behind him in London the coolnesse arose, he persists and should I have altered I had been a very poor man.

[1110]According to Lord Perceval's account of the debate Grey Neville had said of the Irish protestants that 'there is no doubt but that they are in a fair disposition to shake off their dependency' (BL, Add. MS 47029, ff. 22–5: Perceval to Daniel Dering, 5 Mar. 1719/20).

[1111]From the duke of Bolton. Ormond's pension of £5,000 p.a., granted for 15 years in 1728, had, with the rest of his property, been vested in commissioners following his outlawry. His brother Charles, earl of Arran, would subsequently purchase the entire estate, including the pension rights (*CTP, 1720–8*, p. 295).

394. *Thomas to Alan I, Dublin, 10 Mar. 1719[/20]*[1112]

(1248/4/232–3)

I have just now yours of the 5th, which I choose to own assoon as possible, though I can doe noe more. I have been four dayes below stairs, butt soe weake that I cannott foresee when I shall bee able to attend the house; Mr Allisson[1113] (whoe has this minute left mee) sayes that the Irish Bill is gone through the Committee,[1114] whoe had left out the severe imputation of a generall affectation of independency, and that of attempts to that end; had I been there I should nott have faild speaking freely as to that part, which however was lesse necessary, because when I was arguing for the linnen, I tooke notice of that false and groundlesse report spread abroad (for twould have been against order to have mentioned a bill nott then come to us) of a desire or inclination to Independency, att the same time desiring to bee understood as speaking of the Protestants onely, I thinke I was very well heard, and have reason to thinke, from what freinds have told mee, that itt has had its effect. Lord M[olesworth] I heare left the house assoone as they went into the Committee, nor doe I heare that any of the other Lords stayd, which I am nott surprizd att, for twould have been to noe purpose; The Peticion was delivered by his Grace and Lord H[illsborough][1115] privately in the closett, I beleive they were convinct, doing otherwise, might have been attended with ill consequences.

395. *Thomas to Alan I, 26 Mar. 1720*

(1248/4/438–9)

The adjournd debate uppon the Rider offered to the Irish Peerage Bill, was this day (according to order) resumed.[1116] I own I thought from the beginning such a clause impracticable, or of noe use, twould bee ridiculous to confirme by a clause what the scope of the Bill enacted to bee *coram non judice*; and a flattering saving, leaving the Lords Judgments in Ireland as they found them would surely have been of noe use, for can any body thinke butt that the inferior Courts (the reversals by the Lords being declared *coram non judice* and consequently null and void from the beginning) would nott have in fact the execution of their own former judgments? Wherfore I told Mr Ward (whoe concurd in opinion) that if any thing of this kind could bee attaind, itt must bee by setting forth (as was done here after the Restauration) the many inconveniences which would bee occasioned by altering pos-

---

[1112] [Endorsed by Alan I] '... that the bill relating to the Lords of Ireland is passed the Committee; the recitals of affecting independency left out. Lord Molesworth left the House as soon as it went into a Committee.'

[1113] Possibly Charles Allanson, MP [GB] Westbury.

[1114] On 10 Mar. (*CJ*, xix, 299).

[1115] One of the signatories (BL, Add. MS 47029, ff. 15–16: copy of petition).

[1116] John Hungerford had evidently proposed this clause on 22 Mar., to confirm judgments already made by the Irish house of lords, 'so as the bill might have no retrospect'. A motion to adjourn the debate had been carried on a division. (*CJ*, xix, 316; BL, Add. MS 47029, f. 27: Lord Perceval to Archbishop King, 29 Mar. 1720.)

sessions etc in cases long acquiesced under, and then providing (if words could bee found to answer the end) that they should remaine in the same condition as if this act had never passed; butt the rider was very different, I resolvd you know from the beginning nott to concerne my self in this affair either by speaking or voting, in my judgment I could nott bee against the Bill, and resolvd nott to appeare for what so many of my freinds were against butt my long illnesse putt both the one and the other out of my power, I meane as to the reason of nott concerning my selfe in the debate. Butt had the calculating a clause been as easy, as difficult, twould in my opinion have (this day) taken noe place.

The Secretary in the beginning of the debate declaring that hee whoe had been hearty against the imputation of affecting an independency, by the generality, should have been of another opinion if hee could have beleivd there had been soe much reason in itt, as appears by the treatment the Chief Baron mett with through the whole circuit, especially att Longford.[1117] Letter uppon letter has walkt round the house these two dayes, uppon the subject, with the most mallicious remarkes possible. Quos Jupiter vult[1118] – surely your people are mad, and will bring the nation under a treatment accordingly.

Lord M[olesworth] spoake very long butt without much attention, hee you know speakes very low, soe that I could nott well distinguish one word from another, my hearing being (since my illnesse) almost quite lost, Butt as I was told hee insisted on the Irish Lords right, for which reason hee was against the Bill. Mr Hungerford (the onely man besides whoe declared to bee of the same opinion) very well foreseeing that this Rider was as ill drawne and as liable to exception as the former, movd againe adjourning the debate, and divided the house upon the question Yeas 44 Noe 119. Then the Bill passt.[1119]

The Appeale of Arthur against Arthur was yesterday heard, the Decree affirmd unanimously, and £50 costs given.[1120]

I recover strenghth very slowly, butt hope in ten dayes or a fortnight the air may bee soe soft as to allow my going into the country, till when I expect noe releife.

I doubt you will nott bee able to make much of this confusd scrowle, butt I cannott help itt, my head is strangely disordered.

[1117] Chief Baron Jeffray Gilbert claimed that, like the other barons who had complied with the judgment of the British house of lords, he had been subjected to vilification and a campaign of petty persecution in Ireland: at the assizes in Longford in 1719 no inn would accommodate him and he was obliged to find a bed in the local army barracks (Ball, *Judges*, ii, 90). In Apr. 1719 Thomas Prior had reported that Gilbert 'received several slights and insults in the last circuit, particularly at Limerick, where the gentlemen of the country would pay him no honours, and none of them would drink with him but once, and then it was to drink to the prosperity of the house of lords of Ireland and several other healths levelled against the chief baron' (Huntington Library, Hastings MSS, box 34, HA 15576: Prior to Sir John Rawdon, 11 Apr. 1719).

[1118] 'Quos Jupiter vult perdere, dementat prius', the neo-Latin version of the classical Latin saying 'Quos Deus vult perdere, dementat prius' (those whom the Gods wish to destroy [they] first make mad).

[1119] *CJ*, xix, 321, records the sequence of events differently: first, an adjournment motion was defeated and then the rider was rejected, both without a division, then, on the motion that the bill pass, the House voted in favour 119–44.

[1120] *Daniel Arthur* v. *John Arthur et al.* The suit concerned the right to the estate of Dr Thomas Arthur (1593–1675) in Co. Galway, disputed between a grandson (the appellant) and granddaughter (wife of the principal respondent): *LJ*, xxi, 280; Brown, *Reports of Cases*, ii, 143–51.

Lord Wards case has been given att our door 3 days together.[1121] Our Mesesippi has made as many mad as that of France,[1122] and will have the same effect (I thinke) upon the buyers, those who gett early out will make great estates, butt some or other must dearly pay the reckoning.

[*PS*] Lord Inchiquin is to marry Lord Orknyes eldest daughter, hee gives £10000 and the estate of Clifden after his and Lady Orkenyes death,[1123] Lord I[*nchiquin's*] estate is calld £4000 per an.[1124]

396. *Alan I, Dublin, to Thomas, Privy Garden, Whitehall, 28 Mar. 1720*

(1248/4/444–5)

I write this early in the morning without expecting my English letters which probably the pacquett boat which I hear is just come in may bring me: If they require any thing of answer, there will be time enough to add a line to this by way of postscript. Last night I was att the Arch Bishop of Dublins who enquired much whether my Lord Lieutenant would return; I told him (as the truth was) that I had no sort of light or hint from England on that subject, at which he seemed much surprized, as beleiving me to keep a constant correspondence with the Duke. The treatment I have mett in not receiving a line in answer to any one of three letters, or indeed on any other subject, except about the Duke of Ormonds pension which I mentioned in a former letter, is a sort of treatment which I think I have not deserved from him; I also think that as a Gentleman I am intitled to better usage: but it often falls out that when men have served in such a maner and to such a degree that it is not easy to make suitable returns, the shortest way is taken by picking a quarrel and that is supposed to cancel or supersede all former obligations.

Pray let some body send me the copy of the bill relating to the jurisdiction of the Peers here as amended or altered by the Commons …

[1121] In 1699 Frances Ward lodged an appeal with the English house of lords on behalf of her under-age son Edward Ward, Lord Ward (later 8th Baron Dudley), against an adverse decision of the Irish house of lords in a lawsuit against the 4th earl of Meath. The appeal lapsed with Lord Ward's death in 1704 (*HL 1660–1714*, iv, 828–9).

[1122] The 'Mississippi Bubble' in France in 1718–20 paralleled the South Sea Bubble in Britain: it arose from speculation in the shares of the Compagnie des Indes, established by the financier John Law, which among other trading monopolies controlled the development of the French territories in the Mississippi valley. Swift wrote to Charles Ford on 4 Apr. 1720, 'I cannot understand the South Sea mystery, perhaps the frolic may go round and every nation … have its Mississippi' (*Swift Corr.*, ii, 257).

[1123] Inchiquin married, on 28 Mar. 1720, Anne, eldest daughter of the 1st earl of Orkney and after his death *suo jure* countess. The size of the marriage portion is confirmed in NLI, MS 45633/4. Orkney's principal seat was at Cliveden in Bucks.

[1124] In 1723 the rental for the entire Dromoland estate was £3,507 (NLI, Collection List 143 (Inchiquin MSS), 350).

397. *Alan I, Dublin, to Thomas, 28 Mar. 1720*

(1248/4/440–3)

I intended that this letter should have consisted entirely of the particulars which concern the late trial of Mr Cotter (son of Sir James) for a rape;[1125] but an account I just now heard from Brigadier Borre of the treatment Baron St Leger[1126] mett with att Philipstown in his circuit inclines me to transmit it to you while it is fresh in my memorye. He told the story thus, that one Low (who now is or lately was in some employment under the Crown)[1127] came to him (being observed to be familiar with Sir John St Leger) and told him, that no one of the Grand Jury would dine with the Judge, and proposed it to him to acquaint the Judge of it to prevent (I suppose) that indignitye being offered him by his not coming. Borre declined the office, but finding the Sherif (Mr Malone) had been in the Army and was now an half pay Officer,[1128] resolved to speak to Malone to break it to the Judge and told him that it would become him who eat the Kings bread not to offer or suffer any affront to his Commission; the Sherif expressed all respect for the Commission and I think broke the thing to the Judge. It hath been customary for the Judges, Sherif, Grand Jury and Gentlemen to eat together at a publick house: Sir John St Leger resolved not to bespeak a dinner separate from the company, but went to the publick house where there was a publick table (I mean a long table at which the Judges etc used to eat at an ordinary) where were the Grand Jury and a great many Gentlemen; when the dinner came up consisting of about twenty dishes, all withdrew except the Judge, Lord Tullamore, the Sherif, Brigadier Borre, one Hackett a Lawyer who came with the Brigadier,[1129] and one more (whose name I forgett but think it was Low and a person in the Kings service). They who withdrew dined it seems together in another room, and before the end of dinner a waiter came into the room where the Judge was and with a loud voice told my Lord Tullamore the Grand Jury (or Gentlemen in the other room I remember not which) drunk his Lordships health; and then he went out; and came in afterward and told the Sherif they drank his health and said that he was threatned by them that they would cutt his nose off if he did not deliver the message: the morning the Judge left the town there was a cold breakfast and large table prepared; the Judge was advised not to go thither, being assured by Brigadier Borre that by their former treatment he might be convinced none of the Grand Jury would breakfast with him: But he resolved to goe as had been usual to the publick house where a great many Gentlemen were, but they did not stay to breakfast with him but withdrew. It is true that this Judge had better luck in one respect then the cheif Baron had at Longford; where it had been usual to allow the Judge a bed in the house formerly Lord Longfords and now Mr

---

[1125] James Cotter.

[1126] Sir John St Leger, baron of the exchequer [I].

[1127] Samuel Low(e) (c.1690– by 1741), of Dublin, Cloneril, King's Co. and Higginstown, Co. Westmeath, surveyor-gen. of ordnance [I] 1718–30 (*Al. Dub.*, 513; T.U. Sadleir, 'High Sheriffs of the King's County 1655–1915', *Journal of the County Kildare Archaeological Society*, viii (1915–17), 34; Reg. Deeds, 15/457/8088, 26/189/15133; *Lib. Mun.*, pt 2, p. 104; *Hist. Ir. Parl.*, v, 122).

[1128] Henry Malone (*d.*1739) of Litter, King's Co., captain in Viscount Tunbridge's foot until the regiment was disbanded in 1712 (Dalton, *Army Lists*, vi, 246).

[1129] John Hackett (*d.* aft. 1738) of Dublin, admitted to King's Inns in 1714 (*K. Inn Adm.*, 295; Reg. Deeds, 32/321/19855, 89/415/63869).

Cuffes;[1130] and I heard Justice McCartney say Mr Cuffe promised him it should be soe now, but either his mind altered, or there was no room; soe as he was forced to take sanctuary or shelter in the Baracks; no private Lodging being found him. But Sir John St Leger had indeed a Lodging allowed him (as usual) in Lord Molesworths house; to whom the town also belongs. How far this behavior will be of service to our Countrey every body is left to judge for himself: but there is one circumstance in it very extraordinary, that some of these Gentlemen (if I understood the Brigadier right) now eat the Kings bread; but whether he means that they are now in the Army or rather in half pay I cannot tell. Be not too ready to shew this; but the methods taken to inflame people against the Barons are very successful; and I doubt not I have my share of the odium for endeavouring the [*sic*] prevent the doing that which I thought would hurt us.

I come now to Cotters case, who was tryed at Corke on 17th instant for ravishing Elizabeth Squibbe. The Judges of Assise gave the Justices an account of his trial and conviction on the 18th and in their letter not only say that the evidence was very full and satisfactory to them, but say the thing was done with great instances of barbaritye. It is pretty observable that Cotter tho found guilty on Fryday morning, was called to his sentence on Fryday in the afternoon; whereas no other person was called then to receive sentence, and the Judges were not to leave the town till Monday.[1131] You know Sir James Cotter the father, and have heard so much of the sons behavior,[1132] that you will be surprized to find the Grand Juryes both of the County and City and Gentlemen and people of the best figure became intercessors to the Justices for mercy to be extended to him:[1133] and their so doing hath put me upon considering what could be their motives for so doing. In the first place I carefully read over the minutes of the evidence given against and for Cotter (for I had them sent up to me as they were taken in Court) and cannot but say that there was room for the Jury to find as they did; the witnesses for the Crown were consistent and positive; I mean she as to the force, and others as to hearing her cry out, and being in a very ill condition after the Act committed, and being found with her clothes up and very ill and vomiting violently when Cotter left her: this I say with the verdict of twelve honest men (as I take them all to be) gives me reason to beleive the woman was forced: notwithstanding several circumstances in favor of Cotter, as her going from Kilworth[1134] in Mr Cotters company after he had attempted to lye with her there, or kissed or tumbled her; and after being cautioned by the woman of the house to beware of him; and notwithstanding her stopping

---

[1130] Michael Cuffe, MP [I], whose father Francis was a nephew of Francis Aungier (c.1631–1700), 1st earl of Longford, inherited part of the earl's estate in 1720, including a house in Longford town (*Hist. Ir. Parl.*, ii, 563; Reg. Deeds: 30/266/17245).

[1131] Confirmed in BL, Add. MS 46971, f. 32: Berkeley Taylor to Lord Perceval, 18 Mar. 1719/20. Cotter was sentenced to be hanged.

[1132] For the chequered career of James Cotter, jr, see *Oxf. DNB*; *DIB*; Garnham, 'Trials', 337–8.

[1133] Arthur St Leger, MP [I] wrote to Lord Londonderry in England to intercede for Cotter, 'a gentleman of a very good family and a very good estate … accused of rape and upon the same sentenced to die, through the means of a powerful faction of quakers who has exhausted vast sums of money to gain their villainous point'. He added that 'All the gentleman of the country together with the grand jury and the jury before whom he was tried have made a representation to the lord justices for his pardon' (TNA, C 108/421: St Leger to Londonderry, 18 Mar. 1720). This opinion was not universal among county society. Lord Perceval told his agent that 'I have no reason to doubt the justice of the law upon Mr Cotter. If his character is not wronged, there will an ill man leave this world.' (BL, Add. MS 46971, f. 35: Perceval to Berkeley Taylor, 5 Apr. 1720.)

[1134] In Co. Cork, just north of Fermoy.

and drinking her share of two bottles of wine with him at Fermoy, and her putting up his gold watch and snuff box into her pockett, which he gave to her in pledge of a glove of hers which he had taken from her: nay farther tho she lay that night at Rathcormack[1135] she never pretended there she had been injured; on the contrary being asked about it (there being a story to that effect spread by some Carryers who passed by the place where the fact was committed) she denyed it; nay went the next morning toward Corke much about the same time that Cotter left the place; and a witnesse swore she knew of the time of his leaving Rathcormuck. To all these she answered that she thought herself safe in the servant she had with her (tho she after found he had betrayed her) and for that reason was under no apprehension of leaving Kilworth; and she imputed stopping at Fermoy to the same servant. She said she put up the watch and snuff box least some travellers who were coming by might see them in her hand; and as to what she did or did not say att Rathcormuck she imputed it to an apprehension of her being in the hands of her enemyes and resolved to say nothing till she came to Corke. Nay when she came thither, tho she went immediately to her Aunt yet she owned she did not discover it to her nor spoke of it in two dayes, nor till after her Uncle (Ned Fen the Quaker[1136]) having heard of it examined her and then she told what had befallen her; but as far as I can find the fact was done on a Tuesday and no examinacions given before any magistrate till the Monday following. But considering the verdict I must take him for a guilty man: But I have heard from some bystanders (who are far from being freinds to Cotter) that there was not that tendernesse shewn toward him on his trial, as is usual in Cases of Life and death; and it is plain by the Letter of the Judges and otherwise that they have not entertained the same thoughts of compassion toward him that the countrey hath. The circumstances might move some the maner of the trial might affect others; but that to which I cheifly impute their interposing in his behalf is a real conviction of mind that he is a true penitent and will become a good man if received to mercy: In addicion to this the admirable character of his wife, and the forlorn condition of her and fowre infants, together with the having done right to the character of the injured woman, and by their verdict convinced people that facts of that nature are not alway to be turned into jests, but may and will subject people to the sentence of death; these or some other motives have induced the worthiest and most valuable men in the County and City to apply for mercy. The Quakers also joined in this application, she being formerly one of them, but becoming a convert to give her testimony: nay the woman herself hath applyed on his behalf, and owned to have received sufficient satisfaction for the injury done her.

All these things put together I confesse incline me to look on him as an object of his Majestyes mercy; I think rape is justly made a crime deserving death, but I take it that Law was cheifly made to preserve the sex from such violences; and when the wronged party owns to have reparation, I see no reason why this any more then other felonies should be looked on as not fit to be pardoned; as is daily done in case of robberyes, burglaryes and other felonyes where the criminal hath good fortune enough to be recommended for

---

[1135] Rathcormac, Co. Cork, four miles south of Fermoy.

[1136] Edward Fenn (*d.* c.1729), of Cork, a brewer (*A Journal of the Life of Thomas Story* ... (Newcastle-upon-Tyne, 1747), 547; Vicars, *Index*, 164). After Cotter's execution for the rape of Elizabeth Squibb placards abusing quakers had been affixed to walls in the city of Cork: one read 'Fenn, look sharp, and other bursen-gutted dogs besides, the which were instruments of taking Cotter's breath' (quoted in J.A. Froude, *The English in Ireland in the Eighteenth Century* (3 vols, 1906 edn), i. 481).

mercy by the Grand Juryes of the Countyes where they are convicted. But here not only the Grand Juryes of the County and of the City of Corke but all the petty Jury who found the verdict against him, the high Sherif Justices of peace and I beleive most of the Gentlemen of the County of Corke who were at the Assises have unanimously interceded for mercy. On Saturday we signed a repreive for six weeks, but Mr C[onolly] makes it a matter of great weight and nicety; a man descended from the murtherer of Lisle, who hath been guilty of several real acts of violence, and breaches of the peace, and not well affected to his Majestyes Governement hath now justly forfeited his Life:[1137] and why must mercy be extended to him? As to his being an enemye to his Majestyes Governement I beleive if they who allege it were to be put to the proof of it, he must be forced to resort to his being a Papist. You know how near our part of the countrey he lives, and if he had by any particular act of that nature distinguished himself, I think I should have heard of it. But the popular part is to appear zealous for the execution of justice, and not to doe any act of tendernesse to a man of Mr Cotters kind: for my part the representation of those who have appeared in his favor determine my judgement that he is capable of mercy; and as now advised if it lye in my power he shal partake of it. But I fancy by what I heard spoke darkely it is apprehended his estate is not settled: and if that should be so, he would be an unhappy man indeed if having an estate should have any weight against him. This I heard insinuated, but cannot think any mortal capable of being influenced to obstruct his finding mercy on so vile a motive, if he be otherwise an object of mercy. I find your Nephews name among those of his neighbours and freinds Lord Donerayle Mr Boyle[1138] Mr Hyde[1139] Mr Purdon[1140] Mr Jephson[1141] etc on behalf of Cotter; and perhaps his being soe zealous for him makes some people here averse to the thing; for they give it this turn, as if he had interest enough to have been the means of bringing in the rest to subscribe; this I am sure is false, and a most invidious insinuation. No doubt an account of this matter hath been sent into Dover Street by the hands of a person much confided in: if you read over this to his Grace you have my consent. By what I have wrote you see the sense and unanimous wish of our Countrey, as it is represented to me to be, and that ought and alway shal find weight with me.

398. *Thomas to Alan I, 29 Mar. 1720*

(1248/4/446–7)

… The trifling scandalous appeale against Conly was heard yesterday and the decree affirmed with £100 cost.[1142]

[1137] By this time it had become well known that Cotter's father Sir James had been involved in the assassination of the regicide John Lisle (1610–64) in Lausanne in 1664. Unfortunately for Cotter, Lisle's granddaughter was Lady Bolton, the wife of the lord lieutenant (Garnham, 'Trials', 339–40).

[1138] Henry Boyle, MP [I].

[1139] Arthur Hyde, MP [I].

[1140] Bartholomew Purdon, MP [I].

[1141] Anthony Jephson, MP [I].

[1142] *John Bath v. Robert and Ignatius Conly* (for which see Brown, *Reports of Cases*, ii, 151–8), another appeal from a decision in the Irish court of chancery. The Lords dismissed the appeal, with costs (*LJ*, xxi, 282).

Yesterday evening dyed Mr Doddington of an Apoplexcy,[1143] and yesterday came an accountt of Lord Montraths death att Bath.[1144] There is a report that Mr Letchmere intends to lay down his office of Attorney Generall nay tis sayd has already done soe, the latter I am confident is nott true, butt I thinke the other very probable, the cheif reason I take to bee, Mr Yorke being made sollicitor against his consent,[1145] I am told hee proposd Mr Denton[1146] (whose freinds say hee would nott accept itt) but Mr Yorks interest prevaild.

Letchmere had bought twenty sixth thousand pounds south Sea stock, every penny of which hee has sold out, and is gainer thirty odde thousand pounds.

The Lords sent us a message this day, that they agreed to our amendments to the Irish Peerage Bill.[1147]

The callicoe Bill is ordered to bee ingrosed,[1148] I think the passing itt will bee well for Ireland, for could itt have been stavd of by the E. India company this yeare, itt would have been prosecuted the next, when perhaps Ireland might have been included, butt I think twill nott be worth while to attempt that hereafter. Seperate.

I beleive they will oppose itt in the house of Lords butt without successe. I attended this Bill when others (better able and more concerned as to particular interest) thought fitt to leave itt upon mee. Last Sunday the D[*uke*] of Wharton kissed the Prince and Princesses hands, and yesterday, her Grace, the Princesses. P[*rince*] Frederick has been dangerously ill, butt tis hoped the worst is over.

399. *Alan I, Dublin, to Thomas, at his lodgings in the Privy Garden, Whitehall, 1 Apr. 1720*

(1248/4/244–5)

Yesterday I received yours of the 26th which I resolve to answer by the boat which is just ready to sail. Whether some sanguine people stil hope against hope; and as they formerly flattered themselves that the Peerage bill would meet great opposition in each house, so as not to passe: and on carrying the question for the rider, beleived when it was debated it would be carryed and would make such an alteration in the bill that the Lords would not passe it: I say as they formerly fancyed these things whether they may not now be foolish enough to expect the royal assent will be refused I cannot tell: but by their saying (considering what we have done and how little we are regarded) that we might have expected better treatment, I beleive their principals from the other side of the water have told them they have no hope of any thing of that kind. What effect this will have in time I cannot tell; at present they seem very sullen and displeased; but the nine dayes wonder will be over; and I am sure it will not be prudent in us to provoke those who can doe what they find

---

[1143] George Dodington (c.1658–1720), of Eastbury, Dorset, MP [GB] Bridgwater and former chief sec. [I]. The date of his death is given as 28 Mar. in *HC 1690–1715*, iii, 889.

[1144] The 5th earl of Mountrath died at Bath on 27 Mar. (*Evening Post*, 29–31 Mar. 1720).

[1145] Philip Yorke (1690–1764), of Lincoln's Inn, MP [GB] Lewes, later 1st earl of Hardwicke.

[1146] Alexander Denton, MP [GB] Buckingham.

[1147] The Declaratory Bill.

[1148] The bill 'for preserving and encouraging the woollen and silk manufactures of this kingdom' by preventing the use of all imported calicoes and linens (not including Irish linens).

reasonable (who can gain say them?) and may being incensed go greater lengths then they ever intended, till irritated by our indiscreet behavior.

I cautioned you not to shew the account I gave you of Sir John St Legers treatment; and repeat it, considering the ill effects the treatment of the Cheif Baron at Longford occasioned in St Stephens Chappel.[1149] I wish our freinde Lord T[*ullamore*][1150] had not too deep an hand in the thing; for it was plainly a sett thing at Philipstowne.

400. *Alan I, Dublin, to Thomas, 20 Apr. 1720*

(1248/4/247–8)

I hope this will find you returned well from Newmarkett ... Mr Hoare tells me exchange is now about £12 from Corke and cannot hold so long: your South Sea hath done us the prejudice to raise our exchange, some of our people having drawn from London at £15 to have some thing to venture in that lottery ...This letter will come soe soon after the time, that it will be easy for you to recollect whether the Duke of Bolton went from Newmarkett back to London in two dayes after his first going to Newmarkett, or staid there till the fourteenth instant on which day I know he gott to London: My meaning is to know whether a Letter which he dated as from Dover Street on the eighth was signed by him in London as it imports, or from Newmarkett as I take the truth to have been. It is a letter in which he incloses to us Mr Craggs his answer to him about Mr Cotter; I stated that matter to you at large; your letter came to hand just as you were going to Newmarkett and you had not time to talk with the Duke. I suppose his Grace was in too much hast to read over the many papers relating to that affair before he went away, and ordered Webster to lay them before the Secretary: or perhaps some letters went from people hence to obstruct Cotters finding mercy. A certain person said in my hearing when the first news of his conviction came up that his estate was not[1151] settled; which by the way proves to be otherwise; it is true he marryed under age and made no settlement then nor since: but I hear his father made him tenant for life with remainders over, and left him a power to make a jointure, which power indeed he hath not executed: but certainly the man is not in a condition to raise money: for if he were I cannot but think he would have done it when his life is not only in danger, but I think without any hope. The Secretaryes letter looks something like a reproof to the Justices for repreiving Mr Cotter; his Majestyes sense of the matter must determine me: but till I knew that would have been his pleasure I thought my self to have gone on very good grounds in extending his Majestyes mercy to one recommended for mercy by the whole County, City, Grand Juryes and the petty Jury who tryed him, nay by the person ravished: and beleive the thing might have been laid before the King in such a maner as would at least have skreened us from falling under any severe opinion of his Majestye. The best of it is every body must know, it was not in the power of any one of the Justices to have repreived him alone, so as my colleague must take his share, if there was any thing done amisse. By this and several other passages I see how I am treated by one who

---

[1149] That is to say in the British house of commons.
[1150] John, Baron Moore of Tullamore (see Appendix 3).
[1151] The word not is repeated in the original.

owes me other usage, and that I could convince the world of if there were occasion. Have you never had any answer from him, after promising it so often concerning what you have discoursed with him: But I suppose you are as faulty as I am considering the part you took in the Peerage bill and South Sea affair.

[PS] We have ten thousand storyes about this town; I mentioned that of our Privy Councel; I now find Lord Molesworth and Mr St George[1152] are also named in the number of those to be dismissed: from whom these accounts come I know not, but there are several letters in town to much the same purpose as I am told. Nay a certain Lady said in a publick assembly lately that the English Parliament at their next meeting would lay 4s on each stone of wool manufactured here, and this she said came from very good hands. Perhaps you may think her a little inclined to Jacobitism by her news, but a good deal of disaffected news is stirring.

401. *Alan I, Dublin, to Thomas, at his lodgings in the Privy Garden, Whitehall, 23 Apr. 1720*

(1248/4/251–2)

A pacquet came in last night, but no letter from you; so I conclude you were not returned from Newmarkett when the letters left town. Sure my Lord Lieutenant will have oportunityes enough to reward merit and gratifye particular freinds in the Church as well as Army. Beside Dean Jephson[1153] and the Bishop of Elphin of whose death his Grace hath had a late account[1154] I hear the Bishop of Leighlin is either dead or dying:[1155] whether my colleague hath any body in his eye I cannot tell, but am sure there need little care to be taken least fit persons should not be nominated to his Grace: Mr Webster, his Chaplain Dean Cob,[1156] and his other Chaplain Dean Crosse,[1157] in concert with Dean Hort[1158] now in Ireland and Mr Manley and others (not to mention the Bishop of M[1159]) will take effectual care to have such as they think most deserving to be in his thoughts. These continued rumors of alterations in the Councel here must have some foundation; and we now are told Lord Carpenter[1160] is to succeed Lord Tyrawlye;[1161] if soe it is probable he may be also thought on as fit to be added to another Commission:[1162] I am sure the Souldiers will be of opinion it were very good to have one of that cloth in the Civil power.

[1152] Probably Oliver St George, MP [I], since his namesake Richard St George, MP [I] would have been referred to by his military rank.
[1153] William Jephson, dean of Lismore died on 11 Apr. 1720 (Cotton, *Fasti*, i, 170).
[1154] Simon Digby died on 7 Apr. 1720.
[1155] Bartholomew Vigors, bishop of Ferns and Leighlin, lived on until 3 Jan. 1722.
[1156] Charles Cobbe.
[1157] William Crosse (d.1749), dean of Ferns, who succeeded Jephson as dean of Lismore (Cotton, *Fasti*, ii, 351; v, 189; Brady, *Records*, i, 233).
[1158] Josiah Hort, then dean of Cloyne.
[1159] John Evans, bishop of Meath.
[1160] George Carpenter (1657–1732), MP [GB] Whitchurch, 1st Baron Carpenter in the Irish peerage; a career army officer, and currently c.-in-c. Scotland.
[1161] As c.-in-c. [I] Tyrawley was indeed replaced, but by the earl of Shannon.
[1162] As a lord justice [I].

Pray give me some hints what turn our affairs are like to take; I confesse I am weary of the treatment I find from a certain person, and would be advised by you in what maner I should expresse my thoughts: for I cannnot but beleive the intent is to provoke one to quit whom perhaps they would not now directly remove: for it would be like what Erasmus wondred at in England in Henry the eights time when he saw men hanged for denying the Kings Supremacy and burnt for denying transubstantiation and Popery.[1163]

402. *Thomas to Alan I, 29 Apr. 1720*

(1248/4/255, 258)

… I am ill able to make any guesse what turne your affairs are like to take, being wholly in the darke, I know there has been a whisper of a higher remove then that of Privy Counsellors; and have heard this expression on the subject, What doe people thinke to talke a man out? the thing however has probably been aimed att, and my opinion is, that a successor is the difficulty. There can bee noe doubt I thinke in what more immediately relates to your self, act as you allways have done, with zeale for his Majestys interest, justice and candour in your post, with respect to the good of your country, and waite with patience the event of things, without giving opertunity for gratifying some peoples wishes, without which, they may find themselves att a losse, This is the part I would act, and what I would advise you, though I know twill be irksom.

403. *Thomas, Peper Harow, to Alan I, 29 Apr. 1720*

(1248/4/256–7)

… I told you in my last, that I had nott shewn your letter, as I once intended, thinking on second thoughts, nott advisable to doe itt, nor has there been att any time the least mention made to mee, of the subject on which twas principally wrote, you judge very rightly of my being in the black booke, and consequently nott consulted. Mr Secretary is allways mute, and I can act the same part, leaving them to doe as they see best … The Duke of Bolton came to Newmarkett Wensday the 6th instant, and returned nott to London till the day you mention; to the best of my remembrance hee told mee hee had receivd a letter from you just before, butt sayd noe more. I can make noe judgment whence the resolution of nott extending mercy to Cotter proceeded; nor will itt lye in my way to discover whither letters against itt, came from your side, butt am very inclinable to thinke, without any such, obtaining itt would have provd a difficult task, manet alta mente[1164] – The matter promisd to bee talkt uppon, has never been mentioned to mee, nor have I thought the resuming itt,

---

[1163]This seems likely to be a reference to the executions at Smithfield on 30 July 1540, when three catholics were hanged as traitors for refusing to the oaths of succession and supremacy and three reformers, including Robert Barnes, a friend of Martin Luther, were burnt as heretics. The story was told in Foxe's *Book of Martyrs* and in Gilbert Burnet's *History of the Reformation*. Barnes had studied under Erasmus, but since Erasmus died in 1536, he could scarcely have commented on Barnes's fate. If Alan was indeed alluding to this incident, the source of his confusion has not been discovered.

[1164]See below, p. 289.

worth while, for more reasons then one. I have you know been very little in town for some time past, nor did I, even then, goe to Coffee house, or other publique place, soe that town chatt if such there were, (which however I doubt) about any alterations designed in your councill, might escape my knowledge, I rather thinke if any thing of itt bee intended, the intelligence arises from a correspondence with those whoe can speake with more certainty, butt nothing of itt has come to mee. Tis possible you may have an accountt (which my being out of town prevents my being able to give) by whose interposition the happy reconciliation has been brought about, a good worke I am sure itt was.

I found vast benefitt by the air and little exercise I was able to take att Newmarkett, defending my selfe against the sharpnesse of the climate by perfect load of cloaths; I thought therefore this place more likely to contribute to my mending, then that, for which reason, with great regrett, I withstood Lord G[*odolphin's*] earnest desire of my going with him to the second meeting, which continues about ten dayes, for though I am here alone, I find amusements sufficient, which possibly may putt of, for a time, or att least lessen the severity of what is nott to be avoided, for I am nott any one hour togather, free from sharpe paine in my kidnyes, nor expect ever to bee. You may remember I told you of a proposall made to a freind of ours about the middle of the last session; something of like nature was hinted to the same person the beginning of this, and I am convinct with the same designe, as the former, though one would thinke one tryall of that kind sufficient, itt had noe effect, and will probably end as the other did. I am earnestly presst by a very good freind to try whither I can possibly doe a service to a man whose case is such as entitles him to the assistance of honest men; My freind having a noble parke att some distance from his house, has for some years past suffered as many others have done, till att last all his deer almost were destroyd, severall little rogues hee discovered, butt could nott come att the bigger ones, att lenghth hee fell uppon the scent of a supervisor of the excise; (a perfect Basshaw[1165] in the country) in order to his conviction hee was privately advised to summon an excise mans wife, whoe had helped to make several pastyes in the supervisors house, the poore woman having just sence of an oath, with trembling and under the greatest concerne owned the truth; the supervisor suspecting (though utterly without grounds) that the husband had privately given the intimation, soone found an opertunity of turning him out, for some neglect (or rather pretended neglect) in his duty; all the fraternity (like those of another profession) made the cause their own, and thus the man and his family are to starve. Lett mee desire you if possible to gett a promise of some businesse for him, hee is a knowing officer, and I am told of as fair a character as any of his kind, I would nott venture to advise his going over till I hear from you, though I thinke you cannott fail in such a thing.

404. *Thomas to Alan I, 2 May 1720*

(1248/4/259–60)

… I hear the parliament was progrogud last Saturday, onely to this day, a strange method surely (if true) to gett six hundred thousand pounds for making good the deficiency of the civill list,[1166] how itt came to bee soe, God knows, butt nothing is to be wondred att.

[1165] A haughty, imperious person, often an official (an early version of the Turkish title pasha) (*OED*).

[1166] In fact, only adjourned from Friday, 29 Apr. to the following Monday morning (2 May) (*CJ*, xix, 352).

The Callico Bill will hereby fall, which may please some of Ireland, butt I doubt will bee of ill consequence to that kingdom, since I fear a worse will passe att some other time, Mr Ward (to whom my humble service) knows my sentiments in this perticular.

I doe nott thinke unlikely butt that the man may influence the master, for doing soe is [?now] very hard talke, a little time will sett in the light what I am att present an entire stranger to, and possibly things may take an unforeseen turne especially if what is whisperd bee true, that the reconciliation[1167] was brought about by Lord L.[1168] and W[alpole] whoe tis sayd are heruppon throughly peiced up.[1169]

405. *Thomas, Peper Harow, to Alan I, Dublin, 11 May 1720*

(1248/4/261–2)

I have yours of the 5th. You may easily guesse the reason of writing darkly, therefore I doe nott wonder att your nott taking my meaning in every instance, the question what doe men mean etc related to the person himself, whoe askt itt, and nott without a good deale of the piquant, butt I believe twill happen as you guesse.

You take rightly manet alta mente repostum,[1170] possibly that might nott bee the onely motive, butt that twas a great one, I am confident.

The intimation of noe rejoicing might bee thought necessary, I agree twas soe, and am of opinion this might bee thought given with more safety to one then another, since there is difference in mens honour, and this wee cannott butt bee sensible of, nay shew what wee thinke, even against our wills.

Though I owe great obligations to the man, att whose instance I wrote about the excise man, I would nott putt you under the difficulty of asking a favour somewhere, which I did nott consider, for as to the mans enemyes here, they are of soe little weight, as nott to bee considered.

I am very sure my case is what Lord G[odolphin] long since told mee, I have nott crosst a horse butt once since I came hither, and then, of choice walkt half the way to Godlymyn,[1171] to attend the land tax,[1172] a repreive is all I can hope.

406. *Alan I, Dublin, to Thomas, Peper Harow, 22 May 1720*

(1248/4/265–6)

By a letter from the Duke of Bolton of the 13th I find that our recommendation of Mr Gore[1173] to succeed Sir Gilbert Dolben in the Common Pleas, and of Mr Rogerson[1174] to

---

[1167] Between the king and the prince of Wales (*Diary of Countess Cowper*, 128–46; Plumb, *Making of a Statesman*, 285–92).

[1168] Presumably the lord lieutenant, Bolton, who played a part in these court intrigues (*Diary of Countess Cowper*, 144).

[1169] That is to say, have made their peace.

[1170] Virgil, *Aeneid*, i, 26: 'it shall be treasured up in the depths of my mind'.

[1171] Godalming.

[1172] The meeting of the land tax commissioners for Surrey.

[1173] George Gore, MP [I].

[1174] John Rogerson, MP [I].

be Attorney hath taken place; but that of Sennys succeeding to the Sollicitorship is refused,
tho no body yet appointed; but in expresse words the Duke tells me he fears it will not
succeed.[1175] He saith there were two things objected to him; his being the last Session against
giving the dissenters all the ease intended by the Court: that is true, he was one of nine parts
in ten of the house that were of those sentiments: but George Gore was at least as warm
and tenacious in that matter as any one man in Ireland, yet it hath been no objection to his
having a Cushion, and I am very well pleased it hath not. The other objection was his having
the load of laying the 4s in the pound on absent officers and pensioners:[1176] in this he had
no hand as he assures me: in the Duke of Graftons Parliament it was laid on, was intended
to be continued in the first Session under the Duke of Bolton, but in a great measure by
Sennyes undertaking the thing it was laid aside in that Session; but moved again in this,
and as he protests without his knowledge; but not one word offered in the Committee of
wayes and means by the Speaker, Attorney or Sollicitor General, Secretary,[1177] or any other
of the intrusted managers, and so it went without opposition: His crime therefore now was
no more then being silent as well as the rest were. But to tell you the truth of the matter
as I apprehend it, the managers knew they had not interest enough in the house to have
thrown it out and therefore thought fit not to oppose it and at the same time expose their
own weaknesse: and it was also known or apprehended he could have stemmed it and did
not appear in it as he did in the former Session. I am a good deal in doubt whether he had
interest enough in the house without previous concerting with freinds to have stemmed
the current; for at that time the Commons had taken a good deal of pique at the managers
and at a certain persons shewing more regard to the military men and lesse to others then
they thought either of them deserved; but certainly he was under no obligation to propose
the excusing them, when he had never been spoken to nor found any of those who were
in the secrets of the Castle take up the thing. But it was worthy observing that a certain
Gentleman spoke for putting on the 4s in the pound on the military Officers who absented
themselves six months in twelve from their Posts, and likened the Pay of such Officers to
the military Pensions, which were taxed without any opposition. If this Gentleman should
happen to be made Sollicitor, either his and Mr Gores conduct were not represented as
fully as your Nephews or they are sooner forgotten. But I have told the Duke of Bolton
that I cannot but think he labours more under the load and imputation of original then
actual sin. This I took to be intended as a publick declaration to the world in what credit
his father stands with the great ones, and that it is soe understood by every body: without
expressing other dissatisfaction, or writing a word to him whose nose burst out a bleeding
when I could not be either wheedled or bullyed into favourable sentiments of a certain bill

[1175]Rogerson was promoted from solicitor-general [I] to attorney-general [I]. His eventual successor was
Thomas Marlay, MP [I]. It was rumoured in Ireland that St John was to be made solicitor-general if he would
support a repeal of the test, but that he had refused (Wake, Epist. xiii: Bishop Evans to Archbishop Wake, 7 July
1720).

[1176]A tax on income from office, first applied in the 1715–16 parliament to all office-holders who did not
reside in Ireland for at least six months of the year, except for the chief governor and army officers ordered abroad
(A.P.W. Malcomson, *Nathaniel Clements: Government and the Governing Elite in Ireland, 1725–75* (Dublin, 2005),
62).

[1177]Chief secretary.

which you cannot but remember.[1178] My wife is gone into the countrey for a little air and exercise being very far from well …

[*PS*] The Duke hath at large owned the receit of my former letters, is sure he acknowledged them, spoke of them to you (which I know to be true) assures me he hath done me justice to the King and ministry, hath the same kind thoughts for me as ever, that my jealousies etc have no foundation; is satisfyed in the matter of the bill, was only disturbed at the maner of my opposing it (I suppose he means without previously speaking to him of it). Either those professions are forerunners of some things of another nature, or are the effects of a conviction of mind that I have been more unkindly used then he can justifye to himself in his own mind, or an indication that he expects to return: The later seems the most probable, the first possible, the second the least likely of the three.

407. *Thomas, Peper Harow, to Alan I, 29 May 1720*

(1248/4/267–8)

I am nott att all surprizd att the accountt you give (of this day sennights date) of what the D[*uke*] of B[*olton*] told you, in relation to your sonne, tis what I expected, from the consideration of what you are certainly in the right of. Original sinne, for all the other pretences, will scarcely deserve even that name, which I must own I am sorry for, since were those the reall grounds, I should thinke (were the case my own) my charecter thereby better establisht, then probably I should ever have been able to bring about. I know nott butt that you make a reasonable construction uppon his Graces expression of kindnesse, hee may possibly have that in veiwe, butt wee doe nott always judge aright in our own cases; however hee has (most certainly) more good nature, and lesse of artfull designs then other people; which may in great measure answer for what hee says, what ever foote you take itt on; You may I thinke satisfie your selfe in greater measure, then usually happens to men in station, that if continuing you bee resolvd, tis from this consideration, purely, that they foresee the want of your assistance, if nott, that you shall nott want theirs. Whither the ease and quiett which I here enjoy, or the constant use of elder (in every shape) have most contributed to an abatement of my torturing paine, I know nott, butt beleive the one as well as the other has contributed therto, tho I am far from being freed from itt.

I cannott nott butt mention a paragraph of a letter which I nott long since receivd from a freind to this effect. You should come to towne, to be wittnesse of dividing the spoile, if nott to partake of itt; to which my answer was this, Lett them share the booty, whoe can earne their respective proportions by such means as I will nott.

Our neighbours were soe profuse in last nights bonfire,[1179] that wee cannott afford wood for a second this evening, and I beleive they are well contented, for to bee sure their heads ake today, or they have better constitutions then mine.

[1178] The earl of Sunderland, over the Peerage Bill (see above, pp. 245, 253–4).

[1179] To celebrate the eve of Restoration Day, a statutory public holiday.

408. *Alan I, Dublin, to Thomas, Peper Harow, 9 June 1720*

(1248/4/269–70)

… The two pacquets which came in since my coming to town bring nothing of news, at least not to me: tho I fancy from a passage contained in a letter to the Justices which came in this morning that there may be some foundation for the report we have of the Duke of Graftons being to have this Governement, and Horace Walpoole[1180] to be Secretary: the passage was this to loose no time in passing a grant of the mills of Kilmaynham to Mr Farris and his heirs at the yearly rent of £77 = 2 = 6 which is called a rack rent:[1181] but I think I should be no looser if I had them at £200. You know who Farris is,[1182] and sure his name must be in trust for somebody; for such a wretch could not I think pretend to such a grant.

We are told also that every body is going into the countrey to secure his election, the Parliament being to be soon dissolved;[1183] if that should be the case no body can deny they have done a great deal since they sate first, especially in this last Session. Not a word yet who is to be Sollicitor: nor a line in answer to mine of the 19th of May in which I wrote at large on that subject. All the livings which were vacant are filled up by the pacquets; particularly Mr Holt (a noble high flyer) hath a very good exchange given him;[1184] but what is not Mr Manlyes son in Law qualifyed for or intitled to?[1185] And one Mr D'Anvers is to have one of those livings: but who the Sparke is I cannot yet learn;[1186] I hope he is of Lord Galweys recommending. I have hitherto taken infinite pains to doe all the service in my power, and have mett such returns for it as convince me it is possible for a man to intitle himself to better usage by doing lesse for the publick. I will make my self easy, and if doing so will please soe be it: if not I will not make my self any longer a slave to businesse after the discouragements I have mett: I will neither make Court nor throw up; but doe my duty without anxiety for the successe of any thing … Lord FitzWilliams and Gowran are here; and perswade me that you are all running mad in the Exchange Alley.[1187]

[1180] Horatio Walpole (1678–1757), Robert's brother, and MP [GB] East Looe.

[1181] A very high, excessive or extortionate rent (*OED*).

[1182] In Jan. 1720 Bolton had requested a grant of the mills and weirs at Kilmainham Bridge, Co. Dublin (originally forfeited to the crown by one Francis McEvoy for participation in the rebellion of 1641) for his steward William Fariss, and on 2 May the Irish surveyor-gen. had been ordered by the British treasury to make a report (*CTP*, 1720–8, p. 3; John D'Alton, *The History of the County of Dublin* (Dublin, 1838), 635).

[1183] The Irish parliament: a false alarm.

[1184] Samuel Holt (c.1677–1763), prebendary of Lismore. In 1723 he was installed as a prebendary of St Patrick's cathedral, Dublin. (*Al. Dub.*, 408; Cotton, *Fasti*, i, 204, 314; ii, 167.)

[1185] Holt's wife Frances was a daughter of Isaac Manley, MP [I] (*Hist. Ir. Parl.*, v, 190; Swift, *Journal to Stella…*, ed. Williams, 647; *The Boulter Letters*, ed. Kenneth Milne and Paddy McNally (Dublin, 2016), 220–1).

[1186] Arthur D'Anvers (c.1686–1754), son of Thomas D'Anvers 'of Ireland', was an Oxford graduate and previously vicar of Totnes, Devon. He had served as a viceregal chaplain under the duke of Bolton and in Aug. 1720 was installed as rector of Ardagh and Clonpriest in the diocese of Cloyne (Joseph Foster, *Alumni Oxonienses, 1500–1714* (https://www.british-history.ac.uk/alumni-oxon/1500-1714/pp366-405); Brady, *Records*, ii, 22–3).

[1187] An alleyway in the City of London connecting Cornhill (where the Royal Exchange was situated) and Lombard Street. The coffee-houses on Exchange Alley, particularly Jonathan's and Garraway's, were a frequent resort of stock-jobbers. In Mar. 1720 Lady Kinnoull told her father, the earl of Oxford, that 'Exchange Alley is the place of greatest resort now' (HMC, *Portland MSS*, v, 593). Whether accurately or not, newspapers reported especially hectic trading in Exchange Alley in June 1720 (Julian Hoppit, 'The Myths of the South Sea Bubble', *TRHS*, ser. 6, xii (2002), 151, 157).

409. *Alan I, Dublin, to Thomas, Peper Harow, 12 June 1720*[1188]

(1248/4/271–2)

Yesterday I had a letter from the Duke of Bolton of the seventh by which I find he is to be out, tho he will not understand soe entirely; but I take it for granted our next pacquets will bring authentick accounts of the Duke of Grafton[1189] being declared. In the postscript he tells me that he beleives I shal partake of his fate; and indeed I little doubted being removed as soon as it was found to be convenient to their affairs. He whose nose burst out bleeding on my utterly refusing to be for the Peerage bill hath resentment enough mixed with his passion for that bill to seek the ruine of all who opposed it; and there is no withstanding the current of his present power. I beleive too your riding resty this Session hath increased the weight of my sins.

I am preparing for quitting all thoughts of Dublin or publick affairs during my life, and beleive I shal find more happinesse and peace in a private retirement att Peperhara, then I should ever have mett with, if my zeal for his Majestyes service had mett better returns from some who serve him, then they have done: but you and I have not learned to be servile enough, or to bring every body else into a necessity of dancing after the pipe of one sett of men.

[*PS*] Tho my fortune be not great I shal be able to live independant and yet handsomely

410. *Alan I, Dublin, to Thomas, Peper Harow, 14 June 1720*

(1248/4/273–4)

I never was more out of countenance then this morning at Councel, when the Door keeper came in with my Colleagues letters, and those of several Lords of the Councel; but not a line for me. Either his Grace hath altered his mind, or forgott to perform the promise he made me in his last letter to write to me by the very next post, and indeed every post while things were in suspence: or else I have not had right done me in the office. This I am unwilling to suspect, but could have been very well content to have had a line from somebody; I perceived very plainly that the opinion every body conceived at my not having no letters was either that I was entirely neglected, or that my correspondents were unwilling to be the messengers of the dead warrants being signed for me. If you had been in town I should have had intimation of what was done or doing; but a little time will put the matter out of suspence: tho for my part I reckon my self as surely out as if the Great Seal were actually put to my Successors patent who ever shal happen to be the man. One thing I will say, that if he shal be my Successor whom this town mostly agree in, I shal think the Archbishop of D[*ublin*] after his late conduct to be a most fortunate man, who hath the pleasure the man removed whom of all mankind he wishes out, and to see him succeeded by that very man whom of all the world (except himself and perhaps some other favourite Preist) he would have put into that Station … We have so cold weather that surprizes us: Ague begin

---

[1188]Printed in Coxe, *Walpole*, ii, 175.
[1189]Grafton was appointed lord lieutenant on 18 June.

afresh to rage, and abundance relapse who have had them in the Spring and thought they had gott rid of them. The Kings letter constituting Mr Boscawen (my Lord I should call him[1190]) and Sir W[*illia*]m Quintin our Vice Treasurers,[1191] was sent by Sir W[*illia*]m under Mr Conelyes cover, and that was one of the letters he received there and shewed much pleasure att receiving it. Usually things of that nature come under the Secretaryes cover, but he[1192] is a particular freind, and extremely values himself on his English acquaintance.

411. *Thomas, Peper Harow, to Alan I, Dublin, 15 June 1720*

(1248/4/275–6)

I have yours of the 9th, which I can onely acknowledge, having nothing more to say, for wee are here att perfect ease, without enquiring after news of any kind; I intend to goe to towne on Saturday, and to returne in three or four days att farthest, a letter from several Lords and gentlemen relating to a Peticion for establishing a Bank (transmitted by the Justices) is what carryes mee, butt I thinke to noe purpose. I hear nothing of a dissolution, butt wish the report prove true, perhaps the S[*outh*] Sea company may thinke thereby to strenghthen their interest, att less expence, then what creating itt, cost.

Your resolution is certainly right with respect to your future conduct; Lett things take their course, without laying any thing to heart, which you cannott helpe. The days you mention, were as cold with us as you, the weather has been soe of late, insomuch that wee have constant fires morning and evening, however itt has nott yett had its effect in Exch[*ange*] Ally, I am thought a foole for nott taking my share, butt (under the conviction I am) should bee an errant knave, if I did. …

412. *Thomas to Alan I, Dublin, 21 June 1720*

(1248/4/277–8)

I came to towne on Saturday, yesterday morning I waited on D[*uke of*] B[*olton*] and endeavourd doing soe uppon D[*uke of*] G[*rafton*] butt hee was taken up with those of too great figure to admitt of itt, however this day I did itt, (by appointment) when (if I mistake nott) twas thought I would have entred into an Eclercizement,[1193] which I entirely avoided, giving noe handle for entring uppon any particular whatever.

Your freind and mine whoe was the subject of your last, of the 12th instant[1194] acts perfectly right, advise him by all means to pursue those measures, therein mentioned, for that

[1190]The patent creating Hugh Boscawen Viscount Falmouth was dated 9 June 1720.

[1191]A privy seal was issued on 7 June 1720 for a new patent for the office of vice-treasurer [I], on the resignation of Matthew Ducie Moreton, replacing Moreton with Sir William St Quintin. The patent was issued at Dublin Castle on the 16th (*Lib. Mun.*, pt 2, p. 47).

[1192]Conolly.

[1193]*Éclaircissement*: an explanation.

[1194]Alan himself.

course cannott (in my opinion) faile of a good effect, you will surely make him understand mee without saying more.

A letter of the same date, and purport, was shewne mee, I did nott owne knowing any thing, uppon the subject, or that I had receivd any late letter from you; uppon the whole I am of opinion what you expect will nott happen, and for this I could give pretty strong reasons, as well from what I have observed, as from the nature of the thing.

I shall stay in towne till fryday, before which time I may possibly meet with an opertunity of a safe conveyance, if I doe soe, Ile write more att large.

413. *Alan I, Dublin, to Thomas, at his lodgings in the Privy Garden, Whitehall, 23 June 1720*

(1248/4/281–2)

This letter goes by Mr Hill whose occasions call him to London. Possibly the great successe which others have mett in venturing money in the South Sea or some other of the funds may incline him to make a push att increasing his fortune that way too: But his unskilfulnesse in those affairs may subject him to great inconveniences unlesse he hath some freindly advice and assistance from those who are more knowing in those matters. I know you have never concerned your self in those things, but he tells me that Mr Van Hulst[1195] and Mr Gibson[1196] are very knowing in all things of that nature; and your recommendation of him by a line to the former, or if you should happen to be in town by a word to Mr Gibson would be of use to him, and therefore pray give him that assistance …

414. *Thomas to Alan I, 23 June 1720*

(1248/4/283–4)

I have just receivd yours of the 14th … I suppose by last post a coppy of Lord Lieutenants pattent was sent, or att least the transcript of the clause relating to the continuance of the justices till his Graces arrival, which (if what I heare bee true) (and I beleive tis) hee has noe thoughts of, till next yeare, butt this is nott owned; when I waited on him, hee askt when I thought his going necessary, my answer was, that the people of Ireland always were best pleasd when a cheif Governor spent as much time among them as his Majestys affairs would admitt of, to which hee replyed surely they like justices as well, I sayd I thought nott, which possibly was nott the answer expected, butt the baite did nott soe well cover the hooke, as nott to bee discovered.

His Grace sayd hee hoped every thing would bee easy, I sayd that would bee in his power, for that doing what was right would make itt soe, I was sayd hee a white Boy;[1197] I told

[1195] William Charles van Huls (aft. 1649–1722), of Whitehall, Westminster, clerk of the robes and wardrobe, MP [GB] 1722 (*HC 1715–54*, ii, 492).

[1196] Thomas Gibson (1677–1744), of Lothbury, London, a wealthy financier and cashier to the pay office [GB], MP [GB] 1722–34, 1736–*d*. (P.G.M. Dickson, *The Financial Revolution in England: A Study in the Development of Public Credit* (1967), 286, 288; *HC 1715–54*, ii, 62).

[1197] A favourite or pet (*OED*); in this case of the ministers.

him that wee Picture mongers very well understood that a very darke shade always made the next figure appear brighter then twas, and therefore would advise nott relying wholly on that. Mr Secretary[1198] sayd, hear what old Rufler says,[1199] to which the other replyed, assure your selfe tis a just caution, thus our interveiw endid, nothing more passing then compliment.

I think youl nott have a successor soon, when tis, not him you mention.

415. *Alan I, Dublin, to Thomas, 26 June 1720*[1200]

(1248/4/285–6)

I thank you for your letter of the one and twentieth, but cannot be of your opinion in relation to what you fancy will not happen: I have all along taken it for granted I should be removed from the time I could not promise to goe into the darling bill; and you may remember I told you I had it more then hinted to me by Lord S[*underland*] and the D[*uke*] of B[*olton*] what the consequence of persisting in my own sentiments and not going implicitly into that scheme would prove to me. It is impossible for a proud man to forgive being denied the most unreasonable request; and you may be sure it caused no little ferment in his bloud, when it burst out so plentifully att his nose as it did on his finding me immoveable after all the soft and rough arguments had been made use of. But in my opinion the late order from the Lords of the Admiraltye for the Yatcht to attend immediately at Chester, to bring over the Lord Chief Baron Gilbert with his servants, and equipage,[1201] shews he is to return a greater man then he went over: the usual method hath been to apply here for an order for the Yatcht, which would have been granted immediately: but this being new makes the thing more taken notice of and creates the same opinion in the rest of the town that it did in me when Captain Lawson first shewed me the order. It is pretty odd, if it be determined that I am to be removed, that it is kept so much a secret; after its being none that some people have for a good while been preparing the way for doing it. We are not strangers to the offer made Sergeant Pengelly, and the terms of the treaty; nor to the sending for Sir R[*ichard*] L[*evinge*] to return to London: but there is some thing not yet adjusted finally to the satisfaction of the schemists. If my good freinds fancy I will throw up, they shal find themselves mistaken; for tho I know when I am ill used I resolve not to give them an handle for doing what they have only wanted a pretence for doing some time past. If I consulted my own interest I know not that man alive whom I would rather have to succeed me then the person who I think will doe soe: My honest endeavours to prevent our Lords from doing some things in the last Parliament (for which I cannot but think most of them are a good deal concerned, tho they cannot bring their stomachs to own it) rendred me for some time the butt of the rancour and malice of all who were infatuated with a notion that the Lords were doing the Kingdome service, and that those who opposed their

---

[1198] The chief secretary, Horatio Walpole.

[1199] Ruffler: used in the 17th century to mean 'a member of a class of vagabonds and rogues said to operate in the guise of maimed soldiers and sailors' (*OED*).

[1200] Printed in Coxe, *Walpole*, ii, 175–8.

[1201] His retinue: a term more appropriate to a lord chancellor than lord chief baron.

proceedings did it to make their court in England; they and their abettors were Patriots, those who differed from them were betrayers of their countrey; thus I suffered for some time in the opinion of weak men, and you may be sure my personal enemyes took care to blow the coales. Nay I was so injuriously treated that when the Cheif Baron had refused to take any notice of an order of the Lords here on an appeal from a decree in the Exchequer, tho there was no appeal brought before the Lords of Britain, I was said to have been privy to it and to have advised the Cheif Baron to doe soe: tho between you and me I never heard of the thing till after it was done, and Mr Gibbon[1202] told the story at the Cheif Barons table when the Duke of Bolton dined there and I happened to be of the company. I think people begin now to think that they were not so much to blame who told them what the consequence of their hot proceedings would be, as they were once thought to be; and perhaps it may be now thought they meant better to the Kingdome or saw farther into consequences, then some of the furious drivers of that extraordinary proceeding. This is a thing one would wish should come to passe, as I plainly foresaw it would in a little time: but when that man is made Chancellor and sits among the Lords who formerly used him very cavalierly,[1203] I cannot but think it will be looked on as the last indication in how heinous a maner his treatment and some peoples behavior to him is relished in England; and their characters must fall very low who assured people that they were weary of the thing in England, that it was an hot Iron, which they resolved to lett fall etc. An ArchB[*ishop*] and a certain Viscount of your acquaintance,[1204] tho not your freind or mine, were ever harping on this String.

This step therefore cannot I think fail of having this effect, that people will see I advised against doing those things which would never be born in England, but on the contrary would irritate them to the last degree, and acted honestly in giving that advice, and had the prudence [?to][1205] judge better of the event then the managers of that hot headed project. I cannot at the same time but think this step will lay my Lord Lieutenant under a good many unforeseen difficultyes: whether an unacceptable man will be able to doe much service among the Lords I leave you to judge, as well as whether he will be soe: but as to the matter of doing the businesse of a Speaker in the house, or of a Chancellor in preparing the bills at the Councel board, I cannot but think he will by application make himself a master of both. We have it here that our Parliament is to be dissolved and a new one called: If this be soe I cannot dive into the secret, unlesse it be this, that a certain person desires to gett out of a Post in which he may foresee more rubbs then he hath yet mett with or can well remove.[1206] But I fancy the thing is only conjecture; tho Mr Horace Walpoole I know hath sent over for a List of the Lords and Commons.

I will not conclude without telling you that it is given out among the people confided in that I was at the bottom in promoting the proceedings against the Barons: Is this so? If it be, no man on earth was ever more injuriously treated on both sides then I have been.

[1202] Phillips Gybbon.

[1203] On 29 July 1719 the Irish house of lords had passed resolutions condemning the barons of the exchequer for ordering compliance with the judgment of the British upper House in the case of *Annesley* v. *Sherlock*, and had ordered them into custody (after a division). They were only released at the end of the session. (Burns, *Politics*, i, 94–5, 99.)

[1204] Archbishop King and Viscount Molesworth.

[1205] MS blotted.

[1206] Speaker Conolly.

416. *Alan I, Dublin, to Thomas, 20 July 1720*

(1248/4/289)

I have your letter of the tenth with the enclosed paper[1207] ... which I think to be a good deal short of what might reasonably be expected; but your South Sea hath soe overturned every thing that I know not what proporcion Lands now bear to money: Delay in things of this nature is to be avoided, and I thank God I have no occasion to use any, having as much as I intend to part with on such an occasion out upon such securityes as will at any time produce ready money; tho with more difficultye now then ever; you having drained us of every penny we have: in so much that I have too good reason to beleive it to be true that travellers are obliged to run in debt on the roades, the Inkeepers not having silver to give in change for Gold ... I find Mr Crookshanke of Twickenham[1208] is very knowing in the South Sea and hath the character of a very honest man; I wish you may know him or somebody else to act for me if my sister and you shal go into my sentiments of venturing my Lottery tickett money in the new subscriptions.

417. *Alan I, Dublin, to Thomas, 29 July 1720*

(1248/4/292–3)

By a letter from Ally dated the twentieth I have the very disagreeble account of your having had a severe return of the stone, from which and all other miseries God protect and deliver you.

I formerly hinted to you that I had an account from Mr Lake[1209] that he understood from Mr Methuen that the great ones had been pushing att me, but without successe: That Gentleman[1210] hath alway acted toward me with great honour and freindship, and I am much obliged to him for it: he remembers how truly I endeavoured to serve and support his father against his enemyes here. What I infer from this attempt is not that the design is over: perhaps things could not be brought to bear in the short time allowed for considering our little affairs; but by the treatment I have mett with all along, especially since my flatly refusing to goe into the Peerage Bill I am sensible the Lord who spoke to me on that subject will never be at rest till he hath gott me removed: and his power is too great to be withstood, where there is no need of assigning a fault; it is enough that his Majestye hath no longer occasion for ones service to stop ones mouth from complaining; you held att will, and the Kings pleasure is that you continue no longer in your employment must silence any man who happens to fall under a great mans displeasure. But as for shewing in what I have neglected to do my duty, or done any thing contrary to it in the Station I

[1207] A proposal from Robert Monckton (c.1659–1722), of Cavill Hall, Yorks., for terms of marriage of his son John with Alan's daughter Alice. John Monckton eventually married a daughter of the 2nd duke of Rutland.

[1208] John Crookshanks (d.1738) of Heatham House, Twickenham, who was among those borrowing substantial sums of money from the South Sea Company (R.S. Cobbett, *Memorials of Twickenham: Parochial and Topographical* (1877), 67; TNA, PROB 11/693/350; Dickson, *Financial Revolution*, 196).

[1209] Francis Lake, his secretary.

[1210] Methuen.

now hold, I may without vanity or danger defye my enemyes. If Mr C[onelye[1211]] hath not more vanitye then I can imagine him possessed with (tho I own he hath a great deal) he keeps a very familiar correspondence in Bond Street: One day his minions talk of a mighty kind letter received, the next his Lady reads a letter from a certain Dutchesse; att the Lord Mayors last Thursday he pulled out two snuff boxes, offered the choice of the snuffs, and said the snuff in one of the Boxes was a present from his Grace of some just come to him from Holland. Now tho it may be reasonably expected that a letter of complement should find an answer, I doe not think it very proper to have such letters read or publickly shewn; yet that this is done to support an opinion of a great interest is most certain. But this hath been the practice of a long time; and now I will tell you that a certain Gentleman shewed about and read a letter from the D[uke] of B[olton] with words in it to the effect following: That his Majestye had acknowledged and thanked him for the great services he had done him in Parliament here; and then the letter proceeds to subjoin this question; And to whom doe I owe the having done those services but to the good advices given me by my dear freind Mr C[onolly]? You may be sure that I did not see this letter, but you may be as sure that a letter hath been shewn, and the import of it is trumpeted about to be much to the effect I mention: Nay I have it from so good an hand that I cant doubt the truth of it, that he saw a letter in which there were such expressions of Mr C[onolly's] s services, as certainly far exceeded his desert, and consequently were highly injurious to another, who without thanks hath done every thing to carry on the Kings businesse happily, and hath seen another make merit of what his endeavours and advice produced and effected. It is not my businesse to resent my treatment farther then I have already done; but I am sensible the D[uke] of B[olton] toward the end of the Session was misled to beleive unkindly of me, and am confident he then not only did not do me right in representing my services as they deserved, but did all he could in favor of another; and I beleive he now finds and is concerned for having taken such a step, I mean for not having done me justice: for I know the hold which another hath of him by such mean insinuating methods with his dependants and creatures as I abhor the thought of. When you see him pray in a pleasant maner tell him of this letter, and ask him whether he owed all his successe in Parliament to any one mans advice, and whether Mr C[onolly] was that man? My wife desires to have a plan of the now old house at Peperhara, that she may see what rooms and conveniencyes are to be found there, if it should be our lot to sett up our rest there … My Lord Cheif Justice Whitshed is (we are told in town) going for England: he pretends to have a great interest in Lord Sunderland and Lord Townesend. If they will ask one mans opinion, they cannot be long att a losse into whose hands the Great Seal may best be committed if there be occasion for a remove …

418. *Thomas, Peper Harow, to Alan I, 3 Aug. 1720*

(1248/4/298–9)

Yesterday I receivd yours of the 29th of last month, itt came to London on Munday, by the post marke, butt how I cannott imagine, unlesse the male came directly to Chester, or that

---

[1211]Blacked out in original.

you mistooke the date, the former I thinke most probable. I am nott att all surprizd att the correspondence you mention, nor much att the letter you say is shewn and boasted of, you know in one case the writer is a weake man, and the other (I meane the former) a very artfull one.

What you mention from Mr Lake is too well grounded to admitt of doubt, butt still I continue my former opinion that matters are nott ripe, and possibly never may.

You know that what was built by Lord Holles[1212] is a drawing roome, a bed chamber, and a little roome beyond itt, over which there are three rooms, the garrets were never floord, (though admirably timbered), butt may uppon occasion, over the great eating roome are two chambers, this is what that part toward the garden contains, the Hall and remaining part of the house is onely fitt for servants, Mrs C[ourthope] (whoe is gone to London about your lottery tickets) will informe you better as to this part of the house then I can; The S[outh] Sea Directors having last Wensday come to a resolution to take in a moyety of the Redeemables as well as Irredeemables (nott yett writ [?in])[1213] and appointed doing itt by opening books next Thursday, her going was necessary, because your tickets are lockt up, where noe other can come att them, though I question whither itt bee nott already determind, whoe shall (att this time) bee admitted, if soe, I fancy you will nott bee of the number, nor can I pretend to judge whither that may bee for the better or worse, for they are too big to say on what termes, that nott being to bee declared, till they see how people stand affected, butt I suppose after the termes declared any one whoe writes in, may withdraw his subscription, if hee thinks fitt, the option therfore being left, was what induced mee to advise her going to towne, and making an offer. The thoughts of subscribing next time into the stock (which your last letter mentioned) is out of doors, by a resolution of the companyes to admitt none butt those whoe have original stock or were subscribers to the first or second subscription, and these onely in proportion to their stock or subscriptions, butt what the proportion will bee I thinke nott fixt, att least I doe nott know itt, butt am told tis nott to exceed a fifth part. I am entirely att a losse to find what the gentleman means whoe vallues himself uppon the favour of a £2000 subcription att 300 unlesse by thinking people whoe understand nothing of the matter may take this as a signall marke of favour. There have been three subscriptions, the first att 300 the second att six hundred and the last att a thousand, if his were of the first twas a favour which every cobler might have had, bookes being opened for all, and little did they expect its filling soe soone as itt did.

If it bee in either of the other two, itt is indeed a favour, for tis just so much mony given as 300 falls short of the respective prizes; Tis nott in the nature of the thing that the company should make this abatement for that would make five hundred enemyes, by gaining one freind, which I beleive they would think too hard a bargain, if there bee truth in the story, and that without equivocation, itt can be reconciled noe otherwise then thus, that the person making the compliment may have had the subscription in the first, and after seeing to what a price the last rose, might (if hee pleasd which seems very improbable) give the benefitt away, by taking onely his first cost againe, which, as I sayd before, is equivalent to a present of just as much mony as the difference amounts to, this is all I can think of the

---

[1212]Denzil Holles (1599–1680), 1st Baron Holles.

[1213]'Redeemable' and 'irredeemable' annuities on the National Debt: titles to these annuities were to be deposited with the company in readiness for the terms that would be offered to convert them to South Sea stock (Carswell, 161–4).

matter. Collonel Stephens late knight for the county of Gloster … is long since dead, and Lord Berklyes brother chosen in his roome[1214] …

419. *Thomas to Alan I, 13 Aug. 1720*

(1248/4/263a–b)

… Before the receipt of your last my Brother L[*aurence*] shewed mee your letter, I had been presst by Mrs C[*ourthope*] att the instigation of Mrs B.[1215] to come into that matter, as what would bee very advantagious to Ireland, as well as to the undertakers; my answer was that I should never decline what might conduce to the former, even though nothing of the latter were in the case, and thefore would come into itt, uppon that foote, if I saw reason to beleive twould take effect. My Brother's letter (which I returne to you) has stated the matter (in the maine) well enough, I will therfore now tell you my thoughts uppon the whole. I thinke a Company impowered (by charter) to insure against fire, in Ireland, nott very likely to make advantage therof, for that I much doubt whither the number and vallue of houses, thus to be insured, will answer the expence of offices etc. Tis true that in this great opulent citty, tis far otherwise, butt they will I doubt bee mistaken whoe take measures from hence; The danger of a suddaine and great fire, ought to bee ballanced with a probabillity (att least) of proportionable gaine, and this I apprehend will nott prove the case in a poor country; Tis true sayes my Brother if this alone were intended, there would bee force in the objection, butt what is cheifly in prospect as the most likely to prove gainfull, and att the same time advantagious to the kingdom, is, that the company will deale in exchange, by which (allowing they transact that businesse att much a lower rate then usuall) very great gaine may bee made; Butt this will depend uppon what may possibly nott happen; Their Directors as well as those employed by them must bee men of skill, and great integrity, otherwise twill fare ill with the Proprietors; This very consideration has allways created an aversion in mee against going into the stock of great companyes, for every body (whoe observes att all) very well knows, Directors lick their own fingers, too much, to allow considerable profitt to others. I thinke therefore this very liable to the objection, in a very great degree, when I see Sir A[*lexander*] C[*airnes*] intended to be casshier, and other exchangers to bee deeply concernd, will they nott with Demetrius consider that twill sett their craft att nought,[1216] and consequently may bee reasonably supposed to have a good prospect of ballancing that losse some way or other.

[1214]Thomas Stephens (1672–1720), of Lypiatt Park, Gloucs., died on 24 Feb. 1720. Hon. Henry Berkeley (aft. 1682–1736), of Berkeley Castle, Gloucs., was elected in his place on 30 Mar. following. (*HC 1715–54*, i, 243, 456–7; ii, 444–5.)

[1215]Possibly Laurence's wife, Anne.

[1216]Acts 19: 24–7: 'For a certain man named Demetrius, a silversmith, which made silver shrines for Diana, brought no small gain unto the craftsmen; Whom he called together with the workmen of like occupation, and said, Sirs, ye know that by this craft we have our wealth. Moreover ye see and hear, that not alone at Ephesus, but almost throughout all Asia, this Paul hath persuaded and turned away much people, saying that they be no gods, which are made with hands: so that not only this our craft is in danger to be set at nought; but also that the temple of the great goddess Diana should be despised, and her magnificence should be destroyed, whom all Asia and the world worshippeth.' A list of subscribers to this company can be found in SHC, 1248/8/135–7. Several similar schemes were proposed in Dublin at around this time (Rowena Dudley, 'Fire Insurance in Dublin 1700–1860', *Irish Economic and Social History*, xxx (2003), 24–5; Walsh, *South Sea Bubble*, 82).

Mr Brother lett mee into a farther matter, which I chose rather to passe over without remarke, then to make what occured to mee, Lord Lieutenant hee sayes will make (as hee beleives) a favourable Report, butt att the same time intends soe far to lay his hand on itt as to dispose a great number of shares, and by his letter you see his Grace intended to bee Governor with these (as hee tells mee hee apprehends) court is to bee made to the officers of the army; Tis nott to bee imagined butt that the greater number of these, will bee for selling out assoon as they shall bee enabled soe to doe, and thus will itt become a stock jobbing company, the reall bane of all companyes, for though power of transferring bee in every case, absolutely necessary, yett what is originally formed with that veiwe, must in my opinion come to nothing; There remains yett another difficulty which I did nott care to mention to him; In order to obtaine the Act against Bubbles, passt last session,[1217] A question was putt to the Attorney Generall etc[1218] whither persons acting as a corporate body by vertue of a charter could legally deale in any other thing then what the charter appeared originally to intend, I am told they answer negatively, with this addition, that by soe doing the charter becomes forfeited; I was nott in the house during the progresse of the Bill, butt from clauses printed in publique papers (by way of caution) am fully convinct, perticular care has been taken in wording the Act uppon this head, possibly itt may nott extend to Ireland, butt suppose itt does nott, nothing is gaind hereby, butt an exemption from the powers given by the Act for bringing actions, and recovering theruppon by the persons whoe suffer losse by such practice, the opinion as to the forfeiture stands still in force, and what will bee a forfeiture in England, will you may conclude nott bee thought lesse soe in Ireland.

All that I thinke necessary att present to bee done, is following your directions, of taking care that you bee nott excluded, nor yett engaged beyond power of retreate.

Captain Butler is the same you mention to have married the widdow Raines,[1219] I have nott yett seen him, butt beleive (from what my Brother sayd) that I soone shall. Nor have I had the honour of waiting on Lord Lieutenant since my coming to towne, though I have attempted itt, after telling Mr Secretary I intended doing soe, I was yesterday att ten a clock told his Grace was gone abroad, butt that shall nott prevent my going againe, twill bee butt my labour lost, if I have the same answer. The person whose signall favour in giving the two subscriptions is boasted of, made the same compliment to his Apothecary, and to some others of a lower ranke; which argues abundance of good nature, or that wee did nott thinke the thing soe valluable, as itt afterwards proved, thankes to the mad men, whoe made itt soe …

420. *Alan I, Dublin, to Thomas, Peper Harow, 4 Sept. 1720*

(1248/4/304–5)

Last night Justice MacCartney returned from his Circuit and mett a letter from the Lord Cheif Baron Gilbert who was appointed to go the Circuit with him, and for whom a late

---

[1217] The so-called 'Bubble Act' (6 Geo. I, c. 18 [GB]).

[1218] Nicholas Lechmere, attorney-general [E], and the other English law officers.

[1219] Elizabeth, daughter of William Culliford (*d*.1724), revenue commr [I] 1684–8, 1690–2, was married three times: to Boyle Aldworth (*d*.1698), John Raines or Raynes, and finally Captain Butler.

sitting was appointed in one County to intitle him to his hundred pounds;[1220] this letter he shewed me which imported that he should not return again into Ireland as Cheif Baron and hoped he should be provided for in England: that he had spoken and would speak for MacCartney to succeed in the Common Pleas (so that if he be not provided for in England the Chief Justiceship of that Court is not in his view) but that he beleived that Cushion would not be soon disposed of; and that the matters relating to Ireland are not yet settled.[1221] I cannot but think that the provision they intend for him here (if that shal be his case) will be the Great Seal: for I fancy he will not be desirous to exchange for the Kings Bench, which is a post altogether as laborious and very little if any thing more advantagious. By the Duke of G[*rafton*]'s not answering or taking notice of two letters of mine in favor of Justice MacCartney I think I have reason to beleive my self not kindly used; they might deserve being owned, whether they had any effect or not: But I suppose Lord S——[1222] is to bring over the last orders, and I cannot but beleive the Cheif Baron was intended by my fast freind to be my Successor from the beginning. How they will adjust matters among the Gentlemen who happen to be in their good Graces I cannot tell: which I take to be the Chief Justice Cheif Baron Sir Rich[*ard*] Leving and Justice Gore. I really am weary of this treatment and wish it were over; and if other people do not put an end to it, I must take the only method left. I wish when you are in town you would a little expostulate with his Grace.

421. *Thomas, Peper Harow, to Alan I, 4 Sept. 1720*

(1248/4/306–7)

I shall goe to towne sooner then I intended, the S[*outh*] Sea directors having given notice that they would doe something (what I know nott) with the Proprietors of the redeemable funds, that this something is to bee a catch, I thinke very plainly appears from the short time by them limited, viz between the 12th and 17th instant. Your Lottery tickets are of this sort, and Mrs C[*ourthope*] nott being able to goe, on accountt of illnesse, I must, least you bee among the number to bee surprized.

They alwayes expresse themselves in termes capable of very different constructions, and you may bee sure enterpret their meaning in that sence which shall bee most advantagious to them att the time; The mighty and suddaine fall of stock has a good deale surprized them, the plan for its falling, was beyond controversy layd by themselves, in order to bite those whoe had agreed for great summes att 1000 for the opening their bookes, itt has had the designed effect, for those whoe by buying Bulls and Bears[1223] have formerly gott immense summes, must now refund a great part of that gaine, which they (as interlopers) had taken out of the mouths of the favourites for whom the scheme was intended; thus far

---

[1220] His 'travelling charge' on circuit.

[1221] The talk in Ireland was that Alan was promoting the candidature of Macartney to succeed the ailing John Forster as lord chief justice, while Conolly espoused the claims of George Gore (Wake, Epist. xiii: John Pocklington to Archbishop Wake, 9 July 1720).

[1222] Possibly Lord Shannon, recently appointed c.-in-c. [I].

[1223] Speculating that stocks will rise (bull) or fall (bear).

itt goes well with the company, butt they did nott foresee, or att least would nott beleive themselves incapable of putting a stop to the fall of stock, whenever they thought fitt.

However soe itt proves nor will all their skill and power drive itt up againe, without giving greater advantages then ever they intended, for men begin to thinke more coolly, they examine more closely into what figures will bring togather, instead of running with the stream into chimerical calculations. What therfore these fall short of coming something near vallue, must bee made up att the companyes loss, to avoid an irretreivable sinking, which becomes the more likely to happen from the scarcity of mony, The cash of Europe is nott somuch as would answer the bargains now in being, hitherto paper creditt has supplyed the place of specie, and this twill allwayes doe, whilst creditt makes paper equall to mony, butt when that begins to bee made a question, the consequences are very obvious; The vast summe (above 1000000 every body agrees) carryed away lately by a certaine sett of people, that shall bee namelesse, will have itts effect, and this I think will soon bee very vissible.

Wee are told itt is a child of our own begetting, and must therfore bee supported by us; I fancy a little variation in the proposition would make itt a true one; in the case of bastardy the person charged by the mother, is oblidged to keep the brat, though God knowes hee had noe share in getting itt, however hee must maintaine itt and this I truly thinke to bee the case of the nation.

By what methods this Foe Pa[1224] shall bee retreivd I know nott, butt done itt must bee or some of those fatall consequences (which I always dreaded) will fall uppon us, sooner then I expected, God preserve us in peace. The D[uke] of S[omerset] has been inquisitive after your coming over, itt will bee certainly necessary (without losse of time) that you write to him about your election, if you thinke of coming into Parliament nay if you should nott, which I beleive will nott bee the case, twill bee very fitt that you acquaint him with your resolution,[1225] returning your thanks for his past favours, pray loose noe time, for I dare say hee will speake to mee uppon itt, when wee meet att Newmarkett …

422. *Alan II to Alan I, Dublin, 10 Sept. 1720*

(1248/4/316–17)

… We have no news here, but the Countrymen are in great hopes of a new Parliament, that they may make their South Sea of the Candidates …

423. *Thomas to Alan I, 13 Sept. 1720*[1226]

(1248/4/318–19)

I came (as I told you I would) to towne, in order to adjust the matter of your lottery ticketts, pursuant to the advertisement from the S[outh] Sea company; yesterday was the day appointed, butt (as is customary with them) they have putt itt of, and those concernd are

[1224] *Faux pas*: false step.
[1225] Alan did in fact stand for re-election, successfully, at Midhurst in the next general election, in 1722.
[1226] Partly printed in Coxe, *Walpole*, ii, 190–1.

to wait their Leisure, and take such satisfaction as they thinke fitt to give. Wee made them kings, and they deale with every body as such; those whoe submit and subscribe are att their mercy, those whoe doe nott are to bee opprest in such manner as shall make what is due to them of little use, and all this I suppose they are to bee supported in, having engagd the house of Commons soe far in their interest, by wayes obvious to every body, that I thinke the nation will bee to beare such part of the losse sustained by private persons, as the company shall thinke fitt, whilst the gaine obtain by fraude and villanous practises is to turne to their advantage. I foresaw this from the beginning, and have as many witnesses of itt, as persons I convert with, butt I owne I thought they would have carryed on the cheat somewhat longer. Various are the conjectures why they suffered the cloud to breake soe early, I made noe doubt butt twould doe soe when they found itt for their advantage, which nott being the case just att this time some other reason must bee found, and the true one I take to bee stretching creditt soe far beyond what twould beare that specie proves deficient for supporting itt, by circulating paper. Itt is observable that many of their most considerable men, with their fast freinds the Toryes Jacobites and Papists (for these they have allalong hugged) have drawne out, securing themselves by the losses of the deluded thoughtlesse numbers whose understandings were overruled by avarice, and hopes of making mountains of mole Hills. Thousands of familyes will be reduced to beggery, what the consequence of that will bee, time must shew, I know what I thought from the beginning, and feare tis very near att hand. The consternation is inexpressible, the Rage beyond expression, and the case soe desperate, that I doe not see any plan or scheme, soe much as thought of, for averting the blow, soe that I cant pretend to guesse att what is next to be done.

I feare the people of Ireland have nott onely lost all they soe precipitately and madly returned over to bee employed in this chimericall project, butt have likewise run soe far on score[1227] that they will never bee able to shew their heads,[1228] whilst these were pouring in their little, a wiser generation were carrying out what mad men brought in; with great difficulty, and nott without vehemently displeasing I prevented Misses running headlong, our neighbours att Godlymyn gott immense summes and every body did or might doe soe, whose abundant caution did nott make them thinke themselves wiser then the rest of mankind, butt the event has provd whoe judged best, the one sort (though butt few) are where they were, the others cannott shew their heads, some must fly their country, others goe into Goals; for whatever shall bee done to support this favourite company, under the specious pretence of maintaining creditt, those whom they have by their wicked practises brought to beggary, will bee left in that condition, and all this to make a small number (comparatively) great men. Mr Hill told mee last night hee would write to you, from him you may expect a more perticular account then I can give, for hee goes among them, which I hate doing, nott being able to bear itt.

I had by yesterdays post (from Pepper Hara) your letter of the 4th. I know nott whither what you mention might have been intended, butt I thinke this will nott bee thought a proper time.

Before I went out of towne I attempted twice or thrice waiting on the D[uke] of G[rafton] butt had nott the good fortune to find him, I did the same againe uppon my returne, butt

---

[1227] On credit (*OED*).

[1228] For Irish investment in South Sea stock, see Walsh, *South Sea Bubble*, esp. ch. 4.

with like successe; last fryday I saw him on the Tarras[1229] in St James Street, I alight out of my chariott, to tell him how unfortunate I had been, his answer was that hee had heard of my being att his house, that I knew unlesse great men were denyed their doing businesse would bee impracticable, butt that hee thought I had known better then to take that answer, I told him I never thought taking up such mens time reasonable, when I had nothing more to say then that I was their humble servant.

Hee askt mee when I heard from you, I told him nott lately, I had lately sayd hee, a letter from him desiring to bee in my list when the Irish Insurance should bee agreed to,[1230] which you may rallie uppon, I sayd I might then say you should when hee made one; noe sayes hee, for hee may from thence possibly infer the thing in agitation, and in short turnd it into ridicule; Hee went last Saturday to Euston till the kings returne.

424. Thomas to Alan I, 27 Sept. 1720[1231]

(1248/4/320–1)

Last night came yours of the 18th with the inclosed for the D[*uke*] of S[*omerset*] which ile deliver assoone as hee comes to town, hee is hourly expected in his way to Newmarkett.

In speaking of dividends etc you are allways to understand onely capitall stock, nott what is payd for itt.

When I last came to towne in order to demand back your ticketts or a better consideration for them, I found vast numbers of people had been before hand with mee in the like demand, to whom noe positive answer was given, their spoakesman Mr H.[1232] explaind him selfe indeed as you mention, butt little regard was given to what hee sayd, for if hee bee nott foully belyed hee neither says or does any thing for nothing, I mett him in the Ally accidentally crossing itt, for the place I abominate, and gave him to understand what I as well as thousands expected, and I beleive should bee able to obtaine.

The company have yett come to noe determination, for they are in such a wood that they know nott which way to turne, butt tis given out (I suppose by direction) that they will lower the price of the third and fourth subscriptions, and offer more reasonable termes to the Redeemables, leaving to their option the acceptance, or returne of their severall securityes, these to remain on the foote they are, till dischargd by payment in mony. Noe doubt att first they intended nothing lesse, butt as Mr Budgell[1233] told them in the generall Court, since the Mountain would nott come to Mahomet, hee must goe to the Mountaine.[1234]

[1229] Terrace.

[1230] See above, p. 301.

[1231] Partly printed in Coxe, *Walpole*, ii, 191–2.

[1232] Possibly Archibald Hutcheson, MP [GB] (J.H. Plumb, *Sir Robert Walpole: The King's Minister* (1960), 340; Carswell, 179; *HC 1715–54*, ii, 163).

[1233] Eustace Budgell: for his extensive losses in the South Sea Bubble, and its catastrophic effect on his finances, see Eustace Budgell, *Memoirs of the Lives and Characters of the Illustrious Family of the Boyles …*, ed. Donald Brady (Waterford, 2003), ix; and for his own views on the crisis, Eustace Budgell, *The Case of the Annuitants and Proprietors of the Redeemable Debts. In a Letter to the Author of the Several Calculations on South-Sea Stock* (1720).

[1234] Eustace Budgell, *The Speech Made by Eustace Budgell, Esq; at the General Court of the South-Sea Company, in Merchant-Taylor's Hall, on the 20th of Sept. 1720* (Dublin, 1720): 'I am very glad, sir, to find, that since the mountain

You misunderstood mee in thinking I expected a speedy dissolution, that had been considered and layd aside, notwithstanding which, as earnest application was every where making as if elections were to begin within a month, this was begun by the S[*outh*] Sea men, and great sumes have they already spent, butt if I mistake nott they will meet with more disappointments then they expected, for by severall gentlemen lately come to towne I perceive the very name of a South Sea man growes abominable in every country.

Your remarke is very just that if this great Leviathan intended to have been Directors of the whole national affairs, as well as of the company, doe fall, itt will necessarily occasion such a convulsion as no honest man desires; Butt I think there remains a middle way between the two extremes, by supporting their creditt as far as in reason itt ought to bee supported, distinguishing between what ought properly to bee calld creditt, and chimericall calculations, and the one is certainly practicable without running into the other. A great many goldsmiths are already gone of, and more will daily, I question whither one third nay a fourth can stand itt, the cause of which is this, those whoe had either originally, or by buying with mony gott by taking differences, run into pretty considerable quantityes of stock, nott being therwith content, butt resolving to sitt down with nothing lesse then hundred Thousands, in order to obtaine which, gave vast praemiums to the goldsmiths for mony, pawning their stock some att four others att five and six hundred, this being lookt uppon as good as land security, The mony thus lent by the goldsmiths was in cash notes, which whilst paper had creditt, answered the end as well as specie, butt assoon as a run was uppon them, they found (by reason of the stocks sinking) their pledges would nott produce cash to answer their notes, and thus one after another are they every day going of.

From the very beginning I founded my judgment of the whole affair uppon this unquestionable maxim That Ten millions, (which is more then our running cash) would nott circulate two hundred millions, beyond which our paper creditt extended, that therfore where ever that should become doubtfull, bee the cause what itt would, our noble state machine must inevitably fall to the ground, or att best bee brought within soe much a narrower compasse then what was projected that our most sanguine people would find nothing more appositely expressive of their vain hopes then Parturiunt montes.[1235]

I endeavourd with an honest and freindly intention to perswade as many of my freinds as I convarst with to secure the main chance, and nott dip (att least) out of their depth in case they should resolve to goe with the current, some few were prevaild uppon by such arguments as I thought well founded, whose hearty thankes and acknowledgments I have received, butt the far greater part concluding (as I must own I did) that the thing would have been carryed on for some longer time, have on this supposition run themselves aground, which they dearly repent.

Into this were they generally lead by assurances from the Gent whose nose bled,[1236] and whoe himselfe was certainly duped by the honest Directors from whom hee received information, whilst they were all the time (underhand) selling out as fast as they could. That hee was duped I thinke past doubt, from his having by his influence, brought all his

---

[1234] (*continued*) will not come to Mahomet, Mahomet is going to the mountain; or, in other words, that since you cannot raise your stock to your subscriptions, you are prudently bringing down your subscriptions to your stock.'

[1235] 'Parturiunt montes, nascetur ridiculus mus': Horace, *Ars Poetica*, 13 ('Mountains are in labour; a ridiculous mouse will be born').

[1236] Lord Sunderland (see above, pp. 290–1).

perticular freinds, and even his owne family and nearest relations soe far into the mire, as that few of them will during their lives surmount the losse, others of them, soe totally undone, as to bee beyond possibillity of retreiving itt. Possibly before the end of next session I may bee calld a S[*outh*] Sea man, for I shall nott join with those whose losses have soe far exasperated them as to bee desirous out of revenge to run into extremes which may endanger the nation.

425. *Alan I, Dublin, to Thomas, 8 Oct. 1720*

(1248/4/326–7)

… We are here in utmost confusion, through the news from Gibraltar[1237] and the dismal accounts every body receives of the dreadful effects of your South Sea businesse. I beleive, not many of our merchants have directly dabbled there, but God knows how many of the smaller pins the ninth pin may throw down,[1238] if that chance to fall: I mean how many of our merchants may be ruined if a few great ones in London should fail. Here hath been a great run on the Bankers, but they have all hitherto stood it, except one Swift who however is I think an honest man, and able to pay every body.[1239] The good nature of the town hath thought fit to lay his misfortune at the door of Ben. Burton a brother banker;[1240] but really I think with out cause … If greater affairs did not employ the thoughts of our great men, one would think it were time to name a Cheif Justice of the Common Pleas, a Sollicitor General, and that we should have the Exchequer fuller then it hath been of late.

426. *Alan I, Dublin, to Thomas, 18 Oct. 1720*

(1248/4/330–1)

The letters which came in yesterday have brought me the certainty of what you and I have long known was intended;[1241] and I am now uneasy at nothing so much as that I am not yet discharged and at liberty to doe (what I have been forced of late too much to neglect) my own private affairs. But that which truly and to the bottom of my soul afflicts me is that the ill state of my poor wifes health, which hath been rendred a great deal worse by the unfortunate conduct of her younger son, hath I fear been much encreased by the part she takes in my ill treatment: I have done and will doe all in my power to comfort and support her; but by a letter I received from her this morning (for she is now in the countrey but will be in town tomorrow) I have very great apprehensions of her. Other people take comfort in their sufferings when the calamitye is general; but my own private misfortune hath no weight, in comparison of the pressures I lye under by my concern for the general miserye

---

[1237]Rumours in London newspapers that the Spanish monarchy was resolved to insist on the return of Gibraltar as an essential prerequisite for a peace treaty, followed by reports of a build-up of Spanish troops in Andalusia and the issuing of orders that all officers in the Gibraltar garrison return to their posts (*London Journal*, 3–10 Sept. 1720; *London Gazette*, 6–10, 17–20 Sept. 1720).

[1238]From the game of ninepins.

[1239]James Swift (*d.*1749), no relation of Jonathan, ran a private bank in Eustace Street, Dublin (*Letters of Marmaduke Coghill, 1722–1738*, ed. D.W. Hayton (Dublin, 2005), 5).

[1240]Benjamin Burton, MP [I].

[1241]His dismissal as lord chancellor [I].

under which such infinite numbers of people labour and are irretreivably sunk. Advise me what to doe; supposing my wife be able to undertake a Sea voyage and a journey afterward, can I doe better then carry her immediately to the Bath and if I find I may doe it without cruelty to her, after spending some time with her there, take a step to London to shew my self at Court and in the Parliament house after my disgrace. The maner of my removal galls me more then the thing itself: Have I done or suffered soe little for – to be treated with neglect and have marks of displeasure laid on me. When I next endeavour to please I will take the right course, and provided I make my Court well to the first minister may be induced to think I have better consulted my own securitye and advantage then by pursuing what I have hitherto thought it my duty to have cheifly in my eye. What reason have I to blesse God that I have not been carryed on to ruine the acquisitions of a long and painful life by being in the fashion and ruining my self and familye in the common abysse! And how many obligations have I to you for your constant advice to the contrary. This morning at the Castle my Lord FitzWilliams shewed us a list of names which he received out of England, which according to the best of my memorye were as followeth. Kingston[1242] Wharton all the Boltons, all the Scarboroughs,[1243] Carlisle,[1244] Lonsdale,[1245] all the Princes servants men and women, Hillsborough, the Cockburns,[1246] the Foresters,[1247] Ladyes Gainsborough,[1248] Burlington,[1249] Pembroke[1250] Lady Anne Harvey,[1251] Lady Greenvile,[1252] all the Scotch as well in the South Sea as in the York buildings:[1253] I need not say what the condition is to which his intelligencer saith these persons are reduced: he shewed it with true concern. I hope things are not soe ill with any, and beleive they are not with a good many of this number as represented: but alas what is this number to the multitudes who must have suffered in this miserable havock. What can be the end of these things, and what may not a nation in our condition fear if an advantage should be taken of the present scituation of our affairs. Upon my word the person who is now placed at the head of the Treasury hath an ample feild to shew the great man;[1254] and if methods can be found now to extricate us out of our difficultyes, it will redound to the everlasting honour of the instruments. But

---

[1242]Evelyn Pierrepont (1665–1726), 1st duke of Kingston-upon-Hull.

[1243]Richard Lumley (c.1650–1721), 1st earl of Scarbrough.

[1244]Charles Howard (1669–1738), 3rd earl of Carlisle.

[1245]Henry Lowther (1694–1751), 3rd Viscount Lonsdale.

[1246]The Scottish lord of session Adam Cockburn (1656–1735), Lord Ormiston, whose son John was MP [GB] Haddingtons. and a lord of the admiralty.

[1247]William Forester (1690–1758), MP [GB] Much Wenlock.

[1248]Elizabeth (née Chapman) (d.1771), wife of Baptist Noel, 4th earl of Gainsborough.

[1249]Juliana, dowager countess of Cork and Burlington.

[1250]Barbara (née Slingsby) (d.1721), second wife of the 8th earl of Pembroke.

[1251]Lady Anne Harvey (née Montagu) (d.1742), wife of Daniel Harvey, MP [GB] Weymouth and Melcombe Regis.

[1252]Grace Carteret (née Granville) (c.1677–1744), widow of George, 1st Baron Carteret and *suo jure* Countess Granville.

[1253]The York Buildings Company, originally incorporated in 1690 as the company 'for raising the Thames Water at York Buildings', diversified its activities in 1719, acquiring large quantities of forfeited estates and, like the South Sea Company (although on a smaller scale), was the subject of speculative investment which ended in a crash at the same time as the bursting of the South Sea Bubble.

[1254]Robert Walpole. Alan is jumping the gun here, for Walpole did not take up the post of 1st lord of the treasury until Apr. 1721 (on his position at this time, see Plumb, *King's Minister*, 320–3).

at the same time I think he risques very little in undertaking so difficult a province, and tho his successe should not answer his wishes he will be sure not to leave things in a worse condition then he found them. There will need aboundance of temper the next Session, or else we are irrecoverably lost; and if I come to Parliament I resolve to shew it, forgetting the usage I have mett.

427. *Alan I, Dublin, to Thomas, at his lodgings in the Privy Garden, Whitehall, 22 Oct. 1720*

(1248/4/332–3)

Before this can reach London I take it for granted that I shal have received the letter for appointing me a Successor: but I write to you to desire you to send me the earliest account of the steps taken for my governement. It is not usual to appoint a Chancellor of this Kingdome under the Great Seal of Great Britain, and there appeared soe many difficultyes in the doing it, that the Regency would not supersede Sir Constantine Phips in that maner,[1255] altho his having with the Primate and some others of the Councel paid very little respect to their orders in another matter, made some of them inclined to have done it that way.[1256] I doe not beleive Mr Gilbert will be made Chancellor in that unusual maner; but if he should I would willingly have the earliest intimation of it, that I may desist acting the moment I hear his Commission is under the Great Seal of Great Britain: but probably this is an apprehension of mine for which there is no foundation. I should be glad also to have as early an account as may be who are to be Lords Justices; I suppose the new Chancellor and Mr Conollye; that I may know when I shal be again at liberty to attend my own affairs. Neither the Duke of Bolton (tho he promised to doe it) nor my Lord Lieutenant hath given me the least hint of my disgrace; but Delafay was too full of joy to contain it. I thank God I goe out before the nation hath to the full felt the consequences of the South Sea scheme and it is a comfort to me that I find my freinds are they who were deepest in that noble contrivance, which is to pay the Nations debts.

428. *Thomas, Peper Harow, to Alan I, Dublin, 26 Oct. 1720*

(1248/4/336–7)

I have just now yours of the 18th and will nott loose this post, in telling you that I thinke you cannott doe a righter thing then bringing my sister immediately to the Bath, itt will in all probabillity bee of great use to her, and att the same time give you an opertunity of coming to towne, which on all accounts is advisable.

In the meane time assure your selfe that one mentioned in your list, is nott under like circumstances with the others, butt in his stead a vast number more might bee added.

I am oblidged to goe out this minute, and had done soe ere now butt that I waited for the post, I will very soone write to you …

[1255] In 1714.

[1256] In relation to the Dublin mayoralty (see above, p. 149).

429. *Alan I, Dublin, to Thomas, 3 Nov. 1720*

(1248/4/338–9)

I have yours this morning dated the 26th October from Peperhara; and think you advise well that I should go immediately into England: but as I have hitherto born that treatment which would have provoked any body but me to have laid down long since, soe I resolve to continue to doe it for the reason I have done it hitherto; that is, that they who have long had it in their resolution to remove me may not have it to say that I quitted the Kings service: I am sure it was expected the usage I mett would have made me peevish, and prevailed on me to quit without being laid aside: but I doe not owe them soe much, as to furnish them with that pretence for my not being in his Majestyes service: and if they should cast about to find out a reason, perhaps they might be att a losse: for the true one will never be given by my great freind. By this means I know not when I shal be my own master, and possibly a good part of the Session may be over before I am actually removed; but to remain under sentence of death without being put out of pain is more uneasy then death itself. And indeed I think if my wifes state of health would allow of her now crossing the Seas and performing a journey to London, I should be able to find a way to gett free from the uncertainty I am now in as to the time of my being superseded in the Seal and Governement: but this I am firmly resolved of, not to act in the later (except in bare things of course) after being removed from the former; nor to act at all after there shal be two on the spot to act as Justices: but in this particular I suppose I need not be sollicitous; for I take it for granted, I am to be removed from being one of the Justices and to loose the Seal at the same time: But my wife is too weak to undertake such a fatigue yet; and there is no consideration shal induce me to presse or allow her to doe any thing that may endanger her, who is weak beyond what you will easily imagine; and I am sure I owe her too much not to be as tender of her life as of my own; tho I should have only the losse of her person in her death: therefore I passe by the annual income which her jointure produces, because not to be named in comparison of herself: otherwise an additional losse of £1200 a year to that of my place would be considerable. Who is he that hath not suffered equally with the rest of the List? Is it the Duke of B[*olton*] or Lord Hillsborough. There is not a penny of money stirring in the countrey. This time seven years it would hardly have obtained credit, if it had been foretold I should now meet the usage I am like to doe: Pray what did my good freinds doe at that time for the Hanover succession, when I at the peril of my Life and fortune exposed my self to the rage of a party, to whom some now great men paid an entire submission? or at least made very faint and secret opposition. Under Queen Ann [*sic*] Governement I carryed the chair of one house, and seven years after have deserved to loose my seat in another place … I hope my Successor will deserve better.

430. *Thomas, Peper Harow, to Alan I, Dublin, 11 Nov. 1720*

(1248/4/340–1)

I have just now yours of the 3d. I never thought of your coming over till you were superceded, you know I always was of opinion that you ought to putt your enemyes in the wrong, and they find themselves soe.

Surely they will appoint justices when a Chancellor, I am sure if they doe nott, businesse should stand, and lett them answer for the consequences.

Twas nott the D[uke] of B[olton] butt Lord H[illsborough] which I meant.

The weather has been fine beyond conceiving during the whole autumne, butt especially of late, which has given an opertunity of finishing (I hope) what I thought must have been deferd till Spring, for a few dayes will doe itt, I designd staying here till the latter end of next weeke, butt I beleive by the Guns which wee heard very plainly this morning, the king is landed, if I find itt soe tomorrow att Guilford, ile goe as far as Ripley after businesse is dispatcht for the country,[1257] in which case you shall have a letter by Tuesday post …

431. *Thomas to Alan I, 15 Nov. 1720*

(1248/4/346–7)

… I came to towne on Sunday night, a my last told you intended, you will therfore thinke itt strange that I should nott bee able to say wither the order for your delivering the Seale were yett gone, this morning before eleven I endeavourd seeing Lord Lieutenant on noe other account then information herein, butt was told hee was gone abroad, surely wee are grown very secret, or there is some great mistery in this affair, for watt att other times you might bee satisfyd in by any under clerke in the office, I cannot come att from any hand whatever. I have sent a freind to one whoe I know can tell if hee pleases, and hope before I seal this to have an answer, Mr Gilbert I am told is still here. I am told that strong assurances are given of every thing going smoothly on your side, I think both you and I can easily guesse from what quarter, I am sure I heartily wish they may bee in the right, for tis more then enough to leave one kingdom under the inexpressible distraction this labours att present, Tis sayd that when the day comes (the 25th instant) for the parliament meeting, wee shall (by message) adjourn for some days, wiser heads then mine must determine how far doing soe may bee prudent, butt possibly they may thinke some time necessary to consider how and where to begin, I dare confidently say noe mortall can foresee where things will end.

S[outh] Sea stock fell yesterday above twenty per Cent, whither from the Bank having advisd with Councill how far they were bound legally by the agreement for taking what the south Sea was to pay them, in stock att the rate of 400, or that this is a finenesse[1258] of the Directors just before the meeting of the parliament I cannott pretend to judge, butt either case sufficiently shews the perplexity of affairs.

432. *Thomas to Alan I, 18 Nov. 1720*

(1248/4/344–5)

I write this, though not on a post day, to the end I might more perticularly informe you of what just now passed between the Duke of Grafton and mee in the parke, whilst the

---

[1257] In Surrey, seven miles north-east of Guildford.
[1258] Finesse.

whole is fresh in my memory. I told his Grace I had endeavourd waiting uppon him att home, butt misst the honour of seeing him, to which hee replyed, I will tell you how that happened, I was when you calld under Dr Lambs (the corne cutters) hands.[1259] I told his Grace my business was to have beggd the favour of knowing when I might hope to see you; hope replyed his Grace, yes indeed my Lord I can give itt noe other terme, for mankind is generally desirous to have that over, which hee knowes is to bee done; I doe assure you sayd hee, I have nott been spoken to uppon the subject, nor have I askt any question about itt.

I told his Grace hee could nott butt bee sensible that I knew what letter hee had receivd att Newmarkett from Mr Secretary. I receivd none sayd hee there, well my Lord sayd I, that will nott much alter the matter, for if nott there, you had one att Euston either the day or day before you were att Newmarkett, as to that sayd hee, I both wrote and spoake what I thought proper, having nothing to doe with any exception that might bee taken before my time, I told his Grace, I was very sensible this was the case, for that a man of great quallity sayd to mee, (directly) that whoever in the kings service would nott give his vote in the house of Commons as the ministry should thinke reasonable, ought to lay down his employment, the subject of discourse being the Peerage Bill; and therfore I assurd his Grace I was very fully satisfyed with the cause of your removal, to which his Grace replyed, twould bee a jest (that was the word hee used) to putt itt on any other foot.

I then sayd I thought they seemd to make you much more considerable then they ought, for that I could nott butt thinke, and I beleivd many might bee of the same opinion, that the delay was cheifly with intent to prevent your attendance in Parliament to which his Grace replyd that hee did nott thinke they had that in veiw; this was what past, except a short compliment to each other, personally, and I am very sure a good part is repeated verbatim, and the whole in sence.

Mr Gilbert being lately askt by a Gentleman whither hee might wish him joy, replyed, I know nott, for nothing is yet done, and perhaps may nott. Uppon the whole you were to bee turned out, butt without maturely weighing whoe might bee a proper successor; whither this delay proceeds from Mr Gilberts diffidence of his nott being able to carry businesse through, (for something like this I heard) or that others may bee of that opinion, remains (as to mee), in the darke, butt I am nott without hope that this conversation may expedite, what I most earnestly long for, the seeing you in a short time.

Things here are in soe melancholy a scituation, that I avoid making perticular mention of them, onely in generall Ile venture to say that the Ministry have a large feild wherin to display their abilityes, and if they can sett things to rights they will convince the world that they are able and very great men.

[1259] A chiropodist, who was well enough known to be described in 1764 as 'the noted Dr Lamb of corn-cutting memory' (*Public Advertiser*, 13 Apr. 1764), but this may have been owing less to professional skill than to the fact that the eponymous 'corn-cutter' of the *Corn-Cutter's Journal*, a pro-government newspaper of the 1730s possibly written by John, 'Orator' Henley (Michael Harris, *London Newspapers in the Age of Walpole: A Study of the Origins of the Modern English Press* (1987), 117), was one 'D. Lamb, a Caledonian corn-cutter and professed scribbler' (*Corn-Cutter's Journal*, 24 Sept. 1734).

433. *Thomas to Alan I, Dublin, 24 Nov. 1720*

(1248/4/352–3)

The Parliament is to bee prorogued to this day fortnight, I suppose by Proclamation, for there is to bee a Councill this night.

The reason given is the not being ready to lay sooner before the house the scheme proposed, and which is sayd to bee founded uppon an agreement made between the Banke and S[*outh*] Sea companyes, which (as reported) Mr Walpole[1260] has seen, and declares hee thinkes will doe; if the Reporters would change a terme, possibly they may bee in the right, that is, instead of agreement call itt a proposall, for I have very good reason to beleive no agreement is yett concluded, wherfore I thinke a fortnight little time enough for bringing itt to bear, since there is a possibility of its never being effected, youl easily judge the perplexity of affairs.

I cannott say a word more then I have told you, of your own affair, probably their thoughts are fully employd in what is of more consequence.

434. *Thomas to Alan I, 26 Nov. 1720*

(1248/4/354–5)

The Parliament was yesterday prorogued (by Commission) to the eighth of next month,[1261] uppon account (as is sayd) the adjusting matters with the Banke, uppon which the scheme to bee layd before the house must bee founded, would take up a fortnight, which beyond question is true, supposing they were agreed in the most material parts, butt I thinke tis far otherwise, for I am pretty well informd that on Thursday night there was a wide difference touching the Price the Banke should allow for S[*outh*] S[*ea*] stock to be taken from the others, how far the one may comply or the other recede is uncertaine.

I resolved against loosing the opertunity of speaking to the D[*uke*] of G[*rafton*] being pretty sure of finding him att the House of Lords; I desired to know whither orders were yett gone into Ireland, which he answerd in the negative, I told him twas a very cruell thing to keep you there when you ought to bee here, uppon which hee sayd hee beleivd they would goe in three or four dayes, I told him I hoped I might rely uppon their doing soe, notwithstanding I very well knew that Mr Gilbert had absolutely refused accepting the Seals; hee told mee some people had made the king very angry with you, to which I answered, that I was very sorry any ill impressions of you should bee made uppon his Majesty whom you had servd with the utmost fidelity, and nott without pretty good successe, butt that he knew I was very sensible uppon what occasion some great men had taken up their distast, and that I was very sure were the thing to bee done over againe, you would act the same part, being throughly convinct of its being right; since the minute I first heard of Gilberts hesitation, I concluded the game was to bee playd into Mr Whitsheds hand, to facilityte which, (and perhaps by advice from your side) I am confident those whoe are least freinds

---

[1260]Robert.

[1261]By a proclamation of the lords justices [GB] (*CJ*, xix, 377).

to you have been as forward as any in expressing the impracticablenesse of his carrying on the Kings businesse, and have gone soe far as to say Sir C[*onstantine*] P[*hipps*] would have been a fitter man, this latter part I know to bee true, butt the motives I can onely guesse att, though possibly the event may warrant my coniecture, and I am nott free from suspition that the project for a total repeale of the Sacramental Test (with respect to Dissenters) may have great weight with your greatest enemy; nor doe I thinke itt lesse probable that the assurances given from your side, might bee in order to this, as what would bee most likely to attaine the end aimed att; if this should bee soe, I shall as little wonder att a disappointment in this, as I doe att the failure of many other notable projects. I am sure I had suficient reasons for pressing your being soone discharged, butt between ourselves I never mentioned what stuck closest to mee.

Tis now above a fortnight since a whisper has been of a ship from Marseilles directly (and which was driven of our southerne coast by a man of war) being gott into the Isle of Man,[1262] I know orders went last post for guarding your coast with souldiers in order to prevent any landing from that place; this was occasioned by a letter from the shire of Gallaway (in scotland) nott onely confirming that ships arrival then, butt likewise that the plague was actually broake out uppon the Ireland, this letter came on Thursday, I pray God itt bee nott too well grounded, wherfore lett mee begge your coming away immediately, for I thinke the art of man will nott bee able to prevent persons landing in some of your criques whoe will run all hazard to gett out of an infected place, and may carry the infection with them. I need nott caution your nott mentioning this reason, since you have so many other good ones, for your immediate coming away …

435. *Thomas to Alan I, 1 Dec. 1720*

(1248/4/356–7)

The Kings letter lyes still in the hand of one of the clerkes. The Cheif Baron has severall times endeavourd waiting on Lord S[*underland*] butt has as often missed the opertunity of that honour. I have onely my guesses why this is delayd, nor when twill bee thought fitt to putt an end to itt; under this uncertainty you att a distance are as good a judge as wee on the place; The Duke of Grafton is going into the country, even this affords matter of speculation and may proceed from either of two very different sources; hee told mee this morning that hee did soe. I have by this nights post sent your letters to Mrs Courthop, in order to her directing mee where to come att the best Gascoignes powder,[1263] which Ile send assoone as possible, they are all att Pepper Hara, chiefly by my perswasion in order to fit every thing as well as may bee for your reception, for I beleive you will find itt most advisable to goe directly thither, till a fitting house which may please my sister can bee

---

[1262]During the summer of 1720 there had been a serious outbreak of plague at Marseilles which had produced a panic in Britain (C.F. Mullett, 'The English Plague Scare of 1720–23', *Osiris*, ii (1936), 484–7). In September the Irish lords justices and privy council issued a proclamation imposing a quarantine on all shipping coming into Ireland from the Mediterranean (*Proclamations*, ed. Kelly and Lyons, iii, 103–6).

[1263]Gascon's or Gascoigne's Powder, a highly expensive concoction widely used as a 'cure-all' remedy: the ingredients included crab claws, bezoar, pearl, and coral. Reputedly effective against plague.

pitcht uppon, which may bee hard to find, butt as for Lodgings none are to bee had, dead rent[1264] has been payd for all good ones 3 months past.

436. *Thomas to Alan I, 3 Dec. 1720*

(1248/4/365–6)

… This day I spent in the citty, the better to informe myselfe how matters stood there, for a word cannott bee depended uppon which wee are told. I beleive what follows to bee true. The Banke being presst to come into measures with the South Sea company, gave for answer, That when the Parliament mett, they would (if desired) lay their proposalls before the house, butt would nott doe itt elsewhere.

Yesterday a generall Court of the E[ast] India company was held, where twas proposd that a power might bee given their Directors to hear what termes should bee offered them for the advantage of the company, butt this was exploded with bitter speeches, Lett any such proposals (if such can bee) bee layd before the Generall Court, weel delegate noe power, and thus itt ended in the utmost confusion.[1265]

A member of our house sayd publiquely there, that the ministry had agreed to release the 7 millions and a halfe, notwithstanding which stock fell, such is their creditt. An honest west Country member told mee there had been some mobs (I thinke att Tiverton) where they sayd, lett nobody accuse us of disaffection to the Government wee are heartily and with the utmost zeale for itt, butt our trade is entirely lost, wee neither have or can have businesse, and starve wee wont. This is what our noble project has brought things to, and I am afraid the worst is nott yett seen, Those whoe were last session against itt were branded in the beginning with Jacobitisme, which was afterwards turned into other appellations, Grumbletonians and whimsicalls, I pray God the Pretenders interest did nott sitt nearer the hearts of the cheife Promoters of itt, then any other consideration except that of lucre, I fear each had its share, att least tis plaine itt has given more advantage to the enemyes of the Government then all the Jacobites in England could have done, or indeed hoped for, by sowering the minds of itts most steddy freinds, whose despair may prepare them for any thing; another peice of news (which I cannott butt thinke very ill) the same person told mee, that all our Brasse and other heavy Cannon were brought from Gibralter which hee sayd hee had taken notice of to Mr C. Stanhope,[1266] whose answer was that there were more then they had occasion for, how came they then to bee unnecessarily sent? You have generally thought mee over sanguine, I should bee very sorry to have that opinion well grounded, for I owne to mee things appeare very black, I pray God avert the impending storme, and graunt that wee may preserve our happy constitution under his Majestys Government and that of his family, otherwise wee must inevitably bee an undone ruined nation. I am

---

[1264] The term dead rent usually meant 'a fixed rent which remains as a constant and unvarying charge upon a mining concession', irrespective of yield (*OED*). It is used here to mean a rent paid whether or not the property was inhabited by the tenant.

[1265] According to newspaper reports, the meeting of the general court, at East India House in Leadenhall Street, to hear about proposals made to them 'by another great company' agreed to empower the directors to negotiate (*Daily Courant*, 2 Dec. 1720; *Daily Post*, 3 Dec. 1720; *London Journal*, 26 Nov.–3 Dec. 1720).

[1266] Charles Stanhope (1673–1760), of Elvaston, Derbys., MP [GB] Milborne Port and secretary to the treasury [GB].

told (by a good hand I think) that wee shall sitt uppon businesse next Thursday, doing soe will I thinke bee necessary, butt how well prepard our Great men will bee I thinke doubtfull, especially if what is given out prove true, that the miscreants whoe have brought the kingdom into the confusion itt now is, are to bee supported, which alasse say some is nott somuch as thought of; onely say they putt things uppon a good bottom first, for enquiring into mismanagement before that is done will destroy all, if this doctrine prevail I thinke I could readily venture for half a crowne to stand in any of their places, I mean with respect to an after reckoning; wee saw enough of that in the matter of the Report from the Secrett Committee,[1267] though those then att the head of affairs assured us of vigorous enquiryes att a proper season, butt that time never came …

437. *Alan I, Dublin, to Thomas, 4 Dec. 1720*

(1248/4/367–8)

Yesterday arrived a pacquet boat, which brought in nine mails; and among others your several letters of the eleventh, 15th, 18th, 24 and 26 of November …I thank you for the particular account you give me of the conversation you had in the Parke with —.[1268] By it, any body may see that as the removing me was the act of another, and not his; soe his saying he wrote and said what was proper on the subject was saying nothing: he might say every thing to my prejudice and skreen himself from being guilty of a falsitye, by thinking it proper to say soe: but the truth is, he let the things spoken by my enemy to my disadvantage remain on that foot, and that he seems to acknowledge by saying he had nothing to doe with any exception taken before his coming: but truly I beleived he bestirred himself heartily to prevent his being my Successor for whom the letter hath been soe long signed. For his favourites here will be forced to unmask, and will find it impossible to play their double game (as hitherto) with out being discovered and exposed: if they do not strike in with the man whom the great man recommends, they will shew their professions made there hitherto are not soe sincere: if they doe, the people here will know them to be through hypocrites. My sense is, that the party will divide upon this, some will leap over the stick or creep under it as they are ordered;[1269] but others will shew uneasinesse, and they will not draw together as they have done hitherto. Yesterday Sir Rich[ard] Levings letter to be cheif Justice of the Common Pleas was laid before us at the Castle; it was not transmitted by my Lord Lieutenant or Mr Walpole but brought by Sir Ri[chard] Levinges servant to the Office. A certain person asked whether we had not sent back letters which came soe, and seemed desirous at least to have postponed signing a warrant to the Attornye to draw a fiant; I said we had indeed refused to put people on the establishment for pencions on dormant letters which had been kept in peoples pockets from the time of a former Governement and been then brought to us, and that I thought we were warranted so to doe by our instructions till we received his Majestyes farther pleasure; but that I (who resolved and expected to

[1267] The 'committee of secrecy' appointed by the British house of commons on 9 Apr. 1715 to investigate the circumstances surrounding the negotiations leading to the Peace of Utrecht, which led to the impeachments of Lords Bolingbroke and Oxford.

[1268] The duke of Grafton (see above, pp. 312–13).

[1269] A common metaphor for political subserviency, picked up by Swift, for example, in *Gulliver's Travels*, ed. David Womersley (Cambridge, 2012), 58–60, 87.

sign a more unacceptable warrant very soon, meaning for a patent to my Successor) would without delay sign this and immediately did soe, which was followed by my collegue with this expression, that he never signed any thing with a worse will. I had received a very civil and respectful letter from Sir Rich[ard] Levinge on the occasion, which I answer by this pacquet. You will not make this publick, but if the story could be told handsomly to Lord P[arke]r[1270] I should not be averse to it. Yesterday also Mr Marlays[1271] letter came over to be Sollicitor. The Cheif Justice had recommended Mr Parnel his brother in Law[1272] for this place, or a Cushion in case of the removal of any of our puisne Judges; and by what I could observe by his countenance at the Councel he seemed not greatly pleased; for you must knew there is no good bloud between him and his brother that is to be in the Common Pleas.[1273] In your letter of the 26th you tell me that you told the Duke of Gr[afton] you know that Mr Gilbert had absolutely refused to accept the Seals; but doe not say when that refusal was. If things fall out according to what his Grace told you, that in three or fowre dayes after your talking together the orders would go for Ireland I shal know what the end of this affair will be, before you can answer this letter: but possibly your having things of soe much greater weight on your hands may not be at leisure to think of this poor Kingdome. I know that Lord S[underland] thought I did not doe all in my power about the Sacramental test, for in effect he was of opinion I was cool in the matter when I gave him and the other ministers my advice that it would be an impracticable thing to aim at a total repeal of it, as they soon found after they undertook it and will doe so more fully the next time; but this to yourself: for now they are all as they would be. I would be content they should trye their hands and they would then see whether having a willing Chancellor will doe, or whether I was the occasion of the disappointment. We have reason to hope from the paragraph in the Gazette of the 26th and our not hearing any thing of it from Scotland directly to the North of Ireland, that the terrible account of the plague being broke out in the Isle of Man is groundlesse, but we doe all in our power to guard against it[1274] …

438. *Thomas to Alan I, 10 Dec. 1720*[1275]

(1248/4/371–2)

Uppon Wensday night[1276] about a hundred members mett att the Secretarys office, where (according to custom) the kings speech was read,[1277] and a resolution was proposd for an Addresse of thankes.

One of the company sayd hee thought the Directors of the S[outh] S[ea] company ought by name to bee represented as the persons to whom the loss of creditt ought to bee

---

[1270] Baron Parker, lord chancellor [GB].

[1271] Thomas Marlay, MP [I].

[1272] John Parnell, MP [I], was married to Anna, a sister of Lord Chief Justice William Whitshed.

[1273] Sir Richard Levinge.

[1274] The *London Gazette* of 22–26 Nov. 1720 carried a paragraph dated from Whitehall on 26 Nov. reporting that 'Letters from Scotland by the last post contradict the report that the plague was broke out in the Isle of Man'.

[1275] Partly printed in Coxe, *Walpole*, ii, 201–3.

[1276] The day before the parliamentary session opened.

[1277] The practice of inviting ministerial supporters to pre-sessional meetings was in fact a relatively recent innovation (Geoffrey Holmes, *British Politics in the Age of Anne* (1967), 365; *HC 1715–54*, i, 3).

imputed, butt condemning persons unheard (however obnoxious) was nott reasonable, butt that the end might bee attained by generall words, to witt, <u>to enquire into the causes of these misfortunes</u>. This was very vigorously opposd by some few, and a great man sayd itt would instead of retreiving occasion (probably) an utter losse of itt, for that the Directors would run away, butt this did not obtaine, for my own part I thought the words fully agreed to, when on a suddaine twas whisperd about, that they were omitted, which gave occasion to a freind of yours to call to Mr Secretary whoe was reading a subsequent paragraph, to know whither the amendment proposd were incerted, to which hee answered Noe, for you know, says hee, I am to observe directions, and members calling out Read on Read on, I proceeded soe to doe, without incerting them, the other replyed, I thought the words agreed to, and consequently incerted, for surely half a dozen near you are nott to thinke of determining for soe great a number, wee meet here as I apprehend to endeavour soe to understand each other as to bee of one mind in another place, I think itt therfore incumbent on mee to speake plainly, this resolution is to bee proposd to the house, where the words you have thought fitt to omitt, may bee offered, and I doe promise you uppon word they will bee soe, when they will bee fully debated, and if occasion bee, the question determined by a Division. Mr Secretary then sayd, propose your words, which being done, they were without more adoe incerted.

The motion being yesterday made, gentlemen lett them selves into the most bitter invectives against the misexecution of the Act of Parliament[1278] and indeed in great measure against the Act as vesting too large powers in a sett of men whoe are now calld miscreants, the scum of the people, and worse names if possible, thus are wee ashamed of what many of us contended for last yeare with the greatest eagernesse, and that uppon motives nott fitt to bee mentioned. The more moderate few (for that was what butt very few had a right to call themselves) layd the stresse uppon misexecution, butt even uppon this head, they went great lenghts, perticularly Sir J[oseph] J[ekyll] whoe sayd that hee could nott butt thinke, att least hope, that all the Directors were nott equally culpable, butt sure hee was that some were highly criminal, whoe were nott Directors; another sayd the ministry with onely a frowne had been able to putt a stop to all the little bubbles, in order to deepen the water for the great one, whence profitt was to arise. A third concluded thus, This Parliament began with a secret Committee falling uppon a precedent ministry, and why may itt nott conclude with doing soe to another. What your freind sayd Wensday night proves to have been well judged, for uppon reporting the Addresse yesterday Sir J[oseph] J[ekyll] movd an amendment by inserting what you see therein of punishing the authors, which went without opposition, others tooke exception to itt as too tender, this nott being a party cause, arrowes in full vollyes are lett fly from every quarter.[1279]

Thursday is appointed for considering the state of creditt when Mr Walpole has promised us his thoughts, and tho his freinds doe nott love to hear of a scheme being calld his, hee is certainly digesting one, which wee are then to have, the greater part of which all the towne knows already.

Wee are to attend his Majesty with our Addresse this day att two, soe that I suppose little will bee done in the house, if any thing materiall happen ile adde itt, for writing

---

[1278] The original act of 1711 establishing the South Sea Company (10 Anne, c. 37).

[1279] Added to a statement of the Commons' intention to investigate 'the causes of our present misfortunes' (*CJ*, xix, 380).

this in the morning gives an opertunity of saying what will certainly bee more diverting then Parliamentary accounts. An old Atturny (sayd to bee underhand employd by Lord Oxford) has acquainted Lord Conigsby with having found a very antcient booke (wee call itt a record) whereby itt appears that the Mannor of Leompstar (formerly belonging to the Abbott of Reading) was in the nature of a Pallatinate, with power of life and death etc.[1280] His Lordship then, being now Lord of that Mannor must have an acknowledged undoubted right (and a sole right) to all the priviledges to which the Abbott was entitled, and uppon this foote (as I heare) has wrote to Lord Stanhope[1281] praying that a Commission of Oyer and Terminer bee sent him,[1282] and that by this post, for that an hours delay will risque his Lordships life.

You must know that there have been grieveous outrages committed (as disaffected people are pleasd to call them) by forcible entryes, sending men to goale etc and nothing sure can bee more reasonable then putting an end to these disputes, in a legall way, for Gafnying will nott goe down in this country,[1283] nor doe wee desire itt, this Commission would sett all things right, butt whither the multitude of other weighty affairs may nott retard itt, seems very doubtfull, on the other hand his Lordships attendance in Parliament is necessary, for though Proxeyes in some cases may doe well enough, it is nott to bee supposed that in every instance a Proxey is equall to the Constituent, when this matter is determined you may hear of itt, though I hope to see you here before twill bee soe.

Woe bee to Serjeant Birch[1284] and Sir George Caswell[1285] if they presume to stand Candidates att Leomstar att any future election; which however may nott be soe near as some people thinke, for in case wee deserve itt, tis hoped by some, and feard by others that wee may bee longer livd then this session, as well as that 25 Scots Peers, in addition to the two disputed Titles, may bee made Hereditary, leaving out of the Bill[1286] what relates to England, butt I thinke if offered (which I cannott yett bring my self to beleive) twill run the Gautlett as the last did.

Wee have had a little flurry by an unexpected (undigested) motion made by Governor Pitts,[1287] for ordering the Directors to attend on Thursday, with their myrmodons the

[1280] *The First Part of Earl Coningsby's Case, Relating to the Vicaridge of Lempster in Herefordshire* … (1721), relating to his claim to present to the living of Leominster, named Thomas Price, Oxford's steward, together with 'Thomas Rodd, the vilest of all Attornies', as Price's 'coadjutor'. The right of presentation formed part of Coningsby's wider claim to the title to the 'royal franchises within his liberty of Westminster' (*The Abstract of Earl Coningsby's Title* … [1721]; *The Case of the Right Honourable Thomas Earl Coningesby* … [1722]). Enraged by failure of a chancery lawsuit, Coningsby published derogatory remarks about the lord chancellor and in consequence spent six months in custody in the Tower of London in 1721 at the behest of the house of lords. On this episode, see Pat Rogers, *The Life and Times of Thomas, Lord Coningsby: The Whig Hangman and His Victims* (2011), chs 7–8.

[1281] As secretary of state.

[1282] A commission, usually given to an assize judge, to hold courts to inquire into and punish treasons, felonies and misdemeanours.

[1283] It was alleged that as a lord justice in Ireland in 1690–2 Coningsby had ordered the summary execution of one Gaffney, witness to a murder whose perpetrator had escaped justice by bribing the government; hence his opprobrious nickname, 'Gaffney's hangman'. See Rogers, *Coningsby*, ch. 3.

[1284] John Birch (c.1666–1715), of Garnstone Manor, Herefs., MP [GB] Weobley.

[1285] Caswall had been returned for Leominster in a contested by-election in 1717.

[1286] The reintroduced Peerage Bill.

[1287] Thomas Pitt (1653–1726), of Mawarden Court, Wilts., MP [GB] Thirsk, former (1716–17) governor of Jamaica.

Secretary and Treasurer, and if they pleasd with their great Scanderbag,[1288] whoe hee meant by this I know nott, butt the epithet denotes sombody of consideration. The time being come for attending his Majesty with the Addresse, itt was agreed by common consent that this matter bee taken into farther consideration on Munday, without a question putt for adjourning the debate, att which time I apprehend the maine argument on one hand will bee, that unlesse creditt shall bee reestablisht before you fall to finding faults, doing itt will grow more difficult afterwards, on the other side twill bee sayd (and I doubt too truly) that unlesse you probe the sore to the bottom before you enter on remedyes, twill bee onely skinning over what from a corrupt bottom will in a short time breake out againe; and that with more virulence from the expectation of impunity which such a proceeding will give ground for, twill bee I beleive a very smart debate, since upon the successe a great deale depends. I was told (and nott by a very ill hand) that a great man had been heard to say twould bee necessary to adjorn in order to more temper, I thinke such a remedy will onely irritate, butt perhaps the approaching hollidays may bee the avowd reason.

I askt Mr Secretary[1289] (The Duke of Grafton nott being returnd) whither the order were gone over, Hee told mee, nott that hee knew of and hee beleivd nott, itt being his province, wherin nothing was done att any time, but uppon the Lord Lieutenants writing to Mr De Lafay, desiring hee would move the Secretary to know the Kings pleasure.

I sayd I understood that to bee the usuall forme, butt that Sir R[ichard] L[evinge's] letter had been deliverd by a Private hand, which possibly might att another time have been represented back againe, butt that hee might easily guesse why you could nott thinke itt proper, and that therfore a fiant was ordered. Hee askt mee if I desired his doing any thing, I replyed I had nothing to aske. They are most certainly labouring G[ilbert][1290] whoe does nott yett come to … Looke well on the seale for I make noe doubt this will bee opened.

439. *Thomas to Alan I, 13 Dec. 1720*[1291]

(1248/4/373–4)

The motion of Saturday (which I mentioned in my last) was yesterday lickt into better forme as you will see by the votes.[1292] The first question movd was in very strong terms opposd, by three or four, for as I remember, that was the number, on the other hand members spoake with the freedom becoming a Brittish house of Commons, the first whoe spoake on the side of the question was my quondam Colleague Sir R[ichard] S[teele],[1293] hee indeed sett the matter in a clear light, by telling us, that a nation of more wealth and greater creditt then

---

[1288] A rogue or rascal (*OED*).

[1289] Secretary of State James Craggs.

[1290] Jeffray Gilbert, to replace Alan as lord chancellor [I]. Gilbert was certainly not William Conolly's choice, who complained to Grafton about this and about Sir Richard Levinge's nomination as lord chief justice of common pleas (BL, Add. MS 74049: Conolly to [Grafton], 18 Oct. 1720).

[1291] Partly printed in Coxe, *Walpole*, ii, 203–4.

[1292] The motion for a supply, originally made on Saturday, 10 Dec., was considered by a committee of the whole House on Monday, the 12th, and reported the next day (*CJ*, xix, 381–2).

[1293] Sir Richard Steele (1672–1729), of Llangunnor, Carmarthenshire, MP [GB] for Stockbridge alongside Thomas in the 1713 parliament, who now sat for Boroughbridge.

any in Europe, within lesse then two years, was reduc't to what wee see, and too sensibly feel, by a few cyphering Citts,[1294] a species of men of equall capacity in all respects (that of cheating a deluded people onely excepted) with those animals whoe savd the Capitol,[1295] whoe were now to be skreend by those of greater figure, for what reason they best know, others were att liberty to judge.

Another (in answer to an argument against the question that this vindicative justice somuch contended for would nott attaine the end proposd for that you would nott bee able to come att the estates of the delinquents) sayd hee thought all the laws against Bankrupts being enacted into one against the Directors (for soe hee would allways call them as what carryd more of obloquy then any other word could expresse) would in his opinion attaine the end proposd. Abundance spoake with equall bitternesse, and such was the general outcry that the previous question which had been demanded, was nott thought fitt to bee insisted on, and they were too wise to discover their weaknesse by a division uppon the main question.

How far <u>wayes and means</u> will goe towards warding the blow I know nott, that they will bee used I am satisfyd, butt I thinke there is a possibillity of a disappointment.

The warrantt lyes still in the Secretarys office, the game now playing is a Handicap (in our Newmarkett phrase) between G[ilbert] and Sir R[1296] butt as with us, soe in this case, both must agree, or itt comes to nothing, if they doe, I suppose the boote shall bee payd by the nation, and I beleive you thinke one of them skilfull enough (considering the present scituation of affairs) to aske a pretty deale.

I cannott tell you the precise time of the refusal, butt by all I can collect twas haesitated uppon from the very beginning, and grew stronger and stronger when people talkt soe very freely as they did on the subject. Your fast freind was heard to say that you were soe intollerably proud as to bee above submitting your judgment to any other mans whatever, a Courtly way of expressing an unwillingnesse of Leaping over a stick or creeping under itt as directed.

440. *Alan I, Dublin, to Thomas, 14 Dec. 1720*

(1248/4/375–6)

… By our wanting three mailes now, and I might say a fourth, there being another by this time at the Head, we are great strangers to what is done or doing in London: Our men of intelligence (I mean the favourites) continue stil of opinion that such reasons have been sent into England (by them) against giving me the Successor intended, that they will not be perswaded to beleive Mr Gilbert will be sent over: I confesse I think the person (whose scheme the sending him was) will not put himself soe much in the wrong as to recede from the least article of it; and if that point should be weathered by my Lord Lieutenant and his freinds, people will be apt to think it an instance that one mans power is in declension. If

---

[1294]Citizens ('citts') calculating arithmetically (*OED*).

[1295]The sacred geese, whose cackling alerted Marcus Manlius Capitolinus to the surprise attack being made by the Gauls on the Capitoline Hill during the siege of Rome in 390 BC.

[1296]Sir Richard Levinge. He and Gilbert were candidates to succeed Alan in the lord chancellorship.

that should be the case, you will presently see whether the person who assured you he had no concern in this whole affair, and who (you say) spoke as if he desired to be beleived was in earnest, or acted the Courtier: for if the first design is not prosecuted, and another be pitched on, it must be his act: and I beleive the eye of the party is to bring in W[*hitshed*]. But how have I deserved the usage I have for some time past mett with? It would be vanity in me to say how much I did, and how much I suffered to support a certain interest before his Majestyes accession to the throne. I was then thought a proper person to commit the Great Seal to: a place of honour, but which no way hath tended to the making a fortune to me: since beside the obligation it layes me under of being at a greater expence then I needed otherwise to be at, I was by it obliged to quit my profession which brought me in a better income then my emploiment doth.

You know it was Lord S[*underland*] who first moved the making me a Peer to answer the occasions of the Crown and enable me to serve the King in the house of Lords in a better maner then I should have been able to do, by sitting on the wool sack barely as Chancellor: this hath made it not only impracticable to resort to my profession but hath rendred it desirable if not necessary to leave a better estate in my familye then I should have thought sufficient if I had continued a private Gentleman. In this office I have served uprightly, diligently, and I think I may add with general satisfaction; I have never been suspected of being influenced in judgement by fear, favour, or money: and am certain I have to the best of my power served the King at the Councel board and Parliament, and I think I can prove it to have been with good successe and without reproach. But after all this, I have for six months past been continued in my post just till somebody would take it; and no notice given me of my being to be removed, soe as to put my affairs in order: I have too much duty for my Prince to entertain any dissatisfaction at putting another person into my emploiment when he finds it for his service to doe soe: but I am told it hath been usual, when men are not turned out in displeasure and as having very much misbehaved themselves, to give them some notice of it; but mine hath been by the WhiteHall letter, printed newspapers etc soe that I seem to be appointed only to hold the horse till somebody can be found who will mount into the saddle; and am not permitted to attend my own affairs, without doing what I have long thought by some usage I have mett with, it was hoped I would doe, I mean make it my own act to lay down. By this means I loose an oportunitye of shewing by my behavior in the English parliament that no body hath a stronger inclination to serve his Majestye then I have; and I beleive things are on such a foot that those who are well affected to his Majestye will have as fair an oportunitye to shew it now as ever they will have. But perhaps my having been against the Peerage bill is taken by some as a declaration of my inclinations to be as opposite in all other matters: they little know me who make that judgement; for I resolve (whatever treatment I meet with) to act with all zeal for his Majestyes service and interests: and from this resolution the hardest usage shal not remove me; and my doing this will at length convince people that I doe not deserve the displeasure of the Crown, tho by what you wrote to me as spoke by the D[*uke*] of G[*rafton*] (that they had made the K[*ing*] very angry with me) I have great reason to beleive I have had other representations made of my actions then they will be found to deserve, when I have oportunitye to justifye my self.

441. *Thomas to Alan I, 22 Dec. 1720*[1297]

(1248/4/377–8)

I showd your freinds letter[1298] of the 14th to the proper person, hee tooke itt home with him, and returnd itt next day.

I can now informe you that a resolution is taken against sending G[*ilbert*] as your successor, butt the heavy load att this time on the shoulders of our great men, prevents even the thought of another person; Lord Lieutenant would nott owne the knowledge even of thus much. I told him hee then owed mee a peice of news in returne of what I had told him, in the meane time I askt whither hee were free to tell mee who hee intended; his answer was that hee had never somuch as thought of itt, adding what I formerly told you relating to your selfe, I then sayd I would ask a plaine question, is nott W[*hitshed*] the man, nott, sayes hee, that I know of, you may remember the same answer verbatim given you by a former Lord Lieutenant of equall quallity with his Grace[1299] to the question you askt whither there were nott a designe of restoring the Pretender. You will bee happy in a recesse, att a time when the seas run soe high as that noe prudent man would willingly have his ship out of harbour.

Our scheme was yesterday opened by Mr Walpole,[1300] whoe with the greatest skill imaginable intrencht himselfe, by telling us that hee tooke for graunted things were, as they are layd before us – Cuius contrarium[1301] – , and in speaking his thoughts, as hee termd itt, att least six times desired itt might bee remembred that hee argued uppon this supposition. The substance in short was this.

That of the 38 millions now vested in the S[*outh*] S[*ea*] company, nine should by way of ingrafment bee vested in the banke, as many in the E[*ast*] India company and the remaining 20m remaine to the S[*outh*] Sea. The mony account hee sayd hee did nott care to meddle with, and hee was in the right, for when that shall bee discussed (if ever itt bee) twill nott beare an examination, after many long speeches to very little purpose, twas understood that the house would bee ready to receive proposalls from these 3 great bodyes, which wee shall I thinke agree to, bee they what they will, for the same reasons (for they will bee plentifully made use of) which induced us to passe the Bill last session, I then told you what I thought would bee the issue, which to my great greife proves too rightly judged. I will now tell you my fears of this matter.

That Mr W[*alpole*] made the most of every thing is very certaine and supposing his postulata[1302] (to use his owne words) well grounded, his conclusions were right, Butt my opinion is that skinning over the soare without probing the wound to the bottom, will end in its breaking out againe, when possibly the malignity may bee too great, to bee overcome,

---

[1297] Partly printed in Coxe, *Walpole*, ii, 204–5.

[1298] Alan himself; presumably Thomas was attempting to mislead anyone intercepting his letter.

[1299] The duke of Bolton.

[1300] In the committee of the whole House considering the state of the public credit (*CJ*, xix, 392; Cobbett, *Parl. Hist.*, ix, col. 691). Robert Walpole had taken responsibility for piloting through the Commons the new scheme to refinance the national debt (Carswell, 201–15).

[1301] 'Of which the contrary is true'.

[1302] Propositions.

butt wee are for putting of the evill day, and hee is fool or knave whoe joins nott therin. I am told (I beleive by a very good hand) Gibraltar is after all to bee given up to the Spaniard, a supposition which last year argued the utmost disaffection.

When or where our misfortunes shall end, time alone can determine, though I am very inclinable to hope the best, that strong inclination cannott soe far prevaile as to leave mee without fears.

I have gott a recomendation from the Treasury in favour of Peter Smiths being surveyor att the Cove,[1303] this they tell mee is the usuall method, though lookt on by them as a direction. Sir W[illia]m St Q[uintin] writes to your colleague to facilitate the businesse.[1304]

The Lords this day adjourned to Munday fortnight, probably wee may doe soe on Saturday,[1305] after reporting tomorrows resolutions of the Committee, bee itt as twill I goe out of town tomorrow morning my returne will depend uppon the time to which our house shall adjourne.

[*PS*] I am just told the E[*ast*] India company stand of.

442. *Thomas to Alan I, 27 Dec. 1720*

(1248/4/379–80)

The unexpected short adjournment prevented my going out of towne, twould have taken mee two dayes in going, and as many in returning from Pepper Hara, soe that I could have spent butt one day there.

This was occasioned by the E[*ast*] India companys haesitating for twas thought they would have come roundly in, and tis still imagined they will att last comply, however this step shews they are nott very fond of the scheme; I cannott pretend to judge of the event of things, butt tis very plaine that such uncertaintyes occasion great confusion, God send us well out of itt.

Youl see two terrible letters in the inclosed papers, tis whisperd that a noble Lord of our country is the author, and I am told endeavours are using to trace itt, butt to what end I doe nott see, for they take wonderfully, soe that I cannott thinke such an enquiry of any use.

The Divine mentioned in one of them is brother to the D[*uke*] of Bridgwater, and the Lady a daughter of the Dutches Dowager of Portland.[1306]

[1303] Modern-day Cobh, Co. Cork: a port on the south of the Great Island.

[1304] The place of surveyor at Cobh was vacant by the death of the incumbent, Thomas Cole, but on 24 Nov. the revenue commissioners had appointed Alexander Erwin, tide surveyor at Ringsend, Co. Dublin (TNA, CUST 1/15, f. 47: minute, 24 Nov. 1720). On 26 Jan. 1721 Smith arrived at the custom house and presented a letter of recommendation from Secretary Stanhope, only to be told that the place had been filled. The commissioners assured him he would have orders to be instructed in the business of surveying and would be given the first 'proper vacancy' to arise (TNA, CUST 1/15, f. 66: minute, 26 Jan. 1720[/1]). However, in Apr., in obedience to an order of the British treasury, and the receipt of evidence that Smith had been instructed, he was belatedly given the post at Cobh, Erwin being switched to the surveyorship of Cork (TNA, CUST 1/15, ff. 91, 96: minutes, 25 Apr., 9 May 1721).

[1305] On Friday, 23 Dec. the Commons adjourned until the following Thursday, the 29th (*CJ*, xix, 393).

[1306] Henry Egerton (1689–1746), later bishop of Hereford, married on 18 Dec. 1720 Lady Elizabeth Ariana Bentinck, one of the daughters of Hans Willem Bentinck, 1st earl of Portland by his second wife, Jane Martha (1672–1751) (née Temple).

I thinke your affair may lye by some time.

443. *Alan I, Dublin, to Thomas, Peper Harow, 30 Dec. 1720*

(1248/4/383–4)

I confesse I either doe not understand your soe much talked of scheme, or very much doubt how it will in any measure answer the designed end of restoring publick credit: but this I very plainly see by the preparatory resolutions that the annuitants and among the rest those concerned in the Lottery tickets of 1719 are to stand to the courtesy of the general Court of the South Sea company or to take a touch with that Leviathan in Westminster Hall.[1307] Whatever you did for me I will abide by, tho I confesse I never had any stomach to be forced into a company the original forming and formers of which I detested: I thought I had been so fortunate by drawing benefits of £1545 that I should never have lost any part of my principal summe of £900 which I first paid in; but alas! I find my £1545 and the interest of it (amounting to about £1600 in the whole) is to be turned into £400 capital stock in the South Sea, which as I take it is called in our printed papers worth £170 per Cent. soe as I may (if I can gett a ready money chapman which I doubt is not easily to be had) make £880 of my £1545. A pox of all such bargains say I. No doubt these Holydayes have given the great people time to doe every thing that can be done to carry on their grand affairs and have been employed to the best advantage, soe that I little question your meeting in very good temper after New years tide: you cannot but perceive you were come to a pace before you parted: Mr Maddocks[1308] read to me a part of a letter from Mr Pyott[1309] in which he tells him with great triumph and exulting that the vote for not releiving the annuitants etc was carryed by a majoritye of 150 odd;[1310] with this addition that the Toryes to a man voted with the Court in this vote; soe I find it is the Whigs who are at present the naughty people in their opinion where Mr Pyott resorts. Unlesse something is done in relation to the Seal here during the Holydayes I beleive things will remain as they are till the D[uke] of Gr[afton] comes over; But I confesse I expect by every pacquet the dead warrant,[1311] the forerunners being already arrived, I mean that for constituting Lord Shanon commander in Cheif of the forces here in the room of Lord Tyrawly and that for Mr Marlye being Sollicitor General in the room of the now Attornye who was made so on Mr Gores being made a Judge:[1312] now I argue thus with my self; Lord Shanon was made commander in cheif here by the interposicion of his freind my Lord Lieutenant; and I think a Sollicitor

---

[1307] The English court of chancery.

[1308] Charles Maddocks (*d.* c.1756), secretary to the lords justices [I] 1718–24 (Sainty, 'Secretariat', 26–7).

[1309] Richard Pyott (*d.* c.1738), of Streethay, Staffs., formerly a.d.c. to the duke of Bolton as lord lieutenant, appointed in June 1720 as lieut.-col. of the 4th troop of life guards (*Post Boy*, 7–9 June 1720; Dalton, *Army Lists*, vi, 146; TNA, PROB 11/691/78).

[1310] On 20 Dec., the Commons heard the report of the committee considering the state of the public credit, and agreed with the committee's resolution that all subscriptions and contracts made with the South Sea Company remained valid unless altered by a general court of the company or by statute. There was no vote on the resolution as such, but on a previous motion to adjourn, which was defeated 232–88 (*CJ*, xix, 392).

[1311] For his dismissal.

[1312] John Rogerson MP [I], appointed in place of George Gore, MP [I].

would hardly be appointed without his privity, if then he knew what was doing at that time he probably knew all that was doing, and I can assure you that Lord Shanons commission and Mr Marlays letter to be made Sollicitor bear date at Gore on the same day that his Majestyes letter for constituting Mr Gilbert my Successor bears date I mean 13 October. I would not have you beleive that I think the D[*uke*] of Gr[*afton*] had any hand in the affair of G[*ilbert*]. No the alarm was too great from the persons in confidence here to admit of such a step! and indeed it would have been the most unadvised thing in the earth, to do an unnecessary and the most unpopular action in the world meerly to provoke and irritate a people who have been and may hereafter be of service to his Majestye when other people seemed to stand by unconcerned what the event of things might be. You see I speak with regard to his Majestyes service and the good of the Kingdome and quiet of our next Session: for with respect to myself the more unacceptable my Successor is the more the weight will be on those who removed me and by so doing made way for such a Successor. I know the wishes the Cabal have are to have W[*hitshed*] Chancellor; Mr Gore Cheif Justice, and Mr Parnell[1313] Justice of the Common pleas in Mr Gores roome: if this obtain you will judge how far the person who hath not yet had these things in his thoughts is to be relied on. This is a noble high Church scheme indeed; his Grace of D[*ublin*][1314] next to the present possessor wished the Seal might not be in the Cheif Barons hand; and of all men living (beside his own) wished it should be put into W[*hitshed'*]s with whom there hath from an identity of principles and sentiments been a long intimacy and freindship; Mr Parnel is his Gr[*ace'*]s seneschal and marryed to W[*hitshed'*]s sister.[1315] If every thing that is proposed hence be complyed with, they serve very ill whose measures are entirely gone into, if any thing happen amisse under a certain administration: the late French King alway expected that General should take the town he beseiged whom he furnished with such an Army and military provisions as the General demanded. My Lord Cheif [*Justice*] W[*hitshed*] declares he hath not been recommended from this side, will lay £500 to £100 he is not the man, and that it will be somebody from the other side. I had a mighty civil letter from my Lord Cheif Justice Levynge on my giving his patent dispatch. You did not tell me a word what Mr M.[1316] said after giving back my letter to you …

444. *Alan I, Dublin, to Alice, Peper Harow, 30 Dec. 1720*

(1248/4/385–6)

I wish you and all with you many happy new years: you complain of my writing seldome, are not you more liable to have that objected to you? Consider how my time is taken up in publick affairs and my own private ones, when I must have it in my thoughts to goe into a perfectly new course of life and to remove my familye into another Kingdome for good: beside this my own and poor wifes ilnesse have prevented my doing a good deal of what I might have had leisure to doe if we had been in health. Tell your Uncle that the

---

[1313] John Parnell, MP [I].

[1314] Archbishop King.

[1315] Mary Whitshed.

[1316] Probably Paul Methuen.

Cabal mentioned in his letter of this date are C[*onolly,*] W[*hitshed,*] Gore, the Bishop of Meath, Mr Manlye[1317] Dean Hort and a very few more; the later are the persons who I doubt make an ill use of a distinction between the old and new English, that is between those who have estates here and those who have not but come over very hungry and think themselves intitled to every thing till they are filled: ask some of these whether this be not a very ill distinction they own it, but say not they but others brought it up; the truth is it lies between the A[*rchbishop*] of D[*ublin*] and the B[*ishop*] of M[*eath*] but which ever of them it was, better he had been hanged then introduced it; but it is visible who turn it to a very good account to themselves. One of the abovenamed six told me upon occasion of filling the vacant See of Down that he supposed I could not but be sensible none but a man born in England would succeed: and I doubt not this is the constant advice of the three later.

445. Alan I, Dublin, to Thomas, Peper Harow, 2 Jan. 1720/1

(1248/4/387–8)

This will be a very short letter to tell you in how melancholy a maner I have begun the year: Yesterday I expected the death of my dear wife yet she hath survived last night, but I am very apprehensive she will not another. I will not trouble you with saying how well she hath deserved of me, for whom she hath alway shewn an unexpressible tendernesse and care; confidently I may say it, never woman shewed more toward an husband; and I must be ungrateful to the last degree and ill natured beyond what I think I am, not to regret her misery and danger with all the veins of my heart. Now is the time when I wish for the execucion of my enemyes malice against me; for they can take nothing from me which I can value in comparison of that losse which the good hand of providence in mercy to her seems determined forthwith to afflict me with. I am not well my self; my concern hath oppressed my spirits and almost suffocated me. My letter grows to a great length but the subject is too near to me to be soon quitted of choice.

446. Alan I, Dublin, to Thomas, 8 Jan. 1720[/1]

(1248/4/389–90)

I sit down to write just after my poor wife hath taken a vomit, on the good or ill effects of which I apprehend her life depends: this is a sort of Physick of soe rough a nature that I dreaded its being given to one in her weak condition, but all her three Physicians Molineux,[1318] Comyng,[1319] and Robinson[1320] advised it and assured me that in their opinion it was not only no way dangerous but in their judgement like to produce very good effects, if not of absolute necessitye. God Almighty grant it may answer their intentions; and I trust that his goodnesse which hath preserved her contrary to my expectations and indeed every

---

[1317] Isaac Manley, MP [I].

[1318] Sir Thomas Molyneux (1661–1733), of Dublin, MP [I] 1695–8 (*Hist. Ir. Parl.*, v, 265–6).

[1319] Duncan Cumyng.

[1320] Bryan Robinson (c.1680–1754), of Dublin (*DIB*).

bodyes since this day sennight, will stil preserve and restore her. I have the letter written by Charles[1321] on 29 December by your order; and two prints under a cover; a man must have a great deal of charity who doth not suspect there be some ill design contained under that vail of patriotism and concern for the publick: nay may not one without breach of charity say that the most natural tendency of one of them is an hint to the Mob that unlesse those persons are sacrificed whom he denotes to be the Authors of the publick calamityes, and calls horse Leeches and bloodsuckers, all maner of confusion and resentment may be expected as the natural result of their not being proceeded against in the maner the Author points out.[1322] I neither love the persons of the criminal, nor approve their actions, nor am concerned one farthing; but I dread such appeals ad populum,[1323] as those seem to me to be: arguments within doors are fit but I know no end so good to deserve being attained by means which (if I understand the paper right) have no other tendency then to enforce people in a certain assembly to come into the Authors measures. If his honesty be equal to his zeal or the sharpnesse of his style, he is a very honest man: and so I will quit this subject.

Mr Carre the cursitor dying lately,[1324] I gave a certain person with whom you walked in the Parke[1325] an account of it; told him it was an office of great trust and required a man of skill and care; that I would not pretend to name any person to succeed in it, but recommended it that if the new Officer appointed should either act in person or by deputy, he might be a man of skill and who would do his duty carefully: the words of the letter I cannnot charge my memory with. His answer is as follows. I am extreamly obliged to you for your favor of letting me have so early notice of the death of Mr Carre I very much agree with your Lordship that whither this office be to be transacted by deputy or by the person that is to have it they should be enjoined to execute it with care: for as you are so obliging to give me this caution, I shal doe what lyes in me to follow. it. Being My Lord etc.

I am certain my letter had another tendency then to desire the writer of the answer to enjoin the Officer or his deputy to be careful in it: alas the Chancellor for the time being will oblige him to that, and so will his own securitye not to forfeit the Office by negligence; but the truth is I did apprehend the place would be given not to one expert in it, but to some favourite; I also expected the grantee would either set it out to profit to a Deputy, or depute a person at a salary to officiate; now people of the least merit sufficiencye and especially integrity will be the people who will give most, or serve for least wages: men of knowledge will not look on that to be a competent recompence for their service which an ignorant man will be very glad of; and a knave will make more then he ought of it, so will be able to give more then an honest man; and indeed my intent was to guard against ignorance and extortion, by shewing the necessity there was to oblige the patentee (who

[1321]Charles Powell (*d.* c.1653), of St James's, Westminster (TNA, PROB 11/802/510), was a witness in 1744 to the will of Alan II (*Registry of Deeds, Dublin: Abstracts of Wills*, ed. P.B. Eustace and Eilish Ellis (3 vols, Dublin, 1954–84), ii, 14). He was probably identical with the Charles Powell who was one of the six clerks in chancery [I] 1711–46 (*Lib. Mun.*, pt 2, p. 23).

[1322]Archibald Hutcheson, *A Computation of the Value of South-Sea Stock, on the foot of the Scheme as it Now Subsists* ... (1720), esp. 12, 19, 23; Archibald Hutcheson, *Some Computations and Remarks Relating to the Money Subscribers, and the Proprietors of the Public Debts* ... (1720).

[1323]To the people.

[1324]Thomas Carr (1667–1720), MP [I] 1703–13, jt cursitor in chancery [I] (a life patent).

[1325]The duke of Grafton: see above, pp. 312–13.

ever he shal be) to appoint not only a person who will act with care, but who understands
the emploiment and is of such a character as may give reasonable hopes he will discharge
his duty as he ought. Now to have thanks given me for advising that the person to be
appointed be careful, without one word of his being a man of knowledge and fit to be
intrusted in such a place, argues either that he thinks I have done a very impertinent thing
in making so simple a request or that he hath somebody in his eye for whose knowledge
or resolution to appoint an honest knowing Deputy he is not willing to say any thing. And
if the young Gentleman succeed who is talked of for it on this side,[1326] I am sure he knows
nothing of the matter, and probably must putt it into hands who will give most without
regard to any other qualification. My wifes vomit is well over and we hope hath done her
good ...

[*PS*] The man I mean is he who owes £100 etc[1327]

447. Thomas, South Sea House, to Alan I, Dublin, 14 Jan. 1720[/1]

(1248/4/391–2)

Wee have spent this whole day here, in examining a parcell of Gentlemen whose short
memoryes does very justly entitle them to more witt then any so many men in the kingdom
can pretend to, for nott one of them remembers what passt either in publique or private,
They leave us to fish out what wee can, which I thinke will bee enough (from their own
papers delivered to the house) to shew them in their colours, tho wee shall never come att
a twentyeth part of the truth.[1328] The Lords on Thursday came to the following resolution,
That itt is the opinion of this Committee That the Directors of the S[*outh*] Sea company in
the loans by them made of stock and subscriptions have been guilty of a nottorious breach
of Trust, and ought out of their own private estates to make good the Losses the company
have sustained thereby.[1329]

Our house continues very warme.

448. Thomas to Alan I, 19 Jan. 1720[/1][1330]

(1248/4/399–400)

... By an excessive cold which I tooke by sitting last Saturday from nine in the morning
till eleven att night in a large cold roome att the S[*outh*] Sea house, I was on Sunday night
throwne into a violent fitt of the stone, nott after the usuall manner, the torturing paine

---

[1326] A privy seal was issued for a new patent on 20 Jan., in favour of William Conolly (bef. 1706–1754), of
Rathfarnham, Co. Dublin, MP [I] 1727–*d*. and [GB] 1737–*d*. (*Lib Mun.*, pt 2, p. 26).

[1327] The 'young gentleman ... talked of' for the cursitor's place.

[1328] The 'secret committee', chaired by Thomas, investigating the affairs of the South Sea Company; it had
received large numbers of documents submitted to the House by the company's directors (*CJ*, xix, 393–4, 396–7,
399).

[1329] The committee appointed on 10 Jan. to consider papers submitted by the South Sea Company (*LJ*, xxi,
389).

[1330] Partly printed in Coxe, *Walpole*, ii, 205–6.

being in both kidnyes, without any stone passing the Uriters,[1331] then, or since, the paine lasted about four hours, succeeded by great sorenesse, which is almost gone of, butt my cold continues in a great degree; this unhappy accident prevents attending my duty att the Committee, and indeed I foresaw a probabillity of this kind, for which reason I endeavourd excusing my taking the chair, butt was told in such case some one would constantly supply itt, as my worthy good freind Serjeant Pingelly has done since.[1332]

You see by the votes the Bill against the Directors reported and ordered to bee engrossed, I beleive twas this day read a third time and carryed to the Lords.[1333] Itt prohibits their going out of the kingdom for a year, and to the end of the next session of Parliament , requiring their entring into Recognizance of a hundred thousand pounds, with two suretyes in twenty five thousand pounds each for performance of the above condition; itt requires the delivery of an inventory of their estates Reall and personall uppon oath, and enacts that if they shall falsifie therein (being convict) shall suffer as fellons without benefitt of clergy, there is a clause for encouragement of discoverers, and others such as may make the Bill more effectuall. They had the assurance to petition to bee heard by councill against the Bill, which was rejected with the utmost indignation, although supported by some of our great men (which by the way was very ill relisht) nott allyes in favour of the Directors, butt on account of justice, for that noe criminal (how great soever) ought to bee condemnd unheard, to which twas answered that this Bill did nott condemne, the cheife end being onely to secure their standing a tryall, and preventing alienation of their estates till such time as their tryall was over; twas then sayd even thus much would bee inflicting a great punishment, unheard, to which twas replyd that surely gentlemen had nott read over the papers and accounts delivered att the Bar by themselves, for that by these the most nottorious breach of trust (against the tennor and puport of the S[outh] Sea Act as well as against their owne By lawes) were confessed, that therefore the case was noe more or other then committing or requiring bail from a criminal uppon confession, according to the nature of the offence; that from the notoriety of the thing, as well as from the national prejudice sustain thereby, the legislature were now doing what in ordinary cases the Magistrate might and ought to doe; The house were from a coolenesse of temper wrought up to a great heighth, and that (in my opinion) by the earnestnesse of some gentlemen, whoe att last were forct quietly to give up the Point. I have seen strange turnes, butt I thinke this matter incapable of one, what a considerable man began his first speech with (for he spoake with great vehemence a second time) is certainly true, that saying any thing which might bee interpreted as favouring a S[outh] Sea Director would bee very ill heard, and putt the speaker under great disadvantage. I will nott goe abroad (being a good deale feaverish) till I thinke I can doe itt without great hazard, though I own I shall bee very uneasy till I can attend my duty …

[PS] The Bill is ordered to the Lords. That house have had severall Brokers before them this day,[1334] a gentleman is just gon from mee (the Lords being sitting late as itt is) to lett mee know that those sparkes have confessed somuch that their Lordships thinke they will scamper unlesse taken into custody, with a declaration and message sent to the house of

---

[1331] The ureter: the duct leading from the kidney to the bladder.

[1332] Sir Thomas Pengelly was also a member of the secret committee.

[1333] Confirmed in *CJ*, xix, 403.

[1334] Nine brokers had been summoned to attend, alongside the directors and officers of the company (*LJ*, xxi, 399).

Comons acquainting them herewith, and that when and as often as the Comittee shall send for them, their officer shall attend with them, desiring to know my opinion whither the house (whom they would avoyd in any wise disoblidging) may looke uppon this as the least obstruction to the enquiry.

My answer was that I could onely speake as a private man, and as such, did freely own my thoughts, That this proceeding, thus circumstantiated, could nott bee thought in any sort an obstruction to our enquiry. That I know the Committee had in several instances avoided doing things which possibly might administer cause to people without doores to hope for disputes between the houses, nothing being more in their desire then avoiding such. That I verily beleivd the house were of the same mind. For which reasons (though I desired itt might bee remembred I tooke uppon mee to speake onely as a private man) I was of opinion noe exception would bee taken to this proceeding.

449. Alan I, Dublin, to Thomas, Westminster, 22 Jan. 1720[/1], 'Sunday 12 o'clock'

(1248/4/401–2)

Last night the pacquet boat with fowre mailes arrived and brought me your two letters of the tenth and fourteenth: It is certainly very much to your honour that in a matter of soe general concern as the enquiry into the execution of the South Sea bill, you should have more voices to be one of the thirteen then any other Gentleman of the house: those who prosecute that enquiry with intent to come at truth as far as so dark a transaction will allows its being found out, must be sensible that no methods will be left unattempted to suppresse many things from being brought to light, and that consequently the persons to manage such an enquiry ought to be men of understanding, courage, and not capable of being brought to soften matters in favor of vile offenders: and I think it an instance that the persons pitched on were esteemed men duly qualifyed with understanding to find out truth, with courage to tell the truth when they have found it out, and not capable of being softned by the methods usually taken on great occasions by very great offenders. After having said this, you will allow me to tell you my thoughts, that I beleive the offenders are soe many, and soe powerful in freinds and in that which seldome fails to create them, that I rather wish then expect your best endeavours may be attended with the successe you aim att. If I may make a judgement of what may happen on your side of the water from what I have alway observed to be the event of undertakings for the good of the countrey here, I shal be in pain least instead of serving the publick you disserve yourself by raising more and more bitter enemyes then you have already: but I doe not say this, with desire or hope to incline you to be easy (as it is termed) in your enquiry: but when I look over your list I cannot say that I like every <u>one</u> man in it equally; I am sure there is <u>one</u> there, whose sentiments and ours (especially in the grand bill) were as opposite as East is to West; and who you must be sensible is and hath for some time been an utter enemy to our familye: your prudence will restrain your from conversing with any freedome there, unlesse you have a mind to have every thing known where one would not willingly have it: and I think I can convince you that there is a good understanding between that person and another (tho they seem in very opposite interests) whom I will not name, but his nose is apt to bleed upon occasions. We are told you are in the chair of that committee; that layes you under no necessitye of being more personally concerned in this enquiry then the rest of the Committee. I have been very ill, but am much better and soe is my wife: I was not able to go to the Court the first seal day, but hope to go to morrow. My Lord Lieutenant hath in an handsome and obliging maner made Jemmy Barry (my purse bearer) a Captain,[1335] which I will this post acknowledge as I ought, but I must be upon my guard not to doe it improperly; for it is soe long since I have had any thing done toward me which was not done in the most disobliging maner that like a man half starved I shal be apt to fall too eagerly on and to be too full of acknowledgements for the first bit of good usage I meet with. But I doe not here tax my Lord Lieutenant who hath been all along very civil, tho very much at a distance …

[*PS*] I think it will be absolutely necessary for my health (if I were not to be removed) to ask his Majestyes leave to goe for England; on which subject I will soon write more at large.

450. *Thomas to Alan I, 28 Jan. 1720[/1]*

(1248/4/403–4)

By going out (too soone) last Munday uppon the notice wee had of Knights being gone of,[1336] I suffered a good deale, butt I hope I have gott over itt, unlesse doing again the same thing this day, should prove hurtfull to mee. Late last night I received a message desiring (if possible) my attendance this morning uppon a perticular affair. When I was with them, they presst my stay till the two members (whoe were to bee this day heard) should bee taken into consideration; Twas whisperd that Sir Robt Chaplin[1337] would bee given up, butt that the expulsion of Eyles[1338] would bee contested, they therfore layd uppon mee their commands of making the motion against him, which I did, the house were apparently too warme to leave roome for any hope of successe, [?wherefore] they very prudently lett itt goe as they had the former without debate.

The scene of iniquity is too large to bee gone through within any reasonable compasse of time, butt I thinke sufficient will appeare to convince mankind that a great deale is left behind, in doing which I apprehend a great many of our own body will come upon the stage. How far itt may goe farther ile nott venture to guesse, butt that obtaining the Bill cost above a million is very obvious from papers before us, and is noe secrett … Your affair remains in itts former scituation, butt I thinke will nott long; if I am rightly informd the first person thought on in all events is likely to succeed you. I long with impatience its being over, though I am now in great doubt what may bee advisable for you to doe,

[1335]James Barry (1689–1743), of Rathcormac, for whom see Appendix 2. Alan may have been mistaken, as there does not seem to be any record of James Barry being given a captain's commission at this time. However, a David Barry was given a commission in Oct. 1720 as a captain in the 13th Foot (Dalton, *Geo. I's Army*, ii, 96).

[1336]Robert Knight (1675–1744), of Barrells, Warws., cashier of the South Sea Company, who on 21 Jan. had admitted before the secret committee that the company had undertaken widespread bribery which he had disguised by false accounting. However, he refused to divulge the names of those who had accepted bribes, and when the committee adjourned over the weekend he took the opportunity to flee to France (*Oxf. DNB*).

[1337]Sir Robert Chaplin (c.1670–1726), 1st Bt, of Louth, Lincs., MP [GB] Great Grimsby, a director of the South Sea Company, expelled the House on 28 Jan. (*HC 1715–54*, i, 541–2).

[1338]Francis Eyles (c.1679–1735), of Earnshill, Som., MP [GB] Devizes, and a director of the South Sea Company. Also expelled on 28 Jan.

Doctor Hale[1339] having in a late conversation (during my illnesse) expressed himself in the strongest termes, more then doubtfull of the contagion which spread in forreigne parts, reaching us,[1340] to which hee apprehends the present unseasonable temperature of the air will greatly contribute, when in Aprill or May itt shall grow warmer.

If this should happen to bee the case what addition to the present confusion must there necessarily bee, by peoples running out of towne att a time when nott one of twenty is capable of making a judgment of his owne, or the circumstances of his family, God avert itt, the consideration is most dismal … The company have bought in (noe doubt from the Directors) stock att 67 and 800 to replace what they sold out att lesse then a third of those prices to procure the Bill.

451. *Thomas to Alan I, 31 Jan. 1720[/1]*

(1248/4/405–6)

I have just receivd yours of the 22d att my returne from the S[*outh*] Sea house, where our duty is very hard.

Your caution is what was sufficiently in my thoughts, your observations are just, seldome failing, though in this instance they will, for without breach of that secrecy which is enjoynd, and which wee have sollemnly promisd each other, I may in generall tell you, that though a thousand circumstances of lesse moment will unavoidably escape our knowledge, the mistery of iniquity (in the maine) will bee brought to light, and traced to the very origine. Wee see clear day light, and have sufficient ground to stand on. I own my self of your opinion that a greater honour could nott have been done mee; I was nott in the Court list, nor any other except one of our thirteen, nor had hee been chosen butt that hee was in our list likewise.

By this instance you see the good effect of Balloting in some cases, though I am sensible itt may often prove otherwise; The number of Ballots were 395.[1341] Consider then how many whoe tooke the Court list must have torne itt, and made such an one as they liked better. I am nott without my fears that somuch truth as will appeare may bee attended with consequences I dont desire, this therfore is to bee committed to Gods good providence.

452. *Alan II, London, to Alan I, 31 Jan. 1720/1*

(1248/4/409–10)

… The greatest comfort People have now is from the Committee, who have already de-tected many of the Villainous Practices of that vile sett, who thought to have raised them-

[1339]The physician Richard Hale (1670–1728) (*Oxf. DNB*).

[1340]The plague which had broken out in Marseilles in 1720 (see above, p. 315).

[1341]In the ballot for members of the secret committee, on 9 Jan., Thomas had come first with 334 votes (*CJ*, xix, 397, 399). According to Carswell, 220, two of the 13 MPs chosen had been on the court list, Sir Joseph Jekyll (3rd) and Edward Wortley Montagu (4th), a calculation seemingly endorsed in Linda Colley (*In Defiance of Oligarchy*, 196), but according to J.H. Plumb (*King's Minister*, 340), Jekyll was 'one of the fiercest critics of government', a characterisation supported by the biography in *HC 1715–54*, ii, 174–5.

selves upon the Ruin of their Country above the reach of its Laws. But they begin to find they were mistaken, for the Parliament seems resolved to do all in their Power towards recovering the Nation from the Misfortunes and Calamity's it labours under. It is thought all the Directors estates that can be come att, will be thrown into the stock; as many of them are in Custody as can be spared untill some new are chosen. There is a Report that 400000 Pound stock was distributed in the — att the time the bill was depending, and a List of those that took it is handed about[1342]; whether it is an Authentick one, I cannott tell; but be that as it will no doubt but a true one will be made Publick, for Mr Astell (the only one of the Directors that has made any Confession)[1343] named severall att his examination before the Lords. But my Lord the most melancholly news I have heard is that your Lordship and my Lady have been Ill; the best and most comfortable is that you are both on your Recovery. My Uncle's Illness has hindred him from attending the Committee so constantly as he would otherwise have done; but he is now much better ...

453. *Thomas to Alan I, 4 Feb. 1720[/1]*[1344]

1248/4/407–8

Last Tuesday[1345] (when by order the Mutiny Bill was to bee reported) four of us were sent from the S[*outh*] Sea House, to putt itt of for some time; the first order of the day was the call of the house, which was adjourned till Thursday next by common consent. The day movd for the Mutiny Bill was next Tuesday sennight, Mr Secretary uppon that occasion movd for this day sennight[1346] to which wee readily agreed, in speaking to which he was pleasd to say that by the day fixt for the call in the sollemn manner itt was, (meaning the revoking all leaves of absence, and ordering circular letters) hee supposd that about that time the house might expect that <u>important</u> Report, somuch expected.

I spoake after him, taking notice of the intricacy of accounts (affectedly made soe) and the lenghth of time in examining witnesses, whom att present, I would call by noe harder name then that of being very unwilling ones, and that when I was oblidged to acquaint the house that without intermission of a day, (Sundays and the 30th of January excepted) the Committee had satt from nine in the morning till eleven att night, I could nott butt hope the Report <u>so much expected</u>, had been putt in the best forwardnesse the nature of the thing admitted, That as to the Importance, itt must bee referd to the judgment of the house, when itt should come before them, butt that thus much I would take uppon mee to assure the house, and the gent in perticular, that itt would bee a fair and honest one, nott reporting any one fact which was nott well supported, or omitting a tittle that was soe; I was well heard, without a word of Reply made.

Wee are in such forwardnesse as leaves little roome to doubt my having directions (before the house begins to bee calld) that the Comittee are ready to lay before the house an account

---

[1342] *The Skreen Removed; in a List of All the Names Mention'd in the Report of the Committee of Secrecy. With the Sums Wherewith They are Charged, in Relation to South-Sea Stock, As Well on Account of Loans, As Otherwise ...* [1721].

[1343] William Astell (*d*.1740), of Everton, Beds. (Carswell, 274).

[1344] Printed in Coxe, *Walpole*, ii, 206–8.

[1345] 31 Jan.

[1346] Saturday, 11 Feb.

of the progresse they have made in the matters referd to them, being by order to Report from time to time, att such time as the house should please to receive the same, which I beleive may bee the next day, or the Munday following att farthest, Saturday being appointed for taking the Report of the Mutiny Bill.[1347]

Bee itt when itt will perhaps itt may appear of more importance then Mr Secretary imagined at the time hee spoake, for though generally speaking they have been pretty well apprised of what passes among us, from the information of the very persons examined, this insulting speech convinces mee they doe nott receive accounts from any of our number, for wee had the day or two before made some discoverys which I am sure by the way of speaking hee was a stranger to, and these naturally lead us since that time into a more perfect and strict enquiry into some things then hee thought of, and which I must beleive hee thought us strangers to; Your curiosity will in a short time bee satisfyed, and the nation convinct that our enquiry has nott been in vaine.

Five hundred and seventy thousand pound stock was sold by the Company att under rates whilst the Bill was depending, att which time the Company had noe more then twenty five thousand reservd for taking in the annuityes of 1710. Butt this stock was to bee created afterwards, and in fact was soe, and stands in the Companys books as sold to – or fictitious names. Of this great summe wee have hitherto been able to trace onely about two hundred thousand pounds, Mr Knight having either destroyd or secured from us all the secret bookes by which the whole scene of iniquity might have been discovered, I doe nott thinke itt impossible butt wee may come att a good deal more, by crosse examining and putting things togather, butt if wee should faile therin, enoug God knowes is come to light, to shew how the house was curryed, and by what methods that cursed scheme was carryd through to the destruction of the nation. The stock was sold att different prices to different persons as they were favourites, and more or lesse usefull, butt to all att soe low rates as that the difference between the prices delivered to them att, by the Company, and the prices they sold out att exceeds a million, butt the truth is noe stock was ever transferd to them, and consequently they sold none, for both the one and the other was fictitious. The method being to pay these good people the difference between the price when sayd to bee sold to them, and the time when they are to bee supposd to have sold out, which being after passing the Bill amounts (as I sayd before) to above a million.

I know nott whither our Cant words and wicked actions will bee readily understood by you, butt I fancy I have made my selfe intelligible if you revolve the thing in your mind. By these vile means was the Bill carryd, and the Execution was of a peice with its formation, six months would nott suffice to descend into the perticulars, butt probably a second Report may point out some things that are most nottorious and obvious.

454. *Alan I to Thomas, Westminster, 4 Feb. 1720[/1]*

(1248/4/411–12)

I was surprised at not receiving a line from you nor any account about your state of health by the two mails which came in on Thursday and brought us the letters of the 24th and

---

[1347]On 13 Feb. Thomas reported that the committee's report would be ready 'in a few days', and it was appointed to be received on Thursday, 16 Feb. (*CJ*, xix, 421).

26th of January and was in a good deal of pain about the cause of your silence, which my melancholy inclined me to conjecture might proceed from a worse cause then I find it did by your letter of the 28th which I received yesterday. However tell me whether you did not make Charles write a line to me; for I did think the resolutions of the house on Knights withdrawing himself and what followed thereon would have been sent or some hint given of it: but I suppose your ilnesse returning occasioned your silence. My poor wife continues stilll very weak and ill, and tho the Doctors give me great hopes of her recoverye I cannot but be in the last apprehensions for her; she is emaciated to a skeleton and now her Legs swell; but she makes more water then she takes liquids and the Physicians say they think those swellings will be carryed of: and indeed they plainly doe abate … You must know that it is now the discourse among those who are in the Court secrets here, that I am to stand;[1348] at the same time that you give me reason to expect the Coupe de Grace very soon.[1349] But I can hardly think he will be my Successor whom you hint at, if I take you right. I mean the most disagreeable to this Kingdome on earth; but somebody cares not whom he disobliges.

455. *Thomas to Alan I, Dublin, 11 Feb. 1720[/1]*

(1248/4/413–14)

Wonder nott att my silence, being fully employd from nine till eleven att night, fully accounts for itt, this is the first night of a great many when I have gott hence early, for soe I call eight att night, when I receivd yours of this day sennights date.

Wee have just agreed upon the materials for a first Report which the Master of the Rolls[1350] licks into forme, on Munday I take it for graunted the house will bee told wee shall bee ready to make itt, att such time as they shall appoint. When tis taken, I thinke twill make a nose bleed.

There has been a flying Report of Knights escape, butt I can find noe sufficient grounds for itt, and rather thinke people foresee what may possibly happen, then that itt has already; I owne my doubting whither hee will bee delivered to us, as a cleaner way of doing the same thing. Hee is certainly capable of disclosing the whole scene of villany, and being a felon without clergy by going out of the kingdom, his falling into the hands of the Commons may nott (perhaps) bee thought advisable, they gott the start in their Addresse, the Lords being upon one att the same time. Wee have for some days past had what you mention of your men in the secret of affairs, spoake of here, and perhaps the confusion of affairs may bee the ground of itt, for I dare assure you itt proceeds (if true) from nothing else.

The Report of the Mutiny Bill is (againe) this morning put of to this day sennight, on which occasion our whole Committee went into the house, butt itt mett with noe opposition. The Royall Assent was this day given to the Land tax, butt the mault Bill is still behind, in our house.

[1348] That is to say he would remain in office as lord chancellor.

[1349] *Coup de grace*: a blow by which someone mortally wounded or condemned to death is despatched quickly; a finishing stroke (*OED*).

[1350] Sir Joseph Jekyll.

Something should bee done for restoring creditt (if that bee possible) but whither Mr W[*alpole's*] Bill will attaine itt,[1351] I very much question, The error in the first concoction (I mean the S[*outh*] Sea Bill) will with great difficulty bee amended ...

456. Alan I to Thomas, Westminster, 13 Feb. 1720[/1]

(1248/4/415)

As soon as you receive this send the inclosed to Charles Powel, or somebody else who can write and whose hand will not be known,and let it be transcribed fair and doe you compare it and then wrap it up in a fair sheet and seal it up and carry it to the person for whom it is intended and tell him that I wrote to you that I had in a letter to him mentioned an inclosed paper which I had omitted to inclose till the letter was sealed, for which I beg his pardon and desired you to deliver it. I have my reasons for taking this method: for he is mighty great with the contriver of all the roguerye and may perhaps, send over the original to him, which (tho literally true) I would not have come to any other hands then those to whom it is sent ... We have in this town made Lord Carteret sick in the same maner as Lord Stanhope was seised, but have carryed him through it by bleeding at the ear:[1352] and have made Mr Craggs ill and in very great danger.[1353]

457. Thomas to Alan I, Dublin, 28 Mar. [recte Feb.] 1721[1354]

(1248/5/206–7)

Last night I received yours of the 20th. which I can onely acknowledge, being under such perplexity of mind, as leaves noe room for saying or thinking, all brought uppon us by the cursed S[*outh*] S[*ea*] scheme.

When things will end, I thinke noe mortall can uppon probable grounds judge, every thing is in confusion, creditt utterly lost, and the nation in such a ferment as cannott bee expresst. I see noe other way of escape, then the hope that noe body is ready to lay hold of the opertunity, this would be somthing, if a man could promise himselfe security against domestick broyles, which I own I apprehend, God avert the blow, for I thinke itt surpasses humane prudence. I know nott what to advise with respect to your selfe, this you must

---

[1351]The bill to engraft part of the capital stock and fund of the South Sea Company into the stock and fund of the Bank of England, brought into the Commons on 3 Feb. by Robert Walpole, reported, passed and engrossed on 22 Feb., and enacted as 8 Geo. I, c. 21[GB] (the South Sea Company Act) (*CJ*, xix, 416, 456).

[1352]John, Lord Carteret (1690–1763), 2nd Baron Carteret and later 2nd Earl Granville. On 4 Feb. Stanhope had been obliged to return home from the house of lords in the grip of a violent headache after making a passionately angry speech. He seemed to have recovered but died suddenly at home the following evening (Aubrey Newman, *The Stanhopes of Chevening: A Family Biography* (1969), 98–9).

[1353]James Craggs sr (1657–1721), of Charlton, Kent, father of the secretary of state (who had himself died of smallpox on 16 Feb. 1721).

[1354]Date corrected on the basis of the reference to the illness of Craggs, sr.

judge of, butt in generall I thinke a passenger[1355] the best scituation under our present difficultyes. Mr C[*raggs*] remains very ill.

458. *Alan I, Dublin, to Thomas, Westminster, 6 Mar. 1720[/1]*

(1248/4/422–3)

I had not Mr Wards letter of the 25th February with the inclosed abstract of the report by the former pacquet, tho other letters of that date came by it; but by that which came in yesterday and brought in Charles letter of the 28th; by which I see, that is likely to come to passe which I all along apprehended. Defendit numerus.[1356]

Pray let me know how the great men Mr W[*alpole*] my freind Mr M—[1357] and others acted: there must have been a good many who did not vote, or your house is thin considering the nature of the debate and how lately the house was called. I suppose our Northern freinds[1358] were (as usual) a good deal unanimous … When shal you be up, when shal we see Duke of Grafton; we have here made Lord Carterett Secretary. Great rejoicings att a certain house on the successe on Tuesday last.[1359]

459. *Thomas to Alan I, Dublin, 7 Mar. 1720/1*[1360]

(1248/4/424–5)

The paper (which came last night) was coppyed by Charles,[1361] and your directions observed, you will in a little time hear from the person to whom itt was delivered, whoe says hee thought you would easily distinguish a letter of compliment (and intended for noe more) from a designe of complying with an unreasonable request. You have heard of Mr Stanhopes aquittall by a majority of three,[1362] which has putt the towne in a flame, to such a degree as you cannott easily imagine, what consequences itt may have I can nott imagine, these I thinke will bee more or lesse by what shall bee done tomorrow, when Mr Aislebyes case comes on.

[1355] A passer-by, or a bystander.

[1356] There is safety in numbers.

[1357] Probably Paul Methuen.

[1358] The Scottish MPs.

[1359] The vindication of treasury secretary Charles Stanhope in the house of commons from charges of accepting a bribe from the South Sea Company (*CJ*, xix, 462). Presumably the 'certain house' was the residence of Speaker Conolly. Stanhope's cousin and patron, James, 1st Earl Stanhope, was a close friend of Conolly's political associate Henry Maxwell (D.W. Hayton, *The Anglo-Irish Experience: Religion, Identity and Patriotism* (Woodbridge, 2012), 105–6).

[1360] Printed in Coxe, *Walpole*, ii, 208–9.

[1361] Powell.

[1362] By a vote of 180–177 (*CJ*, xix, 462).

Lord Stanhope (sonne to Lord Chesterfeild)[1363] carryed of a pretty many by mentioning in the strongest termes the memory of the late Lord of that name,[1364] between forty and fifty whoe could nott bring themselves to give negatives, were however perswaded to withdraw before the question, on the other hand a great many of the affirmatives are gone out of towne in the utmost rage, many of them nott really displeasd att what happened, since itt affords butt too good a handle for formenting greater discontent in the country; I owne I thinke itt a very bad peice of pollicy, for the whole kingdom are enraged against the S[outh] Sea scheme, and nott lesse soe, against those whoe support their abettors. Youl soone see, by reading the advertisements, the reason of sending the inclosed paper, Mr W[alpole] lives opposite to B. Spars.[1365] The two brothers[1366] were remarkably the most zealous advocates, and perhaps may prove soe tomorrow. Quos Jupiter vult perdere.[1367]

This behaviour (whatever may bee thought) will nott bee forgott, things may for a time bee carryed with a high hand, butt such violences cannott bee long supported; a scalld head is soon broken.[1368] Youl see by your abstract of the Report that the proofe was full as strong as the nature of the thing (Knight being gone) would admitt of, and supported by many concurrent circumstances. Sir J Blunts[1369] evidence was to bee villifyed, for farther reasons which youl easily guesse att; every body see through that …

460. *Thomas to Alan I, Dublin, 9 Mar. 1720[/1]*[1370]

(1248/4/426–7)

Yesterday night past twelve Mr Aislebyes fate was determined, as you will see by the votes, almost the whole time being taken up in examining numbers of witnesses (late Directors) called by him.[1371] The questions proposd were the same to them all, viz. whither they knew or had heard of any fictitious stock taken in, or held for him, or of any stock bought for his use with the companyes money, to every of which they all answerd roundly in the negative, from whence he argued the certainty, and as hee expressed himselfe even to a demonstration of his innocence, for that twas nott to bee conceivd butt they must have known the thing. As to the proceedings of the Directors (to whom hee gave all the hard names hee could thinke of) his plea was ignorance. To the charge of having great dealings in stock (pending the Bill) hee sayd nothing, otherwise then by insinuation that doing soe with his own mony hee hoped would nott bee criminall. His concerting with the Directors taking in the

---

[1363] Philip Dormer Stanhope (1694–1773), MP [GB] St Germans and later 4th earl of Chesterfield.

[1364] The recently deceased James, 1st Earl Stanhope.

[1365] Carl Gustaf (*d.*1741), Baron Sparre, envoy extraordinary and minister plenipotentiary of the king of Sweden.

[1366] Robert and Horatio Walpole.

[1367] See above, p. 278.

[1368] A Scottish proverb, 'A scald man's head is soon broken' (John Ray, *A Compleat Collection of English Proverbs* … (3rd edn, 1738), 278).

[1369] Sir John Blunt (1665–1733), 1st Bt, the originator of the South Sea scheme (*Oxf. DNB*).

[1370] Partly printed in Coxe, *Walpole*, ii, 209–11.

[1371] On 8 Mar. Aislabie was condemned for promoting the South Sea scheme 'for his own exorbitant profit', expelled the House and committed to the Tower (*CJ*, xix, 472–3).

1st subscription att 300 per Cent hee dropt, nott saying one word to the charge; butt an incident happened which gave great disgust to the house. The second Report takes notice of great dealings in stock between him and Mr Hawes (formerly his clerke as Treasurer of the Navy)[1372] whoe had informd the Committee that those accountts were finally adjusted in Nov. last, when Mr Aisleby insisted uppon having Mr Hawes booke (of which hee had a duplicate) delivered him, that noe one might see itt, which was done accordingly uppon his giving Hawes a general release. On Tuesday a motion was made for his laying that book before the house as Yesterday, which hee opposd as what the house could nott demand, for that itt relates onely to his own private account with Hawes, butt was overruled by the house, and ordered to bring the booke, wherwith nott complying, notice was taken of itt in the house.[1373] Hee then desired Mr Hawes might bee examined, whoe sayd att the Bar that when hee deliverd up the booke, both that and the duplicate (in Mr Aislebyes hand) were burnt, of which Mr Haws made noe mention when examined by the Committee, nor did Mr Aisleby on Tuesday, from whence twas concluded that this was an after thought, and the books burnt (if att all) ex post facto. Hee had on Tuesday imprudently enough sayd That if the Committee should have demanded those books, hee would have burnt them before their faces.

After his defence the questions went without other opposition then what was very slender, by Mr Minshall[1374] and Mr Fuller, Sir Richard Steele sayd a little nott very plaine in effect (as I understood him) that the examinations did nott sufficiently support the question proposd, butt itt did nott obtaine Mr W[alpole's] whole corner satt mute as fishes.[1375]

Mr Fuller uppon one question demanded a division, which was very artfully turnd of by the Speaker, and generally understood with designe to obviate the difficulty those in employment might lye under on whatever side they should divide. Thus the matter ended, and in returne for the fatigue the house underwent wee gott a play day, adjourning till tomorrow, when I thinke Sir George Caswell will have the same fate.

I am told his Grace[1376] told a gentleman that hee had very earnestly presst your continuance, butt that the ministry would nott hear of itt, I am pretty sure (if soe) hee might have savd that pains on your account, which I have very often broadly hinted, and indeed spoak itt in plaine termes.

I thinke your writing to desire being discharged very well deserves consideration, and I thinke should bee nott bee long delayd. I beleive I am well informed that G[ilbert] declines returning in any post whatever, choosing rather getting into the Commission of trade or any other employment till an opertunity offers of a cushion here, which may nott soone fall to his share; if soe endeavours are using for promoting G[ore] to the Exchequer.

I heare (and beleive) H[oratio] W[alpole] is to succeed Mr Stanhope as one of the Secretaryes of the Treasury, you may bee sure twill suit his brothers inclination in case (which

[1372] Francis Hawes (*d.*1764), of Purley Hall, Reading, cashier to treasurer of navy [GB] 1716, receiver-gen. of customs [GB] 1717 (Carswell, 279).

[1373] The order on 7 Mar. for Hawes' book to be laid before the Commons was recorded in *CJ*, xix, 469, but not the preceding motion.

[1374] Edward Minshull (b. c.1685), of Stoke, Cheshire, MP [GB] Bramber.

[1375] As mute as a fish: proverbial.

[1376] The duke of Grafton.

is nott doubted) his Brother bee Chancellor of the Exchequer and that Mr Hopkins (your Commissioner) is to bee Lord Lieutenants Secretary.[1377]

Wee have now a very full house, I hope twill continue soe. Severall whoe went away have been prevaild uppon to returne…

461. *Thomas to Alan I, 11 Mar. 1720[/1]*[1378]

(1248/4/428–9)

Yesterday Sir George Caswell had Mr Aislebyes fate, with this further addition, of refunding £250000 as youl see by the votes.[1379] The day was long enough, though nott soe bad as the other, for wee rose just after eight a clock; our time was taken up by an insignificant defence, endeavouring to prove that company loosers by the South Sea, the onely materiall thing insisted uppon by him was a pretence of having given sufficient security for the £50000 stock taken in by Knight for them, in order to gett cleare of a former resolution.

The case (as himself opened itt) stood thus; in January or February 1719 (for wee can never fix them to certain times in any instance) hee and company pawned £70000 stock to the S[outh] S[ea] company, borrowing £105000 uppon itt. The first of March following Knight takes in the £50000 fictitious stock for them, uppon which two questions arose First whither the pawnd stock could (without agreement of partyes) remaine a farther security for the £50000 stock taken in by Knight, even suppose itt would in vallue have answered both. Secondly whither itt would have been sufficient security. The Master of the Rolls differed from his brethren upon the first,[1380] insisting that before they should have been lett in to the redemption uppon payment of the 105,000 they would have been oblidged in equity to have payd for the £50000 stock taken in by Knight. I must here observe that long after, and att the Bar sayd to bee the 13th of May, (though noe witnesse upon oath before the Committee would fix the time) a note under Caswells hand was sent to Mr Knight for £125000 the price of the £50000 stock att 250 per Cent.

As to the second point twas urged (and generally agreed to) That if the S[outh] Sea scheme had failed in our house, the £70000 stock would nott have been near a sufficient security for the £105000 lent thereon. The Masters differing from us was in my opinion what lead the managers into the demand of a division uppon the first question, butt they soon saw their error, The Yeas being 228. The Noes butt 92.[1381] Youl easily beleive the subsequent questions were given up uppon seconding, If I mistake nott the first question was battaild to avoid the consequence of our last question that of refunding, for tis generally thought this stock was in trust for others, and this was in plaine termes spoake strongly to in the debate, even the Master of the Rolls declard freely his being of that opinion, going yett farther, that hee did nott see how any member could justify buying stock (pending the

---

[1377] In April Robert Walpole was made 1st lord of the treasury and chancellor of the exchequer [GB]; and Horatio was made junior secretary to the treasury [GB]. Edward Hopkins, MP [I] succeeded as chief sec. [I] in May. (J.C. Sainty, *Treasury Officials 1660–1870* (1972), 157; Sainty, 'Secretariat', 25.)

[1378] Partly printed in Coxe, *Walpole*, ii, 211–13.

[1379] On 10 Mar. Caswall was expelled the House and committed to the Tower (*CJ*, xix, 476).

[1380] Confirmed by another contemporary report in HMC, *Portland MSS*, v, 618.

[1381] 227–92 in *CJ*, xix, 476.

Bill) although hee should re vera have payd ready mony for itt. Tis nott to bee conceivd what satisfaction these two dayes worke have given, and indeed tis well itt soe happens, for the rage was grown to such heighth uppon the acquittall of Stanhope that noe man can tell where twould have ended; Bonfires were made in the citty the day Mr Aisleby went to the Tower.

Tis sayd an attack uppon the Committee was talkt of in private, and intended, butt wee have acted with such caution and candour as to bid defiance, should any thing of that kind bee attempted, they must have a better posse then appears att present, our creditt through-out the kingdom will sufficiently support us, lett them looke to themselves, they stand on a sandy foundation. In debating the motion for a Bill against Mr Aisleby, Mr W[*alpole*] sayd impeaching (nott Billing Ministers) was the way of Parliament proceeding in time of our Auntcestors, which was very smartly animadverted uppon, perticularly by the Master, hee observed (saying that gentlemen very well knew) that the course of Parliament proceedings was altered, quite inverted, by rendring all prosecutions by way of impeachments ineffec-tuall; That noe greater instance need bee given then in the present case, wherin the Lords have by way of Anticipation entred into the examination of what properly belongd to the Commons, in order to come to a resolution of the legality of that constitution made out by the Treasury appointing the Directors judges where they were beyond possibillity of denyall partyes, by which means all the publique Creditors were imposd uppon and defrauded, and which in truth was the first and cheife source of the misfortunes which have happened.

Last night I found yours of the 6th my last answered the most materiall quaeres of this, the Northern Brigade[1382] went in plum.[1383] Lord M[*olesworth*] went away long before the question, I really thinke out of necessity, for hee labours under a violent Diabetes.

The Master of the Rolls was likewise absent, occasioned by an inflammation in one of his eyes, which I then thought very dangerous, I doe nott yett thinke him safe, though much mended. Mr Sloper went away, hee sayes hee was very ill.[1384]

The sneakers[1385] looke generally out of countenance, some of the most valuable own that twas personal, a poor excuse indeed.

Whither our Session bee drawing towards an end, or will protract into a very long one, is nott in my opinion certaine, though I rather incline to thinke the former, being throughly perswaded wee are nott to expect Knights being brought over. I looke upon this as a two edged sword, and which will give a gash either way, those in whose power itt is, will doubtlesly determine uppon what they thinke least dangerous, in which there can bee noe doubt as to the present; Lett tomorrow looke to itt selfe.

I take itt the D[*uke*] of Graftons going over must necessarily depend uppon the time of the Parliament rising, I meane that hee will have noe thought of doing itt sooner.

[1382] The Scottish MPs.

[1383] Plumb, i.e. as one, in a similar sense as 'voting plumb' (*OED*).

[1384] William Sloper (c.1658–1743), of West Woodhay, Berks, MP [GB] Great Bedwyn.

[1385] Men abandoning their principles or loyalties in order to serve a turn: the most notorious instance in English politics was probably the failure of a contingent of 'moderate' tories in the house of commons to support the 'tack' of the Occasional Conformity Bill to the Land Tax Bill in Nov. 1704. In the *Tatler*, no. 7 (26 Apr. 1709) 'Isaac Bickerstaff' gave 'my courage among all who are ashamed of their distressed friends, all Sneakers in assemblies' (*The Tatler*, ed. D.F. Bond (3 vols, Oxford, 1987), i, 64).

462. *Thomas to Alan I, Dublin, 16 Mar. 1720[/1]*[1386]

(1248/4/430–1)

That part of the Report of the Committee of Secrecy which related to Lord Sunderland, and should have been taken into consideration on Tuesday, was att the pressing instances of Mr W[*alpole*] adjournd to yesterday, uppon suggestion that itt would bee necessary, for the further information of the house, that the severall wittnesses whoe had been examined by the Committee might bee examined att the Bar,[1387] since possibly they might nott come up in every perticular whereof they had informd the Committee, or might soe far explaine their meanings as to give a very different turne from what the words of their examination might possibly import; wee very well foresaw gaining a night was cheifly in veiwe, and itt had (in my opinion its effect) for when they came to bee examined, uppon crosse questions, every one of them strenghtned the Report; among the rest orderd to attend Sir John Blunt was one, butt his Lordships avocates did nott thinke fitt to call him in.[1388] The abstract of the Report which you have will evince the strenghth of the case, which I own I thinke fuller provd (and soe I sayd) then any of the three case which had been under consideration.

The defence made was entirely different from what I expected, there being (as I apprehended) noe room left for denying the fact, wherefore I concluded the sufficiency of the security (His Lordships note sworne to have been shewd Sir J[*ohn*] Blunt by Knight) would have been insisted uppon, butt that point was given up, and his Lordships denyall of any stock taken, or note given, was the subject of three hours debate, after all the papers read and witnesses examined; By way of negative proofe, Mr Pelham Brother to the Duke of Newcastle,[1389] and Mr Walpole, informd the house that his Lordship had empowered them to declare that noe stock had ever been taken in for him by Knight, or note given, soe that the question in truth was neither more or lesse then whither wee should give creditt to that assertion or Sir John Blunts oath, a good deal of paines was taken to falsifie the oath, by asking the witnesses att the Bar whither Knight had told them of this stock being taken in in presence and hearing of Sir John Blunt (as hee had sworne) they ownd Knights telling them of the stock soe taken in for Lord Sunderland, one of them sayd hee was alone with Knight when hee told him of itt, two others ownd Sir Johns being in the roome when hee told itt them, butt did nott beleive him within hearing of what Knight sayd, such trifling stuf never surely was insisted uppon in any other case, and would in any other have been the strongest proofe of the fact; Twas foreseen too well that such a defence was nott to bee relyed uppon, and therefore the sheet anchor was Lord Oxfords play. If you come into this vote against Lord Sunderland the ministry are blowne up, and must and necessarily will bee succeeded by a tory one.[1390]

[1386] Partly printed in Coxe, *Walpole*, ii, 213–14.

[1387] The adjournment was voted on 14 Mar. and the seven named witnesses ordered to attend (*CJ*, xix, 481).

[1388] The serjeant-at-arms was ordered to bring Blunt, who was in his custody (*CJ*, xix, 481).

[1389] Hon. Henry Pelham (1695–1754), of Esher Place, Surrey, MP [GB] Seaford and treasurer of the chamber [GB].

[1390] A tactical argument previously used by Robert Harley, 1st earl of Oxford, during his period as first minister, 1710–14, though in Harley's case what would have been threatened would have been a whig administration.

I really thinke I never heard any thing better debated on the one part, or more weakly on the other, butt Sir J. Walter's argument of Monosillables was the best refuge.[1391] Yeas 172. Noes 233.[1392]

I have sunke nothing, butt tell truly and in short the whole case. I take itt for graunted wee are over the materiall parts of both reports, if what I heard this day in the house prove true; one whoe came out of the citty told mee, hee beleived Mr Craggs dying, if nott actually dead, and gave some circumstances in confirmation of a whisper of his having taken a dose, if soe, itt resembles in great measure Lord Essex's case.[1393]

J[ustice] Pingelly is on the circuite, butt expected soon in towne, when hee comes you shall bee sure of answer to your letter of the 9th. I thinke uppon cursorily reading over your letter last night in the house, itt seems to mee in great measure to resemble what (in my last) I told you was altercated in Caswells case between the Master of the Rolls and Mr Lutwitch[1394] wherein the Master did nott seem to adhere soe positively to his opinion as the other, however this prevents my consulting him, rather choosing to wait the Serjeants Coming[1395] ...

[PS] Wee had againe a great many sneakers. An exact list I am told is made of those whoe voted on both this and the former question.[1396]

463. Thomas to Alan I, Dublin, 18 Mar. 1720/1

(1248/4/432–4)

Tis noe longer a secrett that Mr Craggs tooke a dose of Laudanum sufficient to kill the two strongest men in England,[1397] the circumstance I hinted in my former (told mee in the house) was his having directed his perticular confidant (Mr Huggins[1398]) nott to allow his being blooded, blistered or scarrifyed, all which the phisitian (when hee came) would have ordered, butt was told none of them must bee done, nor indeed would they have been of any use, considering the largenesse of the dose, hee never opened his eyes, movd or spoake after itt began to take effect. You may bee sure his estate will (as far as possible) bee conceald, itt comes to either three or four daughters, and the town says is a million and a halfe, for which calculation I am told there is the authority of a freind of his, to whom he ownd that summe.[1399]

[1391] Sir John Walter (c.1674–1722), of Sarsen, Oxon., MP [GB] Oxford. Described by his friend Jonathan Swift as 'an honest, drunken fellow' (*HC 1690–1715*, v, 788).

[1392] These figures on the division over the motion on 15 Mar. stating that Sunderland had received a bribe of £50,000 are confirmed in *CJ*, xix, 482.

[1393] Arthur Capell (1631–83), 1st earl of Essex, having been arrested in July 1683 after the discovery of the Rye House Plot, was found shortly afterwards in the Tower of London with his throat cut, in what was widely assumed to have been a case of suicide.

[1394] Thomas Lutwyche (1674–1734), of Lutwyche Hall, Salop, MP [GB] Appleby.

[1395] Pengelly.

[1396] No printed division list is known (*British Parliamentary Lists*, ed. Ditchfield et al., 126).

[1397] Craggs died of apoplexy on 16 Mar., though rumours abounded that the cause of death was an overdose of opium (*HC 1690–1715*, iii, 782).

[1398] John Huggins (1645–1745), the notorious warden of the Fleet prison 1713–28.

[1399] Craggs's estate was valued at £1,500,000, or £14,000 p.a. (*Oxf. DNB*).

Yesterday (by order) the farther consideration of the Report was to have been, when, the house were told that by reason of Craggs death, the Committee had nothing farther to trouble them with, that hitherto they had taken uppon them to bee the movers, although they had nothing more to doe in that affair then every other member, that therfore the house being possessed of itt, if any gentleman should thinke fitt to move uppon any perticular part, the Committee (as members) were ready to give their best assistance, That the principal part, unreported, was the list of members (deliverd into the house by the Company) for whom the fictitious stock had been held; of which noe evidence had as yett appeard to them, except that of Surman,[1400] whoe took that list from Knights mouth, and whoe had informd them that Knight had therein omitted many names, putt in several fictitious ones (to cover the reall) and had altered sumes by adding to, and taking from several, That they observd legall proofe was insisted uppon in other cases, which none could give in the manner which had been demanded butt Knight himself, and therfore concluded with the Addresse in the votes, before they proceeded in the farther examination of this matter, the motion seemd to surprize some people, butt there was noe withstanding itt, and soe itt went with a Nem. Cont.[1401]

464. Alan I, Dublin, to Thomas, Westminster, 20 Mar. 1720[/1]

(1248/4/434–5)

Last night yours of the ninth and eleventh arrived here; by which I fin[d] how vilely false the story was which hath been rumoured about this town that Lord Molesworth Sir Joseph Jekyle and you withdrew on the question about Mr Charles Stanhope; that such a thing was whispered among a sett of rascals I am satisfyed; but that it could be true with regard to you I never had the least suspition; nor had I any of the Master of the Rolls, provided his health allowed him to attend; the other I confesse I think too deep a politician and courtier to be soe much depended on. But what you say about him having a diabetes is too good an excuse, I mean too just an one not to be allowed: but the good nature of our town hath put you in the room of Mr Sloper;[1402] and it is very seldom that some peoples private intelligence holds so far true, as it hath done in this case: for two thirds of it holds true. You see I guessed right as to the Northern Brigade, and of the inclinations of another set of men. I find my good freind[1403] continues stil, and for ought I find is like to be (as I think he hath been some time past) the M[inistr]y; for I am sensible it is he that is meant under the name of the m[inistr]y not hearing of something said to have been proposed by the D[uke] of Gr[afton]. The Gentleman cheifly concerned in that affair is under a good deal of difficulty as to the maner of doing it, tho not as to the thing. But after advising with his freinds will soon come to finally resolve, and put in execution what is thought advisable.

[1400]Robert Surman (*d*.1759), deputy cashier (Carswell, 284).

[1401]On 17 Mar., after further consideration of the report from the secret committee, the house of commons resolved, nem con., to address the king for 'the advices his majesty has received, or shall receive, from abroad' relating to the efforts to bring Knight to justice (*CJ*, xix, 484).

[1402]Until 1720 Sloper had been deputy paymaster-gen. [GB].

[1403]William Conolly.

I have been asked by several Gentlemen how they were to distinguish Mr S[*tanhope's*] case from Mr A[*islabie's*]. my answer was that there certainly was a great deal of difference between them, since the proper Judges of both made so different a judgement of them: but was forced to refer them to those who saw farther into matters then I could to learn wherein the difference consisted. I hope and almost beleive my wife is in a mending condition; by the middle of next month the season will be soe far advanced that I may expect her being able (if ever) to undertake an English journey. I came to town on purpose to find out the Bishop of Rapho, only brother and Executor of the late Lord Cheif Justice Forster,[1404] with whom it is as probable the settlement Sir George Markham[1405] enquires after may be found, as with any body: for there was a great intimacy between Mr Forster when he was at the Bar and Mr Ogle,[1406] tho it cooled pretty much before the death of the later, by his going into measures and freindships perfectly opposite to those he seemed in the former part of his life to have embraced. I should be glad to be able to serve Sir George Markham, and to answer Mr Wortleys expectations,[1407] but am told the Bishop is gone out of town, soe that I shal be under a necessitye of writing into the countrey and expecting an answer before I can effectually answer that part of your letter which relates to this affair. In the mean time let me assure you that my Lady Altham hath chosen her third husband not out of the number of men abounding in Land or money, but he is a good agreeable young fellow, of good sense and addresse[1408] and one who neither chose her for youth or beauty: and if the estate was in her power when he marryed her, I doubt not it either is not soe now, or will not long be soe: just as I had wrote the last words Charles Campbel came to see me from whom I thought I should get some light into the matt[er] as having great acquaintance with Mr Ogle. On discoursing him I have reason to beleive there was some settlement made on Mr Ogles marrying Lady Altham, but he saith he beleives the estate was soe limited as (if her Ladyship survived him) that it would be entirely in her own disposal. He adds that tho the Bishop be gone out of town, it is not to Rapho, but to Forest (an house within six miles of Dublin)[1409] soe that I resolve to write to him this night, and will transmit his answer to my letter as soon as I receive it under your cover. I am greatly afflicted at the news my namesake sends me of my sisters great ilnesse: God preserve and restore her. I find by a print of the 14th that Lord S[*underland*] hath been named in the house: that will occasion a bloody nose.

[1404] John Forster.

[1405] Sir George Markham (1666–1736), 3rd Bt, of Sedgebrook, Lincs., MP [GB] 1695–8, 1701, a contemporary of Alan and his brother St John (II) at the Middle Temple.

[1406] Samuel Ogle (*d.*1718) had married Markham's sister Ursula, widow of the 1st Baron Altham, his heir presumptive since Markham was unmarried. Markham's 'intense dislike for most of the Ogles' prompted him to leave his estate away from them (*HC 1660–1715*, iv, 760).

[1407] Edward Wortley Montagu (1678–1761), of Wortley, Yorks, MP [GB] Westminster.

[1408] Dorothy (*d.*1725) (née Davey), widow of Richard (*d.*1701), 3rd Baron Altham (brother of the 1st Baron) married in 1720 William Vesey, MP [I].

[1409] Great Forrest, near Swords, Co. Dublin, which had been John Forster's country seat.

465. *Alan I, Park Lodge, Dublin, to Thomas, Westminster, 22 Mar. 1720[/1]*

(1248/4/436–7)

This morning I received both your letter of the sixteenth and my sisters of the same date: and am in no sort surprised at the event of the affair which was the cheif subject of yours: If you think my letters worth keeping you will find (in the first which I wrote after hearing you were chosen one of the secret committee) what my thoughts were of the determination of that great affair. The things to be enquired into and the persons supposed to be concerned were both strong arguments against the probabilitye of the committees being able to bring things so into the light as to convince in the maner people would expect to be satisfyed.

But I will decline saying any more on a subject of this nature, and proceed to tell you that since my last I have seen the Bishop of Rapho, who assures me that he hath since his brother the Lord Cheif Justice Forsters death had occasion carefully to examine into and inspect such writings as were in his custody at the time of his death; and that he doth not remember or beleive there was any deed paper or writing of any sort among them relating to any settlement made by Mr Ogle and Lady Altham or either of them of her Ladyships estate; or indeed any writing concerning them or either of them: but he promised that he would very soon peruse and look over the writings in his hands, and if he finds any relating thereto, will give me notice of it and not part with it. He adds that he never delivered any writing to Mr Vesey (who is marryed to the Lady) or any other since his brothers death. He is a man of probity and may be depended on in what he affirms or promises. My sisters letter hath a paragraph in it soe full of her apprehensions of the present scituation of affairs, that I have no doubt she thought the last of evils (I am sure I think it soe) not only probable, but like to fall on us and that very soon without any great prospect of being prevented. I never approved the South Sea scheme, and alway beleived it was designed by the first projectors to enrich a few cunning knaves on the ruine of thousands; What the Committee hath brought to light hath convinced the world that very impolitick and indirect means have been taken in the prosecution of that affair. But what the final result of the whole will be God only knows: I wish the discoveries made may have created his Majestye and the present establishment more freinds then they had before the Parliament mett. If I understand my sister right, she fears that what we have alway looked on as the last calamitye is like to fall on these Nations. God avert it: my cheif dependance is on that providence which hath for so many years protected us against the same, when we had reason to fear it as much as we now seem to have. Pray find out the Gentleman to whom the inclosed is directed and let your servant put it into his hands. He never doth me the favor to answer any letter, tho they concern both him and me nearly, relating to money. I will by next pacquet write to his Grace of Grafton and desire my quietus,[1410] which I suppose will now be sent me without delay, since the late triumph …

[1410]Release from suffering, i.e. his dismissal from office.

466. *Thomas to Alan I, Dublin, 30 Mar. 1721*

(1248/5/208–9)

After reading (on Munday) the papers layd before the house by his Majestys order (pursuant to our Addresse) relating to the application made for delivering Knight, an inconsiderate motion was made by one of our Comittee, for addressing to pardon him, in order to encourage his returne, the objections against this were too obvious to need being mentioned, and indeed the gentleman uppon second thoughts acknowledged his mistake; this however gave a very good opertunity to a more regular step, to witt the house resolving itt selfe into a Committee to consider that matter, which was orderd for yesterday, when I thinke the whole procedure in relation to the demanding Knight was exposd beyond what I ever heard, with a freedom becoming a house of Commons; gentlemen were calld upon in sharpe termes, butt yett civill, to say what they could in justiffication of the methods taken, butt nott a man could bee provoked to speake, except Sir Rich[ar]d Steele, whoe I beleive will bee well jobed for his speech.[1411]

Hee sayd two remarkable things, First that surely noe man could wonder att Knights withdrawing to avoid the Torture; The house cryed out wee have noe Rack. Noe replyd hee nott for the body butt the torture of a mans mind is the worst of Racks, suppose then this gentleman should have been privy to secrett transactions which hee did nott thinke to reveale, this hee must have done uppon examination, or have perjured himselfe; this occasioned a good deal of mirth the whole house beleivd itt. His next step was very remarkable, The power of this house says hee, nor of the nation goes noe farther then his Majestys dominions; att which people stared an instance whereof wee late were made sensible of, when all the applications that could bee made were fruitlesse att the Court of Loraine for removing the Pretender,[1412] in answer to which Mr Cooper[1413] agreed the Paralell very exact (as hee beleivd) in every part, for that itt seemed to him more then probable the Ministry in both instances acted with the same veiwe, the neither the one or other should take place; then appeard a prodigious spiritt, by the votes youl see a very home address, couchd in soft dutifull termes; The dissatisfaction mentioned needs noe paraphrasing uppon. Twas a surprize certainly upon some gentlemen whoe expected a renewall of the former motion for a pardon, into which they would readily have gone, as what would very fully have answered their ends by Knights refusing the offer.

I protest I cannott guesse what part they will now act, for this two edged sword cutts soe terribly both wayes, that the choice will I thinke bee very difficult, The nation will expect Knight, bringing him over may bee very unsafe for some people, unlesse hee can bee brought to choose Sir R[ichard] Steels latter way, thinking that the safer and lesser torture, which perhaps hee may have good reason to doubt.

[1411]Rewarded with a 'job', an office or pension. Steele's speech, 'offer[ing] something against obliging Mr Knight to be an evidence, whether he would or no', is noted briefly in Cobbett, *Parl. Hist.*, ix, cols 759–60.

[1412]Efforts by the tory ministry in 1711–14, pressed by the house of commons, to oblige the king of France to assist in securing the removal of the Pretender from his residence in the duchy of Lorraine (H.N. Fieldhouse, 'Oxford, Bolingbroke, and the Pretender's Place of Residence, 1711–14', *EHR*, lii (1937), 289–96).

[1413]Spencer Cowper (1669–1728), of Hertingfordbury Park, Herts., MP [GB] Truro.

After writing last post, I spent my evening with Lord G[*odolphin*] whoe is a good deale out of order, att my returne I found yours with the inclosed to his Grace, whoe told mee this day when wee delivered our Addresse[1414] that hee had communicated your request to his Majesty but receivd noe answer, which however hee thought hee should in a few dayes, and would impart itt to mee assoone as possible, I presume the matter is to bee adjusted with others, bee that as twill I please my self with a speedy determination, without the least concerne for the event, my way of acting is too publique nott to bee thoroughly understood, this may very probably bee under consideration, butt I am nott sure what effect itt may have, perhaps different from what some imagine, nott that I should please my self with its taking that turne.

467. St John III, Cork, to Alan I, 31 Mar. 1721

(1248/5/211–12)

You will probably hear from other hands of a Tryal which has made a good deal of noise here, and about which people are extremely divided in their opinions, and therefore I will, as far as my memory serves me, give you as exact and true an Account of it as I can. Geoffrey Keating and Samuel Ryland were endicted and tryed on Monday last for the Murther and Robbery of Mr Watkins.[1415] The Evidence against them was one Thomas Dart, who swore he was with them at Waterparke, being perswaded by Keating to join in that Robbery. He said he was a servant to one Mr F[*it*]zGibbon who liv'd at a place calld Knockgraffan 5 Mile below Ardfinnan;[1416] that Sunday the 5th of February being the day agreed on, he left his Masters house 2 hours after night, and went directly to a place call'd Knockballyreecy, 3 mile wide of Ardfinnan, and 2 from Knockgraffan, and there met the Prisoners, one Power, James Birne and a Smith whose name he knew not; that when they met there, all but the Smith and the witness smutted their faces, agreed upon the manner of the Robbery, and then went directly to Rylands house at Ardfinnan, and from thence a cross the Mountains thro Arraglin[1417] to Waterparke; He was very particular as to the several circumstances of the Robbery which are not worth troubling you with, and if he were not actually there, must have had a most exact and particular Account from those that were; and yet by his own way of telling the story, and computing the time that must have been employed in riding from Knockgraffan to the place of meeting, from thence to Ardfinnan, and so to Waterparke, which must have been at least 18 Miles, it seemd hardly possible he could be there so early as between 9 and 10 at night, which was the time the whole family agreed the Robbery and Murther were committed; However he was most positive and

[1414] Relating to the apprehension of Knight.

[1415] Isaac Watkins of Waterpark, Co. Waterford, the son-in-law of Dean Davies of Cork (H.W. Gillman, *Index to the Marriage Licence Bonds of the Diocese of Cork and Ross…* (Cork, 1896–7), 38). He and his gardener were murdered in a robbery which occurred shortly after Watkins had taken possession of £200 in cash from a widow for whom he acted as receiver. This was one of a spate of robberies in the area. (BL, Add. MS 46972, f. 17: Berkeley Taylor to Lord Perceval, 9 Feb. 1720/1; SHC, G145/box 98/1: Nicholas Greene to Alan I, 9 Mar. 1720[/1].)

[1416] Possibly John Fitzgibbon (*d*.1731) or his brother Thomas (John O'Hart, *Irish Pedigrees … Second Series* (Dublin, 1878), 333). Knockgraffon was four English miles north of Cahir, Co. Tipperary; Ardfinnan some six English miles to the south.

[1417] Araglin, in the north-east of Co. Cork, on the route to Co. Waterford over the Knockmealdown Mountains.

particular, and gave his Testimony in so plain and simple a manner as perswaded a good many to beleive it true, and that he had not understanding enough to frame and contrive such a story had it been false. The next Evidence was Mr Watkins's son who agreed in almost every circumstance with Dart as to the manner of attempting and breaking open the house, and swore positively Keating was the man who shott Mr Watkins, but could not be positive as to Rylands face. He seem'd to give his Evidence with a good deal of modesty, and when the Prisoners were first taken he would not venture to swear to their faces till they were both smutted, and then was positive as to Keating. There was a particular part of his Evidence, which indeed seem'd very strong, and I beleive determin'd the jury against the Prisoners, and that was, that after Watkins was kill'd and the Rogues were rifling the house, Keating, not finding the Key of a Cabinet, set his foot against the backside of it, and burst in some of the Boards, and his Leg going thro them, swore a great oath that he had broke his shin, and 2 Gentlemen swore they lookt upon his shin when he was first brought into Goale [*sic*] and that there was a scab upon it, and seem'd to have been lately broke. A Nephew of Watkins's, his Butler, and 2 servant maids were then produc'd and all swore directly to Keating, but only one of the maids was positive as to Ryland, and she differd from Dart in 2 material points as to him, Dart swearing he wore a light wig and had only his wastcoat on when he was in the house, and the wench swore he had a dark wig and wore his Coat. Major F[*it*]zGerald[1418] swore when he took them they both absolutely denyed ever having known or been acquainted with Dart, and tho 2 or 3 witnesses were examin'd to this point, there was no other Evidence then that F[*it*]zGibbon his master once sent him to Keatings house for 2 Pound of Hops, he keeping a shop in Cahir; and also, that Dart waited upon him once to Rylands house in Ardfinnan, and attended him there for 2 or 3 hours while he was speeding a Commission. This was the substance of the Evidence against the Prisoners. They in their defence endeavour'd to prove first that Dart was not out of his Masters house the 5th of February, and if he were, twas impossible he could have been at Waterparke at the time he mentiond even by his own way of telling his story. His Master swore he pull'd of his spurs and put him to bed that night between 7 and 8, and that he saw him by 6 the next morning, and was certain the horse Dart pretended to have rode could not have been at Waterparke and back again the night before, which was at least 35 Mile, without being dirty or out of order the next morning, which he was not at all. Mrs F[*it*]zGibbon swore she saw Dart at her own house the 5th of February between 10 and 11, and that she sent him about that time with some warm Ale to a joiner who had workt and then lay sick in her house; Her maid and the joiner swore the same thing, and the joiner said he lay with him that night; they were both very Circumstantial in their Evidence, but differed in some minute particulars, as that Dart pulld of his Masters Boots that night, tho the Master said he wore no Boots, and that he only pull'd off his great Coat and spurs but in all the material parts they agreed exactly. The Prisoners then produc'd a multitude of Witnesses to prove each of them at his own house at the time they were suppos'd to be at Waterparke, and this they did by people of undeniable Credit, that told abundance of particular Circumstances, and did not contradict each other in any one that was material, and concluded their defence with calling a great many Gentlemen to their reputation, who gave each of them a very extraordinary Character, and tis certain that till they were accus'd

---

[1418] Possibly John Fitzgerald (c.1648–1728), of Ballynacot, Co. Cork, MP [I] 1727–*d*., and high sheriff of Co. Cork in 1722 (*Hist. Ir. Parl.*, iv, 152). See also Dalton, *Geo. I's Army*, i, 137.

of this fact, no 2 men of their sort in the kingdom liv'd in better esteem then they did. The Tryal lasted about 12 hours, and the judges being pretty much fatigued did not think fit to sum up the Evidence to the jury, tho twas sum'd up by Mr Purdon[1419] against them (Mr Bernard[1420] and I refusing to do it), and was certainly as nice and doubtfull an Evidence, and left people as much divided in their judgments, as any one that ever was given. However the jury did not think so, and were ready to find them guilty without even stirring from the Bar, and would have done so had not the Court been Adjourn'd for an hour, for decency as one of the judges said. Assoon as they return'd, they were found Guilty and sentenc'd to be Executed on Wednesday which the poor men received with great constancy and with the most solemn professions of their Innocence, and indeed during their whole Tryal they shewed such an Air of unconcernedness and resolution, as nothing but an innocent, or a most harden'd wicked man, could have put on. Tis certain the Evidence of both sides was most full; but, as the Prisoners insisted, that against them, was only the bold swearing of an infamous man as the Approver[1421] was allow'd to be, and of the 5 witnesses who swore to their faces, without any one Circumstance to confirm their Testimony; whereas what was produc'd on their behalf consisted of so many as could not possibly lye, provided and prov'd by people of as good Character as those who swore against them. In short the doubtfullness of the Evidence, the Compassion which every body must have for wreches in their Condition, and their constant solemn denial of the Fact of which they stood convicted, so far wrought upon the minds of the people, that almost every one beleiv'd them innocent, and therefore the Grand jurys both of County and City join'd in a request to the judges to grant them, if no longer time could be obtain'd, a Repreive for 3 days only, but they were so far perswaded of their Guilt as not only to deny what was earnestly askt, but to do it in very angry disobliging Terms, and so the poor men were Executed on Wednesday pursuant to their sentence. I cannot tell you the impression their behaviour at the Gallows made on every one who either saw or heard of it. They shewed not the least concern or fear of death, and behav'd themselves with uncommon spirit and Devotion, and Denyed their Crime in the most solemn manner, and with the highest Asseverations. Keating was first Executed, and just before he was turn'd off the Preist call'd to him, for he was a Papist, and told him, among other things, that if he were really guilty and dyed without confessing and repentance, he would certainly be turn'd off the Ladder into Hell;[1422] the poor man answer'd him, and spoke so loud that all the people heard him; he told him he fully beleiv'd all he said, but knowing himself to be Innocent he was resolv'd with his last breath to declare it; and then lifting up his Eyes and hands he spoke these words; Thou great God of Heaven knowest I am Innocent, and do thou so deal with my soul in the next World as what I here declare is true or false, and dyed the next Moment. Ryland dyed a Protestant, and with the same Professions, and earnestly beg'd to receive the Sacrament at the Gallows, to give, as he said, the most sacred Confirmation of the truth of what he said, but that was

---

[1419] Henry Purdon, MP [I].

[1420] Francis Bernard, MP [I].

[1421] St John evidently means the witness Thomas Dart, but according to another account it was William Lyne, a convicted felon, whose testimony was instrumental in proving the guilt of Keating and Ryland. Lyne admitted after the execution that he, along with James Byrne, his brother Michael Byrne, and another unnamed party 'were the only persons guilty of the said murder and robbery' (John Fitzgerald, *The Cork Remembrancer* ... (Cork, 1783), 155–6).

[1422] Jacob's ladder (Gen. 28: 10–19).

denied him by direction of the Bishop, and the opinion of the Clergy who did not think it proper that a man convict of such a Crime should receive it without Confession; however 5 of them subscrib'd his last speech, which the judges thought was publishing their opinion of his Innocence to the world, and therefore sent for them the next day to Court, and reprimanded them for what I confess I think an imprudent Act.[1423]

These are all the particulars I can at present recollect of this Tryal, which has made a greater noise in the Countrey then you can imagine. There are some others which are not proper to be communicated by letter, and must therefore be reserv'd till I see you, and particularly that part of Keatings defence which related to his accounting for his broken shin, which he said he could have fully explain'd had the length of his Tryal or the impatience of — permitted him. I am afraid I have tir'd you with this long letter, which has kept me so late that I have mist the Post …

468. Alan I, Dublin, to Thomas, Westminster, 1 Apr. 1721

(1248/5/1–2)

… I had … a letter from an unknown female correspondent, with an inclosed print called the London journal; I see by the hand and spelling that it is from a woman, but who the Lady is who favours me with her presents of this kind I cannot guesse. The inclosed paper is very sharply written,[1424] and I am so much in my judgement convinced of the fatal consequences which have attended the South Sea scheme that I could be content to see the projectors and contrivers of that infamous cheat (soe I may call it as it hath been managed) brought to the last punishment and infamy: but I should be sorry to see the nation put into the utmost confusion and our all indangered if that cannot be attained to the heigth of mens wishes and expectations. And yet that paper seems calculated to irritate and inflame the people, to be wrote as an appeal to them, if all the measures be not gone into, which the authors think advisable. I wish you could hinte to me who the supposed Authors are of that weekly paper: for it is plain to me by the last that it is the spawn of a Club: By one expression in it I should be apt enough to beleive a certain Lord of this countrey had an hand in it,[1425] where he mencions the care taken by the ministry lately to make England and Ireland easy. This I think relates to the late affair of the jurisdiction of our house of Lords, for which he was a most zealous advocate and stickler: but then the paragraph which mentions the late offer made to the Commons, which (if it had been accepted) would have inslaved them I take to be meant of the bill brought in, which among others I never could come into;[1426] and the Lord I mean was for that bill. But I hear it said that a certain person

---

[1423]For the practice of publishing 'gallows speeches' in 18th-century Ireland, see James Kelly, *Gallows Speeches from Eighteenth-century Ireland* (Dublin, 2001), 26–41.

[1424]John Trenchard and Thomas Gordon, the authors of the *Independent Whig*, contributed a series of letters to the *London Journal*, usually under the pseudonym 'Cato'. These were subsequently reprinted as *Cato's Letters …* (4 vols, 1724 and subsequent editions). Alan is referring to the letter contained in the issue of 25 Mar. 1721.

[1425]Viscount Molesworth.

[1426]The Peerage Bill.

whom that Lord proposed to an acquaintance of yours for his nearest relacion[1427] is in a club with the other, and one paragraph may be the produce of one head, the other of the other. By all accounts I can hear of, things seem to run very high: God send all concerned more wisdome and temper then to do what may help to bring on the greatest calamitye these nations can fall into.

Mr Ward writes that your Committee are preparing a farther report, whether Knight is sent over or not: I am sure by what is already done, your Committee (and particularly the Chairman) have rendred themselves mighty obnoxious to the displeasure of those who often have oportunity of doing shrewd turns and seldome omit making use of them. I wish you would let me know the Master of the Rolls sentiments of the Case I sent to you to shew Serjeant Pingelly. I find Gilbert was within this fortnight in doubt whether he should come over or no: so said Mr Manly from a letter he had from him; but Mr Ward saith he declares if ever he doth come over, it will be in his former station: soe as I take it W[*hitshed*] is to be the man.

I have never had a line from his Grace in answer to the letter about the living,[1428] in which his Grace will act a poor part if he comply with the unreasonable expectacions of a certain Prelate.[1429] … The murtherers of Isaac Watkins att Waterparke are discovered and executed.

469. *Alan I, Dublin, to Thomas, Westminster, 2 Apr. 1721*

(1248/5/3–4)

I can hardly expresse the terror into which your letter of the 28th of March hath put me: for by it I plainly perceive that you apprehend very ill consequences, from the confusion things have been put into by this damned S[*outh*] S[*ea*] scheme and the execution of it. By some of my late letters you could not but observe that my fears were very great what the event might be of the enquiry which hath lately been made, which hath brought a small part of that work of darknesse to light: for as on one hand people that know the nation and they themselves to have been injured will be apt to presse bringing the causes of the misfortunes to punishments; so on the other, when they have reason to beleive that there are wealthy and powerful persons concerned in the guilt, they cannot but expect that they will rather chuse to see all things brought into the last extremitye and danger, then be brought on the stage and run the risque of undergoing the last infamy and punishment. God Almighty send into the hearts of those to whom the care of the publick is committed, such a spirit of wisdom and temper as may contribute to the pacifying publick discontents and to keep us in quiet and peace and due obedience to his Majestye and the Laws. Let me desire you to caution your Nephews [*sic*][1430] (whose youth hath not allowed him experience enough

---

[1427] This may refer to John Trenchard, whose first wife committed suicide in Nov. 1718, and who married for the second time a year later (*HC 1715–54*, ii, 481).

[1428] Raheny, Co. Dublin (see below, p. 357).

[1429] Archbishop King.

[1430] Alan II.

to be discreet) never to say or doe any thing that may seem to savour of discontent or disaffection.

I have for some time past been of opinion from the numbers of Irish who have endeavoured to ship themselves off for foreign service, and from the more then ordinary frequency of insolencyes and robberyes in this town and in the countrey, that there hath been mischeif brewing among the enemyes of our peace and of his Majestyes Governement: and of this we have given hints to my Lord Lieutenant from time to time. And I cannot say that I ever observed the Jacobites behave with more assurance, or with a greater air of insolence then they have done of late: and they lay hold of this publick calamitye to rail at those whose businesse it was to have prevented it, meaning (as they pretend) the ministry; but perhaps intending to throw dirt farther. And tho I would not have you take notice of it, yet I cannot but think that something which hath lately been set on foot by a great P[relate] with an appearance of charity, may in the consequence increase rather then allay the discontents among poor tradesmen for want of trade. I will not explain my self; for you will guesse at what I mean, when you recollect what was moved in behalf of the poor of one sort of tradesmen here in town: I mean the weavers.[1431] The encouragement that hath been given them thereby will I doubt not only bring the like applications from other trades but I think make them insolent and idle …

470. *Thomas to Alan I, 6 Apr. 1721*

(1248/5/5–6)

Noe answer is yett given; since my last your letter has been shewne to our great men, which I am very well pleasd with. I know as well as themselves what is determined and am noe stranger to the wood they are in, in order to execute their fixt intentions. In the first place a proper Lord Justice comes into consideration; this I suppose will fall to Lord Shannons share, whoe, in order thereto, is to bee sent away, assoone as hee can gett ready, butt determining the other point requires more consideration, and is attended with greater difficulty. A point was last night started which I could nott salve, notwithstanding (to the best of my remembrance) I have formerly heard itt mentioned on occasion of the same nature; To witt, whither a pattent constituting new Justices would nott supercede that of Lord Lieutenant I am promised an account of the solution, if itt can bee had, this night, in which case ile adde itt att the end of this letter. I have talkt the matter very fully and with opennesse, to Lord Lieutenant whoe protests against having had any share in itt and repeated what hee sayd to mee att Newmarkett, that hee had wrote to the cheife person concernd, that hee would have noe hand in itt, butt went farther then hee did att any time before, that hee had from him receivd assurances that the thing should nott bee done, butt hee has altered his

---

[1431] In Mar. 1721 Archbishop King informed Archbishop Wake of Canterbury that he had received a petition from destitute linen, silk and woollen weavers, which he had put before the lords justices and privy council. He had been ordered to investigate the truth of the allegations, and after commissioning parish clergy and churchwardens to make inquiries had concluded that a third of the city's population were in need of poor relief. He had organised church collections and had 'engag'd the clergy to represent their case in the most effectual manner to their people'. The playhouse had also given a benefit performance. (*Swift Corr.*, ii, 369–71; Ehrenpreis, *Swift*, ii, 116–17, 156–8.)

resolution in that particular. After having recapitulated the manner of proceeding, I told him I beleivd hee could nott bee surprisd if, when your owne, as well as my sisters health (nay life) in probabillity might depend uppon both your coming over, you should come away, which nothing butt the last extremity could induce you to doe, having soe long and soe earnestly presst a dismission, for the truth of which I must appeale to himself, to which hee onely answered that hee hoped you would nott doe itt; I see noe other method practicable for obtaining your releasement then by fairly representing what might bee the consequences of these affected delayes, for I make noe doubt of the designe of keeping you on the spott till his Graces arrivall, which will nott probably bee sooner then three months; lett mee hear often from you, and assoone as you can; I presume all my letters are opened, I vallue nott their being soe, nor should I care if they were publisht att the markett crosse, very well knowing that both of us have in every instance acted with duty and true zeale for his Majestys service, butt since nothing will satisfie great men butt leaping over a stick and creeping under itt, as directed, against a mans judgment, and prostituting his charecter,[1432] the sooner wee are disingaged from such like expectancyes, the better. This peice of drudgery I never did, or ever will submitt to. Your being against the Popery Bill, and nott exerting as was expected for Repeale of the Sacramentall Test (the latter much the sorer place) are trumpt up to skreen (for that machine is in great request[1433]) your being against the Peerage Bill and should you bee here, you might possibly prove as restif against giving up the seven millions and the continuance of this parliament beyond the limited time, refusing the former would nip in the bud those advantages which may accrue to some people by playing the late game over, and the latter may administer doubt whither a new Parliament may bee as subservient to some mens commands, as the present. Lord Lieutenant goes tomorrow (for a weeke) into Suffolke, I hope att his returne all difficultyes may bee removd, or very soon after … H[*oratio*] Walpole succeeds Mr Stanhope (whoe the town says is to bee better provided for)[1434] as one of the Secretaryes of the Treasury, and Mr Hopkins is to supply his place under my Lord Lieutenant.

His Grace is this minute gone from mee, hee says there is a clause in his pattent appointing you to hold over till his coming,[1435] and that you may see his pattent in the office, and from thence infers that till his arrivall you cannott bee discharged, looke into itt, consider very well the thing, and lett mee have your directions. I have told him with protestation that unlesse you forbid itt, I will deliver a memoriall in forme to the King, and ile keep my word, for such treatment as you have found is nott to bee borne.

Hee says hee will bee back Sunday sennight, soone after which I hope to hear from you, write soe as if occasion bee I may shew your letter.

[1432]See above, p. 317.

[1433]A reference to the supposed 'screening' of those guilty of corruption in the South Sea affair.

[1434]Charles Stanhope eventually became treasurer of the chamber [GB] in 1722.

[1435]That is to say, the commission of lords justices would remain in place until Grafton arrived.

471. *Alan I, Dublin, to Thomas, Westminster, 7 Apr. 1721*

(1248/5/7–8)

It is now six weeks since I wrote to the Duke of Grafton in behalf of Mr Gibbons[1436] about the living of Raheny: I beleive you expected something would have been done before this time in favour or rather in justice to that honest worthy man: at least that his Grace would have come to a resolution in the affair and not put an entire stop to the Kings suit for a living granted under the great Seal before he was in the Governement; but not one word is come about it tho several directions about other livings for persons whose recommendations are of a later date.

When you see him, you may by way of question remind him of this; for I would not write again, which will be like asking a favour: whereas common justice and not doing things out of all course will answer that Gentlemans expectations. But it is known that I justly value him and he hath the misfortune not to be in the good graces of the Archbishop of D[*ublin*] to whom we pay court; but in the event it will not attain the end. I hope your sister will be able to be put on shipboard in some time, for she seems to me to mend; and the weather coming in warm will I am perswaded contribute a good deal to it. Probably I shal know his Majestyes pleasure in reference to his giving me leave to be absent as soon as I can hope she will be able to travail: but I doubt your delivering my letter just at the time things were in such a ferment on the Emperors answer about Mr Knights[1437] may be looked on as laying down (which no body ought to doe) in discontent: I am sure that was not my design, and my letter to my Lord Lieutenant speaks the naked truth of my design, to carry my wife over.

As I would not meanly sneak to keep a place, which I know some great ones have a long time resolved to have me removed from, so neither would I in a time of dissatisfaction decline the Kings service, if it shal be his pleasure to continue me in it: for I have done him real service and can stil doe soe.

We have a flying report about the town, that the Garter is given the D[*uke*] of G[*rafton*][1438] in exchange for this Governement, and some people offer wagers that he will not come over; but I look on this to be exceeding ridiculous.

Pray if my lottery tickets can be disposed of and turned into money, let it be done. As far as I understand the matter by the prints they are now worth 97=10=0. per Cent. so as I shal loose 2-10-0. per Cent if that be the case pray sell them, and let me find a little ready money at my coming to town, beside what I shal bring over with me. The two men who were executed for the murther of Isaac Watkins are supposed to have suffered innocently.

[1436] Richard Gibbons (1683–1731), chaplain to the Royal Hospital at Kilmainham, had been presented to the rectory of Raheny in Nov. 1719 and installed in Feb. 1720 (*Clergy of Dublin and Glendalough* … , ed. W.J.R. Wallace (Belfast, 2001), 151, 599–600).

[1437] The emperor Charles had replied to George I's request to deliver the person of Robert Knight, then held in custody in Brabant in the Austrian Netherlands, by promising to do what he could but noting possible difficulties 'on account of the known privileges which the States of our Low Countries enjoy'. This and other relevant correspondence was communicated to the Commons on 27 Mar. (*CJ*, xix, 496–8). Edward, Lord Harley, interpreted this as prevarication: 'Yea quoth the E[mperor] but not today.' (*Tory and Whig: The Parliamentary Papers of Edward Harley, 3rd Earl of Oxford, and William Hay, M.P. for Seaford 1716–1753*, ed. Stephen Taylor and Clyve Jones (Parliamentary History Record Series, i, Woodbridge, 1998), 230.)

[1438] Grafton was admitted to the order at a chapter held on 27 Mar. (*London Gazette*, 25–28 Mar. 1721).

I own I much doubt it.[1439] Last night two or three of the rogues that have infested our streets by robbing by night were apprehended; they fought stoutly, and wounded two of the Souldiers who assisted the watch in seising them.

472. *Thomas to Alan I, 11 Apr. 1721*

(1248/5/11–12)

I have formerly told you how very earnestly your sone presst getting him into parliament which I thinke I have a probabillity of effecting by a generous offer of a worthy freind, a member of our house. Hee tells mee wee are to expect opposition from great men, notwithstanding which hee makes noe doubt of having double the votes against any person they shall recommend, butt that the returning officer being under their influence, may very probably make a false returne, if soe I am apt to beleive a good cause will prevaile, uppon a petition, which will bee his onely expence, for my freind tells mee hee shall nott spend a penny in the Burrough; I relish the matter more att this time then I should att another, for more reasons then one, you shall hear againe next post, in the mean time lett him prepare to come away without losse of any time, in case my next give noe reason to the contrary.

I have both your letters of the 1st and 2d, I cannott bee positive, butt thinke you guesse right in every perticular in relation to the weekly prints, which still continue, the misery is, what you say, that desperate men will rather choose bringing every thing into confusion then risque the infamy and punishment due to them; this would make the case desperate, could they propose being supported by any numbers, butt tis far otherwise, the whole nation (like Lord Thomonds cocks[1440]) are on a side, all against them, ways may bee taken for quietting our house, butt alasse wee are butt 558.[1441] Doing that however may avert for a time, butt nott appease an injurd people, unlesse some satisfaction bee made, instead of the methods hitherto taken, by screening, nay justifying the greatest delinquents; bullying may bee tryed, and craft made use of, butt neither nor both togather will prevaile. I understand your meaning of the proposall made in relation to the weavers, and thinke itt may have the ill effect you apprehend. You may I beleive bee assured that Mr W[alpole] judges very right in relation to G[ilbert] nothing of this kind is thought of (att present) by a great man, a greater then him told mee hee could have accesse to his Majesty butt nott to his Lordship. How things will bee managed in our house I cannott foresee, in case the numberlesse petitions from all the quarter sessions throughout the kingdom come up, and that they will is very positively affirmed. The people are quite mad, and noe care that I see taken to appease them; butt directly the contrary. Wee flatter our selves that if wee can gett into all the beneficiall employments etc all will end well, time will allay heats, and mankind come to temper, butt I doubt they misjudge; and will find more substantiall remedyes absolutely necessary. Things are brought to this dilemma, creditt must bee supported, or the nation is undone, this creditt

---

[1439] See above, pp. 350–3.

[1440] A collection of individuals, who though ostensibly all of one side were prone to quarrel, as in the apocryphal story of Lord Thomond's Irish servant who locked all his master's fighting cocks up together the night before a match, believing that they would not fight each other; in the morning most were found killed or lamed (P.R. Wilkinson, *Thesaurus of Traditional English Metaphors* (2nd edn, 2002), K.58b).

[1441] The total number of MPs in the British house of commons.

can have noe other Basis (say they) under our present circumstances butt the S[*outh*] S[*ea*] company, this cannott take effect butt by remitting the 7 millions, youl easily guesse what the nation will thinke and say, wee have been undone by the project (carryd by corruption) and now wee are to bee stript of the onely pretended good, our severe taxes are to continue to releive gamesters and cheats. I take this to bee the most desperate attempt hitherto made, and am convinc't twill prove soe, if carryed.

Surely wee are secure against any designe from Spain, by sending our fleet into the Baltick, the Popes death is seasonable.[1442] Serjeant P[*engelly*] will bee in town this weeke, you shall have his opinion on the case you sent, lett mee have a speedy answer to my last.

[*PS*] Lord Lieutenant bid mee excuse his nott writing about the living, hee says heel nott agree to the recommendation of – till hee and you settle the matter.

473. *Alan I, Dublin, to Thomas, 12 Apr. 1721*

(1248/5/13–16)

I came last night to town upon this occasion: We received letters by post and expresse upon expresse from the magistracy and Inhabitants of Corke, expressing their utmost consternation and terror on the arrival of a ship called the Elizabeth of London, in the harbour of Glendore[1443] in the West of the County of Corke; this ship sailed from Marseilles to Thoulon and from Thoulon into this Kingdome while both those places were infected with the plague, as they stil continue to be (if we may give credit to our prints and publick papers) especially the later, where the plague seems rather to increase then abate. At one or both of these places this ship took in her cargo, and sails directly from places actually infected, laden with goods from the infected places, and therefore we have all the reason in the world to beleive they have infected goods on board; for I suppose it is not expected we should wait for sensible proof of their being soe, by their infecting any of the people here. I believe no body hath had the impudence to bring or send any ship or goods from places actually infected barefaced into England, but the French man by name Vignon concerned with some English merchants in the ship and Cargo very gravely wrote a letter to one Augustine Carrè a French merchant in Corke,[1444] notifying his having sent the ship from Marseilles to Thoulon, there to take in her lading and with orders to sail for Corke harbour, and that she would be ready to sail in 30 dayes from the date of the letter, which was dated (I think) on 24 February new style: This letter Carrè communicated to the Mayor and Collector,[1445] and they to the Governement; the Lords Justices on receit of these letters

---

[1442] Clement XI died on 19 Mar. N.S.

[1443] Glandore.

[1444] Augustus Carré (*d.* c.1747), a Huguenot and one of the sheriffs of Cork city in 1721 (Vicars, *Index*, 78; Lee, *Huguenot Settlements*, 29; David Dickson, *Old World Colony: Cork and South Munster 1630–1830* (Cork, 2005), 379).

[1445] See TNA, SP 63/383/45: Carré to Thomas Corker, 2 Apr. 1721. The mayor was Joseph Lavit(e) (*d.* c.1728), also a Huguenot (*Cork Council Bk*, 415; Vicars, *Index*, 279; Lee, *Huguenot Settlements*, 60; David Dickson, 'Huguenots in the Urban Economy of Eighteenth-century Dublin and Cork', in *The Huguenots in Ireland: Anatomy of an Emigration*, ed. C.E.J. Caldicott et al. (Dun Laoghaire, 1987), 328). The collector of the port of Cork was William Maynard, MP [I], who on 31 Mar. sent Carré's letter to the revenue commissioners in Dublin. Carré had

ordered Captain Townesend commander of his Majestyes ship the Successe,[1446] who was
at that time cruising off Dungarvan to prevent the shipping off Irish men inlisted (under
pretence of Spanish service) for the Pretender, as we have too good reason to beleive, to
cruize between Dungarvan and Corke and to prevent the Elizabeth from putting into the
harbour of Corke. The Justices laid these letters before the Councel and so they did from
time to time all other accounts which they received about this ships being expected, and
I constantly laid before them such private letters as I received from Mr Hoare my correspondent in Corke[1447] on the subject. The Councel apprehending the Justices had done
all that was possible or necessary did nothing farther, but expresse their approbation of the
care the Governement had taken. Now I doe confesse I think we were overseen[1448] in not
then thinking of issuing a proclamation declaring that no ship which should come from
Marseilles, Thoulon or any other place actually infected with the plague should be admitted
to come into any of our harbours or perform quarenteen or land any of her goods. But that
was not done, I presume under a supposition that the Successe would prevent the Elizabeth
from coming into the harbour of Corke and oblige her to put out to sea and go off from
this coast: and I confesse I thought that the most advisable and the most justifiable thing that
we could doe. After we had given these orders to Captain Townesend upon receit of some
letter from Corke (I think from Mr Hoare to me which I communicated to the Councel) I
mentioned in Councel the orders the Justices had given to Captain Townesend as requiring
him to force the ship from off our coast. The Cheif Justice[1449] hapned to be that day at
Councel, and said that was the way to bring infection into the Kingdome, since the ship
if infected and obliged by the man of war to put to sea would take the first oportunity of
making some other unguarded port and land men and goods and consquently infection
there, and he thought the best way to prevent infection was to oblige her to resort to the
place for performing quarenteen where she might be strictly watched and guarded: The
Justices then sent new orders to Captain Townesend (having sent Captain Laurance[1450] to
cruize off Dungarvan) that he should cruize between Capel Island and the Old Head[1451]
and look out sharp for this ship which was very soon expected, and not permit her to go
into Corke harbour. Townesend arrived at Corke a week before the Elizabeth came on
this coast, but she came into the harbour of Glendore on 1 April: and immediately on notice of her arrival we had expresse upon expresse with peticions and applications that she
might not be permitted to perform quarenteen or to unlade any of her goods, because it
was morally impossible to prevent her sending men and goods on shore if she was allowed

[1445] (*continued*) originally notified Maynard in a letter of 12 Feb. that the *Elizabeth* had sailed (TNA, CUST 1/15, f. 85: minute, 3 Apr. 1721).

[1446] Isaac Townsend (c.1685–1765), of Old Windsor, Berks., MP [GB] 1744–54, 1757–d., had been appointed captain of the *Success* frigate in Feb. 1720 (Charnock, *Biographia Navalis*, iv, 85–9).

[1447] Edward Hoare, MP [I].

[1448] Bewitched; or possibly used here in an equally archaic sense of the word oversee, meaning to overlook (*OED*).

[1449] Whitshed.

[1450] Thomas Lawrence (*d*.1747), captain of the *Aldborough* (Charnock, *Biographia Navalis*, iii, 299–300; Patrick Walsh, 'Ireland and the Royal Navy in the Eighteenth Century', in *The Royal Navy and the British Atlantic World, c. 1750–1820*, ed. John McAleer and Christer Petley (2016), 61).

[1451] Capel Island, near Youghal and the Old Head of Kinsale, both in Co. Cork.

to perform quarenteen at Baltimore, and the peticioners farther prayed that the Councel would order the ship to be burned. The terror and confusion which this ships arrival hath put the countrey in is inexpressible. The Councel in general, were, in this case of last necessity and self preservation, for ordering the ship to be burnt: only the Archbishop of Dublin mentioned that on the ships finding orders were come to burn her, they would sail away. My colleague[1452] (as far as he explained himself) and I were for giving orders she should sail away and not come into any harbour of this Kingdome with intimation to her that if she attempted it she should be sunk or burnt; but Lord FitzWilliams was now of Lord Chief Justice Whitsheds opinion that this was the certain way to spread infection into some more unguarded part of the Kingdome then the place is where she was to perform quarenteen (if admitted to doe soe) and therefore he was for burning. I desired to see what power we had to doe soe, and looking on the Act[1453] found it to be that if it should appear to <u>his Majestye his heirs or Successors</u> that any ship came from an infected place, or had taken in any goods from such place, His Majestye might by order in Councel cause the ship and Cargo, or such part of it as was necessary to be burnt. The Act extends to Ireland, but if it must be so literally expounded as that no order can be made with relation to this Kingdome but by his Majestye in person, then it must be by application from hence to his Majestye and the order must be made by the King in Councel in Great Britain: of what avail an order made in case of infected goods coming into Ireland from an infected place or in a ship where the men have the plague, will be after all the delayes and losse of time in procuring such an order every considering man will see. However I had a doubt how far the Governement and Councel here could doe it; the board then said that they from the necessity might doe it as an Act of State and for the preservation of the health of the Kingdome. At length seeing the bent of the Councel and apprehending the ruine that would attend that part of the Kingdome, if an order to that purpose were not made, I consented to sign one drawn up and formed by the Archbishop of Dublin. My Collegue told me he never signed any order with a worse will, or a more unreasonable one. I confesse I am in some pain on this score, least the thing should not be strictly justifiable; and I should be very sorry to fall into the power of some people who have been pleased to professe a more then common resentment toward me: but I consider that what I have done was done with a good intention, for the service of the King and Kingdome and am under no sort of apprehension that I shal be called to an account for any thing done in the maner and on the motives and under the circumstances this was done. I would not have you talk of this, least it may put malicious people upon looking narrowly into the strict legality of what hath been done; but I inform you of this whole matter that you may be able to discourse it if you find occasion. This I can assure you that tho the Councel hath in their order for burning the ship mentioned not only her coming from infected places, but that they have just reason to think she hath infected goods on board her, that they had no other proof of her having such goods on board but that it appeared to them that she took in her loading at Marseilles and Thoulon (which they thought reason sufficient for their making that conclusion) and no letters which came

---

[1452] Brodrick's fellow lord justice, William Conolly.

[1453] The first Quarantine Act of 1709 (9 Anne, c. 2 [GB]) had recently been updated by a second act, rushed through in response to the outbreak of plague in the Mediterranean and given the royal assent on 25 Jan. (8 Geo. I, c. 10 [GB]).

this mornings post from Corke mencion any thing farther to give us reason to think she hath any infected men on board. But Sir Tho[*mas*] Tipping (Nephew to Lord Orford) and his Tutor Mr Wood are on board.[1454] I will every post give you constant accounts of the health of that part of the countrey, and can now say it is perfectly well: least this damned ship coming among us may prevent English ships coming to us, or incline England to oblige ships from Ireland, or at least the West of it to perform quarenteen. I have yours of the 6th and will answer it soon and fully. Yesterday the Archbishop of D[*ublin*] in the closet shewed the WhiteHall letter to this effect that the Court resolved to remit the 7 millions and an half to the proprietors of the South Sea and that there would be a short prorogacion for about 10 dayes to effect soe good a work. I thought the nation had been interested in this money, and that they were to be discharged of so much of the publick debt: If that be soe then I find the writer understands the word Court in his letter to mean the Parliament. But as the short prorogation may be fit to enable the effecting that design, you will have a particular benefit by it; for it will discharge you of the most troublesome, most invidious and (in my opinion) most dangerous affair you were ever engaged in: but perhaps you think nothing that is honest is to be declined on account of danger ...

[*PS*] Our countrey is miserably poor.

474. *Alan II, London, to Alan I, 15 Apr. 1721*

(1248/5/17–18)

... I shall always observe the command att the End of your Lordships last Letter, viz: never to mix with Malecontents, as well in compliance with my own inclination as your Positive Order; and shou'd be Ashamed of the Company of those Men, who (as I fear some of them do) cover the most Villainous designs under the most specious Pretence, and affect the Name of Patriots att the very time when their Countreys Ruin is nearest to their hearts. News is a very scarce Commodity here and I don't doubt but your Lordship sees by the Prints, that Lord Irwin is dead,[1455] that Lord Cobham is to have his Regiment, and to be succeeded by Lord Lumley[1456] ...

[1454] Sir Thomas Tipping (1700–1725), 2nd Bt of Wheatfield, Oxon. The crew and passengers were taken on shore and provided with provisions and new clothes, their own having to be destroyed. Local reports named Tipping, 'a young Englishman travelling abroad', and Mr Wood or Woods, his preceptor (TNA, SP 63/383/43: Henry Vaughan to ——, 3 Apr. 1721; SP 63/380/20–1: John Purcell to [lords justices], 19 Apr. 1721). 'Mr Wood(s)' may have been Lubbridge Woods (c.1688–1763), the younger brother of Thomas Woods ('flogging Tom'), headmaster of Abingdon School. Lubbridge became vicar of East Meon, Hampshire in 1733. (Joseph Foster, *Alumni Oxonienses, ... 1500–1714 ...* (4 vols, Oxford, 1891–2), iv, 1675.)

[1455] Richard Ingram (1688–1721), 5th Viscount Irwin, colonel of the King's Own Regiment of Horse (1st Dragoon Guards), died from smallpox on 10 Apr. 1721.

[1456] Richard Temple (1675–1745), 1st Viscount Cobham, then colonel of the Royal Regiment of Dragoon Guards, replaced Irwin by a commission dated 10 Apr.; Richard Lumley (1686–1740), Lord Lumley, who succeeded his father as 2nd earl of Scarbrough in Dec. 1721, eventually transferred from the 1st troop of horse, Grenadier Guards, to the colonelcy of the Coldstream Guards in June 1722 (Dalton, *Geo. I's Army*, i, 99; ii, 6–7, 199, 269).

475. *St John III, Midleton, to Alan I, at his house in Dublin, 16 Apr. 1721*

(1248/5/19–20)

… I am almost afraid to mention what I now am going to write about, and hope if you dont think fit to grant what I desire, you will at least forgive my asking it. You know I have long had an inclination to get into the English Parliament, and when I last spoke to you about it, you seem'd not to be utterly averse to it. I know my Uncle Brodrick[1457] has it now in his power to serve me if he thinks fit, and am sure he would do it, if you were pleas'd to recommend it to him, which I beg you will be so good as to do. I am sure my being there can be no prejudice to you, and cant but think it will be of service to me. You will therefore give me leave to hope that you will mention this Affair to my Uncle in such manner as you think proper …

476. *Thomas to Alan I, 18 Apr. 1721*

(1248/5/21–2)

Serjeant Pingelly being returned to towne, you will I beleive have his opinion uppon the state you sent, by next post; hee tells mee prima facie the thing according to the aunctient methods of the Court of Chancery, admits of noe doubt, butt the modern practice has pretty materially differed, wherefore hee will make himself master of this, by one whoe is well able to distinguish nicely, and whoe will doe itt faithfully. Hee sayes hee must bee more nice then ordinary, seeing the lawyers with you differ in opinion.

Assoone as I have itt, ile send itt away.

I thinke Sennyes matter will bee carryd through the house.[1458] I send you a very short abstract of the Directors Bill,[1459] I fancy considerable additions will bee made in the Comittee, for the house are soe very warme, as theyle goe readily into any thing that shall bee reasonably proposed. Wee shall in a few dayes know certainly what wee are to expect in relation to Knight, among the papers read yesterday Mr Leathes last letter sayes that next day the states of Brabant were to meet,[1460] and that the M de Prie[1461] would then lay before them the memoriall which hee had delivered, and concludes that hee is nott without some hope of itts being complyd with. Tis really well drawne and in very strong termes, and Lord

---

[1457] Thomas.

[1458] A writ had been issued for Bere Alston on 14 Apr., after Edward Carteret vacated his seat by accepting an office. St John was defeated at the by-election on the 29th, but seated on petition, thanks to the support of the Walpoles: this is presumably Thomas's meaning, that his nephew would carry the election on petition. (*CJ*, xix, 507; *HC 1715–54*, i, 225–6.)

[1459] The bill 'for the relief of the unhappy sufferers in the South Sea Company', presented on 3 Apr., and given its second reading on the 19th, when it was committed to a committee of the whole House (*CJ*, xix, 502, 515).

[1460] William Leathes (1674–1727), ambassador in Brussels. His letter to Lord Townshend, dated 22 Apr. N.S., was presented to the Commons on 17 Apr., stating that the Assembly of Brabant would meet the next day, 12 Apr. O.S. (*CJ*, xix, 511).

[1461] Ercole Giuseppe Lodovico Turinetti (1658–1728), marchese di Priè, governor of the Austrian Netherlands.

Townsends letter uppon which tis founded is soe too,[1462] soe that if all appears above board, I meane if there bee noe secrett will, tis possible wee may have him.

The Prints tell you hee has been examined by M de Prie and Leathes.

[PS] Since writing very hastily the other side, yours of the 7th and 12th are come in. I thinke the orders given for burning the French ship (all circumstances considerd) very justifiable and I beleive twill bee allowd to bee soe, for that the plague rages att Marseilles and Tholoun (especially the latter) is true beyond contradiction.

Your Whitehall letter writer may proves [sic] mistaken in relation to the 7 millions, wee all know that the court (as hee sayes) are for doing itt, and Mr Walpole very earnest therein, butt I thinke nothing but what last year carryd the S[outh] Sea bill can bring this to beare. A little time will determine itt.

477. Thomas to Alan I, Dublin, 22 Apr. 1721[1463]

(1248/5/23–4)

Last night came yours of the 15th and 16. The contents of the latter affords very melancholy considerations, butt tis too late to retract, I wish I had sooner knowne what I doe now, which would have overballant all the inducements which lead mee into giving way to the thing.

This morning I waited on the D[uke] of G[rafton] having first read your letter over and over, wherein I could find nothing either in substance or expression rendring itt unfitt to bee shewne; my constant opinion is, that plaine dealing is honestest, though nott most pollitique, butt all circumstances considered I thinke twas very modest.

With his Grace I found your Cheif Baron, whoe I really did nott know.[1464] Mr St George[1465] and Mr Ward came afterwards in, you may easily judge their errant, which gave mee an opertunity (being desired to speake my opinion) to say what I thought as to the duration of the intended Banke, that part onely being now under consideration, for every thing beside, are I take itt, agreed to.[1466] I thinke a short terme ridiculous, notwith-standing what was sayd of prolonging itt when the terme should bee near expiring, twill either prove beneficiall to the undertakers or nott, if the former their advantage after the expence they shall bee att may bee taken from them by those whoe will bid most, and such people will nott bee wanting, if the latter they will of course lett the thing fall, thinking (and rightly) that the first losse is the best.

We had likewise a little upon the subject of an approaching session, I could nott for-beare what is allways att my heart, the number of unnecessary pensions, especially those of continuance; I wish his Grace well over itt, butt nott att too great an expence to a very

---

[1462] Townshend's letter to Leathes, 10 Apr. 1721, was also laid before the Commons (*CJ*, xix, 511). Townshend had been appointed as secretary of state for the northern department [GB] on 6 Feb.

[1463] Partly printed in Coxe, *Walpole*, ii, 214–15.

[1464] Jeffray Gilbert.

[1465] Oliver St George, MP [I].

[1466] The proposed national bank in Ireland. Two sets of proposals had been received by the Irish government in 1720 and the lords justices had been asked to decide between them. They plumped for the first scheme, put forward by John Irwin and Lord Abercorn, in which Michael Ward and Oliver St George were heavily involved, and through Ward the Brodrick family (Walsh, *South Sea Bubble*, 126–42).

very poore country, considering how little they have deserved from itt, to whom these are graunted. After the company were withdrawn I spoake with freedom (in Mr Hopkins presence) uppon your subject, and gave a coppy of the state of the case, in relation to a new appointment. His Grace promisd speaking to the King (by which I understand the ministry), saying hee doubted whither your request would bee agreed to, Lord Shannon I hear is ill, which may probably prove an obstacle. Wee were told of a very great struggle and long debate which was to bee yesterday uppon the motion for consolidating Mr Aislebyes Bill with that of the Directors,[1467] butt itt provd far otherwise. That motion was lett goe easily, if I mistake nott uppon a surmise that thereby the Lords would have a better handle for arguing itt to bee a tack, since that of the Directors is for vesting and selling their estates, the other onely for rendring an account of vallue, for which a former Bill has passt in relation to the Directors, Butt in this they were well jockyed by the next (unexpected) motion for providing by a clause that his estate bee subjected in like manner as the Directors are, I say unexpected, because Mr W[alpole] could nott forbear owning itt such. Hee had nott spoake before, butt now did with great earnestnesse, calling itt a Bill of Attainder, or equivalent to such, butt the maine bent of his speech was to move the passions, by mentioning over and over againe wife children family etc. You would have been surprizd to have seen how little place this tooke, gentlemen satt like soe many statues without being movd by all this Oratory. I dare confidently affirme there were nott thirty Noes, from whence you will easily conclude them discreet enough nott to divide.

The onely persons beside, whoe spoake against the question, were Sir Richd Steele, Sir James Campbell,[1468] Bishop Nevill, Mr Vernon brother in law to Mr Aisleby[1469] and Arthur Moore;[1470] I am satisfyed twill goe downe like chopt hay[1471] in the other house, they may perhaps send itt back with an amendment by leaving out Mr A[islabie] to which I thinke the Committee will nott agree, even though ways and means should bee found to take some of, for the waters run low in the usuall place for effecting such designes, I conclude the Bill will passe, from beleiving the Lords will nott take the load of loosing itt uppon their shoulders, or rather the ministry, whose influence is allwayes throughly understood, and att whose doore (principally) twill bee layd by the whole nation …

478. Alan I, Dublin, to Thomas, Westminster, 24 Apr. 1721

(1248/5/25–6)

This being the Seal day[1472] hath brought me to town, where I find an account that the pacquet is just come in: but the letters not being sorted, I cannot own the receit of any from you but in a postscript; resolving to give such farther account as I am able in relation

---

[1467] A bill to prevent John Aislabie from going abroad, and to prevent him from disposing of his 'estate and effects' was read a second time, committed to the committee of the whole on the 'directors' bill', who were instructed to merge the two bills (*CJ*, xix, 522).

[1468] Sir James Campbell (c.1666–1752), of Ardkinglas, Argylls., MP [GB] Argyll.

[1469] Thomas Vernon, (bef. 1683–1726), MP [GB] Whitchurch. John Aislabie had married Vernon's sister.

[1470] Arthur Moore (c.1666–1730), of Fetcham Park, Surrey, MP [GB] Great Grimsby.

[1471] In relation to horses, food being swallowed without difficulty (Wilkinson, *Thesaurus*, E.15b).

[1472] Appointed days in which writs were sealed in chancery.

to the affair of Lady Althams children, about which Mr Wortley spoke to you at the desire of Sir George Markham. I have now farther to inform you that since my last on that subject, the Bishop of Raphoe called again at my house and assured me that after strictly examining and looking into the papers of his deceased brother, the late Lord Cheif Justice Forster; he cannot find any settlement or copy of a settlement made by Mr Ogle or Lady Altham, or any writing whatsoever which concerns them or their children except the two inclosed papers; which he left with me, to be made such use of as might be for the service of any persons to whom they may be of use. You'l find them to be two Cases drawn up and stated, and one of them was certainly drawn since Mr Ogles death, and by the quaere's at the end of it seems to have been designed to be laid before Councel for their directions in what maner Lady Altham might act the most for her own benefit, whatever became of the children of Mr Ogle by his former wife.

These papers were certainly drawn out of some settlement or copye of a settlement, for they or one of them mention the partyes, dates, and uses of such settlement; soe as no doubt a settlement there was; but where it now is, the Bishop is wholly a stranger. Sir George Markham will upon advising with councel be informed how far such a settlement as therein is recited will be of service to those for whom he is concerned; for in all probabilitye the settlement is truly recited, since it would have been a folly in them who drew the state of the case for Lady Althams service to be shewn her councel for their opinion, to mistate the case. But you know that it is altogether improper for me to give my thoughts on this subject, and having told you all that the Bishop hath informed me of, I transmit it to be told Mr Wortly and Sir George Markham; but I would not have my letter put out of your hand, tho it doth not more then what I think is very well consistent with my character: for any honest man may enquire after, and inform his freind what he finds about a deed belonging to him, as whether there ever was such a deed, and where it is likely to be found. Our town hath been of late pestered with robbers, and we have caught several of them, and hanged them from time to time, our Sessions at the Tholsel[1473] being held on by adjournement. These disturbances continue to give me suspition that the villains concerned in them expect troubles of a more general and diffusive nature, and I hear they term these robberies lè petit guerre. My wife mends extreamly and I hope will be able in a few weeks to take a voyage and journey toward you; for which we shal make the nimblest preparation, when my dimittis[1474] arrives, which probably some of these mails brings: but I shal close and seal my letter before I have any thing from the Post Office. I shal then know whether there be any thing of truth in the news we have in town, of some very great things to be laid before the house by the Committee of secrecy; of which Lord Molesworth assured the house and moved all leaves of absence to be recalled, and was seconded by the Master of the Rolls. This is among his freinds, and in some publick letters, but you have been wholly silent in the whole affair to me, which makes me doubt.

[1473] In Skinner Row, near Christ Church cathedral, housing the offices of Dublin corporation, the Royal Exchange and the Trinity Guild of Merchants.

[1474] Notice of dismissal.

479. *Alan II, London, to Alan I, 16 May 1721*

(1248/5/27–8)

… The House has been lately very much taken up with the Directors Bill, and the most sanguine Folks hope to see it finished by the end of this week, but 'tis generally beleived it will cost them good part of the next. There is a report about town that there is a design on foot to take four fifth's of the late Directors estates, and allow them twenty per cent: upon a supposition that they have given in true estimates. But there is no certainty in this report.

[*PS*] To day I had the Pleasure of seeing my Uncle[1475] walk across his Chamber; his feaver has quite left him, and his Pain is very much abated.

480. *Alan II, London, to Alan I, 18 May 1721*[1476]

(1248/5/29–30)

I am just come from my Uncle, who is pretty well, but his head won't permit him to write. He has therefore ordered me to lett your Lordship know, that Lord Shannon is to sett out for Ireland on Monday sevennight. He bid me also tell you that he beleived what my Aunt lately hinted by his direction would not take effect, as there is great opposition against him; and is of opinion that it will be in Commission …

481. *Alan I, Dublin, to Thomas, 25 May 1721*

(1248/5/31–2)

On Tuesday Senny sett sail from hence and will I make no doubt have waited on you before this letter can reach your hands: I suppose you will think it proper that he wait upon my Lord Lieutenant and I have advised him to doe the same to Lord Townesend and Mr Walpole, who were his school fellows;[1477] which may intitle him to make them a visit of mere complement and I think he intends noe more. I have put him in mind that it is his duty to wait on his Majestye, but who the person will be that will introduce him I cannot tell, considering how you and I stand at present in the eye of the Court. Pray be soe kind to him to caution him as to his conduct and maner of conversation in relation to publick affairs: for considering the ferment that things are in there is a great deal of prudence necessary and if he could govern himself soe far as to say or intermeddle little, I think it will be the best thing he can doe: and a word from you to him will have its weight. I am apprehensive that his being in London may draw a young man whom you know into such company as

---

[1475] Thomas.

[1476] Endorsed by Midleton: '… Shanon is coming over. That Mr Winnington Jeffryes will not be Chancellor.' The appointment of Edward Jeffreys (for whom see above, p. 74) as Irish lord chancellor had been rumoured in Dublin (BL, Add. MS 34778, f. 44: Thomas Medlycott to [Edward Southwell], 12 May 1721).

[1477] At Eton College, though they were not strict contemporaries.

may not be of any advantage to him: I know one who hath been effectually undone by a near relation of his own, and hath no influence in the matter.

[I] should be very much concerned if the person I mean should by any way be brought into an acquaintance with him who hath already ruined one for whom he must have more regard then for any relation of mine. I should be contented he were in the countrey rather then in town for some weeks to come: You cannot but understand me, but if you doe not I mean him by whose hand you communicated to me that you thought the Seal would be put into Commission. And now I have mentioned that, I confesse I grow more and more desirous to have that matter over, which I make no doubt will soon be determined: you know a great many reasons for my wishing it: but I will add one more, which I should hardly venture to doe to any body but you, least I may expose my self by giving any heed to a paper that ought to be wholly despised. By the mail which arrived this morning I received a letter subscribed Wharton, in a scurvy hand, and I am sure written by some Irish raskally Sollicitor: this I collect from the style, and by his spelling the word spawn as he doth in the following words: I hope I shal see the spane of Oliver Crom[well] sunk under the yoak of misery. In this scurrilous letter the writer is pleased to tax me with giving decrees in favor of those who give the largest bribes, and he adds that you have taken up the same trade in England. He asks me of twenty decrees given by me since I have been Chancellor, from which there have been appeals, how many have stood? and I apprehend by it means to insinuate that upon some late appeal or appeals the Lords have altered or reversed some one or more decree or decrees of my making. I am very easy in that matter, and as they are guided by their consciences in what they doe, I am sure soe was I in what I have done; which gives me as much ease of mind after they have reversed or corrected the errors of my decrees, as they can have when they have done what they thought just: and altho I could have foreseen they would have reversed them, yet I being to judge by the rule of my own conscience should have given the same decree I did: that is what I then thought to be right, tho I might beleive they would be of another opinion.

I know of noe appeal this Session but two, Lord Lanesborough against Elwood:[1478] and Rotchfort against Creswick.[1479]

In the former probably the appellant may succeed, for the course of our Courts of equity here on bills for quieting possessions (of which nature I think the bill in that cause was) hath never been approved in England, and many decrees have been reversed in such cases. I will not doubt but that every order made by the Lords was right; but the rendring bills for quieting possessions wholly uselesse will in the consequence be a prejudice to this Kingdome; I doe not mean that any thing which hath yet been done in any case will be soe, but carrying it a little farther I doubt will be it. The other case may also find successe; for I am sure I was not more clear in my judgement in this cause, then I was in that between Nugent and Rotchfort;[1480] but that decree was reversed tho I was assisted by all the Judges

---

[1478] *Viscount Lanesborough and Laurence Eustace* v. *Eleanor Elwood*, a case heard by Alan Brodrick in 1719–20. Lanesborough petitioned the British house of lords on 26 May 1721 and on 28 June the case was decided in his favour (Brown, *Reports of Cases*, ii, 267–74).

[1479] *Robert Rochfort* v. *Francis and Mary Creswick*. Alan had heard the case in June and November, assisted on this occasion by the lord chief justice of king's bench [I] and two justices of common pleas [I], and had found for Creswick. Rochfort's appeal to the British house of lords was dismissed on 22 May 1721 (Brown, *Reports of Cases*, ii, 296–302).

[1480] See above, p. 189.

of the Kingdome who were unanimously of opinion that the Court ought to decree for Nugent: but indeed a letter of Rotchforts own, which had great weight and was a very strong peice of evidence in the Chancery could not be read before the Lords, for it was not proved in the cause by witnesses examined by commission, but produced in Court and owned by him then in Court to be his hand writing, and upon that allowance it was read; but the Register[1481] omitted to insert into the minutes that he owned the letter in Court; soe the Lords had not the case before them. But in Creswicks case I was only assisted by Lord Cheif Justice Whitshed Justice McCartney and Justice Gore, who were all of opinion against Mr Rotchfort and for the decree which I gave; but he is a lucky man. I do not think it any reproach to have it known my decrees are capable of being erroneous; and hope their being mine …[1482]

482. St John III, London, to Alan I, 27 May 1721[1483]

(1428/5/33–4)

I got hither about 11 last night after a very dusty hot journey, which has put me a good deal out of order, so that I hardly slept a wink last night, and am extremely hot and Feavorish today. I hope a little rest will set me up in a day or two; if not, I resolve to send for a Phisitian, for at present I am very far from being well. When I came to town I drove directly to Whitehall, where I found my Uncle as well as I could reasonably expect him, tho at the same time I think him weak and not perfectly recover'd. The continual Crouds of people that are always with him, and his own uneasinesse at being kept from the House, where indeed he is at this time extremely wanted, do him no service, but I hope in 2 or 3 days these will both be at an end, and that he may then with safety venture abroad.

I waited upon Lord Cheif justice King[1484] this morning with Sir Francis Drake,[1485] who is perfectly conversant in the History of the Burrogh of Beralston, having serv'd many years for it; he has given himself the trouble of drawing up a short skech or heads to prepare Breifs by for the hearing.[1486] He assur'd me that a clearer case never came before the House, but that notwithstanding that, I must expect a very powerfull opposition from the Ministry and their freinds, who espouse Mr Cavendish[1487] with a great deal of warmth and zeal. As far as I can learn mine have not been idle, and have so far divided the Whigs, and made such a party among the Torey and Scoch Members that they seem assur'd of carrying the Election by a very considerable Majority. I wont trouble you with a particular state of the Case in this

[1481] Richard Tisdall, MP [I].

[1482] Remainder of letter missing.

[1483] Partly printed (and misdated as 24 May) in Coxe, *Walpole*, ii, 215–17.

[1484] Sir Peter King (c.1669–1734), of Ockham, Surrey, MP [GB] Bere Alston 1701–15, chief justice of common pleas [GB]; later 1st Baron King of Ockham.

[1485] Sir Francis Henry Drake (1694–1740), of Buckland, Devon, MP [GB] 1715–*d*. His family controlled one seat at Bere Alston (*HC 1715–54*, i, 226, 620).

[1486] Of St John's petition for Bere Alston, which was heard on 6 June. A copy of his case, endorsed by Alan I, is at SHC, 1248/9/115–1.

[1487] Philip Cavendish (*d*.1743), of Westbury, Hants, MP [GB] 1721, 1722–7, 1734–*d*. He had been returned on the Hobart interest and supported against St John's petition by his first cousin John, 2nd Baron Carteret, and other ministers, but not Robert Walpole (*HC 1715–54*, i, 538).

letter, resolving by next Post to send you a Copy of Lord Cheif justice Kings instructions, which are now in the hands of Sir Fr[*ancis*] Drake, in order to prepare his Breifs by.

I was this morning both at Lord Lieutenants and the D[*uke*] of Boltons houses, but had not the good fortune of meeting either of them at home. The former has given some promises of standing neuter in my Affair; the latter I am told will give me a great many fair words, and nothing else but be that as it will, I hope I shall carry my Election without either of their Assistance. I have been so short a time in town, that your Lordship will not expect much news from me and what little I have heard, is far from being agreable, or indeed proper to be communicated by letter. A great man is determined to spend the Sumer at a Countrey seat he has at a very great distance from this place, notwithstanding the orders that were given to fit up a very fine house he has 2 Mile below Kingston, and the Declarations that were made of his resolutions to live there this Summer.[1488] They say when this matter was open'd to some of his freinds, who were call'd together to Advise with upon this occasion, there were very warm Debates about it; and by much the greater part gave their opinions very freely against the journey and the Advisers of it, which however was resolv'd upon by the opinion of 2 or 3 who seem to have a great influence over the Gentleman. This resolution is kept as a very secret, for fear of Applications against it from people, who fancy they have a right to intermeddle in the most secret Transactions of the family, and will in all probability take upon them to do so in this; you may depend upon the truth of what I tell you, and I am sure would do so, if twere proper for me to name the person from whom I received the Account of it.

After all the pains that have been taken to detect the villanys of the Directors and their freinds, I am afraid they will at last slip thro their fingers, and that nothing further will be done as to confiscation, hanging etc. There certainly is a Majority in the House of Commons that are willing to do themselves and the Kingdom justice; but they act so little in Concert together, that they are constantly baffled by a set of men whom Guilt, Money etc have link't in the closest Bond. Tis impossible to tell you of what infinite consequence the absence of a freind of yours is at this time, and how uneasy the generality of mankind is at it.[1489] He is, without Compliment, the spring that gives Motion to the whole body; and the only man that either can or will set matters in a true light and expose and baffle the schemes of the Skreen [1490] etc. The House were 5 hours in a Committee last Friday upon the Directors Bill and were amus'd and Banter'd the whole time by Questions and Amendments propos'd by the Skreen etc so that they rose at last without coming to any Resolution. They were to be upon the same business again this day, but assoon as the House sat Mr Lechmere brought in Mists Paper of this day (which is indeed a most infamous Treasonable Libel)[1491] descanted upon it for $\frac{1}{2}$ an hour, and at last mov'd to Censure it etc which was accordingly order'd.[1492] The Master of the Rolls, Pengelly, Ross and 5 or 6

[1488] The prince of Wales had purchased Richmond Lodge from the forfeited estate of the duke of Ormond in 1719 for £6,000, but his annual expenditure on the property was over £90,000 (Andrew Thompson, *George II: King and Elector* (2012), 63).

[1489] Thomas (absent from the Commons because of ill health).

[1490] Robert Walpole, nicknamed 'Screen-master General' for his role in hiding some prominent public figures from exposure over the South Sea scandal.

[1491] The *Weekly Journal* of 27 May 1721 (*CJ*, xix, 562). Nathaniel Mist (*d*.1737), of Great Carter Lane, London, was a noted publisher of opposition newspapers (*Oxf. DNB*).

[1492] Lechmere's role is confirmed in Cobbett, *Parl. Hist.*, ix, cols 803–4.

others speecht for the Motion,[1493] so that the time was so spun out by this means, tho no body ventur'd to oppose the Question, that when the order of the day was calld for, people seem'd to be tir'd and readily went in to the Adjourning it till Wednesday. In short unless this Affair takes some new turn, and fresh life by that time, you are to expect very little success from the late Enquiry; for the Session is spun out to that vast length, that nothing can keep the Countrey members in Town, and you may be assur'd all proper Arguments have been made use of by the Directors to keep their freinds together. I doubt the Secret Committee are not now so unanimous as they have been, and that there have been at least 2 false Brethren always among them. His Grace of Lancaster is promis'd[1494] and expects mighty things; and you may easily imagine the world is come to a fine pass, and that the Kingdom is like to be very happy, when he, Skreen, and the Gentleman with the bloody nose[1495] act in perfect Concert together.

The Lords have ordere'd the Account of the Charge of the Navy to be laid before them next Thursday, and intend to enquire particularly into the heavy Article of the Baltick Squadron.[1496] This was occasion'd by an Expression of Lord Guilfords[1497] in some Debate, in which he took notice of the vast Expence England was put to by fighting other peoples Battles etc. He was answer'd by no less then 5 Lords who all got up together, and spoke with great warmth against that Expression, and endeavour'd to justifye our sending the Fleet to the Baltick, Mediterranean etc. Assoon as the Debate was over and Question put, Lord Cooper went to Lord Carterett and askt him, if the bare touching that sore made some people so uneasy, what condition they were like to be in when it came to be searcht and prob'd to the Bottom, assoon it must be in a Regular Debate to which no Answer was return'd. This I have from a Lord that was by, and heard the discourse; but I fancy they are under no great Apprehension in the House of Lords, where they have an indisputable Majority and carry every thing.

My Uncle will write at large to you about your own Affairs the Minute he is able. He seems a little recover'd, tho I confess I think him far from well, and wish the Constant Crouds of people that are with him, may not occasion a Relapse; for tho he has spirits, he really has not strength enough to bear the fatigue of so much Company ...

483. *Thomas to Alan I, 30 May 1721*

(1248/5/35–6)

I am under the last difficulty in writing uppon the subject which I am now to doe, being as you may very easily beleive throughly sensible of the treatment you have mett with; I have formerly told you from what quarter itt came, to which I need adde noe more then what I have formerly sayd of Lord Lieutenants being wholly a stranger to every step made

[1493]Cobbett, *Parl. Hist.*, ix, col. 808 names Jekyll, Pengelly and eight other MPs, but not Charles Rosse.
[1494]Probably a reference to Lechmere's office as chancellor of the duchy of Lancaster.
[1495]Sunderland.
[1496]The cost of sending a British fleet into the Baltic in consequence of treaty obligations to Sweden (Cobbett, *Parl. Hist.*, vii, cols. 845–6).
[1497]Francis North (1673–1729), 2nd Baron Guilford.

in that affair till the Kings letter came over, which hee resented, as well hee might, uppon being treated in the manner hee was.

That his Majestys discharging any servant (even without assigning other cause then his service requiring itt) has allwayes been submitted to, and ought to bee soe, is most certaine, butt the manner may be very different, and therfore as you have formerly taken notice, this is what very justifiably may give sufficient ground of resentment, towards the authors of itt, withoutt the least ground for creating even an uneasinesse att his Majestys pleasure, since the thing and method of putting itt in execution are independent of each other. In short, to come closer to the point, I must informe you that I have good reason to beleive from what the Duke of Grafton has told mee that hee thinkes your continuance in his Majestys service would bee of use, att this time more especially, as well as that hee beleives your expressing a readinesse soe to doe, if that shall bee agreeable to his Majestys pleasure would bee entertaind and well receivd by those whoe att present may probably have the direction. I know you are netled, and to tell you the truth I am soe too, butt what a man of honour (a true freind both to you and mee) with whom I tooke the liberty of talking freely on your subject, sayd, has made great impression on mee. The unhappy differences (says hee) which have of late arisen between the kings freinds, whoe meane the same thing have already had ill effects, and worse they will have unlesse by prudence and temper a stop bee putt to these misunderstandings, since those whoe have other veiwes will take advantage. This I am pretty sensible of from what happens to my selfe, I am treated in a very different manner from what I was formerly, by people that I seldom joind with; I will never faile to returne with very gratefull acknowledgments every obligation as far as I can doe itt personally, and that in every instance wherein the good of the whole may nott bee concerned, butt in that case all private obligations are to give way, doing otherwise would bee paying my debt att anothers expence. Things are in more confusion then you can easily imagine, which enforces the necessity of every honest mans giving his best assistance towards extricating us out of the difficultyes wee labour under, you very well know my principles, and I know yours to bee exactly the same, what therfore conduces most to what wee are satisfyed is for the publique good ought to bee pursued, notwithstanding any personall disobligations whatever; I know tis touching you in a tender point where you thinke your honour att stake, butt I whoe am on the place, see, what you can onely hear, consider the whole matter seriously, and lett mee heare from you; bee your resolution what itt will, as to quitting or nott, I am sure that both in the manner of expressing your selfe, as well as your after actions (in either case) will bee such as are most suitable to the duty of a good subject to a gracious Prince. This is the first time I have taken pen in hand since my illnesse, my head is confused, and my heart full, if what I write bee throughly intelligible, tis all I desire, or you can expect.

484. *Alan I, Dublin, to Thomas, 5 June 1721*

(1248/5/37–8)

I returned last night from Mr Campbels,[1498] where fowre or five freinds spent the last five dayes of Whitson week very innocently and agreeably, which is the only time I have

---

[1498] Charles Campbell, MP [I].

employed since my coming last for Ireland otherwise then in his Majestyes and the publick service: and found your letter of the 30th of May. The nature and subject matter of it is of that nicety that would require more time to answer it (as it ought to be) then the pacquets going off this morning allows me; on the other hand I think it requires the speedyest answer possible tho you doe not say soe in expresse terms. You tell me that you were much indisposed when you wrote it, and I find by a letter from Bond Street, that you had wrote it the night before, soe as your letter was written on Monday tho dated on the post day: for your Nephew in Bond Street[1499] mentions your being seised with a fit of vomiting, the day after you had wrote to me, in his letter dated 30 May; which could not be misdated, it being impossible for his letter to have come hither soe soon if wrote any time since Tuesday last. I am a good deal at a losse after reading over and considering your letter to form a judgement whether what you say in it be the result of your own thoughts upon the condition of publick affairs, and from the perfect understanding you have of my hearty and unalterable attachments to his Majestyes interests and services and the present Governement and administration, or whether it took rise from some one or more persons in London: that you may have so favourable an opinion of me as to beleive my continuing in his Majestyes service at this time, may be of use I am not at all surprised; for your kindnesse hath inclined you to overlook my failings, and to beleive that a mans meaning sincerely the service of the Crown goes a great way in enabling him to serve it effectually; I am sensible too you have been of opinion a good while that I have been able to doe it more service then will be readily allowed by those, who for private reasons and out of resentment at my not being able to comply with some expectations, have endeavoured to lessen my services and me, in order to disgrace me; and to make me sensible that what I was told would be the consequence of my being against a certain scheme was in the power of the man who used the menace to effect. That part of your letter I say I can readily beleive to be the result of your own thoughts only, but the next words incline me to beleive you have had discourses with others, and that you write by order, else you would hardly say you have reason to beleive my expressing a readinesse to continue in his Majestyes service (if it shal be in his Majestyes pleasure) would be entertained and well received. If that arise from discourse used to you by my Lord Lieutenant or any of the ministry, why doe you keep me in the dark? If not, pray (without going into the reasonablenesse of the thing) weigh whether the severe and undeserved treatment I have received (to give it no rougher epithet as I justly might) give you the least ground to beleive there can be an intention to continue a man in his Majestyes service, who hath been unnecessarily endeavoured to be mortified, by finding out occasions to doe every thing most disagreeable to him, and that in the most disobliging maner. There remains but one conjecture to solve this difficulty, that perhaps all men are not under a necessity or a disposition to do the same thing which I know I originally owe to one: but this conjecture is not a sufficient reason for me to expresse my self in terms of a desire or readinesse to continue in a post under his Majestye which hath been lessened below the dignity it ought alway to be supported in, meerly to lessen the man who at present fills it. I would give no particular instances beyond the putting little people on a level with me in some things and giving an entire and plain preference in most, as in recommendations etc passing your Nephew by in the Sollicitorship, and granting late

---

[1499] St John III.

emploiment to the Nephew of a favourite[1500] etc. All this done with a view of depressing the interest of one and aggrandizing that of another person: which the party concerned is very sollicitous to render well understood through the Kingdome. But between freinds things here have taken a turn contrary to the expectations of some; and men have for some time past considered what grounds there are for such vehement caressing? To come now to answer the question of your letter; I am like one who by expecting death every hour (for the dead warrant hath been sent out of England to be signed at Hanover in October last if my good freind Mr Delafayes early vaunt and triumph in a publick company on the Sunday after it went away and before it could reach Herehausen[1501] may be credited) hath made it familiar and not at all terrible to him: It is fit and reasonable that when his Majestye thinks his service requires it he should discharge any person from his service, without assigning other reason; but then the maner and method of parting with a faithful and perhaps an useful servant hath not been alway the same as I have mett with: I will not descend to particulars, but refer you to former letters for the treatment I have from time to time received, which have piqued me so much that I doe not think it will consist with my honour and character to seek being continued in his Majestyes service without some mark of his Majestyes Royal favor to wash me from the little imputations of being in his displeasure, disaffected to his service or having acted in opposition to his interest (for my being against the Peerage bill I cannot think a disservice to his Majestyes Crown or interests, but a duty which I owed to both) and without reason to beleive I shal not for the future see a little man (for so he is in all respects but one) be represented as the first mover and promoter of what ever is done for his Majestyes service: of which he takes care to create merit to himself, how little an hand soever he may have in effecting the businesse. And when I may without being trampled on (as of late) continue in that honourable Station in which his Majestye once thought fit to place me with the dignity which ought alway to attend it, I shal with the greatest pleasure and readinesse be encouraged to employ the utmost of my endeavours for his Majestyes service (if it shal be his Majestyes pleasure to think me a person as capable and well disposed to his service as I have been thought formerly) and (tho in no perfect state of health) am ready to venture my life again in another Session of Parliament: And I must call it soe, from an observation I have made of never having passed one Session of the last five without a feavor immediately following it. I ought not to pretend to make terms, or insist on conditions: but when it will be impossible for me without something of this kind either to doe any thing considerable for his Majestyes service, or to act with regard to my own reputation I must be excused for being of these sentiments. If your letter was wrote without direction you know my mind; if it proceeded from a previous discourse with one or more great men, I intreat you to answer for me to the sense contained in this paper, but entreat you also to soften the expressions where my opinion of having been unkindly used may have made it too harsh. Let me hear from you soon, for I long to see you, and shal from your next letter make a judgement when I may have that happinesse. I had almost forgot to tell you, it is now all over the town that a Gentleman man [*sic*] who is called by two sirnames is to be my Successor.[1502] This I hardly beleive, as being perfectly inconsistent

---

[1500] William Conolly, jr, recently appointed cursitor in chancery [I].

[1501] George I's summer palace at Herrenhausen, near Hanover.

[1502] Edward Winnington Jeffreys, MP [GB] Droitwich.

with your sentiments and the occasion of your whole letter; but perhaps the secret may not have reached your ears. If that should be in view how should I be turned into ridicule to make any advances etc but I cannot beleive a thing so dishonourable designed, if you write by direction. What ever turn this affair takes I cannot but have that concern for the Kings service, the good of the Kingdome, and the honour and ease of my Lord Lieutenants Governement to wish and use my best endeavours that it may be a very successeful Session of Parliament which is now approaching here; it is of absolute necessity at this time; for the misfortunes and uneasinesse which have affected England have reached farther. Pray give my Lord Lieutenant my best services and tell him that from a zeal for the publick good and his service I think it highly advisable he begin his journey toward us as soon as is possible, which I know depends on the rising of your Parliament. I am concerned to hear Mr Hopkins declines the Secretaryship: he will [be] serviceable and very acceptable, and will find lesse difficulty then perhaps he expects.

485. *Alan I to Thomas, 5 June 1721*

(1248/5/39–40)

As the subject matter of your letter of the 30th May put you under a good deal of difficulty in what maner to expresse yourself and how you should advise me to act, soe you will find me to have been under as great in what maner to answer it. But I have on the best thoughts I am master of, chosen to take this method, to write two letters one Directly to my Lord Lieutenant; and another to you, but soe framed that I apprehend it may very well be shewn to his Grace, and unless your conversation with him was such that he expects (if I give in to the thing proposed) that I should write to him directly a letter to be shewn and made use of to those who may concur in his opinion and be an handle for them to be the means of revoking what Lord S[*underland*] hath for his own reasons done to my prejudice, I had much rather the letter I send to his Grace inclosed should be intirely suppressed then be made use of; because I may speak my mind more freely and in stronger terms to you, then will be judged proper to be used to him and through him to such of the ministry as he shal [think] it fit to communicate it to, I mean Lord T[*ownshend*] and Mr W[*alpole*] for I take it for granted they draw together. By your maner of writing I cannot but think he expressed himself so plainly to you that he expects a letter from me directly to him self; but you leave me to act according to my own judgement after telling me that he said my expressing a readinesse to serve would be entertained and well received; and there you leave it for my determination in what maner to doe it, if at all. If I should write directly to him in that maner and the thing should not take place my letter may and will be made use of; that at last they had brought me not only to accept, but to ask being continued, and indeed I should hardly think it modest to annex the same terms and condtions in the body of that letter and to expostulate in so strong terms the reasons of my late inhumane treatment as I may venture to use when I am writing directly to you and for your view only. But this puts me under the difficulty of writing three letters, viz. this, that to his Grace and the other to you, to be shewn if on considering it you judge it best to suppresse that to his Grace and not to deliver it and to make use of that directly to yourself; at a time when I have not leisure enough to write one letter as it ought to be wrote on an affair of such nicenesse and difficulty: but that which more sensibly affects me is that I at the same time am giving you in your very weak and ill state of health the trouble of reading over three long letters, and then judging what is advisable to be done, and putting that in execucion. Indeed brother you ought and need take more care of your health then you doe, by all I could ever observe when with you or find from those who now give me an account of your condition, and the ill consequences your late indisposition continues to have on you. But I had almost forgott to insert one motive of writing this letter, which was to let you into the expresse reason of saying some things in my other letter to you, which you will be surprised at till you consider that they were proper to be said if my letter to the Duke shal not be delivered, particularly my expostulating with you for not telling me in plain terms that you had been spoken to by some great man, but had left me in the dark to conjecture whether the sentiments you expresse of my being able to serve the King to his advantage at this time, and the n[ec]essity of every bodyes doing soe in the best maner when things are under such difficulties as they are reduced to at present be your own originally or took rise from others speaking to you. God preserve you and restore you and send us an happy meeting.

[PS] The matter of Mr Winnington Jefferyes I had sometime since in a letter wrote by my Namesake by your order, but I mention it as news, as indeed it is by the last pacquet but one among our people. I doubt I shal not have time to write by this pacquet to my Lord Lieutenant but have wrote a line to him to get the living of Mallow for Mr Murdock.[1503]

486. St John III, London, to Alan I, Dublin, 6 June 1721

(1248/5/41–2)

I have but just time to tell your Lordship that after a hearing of 5 hours, I carried my Election almost without a Negative. I am this Minute going to my Electors and Witnesses, so that I have not time to trouble you with particulars; in general, you will beleive I had a pretty clear case, when after the most warm and personal sollicitation of all the Ministry, except Mr Walpole, I carryed it without a division, or even a Negative.[1504] I am under abundance of obligations to a great many freinds; but those to my Uncle Brodrick and the Doctor,[1505] I can hardly express, and wish I may be ever able to repay. I have the pleasure at the same time to tell you, that there were very few men, if one in England, that could have withstood the power and Application of Lord Carteret, as my Uncle has done; who without Compliment or vanity is the most popular, best regarded man in the House.

I told you in my last the Ministry were broke to peices, which you may depend on; and this was one reason why Mr W[alpole] and his freinds were for me. In a very few days this will be publick; but what turn twill take I dont pretend to guess. Your good freind may perhaps prevail at —, but I dare say no where else.

[1503] Most probably John Murdoch (c.1681–1740), who became vicar of Bregoge in 1728, though possibly his younger brother Benezer (c.1682–1747), who had been appointed to the rectory of Kilshannig, Co. Cork in 1719. In Oct. 1721 the vacant rectory of Mallow was given to George Chinnery.

[1504] The first question, concerning the right of election, was carried in St John's favour, nem. con., the second, declaring Cavendish not duly elected, was carried by acclamation (*CJ*, xix, 579).

[1505] The physician whose ministrations had enabled Thomas to return to the Commons.

Tis now resolv'd, (but no resolution is to be depended upon 2 days) to dissolve this Parliament immediately and to call a new one to sit in october; I think your freind will not be able to stand his ground any where but — …

487. *Alan I, Dublin, to Thomas, 6 June 1721*

(1248/5/43–6)

The subject of your letter of 30th May and one expression in it which seemed to shew you expected a suddain answer induced me to resolve immediately to put pen to paper, before I had given my self time well to consider what resolution was proper for me to take in a matter of that nature and consequence as that you wrote about seems to me to be. This occasions my writing soe soon to you again, and telling you some things which did not soe readily occur to my mind when I wrote last, and informing you of others which I was a stranger to then. I received your letter at my return to the Lodge in Dublin Parke[1506] whither I went directly on Sunday night from Mr Campbels house and by that means was not privy to the accounts which the two last pacquets brought to the rest of the world, but on coming to town next morning I found it in every bodyes mouth, that the Chancellor was to continue, but the men of politick[s] and they who keep and value themselves for a more confiding correspondence then others are admitted into, give it out among their freinds that I am to continue Chancellor till the Session of Parliament is over.

Now from this I infer that nothing hath been said in confidence to you, but what was previously determined on to be done in all events to answer the present occasion, and the limitation of time is a very good explanation of that part of your letter in which you say it is thought my continuance for some time in the Kings service may be of use. See then how you and I are treated; You are spoken to as out of freindship and in confidence by one who pretends not to have any hand in my removal, that it would be well taken If I expressed an inclination and readinesse to continue Chancellor if his Majestye should think fit, and as if my soe doing would enable them who were of opinion I had not been well used to be a means of my being continued, and this I must take as a favour done me and it must therefore be at my seeking: when in truth the place hath been soe long hawked about that no body cares for taking it whom they would put into it: I mean none from your side, for I am noe stranger that it hath been offered to abundance, when Mr Gilbert was too prudent to suffer its being rammed down his throat.

I beleive the person you talked with was not privy to the sending the order to be signed in October appointing the Cheif Baron my Successor and yet the same person shal never perswade me that he ever interposed in preventing my removal; but I beleived he was nettled (and with reason) in having a matter soe directly within his Province topped upon him, as naming him a Chancellor to hold a Session of Parliament with. Beside this intirely thwarted his inclination to have W[*hitshed*] the man, to whom he shewed such countenance when last in the Governement that I never can forgett: But Lord S[*underland*] was and is positive it shal not be one of this countrey. The amends then and reparation intended me for the vilest insolences to which I have been exposed is to be permitted (upon my own

---

[1506] The Phoenix Park.

application) to serve other peoples turns, till they can adjust their scheme in a better maner then the difficultyes they at present lye under will allow at present. I am to slave out another autumn to the impairing and ruine of my health, to carry on a very difficult Session (for soe it will necessarily be, tho I should be forgiving enough to assist as I did in all former Sessions, and if I should act another part, nay be absent or neuter it will be much more soe) and when it is over the merit and credit of what would not have been effected without me, shal be placed to the account of them who have arrogance enough to assume every thing to themselves, and by Sycophantry and insinuating themselves with great men by caressing their little familiars and making court to Secreatries, Postmasters[1507] etc who have accesse to and confidence with great men, perswade them that all is due to their interest and management. This game I have seen plaid twice or thrice since 1714, and once told the person with whom you lately conversed that with a wet finger (notwithstanding the vaunted interest of his great favourite) the whole scheme was capable of being disappointed; he seemed surprized, yet not to beleive it: but the thing was true: and if I had given him then a convincing proof (as I could with all ease) the Idol would not have been adored, as it hath since been. And is it reasonable for me to contribute stil to the support of a character so undeserved?

The poverty of the countrey, and heavinesse of the establishment, the pressures on and discouragement of all trade, with other matters, not necessary nor perhaps fit to be mentioned in a letter, make it appear to me a very desirable thing to see others take the labour in their hand, and to rest a little. I have not had such thanks for past services to engage me to lay out myself for the publick without regard to my quiet, my health or fortune. Witnesse the matter of our proceedings in the last Session, when no one Lord in his Majestyes service but myself endeavoured to prevent what hath since hapned: what return was made me? Hatred from many here, for endeavouring to preserve them; and not the least notice taken from the other side the water that I had done what was approved by the King. But stil Brother I am not determined absolutely to insist on laying down, which I now can doe with honour and ease of mind, tho much inclined to it: Nor is the mark of favor I mentioned in my last a feather to be put in my cap by giving me a farther title; I have enough of that already and will not do what must render it impracticable to your Nephew to follow his profession: If I may have assurances given me that after the Session is over I shal by his Majestyes licence be permitted to retire, and that as a mark of his approbacion of all my services, I mean those already past as well as the new trouble I am to undertake, that I shal be placed on the establishment either for a term of years (which were to be desired) or otherwise, I will sacrifice my ease and quiet to the publick service and venture another feavor, the constant present I have mett with on such occasions: these things are not at all strange, Chancellors elsewhere make greater and other terms before they quit their businesse; and every Officer worn out in service thinks himself to have a right to half pay: And I confesse I doe not see why I have not at least equal pretensions. But after all this I would not be understood to undertake to doe any thing but barely not to withdraw; I am to be at liberty to act as I alway have for the good of my countrey as well as the Kings service, and to oppose whatever I may think not for both: for example I hear people talk of a Land tax, I shal be against every thing of the kind: and I own it to be my sense that it were very

---

[1507] A reference to Isaac Manley, MP [I].

desirable the establishment might have received some ease instead of being increased in the maner it hath been. To speak in few words, if I may be at the same liberty I alway have been (in every station in the Crowns service) to act in Parliament with freedome, and not be ill treated or represented afterward for my having done so; if I shal meet such countenance as a Chancellor ought to expect, and not see little people advised with and confided in about matters out of their spheres, and properly within his, and may depend on being allowed to retire with reputation and under such marks of the Kings approving my whole conduct in his service since my entring into it, as I have mentioned before: I think I may continue to serve with honour; and when I can not doe that I am sure I ought not to serve at all. But if I may not have these marks placed on me of his Majestyes approving my services hitherto I am sure I never shal be able to doe that will intitle me to the good thoughts of those who have laid me under disadvantageous characters for what I have done hitherto, and shal never by a slavish subserviency to the pleasure of others put myself on another foot with them then I now am: and therefore am fixed on retiring now when I can doe it with a clean character. Dear Brother, it will be the lesse difficult for you to speak in this maner on my behalf, for the sentiments are mine and if I am too tenacious in any thing I am to answer for it not you. I will conclude with telling you a secret, that after Lord Galwey had mett Country Gentlemen in the Closet in the D[uke] of Gr[afton's] first parliament and the quantum of the supply to be given and accepted had been adjusted to mutual satisfaction, the Duke of Grafton being at Kilkenny; and at his return it being told him, his Secretary Delafay sett a farther demand on foot, when Gentlemens words were passed the one to the other not to do more, and when they had wrote to that effect to their respective Countyes and boroughs. For this I spoke with warmth to Delafay, and perhaps with too much con-sidering it was in the Dukes presence; and I beleive by soe doing disobliged his Grace. This little wire drawing art of the Secretarye was the first foundation of the breach between the Whigs here, which soon after ensued: for there were some who went in to doe a very little more, while others thought them selves ill treated, and sate mute, tho they could with all ease have overturned the scheme. This breach hath been widened by caressing one party, and looking coolly on the other ever since; very little to the advantage of the Kingdome: and it is more then probable those who have been passive hitherto will not alway continue so. I did all I could to soften them who thought themselves ill used tho I doubt the Duke did not beleive so; and it was at this time I told him that with a wet finger the whole un-dertaking of the persons confided in might be demolished. Toward the end of the Session I had an oportunity of discoursing his Grace so freely on this subject before Lord Shanon and General Palmes[1508] that I did then fancy he had laid aside all impressions to my prejudice: but the coolnesse he treated me with when I went for England soon after and the maner of his writing ever since have given me reason to be sensible it is otherwise. Thus I owe a good deal to that Secretary, and I beleive he hath done me all the good offices in his power with his other Great Master

[PS] On Monday morning Sir Tho[mas] Smith[1509] told me Sir Ri[chard] Levinge had a letter that I was to continue during the Session at least. There were others.

[1508] Francis Palmes, MP [I].

[1509] Sir Thomas Smyth (aft. 1657–1732), of Radcliffe, Bucks., MP [I] 1703–14.

Having compared yours of 30 May with my sisters of 2 June I find it will be altogether improper to write to Lord Lieutenant, and that I am not to understand your letter as wrote by his direction, so have laid aside all thought of writing to him on the subject.

This letter is wrote in too strong terms to be shewn but you will mitigate the expressions.

488. St John III, London, to Alan I, 10 June 1721[1510]

(1248/5/47–8)

I have not had the favour of a line from you since I left Ireland, but hear from my Uncle that both Lady Midleton and your Lordship are very well. I am not out of hope of being in Ireland even before the end of this Term; the Parliament will hardly sit beyond that time, the Ministry seeming as desirous of their rising as the Countrey Gentlemen; The Bill of Credit[1511] and that for Releif of the South Sea Sufferers are both in such a forwardness, that I beleive they will be sent to the Lords by this day sennight at furthest, where they will probably meet with a good deal of dispach, as you may be sure the Malt Bill will, which has been now twice read. If there ever were a design to attempt continuing the Parliament towards the end of the Session, tis laid aside; at least for the present; the great ones being too much divided to enter upon an Affair, where I beleive their united strength will not be sufficient. Lord S[underland] is said to be against the Experiment; W[alpole] and his freinds for it, beleiving he will hardly be able to influence and conduct another as he has this Parliament. Tis certain they are at present in great streights; there is hardly a probability of getting such another set of honest men together as they have at present; and tis not certain but even these may ride Restiff[1512] in case their Lease be renew'd, tho this is what is least apprehended, there being a certain and tryed way of quieting such unruly spirits. These divisions in the great ones made my Affair very easy. Lord Car[tere]t was pleas'd to embark and sollicite personally against me, which made Mr W[alpole] who at first was zealously against me, quit his Countreyman Sir John Hobart,[1513] and engage all his freinds for me, so that I really beleive had they been so hardy as to stand a Division their Numbers would not have exceeded 40, tho both Lords S[underlan]d and C[arleto]n said publickly at their Levee's the morning before my Election came on, that I should loose it by more then 2 to one.

There was a pretty extraordinary Attempt made yesterday in the House. You remember that some time ago there was a very warm Debate and a Close Division in a Committee of the whole house about remitting the remaining 2 of seven Millions to the S[outh] S[ea] Company, which was carryed in the Negative by a small Majority. This Resolution, tho agreed to above a month ago was not reported till yesterday, and most people thought would have been unanimously agreed to, but assoon as the Report was made Sir Ch[arles] Wager, in a very short unintelligible speech mov'd to disagree with the Committee, and

---

[1510] Partly printed in Coxe, *Walpole*, ii, 217–19.

[1511] The bill 'for the Better Establishment of Public Credit, by Preventing for the Future the Infamous Practice of Stock-jobbing'.

[1512] Restive meant indolent or sluggish, and was often used in the context of horse riding, to denote a failure to keep pace.

[1513] Sir John Hobart (1693–1756), 5th Bt, of Blickling, Norfolk, MP [GB] St Ives, who had inherited his uncle Lord Stamford's electoral interest at Bere Alston.

was seconded by Hor[*atio*] W[*alpol*]e. Mr Freeman of Hertfordshire got up and spoke to order; said as this was a most unreasonable so twas a very irregular motion; that there could be nothing more so, then giving money in the Chair, which this in Effect was; for if the 2 Millions, which were now the money of the Publick were remitted, the House must think of another fund to make them good; or at least continue the Dutys on Candles, Soap etc which this money was to pay off. The Question was then put for agreeing etc and carryed only by a Majority of 11, 166 against 155, when very few thought there were so [*many*] in the house would have appear'd on that side the Question.[1514] This extraordinary Attempt was so far resented by the Majority, that while the House was telling I thought twas resolv'd to Attempt to strike off 2 of the 5 Million, in return to their freinds favour, but upon reporting the Division, the Mocion was dropt, which in the Temper the house was, I really beleive might have been carryed if Attempted.

I write this before I go to the House, if any thing worth your Notice happen there to day, I will trouble you with it.

[*PS*] 8 in the Evening.

I am this minute come from the House, where we had a warm Debate about the time to which Aislabies forfeiture should relate.[1515] W[*alpole*] and L[*echmer*]e and all the Court for carrying it only to December 1719; which would have produc'd little or nothing to the publick,[1516] others were for the time of his being Chancellor of the Exchequer, and carryed it 113 against 95. My Uncle propos'd this time and spoke for it.[1517] Sir Jos[*eph*] Jekyl was for going as high as 1714, when he[1518] was appointed Treasurer of the Navy, but this was generally dislik't. The Torys were against him to a man, and there was, as indeed there generally is, a pretty motley Division; The Torys and what they call the old Whigs against the Court. These have generally gone together since I came into the House, and are at present indisputably the Majority so that I think there will hardly be an Attempt this Session to continue the Parliament. That great work must be reserv'd to another, by which time Gentlemen will have leisure to reflect, and consider the Arguments that will certainly be applyed to them. Be it when it will, I think twill hardly meet with success.

I will not close my Letter till I tell you there is a Petition prepar'd and ready to be offer'd to the King by most of the Western Members, to desire his Majestys Instructions to the Duke of Grafton to propose taking off the Duty of 1s-7$\frac{1}{2}$ per stone on wool exported from Ireland to England, to the next Parliament in Ireland; which will of Course oblige us to think of some other fund for the support of our Lord Lieutenant in leiu of the wool licences.[1519]

I should be glad to have your Lordships thoughts upon this subject, which I own I do not foresee any great objection to; and if there be not, I had rather twere done by our Parliament

[1514]Confirmed in *CJ*, xix, 585.

[1515]In the committee of the whole considering the merged bills for the relief of sufferers from the South Sea Company, and for seizing Aislabie's estate (*CJ*, xix, 586).

[1516]Walpole's proposal is confirmed in Cobbett, *Parl. Hist.*, ix, col. 832.

[1517]Confirmed in Cobbett, *Parl. Hist.*, ix, col. 833.

[1518]Aislabie.

[1519]Licences to Irish merchants to export wool to England were granted by the lord lieutenant, who received the fee directly for the support of his office.

then this, which I am perswaded will be the Case if it meet with any obstruction there; for all the Western Men seem extremely intent upon it.

I have already talkt with my Uncle on this subject, and have sent you his thoughts in what I have wrote above …

489. *Thomas to Alan I, 17 June 1721*

(1248/5/49–50)

I need adde nothing to what I have formerly sayd of Lord Lieutenants being an utter stranger to your whole affair, you may bee very sure hee was soe.

I have communicated to him what you desired mee to say in your name, and am pretty sure his Grace has imparted itt to the proper persons, from whom hee bids mee assure you, that you may depend uppon being dismissed his Majestys service (when ever his occasions shall make that necessary) in such manner and on such termes as shall leave noe roome for the worst of your enemyes doubting (much lesse insinuating) that your services have nott found a gracious acceptance, this therfore I perswade my selfe will throughly convince you of the reasonablenese of laying aside the grinding thoughts of the past ill usage you have mett with from others, especially when you consider that you may and will bee capable of doing reall service, and that att a time when tis most wanted.

The accounts your pollititians have receivd, of your being to bee made the Catts foote[1520] during the next session of Parliament are ridiculous, for I am very well satisfyed nothing of that kind is intended, or ever was in their thoughts. Tis true things may change here, and consequently you may bee disappointed of your reasonable expectations, butt if that should prove the case, I am satisfyed you will bee contented to fall with them. If otherwise I thinke you very safe, because I verily beleive they will nott breake faith. I thinke what you desire of coming over before my Lord Lieutenants arrival impracticable, for which reason I have nott mentioned itt, you know his Grace can appoint noe justices, nott being himselfe sworne, and as I told you before, I am still of opinion a pattent from the Crowne to that end, would vacat Lord Lieutenants besides by what I can learne from him, I beleive his stay here will nott exceed a month, probably bee shorter. Hee has very heartily bestird himselfe in relation to Lord Arrans bill, and with good successe, as far as Ireland is concernd therein,[1521] your sonne will I hope give you a more perticular account, for I am a good deale out of order, being this day worse then for some dayes past, butt I hope that a little air and ease will in some measure contribute to my regaining strenghth, which I very sensibly want, to which end I intend going to Pepper Hara on Munday or Tuesday att farthest, having yesterday gott rid of my troublsom post of chairman of the Secrett Comittee, by making a finall Report.[1522] Direct your letters however to mee here, from whence they may bee sent, for tis nott impossible butt I may bee oblidged to returne to towne if any unexpected matter of consequence should happen, though I hope twill nott bee the case, for quietnesse nott violent motion will bee likelyest to give mee releife.

[1520]Cat's paw: a person who is used by another to carry out an unpleasant or dangerous task.
[1521]To enable Charles, earl of Arran, to purchase the forfeited estate of his brother James, 2nd duke of Ormond.
[1522]On 16 June (*CJ*, xix, 593–6).

490. *Alan I, Dublin, to Thomas, Westminster, 17 June 1721*

(1248/5/52–3)

By a letter from Senny which is just come to my hand I find that the West countrey men are endeavouring to take off the great expence of licences for transporting wool out of this countrey; and he desires my thoughts in the matter. I have not leisure to write at large on that subject now, and I chuse rather to doe it to you then to him; but desire you not to use my name as having given my thoughts on the subject. In the first place if the petition they intend to present to the King be of the nature he mentions, that it may be recommended to the Duke of Grafton to endeavour to incline the Parliament here to give some equivalent to the Cheif Governor in lieu of the money accrewing to the Sword[1523] by wool licences, I must own that either they or I much misapprehend the nature of them: They seem to think that the fees on wool licences is by Statute made a part of the support of the Cheif Governor: now I take it to be no more then that it is felony to transport wool hence without licence, and that a certain fee is alway taken on granting such licences, which is a perquisite to the Cheif Governor and hath been of late estimated at £4000 per an. and what it hath at some times fallen short hath been make up out of the revenue of the Crown by vertue of a Kings letter. If this be soe you see that all which is necessary to attain the end of the West countrey men is to repeal the Law which makes transporting it without licence to be felony, provided the wool be stil landed in England; which may be taken care of by bond in the same maner it now is when transported by licence.

But then indeed the Cheif Governor will be to seek for a good part of his income, unlesse some method be taken to make him amends: how this will be done appears to me to be a matter of difficulty; for I beleive the Crown will be unwilling to appropriate any thing to the Governor for the time being, and on the other hand it will be as difficult to bring the Commons to give any addicional hereditary revenue in the room of the wool licences; nor doe I see any need of it, for when the Lord Lieutenants appointment is encreased on the establishment as much as the wool licences added to the present establishment usually make it, the Cheif Governor will be at no losse: but it is true the Crown will annually be obliged to make its demand of a supply by so much greater then now it is. For my own part I think if nothing were paid for wool licences, the English merchant will be able to give us the more for our wool, and that of course will lessen our manufacturing it into yarn here, which is almost the only woollen trade we have left. Soe what to say in the thing or whether it will not rather prejudice then benefit this kingdome you can better judge then I. This I say only to you, but it is certain as the wool licences stand now the whole charge of them falls wholly on the Countyes which produce wool, whereas if the money which the sword may loose by taking them away should issue out of the revenue [?at][1524] large, the whole kingdome would contribute equally …[1525] I am glad to find you are so well recovered to be able [to] goe again to the house. Desire Senny not to be too open in his discourse and letters, especially when he speaks or writes of Great men. Our news Lord

---

[1523] The office of lord lieutenant.
[1524] Word(s) missing.
[1525] Word(s) missing.

Shanon left London last Sunday; if soe probably he may be this night at Holyhead, if he be not landed with this dayes maile.

491. *William, London, to Alan I, 22 June 1721*

(1248/4/279–80)

I … beg youl forgive my mentioning a matter on the success of which a great deal as to me depends, my Nephew[1526] soon after his arrival in discourse with Mr St George[1527] and Mr Ward,[1528] mentiond Mr Justice Boat's lying a dying,[1529] or that He was so ill as to be past hopes of recovery, He mentiond Mr Parnel[1530] and Mr Jephson[1531] as the persons who pushd to succeed him, and that Lord Chief Juistice W[*hitshed*] had wrote pressing to the Duke of G[*raft*]on on the occasion, I know that Mr Jephson has by Dick Turner and Mr Grahme been soliciting Lord Burlington[1532] to use his Interest with Lord Lieutenant supposing that there would be a Vacancy occasiond by removals that have long been Talkd of, the making Mr J[*ustice*] Gore Chief B[*aron*][1533] was as I have been informd their Scheeme, That matter being said with good ground, in case your Lordship consent, to be otherwise settled, tis not improbable that Mr Jephsons agent's he being gone last week by Longsea to Waterford, will on Mr J[*ustice*] Boats death if it should happen renew their Sollicitation on the first notice I Doubt not Lord Chief Justice doing the same in the behalf of Mr Parnel and I am told Mr Tisdale[1534] makes pretensions, My Sole dependence is on your Lordship's favour not having mentioned it to any sould living but my sister If your interposing with Lord Lieutenant in my favour shall be thought Impropper I shall rest satisfied, If your Lordship shall think fit to use your Intrest for me, youl provide for two branches of your family my sister to whom I will most willingly make over £200 per year out of the Proffit's and your Lordships most Obedient Humble Servant …

492. *Alan I, Dublin, to Thomas, at his lodgings in the Privy Garden, Whitehall, 6 July 1721*

(1248/5/55–6)

Last pacquet I received a letter from Lord Lieutenant in the following words date 27 June. My Lord, I hope that what has <u>of late</u> been transacted here is to your satisfaction: and that

---

[1526] St John III.

[1527] Possibly Oliver St George, MP [I].

[1528] Michael Ward, MP [I].

[1529] Godfrey Boate died in England on 24 July 1722.

[1530] John Parnell, MP [I].

[1531] John Jephson, MP [I].

[1532] Richard Turner (1653–1725), of Bandon, Co. Cork, was employed in a legal capacity on the Burlington estate (NLI, MSS 43353, 43940/1, 44017/1–2); Richard Graham was Burlington's secretary (see above, p. 200).

[1533] George Gore, MP [I].

[1534] Michael Tisdall, MP [I].

whatever part has been taken by me you will beleive that I have endeavoured to doe what might be agreeable to you.

Your brother[1535] has given you a more full account <u>then I need</u> of what has passed; and as <u>you did desire</u> the freindship of some people, <u>I can answer for them</u>. And I dare say <u>if we can agree in our measures</u> to carry on the Kings affairs, it will be out of the power of anybody to doe ill offices. I have taken the liberty of assuring the King how ready you alway <u>would be</u> to promote his service (not have been as I think his Grace might and should have said) and that I did not doubt but there would be union of his servants the other side the water. In a little time I shal be able to discourse these things att Dublin and to assure you that I am My Lord etc

The inclosed is the answer I think proper to send which if you approve of I desire it may be sent to his Grace. We have orders to prorogue the Parliament here to 25 August[1536] from whence I conclude yours hath some thing more to doe and will not be up immediately. I have wrote to Senny about kissing the Kings and Princes hands, for if he should not doe soe I can not but think it will give just cause of offence but have received no answer ...

493. St John III, Bristol, to Alan I, 8 July 1721

(1248/5/57–8)

I came to this place late last night with Lord and Lady Hillsborogh, and am this minute going aboard ship, tho the wind is now contrary, so that I am afraid tis hardly possible for us to make a passage: if that prove the case, my Lord is determin'd to make the best of his way to Chester and so on to Holihead, rather then wait for a wind here which we may possibly do these 2 months. This journey of my Ladys seems to have been a sudden thought, at least I knew nothing of it till a very few days before I left London; the reason which I hear given for it is that there is a Cole Mine found upon part of the Estate, and that they are unwilling to trust the management or setting of it to any body, till they have veiew'd and enquir'd about it themselves.

Before I came away I had an Account that justice Boate was so ill that twas hardly possible he should recover; and upon this took an opportunity, with my Uncles advice and consent, to wait upon the Duke of Grafton and recommend my Uncle[1537] for his successor. His Grace received me very kindly, exprest great regard for your Lordship and your family, and told me withal that tho he had been applyed to by other people, and namd W[*hitshed*], he neither had nor would lay himself under any promise, but whenever the vacancy hapned would endeavour to serve my freind, <u>if he could do it with any tolerable Grace</u>. I likewise took the liberty to mention this affair to both the Walpoles; the Eldest said as much or more then I could expect, and promis'd to speak to his freind the D[*uke*] of Grafton for my Uncle; so that I really hope tis now put upon such a foot, that if you thought it proper to

---

[1535]William.

[1536]The proclamation had been issued on 4 July. A subsequent proclamation, dated 9 Aug., extended the prorogation until 12 Sept., when parliament finally met (*LJI*, ii, 68).

[1537]William.

second the Applications that have been already made, by a letter, there would be no danger of the success.

I would not have gone this length without your advice, if I had not known W[*hitshed*] was very pressing for his Brother,[1538] and therefore fear'd his extorting a promise before I could possibly receive your commands, but as that is now in a good measure prevented, so if your Lordship should think fit to make any Application on behalf of your Brother, I hope you will do it by letter as soon as you conveniently can, and not wait for the Dukes going into Ireland, because all delays in these cases are dangerous.

I am calld away to go aboard ship, tho the wind is now no better then North West. If I have the fortune to meet with a good Passage, which I hardly expect, I shall be able to pay the Bill I took the Liberty to draw on you, assoon as it can be sent to Corke, if not, am sure my wife will do it. For Gods sake My Lord be not angry at my doing it. The day before I drew I had a Bill of £173 brought me from Beralston for the Expences in the Countrey, which I knew not one word of before, and which I had no other possible way of paying…

[*PS*] I can venture to assure you that after the utmost endeavours to dissolve this Parliament, there has been a positive Answer returnd against it; and notwithstanding this disappointment — will stand his Ground.

494. *Alan I, Dublin, to Thomas, at his lodgings in the Privy Garden, Whitehall, 13 July 1721*

(1248/5/59–60)

I write by this post to my Lord Lieutenant and in my letter mention the procuring the Proxyes of such Lords as are now in England who will not attend the Parliament here and yet are willing to contribute what is in their power to matters going easily and well. I had great hopes that the discontented angry people would have cooled soe far, as entirely to have forgott what they were soe zealously engaged in the last Session, or at least to resolve not to proceed farther in a thing which I think never could be expected to end to their wish. But I have too much reason to beleive the same restlesse spirit reigns in some of them stil, and that it is in their thoughts to harp on the same string. There are some men here as inflexible as steel and as uncapable of being convinced as a mule: I beleive their numbers will not be soe great as formerly, and know that some of the warmest men the last Session seem to have much more temper then I could observe in them before; but it is impossible for me, who avowedly opposed their whole scheme, to dive into their secrets; but it will be of absolute necessity, or at least very prudent, to make the best provision against our being involved in as great difficultyes as lately. This will be best done by my Lord Dukes endeavouring to prevail with as many Lords as he knows will concur in his measures to come over, and by getting blank Proxyes from others of which the Duke of Bolton had several in the former Session.

I have reason to beleive the same Devil is intended to be raised now in another shape, and remember Lord Grimston told me with concern he had given his Proxy to Lord

---

[1538]John Parnell was Whitshed's brother-in-law, and Whitshed was always anxious to assist him (BL, Add. MS 61639: Whitshed to Sunderland, 17 Nov. 1714). Parnell received a bequest of £500 from Whitshed's will, of which he was one of the executors (Marsh's Library, Dublin, MS Z.2.1.7/64: copy of will, 3 Mar. 1724).

M[*olesworth*] who used it on all occasions as he went himself. Speak to my Lord but I doe not write soe plain to him as I doe now to you. Lord Cadowgan[1539] can influence Lord Blundel and I beleive Lord Lieutenant himself can do so with Lord Ranelagh and Percival.

495. *Alan I, Dublin, to Thomas, at his lodgings in the Privy Garden, Whitehall, 15 July 1721*

(1248/5/61–2)

Your Nephew wrote to me on the first instant, and the subject matter of his letter was only an introduction (by way of news) to his telling me [he] had drawn a bill on me for £220, and gives me for reason that he that moment had settled the bills and accounts relating to his election, which had cost him £500; a summe (saith he) greater then I carryed over with me. The later part I beleive, but from a former letter I received from you I much doubt whether his expence in the election was such as he represents it to have been: and rather fancy that he hath mett with something which suits his fancy in London, and things of that kind he never fails buying, who ever the person is whose money must go to pay for them. I beleive I have wrote to you before to know whether he waited on the King and Prince to kisse their hands; if he did not, he was certainly very much to blame; and such a neglect in the son of one of his Majestyes immediate servants will be construed (with too much reason) a designed affront. But if that should be the case, this is not the first time that his misbehaving himself without my direction nay against it, hath been imputed to me. Pray let me know how this matter was, and how he acted in the house, the little time he sate in it, and whether the conjectures I made in answer to your first letter about his being chosen have not by the event been found to have some foundation.

    You may tell my Lord Lieutenant (but must not name the man) that as the time for our Parliaments meeting draws on, one comes to more knowledge on what heads people design to be uneasy. Since my last I was to see the Archbishop of D[*ublin*] who talking about the method of late taken of the Lord Lieutenants living in England and making the place a sort of a sinecure, said the way to prevent it would be to grant the funds only from year to year: which would necessitate them to come over at least annually, if not to continue here. I told him I had been for giving from year to year when that matter came in Debate in the Parliament held by the late Duke of Ormond, but it being then carryed against us by a majoritye of three,[1540] and having ever since been given for two years, it would look unkind and really be soe, to be of another mind under this Governement then we had been for so many years last past. His answer was that when the inconvenience attending giving for two years is discovered, the thing ought to be discontinued. And he seemed by his discourse to allow he had spoke to this purpose to several Gentlemen, and intended to continue to doe soe.

    I plainly saw that he was more of this opinion now when he had not been left one of the Justices then he had been formerly, when he was one: for at that time this notion was not broached by him. But at the same time I cannot (tho at present one of the Justices) but own

---

[1539] William, 1st Earl Cadogan.

[1540] In the committee of supply on 13 Oct. 1703 (C. I. McGrath, *The Making of the Eighteenth-century Irish Constitution: Government, Parliament and the Revenue, 1692–1714* (Dublin, 2000), 169).

that I think it would be more for the Kings service and the good of the Kingdome to have the Cheif Governor actually resident in the Kingdome, by which means those who attend their duty in the Kingdome might have personal accesse to him on occasion, which they now have not; but those who attended their pleasure, and other affairs in London have the start and great advantage of those who are doing their duty here. I also found his Grace hath a very indifferent opinion of our Bank;[1541] a thing I very little understand, but I confesse I dread anything of that nature in this countrey where (in case of abuse or mismanagement) we shal not be able to call the offenders to any account; and if they should be questioned for real misbehavior, I doe not see but that it will be very difficult to come at them, tho a great many may mean very well and endeavour to redresse any publick mischeif. The South Sea, and difficultyes in punishing the greatest villains by a British Parliament makes me dread erecting a body of men who may in time be too great to be called in question. But his Grace assuring me that he hath it from a good hand that my Lord Lieutenant and the Governement are purely passive in that matter, and have only gone into it as a thing universally pleasing to the Kingdome, if this be soe, people will not disoblige tho they should not be wholly for the Bank in the maner proposed and intended. When you talk with the Duke observe his inclinations to it, and let me know whether it is pushed on or only gone into as a thing agreeable to the countrey: But I own I am very apprehensive that hereafter we may feel consequences from it which we doe not now foresee.

496. Thomas to Alan I, Dublin, 27 July 1721

(1248/5/65–6)

I have three of your unacknowledged, which requiring noe other answer then that I had done every thing you directed, I deferd writing till I could give you an account of our proceedings in the close of the session.

I was hurryed from Pepper Hara contrary to expectation, and as you will beleive, desire, by repeated alarms of the Lords resolving to send us a mulcting clause (by way of amendment) to the Directors Bill restoring them to their estates reall and personall vested by the Bill in Trustees, upon payment of a summe certaine by each of them respectively,[1542] I own my opinion against that method soe strong, that I should have been for loosing the Bill rather then agreeing to that amendment. The matter however was concerted, and sollicited by some Lords to such a degree as would have a man thinke the welfare of the nation had depended uppon itt, I will nott by post tell you the mistery (for such itt was [)], nor what methods were taken for warding the blow, both the one and the other you shall know by some safe hand, and they will bee worth communicating, itt remaind under uncertainty till Ten on Munday morning, and by twelve their Lordships were pleasd to drop the matter, sending us the Bill[1543] with three literal amendments and a fourth very reasonable one, for prolonging the time of the Directors delivering up their title deeds to the 20th of September instead of the 3d of August, more time having been spent in going through the Bill then

[1541] The proposed national bank.
[1542] Mulct: a fine imposed for an offence (*OED*).
[1543] On 25 July (*LJ*, xxi, 579).

wee expected when wee appointed that day, I can say nothing of Lord Lieutenants setting out, other then that I suppose hee continues his resolution for Tuesday next …

497. St John III, Midleton, to Alan I, 6 Aug. 1721

(1248/5/67–8)

This is the third time I have sat down to answer your last letter, which is wrote in that severe angry unkind manner, that I protest the bare reading it puts me so far beside my self that I am not able to recollect my thoughts so as to write common sense; however since you require it, I will endeavour to answer it in the best manner I can.

In the first place I assure you I neither advis'd nor was consulted about Lord H[*illsborough's*] journey; the secret of which I am to to this minute a stranger to; nor had I any other hand in carrying him and his Brother out of town with me, then being passive when they first made the Proposal of seeing their sister, which you know even common decency would have prevented my opposing, had I been enclin'd so to do.

I do not pretend to justifye, and surely I ought not to account for any bodys behaviour at the Lodge; and yet I am afraid the Resentment of this, was one Inducement to your writing a letter which, as you direct, I have well consider'd and shall not easily forget.

If ever I have exprest any impatience at being put in mind of any thing that has given you just cause of complaint, I can with great truth assure you that it has always proceeded from the manner of your doing it, and not from any positive selfish notion of my being always in the right, or above advice; and when you are pleas'd to do it in a kind freindly manner, I am so far from being uneasy, that I esteem it as the greatest act of freindship, and own my self extremely oblig'd to you for it …

I have obeyed your Commands in answering your letter with freedom; a greater then I ever took before, but such a one as the undeserv'd unkindness of your letter has extorted from me. If you were to read it again and consider several of the Expressions of it, I beleive you would forgive me; but let what will be the consequence, there is no condition so miserable, as to be constantly oblig'd to submit to ill Usage, without ever daring to justifye or excuse ones self. How far this has been my case God Almighty and your Lordship best know.

I have wrote you so much upon this Ungratefull subject, and am now in such a condition by doing it, that I cant answer another part of your letter this Post as particularly as I will by the next. In the mean time you may depend upon my paying the Bill I took the liberty to draw on you, the minute I go to Corke Assizes. I have already told you the difficultys I was under when I drew that Bill, and considering the cause of them, cant yet think I was guilty of any great crime in doing it, even after the former cautions I received on this subject. When I neglect paying it, twill be time to expose me to the world; but to do it before, and to publish the streights I was in for want of money in London, and to magnifye the sum I drew for, of all which I have been told by several people since I landed and which has been done, tho not by your Lordship savours a good deal of that unkindness which I have met with in almost every step of my Election, and particularly the day before I left Ireland.

I will not say I have in every instance acted with that prudence and caution I ought to have done; but as I am not conscious to my self of having ever been guilty of one Undutyfull

Action, it goes to my heart to find my self treated, as I have been of late, like the greatest Enemy and scoundrel upon earth.

This letter carrys my fortune; if it be taken as I intend it, only a complaint of what I think hard usage, I shall be happy; if otherwise, I can but say, my heart was too full not to venture, once in my life, to write my mind freely upon a subject that has made it perfectly uneasy to me.

If there be any Expression in it that gives you offence, I beg you will impute it to the concern in which I write, which is greater then I can express or you conceive; for let your opinion of me be what it will, I have the satisfaction to know I always have been and resolve to continue My Lord, Your truly Dutyfull son and faithfull servant …

498. *Thomas, Bath, to Alan I, 15 Aug. 1721*

(1248/5/69–70)

I came hither last Saturday, through Glostersheer, where I spent two days with the Duke of Bolton and Lord Godolphin. Yesterday I began the waters, which hitherto agree very well with my stomach, soe that I hope for a good effect of them, since the very beginning is most liable to give disturbance by affecting the head, of which I have noe symptom.

Yesterdays post brought yours of the 2d and 4th.

Though you say you have nothing butt conjecture in relation to the Act of Grace (for there is a distinction (as is sayd) between that an an Act of Indemnity)[1544] the intent of itt is soe very obvious, that you cannott possibly mistake itt.

Assoone as I returne to London ile settle the matter of your Lottery tickets, by subscribing which you will bee a great looser, butt nott somuch in my opinion as people generally thinke; least the Redeemables should nott bee sufficiently naild downe by the resolutions come to in the house, care was taken more explicitly to doe itt by the Bill, which you may easily beleive was carryed through in a house of about 120. I confesse I was under great difficultyes as to my behaviour in relation to my Brother W[illiam] whose conduct has been soe liable to just exception; nor should I have brought my selfe upon his account soe far to have interested my selfe in the matter, as in the common sense of things might very justly have made mee in good measure answerable for his future deportment which I can by noe means rely uppon, I therfore tooke itt by another handle; I told his Grace hee was best judge how far his recomendation ought to take place, butt that one of two conclusions were very plaine, either that the interposition in behalf of Mr Marly was of greater weight with him then your recomendation, or his power lesse then I was willing to beleive itt, that I should however say little uppon either, but that hee must pardon the freedom I should take uppon another Topick, that of the customary right a Lord Chancellor has allways had in recomending to the Bench, I desired his consulting ours what hee would thinke in a like case. I spoke my mind very freely in relation to other peoples taking uppon them to recommend without the least colour of right soe to doe, otherwise then as favourites

[1544] An act of grace pardoned an offender for a crime committed; an act of indemnity merely protected an offender from punishment. The act of grace, introduced in the Lords by Lord Townshend on behalf of the king, and intended to put an end to legal proceedings relating to the South Sea Company, passed both houses the same day (*LJ*, xxi, 582–3; *CJ*, xix, 646).

behind the curtaine; that I was nott surprizd att my nephews disappointment when you were to bee removd after soe unpresedented a manner, and therefore should pray his Graces plaine answer to a question, Whither you were to remaine in the same scituation of creditt as then; if soe I would say noe more, or give him further trouble; if nott I should recur to my former assertion of your right to recommend to him exclusive of all the rest. I drove the matter soe far as to bee earnestly presst to desire your patience till hee gott over, when hee bid mee tell you hee was very sure hee should take those measures as would give you entire satisfaction, I would nott promise to write in his way, however I did really intend doing itt, and certainly had done soe, if what fell from Mr W[alpole] to mee in the house the day before I came out of towne, had nott given (as I thought) very sufficient reason for altering my resolution, of this whole matter I would have given you an accountt butt that I beleivd a letter from hence might more probably come to your hand unopened, then one wrote the post after this happened.

I tooke Mr W[alpole] aside, and stated the matter fully to him, without mincing, in discourse hee lett fall this expression, that the D[uke] of G[rafton] told him that if hee should dispose of the cusshion before the parliament was over, hee should nott bee able to carry the session through, I thankt him for this frank dealing, being now convinct of what I suspected, though his Grace never did or would deale plainly with mee; that I ownd I had thoughts of writing to you in the manner hee desired, butt was now fully determined against itt, on the contrary as far as my opinion would influence, I should without reserve tell you that I thought you now had an opertunity of refuting the malitious and groundlesse insinuations of your enemyes by acting a dutifull and reasonable part in carrying on the Kings businesse in the approaching session, att the same time declaring to his Grace and all your acquaintance that your being Chancellor should end with that of the session, for that you would nott act soe mean a part as to hold longer when twas vissible, meane compliances tooke place of reall meritt, that I ownd having too great a share in prevailing uppon you to beare what you have done, butt that I would nott a second time comitt the same fault. Hee seemd struck, and askt what need so much passion, I told him stating facts, was giving sufficient reasons. I repeated this conversation to one whoe I fancy has acquainted some body, whoe has been usually kept a very great stranger to every thing of this nature.

The two dayes prorogation was occasioned by a Bill having passed (Mr Walpoles Bill of Powers[1545]) by which the seven millions were reenacted for the Publick, soe that the five millions could nott bee released in the same session by repealing soe much of that Act. The remaining two millions is to bee tuggd for next winter ...

499. *Thomas to Alan I, Dublin, 16 Aug. 1721*

(1248/5/71–2)

My head being a little muddy from the waters, I forgott sending you the inclosed from Mr Hillersden.[1546] You will probably remember him by that excellent charecter hee most

---

[1545] Parliament had been prorogued from 29 to 31 July (*CJ*, xix, 640), having passed the Civil List Act, discharging the South Sea Company 'for assurances of part of the money, which they were obliged to pay to his majesty', which received the royal assent on 29 July (*CJ*, xix, 636; *LJ*, xxi, 581, 584).

[1546] William Hillersden (1676–1725), of Elstow, Beds., MP [GB] Beds.

deservedly wears, a worthier man lives nott; I am particularly oblidged to him for his great zeale in my nephewes affair.

Pray lett mee know if you can serve his kinsman, I hope a good deale from the waters, which agree with mee, as they have formerly done.

I suppose my last letter will reach you before the D[uke] of G[rafton] for as I remember hee told mee (I am sure somebody did) that hee should make itt ten or twelve days in getting to the water side, being to stop on the road, probably in Northampton sheer, where hee has an estate.[1547]

Deale plainly and early; observing the Mountebancks frontispeice.[1548] Read, try, and judge as you find.

500. *Thomas, Bath, to Alan I, 2 Sept. 1721*

(1248/5/75–6)

I find apparent advantage by the use of these waters in every instance save that of the paine in my back, which is too firmly fixt to allow any expectation of releif.

I resolve continuing here longer then I intended, since from the early sitting of the parliament the session will probably bee longer then expected, and consequently a greater fatigue, however direct your letters to Whitehall, by which means they will come to my hand wherever I am.

Thursday I receivd yours of the 22d of last month, I know nott what answer to give to what you desire my opinion uppon, your selfe will best judge of that from such observations as may bee easily made of — conduct, butt in general, I thinke your treatment hitherto such, as leaves noe roome for expecting better, unlesse that bee immediately altered, nay the very reverse practised, I told you in a former how plainly I had spoake, if therfore any haesitation bee in that instance, there will need noe explanation of what is farther intended; when ever a private quarrell seems unavoidable, twould bee madnesse nott to give the first blow. The D[uke] of G[rafton] told mee hee would nott labour a land tax, butt leave the Commons to judge of itt, I thought att the time this answer evasive, fancying hee might hope their making itt their own Act, surely they are nott as much infatuated this year, as wee here were the last. I see noe difference between graunting itt for two years and to perpetuity, save in words, for in consequence there can bee no doubt butt twill bee the same thing. Occasions will never bee wanting for its continuance, nor will itt bee long before you will bee told the quantum[1549] must bee augmented, when ever itt takes place. I looke upon the nation undone, therfore have noe hand in itt. I wish another thing you mention may nott prove more prejudiciall then att first sight may appeare, joining the two togather will pin the baskett,[1550] notwithstanding which (how apparent soever) I feare the servile temper of

---

[1547] Wakefield Lodge, Potterspury.

[1548] Possibly a reference to 'The Earl of Rochester's Mountebank Speech, on Tower Hill', printed at the beginning of *The Poetical Works of the Honourable Sir Charles Sedley* ... (1719), 19–23. In another version of his mock mountebank's notice Rochester had likened the politician to the mountebank (*To All Gentlemen, Ladies, and Others, Whether of City, Town, or Country: Alexander Bendo Wisheth All Health and Prosperity* ... [1700], 3–4).

[1549] The amount granted.

[1550] Settle the matter.

some, and covetiousnesse of others may affect what must and inevitably will end in slavery, for I know noe difference between wearing chains of my own putting on, or of anothers; except onely that the first (like the case of the damned) is aggravated by being their owne Act. The onely comfort in such instances an honest man can propose, is having noe share in the guilt.

The great prospect of plenty is like to vanish, by the very unseasonable weather. I question whither one halfe of the years crop will nott bee lost, wee have nott for some time past had a dry day, scarcely four hours togather soe.

501. *St John III, Midleton, to Alan I, Dublin, 5 Sept. 1721*

(1248/5/77–8)

… By not hearing to the contrary from any good hand, I suppose the Parliament will meet to do business the 12th,[1551] and will therefore endeavour to be in Dublin within a day or 2 of that time. I am not yet sure whither my wife will come up with me; if she does, I shall be kept a day or 2 longer; but by what I hear of Parliament business, there is no great occasion for my making any great hast.

Lord Inchiquin, Sir Edw. Obrien[1552] and a great deal more Company are now with me …

502. *Alan I to Thomas, at his lodgings in the Privy Garden, Whitehall, 13 Sept. 1721*

(1248/5/82–3)

The Parliament mett yesterday, and you have above the speech delivered by my Lord Lieutenant;[1553] in which you will observe the maner of mentioning the bank;[1554] which we pretend is not at all espoused here, but left entirely to the option of the Parliament to accept or refuse. But I could not but observe the difficultye shewn at an alteration made by me in the first draught prepared by the Secretary, which recommended it in stronger terms then I thought nec[essary] and at length even my amendment was softned; for I had pro[posed] it thus. After the words to establish a Bank I added But as [it] is a matter of a general and national concern His Majestye leaves it to the wisdom of Parliament whether it may be for the benefit of the Kingdome, and if it should be found to be soe, in what maner it may be settled on a safe foundation etc or to that effect. The words <u>but</u> and <u>if</u> were objected to, and it was said they would not be proper after the King had condescended on the application of Gentlemen of Ireland to direct the granting a Charter etc soe as I was forced to soften it

---

[1551] The date to which the Irish parliament had been prorogued.

[1552] Sir Edward O'Brien (1705–65), 2nd Bt, of Dromoland, Co. Clare, MP [I] 1727–d.

[1553] Not in Alan I's hand. Omitted.

[1554] That the king, out of his concern for Ireland's present difficult economic situation, had been pleased to issue a commission under the great seal for receiving subscriptions to a bank, but left it to parliament to consider what the advantages to the kingdom might be by establishing a bank, and how best this might be settled (*CJI*, iv, 694).

in the maner you see it. I know not what the event will be; but as the thing is represented with us, every body is at entire liberty to consult the good of the Kingdome in accepting or declining it, and I own the longer I consider it the worse I like it; and perhaps a great many in both houses may have their difficultyes. But I think the great contest will be in the upper house, for tho I am sensible a certain person in the Lower[1555] is from the bottom of his heart against it (but perhaps not from the same reasons that other people are) yet he is too good a courtier not to seem in publick for it, but this is of late, and since he hath reason to think it will be well taken in England etc not to reject the Kings favour obtained with so much application of —. The world hath taken up an opinion that a certain person is concerned in the banking trade with Mr H.[1556] and hath been long soe.

503. *Alan I to Thomas, at his lodgings in the Privy Garden, Whitehall, 13 Sept. 1721*

(1248/5/84–5)

After the speech delivered the Lords came to the following resolutions,[1557] moved by Lord Shelburne and FitzW[*illia*]ms; the Archbishop of Dublin, on this ground that he would not have the house to direct the Committee on what heads to addresse but would leave it at large to them to form it: He pretended to think this method of limiting them to the matters upon which the addresse should be founded was perfectly new and never used in England or this Kingdome; our journal shewed his mistake in one part, and I assured him it was perfectly otherwise in England as to the other, especially of late. Whatever my opinion may be of the reasonablenesse of an house coming immediately into a resolution on several particulars contained in a question framed and considered of and digested out of the house by persons who move for the addresse; I am convinced it was necessary in this instance to have it thus: for if the Committee had not been pinned down by instructions I beleive a certain warm affair might have been glanced at if not expressely mentioned, which from the temper I see in the house will not I beleive be stirred this Session. But his Grace was

---

[1555] William Conolly.

[1556] Francis Harrison, MP [I].

[1557] Given in the letter in a different hand: 'That an humble Address be presented to his Majesty to thank him for his Gracious acceptance of the expressions of the Duty and Loyalty of this House in former sessions of Parliament; and for the tender concern he hath for the welfare of this Kingdom and for his readiness to concur with his Parliament in applying such remedies as may restore it to a more flourishing condition; and for his approbation of the care and succesful endeavours of those intrusted with the administration of his affairs in preserving the Nation from the Pestilence which hath so miserably ravag'd a neighbouring Kingdom. And to thank his Majesty for his goodness in leaving it to the choice of his Parliament to have a bank in this Kingdom and to assure his Majesty that this house will with the greatest attention weigh and consider, how far the same may be beneficial to it and will by their conduct and unanimity endeavour to continnue the security of our most excellent church as by Law establish'd; and to strengthen the Protestant interest; and will give his Majesty all further testimonies of their resolution to continue in the same dutiful disposition; which they have att all times shewn to his person and Government; and that nothing shall be wanting on their part to make his reighn easy and his people happy; and to expresse their entire satisfaction in his Majesty's again placing his Grace the Duke of Grafton over us as his Lieutenant whose Person and former conduct have rendred him so acceptable and desirable to the Kingdom.'

not supported by any body but his brother of Tuam.[1558] The house was thin three Earles three Viscounts two Barons eight Bishops.[1559] You see how the Lords thank the King for the Commission for taking subscriptions for a Bank: viz for his leaving it to the choice of his Parliament to have a Bank, and they only promise that they will with attention weigh and consider how far the same may be beneficial to the Kingdome. The Commons seem to me to go farther, for their resolution is in their addresse to his Majestye to return their humble thanks for his readinesse in directing a Commission to passe under the great Seal for receiving voluntary subscriptions to establish a Bank in such maner as may be most beneficial to the Kingdome.[1560] Is not this an acceptance of the Bank offered? But they say they meant no more then to think[1561] the King for putting in their power etc. But I think the drawers of the resolutions who were Sir Ralph Gore the Atturney[1562] and Sollicitor General[1563] and Lord Cheif Justice Whitshed and the Speaker and Secretary meant more. That which I think is most considerable is that it passed in a very thin house consisting not of full 70. Jos[hua] Allen and Dr Worth[1564] were against the resolution as worded and were for adding the words (if it shal be found to be for the general good of the Kingdome) but to no purpose. My next shal carry the Addresses. On the back you have the instructions to the Committee.

504. *Thomas, Peper Harow, to Alan I, 22 Sept. 1721*

(1248/5/87–8)

Wensday night att my returne from Bath (where I spent five weekes) I found here the speech, and resolutions of the Lords to bee the subject of an Addresse; they are very much mistaken whoe thinke this procedure irregular, doing otherwise would bee perfectly un-parliamentary, if the aunctient usage (and indeed the best) bee the rule.

Tis very true that as far as itt relates to the Crowne, the softest and most respectfull words are to bee chosen, since in materiall points those are looked on noe otherwise then the effect of that duty which is due, butt when you come to speake of what more immediately relates to the Country, plaine words without ambiguity are best, since in this case a parliament is supposed to meane neither more nor lesse then they say; The matter of the Banke I take to bee of the last consequence, itt may noe doubt bee of good use, if strictly and well regulated, butt if due care bee nott taken, itt may prove too weildy a body to admitt of

---

[1558]Sir Richard Levinge reported that Archbishop King was the only lord who 'contested', and that the grounds for his opposition to the terms of the address was that the House had received no answer from the king to the representation on the *Annesley v. Sherlock* case (Levinge, *Jottings*, 60).

[1559]The presence list printed for 12 Sept. 1721 in *LJI*, ii, 684 lists one earl, six viscounts (including Midleton himself), three barons and six bishops. Analogous problems with the printed presence lists for the Westminster parliament are discussed in Clyve Jones, 'Seating Problems of the House of Lords in the Early Eighteenth Century: The Evidence of the Manuscript Minutes', *BIHR*, li (1978), 132–45; and in *HL 1660–1714*, i, 42–5.

[1560]An address agreed on 14 Sept. (*CJI*, iv, 701–2).

[1561]Thank.

[1562]John Rogerson, MP [I].

[1563]Thomas Marlay, MP [I].

[1564]Edward Worth, MP [I].

such amendments as may appeare necessary; I thinke this proposition may bee certainly advanced, that in time to come every concession made to them will bee interpreted in the largest and most beneficiall sense for the Company, and indeed soe itt ought, because tis to bee supposed a Parliament have taken due care in nott graunting any such powers as may prove prejudiciall to the whole; An Aggregate body having always the same point of benefitt to themselves in veiwe, will ever bee too hard for the publique, especially in a thing of this nature, where means will bee ever found, for gaining the favour of Government on their side, since in very many instances twill bee in their power to retalliate; in forming the Banke here, the nott advancing mony without consent of Parliament is a condition, and that in the strongest termes, were itt otherwise noe man can tell how soon, and how certainly, the onely valluable power of the Commons may devolve on them. The Banke here has a sollid Bottom by the yearly summs payable during their existence from the publique, by which every body whoe trusts them is in great measure secured against lossse, butt yours wants this, and God forbid itt should ever have itt, for the consequences of any thing of that kind are soe very vissible, that they cannott bee overlookt; itt will therefore bee incumbent on you (I mean the house of Commons) sufficiently to provide for the security of every person whoe shall lodge his mony there, for as paper creditt is certainly usefull under these conditions, itt may prove very dangerous without them; The Banke may and probably will from time too time become possessed of much the greater part of the cash of the Kingdom, if then the security bee nott sufficient in all events, what must become of the whole. Without giving such a body creditt twill come to nothing, on the other hand a creditt beyond what shall bee reasonably secured may prove fatall. The thing is of too nice a nature for mee whoe never had to doe with any thing of the kind, butt there are first principles wherein a man whoe thinks att all cannott mistake.

Itt may deserve consideration whither any Proprietor of stock should nott bee debard transferring for a certaine reasonable time, which will in great measure prevent stock job-bing, for though transferring will bee absolutely necessary after the thing is brought to beare, I thinke those whoe cannott stand what they subscribe till tis soe, have somewhat else in veiwe then publique good, butt this is onely my own notion, which the nature of the thing seems to suggest, without having talkt to any body uppon the subject. Diu deliberandum est, quod statuendum semel.[1565] The thing may prove advantagious, and I am very sure may in ill hands prove very dangerous; I have hitherto cheifly considered the publique; in the next Place the Proprietors are to bee thought uppon, whose gaine or losse (as in every thing of like nature) depends uppon the knowledge and integrity of those that are entrusted, you see what effect the want of both has had on the S[outh] S[ea] Company. Like causes will have like effects and therfore the quallifications of Directors as well as their power ought to bee very maturely considered, and nott theirs onely, butt that of subordinate officers likewise.

If an Act passe (as I take for graunted there must if the thing goe forward) I thinke every thing that can bee foreseen should bee provided for therein, without leaving too great a latitude for by lawes, which may bee made, repealed, or altered to serve particular turnes. I have given some crude thoughts which as far as they goe may serve for hints, having neither time to consider, or opertunity of digesting, when there are soe many talking about mee. I own I feare you are taking a leap in the darke, and know nott where youl light … I doubt

---

[1565]Publius Syrus, *Sententiae*, 158: 'Deliberandum est diu quod statuendum est semel' ('What is once resolved is to be long deliberated upon').

Ireland may bee in att least as much danger as this Kingdom, you will therfore thinke itt necessary to settle accountts with all your tennants getting from them what mony you can …

505. *Alan I, Dublin, to Thomas, at his lodgings in the Privy Garden, Whitehall, 11 Oct. 1721*

(1248/5/95–6)

I write this from the house of Lords where by the late meeting of the house (for indeed we have nothing to do) I have leisure enough to continue the account of the Session, as I began it in two former letters. I said before that we had nothing to doe, but may add to what I then said that our time hath of late been taken up in doing what was much more disagreeable to me then perfect idlenesse, receiving and examining complaints against Lords who to the very great oppression of the Kingdome have obstructed the current of justice by protecting vast numbers of people under the notion of being their menial servants, who had no maner of relation to them, unlesse as Creditors have a relation to their debtors: For several of the persons protected are said to have great summes due from some of their protectors. The Earle of Roscommon and Lord Blessinton appeared to have protected many more then 84 a peice,[1566] but each of them owned they had protected that number, none of which they did or could give the house any satisfaction, were their menial servants or employed about their persons or estates. The Lord Altham protected 21, and if he paid the wages which he certifyed he was to pay them in their respective protections, his income is not sufficient to doe it for the wages amounted to £300 a year and it is vehemently suspected he hath not £100 a year coming in. The Lords were all committed to the black rod;[1567] Lord Roscommon is next door to a —; Lord Blessinton a very unaccountable and extravagant young man; but I will give you no character of the other I will not meddle with it since I cannot give you such an one as will be agreeable to me to write or for you to hear.

The Lords did on Monday discharge Lord Roscommon paying his fees,[1568] which I doubt he is in very ill condition to doe; and I beleive his indigent circumstances were the strongest inducement to the Lords to discharge him soe soon; for if the fees had increased on him by continuing him in custody I am morally certain he never could have paid them.[1569] Lord Blessinton hath not petitioned and I hear intends to stay in during the Session rather then get his liberty by paying the black rod.[1570] Lord Altham petitioned to be discharged but the

[1566] According to Sir Richard Levinge, Blessington had issued 96 protections, Roscommon 76, and Lord Rosse and others smaller numbers (Levinge, *Jottings*, 62–3). Bishop Nicolson gave the number attributed to Lord Roscommon as 95 (BL, Add. MS 6116, f. 112: to Archbishop Wake, 25 Sept. 1721). Philip Perceval numbered Blessington's at 93 and Roscommon's at 84 (BL, Add. MS 47029, f. 71: Philip Perceval to Lord Perceval, 5 Oct. 1721).

[1567] On 2 Oct. Altham, Blessington and Roscommon were all committed to the custody of the gentleman usher of the black rod, William Fisher (*LJI*, ii, 695–7.) Notes by Alan on this debate are preserved as SHC, 1248/5/99–100, and 1248/9/173. The former is misdated 21 Oct., presumably the day on which they were sent to a correspondent.

[1568] On 9 Oct. (*LJI*, ii, 702).

[1569] Evidently Alan had spoken strongly in Roscommon's favour during the debate, 'com[ing] off the woolsack' to do so, but had been vigorously contradicted, and according to Levinge, 'exposed' by Lord Anglesey (Levinge, *Jottings*, 63–4).

[1570] In fact Blessington did petition; his discharge was ordered on 16 Oct. (*LJI*, ii, 704).

Lords would not hear of it,[1571] he having (as was sworn at our bar) put Lord Havershams[1572] hand to a protection without the knowledge of that Lord, for two Moydores and 12 Crowns given him. For this the Lords ordered the Attorney General to prosecute him and seemed resolved not to admit him to sit among them till he should be acquitted of so foul a crime and if he be convicted of it they seem to me to be determined to sequester him from his seat in Parliament during life. He hath been faulty in many other instances in all appearance and the house is extremely incensed against his wicked wayes not his person; tho I think they are not very fond of that nor desirous of his company he having made his brags that as soon as he comes into the house he will set it into a flame by moving to commit the Cheif Baron and thereby bring the old matter of jurisdiction again on the stage. I doe not think this brag of his will at all contribute to his more early inlargement.

14 Oct.

Thus far I wrote in the house of Lords whence I returned to my house very lame and in a weak condicion: by a numbnesse in my Left Leg, which seemed to me to be a paralitical disorder: I sent for Dr Molyneux and Dr Comyng who immediately prescribed me a strong vomit, which I took on Wednesday night and it wrought very well. I slept that night much better then I had done of late: yesterday I take Physick which also did agree with me and purged me six or seven times; I slept better that night then I had done for many past and I have much more strength in my Leg then I had before the vomit and Physick; but it is stil weak. I think plainly my sinew is relaxed, for my foot is apt to slip and give way outward as if my shooe went awry and the joint of my knee is so weak that I am apt almost to fall back, but I gather strength apparently have a very good stomach since my Physick and have no numbnesse nor coldnesse in my Leg, but cannot move my tooes. This I write to let you know the worst of matters; for I make no doubt to see my self dead or at least half soe of a palsye in your next London prints.

Never was I seised at a time that I more regretted being unable to bestir my self in what I apprehend of great service to my Countrey I mean in opposing the Bank which is so earnestly panted after. If I could have gone abroad I should have been able (notwithstanding the eager endeavours of the promoters of it and among them of your Nephew,[1573] who is the most knowing in Banks and most politick in the consequences of one in promoting the trade and benefit of the Kingdome of any man in Ireland, and I suppose he thinks in the world) to have put a spoke into that wheel, but my confinement for these three dayes hath made me lye by and they have employed their time very successefully in proselyting some fools and assuring others great benefit by subscriptions. So that I am apt to think instead of throwing out the heads of the bill this day in the Committee of the whole house, that some Gentlemen who were with me this morning found from what I said to them [?good] reasons not to come into the heads as now prepared, and that they will desire leave to sit again and lick the Cub into better form then they were able to doe in the hurry they were in to bring the bill into the house. I wish you would write a grave letter to that aspiring hot headed young man and in it caution him of being an instrument to erect a society who may in conjunction with others force us into a Land tax and enslave the nation. Look over

---

[1571] Altham petitioned on 11 Oct., but no action was taken (*LJI*, ii, 703).

[1572] Maurice Thompson (1675–1745), 2nd Baron Haversham. The protection had been signed on 10 Sept. 1718 (*LJI*, ii, 698).

[1573] St John III.

my letters and you will find the character which (dealing fairly with you) I was obliged to be true to give you of him least he might deceive and disappoint you. You will find him by his future conduct to make it good f[?or]¹⁵⁷⁴ a title: and run into the measures which shal be most agreeable to his own sentiments (whatever they are) without the least regard to any person but his own or thing but ambition. If he doe not disappoint your expectations (if ever the grand question of continuing — come on the Carpett¹⁵⁷⁵) never trust me again.

506. *Alan I, Dublin, to Thomas, at his lodgings in the Privy Garden, Whitehall, 14 Oct. 1721, eight at night*

(1248/5/97–8)

The Commons after sitting the whole day on the first clause in the Bank bill (which was to this effect that a bank on a solid foundation would be beneficial to the Kingdome) disagreed to that clause: Noes 102 against it. Yeas for the clause 94.¹⁵⁷⁶ It was then moved that the Chairman should leave the chair and report the Committee had made some progresse and ordered him to move for leave to sit again. Which being done Tuesday next was proposed as the day when the house should again resolve itself into a Committee on that matter, but this day two months being also proposed, it was carryed for the later day by 98 against 91.¹⁵⁷⁷ And thus the snare is broken and we are delivered from what a great many honest men feared might have very much other consequences then were yet foreseen from that bill. Truly Mr Speaker and his fast freinds were very zealous for the bill, as was your prudent and most dutiful Nephew;¹⁵⁷⁸ and by it it may be seen whether the sense of the Kingdome was truly represented in England by the late Ambassadors and whether a certain man can carry every thing as he pleases. I wish my Lord Lieutenant may not have given soe much credit to some people to tell his freinds in England it would succeed: because I would not have them think he could be so far deceived. I formerly told you I asked him whether he had the bill at heart, resolving if he had told me he had not to have given it any other opposition then when it came properly in my way to give my sense of the expediency of the bill: and that I should have done at the Councel and in the house of Lords, tho I had been told he was for it, if I had thought it an ill bill. But he eased me of that difficulty by assuring me it was perfectly indifferent to him what the fate of the bill proved; and that he did not desire it should take place except it appeared to be for the good of the Kingdome. And from that time I took the liberty to appear in opposition to it as occasion offered. Pray as soon as you receive this, observe and inform me how people on your side the

¹⁵⁷⁴Remainder of word missing.

¹⁵⁷⁵Come under consideration.

¹⁵⁷⁶Figures confirmed in BL, Add. MS 6116, f. 113: Bishop Nicolson to Archbishop Wake, 14 Oct. 1721. SHC1248/5/105–6 is a list of names endorsed by Alan 'The names of the voters for and against the Bank 14 Oct. 1721 in the house of commons'. The numbers tally with the figures given in this letter with the addition of one teller on each side (the practice in committees, rather than the two tellers in divisions in the House). St John Brodrick was the teller in the minority. The list is printed as Appendix 1, below.

¹⁵⁷⁷Figures confirmed in *CJI*, iv, 780.

¹⁵⁷⁸Though according to Levinge Henry Maxwell 'spoke earnestly against' the bank, while St John 'spoke violently' for it, and in so doing 'abused … Maxwell very much' (Levinge, *Jottings*, 64–5).

water talk of the rejecting a thing by the Parliament after our Plenipo's[1579] had represented it, as the wish of the whole Kingdome. I shal have no occasion for the Bank pamphlets now. I fancy your Nephew[1580] had given some assurances to Mr W[alpole] that it should do. My Lord Lieutenant hath with great unanimity gott the Commons to come into an addresse to the King to add 1d a day to the pay of each private foot Souldier, which I am sure will be a great satisfaction to the King and is much to his honour, being a thing often wished for and aimed at but never attained in former Governements. The debt of the nation att Christmas 1721 is found to be 77261=7⅜ and the supply voted for two years to 25 December 1723 is 331880=14[s. 8d.][1581] The funds will be the continuance of the same addicional dutyes for two years and I think we may have a recesse in lesse then a fortnight, and a very short Session after will finish our bills which be very few and I think pretty insignificant.

507. *Thomas, Whitehall, to Alan I, 31 Oct. 1721*

(1248/5/103–4)

I receivd your two letters of the 11th and 14th last weeke att Newmarkett, and am very well pleasd with the accountt the latter brings of the fate of the Banke project, which I take to have been carryed on by some few skilfull men for private advantage, and whoe imposd on numbers whoe never considered, and perhaps were nott good judges of its consequences, which I thinke must have provd fatall to the Kingdom in generall; tis att an end for this time, and surely gentlemen will a little more maturely consider against another, when itt may possibly bee revived, for tis too sweet a morsell to bee lett fall upon once failing. The procedure of the house of Lords in relation to protections meets with generall applause, as indeed itt ought. I am under very great concerne from the account you give of your indisposition, for notwithstanding what [you] say of your rest returning, and your stomach mending, I thinke your nott moving your toes rather denotes the humour paralettick, then the effect of a relaxation of the Tendons, supposing (as you apprehend) the latter to bee the case, bathing is the onely effectuall remedy, if the former, there can bee noe dispute butt that advice which you may have here, will bee likelyer to remove the cause (in its infancy) then what you can expect elsewhere, taking itt therefore either way, tis plaine your condition requires coming over assoone as possible, and were this entirely out of the case in prudence I thinke doing soe necessary; wee are in a very uncertaine state, what will bee the event God onely knowes; one thing I thinke certaine that matters cannott long subsist upon the disconserted foote they now stand, I cannott say to what party you owe least, I am sure you doe nott much to the one or other; twas indeed incumbent on you as a faithfull subject and honest man to contribute your assistance towards making the Kings affairs easy, att a time when others were endeavouring the contrary, this being compassed (which I beleive without you would nott have happened) I see noe reason why you should continue the cats

---

[1579] Plenipotentiaries.

[1580] St John III.

[1581] Confirmed in *CJI*, iv, 736, 779. The report of the committee of supply was made, and accepted, on 14 Oct.

foote, lett them try how their fast freinds will bee able to carry on business in time to come; Hos ego versiculos feci, tulit alter honores.[1582] You have now an opertunity of holding or quitting with equall honour, which may nott att another time bee the case, wherefore in my opinion you should bring itt to this point, either to hold uppon such termes as your station requires, or lay downe assoone as the session ends, twill bee necessary to determine the one or the other immediately, att the same time declaring positively your resolution, if the former bee treated as a Chancellor ought, if that bee nott done, and sufficient assurance given of the continuance of such treatment, what remains butt with a spiritt becoming a man of honour you resent that usage which ought nott to be borne; I spoake my mind very plainly to the D[*uke*] of G[*rafton*] uppon your recommending to the Bench, a right which noe man ever doubted to bee in the Chancellor, nor is itt ever otherwise here; the least haesitation would att another time have required (in justice to your selfe) laying downe, the onely difficulty arose from timing itt, when by then doing itt the whole would have suffered, butt that is now over, I mention this as one, butt nott the onely thing to bee insisted on, for if there bee nott an entire confidence reposd in you, twere better to part then continue; whatever the result shall bee, you will certainly take care of being att liberty to spend what time you thinke reasonable here, for if there bee a semblance of reason for nailing you down to a constant attendance, twill bee putt in practice.

Your health indispensably requires coming over, besides that tis reasonable on many other accounts. Tis now noe longer doubted butt that this will bee the last session of the present parliament. Your colleague (Mr Knight) dyed last weeke,[1583] the Duke of S[*omerset*] sent for mee yesterday to tell mee soe, and that hee had wrote to Sir Richd. Mills offering his recommendation of him,[1584] butt with this expresse declaration that if in the ensuing parliament there should bee opposition Hee (Sir Richard) must promise to consent (on his part) to your being declared duly elected without poling, for that his Grace would espouse noe interest in opposition to you, after which hee would give him the best assistance in his power, hee has commanded my moving for a writt tomorrow, att parting hee bid mee present his service to Lord Midleton, and tell him I long to see him, you will certainly write immediately to his Grace taking notice of my having acquainted you with what passed. I doe nott thinke wee shall bee up soe soone as is talkt, before Chrismas, butt beleive the session will bee short, in order to have the elections over before the King leaves us, which will bee assoone as well hee can. I have told you my thoughts nott that I thinke they will influence your judgment, or indeed ought, in what soe immediately concernes your selfe, butt because you generally desire my giving them, and att this time there will nott bee an opertunity of writing foward and backward for the matter must bee soone over one way or other.

In relation to my selfe I must acquaint you that I have very lately been acquainted (by a great man) by way of secrett, that there was a great inclination to gratifye mee out of a scence of my ill treatment, I was enjoined nott to take notice of the hint, butt I very well

---

[1582]'I wrote these lines; another has taken the credit'; said to be the first in a series of lines added by Virgil to a verse couplet which he had written anonymously in a public place in Rome in praise of the emperor Augustus, a couplet for which another, inferior, poet had claimed authorship.

[1583]William Knight (c.1668–1721), of West Dean, Sussex, Alan's parliamentary colleague at Midhurst, died on 26 Oct.

[1584]Sir Richard Mill (c.1689–1760), 5th Bt, of Woolbeding, Sussex, was elected to the vacancy on Somerset's interest on 6 Nov.

understand this pumping Cant. I have kept my selfe Independant and told him I resolvd doing soe.

508. Alan I, Dublin, to Thomas, 5 Nov. 1721

(1248/5/107–8)

I know not to what to impute your not writing a line to me for near five weeks together, but hope it proceeds from your finding great benefit from the air and exercise which you found at Newmarkett and that you have been induced to spend more time there then usual, or then you at first intended: but I did promise my self to have had an answer to my letter of the 14th of October in which I gave you a summary account of the proceedings in the Committee of the house of Commons when it had the heads of the bill for erecting a bank under consideration: and did hope to have known your thoughts on that subject and how the news relished and was entertained on your side. It is certain that the managers for the carrying on the scheme were stunned at that unexpected resolucion of the committee, for they promised themselves and others to carry it swimmingly through, but by reason of Mr Uptons mismanagement in moving the question that the Committee had made some progresse and desired leave to sit again whereas (as I told you in a letter of a later date) he might have put it beyond dispute by moving the question I mencion in that letter, which would have been carried by the same majoritye and in consequence the heads of the bill might have then been and would have been rejected. But they began to take heart again in hopes to retreive all when the report from the Committee comes to be made to the house, at which time a certain person whom you will guesse[1585] hath given assurances that people will be brought about and disagree with the Committee and they have been very active and stirring since that time in encouraging and taking subscriptions: and matters have been so ordered by the same person in the lower house that instead of hastning matters for a recesse heads of bills have been much multiplyed of late, and proceeded soe upon that (altho I think it was in my Lord Lieutenants power to have had a recesse long before this if he had inclined to it as soon as the Committee had come to that resolution). I doe not hear the Commons are like to finish what is stil before them till the end of this week at the soonest. Unlesse they shal think it advisable to hasten their pace, which seems to me not unlikely by an accident which they little dreamt of; for I had an intimation given me that probably the house of Lords may take an oportunitye to consider the affair of the Bank by appointing a day to take the Lord Lieutenants speech into consideration, and particularly that part of it which relates to erecting a Bank; and if the managers foresee the Lords are likely to come into any resolutions inconsistent with their scheme, and shewing their sense to be that a Bank will not only not prove beneficial to the Kingdome, but rather tend to the ruine of it; perhaps they may mend their pace and instead of foreslowing businesse may whip and spur and thereby put it into my Lord Lieutenants power to send a message to both houses to adjourn before the evil day comes on which their great Diana is to be taken into consideration.

[1585] William Conolly.

I will now give you a short view of the Session hitherto: The Gentlemen who are in their judgement against a Banke at a great meeting resolved not only not to give any obstruction to the Kings affair, but not to give one negative to the Supply being as large as formerly; they went farther and out of a sense of gratitude to my Lord Lieutenant for appearing and declaring himself indifferent in the matter of the Banke resolved to think of doing something extraordinary and beleiving it would be very agreeable that an addition of 1d per diem to the Common foot Souldier should be made to their former pay, resolved not to give it the least opposition but to go roundly into it and Mr Hopkins was told by one of them that they would doe soe and that they had so resolved, and that it might easily be understood at the Close of the Session to whom the easinesse of the Session was due, by their shewing to the world which part of the house was the majoritye and had the greatest interest those who were for or against the Bank. And I doe assure you my Lord hath not failed to make a prudent and proper use of the two partyes to attain those ends which an honest and prudent Governor ought to aim at, the Kings service and carrying on matters easily and without jarring: and if he shal be soe happy not to fail in his future conduct any more then he hath done hitherto; he will return to London with as much honour as any Cheif Governor hath done these twenty years, and cannot fail to be received well by his Master whom he hath served so successefully. But if the insinuations of Sycophants shal prevail on him to espouse a thing to which the Kingdome hath the utmost aversion, he will owe it to those who would be thought his best freinds that he is deprived of that honour he might otherwise [have] secured to himself. I desire you will employ Charles Powel to find out Randal Clayton[1586] and to deliver the enclosed to that wretched undone youth. Who I hear is fallen into the Claws of that infamous Harpye Mrs Smith, my Lord CastleComers cast[1587] whore who poxed and beggared him. Those who were for the Bank to put themselves upon an equal foot with their Antagonists, moved to take off 4s in the pound on the Officers etc[1588] by young Mr McCartney[1589] into which the others all came very roundly and the struggle hath been who should go fastest.

509. *Alan I, Dublin, to Thomas, Westminster, 6 Nov. 1721*

(1248/5/109–10)

Matters have this day fallen out in the house of Lords in the maner I conjectured in one of my letters of yesterdayes date; for a mocion was made by Lord Tullamore for laying the Commission for taking subscriptions in order to a Bank before the house, which was seconded by Lord Santry: But the Archbishop of Dublin moved that the house would appoint a day to take the Lord Lieutenants speech and particularly that part of it which related to a Bank to be erected here into consideration which was seconded by Lord Montjoy and resolved that tomorrow be the day for doing it. It was farther moved that the Clerk of the Hanaper be ordered to lay the fiant for passing a Commission for taking subscrip-

---

[1586]See Appendix 2. Clayton married Elizabeth Gibbings in 1722 (Green, *Index*, 24).

[1587]Cast-off.

[1588]The absentee tax.

[1589]James Macartney, MP [I].

tions in order to a Bank before the house the same day, but indeed the mocion was for the Commission itself being laid before the house, or the inrolment of it, but it was found the Commission was in the hands of some Gentlemen of the house of Commons who probably would create us more difficulty in coming at it then we desired and I moved the question for the original fiant or warrant for the Commission to be brought in which is ordered also.

Lord Ferard moved that application should be made to my Lord Lieutenant for all such papers as had passed in England or here relating to the Bank, which were in the power of my Lord Lieutenant or copyes of them might be laid also before the house. His Lordship is a great man for the Bank and apprehends there are some papers which will be of use to be shewn in support of the Bank: but I think he hath disserved his cause (I mean the Bank) by that mocion, and that the mocion may put my Lord Lieutenant under some difficultyes which my Lord Ferard did not mean; but that also was ordered. And to morrow the matter will come to a warm debate; the house was pretty full;[1590] and indeed whoever had been in it and had observed how the Lords fired from every corner and the spirit they shewed would be apt to beleive that either the house of Lords is no part of the Kingdome or that if any people have represented it to be the desire of the whole Kingdome to have a Bank erected here they have much misrepresented the Kingdome. I will write to you to morrow and acquaint you how matters goe.

510. *Alan I, Dublin, to Thomas, 9 Nov. 1721*

(1248/5/129–30)

My letters written of late will give you such an insight into the matter now depending before our house in relation to the Bank that tho this paper would be very abrupt in the opinion of one who had not been previously let into that matter, it will not be so to you I am perswaded. Last night the Lords in a committee of the whole house came to the following resolution. Resolved that it is the opinion of this Committee that the erecting a bank in this Kingdome or incorporating any number of persons into a body politick for the management and governement of such bank may in the present circumstances be prejudicial and of extreme ill consequence to this Kingdome. There were in the Committee 37 Lords.

Contents		Not contents.	
	Barons		
	Blaney.		Abercorne
	Santry.		Boyne.
	Tullamore.		Limrick
	Tirawly		Ferard.
	Southwel.		Bishop Dromore[1591]

[1590] The published presence list gives 37 names, including Alan himself (*LJI*, ii, 709–10).
[1591] Ralph Lambert.

	Bishop Downe[1592]
Viscounts [*sic*]	6
Bishops.	
Kilalla.[1593]	
Derry.[1594]	
Elphin[1595]	
Kilmore.	
Raphoe	
Clogher.	
Kildare.	
Tuam[1596]	
Dublin.	
Viscounts.	
FitzWilliams	
Charlemont.	
Strangford	
Montjoy.	
Midleton.	
Donerayle.	
Earles	
Kildare	
Meath	
Barrymore.	
Cavan	
Droghedah. Rosse.	26

You will find by adding them up that the Lords who were for the resolution were only 26 and those who were against it were only six, which makes no more then 32 whereas in the beginning of my letter I tell you the Committee consisted of 37 Lords, which was the number the Clerk told me were that day in the house which makes me beleive that I have forgott the names of some of the Lords who were present, but it occurs now to my memory that my Lord Newtown was in the house at the beginning of the debate, but he was obliged to be carryed out before it was over by reason of indisposition, and so was my Lord Allen but there was no advantage to either side; for Lord Newtown was furiously against the Bank, and Allen as warm for it. These added to the former make the number 34, and if I can recollect who the other Lords were you shal be told before I close this letter.[1597] When the Committee had come to that resolution I moved another question that it was

---

[1592] Francis Hutchinson.

[1593] Charles Cobbe.

[1594] St George Ashe.

[1595] Henry Downes.

[1596] Edward Synge.

[1597] The published presence list gives 34 names: all those listed by Alan, together with Lords Allen and Butler (Newtownbutler) (*LJI*, ii, 712). The six lords listed by Alan as voting against (Strabane (Abercorn), Boyne, Ferrard, Limerick, and the bishops of Down and Dromore) all entered their dissent from the resolutions (*LJI*, ii, 713).

the opinion of the Committee that the house be moved that an addresse to his Majestye be made on the said resolution and that it should be an instruction to the Committee to be appointed to prepare the addresse to thank his Majestye for his goodnesse in putting it into the power of his Parliament to have a Bank erected in this Kingdome, if the erecting one should be thought by it to be for the advantage of it; and to assure his Majestye that after duly weighing and seriously considering the same, it was the opinion of the house that the erecting etc in the words of the resolution, and to beseech his Majestye that no charter of incorporation of any persons into a Bank might passe, and that his Majestye would be graciously pleased to revoke any orders for passing any Charter under the great Seal for erecting a Bank in this Kingdome, if his Majestye had already given such orders. But the Lords who were against the first resolution could not bear the thoughts of any thing of this nature, which I now see proceeded from a fixed resolution taken among some people to endeavour to carry the thing on notwithstanding they knew the sense of the majoritye of the Commons by their vote in the Committee on 14 October, which I gave you a full account of formerly: We say here and I beleive with sufficient ground that Mr Maxwel and Dean Gore[1598] were detached from the Speakers house to a number of the Commons who were mett at a tavern opposite to the Custom house, to encourage them to goe on and to assure them that they would and should be supported in it, and methods taken to soften or make proselytes of some of the 102 who voted against the Bank before the resolution of 14 October came to be reported and that C[onolly] would put himself at the head of them etc till this was done the thoughts of proceeding on the project seemed to be laid aside to the universal satisfaction of the town and I think of the whole Kingdome. But this morning the Speaker with his humble attendants, who never part from him came to the Castle, alarmed the Duke, told him the Commons would on this day come to resolutions in direct opposicion to those of the Lords, which would embroil and embarasse the Session, which might otherwise be a most happy and easy one. I was sent for in all hast to the Castle where I found Lord FitzWilliams with my Lord Lieutenant, who told us what the Speaker had said, and was by all means for stopping our proceeding on the motion I had made yesterday, which mocion I renewed in the house after it was resumed, and a debate arising on it the debate was adjourned till this morning. I said that I did not see what ill consequence could happen from the Commons going on in their own way, and that I very well knew that the Speakers creatures could noe more carry any question in favour of the Bank or in opposition to the Lords resolution then he could carry the house on his shoulders; that the majoritye of the Commons were clearly now against any Banke and that such an attempt would only shew their weaknesse, and put them farther in the wrong then they had already put themselves by some of them proceeding to taking subscriptions since the vote in the Committeee on 14 Oct. which proceeding they endeavoured to justifye them in by voting their soe doing was legal. But there was no perswading a certain person[1599] by any means to hearken to the Commons being left to their own discretion, and indeed in this particular I was not supported by my Lord FitzWilliams who expressed great apprehensions of the consequence of the Commons and Lords coming to a difference. The true secret of this affair was this, C[onolly] knew the weaknesse of his interest and of the

---

[1598] William Gore, dean of Clogher since 1718.
[1599] The duke of Grafton.

Bank party would appear too plain if he was not skreened by the D[*uke*]s interposing to prevent the Lords going on, and his art took place to create a real fear of ill consequences. Soe that all earnestnesse was used with Lord F[*itzwilliam*] and me to interpose our credit with the Lords not to doe any thing this day and a resolution taken to have a speedy recesse; to induce us to doe as desired we had it told us in such a maner as we might understand it; that no charter of incorporation should passe, nor no orders be given for passing any till his Majestyes farther pleasure were signifyed; and we were at liberty to let our freinds understand that we had sufficient grounds to beleive nothing of that kind would happen. I would not come in without saying that the sense of the house of Lords contained in the resolution (if laid before the King) would in my opinion be of great weight with his to prevent any new orders for proceeding with the Charter; and I insisted on a promise that the resolution should be laid before his Majestye in as effectual and strong a maner, as it would have been if laid before him by way of addresse, and assurances to that effect were given that his Majestye should know the Bank was against the sense and inclination of both houses, or to that effect; and it was farther said it was impossible where 19 out of 20 were against a thing (as his Grace said he beleived there were against the Bank) that such a thing should passe. Many promises were given not to countenance or any way support it. And thereupon we two went to the Lords, and they had that confidence in what we told them to adjourn the adjourned debate which [*was*] to come on this day till Monday next. And the resolution taken is to send a message to the house to adjourn on Saturday to 6 December.

11 November.

The houses are adjourned to 6 December: but I have seen so much since last Thursday, that I think I shal hardly interpose at the instance of a Court to make terms etc. The Commons have been going on toward establishing thei[r] Bank, I do not mean the house, but the managers, by carrying on and encouraging and taking subscriptions: and no maner of interposition for fear of creating ill bloud between the houses: that happens only when it is found advisable to prevent the upper house from doing what they think right. You must know I carryed the message of adjournement[1600] and told my Lord Lieutenant that I would not deliver it till after the Commons were actually adjourned, unlesse he gave me expresse orders to doe it before, for I confesse I was unwilling to leave them in a capacitye to act after we had adjourned, and had his permission to deliver it no earlier then after the Secretary delivered the message of adjournement to the Commons and after they were actually adjourned. Much art was used to me by Mr Secretary not to persist in my resolution, he put the case that the Commons should have the same suspicion of the Lords, I told him that I had given the Duke an assurance that if any thing was attempted to be moved by any Lord in relation to the Bank after the Commons were up I would put an end to it by delivering the message of adjornement and that unlesse I were suspected there could be no room for apprehension. I added that I must take leave to be as careful of the Lords honour as he was of the Commons and that since it was a puncto[1601] in whose honour the other party ought to confide I could not but think the Lords ought to be trusted. I then positively told him my resolution was fixed unlesse he had new orders for me from —.[1602]

[1600] Alan, as lord chancellor and Speaker, conveyed to the upper House the lord lieutenant's pleasure that they adjourn to 6 Dec. (*LJI*, ii, 715).

[1601] A fine point of procedure.

[1602] The lord lieutenant.

511. Alan I, Dublin, to Thomas, Westminster, 11 Nov. 1721

(1248/5/136–7)

Our Parliament is now adjourned to the sixth of December: in my former letter I gave you to understand that the Lords finding the drivers of the Bank to proceed in endeavouring to keep life in their project, notwithstanding the Commons had in a Committee of the whole house thrown out that clause (which was for establishing one) upon assurances given by our undertakers and the person who desires that he may be thought able to doe what ever he pleases that members should be brought over to disagree with the Committee before the next meeting and that the Bank should be supported in so much that no lesse then three messages were sent from one house in Capel Street[1603] to incline Gentlemen to proceed in taking subscriptions and in subscribing, and the last of these by a man of noe lesse figure then the reverend Dean Gore Chaplain to Mr Speaker and brother to his dear freind the Chancellor of the Exchequer resolved to take Lord Lieutenants speech into consideration, particularly that part of it which relates to a Bank, and it was moved on Monday by the Bishop of Tuam and seconded by me: We resolved to doe it in a Committee of the whole house on Tuesday and to addresse for such papers as related to it, and were in Lord Lieutenants power: I told the house that one paper viz. the original fiant for a Charter was in the hands of the Clerk of the Hanaper which would supersede the necessity of others: the Bishop of Dromore who was very zealous for the Bank, said there was a necessity of addressing for other papers, nay all that related to it, particularly for the report of the late Lords Justices on which the Charter was cheifly granted, and much was said by him and Lord Abercorne to prevent our entring at all into any consideration of Lord Lieutenants speech particularly of that part of it related to the Bank, because forsooth the Commons had already considered the Speech and had come to a resolucion that a Bank would be advantagious to the Kingdome and they much feared that a rupture might be occasioned by our doing it between the two houses. But the Lords resolved to proceed for they saw that it would be too late to oppose the granting a Charter of incorporacion after they had gott one passed under the Seal which they would be intitled to demand after they had subscribed and paid a proporcion of £500000 according to the Commission for taking subscriptions, which I will hereafter explain more at large to you. The matter was fought with obstinacy by a very small number of Lords who were for the Bank being only Abercorne Boyne Limrick Ferard the Bishops of Dromore (Lambert) and Down (Hutchinson) against 29 Lords viz. six Earles Kildare Meath Cavan Barrymore Droghedah Rosse Viscounts FitzWilliams Charlemont Montjoy Midleton Strangford Donerayle Bishops Dublin Tuam Kildare Clogher Raphoe Elphin Kilmore Derry Kilalla Barons Santry Blaney Tirawly Southwell (I forgett some of them) at length we came to the following resolution that it was the opinion of the Committee that the granting a Charter for erecting a governement of a Bank here in <u>the present circumstances</u> may be prejudicial and of extreme ill consequence to the Kingdome. And upon the resolucion being reported and agreed to by the house I moved a question to addresse the King on the said resolution not to grant any Charter to incorporate the

---

[1603] The Dublin residence of William Conolly.

subscribers or if any directions were already come that the same might be revoked; but much opposicion was given to this question then and it being late the house resolved that a debate arising on that mocion the consideration of it should be delayed to a farther day viz the next which was ordered. In the morning the Speaker with his bosome freinds Vesey, Sir Ralph Gore, General Wyn[1604] and others came to the Castle, told the Duke there would be a rupture between the houses for that the Commons would come to resolutions in direct opposicion to the Lords (which they knew they could not carry) but so far was somebody alarmed or seemed to be soe that he sent Hopkins to me to the house of Lords to come to him instantly and then pressed Lord FitzWilliams and me to stop the Lords from going on with the motion of addressing the King, giving to understand no step should [*be*] made toward any Charter of incorporation till after the two months were out when it might be known whether the Commons would agree with their Committee. We had that credit with our freinds to be able to stop them and made use of it soe as no mocion was made to resumme that debate on Tueday and it was resolved to put it of till Monday next and that we should be adjourned on this day to prevent its coming on. In this whole affair it was pretty plain to me that somebody[1605] leaned more toward one side then he pretended, and in truth it was to skreen the Speaker, the weaknesse of whose party and interest would have appeared on that question. You must know that the Commons (I mean the party) intended to be very smart on me by giving me and Conolly thanks for the report we had made (as they said) for establishing a Bank; I will send you the resolution and my answer, and also the Copy of our letter which they are pleased to say was a letter for establishing a Bank; which plainly it is not, and you wi[ll] see by my answer which perhaps is in print that I call it truly as it was a report about erecting a Bank, sollicited and applyed for by several Lords and others. I will send the Speakers answer also in which he values himself for having been steady in it, and takes on him to say it is for the benefit of the countrey. Time will shew the sense of the Kingdome; if it doth not already appear by 102 Commoners being against it whereas only 94 were for it, and 29 Lords against it and but six for it. This matter hath almost killed me.

512. *Alan I, Dublin, to Thomas, Westminster, 14 Nov. 1721*

(1248/5/142–3)

To shew you that I judged right in my last in saying I would not readily interpose in preventing people from going on their own way, upon hopes of creating a good understanding and preventing pretended quarrels: I doe assure you that our Bankers have not been at all idle since 9 November but they have proceeded to finish their subscriptions, which amount to the summe of £28000, of which the subscribers have paid in £1400, being one twentieth part of their subscriptions, and have given bonds with warrant of Attornye to confesse judgement for 3/20 more when called for by the Governor and directors of the Bank (which is to be) and they have brought a duplicate of those subscriptions to

---

[1604] Owen Wynne, MP [I].

[1605] The duke of Grafton.

me in order to have them inrolled in Chancery pursuant to a clause in their Commission
for taking subscriptions, this being a condicion precedent to their obtaining a Charter of
incorporacion to have those subscriptions inrolled: Upon doing which they may by that
Commission apply to my Lord Lieutenant for a warrant to erect them into a corporation,
and I suppose they intend soon to doe soe; I mean as soon as the subscribers have mett
and chosen a Governor and directors. By this means the Duke will be soon drawn into the
scrape, and have an oportunity of making good his word not to doe any thing toward a
Charter till his Majestyes farther pleasure is known. I formerly commended the prudence
of a certain persons conduct, I must alter my phrase and call it the skil of his management
to attain a certain end: for I cannot shut my eyes soe close not to see that we are not soe
perfectly passive in a certain affair, as we desired to have it understood: but I reckon the
masque will soon be thrown aside: perhaps I may misjudge, and I should be glad to find
I have done soe but I cannot beleive just as I would Pray. Did you ever presse or sollicite
the obtaining the Charter for a Bank: for that hath been insinuated and Mr Hopkins seems
to understand you were mighty fond of it; I am sure when I peruse your letters, in which
I find nothing tending that way I cannot beleive it to have been soe. I will very soon let
you into the secret of the Commons thanking me and Mr Conolly (when Justices) for our
report about the Bank; By it they would insinuate I had altered my mind in relation to
that affair; but I have been perfectly consistent with myself tho I am sure erecting a Bank
and the influences such a thing may have on the Kingdome are matters of so intricate a
nature, that a man may very well without levity alter the opinion, he had first taken up, on
more mature consideration; and the consequences which may attend one are too great, to
leave room for a man to adhere to a mistake or ill formed judgement because it was once
my opinion where adhering may tend to ruine his countrey. In the debates on Wednesday
last the Archbishop of Tuam gave this definition or rather description of a Bank. A Bank
(saith he) is a body incorporated to turn the ready money of the Kingdome to its own
private profit, while they circulate their own paper on pretence of[1606] the publick good.
We have a whimsical ballad here on the Banks being disapproved on 14 October.[1607] You
will not allow it to come up to your London performances of that nature, yet I cannot
but think there are some things in it, not much amisse. When you read it you will be at
a losse what the meaning is of Ba-ba-bank lesse you know that Jos[*hua*] Allen is one of
the most eminent speechers for a Bank, and recollect how unhappy he is in stammering
to a great degree; but that doth not prevent his exerting his talent in rhetorick in favour
of the project.[1608] If your freinds in Bond Street be in town, and should have one of these
Ballads sent to them, they may want this comment. The great patriot Cato is a subscriber
to the Tune of £2000:[1609] I have looked over the book of subscriptions but do not find
his name.

[1606] Superscript: for.

[1607] *The bank thrown down. To an excellent new tune* (Dublin, [1721]).

[1608] Swift made great play with this, repeatedly referring to Allen as 'Traulus', from the Greek *traulos*, 'stutterer'.

[1609] Viscount Molesworth.

513. *Thomas to Alan I, Dublin, 18 Nov. 1721*

(1248/5/144–5)

I doubt the inclosed will come too late, for Collonel Middleton[1610] tells mee my nephew was gon into Munster, before his leaving Dublin, in order to take passage for Bristoll, this poor womans case[1611] is very hard, I was forced to supply her for buying necessaryes, or she must have wanted them, having very imprudently (against my advice and unknown to mee) dipt into the S[outh] Sea att six hundred, uppon the perswasion of Charles Stewart, to the amount of the better part of what shee sold her house for; you will doe what you can to secure her for the future. Tomorrow I goe to Cobham in order to dine att Gilford att the Bailifs feast on Munday, when I designe offering my service in forme, telling them that I never sold or will sell my vote, and therefore will nott buy a seate, if they thinke fitt to choose mee on these termes, well and good, otherwise they may please themselves,[1612] this place has never hitherto been corrupt, butt like Tewksbury may possibly, (though I think twill nott) goe into the new mode, of taking mony, which ile nott give.[1613] Lett mee prevaile uppon you to come over assoone as possible, I am sure your condition requires itt … The Duke of Somersett is nott yett come to towne.

514. *Alan I, Dublin, to Thomas, Westminster, 19 Nov. 1721*

(1248/5/146–7)

No pacquet hath come in hither since the 7 of this month soe that I send the inclosed under this cover; the same boat which carryes this letter will also bring you two of mine in reference to the proceedings of the Lords in relation to the Bank, in which businesse there hath been a great deal of double dealing: and I have too much reason to doubt that after all the intinations given to my Lord FitzWilliams and me that the sense of the Lords in that matter should be laid before the King in as strong a maner as if the Lords had done it themselves by way of address that yet nothing of that sort hath been done. I doubt a certain person[1614] will be farther embarassed by following the advice of those who promote the Bank rather then of those who are against it, which is undoubtedly the much greater part of the Kingdome; and I am not clear whether a warrant will not be signed for preparing a fiant for a Charter of incorporacion: which will put me under the last difficultyes, but in all events I will chuse to lay down the Seal rather then passe it, after the King hath declared in full Parliament he left the consideration of it to the Parliament, and after the majoritye

---

[1610]John Middleton (1678–1739), of Seaton, Aberdeenshire, MP [GB] Aberdeen Burghs.

[1611]Possibly Martha Courthope. For her disastrous investment in South Sea stock, see Walsh, *South Sea Bubble*, 57, 76, 79, 106.

[1612]The franchise in Guildford was in the freemen and freeholders paying scot and lot, and the electorate numbered around 200. Thomas was chosen there in 1722 after a contest (*HC 1715–54*, i, 329).

[1613]The franchise in Tewkesbury lay in freemen and inhabitant householders (some 500 in all). The members of the corporation 'prided themselves on being "above corruption"', but a candidate in 1727 considered that 'money will not be less prevailing in this corporation than in others' (*HC 1715–54*, i, 247).

[1614]The duke of Grafton.

of the Commons in a Committee of the whole house, and also the Lords have shewn their opinion to be against a Bank, as you will see by my former letters. I think I mend, yet it is but slowly, and I heartily wish I were with you in Surry.

515. *Thomas to Alan I, 2 Dec. 1721*

(1248/5/150–3)

Very late on Thursday night I receivd yours of the 19th of last month, and the others of a prior date;[1615] I am in noe wise surprised att the endeavours of some to bring their job to beare, for tis now become fasshionable to avow things under colour of publique good, when God knowes veiwes of selfe interest are the cheife (nay onely) motives; butt uppon the whole I fancy this will bee disappointed, may every thing of the kind meet with like fate; Putting togather all circumstances, I agree with you, that the pretended indifferency of some people was founded upon a strong expectation of the matter being soe layd as to meet with successe, without a bare fac't interposition, which otherwise probably had been the case.

Where I have been deceivd itt has generally proceeded from an over credulity of sincerity; where nothing lesse is intended, Hobb's maxim rarely fails, and from thence proceeds the misjudging of honest men.[1616]

Neither of us can with certainty say how far faith has been kept in laying before the King the sence of the Lords, intended to have been effectually done by way of Addresse, butt I am pretty fully informed that noe more or other has been sayd of the Bills transmitted then the letter of forme, whereas itt has been usuall by a private letter to recommend some one (att least) or more Bills which would bee most acceptable, nor has the person whoe brought them over, or any other that I can heare of, given themselves the trouble of explaining (if they were able to doe itt) the reason or expediency of any Bill, for want of which as I am informed the onely two valluable ones are left behind, however I suppose a large allowance will bee given to the messinger.

I cannott doubt (and am sure I am very well pleasd with) your resolution of laying down rather then putting the seale to what will (if compased) fully convince half sighted people of the fatall consequences of what (with private veiwes) is soe earnestly and artfully contended for. You say itt has been insinuated that I had earnestly pressed and sollicited the obtaining a charter, and that Mr Hopkins seems to understand my having been very fond of itt. Tis nott the first time my sincere endeavours to serve the country have been misrepresented, nay malliciously and falsely turnd uppon mee, butt that has never slackned my zeale for the good of itt. Ile tell you in as few words as I can the part I have acted on this occasion from first to the very last.

[1615] The atrocious weather then obtaining in the Irish Sea is vividly described in HALS, DE/P/F54/23: Robert Dixon to Lord Cowper, 21 Nov. 1721.

[1616] 'For words are wise men's counters — they do but reckon by them; but they are the money of fools …' (Thomas Hobbes, *Leviathan*, iv, 13).

Some time after the gentlemen came over,[1617] they did mee the favour of a visitt, acquainting mee with their errant, att the same time assuring mee that uppon mature deliberation itt was the generall and most earnest desire of the whole Kingdom, which was indeed very surprising, however you may easily beleive such a declaration putt mee sufficiently on my guard in nott opposing what all others unanimously agreed on. Butt if you looke over my letters you will find what were my sentiments, since I knew I could write them to you with security, and indeed I did itt to you with plainnesse least you might unwarily bee drawne into itt, without fully weighing the ill consequences, the most dangerous of which presently struck mee, to witt, putting into the power of that body of men, in conjunction with any or every Government to become entire masters in all times to come of the house of Commons; butt you may bee sure this was too nice a point to bee plainly uttered, under the then circumstances; The first formation of the S[*outh*] Sea company, and the steps taken were too fresh in my memory nott to sufficiently alarme mee in a case of like nature.

I doe not remember ever to have talkt in publique of this matter, save once att Lord Lieutenants Levy (and am sure Mr Hopkins was nott there, and therfore cannott imagine from whence hee should collect my being fond of itt) when his Grace told Mr St G[*eorge*] and Mr W[*ard*] that something (the perticular I protest I have forgott) would nott bee graunted, which gave mee an opertunity of speaking; standers by thought I did itt with warmth, and I beleive them in the right, for I very well remember I concluded thus. I am very sure that if such things are insisted uppon twill bee vissible to every body that itt must prove prejudiciall to that poore Kingdom, for I cannott say I am cleare of itt being advantagious in any shape. I thought this going far enough, and am sure others thought twas going too far. However itt had this effect that point (whatever twas) was receded from; The matter concerted between them butt still to bee under and subject to a discusshion in Parliament which I thought a good point, for that if they would goe into itt, my opinion whatever itt was, neither would nor ought to have weight; things standing thus I did earnestly presse their consulting Mr Lownds whose skill every body allowes, and uppon long experience I never saw reason to question his integrity. Hee was entirely master of the proceedings in forming the Banke here, in doing wherof that man has obviated a greate many dangers which excesse of power might produce, hee was always jealous of great bodyes and their influence, uppon which wee have often talked, therfore thought I if the Parliament will goe into this hee will open their eyes in things which they may nott otherwise see, and I dare say as far as was consistent with the duty of his place hee has done itt; if the question might bee properly askt, I am of opinion hee and I had the same thoughts of this matter, butt this I collect from that delatorinesse which I have often heard him charged with in this affair, for though hee has a great deale of businesse uppon his hands, hee can dispatch a great deale when his heart goes with the thing hee is about. I own this thing has taken a better turne then I expected, for I made noe doubt (uppon what was sayd) butt that the Parliament would hastily have run into the project in order to supply the present defect of coine, (which was represented as nott to bee borne) without considering how much worse the remedy would prove then the disease, I hope itts neck is broake, which may bee recorded as a deliverance. I broake my mind to the people of Guilford as I told you I would, telling them in somany words

[1617]Those projecting a national bank in Ireland. The reference may be to the lobbying of successive lords lieutenant, Bolton and Grafton, in London in May/June 1720 (Burns, *Politics*, i, 121; Walsh, *South Sea Bubble*, 133–4).

that I had never or ever would sell my vote, and therfore would nott buy a seat, if they chose mee I would serve them faithfully. All the people of vallue in the towne are for mee, and very heartily and openly declare themselves, whither Mr Randyll[1618] (whoe sayes hee will stand) or any other will buy the meaner sort I know nott, nor am I sollicitous about itt, since I am sure being out of the house, will contribute to a little longer continuing a broken constitution then the great fatigue which constant attendance will admitt of, I have discharged my duty by postponing that consideration and shall bee entirely satisfyd with the event … I sent your letter to the Duke of S[omerset] assone as I receivd itt, having att my returne to towne reade that part of yours to mee which related to him, hee bid mee give you his hearty service, with assurance of his persevering in the resolution hee had taken.

516. Alan I, Dublin, to Thomas, 3 Dec. 1721

(1248/5/154–5)

Yesterday about noon when we almost despaired of hearing any more from England and were under great apprehensions of all our pacquet boats being lost, there came in one of them with ten mails on board; among the letters it brought were yours of the 4th and 14th instant. The account is very true that the joy of the Kingdome was universal when the Bank project received the baffle it mett on 14 October in the Committee of the house of Commons and it is as certain that bonefires were made in Corke on that occasion, and great rejoicings in other places: but there were a sett of men as much dejected as the others were elevated, and I doe assure you they are in great credit at a certain place: The letter you received by Mr Fisher[1619] will have let you into the conduct used here in reference to this affair. We endeavoured to appear perfectly indifferent in the matter at the beginning, and took occasion to declare soe upon every oportunitye which offered; nay I went soe far to ask the question directly declaring that tho I would in voting follow my own sentiments, altho they should happen to be different from those of a certain person, yet that one would and might justifyably take another way in doing the same thing, for that usually it is the maner of doing a thing which is disobliging: In answer to this question I was in words told the thing was perfectly indifferent both on this and on the other side of the water, yet by the maner of delivery I plainly saw there was in this case a secret and a revealed will, contradictory to each other and that the secret was intrusted only to particular freinds, of which number I was not thought proper to be allowed to be one: By this means I was discharged from the difficultye I should have been put under, if I had been confided in and told that the carrying on the Bank was one of the things the King, the Governement and ministry had at heart: The part I must have taken if I had been confided in, would have been to have told my Lord Lieutenant my judgement was against the Bank and that he must not depend on my contributing to the erecting one here: but I should have been represented as an impracticable man, and not capable of being brought into the measures of

---

[1618]Morgan Randyll (1649–aft. 1735), of Chilworth, Surrey, MP [GB] Guildford. He stood for re-election against Thomas in 1722 but was defeated.

[1619]William Fisher, gentleman usher of the black rod, who had been given leave on 16 Oct. to go into England for a month (*LJI*, ii, 704, 711).

the Governement; from which difficultye I have been happily delivered by their not trusting their darling secret with me: and by their professions of indifferency to the things succeeding or not leaving me at perfect liberty in the matter. The Duke had in one of his letters told me that if we could agree in measures all would doe well: When about three weeks of the Session was over, I told him that he had not explained himself what the measures were in which he expected my concurrence: that by them I understood facilitating the supply and preventing heats in the house of Lords about the point of jurisdiction; both which I thought were at that time past danger, and desired to know if he had any other thing in which he expected I should cooperate with him under the notion of our agreeing in measures: I never was in more concern least I might have extorted the black secret and laid my self under the difficultye of immediately breaking with him then, as I certainly would have done; but he had too honourable thoughts of me to think my bosom could be a fit repository for a design so mischeivous to this poor Nation: and if that was his motive of concealing it from me, it is the most obliging act I ever have had done to me by his Grace. But by the people in whom he reposes confidence, perhaps he might doubt whether the grand secret was to be trusted in the power of one of whom they had no maner of hope. Perhaps they told him I would make an indirect use of the knowledge I might arrive at by this means: and if this was his inducement to keep in reserve, he had poorer thoughts of me then any body who knows me well would ever entertain of me; for I should have scorned to make an ill use of any confidence reposed in me. I have lately found out a secret, of some names who were to be considerable subscribers, and by a very great accident the secret is come to my knowledge. A list of the subscribers was seen in the hand of one of the great managers of this project in which some names were contained, which perhaps may come in a loose paper under cover to the Master Carter (you know him) which if he receive he will not know what to make of, but if you order him to send you such a paper if he receives such an one it will explain things.

Sir Ralph Gore said on the first day of the term expressed himself in this maner that indeed he could not say it as of his own knowledge, but that my Lord Lieutenant had said in his hearing you had sollicited the Bank as much as any body. I told him I would lay him £10 the Duke would not say soe: I asked the Duke about it, and truly he did not come to Sir Ralphs assertion; but seemed to think that you appeared to him to be for it in London. And Mr Hopkins was in much the same sentiments. You will see by one of my former letters that by something I hear fall from him none of our familye were much obliged to him, the expression must not ever be mentioned but it was this that our family had appeared in ten shapes; you know what part my son[1620] took in this matter at the beginning and he drew his unhappy Uncle in: I thought it my businesse to bring both over from contributing to the ruine of the Kingdome, and forsooth the letter I joined in with Conelye (as one of the Justices) is construed as recommending the settling a Bank here; and my appearing now zealously against it is now imputed as taking on me a different shape: And you see how you are to be brought in also. If I had changed my mind (which I never did) it is no more then what every honest man ought doe when convinced of a mistake. Pray write to me a letter on this subject such as I may shew.

[1620] St John.

517. *Alan I, Dublin, to Thomas, Westminster, 9 Dec. 1721*

(1248/5/157–8)

The Parliament met according to adjournement on the sixth and were farther adjourned by message to this day, none of our bills being come over (which is extraordinary if any thing to protract the Session at this time can be thought soe when the reasons for doing the thing are soe visible). You must know we value ourselves much upon not directing a farther adjornement beyond this day, on which the matter of our Bank is to come on by order in the house of Commons: But people without doors say that possibly the message if it had been sent would hardly have put the house off from proceeding on the order about the Bank, and that to avoid that difficulty or giving a general distast to the Commons, the persons confided in were not hardy enough to advise an adjornement to a farther day then this. You may depend on it the heads of the bill about the Bank will be rejected, and that the house will come to votes against a Bank in general and that in particular of which a scheme is laid in the heads of the bill. But what is vehemently laboured by —[1621] and which I was personally pressed to come into was this that the Commons might not address the King not to put the great Seal to a Charter of incorporacion and that he would please to revoke any orders to that effect if granted already (for indeed the letter from the King for granting a Commission to take subscriptions directs a patent of incorporation to passe and promises that he will grant such a Charter, and directs the sealing one when subscriptions are taken, as they now are) now my Lord Lieutenant tells us there will be no need of such address, that it looks like suspecting the Crown or him that any step will be taken farther in the matter; but others apprehend that while the dead warrant is of force and in the Sherifs hand, the partyes life is not safe under a bare repreive without a pardon and a revocation of those orders: that the votes of neither house are the proper methods to inform the King of the sense of his Parliament, and that it is respectful to let the King know the reasons which induced the Parliament not to accept of what was intended to them by the Crown as a favor. I hope and beleive well of the event tho the dilegence used to prevent addressing hath been great.

[*PS*] I have received yours of the 2d and 5th.

518. *Alan I, Dublin, to Thomas, 14 Dec. 1721*

(1248/5/159–60)

You will know by the papers which I sent to you in my brother Will[*iam'*]s letter that I made a right judgement in mine of the ninth, that all the sollicitacion which could be made to prevent it would not prevail on the Commons not to address the King against erecting a Bank. Inclosed come the copyes of the addresse to his Majestye and to my Lord Lieutenant on that subject, with his Graces answers to each; that in answer to the addresse to himself seems to many to indicate how far the subject matter of it I mean his being perfectly indifferent in the matter of the Bank was well grounded or agreeable to him to

---

[1621] The duke of Grafton.

be told he was soe. Gentlemen think that part of the answer which relates to the Bank to be pretty dry, and to leave him a latitude to act clear otherwise then they pray he will if he thinks that to be for the good of the Kingdome which they think to be otherwise. I think the Lords will on Saturday apply in at least as strong terms to cut up the remaining fibres of this Bank, as the Bishop of Tuam expressed himself not long since in the house. Sure the nature of this thing may make the addresses containing the true sense of the Nation deserve to see the light and not to be kept (as every thing of the kind hath been) perfectly from the knowledge of every body but those who live here.

519. *Alan I, Dublin, to Thomas, Westminster, 17 Dec. 1721*

(1248/5/121–4)

On reading the first of the above resolutions[1622] you will find that it is the same which I formerly sent to you as the sense of the Committee of the whole house of Lords when they took that part of the Lord Lieutenants speech relating to the Bank into consideration, to which resolution of the Committee the house agreed. By a letter wrote yesterday sennight by my order you received the Commons addresses both to the Lord Lieutenant and to the King in relation to the Bank;[1623] and by them found that I made a right judgement that it would not be in any bodyes power to stem the thing: If I might have found so much credit as to have been beleived to understand peoples sentiment as well as others who were (I suppose) advised with, I cannot but think it would have been of service to the person to whom I gave the advice with sincerity and freindship: for you cannot think but that a disappointment in a matter of that nature must lessen a man a good deal. The truth is the credit I have had hath been generally to be consulted, and the contrary thing determined to be done to that which I thought most for the service. I told you early that I doubted one mans leaning to a certain side, who professed indifference and neutralitye all along, and whose businesse it was to have exactly practiced both, would make him lesse valued then he otherwise would be:[1624] I perceived the bent of inclination early and cautioned against its being prosecuted, but I confesse (notwithstanding the Commons addresse) I doubt people are not soe wholly convinced of the indifferency as they once were. A late visit to Castletown seems to have had strong influence: tho indeed before going thither I must say I saw plainly what was at heart: The neglecting to doe any thing to hasten the businesse in the house of Commons in order to a recesse after the matter of the Bank

---

[1622] At the top of this letter are written out, in a different hand, a resolution proposed by the house of lords committee, and agreed by the House on 8 Dec., 'that the Erecting a Bank in this Kingdome or Incorporating any number of Persons into a Body Politick for the Management and Government of such Bank may in the Present Circumstances be Prejudiciall and of Extreme ill Consequence to this Kingdom' (*LJI*, ii, 712–13); then a further resolution, agreed by the Lords on 16 Dec., 'that if any Lord Spirituall or Temporall of this Kingdom shall sollicit or Attempt the erecting of a Publick Bank within the same or the Procuring a Charter for incorporating any Number of Persons for that Purpose, or shall be any way aiding or assisting thereunto without the Consent of Parliament first had, he shall be judged to obstruct his Majesties service and shall be deemed a Contemner of the Authority of this House and a Betrayer of the Liberty of his Country' (*LJI*, ii, 720).

[1623] Agreed on 11 Dec. The committee appointed two days earlier to draw up the addresses had included St John Brodrick (*CJI*, iv, 832–5).

[1624] The duke of Grafton.

was looked on to be wholly over by the resolution of the Commons in the Committee of the whole house on 14 October against the first clause of the bill for erecting a Bank and by the adjourning the farther consideration of those heads of a Bill for two months, which was done and so understood to be done out of a prospect the parliament would have been prorogued before that time, notwithstanding my giving an hint how proper it would be to have the recesse as soon as possible, to avoid some difficultyes which might occur if the houses continued sitting and would be avoided by a recesse (particularly the matter of Boroughs[1625]) which I did by letter dated 17 October to which the answer was given to my servant who delivered it that it needed none. This proceeding I say I know not how to account for, but as the effect of those peoples advice who hoped that might be obtained in a thin house which they were sure never could be carryed in a full one: and who did intend to protract the considering the heads of the Bank bill in such a maner, as not to goe fully through with it nor to report it till after Christmas, when they were certain most of the Countrey Gentlemen (except from one quarter of the Kingdome,[1626] and the dependants on the Custom house etc) would be gone into the countrey; and then nothing would have been more easy then in an house consisting of about the same number of members as it did on 29 September when they voted a Bank would be useful, or when they thanked me for contributing to the erecting a Bank; would easily have overturned all that was done 14 October in a full Committee and might have represented the Bank to be the darling and desire of the Nation. This and some other steps have convinced me how far from indifferency some people were in this matter. Add to this, that fox hunting or taking the air was alway thought of when the patrons of the Bank were in their career and going furiously with their project, insomuch that I lay under the difficulty (when pressed by Sir Tho[mas]Taylor and Mr Coote on 13 November to order the duplicate of subscriptions to be inrolled in order to obtain a Charter of incorporation) of sending an expresse to his Grace to Castletown with a Copy of the paper left with me, and an account what the Gentlemen had insisted on, to which I received a short answer intimating he would be soon in town, and till then I saw I was to expect no orders: But when the Lords came to their resolution 8 November the earnestest sollicitations and instances were used to prevent the house from coming into an addresse to the King against any Charter to be granted for erecting a Bank, or to revoke orders for such Charter if given. The same zeal hath been shewn to prevent the Lords from proceeding to censure such members of their house as had since 8 November acted any way in opposition to the vote of that day, and particularly my Lord Abercorne: who doubled his subscription and was chosen Governor of the intended Bank after that time.[1627] Nay yesterday morning there were at the Castle the Bishops of Kildare, Elphin, and Londonderry; the later two were yesterday in the house against the resolution which the house came to yesterday, that those who should proceed etc should be esteemed betrayers of their country: for they thought it unnecessary and that it would continue animosityes. And I think the Bishop of Kildare kept out of the house but the two former speeched against the resolution: yet I am unwilling to attribute their doing soe to their having been at the Castle: but it is observable that the other English Bishop of Kilmore,

---

[1625]The decisions to be taken by the lord lieutenant and privy council in approving (or disapproving) the election of chief magistrates and other officers in the borough corporations covered by the 'new rules' of 1672.

[1626]The province of Leinster.

[1627]Abercorn was elected on 20 Nov. (Walsh, *South Sea Bubble*, 170).

agreed in voting against the resolution, tho all three had been zealous at first against the Bank. It is visible that nothing is soe much guarded against as letting it be known how truly detestable this projected Bank is to the Kingdome in general, and therefore I beleive the motion for printing the two resolutions which I now send you (which will certainly be made tomorrow) will find opposition in our house, tho to no purpose. But sure some of our news papers or prints would think what we have done might deserve a place in their daily sheets, as many other articles; and I confesse I doe think it will be of service to let the world know our thoughts and see that we are not in the power of a certain little fellow,[1628] who among your great men is beleived to carry everything before him by his own interest. I am mistaken in saying the Bishop of Kildare was not in the house; he was and voted for the resolution in every question proposed for amending it.[1629]

520. *Thomas to Alan I, 2 Jan. 1721[/2]*

(1248/5/163–4)

I desired my nephew to excuse my nott owning directly to your selfe the receipt of your several letters, having att that time a violent Rhumatisme, occasioned (as I apprehend) by cold taken going to and from Pepper Hara in bad weather, which however I thought necessary a little to comfort those there, whoe were all in a very ill state of health, the paine I endured was excessive, chiefly in my right shoulder and arme, before that went of I had the symptoms of an approaching fitt of the stone, which I thanke God did nott last very long, for on Sunday morning a large stone came away, and I am now easy, save onely the paine which alwayes followes.[1630]

This day I went for a little while, abroad, judging itt necessary to doe soe (though wee have a cold easterly wind) in order the better to prepare for attending the house (if I can) on Munday. Last night I receivd yours of the 23d of last month, and had before all the others itt mentions.

I will doe what is necessary in relation to Midhurst (if there bee occasion, as I sup-pose there will, notwithstanding a continuance of the towne whisper of prolonging this parliament which I thinke will nott bee attempted, because I beleive twould bee found impracticable in a full house, and a bill of that nature cannott bee whipt through soe fast as nott to give time for filling uppon soe extraordinary a point, a great many may wish the thing whoe I thinke will scarcely adventure bare fact[1631] owning itt, for feare of miscarrying.

L[ord] O[nslow] whoe came to see mee, askt whither you were coming over, my answer was that I had long advisd itt, and hoped I might att lenghth prevaile, since his Majestys affairs in your Par[liament] were now drawing towards a conclusion; upon receipt of your letter I apprehend that question might arise from what possibly shee might have heard att

---

[1628] William Conolly.

[1629] The published presence list confirm all three bishops attended (*LJI*, ii, 719).

[1630] Shortly afterwards Lord Cowper was informed by a correspondent in Dublin that Alan 'has been seized some time with a paralytic disorder that deprives him in a great manner of the use of his limbs and one hand. 'Tis said he is to go soon for England to advise about his health' (HALS, DE/P/F54/24: Robert Dixon to Cowper, 13 Jan. 1721/2).

[1631] Bare-faced.

Court, or in conversation with some of the ministry. You mention the great majority against the favourite scheme without expressing the number, which pray lett mee know. I thinke our session as well as yours might ere now have been ended, if wee had nott had somthing behind which was nott thought fitt to bee talkt of, if this bee the case I fancy twill have like successe as with you. Mr W[alpole] before the Holydayes went into Norfolke being just gott over an ugly intermitting feavor; the Master of the Rolls[1632] told mee two days since (from Horace W[alpole]) that the feavor was returned, which had necessitated a repetition of the Barke,[1633] if this prove true itt may bee dangerous for hee went very weake away, before which the towne sayes hee very earnestly presst for his Majestys leave to lay downe, and they goe soe far as to mention the Speaker for his successor,[1634] as well as talke of severall removes, the first part I am in doubt of, the latter is always the town cant towards the close of every session.

Our merchants are in paine for feare of a rupture with Portugal, where they have above halfe a million effects; you have certainly heard of the confinement and seizure of his books and effects, the case as I apprehend stands thus.

One Winkefeild (sonne of a yorksheer gentleman of a very good estate) having been betrayed by a partner whoe turnd papist, had a seizure made of a great quantity of gold dust found conceald in his house, his bookes were likewise seizd, which latter is (say wee) against the law of nations.[1635] You must know that all gold dust imported from the Braseels[1636] payes a duty of seven per Cent to the crowne, and is to bee entred and coined, or run into Ingots, and may afterwards bee reexported, the seizure made was nott entred, nor payd the duty, the books (say the Port[uguese]) by the same law are seasable in order to facilitate the discovery, and therfore wee have acted according to law.

Wee on the other hand say this trade has been connivd att, and wee deny that bookes may bee seizd; hitherto the King of Portugal has appeard obstinate, butt I hope a messinger newly gone hence may have carryd such instructions as may accomodate the affair, for speaking fairly I doubt a trade connived att, will bee butt a bad plea against a sovereigns executing the law of his country. War (except in cases of the utmost necessity) is to be avoided especially under circumstances like ours, for certainly wee are in noe condition to enter unnecessarily into itt.

I trouble you with this accountt which I beleive a true state of the case, because probably itt may bee a subject of discourse.

There is (if fame may bee credited) another broyle upon the coast. Tis sayd that Port Mahon and Gibraltar are given in part of Dowry to the Infanta, and this grounded uppon

[1632] Sir Joseph Jekyll.

[1633] 'Jesuit's Bark' or 'Peruvian Bark': a remedy against fever made from the bark of the cinchona.

[1634] Hon. Spencer Compton (c.1674–1743), of Compton Place, Sussex, MP [GB] Sussex; later 1st earl of Wilmington.

[1635] In Sept. 1721 an English merchant in Lisbon, Ferdinand Wingfield, had been arrested and charged with exporting gold abroad illegally in the form of dust. His case was pursued by the English envoy to Portugal, and although sentenced to death Wingfield was eventually pardoned and released (*Post Boy*, 21 Oct. 1721; *Weekly Journal*, 30 Dec. 1721; H.E.S. Fisher, *The Portugal Trade: A Study of Anglo–Portuguese Commerce 1700–1770* (1971), 93; David Francis, *Portugal 1715–1808* ... (1985), 37). The actions of the Portuguese government were thought in some quarters to have violated treaty agreements.

[1636] Brazil.

promise of being redeliverd to [*the*] crowne of Spaine, nay they goe soe far as saying this to have been notifyed to our ministers, butt I hope neither the one nor the other is true.[1637]

You may remember what fell from the late Secretary Craggs in the house of Commons; That perhaps the matter might have been mentioned in conversation as what might bee treated of in time to come uppon giving an equivalent, butt positively affirmd nothing had been agreed and as a proof hee would att a convenient time make a motion about Minorca which would furnish an opertunity of knowing the sence of the house in relation to Gibraltar, butt hee never did itt, perceiving very plainly that the generall bent of the nation was against parting with itt, and I think they continue soe.

521. *Alan I, Dublin, to Thomas, 5–6 Jan. 1721[/2]*

(1248/5/165–6)

… Our Lord Lieutenant spent his Christmas as I told you at Conelyes; I cannot tell you the names of all the good company but Mr Maxwel was one of them, and he in his Cups (as I hear) said in his Graces hearing, or to this Grace, that he would have a slap at the Chancellor. Of this I had not the least intimation from the person who might most reasonably have put me on my guard, but indeed I had nothing of that kind, only he said Maxwell being drunk talked wild things without mentioning what or of what nature, and added that he had said to Mr Maxwel, that he hoped he would consider that he (the Duke) was one of them: from which words it is plain the previous discourse of Maxwel must refer to something to which the Duke was a party, which probably must be in Councel: I resolve as soon as he can be seen (for it is now past one of the Clock, and I am just come from the Castle being told among others who attended the Dukes Levee that he was in bed and in a sweat and should not rise in an hour, having been up dancing till seven this morning) to let him know I have heard of this passage in his presence at Mr Conelyes house. This story seems to me the properest introduction to explain the meaning and reasons of a pretty observable resolution which the house of Commons came to at their meeting in a very thin house on Wednesday last. After the bill about Hawkers and Pedlars was read,[1638] Mr Maxwel stood up and told the house that he had reason to beleive that bill and many other very good ones framed by the Commons had been altered at a certain place (I do not know that he named the Councel[1639]) under the pretence of having a power so to doe; that he thought that board had more power already by Law then consisted with the good of the Kingdome but that he beleived they exceeded the power which they legally had and therefore moved that the house would come to a resolution that a Committee be appointed to examine what alteration have been made in the heads of Bills sent from that House this session of Parliament and where the same have been soe made and it was ordered accordingly and a Committee was named and the bill was ordered a second reading on Tuesday next (by which day I suppose they calculated the Committee would be able to make their report).

[1637] On the proposed marriage of the infanta of Spain, Mariana Victoria (1718–81), with Louis XV of France.

[1638] The engrossed bill 'for licensing hawkers, pedlars and petty chapmen', which having passed the British privy council and was presented to the Commons on 3 Jan. (ILD).

[1639] The Irish privy council.

Every body sees the tendency of this resolution to the asserting a right in the Commons to have their crude undigested thoughts transmitted in the form of a bill by the Councel without amendment, and to oblige the Councel to certifye under their hands that the bill so certifyed by them is not only fit but necessary to be passed into a Law: for soe is the form of our transmitting bills into England. And to enable the Committee to make their enquiry they voted an addresse to my Lord Lieutenant to order Copyes of the bills transmitted by the Councel into England to be laid before them; The same day a Bill about making malt was read[1640] and Mr Norman (of Londonderry a certain persons creature[1641]) stood up and said the bill then read was no more the same with the heads of the Bill by him brought in then any other bill was, and that was very true for the Councel found the heads as Mr Norman had framed them were not only not fit to passe into a Law but of most destructive consequence to the Countrey. And this bill was ordered likewise a second reading on Tuesday next as likewise was another favourite bill of the party, for encouraging the hempen and flaxen manufacture: which Mr Maxwels zeal put him on moving the rejection of because of alterations made at a certain place. Now you must know that as the heads of that bill came from the Commons they had given the Commissioners for the Governing the linen manufacture here, power to make by Laws (which by those Heads of a bill would have had the force of an Act of Parliament) but it was moved (as an amendment to those heads of a Bill) and made part of the bill that the By laws should not have that force unlesse approved by the Cheif Governor and Councel and indeed I proposed the amendment; for I am not fond of devolving a Legislative power on any particular sett of men and of all men in the Kingdome would not entrust the Linen board with it, whose wisdome hatched our late intended bank and whose prudence carryed it on soe far as it was carryed after the sense of the Kingdome was known to be against it: for it was begott and nursed up at that board. And truly a story which I heard on Wednesday last in the house of Lords from the Archbishop of Dublin and which he yesterday repeated before my Lord Lieutenant the Archbishop of Tuam the two Cheif Justices and me in the Closet gives me a worse liking of them then I had before which was to this effect that his Grace had been in discourse with one of the linen board (who was had been [sic] a zealous promoter of the Bank scheme[)], about the alteration made to the hempen bill[1642] which restrained the by laws to be made by the linen board to have the force of Laws unlesse approved and confirmed in Councel and his Grace in justifying the addicion said that as the bill was sent by the Commons it devolved a Legislative power in the linen board; the other said he did not know where it could be better lodged, I cannot recollect the very words, but they imported his desire that it were soe and his opinion that it could not be in better hands. Now if that were the case, we should not now want the blessing of a Bank, nor a certain bill which was unfortunately attempted once within these two years, if I judge right; and whether the hopes of obtaining the later by means of the power of a Bank was not in the view of some of our great Bank men, I am a good deal in suspence: but I confesse I think the wisest of them had at least as distant views. I shal not be at all surprised if (now the house

---

[1640]'To prevent frauds and abuses in the making of malt'; amended by the British privy council and presented to the Commons on 3 Jan. (ILD).

[1641]Speaker Conolly's.

[1642]'For amending several laws now in force for encouraging the hempen and flaxen manufacture in this kingdom'; amended in the British privy council and presented to the Commons on 3 Jan. (ILD).

is so very thin, not fifty members in town) the warm Gentlemen prevail in a majoritye to come into some resolution, in relation to our framing bills not altogether agreeable to that exposition which Poynings Law hath alway had, nor conformable to the practice since the passing of it and probably they will endeavour to name a freind of yours; which must tend more to his character and reputacion then any other thing can. Therefore you may be sure if he be concerned at these steps it is on the publick account least in addicion to what was suggested from the proceedings in our house in the former Session (of our affecting an independencye) acquire strength and credit by any farther step that may be made in the other which in England may be construed to look that way. I will (if possible) make a certain person sensible how little such a step will tend to establish the credit of his administration, that a thing which hath hitherto passed unquestioned for so long time should be sett on foot during his Governement and by people to whom he hath shewn great countenance …

522. *St John III, Midleton, to Alan I, 9 Jan.* 1721/2

(1248/5/254–5)

In my last I told you how much this Countrey was alarm'd at the Numbers and insolence of those who are publickly listed for the service of the King of Spain or Pretender, and at the same time surpriz'd that the Government has not yet thought fit to issue any orders for suppressing that dangerous practice. Since that time (whither from the lenity of the Government or what other cause I know not) they have appear'd more publickly, 2 or 300 in a Gang with their officers and several of their men arm'd, and have marcht regularly thro the Countrey at noon day, in their way to the sea side in order to be shipt off. This I heard from Collonel F[it]zGerald[1643] to day, who assur'd me Alderman Knap[1644] told him that he saw at least 200 of them march by his house within these 3 days, in the manner I have describ'd and did not dare interrupt or askt one of them a Question. Standish Barry[1645] din'd with me to day, and assur'd me there were at least 500 of them quarter'd about his part of the Countrey, waiting for the word of command; they live upon free Quarter, and are so insolent that he and a great many of his neighbours are determin'd to remove immediately with their familys to Corke for fear of being plunder'd or Murther'd. If the Papists are under these apprehensions from them, your Lordship will easily judge what condition the Protestants are in. In short we were not half so much alarm'd upon the Queens death[1646] or when the Pretender was in Scotland,[1647] nor at any time since 88 as I have heard from those who liv'd in those times.[1648] No body ventures to stir abroad after night=fall, or to lye a night without a strong Guard about his house; and I give you my word that the common

---

[1643] Possibly John Fitzgerald of Ballynacot (see above, p. 351).

[1644] Edmond Knapp, MP [I].

[1645] Standish Barry (*d.*1741) of Leamlara, Co. Cork, who later in the year would be arrested for involvement in recruiting catholics for the Irish regiments in Spain (Dickson, *Old World Colony*, 265, 273, 580).

[1646] Queen Anne's death in 1714.

[1647] In the Fifteen.

[1648] St John was born in about 1685.

people of the Countrey are so much afraid of them, that tho I had an Account within these 48 hours that 70 of them were assembled at an Alehouse near Carricktohil[1649] in order to go aboard ship that night, I could not prevail with even our own Tenants and neighbours to go with me to disperse them, and had this reason given me, which I confess seems to have some weight, that since the Government did not think fit to take notice of them, they saw no reason why they should officiously run the risque of being murther'd or having their houses burn't, for doing what they thought was more properly the business of others.

If the Government had received true Accounts of the proceedings of these people of late, I think tis impossible but that some sort of care would have been taken to prevent them; and I do assure you they are come to that height in this Countrey now, that unless something of the kind be done soon, the Gentlemen of the Countrey will find themselves oblig'd to apply to the Parliament. How acceptable this will be at a certain place is not difficult to guess.

I write this at the request of several of your freinds and my neighbours who are now with me, and desire this Account may be sent your Lordship, of the truth of every particular of which you may certainly depend. I have no doubt of your doing what is proper upon the occasion, but beg my name may not be made use of for many reasons. In short people may make as light of this matter as they please; but I cannot think it can be for his Majestys service or the Interest of this Countrey, to suffer no less then 20000 Irish Papists (which is a moderate Computation) to be enlisted and transported for the service of our good freind the King of Spain …

[*PS*] My Uncle Will is here, and gives you his humble service. If you can do any thing further for him, I entreat you will, for he is an undone man if this affair miscarrys.[1650]

523. *Thomas to Alan I, 9 Jan. 1721[/2]*

(1248/5/168–9)

Your letter of the 30th past (which I beleive came on Fryday) lay lockt up att the house[1651] till itt mett yesterday.

I am heartily glad that you have resolvd coming away assoone as possible, and hope you have and will employ some time in setling your affairs soe as to suffer as little as may bee by your absence, for I thinke you may bee very sure that the scheme you mention, or som other of like nature will bee putt in execution, a particular freind of yours will take care that bee done.

I told you in a former, I had desired my nephew (to whom I wrote a very short letter) to owne from mee the receipt of your severall letters, nott being then able to write more, they are constantly lookt into, and are generally soe made up as that may easily bee done even without the artificiall way of taking of the seale … Our session as well as yours has been protracted, probably with like veiwes. Hints have been given (as I hear) of the uncertainty

---

[1649]Carrigtohill, Co. Cork.

[1650]The vacancy in king's bench [I] likely to arise from the expected death of Godfrey Boate: this was given to John Parnell, MP [I].

[1651]In the parliament buildings: letters sent to MPs at Westminster were kept in 'boxes at the lobby door' (*HC 1690–1715*, ii, 367).

of a new parliament and yett I thinke wee shall have one, the matter I take gone too far to bee recalled; itt seems the generall expectation of the kingdom, interest is making with great application every where, and equally on both sides, wherfore an attempt of prolonging would (in my opinion) bee making a very long step, and yett daring men may adventure att itt as well as other things, butt I still thinke they will nott. Lett mee know assoone as possible the time you fix for coming away … The Duke of Bolton has been dangerously ill of a pluretique feaver, butt this night the Doctors hope the worst is over.[1652]

524. *Alan I, Dublin, to Thomas, 10 Jan. 1721[/2]*

(1248/5/170–3)

In my last I gave you an account of what passed from Mr Maxwels mouth at Mr Conelyes house and in whose presence; you see how that resolution was pursued in the votes of the Commons of the 3d instant, by appointing a Committee to examine into what alterations had been made of the heads of bills which arose in the Commons house and where the alterations were made.[1653] I having more regard to some body then he hath deserved at my hands, told him that I apprehended that enquiry would not be for his service or interest in England, and advised him to put a stop to it as far as he could; and it was plainly in his power for the thing was concerted by those to whom only he gives countenance and in whom only he reposes confidence. Truly the method taken (as it appears by the event) was that the Committee should not make any report nor the Committee meet, but Maxwel the chairman was to be absent and so no report could be made: and indeed this was the scheme of my Lord Cheif Justice Whitshead, but not with any view of the turn it hath taken; for yesterday the Commons threw out three bills the Hawkers and Pedlars bill, that for the hempen and linen manufacture and that about malt;[1654] you know the house never gives the reasons of a bill, but the members in debating shew the grounds they goe upon. Now I had shewn my Lord Lieutenant how very fatal it might be to the Kingdome for a few hot headed people to doe an act which would give an handle to those who wish ill to this Kingdome to suggest that there was a disposicion in it to throw off the dependency of it on England, and that he would be very cooly received at his coming to St James[1655] if any thing of this nature should happen during his administration, especially if he no way endeavoured to prevent it, and much more if he was any way apprized of the design of the managers of this affair. And truly the use that was made of this hint was that the persons confided in waved their first design of falling on the power of the Councel, which they in words owned, but with great reluctance and regret at the Councel having that power which they

---

[1652] He died 21 Jan. 1722.

[1653] Maxwell was named first to the committee, indicating that he was the proposer, and Clotworthy Upton appeared next, a likely indication that he was the seconder (*CJI*, iv, 846–7; above, i, 187).

[1654] All bills were rejected on account of amendments made by the Irish privy council: in the case of the Hawkers and Pedlars Bill and the Linen Bill the Commons objected to the fact that the council had given itself a supervisory authority (BL, Add. MS 6116, f. 104: Bishop Nicolson to Archbishop Wake, 13 Jan. 1721/2; HALS, DE/P/F54/24: Robert Dixon to Cowper, 13 Jan. 1721/2). In his account of parliamentary proceedings that day Bishop Nicolson observed that 'The lord chancellor faltered very much towards the conclusion of the day's debate, and in appearance is sinking apace' (BL, Add. MS 6116, f. 104: Nicolson to Wake, 13 Jan. 1721/2).

[1655] St James's Palace, that is to say returning to the royal court.

have by Poynings Law: and instead of it Mr Jos[*hua*] Allen a man whose head doth not alway stand right, Mr Upton[1656] (who hates the Councel since they sent over the bill in relation to giving the dissenters ease, but not according to the heads framed by the Commons but those formed by the Lords[1657][)] Mr Maxwel (who hath lost his wits since his elaborate noice about the Bank did not convince men) and Mr Singleton (according to his constant good will and affection to those who derive their power from King G[*eorge*][1658]) took oportunitye to say the Councel had alway misused their power, without giving one instance wherein they had so done; save that the Later was very angry with their executing the power they have in disapproving or approving magistrates in corporacions; which indeed the Councel hath used to very great effect in suppressing the party in which he hath alway appeared. Now this they could not have done if the Committee had proceeded to make their report, for they could not have given one instance where the alterations of the heads of bills from the Commons, which were made at the Councel could be found fault with; such language was never used toward men (as what I heard Lord Tullamore say was used by some of them of the Councel) nay Maxwel said nothing skreened the particular members of the Councel from very severe resolutions but the sense he had that nothing could be done there without the consent of the Duke of G[*rafton*]. Now for my part God damn all skreens say I, and the scoundrels who need them; so I think this story will pretty plainly indicate what terms his Grace made with Mr Maxwel for himself, and that the Councel were left to the discretion of wolves, for I cannot give the fowre a softer name. This puts me in mind of the late Duke of Ormond treating the Allyes toward the end of his infamous campaign.[1659] Somebody hath made a special Kettle of fish of his favourite Bank[1660] and hath paved the way for a very easy Session at the next meeting; if the house had been full, as it was on 9 December when the majoritye against the Bank was 170 against 80 (which you tell me I forgot to tell you in my former letter but I am sure I sent the numbers either to my sister or Ally) we should have had some Gentlemen of spirit and candor enough to have expected the Gentlemen who treated the Councel in the most vile maner, should have given some instances wherein they had misbehaved themselves which none of the members of the Councel who were of the house had the spirit or honour to doe; and indeed their silence ought in all reason to be taken as a tacite owning the truth of all which was said of the Councel as far as it related to themselves; else it is natural for people who hear things laid to their charge of which they know they are not guilty to justifye themselves, and in honour one might expect the same thing should have been on behalf of their brethren who by not being in the house were not capable of vindicating them selves. But truly they were mute, Sir Ralph Gore,

---

[1656] Probably Clotworthy Upton, rather than his brother Thomas, since Clotworthy was the most prominent advocate of the presbyterians' cause, although he was more usually referred to as 'Colonel Upton' (his militia rank).

[1657] The Toleration Act of 1719 (6 Geo. I, c. 5 [I]). In fact, the Irish privy council had been evenly divided and the casting vote of the lord lieutenant, Bolton, had ensured that the Commons bill was accepted in its entirety and transmitted to England. Only afterwards did the Lords produce their own bill, but Bolton insisted – to the disgust of King and other bishops – that the Commons' bill retain primacy (O'Regan, *Archbishop William King*, 248–61).

[1658] Probably Henry rather than Edward Singleton. The statement is ironical.

[1659] In 1712, when Ormond, as c.-in-c. Flanders, was obliged to operate under the so-called 'restraining orders'.

[1660] Maxwell had published two pamphlets in favour of the Bank project: *Reasons Offer'd for Erecting a Bank in Ireland; in a Letter to Hercules Rowley, Esq* (1st and 2nd edns, Dublin, 1721), and *Mr Maxwell's Second Letter to Mr Rowley; wherein the Objections against the Bank are Answered* (Dublin, 1721). For the complexities in his position with regard to the Bank, see Hayton, *Anglo-Irish Experience*, 114–15.

Mr St George[1661] Sir Gustavus Hume Mr Parry Mr Tynte Sir Edward Crofton and more especially Mr Secretary Hopkins. I say his Grace hath cut out fine work for a Successor to hold an easy Session; but I fancy this must have one good effect; and since our Parliament hath been already as long lived as yours I see no reason why it should survive it.

525. *Alan I, Dublin, to Thomas, at his lodgings in the Privy Garden, Whitehall, 19 Jan. 1721[/2]*

(1248/5/174–5)

This letter will certainly come to your hand unopened, being sent by Mr Acton who goes over on account of an appeal from a decree pronounced for him in Chancery without very good reason I thought when I gave it, and continue of the same mind.[1662] I have your letter of the 9th. and am sorry not to be able to fix the day for my leaving this place; but that depends on my Lord Lieutenants granting me a licence of absence; the Dutchesse goes the beginning of next week; but his Grace not soe soon; we say not till the middle of February.[1663] Instead of being used with confidence I am kept a stranger to every thing, even to the disposal of the Judges place now vacant about which I wrote soe long since and you spoke so much before he came over. Yesterday an end was putt to our Session by a prorogation to 13 February; which was managed with as much trick and as little skil as ever was used in any Session on either side the water. I thank God I am a good deal better then I have been and recover strength in my limbs … My humblest services to my Lord Duke of Somersett.

526. *Thomas to Alan I, 25 Jan. 1721[/2]*

(1248/5/176–7)

… tis sayd the D[uke] of G[rafton] is expected in a fortnight att farthest, butt upon what grounds I can nott imagine, for yours of the 10th which I found att my returne on Saturday night, does nott looke like giving any expectation of his being here soe soone; I owne I am glad, and thinke you did very right, with respect to your country, in giving the necessary caution to his Grace of the consequences of the wise step made by those in whom hee confides, for the nation would have dearly payd for their hott headed actions, nor am I satisfyed that the lenghth they have gone will nott have an ill effect, although they stopt short, for I have heard the story represented with a great deale of bitternesse by one whoe seldom fails laying hold of every occasion to insinuate a generall inclination towards endeavouring

[1661] Oliver St George.

[1662] Thomas Acton (*d.* c.1750), of Bride Street, Dublin (Vicars, *Index*, 2; Reg. Deeds, 38/438/24920; *The Vestry Records of the Parishes of St Bride, St Michael Le Pole and St Stephen, Dublin 1662–1742*, ed. W.J.R. Wallace (Dublin, 2011), 174, 334), in a case against Walter Byrne and John Byrne, who had appealed to the British house of lords. Acton had brought a bill into the Irish court of chancery in Jan. 1721 and Alan had found in his favour on 20 Nov. following. On 23 Feb. 1722 the Lords reversed the decree (Brown, *Reports of Cases*, ii, 390–6).

[1663] It was reported in London on 3 Feb. that the duchess had arrived at Holyhead en route for London (*Daily Journal*, 3 Feb. 1722). News from Dublin on the 11th suggested that the duke intended to embark around the 20th. He arrived at Parkgate on 23 Feb. (*London Gazette*, 17–20, 24–27 Feb. 1722).

an independency, and am confident I may (without the spiritt of prophesy) foretell that this matter will bee some time or other trumpt up to its disadvantage. They are (or fancy themselves) able and great men when on their own dunghill, butt would appear very insufficient in stemming the tide uppon this, or cases of lesse consequence, for if an absolute and positive disavowing every such thought will scarcely bee credited (which experimentally I know to bee true) whoe thinke you can withstand the force of such an instance? His Grace surely has few freinds about him, or those of very little foresight, otherwise they must have told him plainly that hee in the first place would bee affected, though the nation would in the end bee the fatall sufferers.

I would recommend reading the late Comedy of Aesop to these worthy patriots and statesmen, where they will find their owne pictures drawne to the life.[1664]

Ten righteous would have savd Sodom,[1665] I wish a lesser number doe nott lay the foundation of ruine to the English interest of Ireland, for beleive itt this matter will nott dye, nor will itt bee enough to say that the ill execution of the powers committed to the Lord Lieutenant and Councill was what they complaind of, since they did nott thinke fitt to give instances, Noe noe twill bee sayd (as often and often itt has) that P[*oynings*] law is what sticks in their stomach, and this will obtaine.

I thinke our session will end in a month att farthest, and writts for a new Parliament issue in a very few dayes after itt.

I was sent for by the late D[*uke*] of Bolton before my going into Surry and spent an hour with him att my returne the night before hee dyed, hee was then perfectly sensible, and has made (as I heare) a very just and honourable disposition of his estate, which is very great.

527. *Thomas to Alan I, 30 Jan. 1721[/2]*

(1248/5/178–9)

Yesterday came yours of the 24th. I will endeavour being able to give you an accountt by next post of what you desire to bee informed, though probably my coming att the knowledge will bee difficult. The other matter you mention may bee denyed, butt that must bee evasively, for I thinke I am very well informd the thing was done uppon the application of a certaine person (whom youl guesse) whoe would nott have interposed without the privity of some body, and thus may his assertion litterally speaking bee true, though nott as desired to bee understood.

Every step now made plainly (I thinke) indicates our session drawing towards a conclusion, I thinke every thing before us may bee finished in three weekes, beyond which time I beleive wee shall nott sitt.

[1664]Sir John Vanbrugh's *Aesop: Or, The Politick Statesman*, which had been staged in Dublin in 1696–7 (John C. Greene and Gladys L.H. Clark, *The Dublin Stage, 1720–1745: A Calendar of Plays, Entertainments and Afterpieces* (1995), 422).

[1665]The story of Abraham's plea for God to spare the destruction of Sodom (Gen. 18:23).

I intend in a day or two waiting on his G[*race*][1666] to receive his commands touching the time of treating,[1667] which I mentioned when last I saw him, his answer was nott till the mony hee had sent to the several publique houses were expended, of which hee would give mee notice, if hee resolve to push for both, there will bee strong opposition, otherwise none, I hope hee will nott, though from some circumstances I doubt hee may.

528. St John III, Midleton, to Alan I, 31 Jan. 1721[/2]

(1248/5/180–1)

… You cannot imagine the confusion and dread that every body in this Countrey is in on Account of the vast Numbers of men that are daily enlisted and transported for the service of the King of Spain.[1668] They appear publickly in great Numbers, 60, 80, 100, in a Gang, with their officers at the head of them, and when the wind is fair they march down to the sea side, and are shipt off; when tis not, they skulk up and down the Countrey till another opportunity. They brag there have been no less then 15 or 20000 sent away within these 3 months, which upon the best enquiry I verily beleive to be true, and am therefore surpriz'd the Government does not think it necessary to take the proper methods to prevent so dangerous a proceeding.

I am glad to hear as I do by a letter from Dr Cummynge that Lady Midleton and you are much better.

529. Alan II, London, to Alan I, 8 Feb. 1721/2

(1248/5/182–3)

… I came to town last night with my Aunts and Sister, and return to Guildford tomorrow with my Uncle, (where he is obliged to be in the Evening) and go from thence to Midhurst by his and the Duke of Somersets Direction, to appear in your Lordships Behalf.[1669] Not that Either of them apprehend any Danger from that Quarter, but they think this the proper time to send me thither. I hope your Lordships Cause wont suffer much by your Absence, since his Grace is so active and sincere in your Interest. I beleive my Uncle is secure att Guildford,[1670] but his Journey thither is on the same Account, with mine into Sussex …

[PS] I thank your Lordship for the Verses …

[1666] The duke of Somerset.

[1667] The so-called 'Treating Act' of 1696 (7 & 8 Will. III, c. 4 [E]) forbade the provision of food and drink to voters after the election writ was issued.

[1668] Lord Perceval's agent estimated the numbers at 18,000 (BL, Add. MS 46973, f. 19: Berkeley Taylor to Perceval, 24 Feb. 1721[/2]. Recruiters and recruited came before the assizes in March and were then tried by a special commission of oyer and terminer in May (BL, Add. MS 46973, ff. 29, 35, 49: Taylor to Perceval, 27 Mar., 7, 22 May 1722). According to Bishop Nicolson, the recruits were all 'bigoted papists', who were leaving Ireland in the confident expectation of returning shortly to fight for the Pretender and their religion (BL, Add. MS 6116, f. 125: Nicolson to Archbishop Wake, 20 Jan. 1721/2).

[1669] At the general election.

[1670] Thomas was returned for Guildford on 26 Mar., taking second place in the poll behind Arthur Onslow (*HC 1715–54*, i, 329).

530. *Thomas to Alan I, Dublin, 8 Feb. 1721[/2]*

(1248/5/184–5)

I am told that the ArchBishop of Dublin, Lord Shannon and Mr Conelly were by the Duke of Grafton recomended for Justices, and that his Majestys approbation went hence,[1671] when leave was given for your coming over, the person from whom I had itt (a man of high station) sayd hee supposd you were left out your health requiring your absence during the summer, and your attendance in parliament would doe soe for the winter, you will easily collect from hence what may bee most proper for you to doe.

Wee shall bee up in a fortnight att farthest, I beleive two or three dayes sooner.

531. *Alan I, Dublin, to Thomas, 15 Feb. 1721[/2]*

(1248/5/188–9)

I make no doubt you have seen a letter I wrote before my going to Court on Tuesday morning. I went first to the Castle and told his Grace that I heard there were three Commissions come over under the great Seal of England one constituting Keepers of the Seal, another appointing Justices and another giving me his Majestyes leave to be absent without prejudice to my patent of Chancellor and desired to see them, because probably that appointing others to keep the Seal superseded my patent of Chancellor, at least so far that after I had intimation of it I could not sit again in Court as I had resolved to doe that morning with intent to doe the businesse depending in Court and had declared my resolution at the rising of the Court the day before; but that I might render my self very obnoxious to censure and severe usage if I should doe any thing not strictly justifiable which I resolved not to doe, for you know my past usage gives me little prospect of better treatment if I by misbehavior should put my self into some peoples power. I should have told you that when I came first into the room I said nothing but cursory discourse, resolving he should first break the matter to me about our new intended Justices. Which fell out accordingly; for he told me he was to acquaint me with a matter which had not been communicated to anybody living here yet, which he did not know how I should take tho he hoped and thought I would not take it ill, because not soe intended. He said it would have been <u>monstrous</u> to have left me out of the Commission if my health and businesse in Parliament would allow my being on the spot, as on the other hand he beleived I would allow that it would be in no sort advisable to leave the administration in the hands of Lord S[*hannon*] and Mr C[*onolly*] only, and appealed to me in that particular; I owned to his Grace I did think it would have been an extraordinary Commission that had constituted only them two to govern the Kingdome; but I confesse I was surprised to hear him who had recommended them to be two of the Justices and who knew or might have known that the Commission to three alway runs to them or any two of them make this observation. He added that he had recommended a third to obviate that objection whom he would name to me; I told him I was not so wholly a stranger to this transaction and put your letter of the eighth instant

---

[1671] These three comprised the commission appointed on 24 Feb.

into his hand on reading which he seemed to be under some surprize but said it was a mistake that he had recommended Justices when he wrote for liberty to give me a licence of absence. One thing is pretty observable that the person whom he named to have three on the spot, is so indisposed in his health as to be under a necessity and (I fancy) a resolution to goe to the Bath, and I am told by Arthur Hill that he had it from the Archbishops[1672] own mouth that his Grace knew that resolution. His Grace told me nothing but my being out of the Kingdome prevented my being one of the Justices and that to obviate all other constructions and insinuations to my prejudice he would say soe in all publick places. A very pretty way of salving reputation. I should not omit that the Archbishop of Dublin was absent five months together during his being last in the Governement, and that I was made one of the Justices by the Duke of Bolton and went into England in the same ship with him. I shal see the Archbishop this morning and beleive he is resolved not to accept the Governement having never been previously consulted in it or spoken to about the matter. There were no Commissions sent over but the letters to give me a licence of absence and appointing Commissioners in my absence etc being under the Privy signet were mistaken for matters under the great Seal. I doubt his Grace will not be able to goe away as soon as he intended I mean next Monday. I am in readinesse to goe and so is my wife.

[1672] King of Dublin.

Appendix 1: The Division in the Irish House of Commons on the Bank, 14 Oct. 1721

This division list, to be found at SHC, 1248/5/105–6, is endorsed by Alan I 'The names of the voters for and against the Bank 14 Oct. 1721 in the House of Commons'. It was previously transcribed in Joseph Griffin, 'Parliamentary Politics in Ireland during the reign of George I', University College Dublin MA, 1977, pp. 190–3. Here the spelling of names has been standardised, and the MPs on each side are given in alphabetical order, except for the tellers, who are listed first and marked with an asterisk.

For the bill
St John Brodrick (Co. Cork)★
Joshua Allen (Co. Kildare)
Richard Allen (Athy)
Robert Allen (Co. Wicklow)
Richard Ashe (Athboy)
William Balfour (Augher)
Thomas Bellew (Mullingar)
Francis Bernard (Bandon)
Richard Bettesworth (Thomastown)
Samuel Bindon (Ennis)
Henry Bingham (Castlebar)
Thomas Bligh (Athboy)
William Boyle (Charleville)
William Brodrick (Mallow)
William Brownlow (Co. Armagh)
Thomas Burdett (Co. Carlow)
Thomas Burgh (Naas)
Sir Walter Burrowes, 4th Bt (Harristown)
Francis Burton (Coleraine)
Jephson Busteed (Rathcormac)
Brinsley Butler (Belturbet)
David Chaigneau (Gowran)
Robert Clements (Newry)
Theophilus Clements (Cavan)
Marmaduke Coghill (TCD)
Caesar Colclough (Taghmon)
William Conolly (Co. Londonderry)

Joshua Cooper (Co. Sligo)
John Corry (Co. Fermanagh)
David Creighton (Lifford)
Thomas Crosbie (Dingle)
William Crosbie (Ardfert)
Silvester Crosse (Armagh)
John Cuffe (Thomastown)
Maurice Cuffe (Kilkenny)
Michael Cuffe (Co. Mayo)
Robert Edgeworth (St Johnstown)
Eyre Evans (Co. Limerick)
Edward Eyre (Galway)
John Folliott (Longford)
James Forth (Philipstown)
Samuel Freeman (Ballinakill)
Sir Ralph Gore, 4th Bt (Co. Donegal)
Alexander Graydon (Harristown)
Hon. Gustavus Hamilton (Co. Donegal)
Henry Hawley (Kinsale)
Arthur Hill (Hillsborough)
John Ivers (Co. Clare)
Anthony Jephson (Mallow)
Edmond Knapp (Cork)
Charles Lambart (Kilbeggan)
Francis Lucas (Monaghan)
Edward Lyndon (Carrickfergus)
George Macartney, sr (Belfast)
George Macartney, jr (Belfast)
James Macartney (Longford)
Isaac Manley (Limavady)
Thomas Marlay (Limavady)
Sir Robert Maude, 1st Bt (St Canice)
Henry Maxwell (Donegal)
William Maynard (Tallow)
Audley Mervyn (Co. Tyrone)
Hon. Richard Molesworth (Swords)
Charles Monck (Newcastle)
Thomas Nesbitt (Cavan)
Brockhill Newburgh (Co. Cavan)
Brabazon Newcomen (Kilbeggan)
John Parnell (Granard)
Benjamin Parry (Tallow)
Thomas Pearson (Killybegs)
John Pratt (Dingle)
John Preston (Co. Meath)
Nathaniel Preston (Navan)

George Ram (Gorey)
William Richardson (Co. Armagh)
Henry Rose (Ardfert)
Robert Ross (Killyleagh)
Henry Rugge (Youghal)
Oliver St George (Dungannon)
Anthony Sheppard (Co. Longford)
Henry Singleton (Drogheda)
James Stevenson (Randalstown)
Robert Taylor (Tralee)
Sir Thomas Taylo(u)r, 1st Bt (Kells)
James Topham (St Johnston)
Thomas Trotter (Duleek)
Thomas Upton (Co. Antrim)
William Vesey (Tuam)
Michael Ward (Co. Down)
Samuel Waring (Hillsborough)
Patrick Weymes (Co. Kilkenny)
Richard Whaley (Athenry)
Hugh Willoughby (Monaghan)
Owen Wynne, sr (Ballyshannon) or Owen Wynne, jr (Sligo)

Against the bill
Robert Pigott (Maryborough)★
James Agar (Callan)
Thomas Ashe (Clogher)
William Aston (Dunleer)
James Barry (Kildare) or James Barry (Dungarvan)
Redmond Barry (Dungarvan)
John Beauchamp (Old Leighlin)
Theobald Bourke (Naas)
James Boyse (Bannow)
Kilner Brasier (Kilmallock)
Robert Bray (Lanesborough)
Henry Brooke (Dundalk)
Richard Buckworth (Cashel)
Benjamin Burton (Dublin)
Samuel Burton (Sligo)
John Bury (Askeaton)
Sir Alexander Cairnes, 1st Bt (Monaghan)
Charles Campbell (Newtownards)
Thomas Carter (Trim)
Hon. James Caulfeild (Charlemont)
Thomas Caulfeild (Tulsk)
Thomas Christmas (Waterford)
John Cliffe (Bannow)

John Cole (Enniskillen)
Richard Cole (Enniskillen)
Robert Colvill (Killybegs)
Edward Corker (Midleton)
Dudley Cosby (Queen's Co.)
Richard Cox (Clonakilty)
Ephraim Dawson (Queen's Co.)
Edward Deane (Inistioge)
Robert Dixon (Randalstown)
Philip Doyne (Clonmines)
Henry Edgeworth (St Johnstown)
Archibald Edmonstone (Carrickfergus)
Cadwallader Edwards (Wexford)
John Eyre (Armagh)
William Flower (Co. Kilkenny)
William Foord (Limerick)
Patrick Fox (Fore)
John French (Tulsk)
Richard Geering (Jamestown)
Sir Arthur Gore, 2nd Bt (Co. Mayo)
William Gore (Co. Leitrim)
Wentworth Harman (Lanesborough)
Francis Harrison (Co. Carlow)
Hugh Henry (Antrim)
Edward Hoare (Cork)
George Houghton (Clonmines)
Sir Gustavus Hume, 3rd Bt (Co. Fermanagh)
Edward Jones (Wexford)
Maurice Keating (Athy)
Richard Lehunt (Enniscorthy)
Thomas Lestrange (Banagher)
Nicholas Loftus (Co. Wexford)
Peter Ludlow (Co. Meath)
John Mason (Waterford)
Edward May (Co. Waterford)
Thomas Meredyth (New Ross)
Humphrey Minchin (Co. Tipperary)
Stephen Moore (Fethard)
Hon. William Moore (Ardee)
Charles Norman (Derry)
Matthew Pennefather (Cashel)
James Peppard (Granard)
Robert Perceval (Trim)
Henry Percy (Co. Wicklow)
Hon. Charles Plunket (Banagher)
Plunket Plunket (Swords)

Hon. Henry Ponsonby (Inistioge)
Abel Ram (Gorey)
Daniel Reading (Newcastle)
Hercules Rowley (Co. Londonderry)
John Rochfort (Ballyshannon)
John Rogerson (Dublin)
William St Lawrence (Ratoath)
John Sale (Carysfort)
Robert Shaw (Galway)
John Short (Portarlington)
Edward Singleton (Drogheda)
Hon. John Skeffington (Antrim)
William Smyth (Fore)
James Stopford (Co. Wexford)
Edward Stratford (Baltinglass)
Richard Tenison (Dunleer)
Richard Tighe (Limavady)
James Tisdall (Dundalk)
Michael Tisdall (Ardee)
Richard Tisdall (Co. Louth)
Blayney Townley (Carlingford)
James Tynte Worth (Rathcormac)
Clotworthy Upton (Co. Antrim)
William Wall (Knocktopher)
William Wall (Maryborough)
Richard Warburton (Portarlington)
Edward Warren (Kilkenny)
Richard Warren (Kildare)
Samuel Whitshed (Wicklow)
Richard Wolseley (Carlow)
Edward Worth (Knocktopher)
Edward Worth (New Ross)

Appendix 2: Brodrick Family Members and Connections Mentioned in the Text

Barry, James (1659–1717), of Rathcormac, Co. Cork, 1st s. of Redmond Barry of Rathcormac, and bro. of Catherine Barry, 1st w. of Alan I; m. (1) Mary, da. of Abraham Anselm of London, 2s. 1da. (2) Susanna, da. of John Townsend of Castletownsend, Co. Cork; MP Rathcormac 1689, 1692–9, 1713–14, Dungarvan 1703–13, 1715–d.; capt. of foot by 1692, col. 1699.

Barry, James (1689–1743), of Rathcormac, Co. Cork, 1st s. of James Barry of Rathcormac (*q.v.*); unm.; MP Dungarvan 1713–14, 1721–7, Rathcormac 1727–d.; capt., Stanwix's regt. of foot 1706–12, Wittewrong's foot c.1715–16, Lord Tyrawley's foot, 1716.

Barry, Redmond (bef. 1696–1750), of Rathcormac, Co. Cork, 2nd s. of James Barry (1659–1717) of Rathcormac (*q.v.*); m. 1727, Anne Smyth of Coolmore, Co. Cork, *s.p.*; MP Dungarvan 1717–27, Tallow 1727–d.

Brodrick, Alan I (1656–1728), of Dublin, 2nd s. of St John I; *cr.* Baron Brodrick 1715, Viscount Midleton 1717; m. (1) by 1684, Catherine, da. of Redmond Barry of Rathcormac, Co. Cork, 1s. (2) 1695, Lucy Courthope (*q.v.*), 1s. 1da. (3) 1716, Anne Hill (*q.v.*), *s.p.*; MP [I] Cork 1692–10, Co. Cork 1713–14, and MP [GB] 1717–d.; recorder, Cork 1690–5, 3rd serjeant [I] 1690–2, solicitor-gen. [I] 1695–1704, privy councillor [I] 1695–1711, 1714–d., Speaker of the house of commons [I] 1703–10, 1713–14, attorney-gen. [I] 1707–9, chief justice of queen's bench [I] 1709–11, lord chancellor [I] 1714–25, lord justice [I] 1717–19, 1719–21, 1722–3, 1724–5.

Brodrick, Alan II (1702–47), 2nd but 1st surv. s. of Alan I by his 2nd w.; m. 1729, Lady Mary Capell (*d.* 1756), da. of Algernon, 2nd earl of Essex, 2s. (1 *d.v.p.*); commr of customs [GB] 1727–30, jt comptroller of army [GB] 1730.

Brodrick, Alice (1697–1780), only da. of Alan I by his 2nd w.; m. 1737, Rev. John Castleman, fellow, All Souls' College, Oxford.

Brodrick, Katherine (bef. 1665–1731), 1st and o. surv. da. of St John I; m. William Whitfield (c.1658–1717), rector, St Martin's Ludgate 1691–1714, prebendary, St Paul's 1695, Canterbury 1710, vicar, St Giles Cripplegate 1714–d.

Brodrick, Laurence (c.1670–1747), 6th but 5th surv. s. of St John I; m. 1710, Anne Humphreys, 2s. (1 *d.v.p.*) 3 da.(2 *d.v.p.*); vicar, Sandon, Herts. 1697–1711, chaplain to house of commons [GB] 1708, prebendary of Westminster 1710–46, rector, Dauntsey, Wilts. 1712–14, Mixbury, Oxon. 1713–43, Turweston, Bucks. 1713–41, Islip, Oxon. 1741–8.

Brodrick, St. John III (1684–1728), 1st s. of Alan I by his 1st w.; m. 1710, Anne Hill, jr (*q.v.*), 4 da.; MP Castlemartyr 1709–13, Cork 1713–14, Co. Cork 1715–d., and MP [GB] 1721–7; recorder, Cork 1708–d., privy councillor [I] 1724–d.

Brodrick, Thomas (1654–1730), of Wandsworth, Surr. and Ballyannan, Co. Cork, 1st s. of St John I; m. Anne, da. of Alexander Pigott of Innishannon, Co. Cork, 1s. *d.v.p.*; MP Midleton 1692–3, 1715–27, Co. Cork 1695–1713 and MP [GB] 1713–27; comptroller of salt duties 1706–11, jt comptroller of army accounts 1708–11, privy councillor [I] 1695–1711, 1714–27, [GB] 1714–*d.*

Brodrick, William (c.1666–aft. 1733), of Spanish Town, Jamaica and the Inner Temple, 5th but 4th surv. s. of St John I; m. (1) 1693, Hannah (*d.*1703), wid. of Capt. John Toldervey and Major Thomas Ballard (2) by 1705, Ann (*d.* 1707), 1s. *d.v.p.*, 1da. (3) 1707, Sarah Ivey; attorney-gen. and judge admiral, Jamaica 1692–8, 1715, attorney-gen., Leeward Is. 1694, member of council, Jamaica 1695, Speaker of house of assembly, Jamaica 1711–13, 2nd serjeant [I] 1718–21.

Clayton, Laurence (1655–1712), of Mallow, Co. Cork, s. of Randal Clayton of Mallow, cousin of Alan I, St John II and Thomas; m. (1) Catherine, da. of Sir Henry Tynte, 1s. *d.v.p.* (2) 1698, Ann Courthope (*q.v.*), 3s.; MP Mallow 1692–*d.*; capt., Lesley's foot 1689, St George's foot 1689, queen's foot 1690–1.

Clayton, Randal (*d.* 1725), of Mallow, Co. Cork, 1st surv. s. of Laurence Clayton (*q.v.*) by his 2nd w.; m. Elizabeth, da. of Simon Gibbings (*d.* 1721), rector of Mallow, *s.p.*

Courthope, Martha (*d.* c.1730), sis. of Sir Peter Courthope of Little Island, Co. Cork; unm.

Courthope, Rachel, da. of John Codrington of Codrington, Gloucs.; m. 1686, John Courthope (*d.* 1695) of Little Island, Co. Cork, *s.p.*

Hill, Anne (*d.* 1747), da. and eventual h. of Sir John Trevor (*d.* 1717) of Brynkinalt, Denbighs., Speaker of the house of commons [E]1685–7, 1690–5; m. (1) 1690, Michael Hill (1672–99), of Hillsborough, Co. Down, MP [I] 1695–9, 2s. 1da. (2) Alan I, *s.p.*

Hill, Anne (b. aft. 1690), da. of Michael Hill of Hillsborough, Co. Down, and Anne Hill (*q.v.*); m. 1710, St John III, 4da.

Hill, Arthur (c.1694–1771), of Belvoir, Co. Down; MP Hillsborough 1715–27, Co. Down 1727–66; keeper of records, Dublin Castle 1719–33, registrar of deeds [I] 1734–48, privy councillor [I] 1750, 1753–*d.*, chancellor of exchequer [I] 1754–5, revenue commr [I] 1755–*d.*; cr. Viscount Dungannon 1766; 2nd s. of Anne Hill (*d.*1747) (*q.v.*) by her 1st husband.

Hill, Trevor (1693–1742), of Hillsborough, Co. Down; MP Hillsborough 1713–14, Co. Down 1715–17, MP [GB]1715–22; privy councillor [I] 1717–*d.*; cr. Viscount Hillsborough 1717; 1st s. of Anne Hill (*d.*1747) (*q.v.*) by her 1st husband.

Appendix 3: Members of the Irish House of Lords Mentioned in the Text

Temporal Lords

Abercorn – see Strabane.

Altham, 14th baron: Arthur Annesley (1689–1727).

Allen: John Allen (1661–1726), of Stillorgan, Co. Dublin, *cr*. Viscount Allen 1717; MP Co. Dublin 1692–3, 1703–13, 1715–17, Co. Carlow 1695–9, Co. Wicklow 1713–14; privy councillor [I] 1714–*d*.

Anglesey – *see* Valentia

Athenry, 14th baron: Francis Bermingham (1692–1750).

Barry, 3rd baron, of Santry: Henry Barry (1680–1735); privy councillor [I] 1714.

Barrymore, 4th earl of: James Barry (1667–1748); MP [GB] 1710–13, 1714–27, 1734–47; privy councillor [I] 1714–*d*.

Blayney, 7th baron: Cadwallader Blayney (1693–1733).

Blessington, 2nd viscount: Charles Boyle (aft. 1673– 1732); MP [I] Blessington 1711–18.

Blundell: Sir Montague Blundell (1689–1756), 4th Bt, of Blundell Manor, King's Co., *cr*. Viscount Blundell 1720; MP [GB] 1715–22.

Boyne – *see* Hamilton

Brodrick: Alan Brodrick I – *see* Appendix 2.

Butler of Newtownbutler: Theophilus Butler (1669–1724), of Belturbet, Co. Cavan, *cr*. Baron Butler of Newtownbutler 1715; MP [I] 1703–14; jt clerk of the pells [I] 1678 (life), privy councillor [I] 1710–*d*.

Carbery: George Evans (c.1680–1749), of Bulgaden Hall, Co. Limerick, *cr*. Baron Carbery 1715; MP [I] 1707–14 and [GB] 1715–27; privy councillor [I] 1715–45.

Castlecomer, 2nd viscount: Christopher Wandesford (1684–1719), of Kirklington, Yorks., and Castlecomer, Co. Kilkenny; MP [I] 1707 and [GB] 1710–13, 1715–*d*.; privy councillor [I] 1710–*d*.

Catherlogh, 2nd marquess of: Philip Wharton (1698–1731); also 2nd marquess of Wharton [GB], *cr*. duke of Wharton [GB] 1719; outlawed 1729.

Cavan, 4th earl of: Richard Lambart (*d*. 1742); lieut., Viscount Charlemont's foot 1694–8, capt., Gustavus Hamilton's foot 1703, lieut. col., Dormer's foot 1715–26.

Charlemont, 2nd viscount: William Caulfeild (*d*. 1726); col. of foot 1694–7, 36th foot 1701, brig.-gen. 1704, major-gen. 1708, privy councillor [I] 1726–*d*.

Doneraile, Arthur St Leger (1657–1727), *cr*. Viscount Doneraile 1703; MP [I] 1692–3; privy councillor [I] 1715–*d*.

Drogheda, 4th earl of: Henry Moore (1700–27); MP [GB] 1722–7.

Ferrard: Sir Henry Tichborne (1662–1731), 1st Bt, of Beaulieu, Co. Louth, *cr.* Baron Ferrard 1715; MP [I] 1715; privy councillor [I] 1715–*d.*, commr of great seal [I] 1716, 1717, 1721.

Fitzwilliam, 5th viscount: Richard Fitzwilliam (c.1677–1743); privy councillor [I] 1715–*d.*

Gowran: Richard Fitzpatrick (c.1662–1727), of Tintore, Queen's Co., *cr.* Baron Gowran 1715; MP [I] 1703–14; commander, Royal Navy 1687, capt. 1688–1703; privy councillor [I] 1715–*d.*

Granard, 2nd earl of: Arthur Forbes (c.1656–1724); cornet, King's own troop of horse [I] 1676, lieut. col., Tyrconnell's regiment 1686, col., Royal Regiment of Foot [I] 1686–8, brig.-gen. 1686–8.

Grimston: William Grimston (c.1683–1756), of Gorhambury, nr St. Albans, Herts., *cr.* Viscount Grimston 1719; MP [GB] 1710–22, 1727–34.

Hamilton: Gustavus Hamilton (1642–1723), of Rosguile, Manorhamilton, Co. Leitrim, *cr.* Baron Hamilton of Stackallan 1715, Viscount Boyne 1717; MP [I] 1692–1714; capt. Mountjoy's foot, 1685, privy councillor [I] 1685–8, 1710–*d.*, col. 20th foot 1689–1706, brig.-gen. 1696, major-gen. 1706.

Hillsborough: Trevor Hill – *see* Appendix 2.

Inchiquin, 3rd earl of: William O'Brien (1666–1719); privy councillor [I] 1702–*d.*, col. of foot 1706–by 1710.

Kerry, 5th baron of: Thomas Fitzmaurice (c.1669–1742), *cr.* earl of Kerry 1723; MP[I] 1692–7; privy councillor [I] by 1711–1714, 1727–*d.*

Kingston, 3rd baron: John King (c.1664–1728).

Kildare, 19th earl of: Robert Fitzgerald (1698–1744); privy councillor [I] 1710–*d.*, lord justice [I] 1714–15.

Limerick: James Hamilton (c.1691–1758), of Tollymore, Co. Down, and Dundalk, Co. Louth, *cr.* Viscount Limerick 1719, earl of Clanbrassil 1756; MP [I] Dundalk 1715–19 and [GB] 1727–34, 1735–41, 1742–54; chief remembrancer of exchequer [I] 1742–*d.*, privy councillor [I] 1746–*d.*

Loftus, 3rd viscount: Arthur Loftus (1644–1723).

Meath, 6th earl of: Chaworth Brabazon (1686–1763), MP Co. Dublin 1713–14; privy councillor [I] 1716–*d.*

Midleton – *see* Brodrick, Alan I.

Molesworth: Robert Molesworth (1656–1725), of Brackenstown, Co. Dublin and Edlington, Yorks., *cr.* Viscount Molesworth 1716; MP[I] 1695–9, 1703–14 and [E & GB] 1695–8, 1705–8, 1715–22; envoy extraordinary to Denmark 1689–92, privy councillor [I] 1697–Jan. 1714, Oct. 1714–*d.*

Moore of Tullamore: John Moore (bef. 1676–1725), of Croghan, King's Co., *cr.* Baron Moore of Tullamore 1715; MP [I] 1703–14; privy councillor [I] 1715–*d.*, commr of great seal [I] 1721.

Mount-Alexander, 2nd earl of: Hugh Montgomery (1651–1717); privy councillor [I] 1685–8, 1693–1714, lieut. of ordnance [I] 1698–1705, brig-gen., lord justice [I] 1701, 1702–3, 1704–5.

Mountcashell: Paul Davys (*d.* 1716), of St Catherine's, Dublin, *cr.* Viscount Mountcashell 1706.

Mountjoy: William Stewart (1675–1728), 2nd viscount; col. of foot 1694–8, 1701–13, dragoons 1715, brig.-gen. 1703, major-gen. 1707, lieut.-gen. 1710, master-gen. of ordnance [I] 1714–*d.*, one of keepers of great seal [I] 1721.

Mountrath, 5th earl of: Henry Coote (1684–1720).

Perceval: Sir John Perceval (1683–1748), 5th Bt, of Burton House, Co. Cork, *cr.* Viscount Perceval 1723, earl of Egmont 1733; MP [I] 1703–14 and [GB] 1727–34; privy councillor [I] 1704–*d.*

Ranelagh: Sir Arthur Cole (1664–1754), of Newlands, Co. Dublin, *cr.* Baron Ranelagh 1715; MP [I] 1692–9; privy councillor [I] 1715–27, 1733–*d.*

Roscommon, 7th earl of: Robert Dillon (*d.*1722); cornet, 4th dragoon guards 1715.

Rosse, 2nd earl of: Richard Parsons (*d.*1741).

St George: Sir George St George (c.1640–1735), 2nd Bt, of Carrickdrumrusk, Co. Leitrim, *cr.* Baron St George 1715; MP [I] 1692–14; vice-admiral, Connacht 1696–*d.*, privy councillor [I] 1715–*d.*

Santry – *see* Barry.

Shannon, 2nd viscount: Richard Boyle (c.1675–1740); MP [GB] 1708–11, 1712–34; cornet, Horse Guards 1693, major 1696–1702, col. of marines 1702–15, brig.-gen. 1704, major-gen. 1708, jt comptroller for clothing the army [GB] 1708, lieut.-gen. 1710, col., 25th foot 1715–21, lieut.-gen. of forces [I] 1716, c.-in-c. [I] 1720–*d.*, col., 6th dragoons 1721–7, Life Guards 1727–*d.*, privy councillor [I] 1721–*d.*, lord justice [I] 1722–3, 1724, gen. 1735, field marshal 1739.

Shelburne: Henry Petty (1675–1751), of Wycombe, Bucks., *cr.* Baron Shelburne 1699, earl of Shelburne 1719; MP [GB] 1715–27; jt prothonotary of common pleas [I] 1692–1700, jt ranger of Phoenix Park 1698–*d.*, privy councillor [I] 1701.

Southwell: Sir Thomas Southwell (1665–1720), 2nd Bt, of Castlematrix, Co. Limerick, *cr.* Baron Southwell 1717; MP Co. Limerick 1695–1717; revenue commr [I] 1697–1714, 1714–*d.*, privy councillor [I] 1710–*d.*, [GB] 1714–*d.*

Strabane, 1st viscount: James Hamilton (*d.* 1734), of Baronscourt, Co. Tyrone, 6th earl of Abercorn in the Scottish peerage, *cr.* Viscount Strabane 1701; privy councillor [I] by 1711–*d.*

Strangford, 3rd viscount: Endymion Smythe (*d.* c.1724), of Westenhanger, Kent.

Thomond, 7th earl of: Henry O'Brien (1688–1741); MP [GB] 1710–14; privy councillor [I] 1714–*d.*

Tyrawley: Charles O'Hara (*d.* 1724), of Dublin, *cr.* Baron Tyrawley 1706; capt., duke of York's regiment 1678–9, Dutch service 1679, 1st foot 1687, col. of foot 1689–96, 7th foot 1696–1713, of foot regiment 1716–17, brig.-gen. 1695, major-gen. 1702, lieut.-gen. 1704, privy councillor [I] 1710–*d.*, c.-in-c. [I] 1714–20; governor, Royal Hospital, Kilmainham.

Tullamore – *see* Moore.

Valentia, 6th viscount: Arthur Annesley (c.1678–1737); also 5th earl of Anglesey [E]; MP [I] 1703–10, and [E & GB] 1702–10; gentleman of the privy chamber [E] 1689–1702; jt vice-treasurer and paymaster-gen. [I] 1710–16, privy councillor [GB] 1710–*d.*, [I] 1711–*d.*, lord justice [GB] 1714.

Wharton – *see* Catherlogh.

Spiritual Lords

Ashe, St George (1658–1718), bp of Cloyne 1695–7, Clogher 1697–1717, Derry 1717–*d.*

Browne, Peter (c.1665–1735), bp of Cork and Ross 1710–*d.*

Carr, Charles (c.1672–1739), bp of Killaloe 1716–*d.*

Crowe, Charles (c.1656–1726), bp of Cloyne 1702–*d.*

Downes, Henry (c.1667–1735), bp of Killala 1717–20, Elphin 1720–4, Meath 1724–7, Derry 1727–*d.*

Ellis, Welbore (c.1661–1734), bp of Kildare 1705–32, Meath 1732–*d.*

Evans, John (c.1652–1724), bp of Bangor 1701–16, Meath 1716–*d.*

Fitzgerald, William (c.1641–1722), bp of Clonfert 1691–*d.*

Forster, Nicholas (c.1673–1743), bp of Killaloe 1714–16, Raphoe 1716–*d.*

Godwin, Timothy (c.1670–1729), bp of Kilmore 1715–27, abp of Cashel 1727–*d.*

Hartstonge, John (1659–1717), bp of Ossory 1693–1714, Derry 1714–*d.*

Hutchinson, Francis (1660–1739), bp of Down and Connor 1721–*d.*

King, William (1650–1729), bp of Derry 1691–1703, abp of Dublin 1703–*d.*

Lambert, Ralph (c.1666–1732), bp of Dromore 1717–27, Meath 1727–*d.*

Lindsay, Thomas (1656–1724), bp of Killaloe 1696–1713, Raphoe 1713–14, abp of Armagh 1714–*d.*

Milles, Thomas (1671–1740), bp of Waterford and Lismore 1708–*d.*

Smyth, Edward (c.1662–1720), bp of Down and Connor 1699–*d.*

Smyth, Thomas (1650–1725), bp of Limerick 1695–*d.*

Stearne, John (1660–1745), bp of Dromore 1713–17, Clogher 1717–*d.*

Synge, Edward (1659–1741), bp of Raphoe 1714–16, abp of Tuam 1716–*d.*

Vesey, John (1638–1716), bp of Limerick 1673–9, abp of Tuam 1679–*d.*

Vesey, Sir Thomas (c.1672–1730), 1st Bt, bp of Killaloe 1713–14, Ossory 1714–*d.*

Appendix 4: Members of the Irish House of Commons Mentioned in the Text

Allen, John – *see* Appendix 3 (Allen, Viscount).

Allen, Joshua (1685–1742), of Stillorgan, Co. Dublin, MP Co. Kildare 1709–26; 1st s. of John Allen (*q.v.*); suc. as 2nd Viscount Allen 1726.

Allen, Richard (1691–1745), of Punchestown, Co. Kildare, MP Athy 1715–27, Co. Kildare 1727–*d.*; capt. 4th dragoon guards 1715; 3rd s. of John Allen (*q.v.*).

Allen, Robert (1687–1741), of Old Court, Co. Wicklow, MP Carysfort 1713–14, Co. Wicklow 1715–*d.*; sec. to revenue commrs [I] 1736–*d.*; 2nd s. of John Allen (*q.v.*).

Bernard, Francis (1663–1731), of Castle Bernard, Co. Cork, MP Clonakilty 1692–3, Bandon 1695–1727; solicitor-gen. [I] 1711–14, prime serjeant [I] 1725–6, judge of common pleas [I] 1726–*d.*

Bingham, Henry (1688–1743), of Foxford, Co. Mayo, MP [I] Co. Mayo 1707–14, Castlebar 1715–*d.*

Bladen, Martin (*c.*1680–1746), of Aldborough Hatch, Essex, MP Bandon 1715–27 and MP [GB] 1715–*d.*; ensign, Fairfax's regiment 1697, capt. Hotham's regiment 1705, col. of foot 1709–10, comptroller of the mint [GB] 1714–28, sec. to lords justices [I] 1715–17, privy councillor [I] 1715–27, 1733–7, 1739–42, 1745–*d.*

Boyle, Henry (1682–1764), of Castlemartyr, Co. Cork, MP Midleton 1707–13, Kilmallock 1713–14, Co. Cork 1715–56; Speaker of house of commons [I] 1733–56, chancellor of exchequer [I] 1733–5, privy councillor [I] 1733–*d.*, revenue commr [I] 1735–54, lord justice [I] with intervals 1734–*d.*; cr. earl of Shannon 1756.

Brodrick, St John III – *see* Appendix 2.

Brodrick, Thomas – *see* Appendix 2.

Budgell, Eustace (1686–1737), MP Mullingar 1715–27; under-sec. [I] 1714–18, accountant-gen. of the revenue [I] 1717–18.

Burton, Benjamin (bef. 1665–1728), of Dublin and Burton Hall, Co. Carlow, MP Dublin 1703–27.

Butler, Brinsley (1670–1736), of Belturbet, Co. Cavan, MP Kells 1703–13, Belturbet 1713–24; lieut. Battle-axe Guards 1704, capt. 1714, gent. usher of black rod [I] 1711; suc. elder bro. Theophilus (*see* Appendix 3) as 2nd Baron Newtownbutler 1724.

Cairnes, Sir Alexander (1665–1732), 1st Bt, of Co. Monaghan, MP Monaghan 1710–13, 1715–27, Co. Monaghan 1713–14, 1727–*d.*; keeper of Phoenix Park 1712–28.

Campbell, Charles (bef. 1640–1725), of Donaghadee, Co. Down, MP Newtownards 1695–*d.*

Chichester, Hon. John Itchingham (aft. 1660–1721), of Dunbrody Park, Co. Wexford, MP Gorey 1692–1713, Belfast 1715–21; ensign, Edgeworth's regiment 1689, lieut., Hale's regiment 1692, half-pay 1710, major, Keane's foot 1716; s. of the 2nd earl of Donegall.

Clayton, Laurence – *see* Appendix 2.

Conolly, William (1662–1729), of Capel St., Dublin and Castletown, Co. Kildare, MP Donegal 1692–9, Co. Londonderry 1703–*d.*; customer, Derry and Coleraine, 1697–*d.*, revenue commr [I] 1709–10, 1714–*d.*, privy councillor [I] 1710–11, 1714–*d.*, Speaker of the house of commons [I] 1715–1729, lord justice [I] 1717–19, 1719–21, 1722–4, 1726–7, 1728–*d.*

Coote, Charles (bef. 1694–1761), of Mount Coote, Co. Limerick, MP Castlemartyr 1715–27.

Cox, Richard (1677–1725), of Dunmanway, Co. Cork, MP Tallow 1703–14, Clonakilty 1717–*d.*

Crofton, Sir Edward (*c.*1662–1729), 2nd Bt, of Mote Park, Co. Roscommon, MP Boyle 1695–9, Co. Roscommon 1703–*d.*; privy councillor [I] 1714–*d.*

Crofton, Edward (1687–1739), MP Roscommon 1713–*d.*; s. of Sir Edward Crofton, 2nd Bt (*q.v.*).

Cuffe, Michael (1694–1744), of Ballinrobe, Co. Mayo, MP Co. Mayo 1719–27, Longford 1727–44.

Delafaye, Charles (1677–1762), of London, MP Belturbet 1715–27; clerk in secretary of state's office [E] 1697–1706, chief clerk 1706–13, second sec. [I] 1713–15, gentleman sewer [GB] 1714–27, jt sec. to lords justices [I] 1715–17, jt chief sec. [I] 1717, under-secretary of state [GB] 1717–34.

Dopping, Samuel (1671–1720), of Dublin, MP Armagh 1695–14, TCD 1715–*d.*; privy councillor [I] 1711–14.

Freke, George (bef. 1682–1730), of Upway, Dorset, MP Clonakilty 1703–27, Bandon 1727–*d.*; ensign, Erle's foot 1691, capt. 1696, lieut.-col., col. 1709, brig.-gen. 1711.

Freke, Sir Percy (1700–28), 2nd Bt, of Castle Freke, Co. Cork, MP Baltimore 1721–*d.*

Freke, Sir Ralph (1675–1717), 1st Bt, of Rathbarry, Co. Cork, MP Clonakilty 1703–*d.*

Geering, Richard (bef. 1682–1742), of Dublin, MP Ballyshannon 1703–13, Jamestown 1721–7; one of the six clerks in chancery [I], 1701–34.

Gore, George (1675–1753), of Tennalick, Co. Longford, MP Longford 1709–20; attorney-gen. [I] 1714–20; judge of common pleas [I] 1720–45.

Gore, Sir Ralph (1675–1733), 4th Bt, of Manor Gore, Co. Donegal, MP Donegal 1703–13, Co. Donegal 1713–27, Clogher 1727–*d.*; privy councillor [I] 1714–*d.*, chancellor of exchequer [I] 1717–*d.*, Speaker of the house of commons [I] 1729–*d.*, lord justice [I] 1730–1, 1732–*d.*

Harrison, Francis (1677–1725), of Dublin, Lisburn, Co. Antrim and Castlemartin, Co. Kildare, MP Knocktopher 1703–13, Lisburn 1713–14, Co. Carlow 1715–*d.*

Hartstonge, Sir Standish (*c.*1672–1751), 2nd Bt, of Bruff, Co. Limerick, MP Kilmallock 1695–9, Ratoath 1703–13, St Canice 1713–27.

Hill, Arthur – *see* Appendix 2.

Hill, Trevor – *see* Appendix 2.

Hoare, Edward (c.1678–1765), of Dunkettle, Co. Cork, MP Cork 1710–27.

Hopkins, Edward (1674/5–1736), of Coventry, Warws., MP TCD 1721–7 and MP [GB] 1701–2, 1707–10, 1713–27; revenue commr [I] 1716–22, chief sec. [I] 1721–4, privy councillor [I] 1721–7, 1733–*d*., master of the revels [I] 1722–*d*.

Houghton, George (c.1671–1733), of Borrmount, Co. Wexford, MP Clonmines 1713–27, Fethard (Co. Wexford) 1727–*d*.; clerk, comptroller and surveyor-gen. of ordnance [I] 1704–18.

Hume, Sir Gustavus (c.1670–1731), 3rd Bt, of Castle Hume, Co. Fermanagh, MP Co. Fermanagh 1713–*d*.; privy councillor [I] 1714–*d*.

Hyde, Arthur (bef. 1674–1720), of Castle Hyde, Co. Cork, MP Tralee 1703–13, Midleton 1713–14, Youghal 1715–*d*.

Jephson, Anthony (c.1689–1755), of Mallow Castle, Co. Cork, MP Mallow 1713–*d*.; cornet, Wharton's dragoons 1710, half-pay 1713, capt. Fielding's dragoons 1716, lieut.-col. Lord Doneraile's dragoons 1716, col. 1740.

Jephson, John (1652–1724), MP Blessington 1703–*d*.; commr of appeals in revenue [I] 1706–10.

Jephson, William (bef. 1686–1716), of Mallow Castle, Co. Cork, MP Mallow 1713–16; capt. Wittewrong's foot 1708–12, half-pay 1713; elder bro. of Anthony Jephson (*q.v.*).

Knapp, Edmond (1659–1747), of Killycloin, Co. Cork, MP Cork 1715–27.

Ludlow, Stephen (bef. 1648–1721), of Ardsallagh, Co. Meath, MP Boyle 1692–3, Charlemont 1695–9, Dunleer 1703–13, 1715–*d*., Co. Louth 1713–14; one of the six clerks in chancery [I] 1669–1711, revenue commr [I] 1711–14.

Macartney, James (1692–1770), of Hansborough, Co. Cavan, MP Longford 1713–27, Granard 1727–60.

Manley, Isaac (bef. 1682–1735), of Dublin and Manley Hall, Staffs., MP Downpatrick 1705–13, Limavady 1715–*d*.; postmaster-gen. [I] 1703–*d*.

Marlay, Thomas (c.1678–1756), of Celbridge, Co. Kildare, MP Limavady 1717–27, Lanesborough 1727–30; king's counsel [I] 1715, solicitor-gen. [I] 1720–7, attorney-gen. [I] 1727–30, chief baron of exchequer [I] 1730–42, privy councillor [I] 1730–*d*., chief justice of king's bench [I] 1742–51.

Maxwell, Henry (1669–1730), of Finnebrogue, Co. Down, MP Bangor 1698–1713, Killybegs 1713–14, Donegal 1715–*d*.

May, Humphrey (bef. 1674–1722), MP St Johnston 1695–9, Charlemont 1715–22; 2nd sec. [I] 1695–6, 1697–9, chief sec. [I] 1699–1701, comptroller of customs, Limerick 1698–1702, clerk of crown and peace, Ulster 1700–2, 1714–15, searcher, Waterford 1716–22.

Maynard, William (1690–1734), of Curryglass, Co. Cork, MP Tallow 1713–*d*.; collector of revenue, Cork port 1717–*d*.

Meredyth, Thomas (1665–1719), of Dollardstown, Co. Meath, MP Navan 1703–13, Lismore 1715–*d*., MP [GB] 1709–10; capt. Schomberg's regiment 1691, adjutant-gen. [I] 1701, col. 37th foot 1702–10, Scots fusiliers 1710–14, 20th foot 1714, brig.-gen. 1704, major-gen. 1707, lieut.-gen. 1709, privy councillor [I] 1714–*d*.

Miller, Robert (bef. 1689–1725), of Milford, Co. Mayo, MP Donegal 1716–*d*.

Molesworth, Richard (1680–1758), of Swords, Co. Dublin, MP Swords 1715–26; ensign, royal regiment of foot 1702, capt. Coldstream Guards 1705, col. of foot 1710–13, lieut. of ordnance [I] 1714–18, col. of dragoons 1715–19, col. of foot 1725–32, 9th dragoons 1732–7, major-gen. 1735, sec. to general officers [I] 1736, commr of great seal [I]

1736, lieut.-gen. 1739, master-gen. of ordnance [I] 1740–*d*., c.-in-c. [I] 1751–8, field marshal 1752–*d*.; 2nd s. of Robert Molesworth, Viscount Molesworth (*see* Appendix 3).

Molesworth, William (1681–1770), of Dublin, MP Philipstown 1717–60; surveyor-gen. [I]1714–*d*.; yr bro.of Richard Molesworth (*q.v.*).

Norman, Charles (1666–1731), of Derry, MP Derry 1703–27.

Palmes, Francis (*d*. 1719), of Charlton, Kent, MP Youghal 1715–19 and MP [GB] 1707–8; capt. Lord Cavendish's horse 1688, Schomberg's horse 1693–4, Wyndham's horse 1694, col. 1706–13, col. of dragoons 1716–17, brig.-gen. 1704, major-gen. 1707, lieut.-gen. 1709, envoy extraordinary to the Emperor 1707–8, 1709–11, Brunswick-Lüneburg 1708, Prussia 1708, Savoy–Sardinia 1708–10, Poland 1718–*d*., envoy to United Provinces 1708, master, Royal Hospital, Kilmainham 1715, privy councillor [I] 1715–*d*.

Parnell, John (1680–1727), of Rathleague, Queen's Co., MP Granard 1713–22; counsel to barracks board and revenue commrs [I] 1714, king's counsel [I] 1715, justice of king's bench 1722–*d*.

Parry, Benjamin (1672–1736), of Dublin, MP Killybegs 1703–13, Limavady 1713–14, Tallow 1715–27, Dungarvan 1727–*d*.; register of memorials of deeds [I] 1707–*d*., privy councillor [I] 1714–*d*., keeper of Phoenix Park, Dublin 1722–*d*.

Pearson, Thomas (1678–1736), of Beamore, Co. Meath, MP Killybegs 1710–27, Ballyshannon 1727–*d*.

Pennefather, Matthew (1675–1733), of Rathsallagh, Cashel, Co. Tipperary, MP Cashel 1710–*d*.; ensign, Ingoldsby's foot 1695, lieut. 1701, capt. 1704, commissary-gen. of musters [I] 1709, muster-master gen. [I] 1709–?

Pratt, John (1670–1741), of Cabra Court, Kingscourt, Co. Cavan, MP Dingle 1713–27; deputy vice-treasurer [I] 1716–25.

Preston, John (1677–1732), of Balsoon, Co. Meath, MP Co. Meath 1709–*d*.

Purdon, Bartholomew (1675–1737), of Ballyclogh, Co. Cork, MP Mallow 1699–1713, Doneraile 1713–14, Castlemartyr 1715–*d*.

Purdon, Henry (c.1688–1737), of Little Island, Co. Cork, MP Charleville 1721–7; king's counsel 1716.

Rochfort, George (1683–1730), of Gaulstown, Co. Westmeath, MP Co. Westmeath 1707–*d*.; chief chamberlain of the exchequer [I] 1708–*d*.

Rogerson, John (1676–1741), of Glasnevin, Co. Dublin, MP Granard 1713–14, Dublin 1715–27; recorder, Dublin 1714–27, solicitor-gen. [I] 1714–20, attorney-gen. [I] 1720–7, chief justice of king's bench [I] 1727–*d*., privy councillor [I] 1727–*d*.

Rose, Henry (1675–1743), of Mountpleasant and Morgans, Co. Limerick, MP Ardfert 1703–34; judge of king's bench [I] 1734–*d*.

St George, Oliver (1661–1731), of Carrickdrumrusk, Co. Leitrim, MP Carrick-on-Shannon 1703–13, Dungannon 1713–*d*.; capt. of a troop of dragoons 1685, capt. Queen's regiment of dragoons 1685–8, privy councillor [I] 1714–*d*.

St George, Richard (1670–1755), of Kilrush, Co. Kilkenny, MP Galway 1695–9, Carrick-on-Shannon 1715–*d*.; adjutant, St George's foot 1690, capt. 1691, major, Lord Slane's foot 1708, lieut.-col. 1711, lieut.-col. Macartney's horse 1727; col. of foot 1737; col. of dragoon regiment 1740, major-gen. 1744, lieut.-gen. 1747, major-gen. of staff [I] by 1755.

St Leger, Arthur (1695–1734), of Doneraile, Co. Cork, s. and h. of 1st Viscount Doneraile, MP Doneraile 1715–27.

Sandford, Henry (bef. 1671–1733), of Castlereagh, Co. Roscommon, MP Roscommon 1692–*d.*; collector of excise, Dublin 1715.

Saunders, Anderson (c.1653–1718), of Newtown Saunders, Co. Wicklow, MP Taghmon 1692–*d.*; one of the six clerks in chancery [I] 1682–1715.

Shaen, Sir Arthur (aft. 1650–1725), 2nd Bt, of Malahide Castle, Co. Dublin, MP Lismore 1692–*d.*

Singleton, Edward (c.1674–1726), of Drogheda, MP Drogheda 1717–*d.*

Singleton, Henry (1682–1759), of Drumcondra, Co. Dublin, MP Drogheda 1713–40; prime serjeant [I] 1726–39, chief justice of common pleas [I] 1740–52; privy councillor [I] 1740–*d.*, yr bro. of Edward Singleton (*q.v.*).

Southwell, Edward (1671–1730), of Kings Weston, Gloucs., Kinsale, Co. Cork, and Spring Garden, Westminster, MP Kinsale 1692–9, 1713–*d.*, TCD 1703–13, and MP [E & GB] 1702–8, 1713–15; clerk of privy council [E] 1693–*d.*, jt prothonotary of common pleas [I] 1698–1717, judge of admiralty court and vice-admiral, Munster [I] 1699–*d.*, jt commr of privy seal [E] 1701–2, [GB] 1715, 1716, sec. of state [I] 1702–*d.*, privy councillor [I] 1702–*d.*, chief sec. [I] 1703–7, 1710–13, prothonotary of king's bench [I] 1715–17.

Southwell, Sir Thomas – *see* Appendix 3 (Baron Southwell).

Southwell, William (bef. 1682–1720), of Dublin, MP Kinsale 1703–13, Castlemartyr 1713–14, Baltimore 1715–*d.*; lieut. Hamilton's foot 1693, capt.-lieut. 1694, major, Rivers' foot 1702, lieut.-col. 1703, col. of foot 1706–8, col. 6th foot 1714–*d.*, capt. battle-axe guards [I] 1714–*d.*

Stewart, Hon. Charles (1681–1741), of West Malling, Kent, MP Co. Tyrone 1715–27, MP [GB] 1723–7, 1737–*d.*; capt. Royal Navy 1704, plenipotentiary to Morocco 1720–1, c.-in-c. Jamaica station 1729–32, adm. 1729, vice-adm. 1734.

Stewart, Hon. Richard (1677–1728), of Ballycastle, Co. Antrim, MP Co. Tyrone 1703–14, 1727–*d.*, Strabane 1715–27; capt. Price's regiment (disbanded 1712).

Taylo(u)r, Sir Thomas (1662–1736), 1st Bt, of Kells, Co. Meath, MP Kells 1692–9, 1713–*d.*, Belturbet 1703–13; privy councillor [I] 1726–*d.*

Tighe, Richard (1678–1736), of Dublin, MP Belturbet 1703–13, Newtownards 1715–27, Augher 1727–*d.*; privy councillor [I] 1718–*d.*; keeper of records in Bermingham Tower, Dublin Castle 1734–*d.*

Tisdall, Michael (1672–1726), of Mount Tisdall, Co. Meath, MP Ardee 1713–*d.*; commr of appeals in revenue [I] 1709–*d.*, advocate-gen. [I] 1714–*d.*

Tisdall, Richard (c.1698–1742), of Bawn, Co. Louth, MP Dundalk 1707–13, Co. Louth 1713–27; usher in chancery [I] 1714, 1734–5, registrar, chancery [I] 1716–44.

Topham, James (1677–1724), of Newtown, Co. Dublin, MP Strabane 1703–13, St Johnston 1713–*d.*; jt clerk of quit rents [I], register of forfeitures [I] 1715.

Trotter, Thomas (1684–1745), of Duleek, Co. Meath, MP Duleek, 1715–27, Old Leighlin 1727–*d.*; commr of appeals in revenue [I] 1728–*d.*, master of chancery [I] 1732–42.

Tynte, James – *see* Worth.

Upton, Clotworthy (1665–1725), of Castle Upton, Templepatrick, Co. Antrim, MP Newtownards 1695–9, Co. Antrim 1703–*d.*

Upton, Thomas (1677–1733), MP Antrim 1713–14, Co. Antrim 1716–27, Derry 1727–*d.*; king's counsel [I] 1715, commr of appeals in revenue [I] 1717–*d.*, counsel to barracks commrs [I] by 1721–*d.*, customer, Derry and Coleraine 1723; yr bro. of Clotworthy Upton (*q.v.*).

Vesey, Agmondisham (1677–1739), of Lucan, Co. Dublin, MP Tuam 1703–*d*.; comptroller- and accountant-gen. [I] 1734–*d*.

Vesey, William (1687–1750), of Dublin, MP Tuam 1715–*d*.; king's counsel [I] 1728, master in chancery [I] 1731–42; yr bro. of Agmondisham Vesey (*q.v.*).

Ward, Michael (1683–1759), of Castle Ward, Co. Down, MP Co. Down 1713–27, Bangor 1727; judge of king's bench [I] 1727–*d*.

Webster, Edward (bef. 1691–by 1755), MP Carysfort 1717–27; clerk, treasury [E] 1691–1755, chief sec. [I] 1717–20, searcher, packer and gauger, Dublin and outports 1718–43.

Worth, James (1682–1758), of Old Bawn, Co. Dublin, and Dunlavin, Co. Wicklow, MP Rathcormac 1716–27, Youghal 1727–*d*.; privy councillor [I] 1715–*d*.; assumed the name of Tynte on inheriting estates.

Wynne, Owen (1665–1737), of Hazelwood, Co. Sligo, MP Carrick-on Shannon 1692–3, Ballyshannon 1713–27, Co. Sligo 1727–*d*.; capt. Roscommon's foot 1689, major, Royal Irish Dragoons 1694, lieut.-col. Ross's dragoons 1695, col. of foot 1705–13, of dragoons 1715, of 4th Royal Dragoons 1727, of 5th Royal Irish Dragoons 1732, of dragoons 1734–6, brig.-gen. 1706, major-gen. 1709, lieut.-gen. 1727, privy councillor [I] 1726–36, lieut.-gen. of forces [I] 1735–6.